THE LAW AND PRACTICE OF PIRA

This collection of essays provides a comprehensive assessment ~. ... ..gai and policy approaches to maritime counter-piracy adopted by the EU and other international actors over the last few years.

This book adopts a holistic approach to the topic, examining approaches to piracy as these emerge in different geographical areas, as well as tackling the central issues which counter-piracy raises in terms of the most topical aspects of international law (international humanitarian law and armed conflict, piracy and terrorism, use of force). It also focuses on the approach of the EU, placing counter-piracy in its broader legal context. Providing a detailed doctrinal exploration of the issues which counter-piracy raises, and discussing policy alternatives, it emphasises and draws upon the insights of the practice of counter-piracy by bringing together academic lawyers and legal advisers of the main actors in the area (EU, US, NATO, UK, Germany).

As the migration crisis in the Southern Central Mediterranean is unfolding, and the EU designs its policy for the disruption of the business model of human smuggling and trafficking networks, the book offers an excellent analysis on the practices of the international community for the disruption of the business model of Somali piracy.

The book will be of interest to legal scholars, political scientists and international relations theorists, as well as policy makers and students of law, politics and international relations.

The Law and Practice of Piracy at Sea

European and International Perspectives

Edited by
Panos Koutrakos and Achilles Skordas

·H A R T·
PUBLISHING

OXFORD AND PORTLAND, OREGON
2015

Published in the United Kingdom by Hart Publishing Ltd
16C Worcester Place, Oxford, OX1 2JW
Telephone: +44 (0)1865 517530
Fax: +44 (0)1865 510710
E-mail: mail@hartpub.co.uk
Website: http://www.hartpub.co.uk

Published in North America (US and Canada) by
Hart Publishing
c/o International Specialized Book Services
920 NE 58th Avenue, Suite 300
Portland, OR 97213-3786
USA
Tel: +1 503 287 3093 or toll-free: (1) 800 944 6190
Fax: +1 503 280 8832
E-mail: orders@isbs.com
Website: http://www.isbs.com

British Library Cataloguing in Publication Data

Data Available

ISBN: 978-1-84946-968-5

Typeset by Forewords, Oxon
Printed and bound in Great Britain by
CPI Group (UK) Ltd, Croydon CR0 4YY

Acknowledgements

Most of the chapters of this book are based on papers presented at a workshop which took place at the University of Bristol on 12-13 July 2012. The organisation of this workshop was possible due to the funding provided by the European Commission under the Jean Monnet Chair in European Law held, until 2012, by Panos Koutrakos.

We are grateful to Niall Coghlan for his editorial assistance.

Contents

List of Contributors

SONJA BOELAERT is Legal Adviser at the Legal Service of the Council of the European Union.

ROBIN CHURCHILL is Professor of International Law at the University of Dundee.

RICARDO GOSALBO-BONO is Director at the Legal Service of the Council of the European Union and Part-time Professor of Law, PILC, Free University Brussels (VUB).

EDWIN EGEDE is Senior Lecturer in International Law and International Relations at the Department of Politics, Cardiff University.

MALCOLM EVANS OBE is Professor of Public International Law at the University of Bristol.

SOFIA GALANI is a PhD candidate at the University of Bristol.

DOUGLAS GUILFOYLE is Reader in International Law at University College London.

JAN KLABBERS is Academy Professor (Martti Ahtisaari Chair) and Professor of International Law at the University of Helsinki.

DORIS KÖNIG is Claussen Simon Professor of International Law at, and the President of, the Bucerius Law School, Hamburg.

PANOS KOUTRAKOS is Professor of European Union Law and Jean Monnet Professor of European Union Law at City University London.

THILO MARAUHN is Professor of Public, International and European law at Justus Liebig University, Giessen.

ANDREW MURDOCH is Legal Adviser at the Foreign and Commonwealth Office, London.

PETER M OLSON is Director of Legal Services and Legal Adviser at NATO Headquarters, Brussels. He is the principal legal adviser to Secretary General Anders Fogh Rasmussen, and the Organization's senior legal officer.

DAVID M ONG is Professor of International and Environmental Law at Nottingham Law School, Nottingham Trent University.

ALEXANDER PROELSS is Professor of Public International Law and European Law at the University of Trier.

TIM RENÉ SALOMON is an Associate at the IMPRS for Maritime Affairs at the International Max Planck Research School for Maritime Affairs and worked as a research fellow for the Claussen Simon Chair of International Law.

ACHILLES SKORDAS is Professor of International Law at the University of Bristol.

GABRIEL SWINEY is an Attorney Adviser at the US Department of State.

DANIEL THYM is Professor of Public, European and International Law at the University of Konstanz.

Table of Cases

Numerical

EUROPEAN COURT OF HUMAN RIGHTS

EUROPEAN GENERAL COURT (FORMERLY COURT OF FIRST INSTANCE OF THE
EUROPEAN COMMUNITIES)

GERMANY

HAGUE ARBITRAL TRIBUNAL

HUMAN RIGHTS COMMITTEE

INTER-AMERICAN COMMISSION OF HUMAN RIGHTS

INTERNATIONAL ARBITRAL AWARDS (UN)

INTERNATIONAL COURT OF JUSTICE

SEYCHELLES

UNITED KINGDOM

UNITED STATES OF AMERICA

Table of Legislation

Common Positions

Decisions

Regulations

FRANCE

GERMANY

International Legal Instruments

Introduction

THIS COLLECTION OF essays aims to provide a comprehensive assessment of the legal and policy issues pertaining to the maritime counter-piracy approaches adopted by the UN, the EU and other regional actors over the last few years. In view of the social structure, global dimensions and repercussions of contemporary piracy, the present volume has set itself the objectives of rethinking the conceptual framework of international and European law and exploring the current practice of states and international organisations. The recent decline in piracy incidents off the Somali coast makes the present analysis even more topical, as the contributors had the opportunity to observe the entire cycle of the phenomenon, and draw conclusions regarding the legality and effectiveness of the instruments, methods and policies employed for the repression of piracy.

Piracy at sea is a phenomenon that has been steadily brought to the top of the agenda of international policy-makers. This is due to economic and security factors. On the one hand, the financial cost of piracy for the maritime industry and world economy as a whole (estimated to be about $18 billion by 2010 in the 2013 World Bank Report on Somali piracy)[1] as well as, more specifically, the cost of tackling the phenomenon effectively (including, but not confined to, the protection of vessels, the prosecution and imprisonment of pirates, and the process of building national and regional capacity to fight piracy) is considerable. On the other hand, piracy may be linked to state failure and collapse, and adds a significant dimension to other pathologies bred by it, such as organised crime and terrorism. In parts of Somalia, in particular, a pirate economy took hold over a certain period of time, and piracy evolved into a transnational criminal business activity based on hostage-taking and ransom, with links and support outside the country. The film industry's stereotypical and plot-generating figure of the romanticised pirate with his antics has to be replaced by the more sophisticated persona of the ruthless and media-savvy pirate leader as a businessman acting on the invisible side of world society's economic and political systems.

The emerging significance of piracy is illustrated by the increasing attention it has attracted by international actors. The EU, for instance, in its Security Strategy, adopted in 2003, well before piracy at the Horn of Africa became an issue of international concern, highlights it as a new dimension of organised crime.[2] Five years later, in its 'Report on the Implementation of the European Security Strategy', the Union elevates piracy as one of the main issues in its effort to build stability in Europe and beyond (along with development and the proliferation of small arms and light weapons).[3] The

---

[1] World Bank, 'The Pirates in Somalia: Ending the Threat, Rebuilding a Nation' (2013) 15, available at http://siteresources.worldbank.org/INTAFRICA/Resources/pirates-of-somalia-main-report-web.pdf (last accessed on 28 September 2013).

[2] 'A Secure Europe in a Better World—European Security Strategy' (Brussels, 12 December 2003).

[3] 'Report on the Implementation of the European Security Strategy' (Brussels, 11 December 2008).

UN Security Council has been adopting resolutions regularly since 2008 urging the international community to tackle piracy and the UN General Secretary has adopted a number of reports on the matter.[4]

However, it is not only in rhetoric that international actors focus on piracy. The EU has been carrying out a maritime mission off the coast of Somalia since 2008 in its efforts to tackle the spread of piracy in the area (EU NAVFOR Operation Atalanta). It was the intensity of the incidents in that area in the late 2000s that attracted greater attention to the phenomenon of piracy: NATO has been deploying missions in the area too since 2008; the US has been leading combined maritime forces from a number of states and covering a very wide zone; China has been carrying out its first overseas mission in the Gulf of Aden since 2009; a number of individual states maintain vessels patrolling the area, including India, Russia and Japan.

Piracy off the coast of Somalia has brought attention to the phenomenon of piracy more generally and also some urgency in international efforts to tackle it. This is due to the large area in which such incidents occur, as well as its significance for maritime transport. This sense of urgency may also be explained in the light of the disintegration and fragility of Somalia, which makes the link between state failure and piracy all the starker. However, piracy is by no means confined to the area off the Horn of Africa, and the emphasis on that region should not underestimate its presence and perseverance in other areas, such as the Gulf of Guinea or Southeast Asia.

In the light of its increasing topicality and the ongoing efforts of the international community to tackle the phenomenon, piracy at sea has attracted the interest of international law and EU law scholars as well as policy-makers. This inter- and intra-disciplinary appeal is reflected in the approach of this book to both its subject matter and its contributors.

First, in terms of its subject matter, this collection of essays examines the approaches to piracy as these emerge in different geographical areas. For instance, in addition to the Horn of Africa, it also examines piracy in Southeast Asia, a case of significance due to the advanced level of regional cooperation achieved in order to tackle the problem.

Secondly, the focus of the book is broad as, in addition to the law of the sea, it also tackles the central issues which counter-piracy raises in terms of the most topical aspects of international law, such as international humanitarian law and armed conflict, piracy and terrorism, and use of force. It also focuses on the approach of the EU, given the increasing prominence which counter-piracy at sea has taken in the Union's external action. Therefore, the book places counter-piracy in its broader legal context.

Thirdly, the book brings together two different perspectives: on the one hand, it provides a detailed doctrinal exploration of the issues which counter-piracy raises; on the other hand, it emphasises and draws upon the insights of the practice of counter-piracy. The broad approach of this book is also reflected by the different perspectives which the contributors bring in order to explore piracy. Academic lawyers from different backgrounds (EU and international law) and legal advisors of the main actors in the area are brought together in order to highlight the multifarious aspects of a phenomenon which has challenged traditional and unilateral approaches to the

[4] For a recent report see S/2012/45 on piracy in the Gulf of Guinea (19 January 2012).

development of the law as well as policy-making in the area. Therefore, the book examines piracy not only in its broader legal framework, but also in its policy context.

The analysis starts off by placing piracy within the framework of public international law. Churchill explores its defining elements in the light of the United Nations Convention on the Law of the Sea (UNCLOS) and explores whether customary and treaty rules on piracy are identical, and whether they are still important for contemporary counter-piracy policies. He articulates the problems raised by the definition of piracy under UNCLOS rules and focuses on the issue of jurisdiction for persecuting pirates as the main shortcoming. This conclusion ties in with the distinct reluctance of states participating in counter-piracy operations to prosecute and the practice of concluding international agreements between them and states in the region where piracy takes place in order to enable the latter to assume this function. The relevant questions of law and practice are examined later in the chapter by Thym.

Once its conceptual parameters under the law of the sea have been set out, Guilfoyle examines whether pirates can be normatively treated as terrorists. This question arises in the context of interpretation of the 1988 Convention for the Suppression of Unlawful Acts against the Safety of Maritime Navigation, which aims to ensure safety of maritime navigation against acts of violence that may be subsumed under the concept of piracy, but are also considered as acts of terrorism. In the post-9/11 environment, the 'person' of the pirate has been differentiated from that of the terrorist in terms of affiliation to or membership of different violent non-state groups, but this is not necessarily true for each relevant act of violence in terms of law; thus the broader question whether counter-terrorist policies should be employed against acts of piracy becomes all the more pertinent. Guilfoyle's analysis engages in a historical and contextual examination of the terms 'piracy' and 'terrorism', and suggests that a strict, exclusive and inflexible categorisation is neither warranted nor necessary.

In his chapter, Proelss discusses piracy in relation to the use of force. The legality of recourse to force against pirates has to be assessed, inter alia, on the basis of the law of interstate force, as provided for by the UN Charter and customary international law, as far as the territorial integrity or political independence of the state where pirates have established their basis of operation is affected. For instance, taking into account the consent of the Somali authorities, the UN Security Council has authorised the use of force in the territorial waters and on the land in Somalia under a number of resolutions adopted pursuant to Chapter VII of the UN Charter. Proelss argues that such measures may not substantiate an authorisation to disregard the prohibition of the use of force, and no state engaged in counter-piracy operations has invoked its right to self-defence under Article 51 UN Charter. However, he discusses the question whether international law prohibits recourse to military force in an absolute manner, and concludes that enforcement measures against private actors that are a priori not covered by the *jus ad bellum* may lawfully involve the exercise of force, subject to legal limits set out in international human rights law.

Another issue raised by the proliferation of piracy in areas of weak governmental structures and regional tension is the relationship between counter-piracy practices and international humanitarian law. Marauhn discusses the issue of application of international humanitarian law in the course of counter-piracy operations. This matter is intimately connected with the question whether the increased level of piracy activities in areas such as the Gulf of Aden could generally reach the threshold of an 'armed conflict' between pirates and the international naval forces. Marauhn answers in the negative, considering that counter-piracy operations have a law enforcement character, and their legality should be measured on the basis of human rights law. However, he does not exclude the possibility of an overlap between human rights law and humanitarian law in counter-terrorism and counter-piracy operations.

Following the conceptual analysis of piracy and its examination within the context of public international law, Part II of the book looks in detail at the ways in which national, regional and international actors have tackled piracy. Reflecting the subtitle of the book (*European and International Perspectives*), this part starts with an assessment of the approach adopted by the EU. Gosalbo Bono and Boelaert highlight the dual focus of the EU's approach. On the one hand, in the context of its security and defence policy, the EU has been carrying out its only maritime operation (EU NAVFOR Atalanta) off the coast of Somalia since 2008. Its mandate was expanded in March 2012 to cover attacks on targets on Somalia's coast. Extended until December 2014, this is a high profile mission which has raised the visibility of the Union in the area. On the other hand, the fight against piracy has also been an increasingly prominent objective of other EU policies, such as development cooperation. This chapter explores both the ways in which these approaches have developed and how they interact in legal and policy terms.

A particular issue that was raised in the context of the EU's maritime operation is the prosecution of alleged pirates. As the general parameters of this problem under international law have been examined by Churchill, the specific practice developed by the Union is analysed in Thym's chapter. He focuses on the transfer agreements concluded by the Union with countries in the area, and explores their modalities and implications, not least in terms of protection of fundamental human rights. Whilst he concludes that all the requirements set out by the European Convention on Human Rights have been met, he points out that the application of the EU Charter of Fundamental Rights is bound to raise significant issues in the light of the exclusion of the jurisdiction of the Court of Justice of the European Union from the areas of common foreign and security policy and common security and defence policy. In the light of this state of affairs, he suggests that national courts and parliamentary fora are bound to be tempted to play a more intrusive role in the field.

In his analysis of NATO's approach to piracy, Olson assesses the organisation's operation off the coast of Somalia. He points out that NATO's capacity to launch and sustain an extended policing operation is effective, even though it may be of lower visibility. This highlights an interesting dimension of the role of NATO, all the more so in the light of the ongoing debate about the limits of its operational capacity and, therefore, its ultimate function.

What follows is an examination of the approach of three national actors, namely the US (by Swiney), the UK (by Murdoch) and Germany (by König and Salomon). Each of these contributions provides a useful illustration of the different issues which national authorities face in their effort to design and implement counter-piracy policies and operations. Swiney outlines the approach of the US and refers to recent case law, as well as to the objection of the US administration to the establishment of an international tribunal for the prosecution of suspected pirates. Murdoch explores the efforts of the British government to articulate a comprehensive approach with increasing emphasis on tackling the long-standing pathologies of the areas where piracy-related problems are the most acute. He explains the internal challenges which such an approach raises and places it in the broader context of the interactions between the UK and other national and international approaches. König and Salomon explore the legal complexities and constitutional law background of Germany's participation in international military operations, and discuss the implications for the country's involvement in the fight against piracy. Their chapter also analyses the development of criminal law in order to deal with different types of piracy-related crimes that fall under German jurisdiction and explores the legal regime governing private security providers.

A common thread of the chapters of Part II is piracy off the coast of Somalia. In his chapter, Egede offers an African perspective by highlighting the main parameters of the genesis and development of piracy in East Africa and by reflecting on the role of both regional states and approaches to tackling this problem. Ong then engages in a comparative analysis of how piracy is approached off the Horn of Africa and in the Southeast Asian Waters. The latter is a topic which is not often explored in the literature. This chapter offers an in-depth compare-and-contrast analysis which sheds light on the differences between the characteristics of piracy as it emerges in the two areas, but also points out certain common threads which underpin their tackling as a matter of both law and policy.

Instead of a conclusion bringing together the themes developed in the contributions in this book, we thought that it would be more interesting to develop the debate about piracy further and open it up by enquiring about its development within the broader international law and policy conceptual framework. This is the main objective of the three chapters in Part III. Skordas explores issues of legal policy and attempts an assessment of the instruments employed for the repression of piracy. He emphasises the inadequacies of the military and law enforcement approaches, and considers that the maritime business should be prompted to take measures of self-help, such as the regular use of private maritime security companies, which can also function as deterrents taking pirates out of business even in the absence of successful nation-building.

Klabbers reflects on the proliferation of regional and international initiatives to tackle piracy and concludes that, for all the range of their legal bases and participants, they may not be seen as giving rise to a body of global law. However, these approaches do form part of what global governance is about—a development which raises serious questions about accountability.

Finally, Evans and Galani explore the issues of jurisdiction, human rights (including rights of pirates and rights of victims) and soft law, and question the prevailing regulatory and jurisdictional mechanisms for tackling piracy and their focus on the latter as a law of the sea problem. They argue that this is too narrow an approach, which distorts the main feature of piracy as a challenge to statehood itself.

Due to the multifarious issues which it raises across a number of areas of national, transnational and international law and policy, piracy will keep attracting the interest of scholars, practitioners and policy-makers. This book aims to contribute to this ongoing conversation by seeking to disentangle different conceptual elements of this phenomenon, highlighting the national, regional and international counter-piracy approaches, placing the emerging legal issues in their policy context, and raising broader questions about the direction of both the relevant law and policy.

Panos Koutrakos and Achilles Skordas
London and Bristol, September 2013

Part I

Piracy and International Norms

1

The Piracy Provisions of the UN Convention on the Law of the Sea—Fit for Purpose?

ROBIN CHURCHILL*

I. INTRODUCTION

MOST UN SECURITY Council resolutions of the past few years concerned with piracy affirm in their preambles that 'international law, as reflected' in the UN Convention on the Law of the Sea (UNCLOS),[1] 'sets out the legal framework applicable to combating piracy'.[2] The aim of this chapter is to analyse and critique this 'legal framework' and to consider whether it is adequate for combating piracy in the contemporary world, as the Security Council perhaps appears to assume. Unlike much of the recent, voluminous literature on piracy, this chapter does not focus primarily or exclusively on piracy in specific regions, such as the Indian Ocean or Southeast Asia, but considers piracy from a general perspective.

The provisions of UNCLOS dealing with piracy (Articles 100–07) in essence do two things. First, they define the crime of piracy for the purposes of international law, although it should be noted that the word 'crime' (or any synonym) is nowhere used in these provisions. Secondly, they provide for universal enforcement jurisdiction to suppress piracy. It is possible for states to label offences as 'piracy' under their national law that do not correspond to the UNCLOS definition of piracy, and some states have done so;[3] but if they do this, they will not be able to enforce such offences through

---

* I am grateful to the editors of this book and my colleague, Dr Jacques Hartmann, for their helpful comments on a previous draft of this chapter. The usual disclaimer applies.

[1] United Nations Convention on the Law of the Sea (adopted and opened for signature 10 December 1982, entered into force 16 November 1994) 1833 UNTS 396.

[2] See, most recently, UN Security Council Resolutions 2039 (2012), fifth preambular paragraph (on piracy in the Gulf of Guinea) and 2077 (2012), seventh preambular paragraph (on piracy off Somalia). The resolutions on Somalia invariably use the phrase 'combating piracy'; those on the Gulf of Guinea 'countering piracy'. The texts of all the UN Security Council resolutions referred to in this chapter may be found on the UN website at http://www.un.org/en/sc/documents/resolutions/ (accessed on 6 January 2013).

[3] DP O'Connell, *The International Law of the Sea*, vol II (Oxford, Clarendon Press, 1984) 979–83; I Shearer, 'Piracy', *Max Planck Encyclopedia of Public International Law* (Oxford, Oxford University Press, electronic version, 2010) para 4. For examples, see South Africa, Defence Act 2002, s 24 and Greece, Code

universal jurisdiction, but will instead need to find some alternative basis of jurisdiction, such as the territorial, flag state or nationality principles.

UNCLOS, or at least the section of it dealing with piracy, belongs to a group of treaties that define various criminal offences but provide for the imposition of criminal liability for such offences to be effected through national law and for alleged offenders to be prosecuted solely before domestic courts. Such offences are labelled 'transnational crimes' to distinguish them from 'international crimes', which international law not only defines and imposes obligations directly on natural and legal persons not to commit, but also provides for their prosecution before international courts, such as the International Criminal Court.[4] In addition to piracy, transnational crimes include, inter alia, the hijacking of aircraft,[5] unlawful interference with aircraft,[6] hostage taking[7] and, most relevantly for this chapter, unlawful acts against the safety of maritime navigation.[8] The treaties defining these crimes provide for a wide range of states to have jurisdiction over alleged offenders, but piracy is unique among transnational crimes in being subject to truly universal jurisdiction.

The piracy provisions of UNCLOS are almost identical to Articles 14–21 of the Convention on the High Seas, 1958.[9] At the Third UN Conference on Law of the Sea, held between 1973 and 1982, at which UNCLOS was drafted and adopted, only limited attempts were made to resist the incorporation, without substantive change, of Articles 14–21 of the High Seas Convention into UNCLOS. Those attempts were uniformly unsuccessful,[10] presumably because of general satisfaction with the provisions of the High Seas Convention and because piracy was not a major practical problem at the time of the Conference. Articles 14–21 of the High Seas Convention were based on, and are largely the same as, the draft articles put forward by the International Law Commission (ILC) in 1956.[11] It therefore seems permissible to regard the ILC's commentary on its draft articles and consideration of those articles at the First UN Conference on the Law of the Sea, which produced the High Seas Convention, as

---

on Public Maritime Law (Law 187/1973), Art 215, as quoted in N Boister, *An Introduction to Transnational Criminal Law* (Oxford, Oxford University Press, 2012) 32.

[4] See further R Cryer, H Friman, D Robinson and E Wilmshurst, *An Introduction to International Criminal Law and Procedure*, 2nd edn (Cambridge, Cambridge University Press, 2010) 3–6, 334–36; Boister, ibid, ch 2, especially 18–19; N Boister, 'Transnational Criminal Law?' (2003) 14 *European Journal of International Law* 953.

[5] Defined by the Convention for the Suppression of Unlawful Seizure of Aircraft (adopted 16 December 1970, entered into force 14 October 1971) 860 UNTS 105 (hereafter Hague Convention).

[6] Defined by the Convention for the Suppression of Unlawful Acts against the Safety of Civil Aviation (adopted 23 September 1971, entered into force 26 January 1973) 974 UNTS 177 (hereafter Montreal Convention).

[7] Defined by the International Convention against the Taking of Hostages (adopted 17 December 1979, entered into force 3 June 1983) 1316 UNTS 205 (hereafter Hostages Convention).

[8] Defined by the Convention for the Suppression of Unlawful Acts against the Safety of Maritime Navigation (adopted 10 March 1988, entered into force 1 March 1992) 1678 UNTS 222 (hereafter SUA Convention).

[9] Convention on the High Seas (adopted 29 April 1958, entered into force 30 September 1962) 450 UNTS 82 (hereafter High Seas Convention).

[10] S N Nandan and S Rosenne (eds), *United Nations Convention on the Law of the Sea 1982: A Commentary,* vol III (The Hague, Martinus Nijhoff Publishers, 1995) 182–223 *passim* (hereafter Virginia Commentary).

[11] Draft articles on the law of the sea, [1956] II *Yearbook of the International Law Commission* 253, 282–83. For detailed discussion of the debates in the ILC leading to the adoption of the draft articles, see AP Rubin, *The Law of Piracy* (Newport, RI, US Naval War College, 1988) 319–37.

being part of the 'preparatory work' of UNCLOS within the meaning of Article 32 of the Vienna Convention on the Law of Treaties (VCLT)[12] when it comes to interpreting the piracy provisions of UNCLOS. As will be seen, such interpretation is, at times, particularly necessary because of a lack of clarity in those provisions. In preparing its draft articles, the ILC was 'greatly assisted by the research carried out at the Harvard Law School, which culminated in a draft convention of nineteen articles with commentary, prepared in 1932 . . . In general, the [ILC] was able to endorse the findings of that research.'[13] While the Harvard draft articles and commentary probably cannot be considered as 'preparatory work' within the meaning of Article 32 of the VCLT, it is nevertheless still useful to refer to them.

In interpreting the piracy provisions of UNCLOS, one must also, as the VCLT directs in Article 31(1), consider their ordinary meaning, their context, and the object and purpose of UNCLOS—indeed, one should do so before examining the preparatory work. The context includes the provisions of UNCLOS relating to the high seas in general. One may also take into account, along with the context, 'any subsequent practice in the application of the treaty which establishes the agreement of the parties regarding its interpretation'.[14] It is arguable that such practice includes action taken by the international community in respect of Somali piracy in the past few years, especially the resolutions of the UN Security Council and the Assembly of the International Maritime Organization (IMO). That practice is discussed at appropriate points below. The object and purpose of UNCLOS include, according to its preamble, the desirability of establishing a legal order that will facilitate international communication and promote the peaceful use of the sea. When interpreting a treaty, Article 33 of the VCLT requires regard to be had to all the authentic language versions of the treaty concerned. In this chapter, references to the authentic languages of UNCLOS other than English will be confined to the French and Spanish texts because of the language limitations of the author. The piracy provisions of UNCLOS and the High Seas Convention have yet to be considered by an international court. They have, however, increasingly been interpreted by national courts in recent years. Unlike interpretation by an international court, interpretation of a treaty by a national court cannot be considered as authoritative because national judges usually have less knowledge and familiarity with international law than their international counterparts. Nevertheless, interpretations of UNCLOS by national courts are not without interest, and will be referred to at appropriate points below.

The High Seas Convention is described in its preamble as being 'generally declaratory' of customary international law. At the time that the Convention was adopted, that statement was probably true as regards its provisions on enforcement jurisdiction relating to piracy.[15] However, it is doubtful whether the definition of piracy in the Con-

---

[12] Convention on the Law of Treaties (adopted 23 May 1969, entered into force 27 January 1980) 1155 UNTS 331.

[13] Above n 11, 282. The Harvard Draft Articles and Commentary may be found at (1932) 26 *American Journal of International Law* Supplement, 739. For detailed discussion of the Harvard draft, see Rubin, n 11 above, 308–17.

[14] VCLT, Art 31(3)(b).

[15] For example, in the *Lotus* case in 1927 Judge Moore stated in his dissenting opinion, without any qualification, that piracy was a crime of universal jurisdiction: *The Lotus Case (France v Turkey)*, Permanent Court of International Justice, Series A No 10, 70. The Court said nothing on the matter as the point was obiter.

vention represented a codification of customary international law. In its commentary on its draft article defining piracy, the ILC said that it had had 'to consider certain controversial points as to the essential features of piracy'.[16] Likewise, the Harvard commentary stated, seemingly almost with relish, that there was 'a chaos of expert opinion as to what the law of nations includes, or should include, in piracy. There is no authoritative definition.'[17] Since the High Seas Convention was adopted in 1958, the position has changed, and it is probable that the definition of piracy in that convention and UNCLOS is now part of customary international law. First, there is a tendency to regard the whole of UNCLOS, apart from parts XI and XV (on deep sea mining and dispute settlement, respectively), as representing customary international law. Secondly, the fact that the UNCLOS definition has been used in a number of other instruments[18] and the formulation in the Security Council resolutions referred to above that the international law on piracy is 'reflected' in UNCLOS both suggest that the international community now regards the UNCLOS provisions on piracy as representing customary international law.[19] In any case, the provisions of the High Seas Convention and UNCLOS are very widely binding as treaty law. As at 31 December 2012, UNCLOS had 164 parties. In addition, six of its non-parties (including, most importantly, the USA) were parties to the High Seas Convention. Thus, only 26 of the UN's 193 Member States are not bound by the piracy provisions of the two conventions;[20] the majority of those states are landlocked.

This chapter consists of two main parts. The first part (Section II) examines the definition of piracy contained in UNCLOS. The second part (Section III) considers various jurisdictional issues relating to the suppression of piracy.

II. DEFINING PIRACY

This section deals with the definition of piracy. As piracy is a criminal offence, the section analyses it as one might any criminal offence by considering first its *actus reus* (Subsection A), then its *mens rea* (Subsection B) and, finally, related inchoate offences (C). This is followed by some criticisms of the definition (D).

---

[16] Above n 11, 282.

[17] Above n 13, 769. See also D Guilfoyle, Chapter 2 below; M Halberstam, 'Terrorism on the High Seas: The Achille Lauro, Piracy and the IMO Convention on Maritime Safety' (1988) 82 *American Journal of International Law* 269, 272–76; Rubin, n 11 above, 32–26 and 343–45.

[18] See IMO Assembly Resolution A.1025 (26) (2009). Code of Practice for the Investigation of the Crimes of Piracy and Armed Robbery against Ships, para 2.1, available at http://www.imo.org/OurWork/Security/PiracyArmedRobbery/Guidance/Documents/A.1025.pdf (accessed on 12 January 2013); Regional Cooperation Agreement on Combatting Piracy and Armed Robbery against Ships in Asia (adopted 11 November 2004, entered into force 4 September 2006) 2398 UNTS 199, Art 1(1); Code of Conduct concerning the Repression of Piracy and Armed Robbery against Ships in the Western Indian Ocean and Gulf of Aden, 2009, reproduced in AV Lowe and S Talmon, *The Legal Order of the Oceans: Basic Documents on the Law of the Sea* (Oxford, Hart Publishing, 2009) 896, Art 1(2).

[19] See further M Gardner, 'Piracy Prosecutions in National Courts' (2012) 10 *Journal of International Criminal Justice* 797, 812–16.

[20] For any reader who thinks that there is a simple mathematical error here, it needs to be remembered that three parties to UNCLOS (the Cook Islands, Niue and the EU) are not members of the UN.

A. The *Actus Reus* of Piracy

According to Article 101(a) of UNCLOS, for an act to constitute piracy, the following conditions must be fulfilled. There must be (1) an 'illegal act of violence or detention, or an act of depredation', (2) 'committed for private ends', (3) 'by the crew or passengers of a private ship or aircraft', (4) directed against another ship or aircraft or against persons and property on board such ship or aircraft, (5) on the high seas or 'in a place outside the jurisdiction of any state'. Article 15 of the High Seas Convention contains an almost identical list of conditions.[21] Each of these five conditions requires some comment. As will be seen, the meaning of a number of these conditions is not altogether clear and requires interpretation. In engaging in such interpretation, one should be cautious of labelling as 'piracy' conduct that would not traditionally be regarded as piracy and justify the application of universal jurisdiction. Piracy is usually regarded as a serious criminal offence, punishable with severe penalties. It is the only maritime offence attracting universal jurisdiction (unlike, say, slave trading or drugs trafficking), justified because it is the use of indiscriminate and often savage violence to disrupt and menace international navigation and commerce on the high seas for purely mercenary ends: in that hackneyed phrase, pirates are the enemies of all mankind.[22] The fact that what may be regarded as undesirable conduct at sea is not, legally speaking, piracy does not necessarily mean that it is not susceptible to being effectively tackled in the absence of universal jurisdiction, as will be shown.

(i) An Illegal Act of Violence or Detention or an Act of Depredation

The first requirement for piracy is that there must be an illegal act of violence or detention or an act of depredation. These acts appear to be in the form of alternatives, ie to constitute piracy, either there must be an illegal act of violence or detention or there must be an act of depredation. As regards the first alternative, neither UNCLOS nor the High Seas Convention indicates the criteria by which an act of violence or detention is to be considered as illegal.[23] In the absence of such criteria, whether an act is legal or not must perforce be determined by national law. In the first instance, this will be the law of the flag state of the ship that arrests the alleged pirates; ultimately, it will be the law of the state where the alleged pirates are prosecuted, if different.[24] In practice, the issue is probably not very significant as it is difficult to contemplate how an act of violence by a private ship could be lawful—except, perhaps, where force was used in self-defence.

A much more important question is whether any illegal act of violence would constitute piracy (assuming the other four conditions listed above were fulfilled), or whether there needs to be a minimum level of violence. This issue has particularly arisen in

---

[21] The only difference is that, in relation to the first condition, the High Seas Convention, n 9 above, speaks of 'any illegal acts of violence, detention or any act of depredation'.

[22] See further the Harvard Commentary, n 13 above, 782 and 786–87; Halberstam, n 17 above, 288; P Birnie, 'Piracy: Past, Present and Future' (1987) 11 *Marine Policy* 163, 164 and 178.

[23] In this, UNCLOS and the High Seas Convention are like other treaties creating transnational crimes (see nn 5–8 above and accompanying text).

[24] This is the position of the Virginia Commentary, n 10 above, 200–01, a position that is said to follow from a brief debate in the Second Committee at the First UN Conference on the Law of the Sea, when a proposal to delete the word 'illegal' was rejected.

two specific contexts, hostilities between fishing vessels and what is often dubbed 'eco-piracy'. The latter is an undesirable term as it presupposes that the conduct in question is piracy, although that may often turn out not to be the case. Therefore a different term, environmental protest, will be used in this chapter. Hostilities between fishing vessels are not unknown, usually where one fishing vessel wishes to discourage another from fishing in the same area. For example, between 1994 and 1999 there were around 50 incidents in the Irish 200-mile zone and adjacent high seas, mainly in the form of foreign fishing vessels deliberately ramming Irish vessels or cutting their nets.[25] In response, the Irish government in 2001 drafted a bill to incorporate the UNCLOS definition of piracy into Irish law, there having been no Irish legislation on piracy before this point, and made it clear that it considered that the types of incident described above fell within the UNCLOS definition of piracy.[26] The bill was, however, eventually dropped. It is debatable whether the Irish government's position was correct or desirable. The incidents described hardly deserve the moral opprobrium tradition-ally reserved for piracy. Furthermore, few coastal states would be likely to welcome other states being able to enter their exclusive economic zone (EEZ) to arrest a fishing vessel, possibly having the nationality of the coastal state, for engaging in an act of violence against another fishing vessel. Instead of dealing with such incidents under the law of piracy, they can probably be addressed under the coastal state's general powers to regulate fishing in the EEZ. On the high seas fishing incidents are better dealt with under the SUA Convention than under the law of piracy. Although only the flag state of the offending vessel will have jurisdiction to arrest it on the high seas, the flag state of the victim vessel, in practice the only state likely to have an interest in the matter, will have adjudicative jurisdiction and may seek extradition of the alleged offenders if the flag state does not prosecute them.[27]

Turning to environmental protest, the most common form of such protest has been action to try to disrupt Japanese 'scientific' whaling in the Antarctic. Some of this action has involved acts of violence.[28] There has also been some use of violence by Japanese whaling ships against protesters. The Japanese government apparently does not regard such environmental protest as piracy, although it is not clear whether that is because in its view the violence used does not reach the necessary threshold to be considered piracy or because the protesters are not acting for 'private ends' (a matter discussed below).[29] It seems correct not to label such environmental protest as piracy because it does not fall within the rationale discussed earlier for treating piracy as a serious crime of universal jurisdiction. However, in a case decided in 1986, Belgian courts determined that protests by Greenpeace against the dumping of toxic wastes by

---

[25] CR Symmons, 'Use of the Law of Piracy to deal with Violent Inter-Vessel Incidents at Sea beyond the 12-Mile Limit: The Irish Experience' in CR Symmons (ed), *Selected Contemporary Issues in the Law of the Sea* (Leiden, Martinus Nijhoff Publishers, 2011) 169–70.

[26] The bill is discussed in considerable detail by Symmons.

[27] SUA Convention, n 8 above, Arts 6(1) and 10–11.

[28] For examples of such action, see Symmons, n 25 above, 192–93; A Kanehara, 'So-called "Eco-Piracy" and Interventions by NGOs to Protest against Scientific Research Whaling on the High Seas: An Evaluation of the Japanese Position' in Symmons (ed), n 25 above, 195, 196–97; SP Menefee, 'The Case of the *Castle John*, or Greenbeard Pirate?: Environmentalism, Piracy and the Development of International Law' (1993) 24 *California Western International Law Journal* 1, 7–10.

[29] Kanehara, ibid, 206.

Belgian vessels did amount to piracy.[30] The case turned largely on whether the 'private ends' requirement for piracy was satisfied, a question discussed below. Whether there was an illegal act of violence appears simply to have been assumed. The only acts of violence mentioned in the report of the case are boarding, occupying and causing some damage to the vessels engaged in dumping.[31] It is debatable whether this was violence on a sufficient scale for piracy.[32] In 2013 a US court of appeals, dealing with allegations of piracy relating to protests by an environmental NGO, Sea Shepherd, against Japanese whaling, unequivocally held that certain acts of violence by Sea Shepherd, which included ramming Japanese ships, fouling their propellers and hurling fiery and acid-filled projectiles at them, 'easily' qualified as 'illegal acts of violence' within the meaning of UNCLOS.[33]

What the discussion so far suggests is that for conduct to constitute piracy there must be a minimum threshold of violence, probably of a fairly serious nature (as in the *Sea Shepherd* case), otherwise there is a risk that the conduct will be labelled as piracy even though that label is not appropriate, given the rationale (explained above) for creating piracy as a crime of universal jurisdiction.[34] Furthermore, to label environmental protest as piracy risks stifling legitimate environmental protests at sea altogether.[35] There are ways of addressing violence at sea below the level that ought to be required for piracy, either through the SUA Convention or by other means.[36] However, in the case of Somali piracy, some domestic courts have accepted a relatively low threshold of violence as sufficient for piracy, such as the firing of shots at the victim vessel without causing injury to those on board or damage to the vessel.[37]

Turning to the alternative form of act, an act of depredation, the conventions offer no definition or guidance as to what is meant by depredation in this context. The French and Spanish texts appear to offer no assistance either, as they use the

---

[30] *Castle John and Nederlandse Stichting Sirius v NV Mabeco and NV Parfin*, Belgian Court of Cassation, (1986) 77 *International Law Reports* 537. The case was not a prosecution against Greenpeace but was concerned with whether an injunction could be granted to order Greenpeace from obstructing the dumping of waste on the high seas.

[31] Menefee, n 28 above, 11, relying on a different report of the case, mentions Greenpeace activists diving in front of the dumping vessels, attaching themselves to the vessels' discharge pipes, painting over windows on the bridge of the vessels and threatening to drop the anchors.

[32] This is also the view of two commentators quoted by Symmons, n 25, 177: see E David, 'Greenpeace: Des Pirates!' (1989) 22 *Revue Belge de Droit International* 295; G Starkle, 'Piraterie en haut mer et competence pénale internationale' (1987) *Revue de Droit Pénale et de Criminologie* 735.

[33] United States Court of Appeals for the Ninth Circuit, *Institute of Cetacean Research et al v Sea Shepherd Conservation Society*, available at http://cdn.ca9.uscourts.gov/datastore/general/2013/02/25/1235266. pdf (accessed on 28 August 2013).

[34] This is also the position of Kanehara, one of the very few writers to discuss this issue: see Kanehara, n 28 above, 211.

[35] See further J Teulings, 'Peaceful Protests against Whaling on the High Seas—A Human-Rights Based Approach' in Symmons (ed), n 25 above, 221, especially 229–31 and 235–45.

[36] Kanehara, n 28 above, 204–19.

[37] High Court of Kenya, *Hassan M Ahmed v Republic* [2009] eKLR, available at http://kenyalaw.org/ CaseSearch/view_preview1.php?link=66028601162227766885163 (accessed on 13 January 2013) (in this case the crew of the victim ship were described as also having been 'roughed up' by the pirates); Supreme Court of Seychelles, *Republic v Dahir and 10 others* [2010] SCSC 81, available at http://www.seylii.org/ sc/judgment/supreme-court/2010/81 (accessed on 13 January 2013), para 51; US Court of Appeals (Fourth Circuit), *United States v Dire et al* (23 May 2012), available at http://www.ca4.uscourts.gov/opinions/ Published/114310.p.pdf (accessed on 13 January 2013). In *Dahir*, which is discussed by Gardner, n 19 above, 799–800, the applicable law was the English law of 1976 rather than subsequent Seychelles law incorporating the UNCLOS definition of piracy. In the other cases the courts based themselves on the UNCLOS definition.

terms 'déprédation' and 'depredación', respectively. Therefore the term presumably has the meaning to be found in a dictionary. However, not all dictionary definitions have quite the same shade of meaning. The *Concise Oxford Dictionary*, for example, defines depredation as 'an act of attacking or plundering',[38] whereas the *Chambers English Dictionary* defines it as 'act of plundering'.[39] Their definitions of 'plunder' are, however, similar, the *Concise Oxford Dictionary* defining it as to 'forcibly steal goods from'[40] and *Chambers* as 'to carry off the goods of by force: to pillage: to carry off as booty: to carry off booty from'.[41] Thus, depredation in the context of piracy appears to mean stealing goods from a ship by force, and possibly also merely attacking a ship. Since both involve some force, there is a substantial overlap with the alternative requirement of an act of violence.

(ii) Private Ends

Turning now to the second element of the crime of piracy, the act of violence, detention or depredation must be for 'private ends'. The conventions give no definition of 'private ends', nor do their drafting histories give any real guidance as to the meaning of the phrase. The French and Spanish texts shed no light, either. The French text has the phrase 'fins privés', which is identical to the English. The Spanish 'propósito personal' translates as 'personal purpose', which probably means almost the same as the English and French texts. Likewise, the Harvard draft convention required an act of violence or depredation to be for 'private ends' to constitute piracy, but also did not define that phrase. In the commentary it was argued that piracy did not include acts of violence or depredation for 'political ends, whether they are made on behalf of states, or of recognised belligerent organisations, or of unrecognised revolutionary bands'.[42]

In the contemporary literature it seems generally agreed that acts of violence or depredation committed for purely mercenary reasons fall into the category of 'private ends', but that acts carried out on the authority of states or by recognised or unrecognised insurgents (at least insofar as acts are directed only against ships of the state against which the insurgency is taking place) are not for 'private ends' and therefore cannot constitute piracy. At the present day most attacks on shipping come into the former category (ie they are carried out for purely mercenary reasons). Nevertheless, there are some acts that fall between that category and the latter category of acts authorised by a state or carried out by insurgents, notably environmental protest and acts carried out by terrorists, each of which has some form of political or ideological motive. Some writers argue that any act of violence or depredation against a ship not authorised by a state or carried out by insurgents is for 'private ends', including therefore attacks by terrorists and environmental protesters.[43] Other writers, however, argue

---

[38] *Concise Oxford Dictionary*, 10th edn (Oxford, Oxford University Press, 1999) 385.
[39] *Chambers English Dictionary* (Cambridge, Cambridge University Press, 1988) 380.
[40] *Concise Oxford Dictionary*, n 38 above, 1101.
[41] *Chambers English Dictionary*, n 39 above, 1122.
[42] Above n 13, 786. See also 798 and 857.
[43] See, eg Boister, n 4 above, 30–31; ED Brown, *The International Law of the Sea*, vol I (Aldershot, Dartmouth, 1994) 301; D Guilfoyle, 'Piracy off Somalia: UN Security Council Resolution 1816 and IMO Regional Counter-piracy Efforts' (2008) 57 *International & Comparative Law Quarterl* 690, 693–94 and

that any act with some form of political motive, including therefore terrorist acts and environmental protest, is not for private ends and so cannot be piracy.[44]

It is debatable whether either of these positions is correct. It is useful to distinguish between acts by terrorists and environmental protest. As regards the former, the Supreme Court of Seychelles has suggested that terrorism, at least for the purposes of the law of Seychelles, usually involves indiscriminate violence with the objective of influencing governments for political ends. Such acts could not be for 'private ends'.[45] It is questionable whether this view is correct. Insofar as the rationale for labelling conduct as piracy is that it constitutes an indiscriminate and violent menace to international shipping and commerce (as argued above),[46] terrorist acts generally fall within such conduct. Furthermore, it is difficult to see how a warship, contemplating the arrest of, say, a foreign skiff that was attacking an oil tanker on the high seas in the Gulf of Aden, could distinguish between whether those in the skiff were acting for purely mercenary ends or for a terrorist purpose. If it subsequently turned out to be the latter, the view that terrorist acts are not to be regarded as being for 'private ends' would mean that the arrest would be unlawful and the flag state of the warship would be liable to the flag state of the skiff for any loss or damage caused by the arrest and seizure of the skiff, in accordance with Article 106 of UNCLOS. Such a result seems absurd, and contrary to the object and purpose of UNCLOS. It would therefore seem preferable to regard acts carried out by terrorists as being for 'private ends' as far as the law of piracy is concerned.[47]

However, the opposite position should be taken as far as environmental protest is concerned, since such protest is not an indiscriminate menace to international shipping but is instead directed at a very specific object, such as Japanese whaling, the dumping of toxic waste or oil exploration in environmentally sensitive areas. Thus, environmental protests should not be regarded as being committed for 'private ends' and therefore potentially piracy.[48] However, this position is contradicted by the decision of the Belgian Cour de Cassation (Belgium's highest court in general cases) in the *Castle John* case.[49] The court held that the acts of members of Greenpeace

---

699; D Guilfoyle, *Shipping Interdiction and the Law of the Sea* (Cambridge, Cambridge University Press, 2009) 32–42; Chapter 2 below.

[44] See, eg the Virginia Commentary, n 10 above, 200; Birnie, n 22 above, 177; I Bantekas, *International Criminal Law*, 4th edn (Oxford, Hart Publishing, 2010) 301; P Campbell, 'A Modern History of the International Legal Definition of Piracy' in BA Elleman, A Forbes and D Rosenberg (eds), *Piracy and Maritime Crime. Historical and Modern Case Studies* (Newport, RI, Naval War College Press, 2010) 19, 24; R Collins and D Hassan, 'Application and Shortcomings of the Law of the Sea in Combating Piracy: A South East Asian Perpsective' (2009) 40 *Journal of Maritime Law and Commerce* 89, 98–99; IMO Secretariat, 'Piracy: Uniform and Consistent Application of the Provisions of International Conventions Relating to Piracy', IMO Legal Committee document LEG 98/8 (18 February 2011), attached to IMO Circular Letter No 3180 (17 May 2011) 3, available at http://www.un.org/Depts/los/piracy/circular_letter_3180.pdf (accessed on 11 January 2013).

[45] *Republic v Dahir and 10 others*, n 37 above, para 37. This aspect of the case is discussed by Gardner, n 19 above, 811.

[46] See text at n 22 above.

[47] Halberstam reaches the same conclusion, following in part the reasoning here: see Halberstam, n 17 above, 282–83 and 290. So, too, Guilfoyle, Chapter 2 below.

[48] So, too, JL Jesus, 'Protection of Foreign Ships against Piracy and Terrorism at Sea' (2003) 18 *International Journal of Marine and Coastal Law* 363, 379.

[49] Above n 30.

protesting against the dumping of noxious waste were carried out for 'private ends', observing that Greenpeace had not argued that

> the acts at issue were committed in the interest or to the detriment of a state or a state system rather than purely in support of a personal point of view concerning a particular problem, even if they reflected a political perspective.[50]

The decision has been strongly criticised,[51] and should probably be regarded as incorrect. Nevertheless, the same position as the Belgian Cour de Cassation has recently been taken by a US court of appeals in the *Sea Shepherd* case, referred to earlier. The court held that '"private ends" include those pursued on personal, moral or philosophical grounds, such as Sea Shepherd's professed environmental goals. That the perpetrators believe themselves to be serving the public good does not render their ends public.'[52]

The conclusion that emerges from the above discussion is that acts of violence or depredation against shipping that are carried out for purely mercenary reasons or by terrorists are committed for private ends. On the other hand, such acts that are carried out by insurgents or are authorised by a state are not committed for private ends and so cannot constitute piracy. Environmental protest has been considered by two national courts to be for private ends, but it is debatable whether that is the correct position.

(iii) Commission by the Crew or Passengers of a Private Ship or Private Aircraft

The third condition for piracy is that an act of violence, detention or depredation must be committed by the crew or passengers of a 'private ship or private aircraft'. The term 'private ship' is not defined in the conventions, nor is it a term of art. The implication from Article 102 of UNCLOS and Article 16 of the High Seas Convention, which are discussed shortly below, is that a private ship is any ship that is not a warship or otherwise used for governmental purposes.[53] Similarly, a private aircraft is any aircraft that is not a military aircraft or one used for governmental purposes.[54] Although the conventions provide that piracy may be committed by a private aircraft, there appear to be few, if any, recorded instances of piracy by aircraft. The ILC rejected the possibility of piracy being committed by warships or other government ships because their immunity from the jurisdiction of states other than the flag state on the high seas meant that any attempt to seize such ships 'might involve the gravest consequences' and would be 'prejudicial to the interests of the international community'.[55] However, Article 102 of UNCLOS and Article 16 of the High Seas Convention provide that, where the crew of a warship or other government ship has mutinied and taken control of that ship, the latter is assimilated to a private ship for the purposes of piracy. It is reported that in some parts of the world government-owned launches are taken out unofficially to engage in acts that if committed by

---

[50] Ibid, 540.
[51] See, eg Menefee, n 28 above, 14–16; David and Starkle, n 32 above.
[52] See n 33 above.
[53] Warships are defined in Art 29 of UNCLOS, n 1 above.
[54] There appears to be no official definition of military aircraft in international law.
[55] Above n 11, 282. For the immunity of such ships, see Arts 8 and 9 of the High Seas Convention, n 9 above; Arts 95 and 96 of UNCLOS, n 1 above.

private ships would be piracy.[56] For example, in 1997 the UAE complained of such acts by Iranian launches.[57] Where the flag state of a launch disavows such acts, it would be reasonable to regard the crew of the launch as having mutinied and for their acts, therefore, to amount to piracy.[58]

(iv) The Victim

The fourth condition for an act to be piracy is that it must be committed by one ship or aircraft against another ship or aircraft. The possibility of an aircraft being the victim of a piratical attack was not included in the ILC's draft articles,[59] but was added at the 1958 Conference. The Virginia Commentary states that, for an aircraft to be the victim of a piratical attack, it must actually be on the surface of the sea, for example a floating seaplane.[60] It is questionable whether this view is correct. It appears to be based partly on the ILC's comment that an attack by one aircraft on another 'in the air' would not be piracy, and partly on the fact that piracy must occur 'on' the high seas. As to the first, probably not too much should be read into the ILC's commentary since it did not propose that an aircraft could be the victim of piracy in any circumstances. As for the Virginia Commentary's second justification, the phrase 'on the high seas' is used frequently in the conventions but it is clear that it does not usually mean literally on the surface of the sea. If it did, there would be no high seas freedom of navigation for submarines nor would vessels be entitled to fish below the surface of the sea. Nevertheless, even if an attack on one aircraft by another in the air does constitute piracy, such attacks are in practice probably better dealt with under the Montreal Convention,[61] within whose scope they will generally fall, rather than under the law of piracy. Interestingly, the Regional Cooperation Agreement on Combatting Piracy and Armed Robbery against Ships in Asia excludes attacks on aircraft from its definition of piracy.[62]

The Virginia Commentary also states that to be the victim of a piratical act a ship or aircraft must be a private one.[63] There is no support for such a position in the text or drafting history of the conventions, and it is contradicted by the decisions of municipal courts.[64] Nor is the position desirable on policy grounds. If an attack on a government ship or aircraft did not constitute piracy, it would not be possible to arrest the attacking ship or aircraft under the universal jurisdiction that is applicable to piracy. Some other basis would have to be sought, such as self-defence, the conditions for the application of which might not always be fulfilled.

---

[56] RR Churchill and AV Lowe, *The Law of the Sea*, 3rd edn (Manchester, Manchester University Press, 1999) 210.

[57] (1997) 33 *Law of the Sea Bulletin* 91.

[58] Churchill and Lowe, n 56 above, 210. Shearer, however, cautions against considering disobedience to orders by the crew of government ships as mutiny: see Shearer, n 3 above, para 17.

[59] In its commentary on its draft articles the ILC expressed the view that an attack by one aircraft on another 'in the air' would not be piracy: n 11 above, 282.

[60] Above n 10, 201.

[61] See n 6 above. See also Campbell, n 44 above, 25; Rubin, n 11 above, 326.

[62] Above n 18, Art 1(1).

[63] Above n 10, 200.

[64] See, eg *Dahir*, n 37 above (the victim ship was a Seychelles coastguard patrol vessel); *United States v Dire*, n 37 above (the victim ship was a US frigate).

(v) Place of Commission

Lastly, to constitute piracy, an act that meets the preceding conditions must take place on the high seas or 'in a place outside the jurisdiction of any state'. According to the ILC, the latter phrase means a terra nullius.[65] In practice, the only terra nullius today is in Antarctica. It certainly includes the unclaimed part of Antarctica (Marie Byrd Land). Whether it includes the parts of Antarctica claimed by certain states is debatable, and depends on how one interprets the Antarctic Treaty, 1959.[66] It does not seem worth discussing this question here as piracy in the Antarctic would seem extremely unlikely in practice.

Of much greater significance is the fact that Article 58(2) of UNCLOS provides that Articles 88–115 (which include the provisions dealing with piracy) apply in the 200-mile EEZ to the extent that they are not incompatible with the regime of the EEZ. There is no such obvious incompatibility in the case of piracy. Therefore, if an act that otherwise fulfils the conditions for piracy is committed in the EEZ, it will constitute piracy.[67] Here there is a difference with the High Seas Convention. The EEZ did not exist at the time that the Convention was adopted. However, even before the entry into force of UNCLOS, the EEZ was recognised as being part of customary international law.[68] If Article 58(2) is accepted as being part of customary international law, as seems likely, that means that, even in respect of non-parties to UNCLOS, piracy may be committed in the EEZ. On the other hand, acts that would otherwise fulfil the conditions for piracy will not be piracy if committed in the territorial sea. However, that does not mean that there is necessarily a gap in the law. There is nothing to stop a coastal state criminalising acts committed in its territorial sea that if committed on the high seas or EEZ would constitute piracy; indeed, many states have undoubtedly done so. The term 'armed robbery' is usually used to label such acts.[69]

B. *Mens Rea*

The *mens rea* for transnational crimes other than piracy is explicitly stated by the treaties establishing those crimes as being intent.[70] The *mens rea* of piracy is not explicitly stated in UNCLOS and the High Seas Convention, but appears also to be intent. That seems to follow from Article 101(b) of UNCLOS and Article 15(2) of the High Seas Convention, which provide that piracy includes any act of 'voluntary par-

---

[65] Above n 11, 282.

[66] Antarctic Treaty (adopted 1 December 1959, entered into force 23 June 1961) 402 UNTS 71.

[67] This is the view of virtually all commentators: see, eg the Virginia Commentary, n 10 above, 184 and 202; Shearer, n 3 above, para 19; JA Roach, 'Countering Piracy off Somalia: International Law and International Institutions' (2010) 104 *American Journal of International Law* 397, 398–99. This position has also been taken by the Supreme Court of Seychelles, n 37 above, para 57.

[68] Churchill and Lowe, above n 56 above, 161.

[69] See IMO Assembly Resolution 1025, n 18 above, para 2.2; Regional Cooperation Agreement on Combatting Piracy and Armed Robbery against Ships in Asia, n 18 above, Art 1(2); Code of Conduct concerning the Repression of Piracy and Armed Robbery against Ships in the Western Indian Ocean and Gulf of Aden, above n 18, Art 1(2). The UN Security Council frequently uses the term 'armed robbery' in its piracy resolutions but has never defined it. It is generally assumed that the term is intended to have the same meaning as in the instruments just referred to.

[70] See, eg Montreal Convention, n 6 above, Art 1(1); SUA Convention, n 8 above, Art 3(1).

ticipation in the operation of a ship or an aircraft with knowledge of facts making it a pirate ship or aircraft': a 'pirate ship' is defined in the conventions as a ship 'intended by the persons in dominant control' to be used for committing acts of piracy or which has already committed such acts and is still under the control of the persons who committed those acts.[71] It is difficult to see how a person could voluntarily participate in the operation of a pirate ship without doing so with intent. One form of *mens rea* which is not required, according to the ILC, is an intention to rob.[72]

C. Related Inchoate Offences

Inchoate offences typically include attempt, conspiracy, and encouraging and assisting a crime. Although using slightly different language, the conventions make the last of these part of the transnational crime of piracy. Article 101(c) of UNCLOS and Article 15(3) of the High Seas Convention provide that 'any act of inciting or of intentionally facilitating' an act of the kind analysed in Section A above is part of the crime of piracy. Unlike the principal offence, there is no geographical limitation on where these inchoate offences may be committed. On the other hand, the conventions do not mention attempt or conspiracy. A proposal at the 1958 Conference to include attempted piracy as an offence was rejected.[73] Given that history, and the fact that international human rights law requires that for an act to constitute a crime it must be explicitly and clearly spelt out in the law, attempted piracy and conspiracy to commit piracy cannot be regarded as part of the transnational crime of piracy.[74] There is, however, nothing to prevent individual states criminalising such acts under their domestic law—and, indeed, a number of states have so legislated[75]—but such national crimes will not be subject to universal jurisdiction.[76]

D. Criticisms of the LOSC Definition of Piracy

The definition of piracy in the High Seas Convention and UNCLOS has frequently been subject to considerable criticism. One of its harshest critics, O'Connell, described the definition as 'one of the least successful essays in Codification in the Law of the

---

[71] UNCLOS, n 1 above, Art 103; High Seas Convention, n 9 above, Art 17. A 'pirate aircraft' is not defined, but presumably the same definition applies *mutatis mutandis*. The definition of a pirate ship is not wholly free of difficulties, especially the first limb of the definition. In practice it may be difficult to know, especially by a warship contemplating exercising universal enforcement jurisdiction, whether a ship is intended by those in control of it to be used for committing an act of piracy.

[72] Above n 11, 282.

[73] United Nations Conference on the Law of the Sea, Official Records, vol IV (1958), 84 and 137.

[74] The Virginia Commentary takes the contrary view as regards attempts: see n 10 above, 202.

[75] See the collection of national legislation on piracy at http://www.un.org/Depts/los/piracy/piracy_national_legislation.htm (accessed on 11 January 2013). One of the Security Council's resolutions on Somali piracy calls on states to make attempted piracy a criminal offence: see Resolution 1976 (2011), para 13.

[76] This is also the position taken by DOALOS. See DOALOS, 'Piracy: Elements of National Legislation Pursuant to the United Nations Convention on the Law of the Sea, 1982', IMO Legal Committee document LEG 98/8/1 (18 February 2011), attached to IMO Circular Letter No 3180 (17 May 2011), 5, available at http://www.un.org/Depts/los/piracy/circular_letter_3180.pdf (accessed on 11 January 2013).

Sea' because of its 'elliptical nature'.[77] One set of criticisms goes less to the elliptical nature of the definition but rather focuses on the perceived narrowness of the definition.[78] A first criticism is that the definition does not cover illegal acts committed against a ship or its crew by persons on board the ship. Such criticism was prompted, at least in part, by events such as the *Achille Lauro* incident (1985), where members of the Palestine Liberation Front, posing as passengers, took control of the eponymous Italian cruise ship on the high seas, held the crew and passengers hostage while demanding the release of Palestinian prisoners from Israeli jails, and threw a disabled American passenger overboard in his wheelchair.[79] There was originally some force in this criticism of the definition of piracy, but illegal acts committed against a ship by those on board are now covered by the SUA Convention, although they are not subject to universal jurisdiction.[80] Even though the SUA Convention was not widely ratified in the years following its adoption, it has now received almost as many ratifications as UNCLOS, having 160 parties as at the end of 2012.

A second criticism of the definition of piracy in the conventions is that it is limited to acts for 'private ends'. This criticism has force if the view is taken that private ends exclude acts of violence committed with any kind of political motive. However, it was suggested above that this view is not correct— and even if it were correct, most political acts of violence against ships would be offences under the SUA Convention as the latter has no 'private ends' or similar requirement. What can certainly be criticised is the lack of clarity as to the meaning of the phrase 'private ends' as used in UNCLOS and the High Seas Convention.

A third criticism is that piracy is limited to acts taking place on the high seas or in the EEZ. This criticism seems misplaced. If piracy could be committed in the territorial sea and was subject to the universal enforcement jurisdiction that applies to piracy committed on the high seas or EEZ, it would cause potentially serious conflict with the rights and jurisdiction of the coastal state.[81] In 2008 the UN Security Council adopted a resolution in which it authorised the ships of states other than Somalia to enter Somalia's territorial sea 'for the purpose of repressing acts of piracy and armed robbery at sea, in a manner consistent with such action permitted on the high seas with respect to piracy under relevant international law'.[82] There seems to be no intention with this resolution to change the traditional definition of piracy.[83] Rather, the intention seems to be to permit a kind of inverted hot pursuit where foreign warships

---

[77] O'Connell, n 3 above, 970. Another harsh critic is Rubin, n 11 above, 333.

[78] See, eg Collins and Hassan, n 44 above, 97–100.

[79] See further Halberstam, n 17 above, 269–70.

[80] Above n 8. In 2005, the SUA Convention was extensively amended, but those amendments do not affect the point being made here.

[81] See further Gardner, n 19 above, 810.

[82] Resolution 1816 (2008), para 7. The authorisation given by this resolution, which is discussed in more detail below (see text at nn 96–103), has subsequently been extended. See n 97 below.

[83] However, the Institute of International Law and Treves appears to consider, though not without some ambiguity, that it does: see, respectively, Institute of International Law, Naples Declaration on Piracy, 10 September 2009, para 4, available at http://www.idi-iil.org/idiE/declarationsE/2009_Naples_EN.pdf (accessed on 12 January 2013); T Treves, 'Piracy and the International Law of the Sea' (2009) 20 *European Journal of International Law* 399, 404. The position taken in the text is supported by Guilfoyle, 'Piracy off Somalia', n 43 above, 696; JA Roach, 'General Problematic Issues on Exercise of Jurisdiction over Modern Instances of Piracy' in Symmons (ed), n 25 above, 119, 123.

may follow suspected Somali pirates into Somalia's territorial sea and arrest them there, without this being a violation of Somalia's sovereignty.

There are a number of other criticisms of the conventions' definition of piracy, going more to its 'elliptical nature', that follow from the discussion above but that do not often appear to be made. They include uncertainty as to the criteria by which the legality or otherwise of an act of violence or detention is to be established and uncertainty as to whether a minimum level of violence is required; the precise meaning of depredation; uncertainty as to the circumstances in which an aircraft, or a state-owned ship, may be either the perpetrator or the victim of an act of piracy; and a lack of clarity concerning the *mens rea* required for piracy. In practice, these matters will fall to be determined by national courts. That may well lead to diverging or incorrect interpretations—as, indeed, has already happened to some degree. It is also a weakness that the conventions do not include attempted piracy and conspiracy to commit piracy as part of the transnational crime of piracy.

III. JURISDICTIONAL ISSUES RELATING TO THE SUPPRESSION OF PIRACY

UNCLOS and the High Seas Convention are concerned only with enforcement jurisdiction in respect of piracy. Even then, they do not deal comprehensively with the issue. It is therefore desirable to consider the matter in rather more detail than the conventions do; and this is done in Subsection B below. It is also desirable, indeed necessary, to say something first about legislative jurisdiction in relation to piracy (Subsection A), a matter on which the conventions are conspicuously silent, and finally to consider adjudicative jurisdiction (Subsection C).

A. Legislative Jurisdiction

It is not so strange that the High Seas Convention has nothing to say about legislative jurisdiction in relation to piracy since that convention was adopted before the modern wave of conventions creating transnational criminal offences. It is rather more surprising that UNCLOS has nothing to say about legislative jurisdiction, given that, shortly before and during the Third UN Conference on the Law of the Sea at which UNCLOS was drafted, the first treaties creating transnational crimes were adopted.[84] Those conventions require their parties to establish legislative jurisdiction over the crimes in question and to make those crimes punishable by severe penalties.[85] The fact that UNCLOS does not include similar provisions may probably be explained by a general desire among participants at the Third UN Conference on the Law of the Sea not to change the status quo and simply incorporate the High Seas Convention's provisions on piracy into UNCLOS without making any substantive changes, and possibly also by a lack of awareness of the conclusion of the trans-

---

[84] See the treaties listed in nn 5–7 above as well as the Convention on the Prevention and Punishment of Crimes against Internationally Protected Persons, including Diplomatic Agents (adopted 14 December 1973, entered into force 20 February 1977) 1035 UNTS 107 (hereafter the Diplomats Convention).

[85] See, eg Montreal Convention, n 6 above, Arts 3 and 5; Diplomats Convention, Art 3; Hostages Convention, n 7 above, Art 2.

national crime conventions mentioned. The omission of any provisions in UNCLOS on legislative jurisdiction concerning piracy is regrettable as it has become apparent that a significant number of states currently do not have any legislation on piracy or do not have legislation that fully incorporates the provisions of UNCLOS.[86] This has led the IMO, the UN General Assembly and the UN Security Council to urge states that currently do not have any, or comprehensive, legislation on piracy to make good this omission.[87] Without such legislation it is not possible for states to arrest and prosecute alleged pirates, at least on the basis of universal jurisdiction.[88] Roach has argued that Article 100 of UNCLOS, which provides that states are to cooperate in the repression of piracy (and is discussed in more detail below), requires states to enact the necessary legislation.[89] This is debatable, and does not seem to be supported by other writers.[90]

B. Enforcement Jurisdiction

Turning now from legislative jurisdiction to enforcement jurisdiction, Article 105 of UNCLOS provides that '[o]n the high seas, or in any other place outside the jurisdiction of any state, *every* state may seize a pirate ship or aircraft, or a ship or aircraft taken by piracy and under the control of pirates, and arrest the persons and seize the property on board' (emphasis added). In other words, enforcement jurisdiction is universal. Article 19 of the High Seas Convention is to similar effect.[91] Articles 105 and 19 are exceptions to the principle that on the high seas a ship may normally be arrested only by its flag state.[92] Allied to the right of arrest under Articles 105 and 19, there is a power under Article 110 of UNCLOS and Article 22 of the High Seas Convention for warships to board other ships if there is 'reasonable ground for suspecting' that they are 'engaged in piracy'.

UNCLOS and the High Seas Convention set out a number of conditions that must be met in order for an arrest to be valid. These conditions are supplemented by certain other requirements deriving from other sources of international law. First, the arrest of an alleged pirate ship must be effected by a warship, military aircraft or other ship/aircraft on government service and authorised to this effect.[93] As a quasi-exception to this condition, the ILC suggested, in its commentary on what became Article 21 of the

---

[86] IMO Secretariat, n 44 above, 1; UN Security Council Resolutions 1918 (2010), preambular paras 13 and 14, and 2077 (2012), preambular para 14; Roach, n 83 above, 132–34; H Tuerk, *Reflections on the Contemporary Law of the Sea* (Leiden, Martinus Nijhoff Publishers, 2012) 75 and 84.

[87] See, inter alia, IMO Assembly Resolutions A.1025(26) (2009), n 18 above, para 3.1 and A.1044(27) (2011), para 8(n), available at http://www.imo.org/OurWork/Security/PiracyArmedRobbery/Guidance/Documents/A.1044_27.pdf (accessed on 14 January 2012); UN General Assembly Resolution 65/37 (2010), paras 85–86; UN Security Council Resolutions 1918 (2010), para 2, 2018 (2011), para 2 and 2077 (2012), para 18. Resolution 2015 (2011), para 11 calls on UN members to report to the UN Secretary-General on the measures that they have taken to criminalise piracy.

[88] See further Gardner, n 19 above, 802–03.

[89] Roach, n 83 above, 121 and 132.

[90] See, eg A Murdoch, 'Recent Legal Issues and Problems Relating to Acts of Piracy off Somalia' in Symmons (ed), n 25 above, 139, 150.

[91] The only difference is that the second 'or aircraft' in UNCLOS was not included in the High Seas Convention.

[92] See Art 92(1) of UNCLOS, n 1 above; Art 6(1) of High Seas Convention, n 9 above.

[93] UNCLOS, ibid, Art 107; High Seas Convention, ibid, Art 21.

High Seas Convention, that it would be possible for a vessel that was attacked by a suspected pirate ship to overpower the latter as an exercise of 'its right of self-defence' and hand it over 'to a warship or to the authorities of a coastal state'.[94]

Secondly, the arresting ship must reasonably suspect that the ship that it intends to arrest is a pirate ship. This condition is not explicitly stated in the conventions but appears to be implicit in two of their provisions. First, Article 106 of UNCLOS and Article 20 of the High Seas Convention provide that, where the seizure of a ship on suspicion of piracy has been made 'without adequate grounds', the seizing state is liable to the flag state of the seized ship for any loss or damage caused by the seizure. 'Adequate grounds' in this context would seem to include a requirement of reasonable suspicion. Secondly, as mentioned above, Article 110 of UNCLOS and Article 22 of the High Seas Convention stipulate that a warship may only board a suspected pirate ship where it has 'reasonable ground' for its suspicions. If boarding requires reasonable suspicion that the ship to be boarded is a pirate ship, that must apply *a fortiori* to arrest.

A third condition for the arrest of a suspected pirate ship is that the arrest must take place on the high seas or in a place outside the jurisdiction of any state. As seen earlier, the high seas also include the EEZ for the purposes of piracy.[95] As mentioned above, the UN Security Council has created a temporary exception to this condition in the case of Somali pirates. The Council, acting under Chapter VII of the UN Charter, has decided that states cooperating with the Transitional Federal Government of Somalia (TFG) (since August 2012 the Federal Government of Somalia—FGS) in the fight against piracy off the coast of Somalia, for which advance notification has been provided by the FGS to the UN Secretary-General,

> may enter the territorial waters of Somalia for the purpose of repressing acts of piracy and armed robbery at sea, in a manner consistent with such action permitted on the high seas with respect to piracy under relevant international law; and use, within the territorial waters of Somalia, in a manner consistent with action permitted on the high seas with respect to piracy under relevant international law, all necessary means to repress acts of piracy and armed robbery.[96]

Not only is this authorisation temporary, although the six-month period for which it was originally given has been continuously extended by 12-month periods down to the time of writing (December 2012),[97] it is hedged about with various caveats—it applies only to Somalia, it does not affect the rights or obligations of UN members under international law, it does not create customary international law, it is given with the consent of the FGS, and its exercise must not deny or impair the right of innocent passage in Somalia's territorial sea.[98] Treves has argued that the fact that the entry of foreign warships to Somalia's territorial sea to suppress piracy requires the consent of the TFG/FGS/Somali authorities means that, strictly speaking, the authorisation of

---

[94] Above n 11, 283.
[95] See text at n 67.
[96] UN Security Council Resolution 1816 (2008), para 7.
[97] See Resolutions 1846 (2008), para 10, 1897 (2009), para 7, 1950 (2010), para 7, 2020 (2011), para 9 and 2077 (2012), para 12. With the last resolution the term TFG has been replaced by 'Somali authorities'. On this change, see Resolution 2067 (2012), para 14.
[98] Resolution 1816, paras 8 and 9. These caveats are repeated in all the resolutions referred to in the previous footnote.

the Security Council was not required, but he suggests that it was given for political reasons.[99] One such reason may be related to the doubt as to what is meant by Somalia's territorial sea in the context of the Security Council's resolutions. At the time that Resolution 1816 was adopted, Somalia claimed a 200-mile territorial sea, in clear violation of UNCLOS, which permits a maximum breadth of 12 miles.[100] It seems that other states and the Security Council treat Somalia's territorial sea as being no more than 12 miles in breadth for the purposes of suppressing piracy.[101] The Security Council has urged Somalia to delimit its maritime spaces in accordance with UNCLOS and to enact legislation to provide for a 200-mile EEZ (and presumably therefore a 12-mile territorial sea).[102] Whether Somalia has yet heeded this call, the writer does not know. In practice, it appears that little use has been made of the authorisation to arrest pirates in Somalia's territorial sea.[103]

Elsewhere than Somalia, the consequence that an arrest must take place on the high seas or in the EEZ is that a pirate ship could seek to evade arrest by fleeing to a territorial sea, whether of its flag state or another state. However, it would not necessarily evade arrest by so doing. Such a ship would almost certainly not be exercising a right of innocent passage in the territorial sea, because the ship would not be in 'passage' as defined by Article 18 of UNCLOS, ie navigating in the territorial sea 'for the purpose of traversing that sea without entering internal waters' or 'proceeding to or from internal waters'. Furthermore, in the unlikely event that it was in 'passage', the ship's passage would probably not be 'innocent' because it would threaten the 'peace, good order or security' of the coastal state by engaging in an activity (evading arrest) 'not having a direct bearing on passage', as provided for in Article 19(2)(l) of UNCLOS. If the alleged pirate ship was not in innocent passage, it would be subject to the full enforcement jurisdiction of the coastal state. The latter would therefore have the right to arrest the ship. Whether it had an obligation to do so is debatable. Article 100 of UNCLOS and Article 14 of the High Seas Convention, which are discussed in more detail below, require all states to cooperate to the fullest possible extent in the repression of piracy, but this obligation applies only on the high seas and in places outside the jurisdiction of any state. However, it could be argued that the spirit of Articles 100 and 14 requires states to give effect to their obligation to cooperate to repress piracy in any area, including their territorial sea. This point is explored further below in the context of adjudicative jurisdiction.

The other conditions governing the arrest of suspected pirate ships are found not in UNCLOS or the High Seas Convention but in other sources of international law. First, under customary international law, when one ship is trying to arrest another at sea, the use of force must be avoided as far as possible; however, where the use of force is unavoidable, 'it must not go beyond what is reasonable and necessary in the circumstances'.[104] Secondly, in effecting the arrest of a suspected pirate ship, the arresting

[99] Treves, n 83 above, 406–08.

[100] UNCLOS, n 1 above, Art 3.

[101] Roach, n 67 above, 402; Treves, n 83 above, 408. See also Roach, n 83 above, 123.

[102] See Resolutions 1976 (2011), para 6, 2067 (2012), para 13 and 2077 (2012), para 4.

[103] D Guilfoyle, 'Counter-piracy Law Enforcement and Human Rights' (2010) 59 *International & Comparative Law Quarterly* 141, 147.

[104] International Tribunal for the Law of the Sea, *Saiga No 2 case (St Vincent v Guinea)* [1999] ITLOS Rep 10, para 155. See also paras 156–59; D Guilfoyle, 'Prosecuting Somali Pirates: A Critical Evaluation of the Options' (2012) 10 *Journal of International Criminal Justice* 767, 773–74; Treves, n 83 above, 412–14.

ship or aircraft must observe the international human rights obligations by which its flag state is bound. It is significant, and welcome, that this has been recognised by the UN Security Council in its resolutions on piracy of the past few years.[105] The human rights obligations most relevant in this context are that no one may be arrested and deprived of their liberty except on such grounds as are established by law; and that anyone who has been arrested must be informed of the reasons for their arrest and brought promptly before a judge.[106] The only case law of international human rights courts and treaty bodies relating to the application of these obligations at sea appears to be that of the European Court of Human Rights. In 2010, in *Medvedyev v France*, which concerned the arrest by a French warship of a Cambodian ship suspected of drugs trafficking on the high seas off Cape Verde, the Grand Chamber of the Court began by finding that the ECHR could apply at sea, previously a matter of some uncertainty as the Court's earlier case law had emphasised the primarily territorial application of the ECHR. In this case, the Grand Chamber held that the ECHR applied because France had 'exercised full and exclusive control' over the ship and its crew from the time of their arrest until they were brought before a French court.[107] It thus follows that, whenever a warship of a state party to the ECHR arrests suspected pirates, the ECHR will apply. In *Medvedyev*, the Grand Chamber found that the arrest was unlawful because there was no right under international law for a warship to arrest a foreign ship on the high seas for drugs trafficking. The Grand Chamber contrasted this position with that of a suspected pirate ship, where there was a universal right of arrest.[108] It would therefore seem that the arrest of a suspected pirate ship on the high seas will be lawful under the ECHR. This is confirmed by the judgment of the Rotterdam District Court in the *Cygnus* case.[109] Finally, in *Medvedyev*, the Grand Chamber found that the 13 days that it took to bring the suspected drugs traffickers before a court following their arrest on the high seas was sufficiently prompt, given the circumstances, and there was therefore no breach of Article 5(3) of the ECHR.[110] By contrast, in the *Cygnus* case, the Rotterdam District Court found that a 40-day delay in bringing the suspects to court following their arrest was not justified by the circumstances and there was therefore a breach of Article 5(3).[111]

---

[105] See, eg Resolution 1976, para 16.

[106] International Covenant on Civil and Political Rights (hereafter ICCPR) (adopted 16 December 1966, entered into force 23 March 1976), Art 9, 999 UNTS 171. Similar obligations are found in the European Convention on Human Rights (hereafter ECHR) (adopted 4 November 1950, entered into force 3 September 1953), Art 5, 213 UNTS 221; American Convention on Human Rights (hereafter ACHR) (adopted 22 November 1969, entered into force 18 July 1978), Art 7, 1144 UNTS 143; African Charter on Human and Peoples' Rights (hereafter ACHPR) (adopted 27 June 1981, entered into force 21 October 1986), Art 6, 1520 UNTS 363.

[107] ECtHR, *Medvedyev and Others v France*, Application No 3394/03, Judgment of the Grand Chamber of 29 March 2010, para 67. The same principle was subsequently applied in ECtHR, *Hirsi Jamaa and Others v Italy*, Application No 27765/09, Judgment of the Grand Chamber of 23 February 2012, paras 70–82.

[108] *Medvedyev*, ibid, paras 85 and 101.

[109] *The 'Cygnus Case (Somali Pirates)*, Judgment of the Rotterdam District Court of 17 June 2010, 145 *International Law Reports* 491, 499.

[110] *Medvedyev*, n 107 above, paras 132–34.

[111] *Cygnus* case, n 109 above, 499–500. However, the court found that the breach of Art 5(3) did not invalidate the suspects' right to a fair trial (at 501). For further discussion of *Medvedyev* and human rights obligations relating to the arrest of pirates, see SP Bodini, 'Fighting Maritime Piracy under the European Convention on Human Rights' (2011) 22 *European Journal of International Law* 829, 829–40 and 843–45; Guilfoyle, n 103 above, 153–60.

Finally, it may be asked whether, if all the conditions for a valid arrest set out above are met, a competent vessel that is in a position to do so is obliged to arrest a suspected pirate ship. As mentioned above, Article 100 of UNCLOS and Article 14 of the High Seas Convention require their states parties to 'cooperate to the fullest possible extent in the repression of piracy' on the high seas and in an EEZ or in places outside the jurisdiction of any state. In its commentary on what became Article 14 of the High Seas Convention, the ILC observed that any state having an opportunity to take measures against piracy and neglecting to do so would be failing in an international duty. However, the ILC added, a state 'must be allowed a certain latitude as to the measures it should take to this end in any individual case'.[112] This suggests that the flag state of a warship or military aircraft in a position to arrest a suspected pirate ship but failing to do so would be in breach of Article 100 of UNCLOS or Article 14 of the High Seas Convention unless it were able to show good reasons to justify its failure to arrest, such as the existence of other steps that were being taken to repress the piracy in question.

C. Adjudicative Jurisdiction

That adjudicative jurisdiction, like arrest jurisdiction, is universal is stated somewhat obliquely in the conventions. Article 105 of UNCLOS and Article 19 of the High Seas Convention both provide that

> [t]he courts of the state which carried out the seizure [of the pirate ship] may decide upon the penalties to be imposed, and may also determine the action to be taken with regard to the ships, aircraft or property, subject to the rights of third parties acting in good faith.

This provision raises two questions. The first is whether only the arresting state may try suspected pirates or whether, instead, it may hand them over to another state for trial. Some writers have argued that the former is the correct position.[113] In support, they refer to a comment by the ILC that its draft article that became Article 19 of the High Seas Convention gives 'any state the right to seize pirate ships . . . and to have them adjudicated upon by its courts. This right cannot be exercised at a place under the jurisdiction of another state.'[114] Other writers, who take the view—correctly, it is submitted—that the arresting state is not precluded from transferring suspected pirates to another state for trial, argue that the ILC's comment has been misunderstood, and that what the ILC was really trying to emphasise was that a state may not exercise the right of arrest within the jurisdiction of another state; this is, of course, an established proposition in international law.[115] While it is true that the text of Articles 105 and 19 refers only to adjudication by the courts of the arresting state, it does not explicitly prohibit that state from transferring or extraditing alleged pirates to another state for trial. That such transfer or extradition is permissible is supported by state practice.

---

[112] Above n 11, 282.
[113] See, eg Bantekas, n 44 above, 297; E Kontorovich, 'International Legal Responses to Piracy off the Coast of Somalia' (2009) 13(2) *American Society of International Law Insight* 1, 4.
[114] N 11 above, 283.
[115] See, eg Gardner, n 19 above, 803–08; Guilfoyle, n 104, 775; Roach, n 67 above, 404–05; Treves, n 83 above, 402.

Such practice includes a number of agreements between Western states and various Indian Ocean states (including Kenya, Mauritius and Seychelles) for the transfer of suspected Somali pirates from Western warships to Indian Ocean states for trial;[116] the decisions of a number of domestic courts that they are competent to try alleged pirates arrested by a foreign state;[117] and explicit recognition of the possibility of transfer and extradition by the Code of Conduct concerning the Repression of Piracy and Armed Robbery in the Western Indian Ocean,[118] the IMO[119] and the UN Security Council.[120] The degree of this practice is such that it would seem to amount to 'subsequent practice in the application' of a treaty (here UNCLOS) that 'establishes the agreement of the parties regarding its interpretation', as provided by Article 31(3(b) of the VCLT.

In order to facilitate prosecution by the Indian Ocean states to which suspected Somali pirates may be transferred, some of the agreements between those states and Western states, as well as the Code of Conduct concerning the Repression of Piracy and Armed Robbery in the Western Indian Ocean,[121] provide for the use of 'shipriders', ie law officers from Indian Ocean states who travel on Western warships that are likely to arrest suspected pirates.[122] Such agreements have also been encouraged by the Security Council.[123] Any transfer or extradition of suspected pirates from the arresting state to another state is subject to the obligation of 'non-refoulement' imposed by various human rights treaties. Thus, under the UN Torture Convention,[124] the ICCPR[125] and the ECHR,[126] alleged criminals may not be extradited or transferred to a state where there is a risk of torture.[127] For those state parties to the ECHR that have accepted Protocols 6 and 13 providing for the abolition of the death penalty (which is nearly all

[116] For details of such agreements, see Roach, n 67 above, 403–04; Murdoch, n 90 above, 152–53. The only such agreements that appear to have been published are the EU's agreements with Kenya, Seychelles and Mauritius, [2009] OJ L79/51, [2009] OJ L323/14 and [2011] OJ 254/3. See further D Thym, Chapter 6 below.

[117] See, eg *Hassan M Ahmed v Republic*, n 37 above; *Cygnus*, n 109 above, 494.

[118] Above n 18, Art 4(7).

[119] IMO Assembly Resolution 1025 (26) (2010), n 18 above, para 3(1).

[120] See, eg Resolution 1976 (2011), para 20.

[121] Above n 18, Art 7.

[122] See further, Guilfoyle, 'Piracy off Somalia', n 43 above, 698–99; Guilfoyle, n 103 above, 149–50; Treves, n 83 above, 411.

[123] See, inter alia, Resolutions 1851 (2008), para 3 and 1897 (2009), para 6.

[124] UN Convention against Torture and Other Cruel, Inhuman or Degrading Treatment or Punishment (signed 10 December 1984, entered into force 26 June 1987) 1465 UNTS 85, Art 3.

[125] There is no explicit provision to this effect in the ICCPR, but the obligation has been found to be implicit by the Human Rights Committee: see General Comment No 20 (Article 7) (1992), para 9, available at http://www.unhchr.ch/tbs/doc.nsf/(Symbol)/6924291970754969c12563ed004c8ae5?Opendocument (accessed on 21 January 2013).

[126] There is no explicit provision to this effect in the ECHR, but the obligation has been found to be implicit by the European Court of Human Rights: see, eg *Soering v United Kingdom*, Application No 14038/88, (1989) 11 EHRR 439; *Chahal v United Kingdom*, Application No 22414/93, (1997) 23 EHRR 413. See further J Hartmann, 'The European Convention on Human Rights and Extradition' in KH Kaikobad and M Bohlander (eds), *International Law and Power: Perspectives on Legal Order and Justice* (Leiden, Martinus Nijhoff Publishers, 2009) 25.

[127] The obligation of non-refoulement also applies extraterritorially: see *Hirsi Jamaa v Italy*, n 107 above, paras 134–35; UN High Commissioner for Refugees, Advisory Opinion on the Extra-Territorial Application of Non-Refoulement Obligations under the 1951 Convention relating to the Status of Refugees and its 1967 Protocol (2007), available at http://www.unhcr.org/refworld/pdfid/45f17a1a4.pdf (accessed on 21 January 2013).

of them), there is almost certainly a further obligation not to extradite or transfer a suspected pirate to a state where there is a risk of the death penalty being imposed.[128]

The second question raised by Article 105 of UNCLOS and Article 19 of the High Seas Convention is whether a state having suspected pirates in its custody is obliged to prosecute them. The use of the word 'may' in Articles 105 and 19 suggests that there is no such obligation. On the other hand, it could be argued that the obligation in Article 100 of UNCLOS and Article 14 of the High Seas Convention to repress piracy, discussed above, does require a state having custody of suspected pirate to prosecute them.[129] However, this is probably reading too much into Articles 100 and 14,[130] and is contradicted by practice in the Indian Ocean, where the overwhelming majority of Somali pirates that have been seized have been released without being brought to trial[131]—a situation that has been regretted by the Security Council.[132] The fact that there appears to be no obligation on a state that has seized a suspected pirate to prosecute or extradite the suspect arguably compares unfavourably with the various treaties establishing transnational crimes referred to at the beginning of this chapter, where a state having a suspect in its custody must either submit the suspect to its competent authorities for the purpose of prosecution or extradite the suspect, ie the principle of *aut dedere, aut judicare*.[133]

In practice, trials of pirates on the basis of universal jurisdiction appear to be infrequent. Kontorovich and Art report that, during the period 1998–2009 inclusive, there were 1,158 reported instances of piracy worldwide, 17 of them leading to prosecutions on the basis of universal jurisdiction, the overwhelming majority of which took place in Kenya and involved Somali pirates.[134] They suggest that the reasons for the low number include the costs of finding and arresting pirates on the high seas and EEZ; problems of obtaining sufficient evidence; and the reluctance of states to prosecute unless they have a direct interest in the matter because of the costs of prosecution and imprisonment if a conviction is secured.[135] However, there have been trials on jurisdictional bases other than universal, such as trials by the flag state of the pirate ship or trials by the states of the nationality of the pirates or their victims (ie the active and passive personality principles). According to a report from the UN Secretary-General,

---

[128] See further Hartmann, n 126 above, 31–33. Such an obligation, as well as the obligation not to torture, is explicitly recognised in the EU–Kenya agreement, n 116 above, Annex, paras 3(a) and 4.

[129] JT Gathii, 'Kenya's Piracy Prosecutions' (2010) 104 *American Journal of International Law* 416, 425. He argues that such an obligation was suggested in *Hassan M Ahmed v Republic*, n 37 above.

[130] So, too, Guilfoyle, n 104, 775; Roach, n 67 above, 405–06; Treves, n 83 above, 402. A proposal at the 1958 Conference on the Law of the Sea to require states to prosecute suspected pirates was defeated: see United Nations Conference on the Law of the Sea, Official Records, vol IV (1958), 84 and 128.

[131] For figures on the number of pirates released and the reasons therefor, see, inter alia, Guilfoyle, n 104, 770; Murdoch, n 90 above, 149–51 and 156.

[132] See, eg Resolutions 2020 (2011), preambular para 5 and 2077 (2012), preambular para 5. The same resolutions call on states to consider favourably the prosecution of suspected Somali pirates: see paras 15 and 18, respectively.

[133] See, eg Hague Convention, above n 5, Art 7; Montreal Convention, n 6 above, Art 7; Hostages Convention, n 7 above, Art 8; SUA Convention, n 8 above, Art 10. See further International Law Commission, Survey of multilateral conventions which may be of relevance for the work of the International Law Commission on the topic 'The obligation to extradite or prosecute (*aut dedere aut judicare*)'. Study by the Secretariat, UN Doc A/CN.4/630 (18 June 2010), available at http://untreaty.un.org/ilc/guide/gfra.htm (accessed on 21 January 2013).

[134] E Kontorovich and S Art, 'An Empirical Examination of Universal Jurisdiction for Piracy' (2010) 104 *American Journal of International Law* 436, 444–45.

[135] Ibid, 449–51.

during the period 2006–11 inclusive there were 1,063 prosecutions of Somali pirates, 612 of which resulted in convictions.[136] However, the report does not say what the bases of jurisdiction were for those prosecutions.

Finally, it must be emphasised that the trial of any suspected pirates must observe the requirements of international human rights law for a fair trial, as acknowledged by the UN Security Council.[137] Such requirements include a fair and public trial by an independent and impartial court without undue delay; the presumption of innocence; adequate time and facilities for the accused to prepare their case; and the free assistance of an interpreter, where necessary.[138]

IV. CONCLUSIONS

An attempt must now be made to sum up the discussion in this chapter and provide an answer to the question asked at the outset: namely, whether the piracy provisions of UNCLOS are adequate for combating piracy in the contemporary world. Sometimes this question receives a fairly emphatic negative answer.[139] The limitations of UNCLOS that proponents of this view usually point to are the two ships requirement (a pirate ship and a separate victim), the exclusion of piratical attacks by terrorists from the scope of piracy and the non-applicability of the UNCLOS piracy provisions to the territorial sea. However, these matters do not seem to be the most important limitations of UNCLOS. As regards the two ships requirement, most attacks on shipping in practice are by one ship against another. Where an attack emanates from within a ship, the SUA Convention will usually be applicable. It is therefore not necessary to consider extending UNCLOS to cover such attacks. It is true that universal jurisdiction is not available under the SUA Convention, but in practice few, if any, states other than the flag state are likely to have an interest in exercising enforcement jurisdiction. However, if they do, they can seek the consent of the flag state. As for piratical attacks by terrorists, it was suggested in Section II(A)(ii) above that the 'private ends' requirement of UNCLOS could and should be interpreted to include acts by terrorists. The suggestion that piracy should be extended to the territorial sea seems fraught with difficulty. If such an extension took place, it would mean the possibility of foreign warships entering a coastal state's territorial sea without its consent to arrest pirates. Such a situation seems a recipe for conflict. Extending piracy to the territorial sea is also unnecessary as there is nothing to stop a coastal state from criminalising quasi-

---

[136] Report of the Secretary-General on specialised anti-piracy courts in Somalia and other states in the region, UN Doc S/2012/50 (20 January 2012), 4–5, available at http://www.un.org/ga/search/view_doc.asp?symbol=S/2012/50 (accessed on 21 January 2013).

[137] See, eg Resolutions 1816 (2008), para 11, 2018(2011), para 5, 2020(2011), paras 14 and 15, and 2077 (2012), paras 17 and 18. See also the EU–Kenya Exchange of Letters, n 116 above, Annex, paras 2(c) and 3. According to the report of the UN Secretary-General, ibid, 2, all the agreements between Western states and Indian Ocean states providing for the transfer of suspected Somali pirates contain human rights provisions.

[138] ICCPR, n 106 above, Art 14; ECHR, n 106 above, Art 6; ACHR, n 106 above, Art 8; ACHPR, n 106 above, Art 7. See also Bodini, n 111 above, 840–41; Guilfoyle, n 103 above, 153–67.

[139] See, eg Collins and Hassan, n 45 above, 105–06 and 112–13; Jesus, n 48 above, 368, 380–87 and 399–400.

piratical acts (ie armed robbery) in its territorial sea and arresting suspected offenders. Furthermore, the SUA Convention may also be applicable.[140]

There are some uncertainties in the definition of piracy and the scope of associated inchoate crimes, as detailed at the end of Section II(C). However, they are unlikely in practice to be significant limitations in the effectiveness of UNCLOS as a legal tool for combating piracy. The real shortcomings of UNCLOS lie in its jurisdictional provisions. First, unlike other treaties establishing transnational crimes, UNCLOS does not require its parties to make the crime at issue, piracy, an offence under their national law. However, at the prompting of the UN Security Council and the IMO, those states with no or inadequate legislation relating to piracy are gradually closing this legislative gap.[141] Secondly, again unlike the other transnational crime treaties, there is no obligation on a state having custody of a suspected pirate to prosecute or extradite. Consequently, many suspected pirates, especially those operating from Somalia, have been released without charge following their arrest.

It needs to be remembered, however, that whatever shortcomings there may be in the piracy provisions of UNCLOS, they are only part of the reason why the international community has so far failed to eradicate the modern scourge of piracy. Other factors include the difficulty and cost of identifying and arresting suspected pirates at sea; the lack of political will and/or resources to put all arrested pirates on trial and pay for their incarceration if convicted; and inadequate efforts to tackle the conditions on land that breed and support piracy.

---

[140] On the application of SUA Convention (n 8 above) to the territorial sea, see its Art 4.

[141] See, eg the report of the UN Secretary-General, n 136 above, 14, 18, 23 and 27, which refers to Kenya, Mauritius, Seychelles and Tanzania as all having recently updated their piracy legislation in line with UNCLOS.

2

Piracy and Terrorism

DOUGLAS GUILFOYLE

An investigator finds that instead of a single relatively simple problem [defining piracy], there are a series of difficult problems which have occasioned [at different times] a great diversity of professional opinion.[1]

I. INTRODUCTION

HISTORICALLY, THERE HAS been some difficulty in defining the terms 'pirate' and 'terrorist'. They are both quintessentially words that stigmatise someone as other: a violent, outlaw actor who seeks to impinge upon states' legitimate monopoly over violence. As a matter of legal usage, the controversial relationship between piracy and terrorism springs from three words in the modern definition of piracy, which requires that piracy on the high seas must involve an act 'for private ends'. That is, both the 1982 UN Convention on the Law of the Sea (UNCLOS) and the 1958 Geneva High Seas Convention (HSC) tell us:

> Piracy consists of any of the following acts: . . . any illegal acts of violence or detention, or any act of depredation, committed *for private ends* by the crew or the passengers of a private ship or a private aircraft, and directed . . . on the high seas, against another ship or aircraft, or against persons or property on board . . .[2]

This immediately suggests a distinction between private piratical acts and some other class of public or political acts. A common view of the effect of these words is that: 'by limiting the definition to acts committed for "private ends" any actions taken for political motives such as terrorist attacks are excluded'.[3]

However, even if this is a correct statement of the law today (a proposition on

---

[1] Harvard Research in International Law, 'Part IV: Piracy' (1932) 26 *American Journal of International Law Supplement* 739 (hereafter Harvard Research), 764.

[2] Geneva Convention on the High Seas (adopted on 29 April 1958, entered into force 30 September 1962) 450 UNTS 82 (hereafter High Seas Convention), Art 15; United Nations Convention on the Law of the Sea (adopted 10 December 1982, entered into force 16 November 1994) 1833 UNTS 3 (hereafter UNCLOS), Art 101. Emphasis added.

[3] DR Rothwell and T Stephens, *The International Law of the Sea* (Oxford, Hart Publishing, 2010) 162; for a more nuanced view, see R Churchill, Chapter 1 above (arguing terrorism could be classed as piracy, but not political protest).

which this chapter will cast doubt), it is far from clear that this was the uniform intention of those who were early advocates of this definition. It is also less than entirely
clear when the words 'for private ends' first entered commonly used legal definitions
of piracy. Their earliest use in any textbook definition appears to date to 1892, where
they were used in the phrase 'for gain or other private ends of the doers', seemingly
as a synonym for piratical intent to plunder (discussed below).[4] Earlier sources do
not appear to use any directly equivalent term at all.[5] Piracy had, traditionally, simply
been defined as robbery on the high seas (often with the further qualification that
the robbers lacked a government commission or letters of marque). So why were the
words 'for private ends' thought necessary? As Lauterpacht put it in 1937:

> Piracy in its original and strict meaning is every unauthorised act of violence committed
> by a private vessel on the open sea against another vessel with intent to plunder (*animo
> furandi*) . . . But there are cases possible which are not covered by this narrow definition . . .
> [I]f unauthorised acts of violence, such as murder . . . are committed on the open sea
> without intent to plunder, such acts are in practice considered to be piratical . . . Therefore,
> several writers, correctly, I think, oppose the usual definition [as too narrow] . . . But yet
> no unanimity exists . . . concerning a fit definition . . . and the matter is . . . controversial.[6]

Lauterpacht clearly considered the traditional definition both too restrictive and at
variance with practice, so proposed a broader definition of piracy based on the unauthorised character of the violence. Similarly, the UK Privy Council in 1934 held that
the definition of piracy 'nearest to accuracy' was 'any armed violence at sea which
is not a lawful act of war'.[7] Such approaches emphasise that legitimate violence on
the high seas is the province of states and, historically, state-licensed privateers and
perhaps civil war insurgencies. In the present author's view, Lauterpacht's would have
clearly been the clearer definitional approach to take. Instead, the ambiguous words
'for private ends' won out in the academic struggle over how to define piracy.

The debate has had a number of phases. In the period 1926–52 work to codify
the law of piracy was undertaken successively by the League of Nations, the Harvard
Research Project and the International Law Commission. For each of these bodies, the
words 'for private ends' were meant to be limiting and exclusionary, but not necessarily in the sense commonly thought now. The debate in this early phase, although
touching tangentially on whether anarchist terrorism could be assimilated to piracy,
was far more concerned with whether civil war insurgents could be considered pirates.
The development of law tends to be shaped by the live controversies of the day, and
the question of the status of insurgent vessels in Latin American conflicts and the

---

[4] See JP Bishop, *New Commentaries on the Criminal Law*, 8th edn (Chicago, TH Flood & Co, 1892)
vol 1, 339, § 553 and vol 2, 617, § 1058; JP Bishop (C Zollmann, ed), *Bishop on Criminal Law*, 9th edn
(Chicago, TH Flood & Co, 1923) 406, § 553. This appears to be Bishop's first use of the phrase. It does not
seem to appear in previous editions under different titles. See, eg JP Bishop, *Commentaries on the Criminal
Law*, 6th edn (Boston, Little, Brown & Co, 1877). The author cites two authorities for his definition: *US v
Palmer* 16 US (3 Wheaton) 610 (1818) and *US v Terrell*, Hemp 411. The former does not use the phrase 'for
private ends'. I have been unable to locate the latter.
[5] The copious review of classical authorities in the 18 page footnote in *US v Smith* 18 US (5 Wheaton)
153 (1820), 163–80 does not contain the phrase or, it seems, an equivalent in French or Latin. The quotes
tend to focus on either the lack of state sanction or intention to plunder (*depredendi causa*, *pour piller*, etc).
[6] H Lauterpacht, *Oppenheim's International Law*, 5th edn (London, Longmans, Green & Co, 1937) 486.
[7] *In re Piracy Jure Gentium* [1934] AC 586, 598; compare the reference to 'unauthorised warfare' in *US v
The Ambrose Light*, 25 Fed 408, 413 (SDNY 1885).

Spanish civil war were still very much in the forefront of legal thought on questions of piracy at this time. Indeed, the very origins of the words 'for private ends' as part of the definition of piracy can only be understood in this context.

High-profile maritime incidents of insurgency or terrorism, starting as early as 1955 but particularly in the 1960s and 1980s, reignited the debate, with a number of scholars calling for 'terrorists' to be assimilated to 'pirates' for the purposes of universal jurisdiction. In this phase, discussion usually centres around the *Santa Maria* and *Achille Lauro* incidents. The latter, in particular, culminated in the conclusion of the 1988 Convention for the Suppression of Unlawful Acts against the Safety of Maritime Navigation (the SUA Convention or SUA). The SUA Convention leaves us with a new doctrinal debate: are SUA 'terrorist' offences mutually exclusive with acts of piracy or are they 'gap-curing' in such a way that some forms of piracy might also fall within the SUA Convention?

Finally, since the 1960s, and especially since 11 September 2001, there have been various attempts to assimilate terrorism to piracy either rhetorically or for more practical legal effect. It has been common since at least 1961 to describe aircraft hijacking as 'air piracy';[8] more recently, some have asked whether piracy fits into—or shares characteristics with—the so-called 'war on terror', suggesting:

> Many of the legal issues that prevent states from effectively suppressing pirates also plague responses to international terrorism. Pirates and terrorists fall in the gray zone between military combatants and civilians. Thus the antipiracy campaign and the so-called War on Terror both raise questions about the legal status of conflicts between states and diffuse armed networks with international operations. Issues that have impeded countries' efforts on both these fronts include . . . rendition of suspects to countries with poor human rights records, claims of abuse by detainees . . . and the legality of 'targeted killings' of suspected hostile civilians.[9]

Many navies presently engaged in countering piracy off Somalia would recoil from the suggestion that there is any ambiguity as regards the status of pirates. The unequivocal position of the EU Naval Force, for example, is that counter-piracy is a constabulary operation directed against criminals.[10] Nonetheless, the quote highlights a debate that will not go away as to the precise relationship between piracy, war and terrorism. While the issue can be resolved at the level of positive law (as discussed below), the historical debate tells us something about the changing and sometimes nebulous nature of the categories under discussion. Pirates and terrorists are almost always presented as the stigmatised other. It was thus common for sixteenth- and seventeenth-century sovereigns to refer to political allies as 'privateers' and to enemies as 'pirates'[11] in much the same way that modern political rhetoric has sometimes used the terms 'freedom

---

[8] The earliest reference to 'air piracy' I have found so far is in SA Bayitch, 'International Law' (1961) 16 *University of Miami Law Review* 240, 262.

[9] E Kontorovich, ''A Guantanamo on the Sea': The Difficulties of Prosecuting Pirates and Terrorists' (2010) 98 *California Law Review* 243, 245.

[10] House of Commons Foreign Affairs Committee (UK), 'Piracy off the Coast of Somalia', HC 2010–12, 1318 (5 January 2012), Evidence Annexe, 14, available at www.parliament.uk/business/committees/committees-a-z/commons-select/foreign-affairs-committee/publications/.

[11] A Rubin, 'The Law of Piracy' (1986–87) 15 *Denver Journal of International Law and Policy* 173, 198; although one should note that piracy has not always had a strong pejorative sense in English: A Rubin, *The Law of Piracy*, 2nd edn (New York, Transnational, 1997) ch 1. See also Harvard Research, n 1 above, 803.

fighter' and 'terrorist'. It is also often assumed (as the quote above demonstrates), erroneously, that both categories must have some relationship to the laws of war. Notably, any close examination of the record shows that piracy has historically been a somewhat loose label, applied over time to a multitude of phenomena rather than to a single activity that is stable across time.[12] Further, even the current textually stable definition may capture a number of different practices: Somali hostage-taking piracy is not the stick-up or smash-and-grab piracy of the Malacca Strait. It is never really accurate to speak of piracy, only of piracies.

The remainder of this chapter will attempt to tease apart the relationship between the concepts along historical and functional lines, before making some observations about the present state of the positive law.

II. PIRACY AND TERRORISM: EARLY CODIFICATION EFFORTS (1926–52)

A. Introduction

The currently accepted definition of piracy found in UNCLOS is taken, with only minor changes, from the HSC definition. The HSC definition, in turn, was taken with very few modifications from the ILC's articles on the law of the sea.[13] The ILC was strongly influenced in its work by the work of the Harvard Research in International Law project on piracy, and its resultant draft convention and commentaries (the Harvard Research).[14] Much of the Harvard Research is an enormous compilation of loosely organised quotes from sources with additional commentary by the authors. This methodology (or lack of it) has the virtue of making the sources upon which the authors relied transparent. Outside of the Harvard Research authors' commentary and draft articles, the words 'private ends' appear among their original sources only eight times in three contexts: several references to the work of the League of Nations (discussed below);[15] a translated portion of the criminal code of Spain;[16] and a twice-repeated quote from the American jurist Bishop,[17] whose works were highly influential and who appears to have been the first to include these words in a definition of piracy.[18] The Harvard Research appears to have lifted the words 'for private ends' for use in its own draft convention from the reports of the League of Nations on

---

[12] See further Harvard Research, ibid, 787 ('The facts that piracy has had a distinct place in law and that the foreign private pirate has been treated with universal public enmity continuously from ancient times, should not mislead us into assuming that the law of piracy in its basic principles, or in its definition of the offence, or in the details of state authority to act in the interest of suppressing it always has been the same').

[13] [1956] II *Yearbook of the International Law Commission* 253.

[14] See [1955] I *Yearbook of the International Law Commission* 40ff, [1956] II *Yearbook of the International Law Commission* 253, 282–84.

[15] Harvard Research, n 1 above, 775, 802, 808 and 873–74.

[16] Ibid, 781.

[17] Ibid, 791 (quoting *Bishop on Criminal Law*, n 4 above, § 533; G Schlikker, *Die Völkerrechtliche Lehre von der Piraterie und den ihr Gleichgestellten Verbrechen* (Borna, Leipzig, Buchdruckerei R Noske, 1907) 43, quoting Bishop.

[18] On Bishop's influence as a scholar see CS Bishop, 'Joel Prentiss Bishop. LL.D' (1902) 36 *American Law Review* 1, 5–8. On his definitions of piracy, see n 4 above.

the topic. Therefore, even though the Harvard Research was more influential on later developments, we must begin with the work of the League.

B. The League of Nations Committee of Experts for the Progressive Codification of International Law 1926

The League of Nations Committee of Experts' work on piracy was brief. Ambassador Matsuda prepared a brief set of draft articles for discussion (without scholarly references or detailed explanation of his drafting choices), which provoked a significant volume of responses from government and a brief report from the Committee of Experts itself, before the topic was dropped from the League agenda as not being of sufficient practical interest.[19] The key text is Ambassador Matsuda's draft Article 1, which provided:

> Piracy occurs only on the high sea and consists in the commission for private ends of depredations upon property or acts of violence against persons.
>   It is not required . . . that [such] acts should be committed for the purpose of gain, but acts committed with a purely political object will not be regarded as constituting piracy.[20]

This approach, at first glance, accords with the common contemporary understanding and divides 'piracy' and 'terrorism' into two mutually exclusive, watertight compartments. Matsuda thus appears to focus on the subjective intentions of the potential pirate, though he sets a high bar before political motives will prevent an act being considered piracy (requiring a 'purely political object'). He thus appears to favour what is now the conventional view that the distinction inherent in piracy is one between private and political motives. This, however, was not what was intended. In his fuller memorandum, Matsuda observed: 'According to international law, piracy consists in sailing the seas for private ends without authorization from the Government of any state with the object of committing depredations upon property or acts of violence against persons'.[21]

   This seems to divide the realm of acts of violence at sea into those authorised by a state and those not authorised by a state. This, in a seeming contradiction, appears to favour what is now the minority Lauterpachtian view: that the dividing line is one between private and public acts characterised objectively and without reference to the actors' motives. However, Matsuda (and perhaps the broader Committee) was in fact quite equivocal on the point of terrorism and political motives. Elsewhere he observed:

---

[19] See Rubin, n 11 above, 331–35; and 'Report of the Committee of Experts for the Progressive Codification of International Law', 13 June 1927 reproduced in (1928) 22 *American Journal of International Law* Special Supplement 216, 222.

[20] As reproduced in Harvard Research, n 1 above, 873; (1926) 20 *American Journal of International Law* Special Supplement 228–29; S Rosenne, *League of Nations Committee of Experts for the Progressive Codification of International Law (1925–1928)* (Dobbs Ferry NY, Oceana, 1972) vol 2, 145.

[21] League of Nations Document C.48.M.25.1926.V, Annexe (emphasis added); as reproduced in Rosenne, ibid, vol 2, 142; (1926) 20 *American Journal of International Law* Special Supplement 223. Quoted in Harvard Research, n 1 above, 775.

It is better, in laying down a general principle, to be content *with the external character of the facts* without entering too far into the often delicate question of motives. Nevertheless, when the acts in question are committed from purely political motives, it is hardly possible to regard them as acts of piracy.[22]

It is difficult at first to see why the political motive requirement has been reintroduced in the second sentence, given the general conceptual approach of the first. The answer appears to be to deal with a particular historical difficulty. Matsuda's Article 4 provided: 'Insurgents committing acts of the kind mentioned in Article 1 must be considered as pirates unless such acts are inspired by purely political motives'.[23] This appears to indicate that civil war insurgencies who commit acts of violence at sea were the class of actors principally targeted by the words 'for private ends'. (This reading is borne out by the review of contemporary debates conducted by the Harvard Research, discussed below.) Matsuda's approach appears to have been that even civil war insurgents (who certainly should be considered political actors) would ordinarily be pirates if they commit such acts unless there was some particularly close connection between the crime and their political goals. This reading is borne out by the Committee President's (uncontested) summation of Matsuda's position:

> In the general case, whether the crime of piracy has been committed follows from the character of the acts. If acts of violence or depredation are committed, there is piracy, regardless of the motives for those acts. Nevertheless, the rapporteur has admitted an exception for acts committed for a purpose which is political and *solely political*.[24]

The Committee President went on to add that the drafting of Article 4 must be read alongside the Article 1 definition of piracy: '*not as an exception to the latter*, but as an *extension* of the idea of acts of piracy to [cover] certain acts of insurrection'.[25]

Thus, in the final analysis, the Committee appeared to concede that '*purely* political motives' would exclude an act from being piracy and thus agreed with Matsuda, though only in the narrow context of certain acts committed during a civil-war insurgency.[26] As discussed below, the principal contemporary debates concerned less terrorism than the laws of armed conflict. This distinction is more apparent in the work of the Harvard Research, which, though contemporaneous, notably had nothing to say about terrorism.

Terrorism was absent from the debate at the League of Nations Committee of Experts. Yet one authoritative contemporary commentator thought the formulation adopted did have implications for terrorism—anarchist terrorism. In his 1926 Hague Academy lectures on piracy, Vespasian Pella contended that the Matsuda formulation

[22] League of Nations Document C.48.M.25.1926.V., Annexe; as reproduced in Rosenne, ibid, vol 2, 143; (1926) 20 *American Journal of International Law* Special Supplement 224 (emphasis added throughout).

[23] Rosenne, ibid, vol 2, 145; (1926) 20 *American Journal of International Law* Special Supplement 229; Harvard Research, n 1 above, 873.

[24] Minutes of the League of Nations Committee of Experts for the Progressive Codification of International Law, Second Session, 14th Meeting, 20 January 1926, reproduced in Rosenne, ibid, vol 1, 124. Author's translation and emphasis ('D'une manière générale, c'est d'après le caractère des actes que l'on peut déterminer le crime de piraterie. Si des actes de déprédation ou de violence sont commis, il y a piraterie, quel que soit le motif de ces actes. Toutefois, le rapporteur a admis une exception pour les actes commis dans un dessein politique et uniquement politique').

[25] Ibid, 126. Author's translation ('non pas comme une exception à cette dernière, mais comme une extension de la notion d'actes de piraterie à certain faites d'insurrection').

[26] See generally the debate reproduced in ibid, 124–26.

would actually bring within the definition of piracy any acts of anarchist violence per-petrated on the high seas.[27] Pella's line of argument to this end was that the dangers posed by anarchist terrorism have a general character and, despite appearing to be targeted at a single government, in fact attack the social foundations of civilised socie-ties everywhere.[28] Thus '[t]errorist attacks do not have an *anti-governmental* character, but an *anti-social* one. They reach the public and legal order of all states . . .'[29] On a strict understanding of the League of Nations approach, this is perhaps correct: the class of political actors potentially excluded from being pirates was limited to those wishing to overthrow a particular government and not a general social system. Pella thus thought: (i) that the consequence of introducing the words 'for political ends' would be the inclusion of anarchist terrorism, effectively violence outside politics, within the definition of piracy; and (ii) that this showed that definitions moving away from a strict focus on intention to rob were too elastic.[30] The point is not whether we agree with Pella's line of reasoning or not; it is simply worthwhile noting that at least one eminent commentator of the time considered that the words 'for political ends' could result in certain types of terrorism (constructed as apolitical or radically antisocial) being classed as piracy.

C. Harvard Research in International Law 1932

The objective of the Harvard Research was to assemble the legal sources relevant to piracy (largely the opinions of commentators, but also national legislation and judicial decisions) and to formulate a draft convention on the topic. Theirs was a codification effort, and in the course of this they had to confront historic cases falling outside the narrow definition of piracy (ie robbery at sea), which had nevertheless been treated as piracy. The main examples were cases in which insurgent vessels in a civil war had been treated as pirates when interfering with the shipping of third states. Such cases obviously involved a choice as to classification. Such cases could be: distinguished as simply misinterpreting or misapplying the law (ie to preserve the narrow definition); integrated into an expanded definition of piracy (ie reformulating the theory to better reflect practice); or excluded as being evidence not of the content of the law of piracy but of some separate rule of international law. The authors of the Harvard Draft put it this way:

> It may be useful to explain the paucity of pertinent cases and of evidence of modern state practice on most of the important moot points in the law of piracy. Except for a few international cases, *chiefly concerning the status of insurgent vessels or of irregular privateers*, and a few municipal law cases, there are no official determinations which will help an investigator to cut a way through the jungle of expert opinion. Indeed the lack of adjudicated cases and of pertinent instances of state practice is the occasion for the chaos of expert opinion. Most of the municipal law cases on piracy are of little value in solving

---

[27] V Pella, 'La Répression de la Piraterie' (1926) 15 *Collected Courses of the Hague Academy of International Law* 149, 218.

[28] Ibid, 217.

[29] Ibid, 217. Author's translation, emphasis in the original ('Les attentats terroristes n'ont pas un caractère *anti-gouvernemental* mais *anti-social*. Ils atteignent l'ordre public et légal de tous les États').

[30] Ibid, 218.

the international problems, because municipal law covers a different field, as a preceding part of this introduction explains, and the judicial opinions are colored by the national legislation.[31]

Once again, as before the League of Nations Committee of Experts, the controversial case for inclusion or exclusion from the definition of piracy was thus not the terrorist but the civil war insurgent.[32] Nonetheless, despite confronting the same problem, the Harvard Research did not entirely adopt the Matsuda approach.

The Harvard Research's draft Article 3 defined piracy as involving various acts committed '*for private ends* without bona fide purpose of asserting a claim of right'.[33] While the words 'for private ends' might be thought to show a debt to Matsuda, Matsuda's further explanatory sentence ('acts committed with a purely political object will not be regarded as constituting piracy') is absent. It is not entirely obvious what the words 'without bona fide purpose of asserting a claim of right' are intended to exclude from the definition of piracy. It is hard to think of private individuals having a 'claim of right' which would allow them to take violent action against another private vessel on the high seas, but this was apparently what the authors of the Harvard Research had in mind (giving as their sole example 'quarrels [between] fishermen of different nationalities').[34] We are left, then, only with the task of determining what the authors intended by the words 'private ends'.

One might think it telling that in its review of the acts under consideration for inclusion in the definition of piracy (on the basis of various authorities) the commentary to the Harvard Research groups together the following examples:

(12) Using a ship to attack another for some political purpose provided the attack is not made under the authority or protection of any state or recognized belligerent government.

(13) Attacks on commerce by illegitimate privateers during a war or revolution.

(14) Participation in privateering attacks of a foreign belligerent on commerce of a nation with which the offender's state of nationality is at peace.[35]

These are not necessarily separate categories. If item 12 is understood narrowly (that is, as referring only to the acts of unrecognised belligerents[36]), then these are all cases of what we would now call illegal participation in hostilities by civilians. They are acts of unauthorised violence lacking public sanction which could, on the Lauterpacht approach, readily be classed as piracy. Indeed, the impression that this might be what the authors of the Harvard Research intended is only reinforced by the authorities referred to in the following pages: every single one deals with questions arising under the laws of armed conflict.[37] However, despite the authorities they marshal, the authors

---

[31] Harvard Research, n 1 above, 764 (emphasis added).

[32] See eg JP Bishop, *Commentaries on the Criminal Law*, 3rd edn (Boston, Little, Brown & Co, 1865) vol 2, 548–49 at § 1018–19.

[33] Harvard Research, n 1 above, 769 (emphasis added).

[34] Ibid, 809. This first appears to have been a concern of Matsuda's: Rosenne, n 20 above, vol 2, 143; (1926) 20 *American Journal of International Law* Special Supplement 224.

[35] Harvard Research, ibid, 777.

[36] This appears to have been the understanding of Matsuda: Rosenne, n 20 above, vol 1, 126 (reproducing the Committee minutes referred to in n 24 above).

[37] Harvard Research, n 1 above, 777–79; see similarly the commentary at 798–802.

of the Harvard Draft eventually favour a motives-based approach over the 'unauthorised violence' approach. In their commentary to the words 'for private ends' they state:

> Although states at times have claimed the right to treat as pirates unrecognized insurgents against a foreign government who have pretended to exercise belligerent rights on the sea against neutral commerce . . . *and although there is authority for subjecting some cases of these types to the common jurisdiction of all states*, it seems best to confine the common jurisdiction to offenders acting for private ends only.[38]

To the modern reader, this may seem a rational enough effort to separate a question of the laws of war from the laws of piracy. The point, however, requires further unpicking. Did the authors of the Harvard Draft mean this in the same sense as the League of Nations Committee of Experts—that the only political 'other' excluded from the definition of piracy were certain categories of acts committed by civil war insurgents?

We have noted already the peculiar historical question regarding the status of unrecognised insurgents in a civil war purporting to exercise rights arising under the law or armed conflict and whether such illegal participation in hostilities should be classed as piracy. Simply put, the doctrine of belligerency held that insurgent forces in a civil war could be given the rights of lawful combatant forces through recognition of their belligerent status by the government they sought to overthrow or by foreign governments.[39] Such recognition could be objectively construed from the conduct of the parties, and the rights it conferred were opposable only to the recognising state. Simply put: '[i]nsurgents (as non-state actors) had no right to take action against neutral vessels [eg by enforcing a blockade or searching the vessel for contraband destined to the enemy] and were liable to be treated as pirates unless the [relevant] flag state had recognised their belligerency'.[40] While the doctrine of recognition of belligerency has now fallen into desuetude,[41] this should not obscure the fact that the words 'for private ends'—despite their seeming generality—appear once again to have been used by the authors of the Harvard Draft to distinguish questions arising under the laws of war.

The Harvard Draft concluded, as indicated above, that such acts by insurgent forces were not piracy. The power to take action against such offenders was instead addressed in a separate Article 16, based on the idea that such illegal attacks vested a special jurisdiction in the flag state of attacked vessels. This article provided:

---

[38] Ibid, 798 (emphasis added).

[39] See generally YM Lootsteen, 'The Concept of Belligerency in International Law' (2000) 166 *Military Law Review* 109; L Moir, *The Law of Internal Armed Conflict* (Cambridge, Cambridge University Press, 2002) 4–18; H Lauterpacht, 'Insurrection et Piraterie' (1939) 46 *Revue Générale de Droit International Public* 518; DP O'Connell (IA Shearer, ed), *The International Law of the Sea*, vol 2 (Oxford, Clarendon Press, 1984) 975–76. See also *The Prize Cases* 67 US 635 (1863); *The Ambrose Light* 25 Fed 408 (SDNY 1885); and the arguments of counsel in *The Three Friends* 166 US 1 (1897). Some authors considered that recognition was not relative and there existed a duty of granting such recognition: T-C Chen, *The International Law of Recognition* (London, Stevens & Sons, 1951) 350–51 (powers arise from the fact of war and there may be a duty of recognition); H Lauterpacht, *Recognition in International Law* (Cambridge, Cambridge University Press, 1953) 250–53.

[40] D Guilfoyle, 'The Mavi Marmara Incident and Blockade in Armed Conflict' (2011) 81 *British Yearbook of International Law* 171, 192.

[41] Moir, n 39 above, 19–21; Lootsteen, n 39 above, 110–11, 125.

The provisions of this convention do not diminish a state's right under international law to take measures for the protection of its nationals, its ships and its commerce against interference on or over the high sea, when such measures are not based upon jurisdiction over piracy.

The relevant commentary notes that this provision:

> covers inter alia the troublesome matter of illegal forcible acts for political ends against foreign commerce, committed on the high sea by unrecognized organizations. For instance a revolutionary organization uses an armed ship to establish a blockade against foreign commerce, or to stop and search foreign ships for contraband . . . These acts are illegal under international law, at least if the revolutionary organization has not been recognised as a belligerent by the offended state . . .
>
> Some writers assert that such illegal attacks on foreign commerce by unrecognized revolutionaries are piracies in the international law sense; *and there is even judicial authority to this effect.* It is the better view, however, that these . . . are special cases of offences for which the perpetrators may be punished by an offended state as it sees fit.[42]

The point being made here is that Article 16 was intended to define the scope of 'private ends' used in the definition of piracy provided in Article 3. The only class of persons acting for 'private ends' under consideration were 'unrecognised' or 'revolutionary' organisations involved in a civil war insurgency.[43] Nonetheless, the authors still assume there is a clear division involved: the narrow class of belligerent acts excluded as being 'for private ends' from Article 3 are excluded because they are regulated by a rule of the laws of war (here, belligerency and neutrality), as indirectly acknowledged in Article 16. The Harvard Research thus, it seems, intended to adopt an approach broadly similar to that of the League of Nations Committee of Experts.

However, the authors of the Harvard Draft appear to have placed much stronger emphasis on the question of motives as the primary distinction involved than did Matsuda or the Committee of Experts. As discussed above, Matsuda appears to have assumed that all violence by unrecognised insurgencies against third states would be piracy unless it fell within an exception for acts committed with exclusively political motives. The Harvard Draft appears, conversely, to have assumed the acts of unrecognised insurgencies would generally not be piracy unless committed for private ends. On either approach the introduction of questions of subjective motives was not strictly necessary. Lauterpacht considered that 'in general, the attitude of governments consists of refusing to treat as pirates the vessels of [even] *unrecognised* insurgents, so long as their depredations are limited to the [vessels] of their state of origin'.[44] The relevant consideration then becomes not the political motives of the insurgency 'but the class of vessel attacked, being those that are legitimate targets for insurgents in the course of a civil conflict'.[45] Put another way, there is no conflict between the state practice the

---

[42] Harvard Research, n 1 above, 857 (emphasis added) and see also 786.

[43] In accord see M Halberstam, 'Terrorism on the High Seas: The *Achille Lauro*, Piracy and the IMO Convention on Maritime Safety' (1988) 82 *American Journal of International Law* 269, 279.

[44] Lauterpacht, n 39 above, 518 (emphasis added) ('En général, l'attitude des gouvernements consiste à refuser de traiter comme pirates des navires d'insurgés non reconnus, tant que leurs déprédations se limitent à leur Etat d'origine') and compare 515, 516, 521 and 523. In agreement see LC Green, 'The Santa Maria: Rebels or Pirates?' (1961) 37 *British Year Book of International Law* 496, 501–02.

[45] D Guilfoyle, *Shipping Interdiction and the Law of the Sea* (Cambridge, Cambridge University Press, 2009) 33.

codification efforts were attempting to account for and Lauterpacht's unauthorised violence conception of piracy, so long as

> one accepts that insurgents attacking legitimate targets [ie the government they seek to overthrow] in an internal conflict are exercising a limited form of public power . . . Insurgents can thus be distinguished from both pirates and terrorists on the basis that they have the [expressly] recognised capacity at international law to become a lawful government.[46]

However, on Lauterpacht's unauthorised violence approach, there is no reason to suggest that such acts could not constitute both an illegal assertion of belligerent rights and piracy in the proper sense. An act breaching the law of armed conflict (for example, by targeting vessels taking no part in the conflict and not flagged or belonging to a party to the conflict) is inherently an act of unauthorised violence. It is also piracy if that act of violence against a vessel is committed by a private vessel, such as those used by unrecognised insurgencies. This is not to suggest that any breach of the law of armed conflict could constitute piracy, for the simple reason that piracy (at least under the modern definition) must be 'by the crew or the passengers of a private ship . . . and directed . . . on the high seas, against another ship'.[47] Thus it is quite clear that state warships and vessels cannot commit piracy unless their crews mutiny.[48] However, the vessels of an unrecognised insurgency would remain 'private' vessels capable of committing piracy unless and until they achieved recognition as belligerents (and thus legitimate combatants).

Ultimately, the approach of the Harvard Research was not to attempt to come up with a rule that could be reconciled with actual state practice and judicial pronouncements but to propose a rule based on (in their view) analytical clarity. The Harvard Research may also have been influenced by the authors' seemingly heavy reliance on the German jurist Steil, who defined piracy as 'a non-political [*unpolitisches*] professional course of robbery'.[49] The suggestion can only have been intended *de lege ferenda*.[50]

D. The International Law Commission Articles on the Law of the Sea 1950-56

It is unclear whether the ILC, in its heavy reliance on the work of the Harvard Research, fully appreciated that the latter had been engaged in, at best, a work of progressive development of the law. Nonetheless, it appears that the ILC simply lifted the words 'for private ends' straight out of the Harvard Research Draft Convention into its own articles on the law of the sea. The commentary to the ILC articles contains no explanation of the reasons for including the term or its intended meaning.[51] The ILC rapporteur JPA François made the point that requiring intention to rob (*animo furandi*) would overly narrow the definition and, after reviewing various authorities, he appeared to endorse the position of the Harvard Research that 'it seems best

---

[46] Ibid, 35.
[47] HSC, Art 15; UNCLOS, n 2 above, Art 101.
[48] See now HSC, ibid, Art 16; UNCLOS, ibid, Art 102.
[49] Rubin, n 11 above, 339, quoting P Steil, *Der Tatbestand der Piraterie nach geltendem Völkerrecht* (Leipzig, Verlag von Duncker & Humblot, 1905) 28. The passage quoted by Rubin and reproduced here, however, does not appear anywhere in the copious compilation of quotes in the Harvard Research.
[50] Rubin, n 11 above, 339.
[51] [1956] II *Yearbook of the International Law Commission* 253, 282.

to confine the common jurisdiction to offenders acting for private ends only', thus excluding cases involving government warships or civil war insurgencies.[52] The point did not otherwise receive detailed consideration in the ILC debates. A great deal of time, however, was spent in ILC debates on the question of whether states could commit piracy, largely due to incidents involving Nationalist China's seizure of Polish ships.[53] As noted above, that proposition has been widely rejected and is expressly ruled out in the modern treaty law.[54]

Ultimately, the ILC adopted a definition of piracy, being a simplified version of the Harvard Research draft Article 3, which included a 'for private ends' requirement. That ILC definition is the one now found almost verbatim in the treaty law definitions reproduced at the beginning of this chapter.

III. THE TERRORISM DEBATE 1955–88

A. 'Terrorist' Hijacking and Piracy

Aircraft and ship hijacking incidents from 1955 onwards[55] resulted in calls for an assimilation of such incidents to piracy, or assertions that universal jurisdiction extended to such crimes on a similar basis as such acts are universally condemned.[56] Pella had said of such calls regarding anarchist terrorism in the 1920s that it would be preferable to conclude 'a special convention' dealing with such crimes than to assimilate them to piracy.[57] Somewhat belatedly, given the failure of the 1937 League of Nations Terrorism Convention to enter into force,[58] Pella's wish was granted in the so-called terrorism suppression conventions of 1970–2010.[59]

The history of these conventions is too well known to warrant detailed repetition here. The usual historical account runs that, in the absence of general agreement within the UN system on a single universal definition of terrorism, it was easier to conclude issue-specific treaties which criminalised certain acts or tactics associated with terrorism.[60] Many of these treaties criminalise particular acts without any express

---

[52] [1955] I *Yearbook of the International Law Commission* 40.

[53] [1955] I *Yearbook of the International Law Commission* 37; see also Halberstam, n 43 above, 280–81. On the widely misunderstood Nyon Arrangement on Submarine Warfare 1937 (181 LNTS 135), which could be taken to suggest certain state acts constitute piracy, see Guilfoyle, n 45 above, 37–38.

[54] HSC Art 16; UNCLOS, n 2 above, Art 102.

[55] Shubber records over 100 aircraft hijacking incidents from 1955 to 1969: S Shubber, 'Is Hijacking of Aircraft Piracy in International Law?' (1968–69) 43 *British Yearbook of International Law* 193, 193–94, note 1.

[56] Eg RA Friedlander, *Terrorism: Documents of International and Local Control*, vol 1 (Dobbs Ferry, NY, Oceana, 1979) 11–13 and see the materials cited at note 37; Halberstam, n 43 above, 289; KC Randall, 'Universal Jurisdiction under International Law' (1988) 66 *Texas Law Review* 785, 788–89 and 828–31. Against such approaches see Shubber, ibid.

[57] Pella, n 27 above, 219.

[58] See KN Trapp, *State Responsibility for International Terrorism* (Oxford, Oxford University Press, 2011) 292–93.

[59] See generally MN Shaw, *International Law*, 6th edn (Cambridge, Cambridge University Press, 2008) 1159–60 and note 212; see also the useful list of relevant treaties at treaties.un.org/Pages/DB.aspx?path=DB/ studies/page2_en.xml. Neither includes the Convention on the Suppression of Unlawful Acts Relating to International Civil Aviation 2010 (Beijing, 10 September 2010, not yet in force).

[60] Trapp, n 58 above, 15–23; R Cryer, H Friman, D Robinson and E Wilmshurst, *An Introduction to International Criminal Law and Procedure*, 2nd edn (Cambridge, Cambridge University Press, 2010) 339–40;

requirement of a special 'terrorist' motive. Thus the offences envisaged could, prima facie, equally apply to non-politically motivated crimes (as further discussed below). The term 'terrorism suppression convention' can therefore be misleading, so such conventions are better referred to as 'suppression conventions' as their aim is to suppress certain defined conduct.

Of more immediate concern is the relationship between piracy and maritime terrorism, which is usually discussed through the prism of the *Santa Maria* (1961)[61] and *Achille Lauro* (1985)[62] incidents. The *Santa Maria* incident of 1961 grew out of the opposition of General Delgado and his supporters to Dr Salazar (Prime Minister of Portugal from 1932 to 1968). The *Santa Maria* was a cruise liner and:

> among the passengers who boarded the liner . . . was a number of persons who subsequently, under the leadership of a Portuguese political dissident, Captain Galvao, took over the liner by armed force. In the course of the seizure one of the ship's officers was killed, while other members of the crew, including the captain, were placed under armed guard . . . Captain Galvao gave the seizure what appeared to be a political complexion by describing it as 'the first step aimed at overthrowing the Dictator Salazar of Portugal'.[63]

Under the HSC definition, this was clearly not piracy, for the simple reason that it did not involve an attack: 'by the crew or the passengers of a private ship . . . and directed . . . on the high seas, against another ship' (the 'two-ship requirement'). The treaty-law definition simply excluded such an incident of mutiny, unless the captured vessel went on to be used to attack other vessels. It was also widely considered that the political motives of Galvao meant the incident could not have been 'for private ends'.[64]

Similarly, in the *Achille Lauro* incident of 1985, Palestinian Liberation Front members posed as tourists, boarded an Italian cruise ship in Port Said and hijacked it from within. They threatened to kill those aboard if the government of Israel did not release 50 prisoners, and they did in fact kill one US citizen outside the Syrian port of Tartus.[65] Once again, this was not piracy as it did not satisfy the two-ship requirement and on the motive-based approach it was not generally considered an act 'for private ends'. Despite the fact that this episode could have been covered by the Hostage Taking Convention,[66] it was widely seen as demonstrating the need for a suppression convention applicable to maritime transport in the same manner that other conventions already covered hijacking and sabotage of airplanes.[67] This eventually led to the conclusion of the 1988 SUA Convention.

G Acquaviva, 'Terrorism' in A Cassese (ed), *The Oxford Companion to International Criminal Justice* (Oxford, Oxford University Press, 2009) 533–34.

[61] See, eg Green, n 44 above; B Forman, 'International Law of Piracy: And the Santa Maria Incident' (1961) 15 *JAG Journal* 143; TM Franck, 'To Define and Punish Piracies—The Lesson of the Santa Maria: A Comment' (1961) 36 *New York University Law Review* 839.

[62] See, eg H Tuerk, 'Combating Terrorism at Sea: The Suppression of Unlawful Acts against the Safety of Maritime Navigation' (2008) 15 *University of Miami International & Comparative Law Review* 337; Halberstam, n 43 above; LA McCullough, 'International and Domestic Criminal Law Issues in the *Achille Lauro* Incident: A Functional Analysis' (1986) 36 *Naval Law Review* 53.

[63] Green, n 44 above, 496.

[64] Green, n 44 above, 503; Franck, n 61 above, 840.

[65] McCullough, n 62 above, 56–57; Halberstam, n 43 above, 269.

[66] International Convention against the Taking of Hostages 1979 (1316 UNTS 205), Art 1(1) and 5(1)(a) (defining the offence and extending its application to events aboard ships).

[67] Convention for the Suppression of Unlawful Seizure of Aircraft 1970 (860 UNTS 105); Convention for the Suppression of Unlawful Acts against the Safety of Civil Aviation 1971 (974 UNTS 177).

The sponsoring governments which first introduced a draft text for the SUA Convention (Austria, Egypt and Italy) cited as part of their reason for doing so the restrictions inherent within the definition of piracy: that it necessarily involved an act for private ends and, in requiring an attack from one vessel against another, could not cover the internal seizure of a vessel.[68] The stated aim of the sponsoring governments was thus to produce a 'comprehensive' convention that did not rest on such arbitrary distinctions.[69]

Another relevant inspiration for the SUA Convention was General Assembly Resolution 40/61, which called upon the IMO to 'study the problem of terrorism aboard or against ships with a view to making recommendations on appropriate measures'. It is important to note, however, that the word 'terrorism' appears only in the SUA Convention's preamble. The consequences of this drafting will be returned to below.

B. The SUA Convention and the Hostages Convention: Can Pirates be Terrorists?

As noted, the current conventional view is that the definition of piracy intrinsically excludes terrorism: a terrorist cannot be a pirate. However, it may still be the case that, under the suppression conventions, a pirate may be guilty of a 'terrorist' offence. The obvious texts to consider are the SUA Convention and the Hostage Taking Convention.

Article 3 of the SUA Convention creates a number of offences. Most relevant for present purposes is Article 3(1)(a), stating that '[a]ny person commits an offence if that person unlawfully and intentionally . . . seizes or exercises control over a ship by force or threat thereof or any other form of intimidation'. There is no express requirement that the seizure be internal or be politically motivated. Thus any act of piracy involving exercising 'control over a ship by force' or its seizure will clearly fall within this definition. Piracy off the coast of Somalia, in which force is often used to compel vessels to stop and permit boarding and in which vessels are seized and diverted to Somalia in order to ransom the vessel and crew, clearly fall within this definition. Attempting, abetting and threatening such an offence are equally crimes under the Convention (Article 3(2)). The SUA Convention does not apply to offences committed solely within a single state's territorial sea, where the vessel was not scheduled to navigate beyond that territorial sea and the suspected offender was subsequently found within that coastal state's territory (Article 4). However, as piracy must be committed outside territorial waters, Article 4 is no obstacle to the SUA Convention's application to acts of piracy. While the SUA Convention clearly does not cover piracy *in toto*, some acts constituting piracy under UNCLOS may also be SUA Convention offences.

As noted, certain forms of piracy may involve taking crews hostage for ransom. Article 1 of the Hostage Taking Convention states that:

> Any person who seizes or detains and threatens to kill, to injure or to continue to detain another person (. . . the 'hostage') in order to compel a third party . . . [including] a natural or juridical person, or a group of persons, to do or abstain from doing any act as an explicit or implicit condition for release of the hostage

---

[68] IMO Doc PCUA 1/3 (3 February 1987), Annexe, para 2.
[69] Ibid.

commits the offence of hostage-taking.[70] This definition is clearly met where a hostage is detained, threatened with continued detention, and a condition of his or her release is that a private person or company pay a ransom. The typical piracy offences being committed off Somalia involving holding crews for ransom could thus clearly fall within the Convention definition.

Two objections may be made against this application of the SUA and Hostages Conventions: first, that these Conventions only apply to terrorism or were only intended to apply to terrorism; or, second, that it would be incongruous to label a mere pirate a terrorist by convicting them under such offences ('fair labelling'). As far as the fair labelling argument goes, it does not apply here. These are not conventions that contain in their title the word 'terrorist', nor do they directly label any offence they create as being a 'terrorist' offence. They are only colloquially referred to as 'terrorism suppression conventions'. One does not label a person a 'terrorist' if they are convicted under national offences created to implement these conventions.

The more serious objection is that these conventions apply only to terrorism or were intended only to apply to terrorism. As discussed, the commonly understood meaning of terrorism hinges on the motive of the criminal: a terrorist is politically motivated. In this context, one may now refer to Article 2(1)(b) of the Terrorist Financing Convention 1999, under which terrorist offences include acts:

> intended to cause death or serious bodily injury to a civilian, or to any other person not taking an active part in the hostilities in a situation of armed conflict, when the purpose of such act, by its nature or context, is to intimidate a population, or to compel a Government or an international organization to do or to abstain from doing any act.

No such language is included in either the SUA or the Hostages Convention. It therefore forms no part of the offence. The reason no such language is included in either convention is obvious: such language was impossible to agree before 1999 due to the long-running (and still continuing) debate over the conditions under which national liberation movements should be exempt from classification as terrorists.[71] Precisely because no agreement could be reached on this element of a general definition, the approach of the suppression conventions was thematic. In the absence of a definition of terrorism (including its special intent element), tactics associated with terrorism were outlawed irrespective of by whom or why they were committed. No argument can be made based on the definition of the offences that these offences are restricted to politically motivated acts.

The final objection is that, even if the text of these conventions contains no express terrorist motive requirement in their operative provisions, they were intended only to be applied to terrorism cases. The argument goes that, while the offence-defining provisions of the treaty are silent on this question of terrorist intent, they are to be interpreted in their context—which includes the references in the preamble to terrorism.[72] The SUA Convention preamble does indeed make five references to terrorism: four references to UN General Assembly Resolution 40/61 (as noted above), as well

---

[70] See n 66 above.
[71] See n 60 above.
[72] Art 31(1) and (2), Vienna Convention on the Law of Treaties 1969 (1155 UNTS 331). Such an argument was put in *United States v Shi*, 525 F3d 709 (9th Cir 2008); see the case note by E Kontorovich, 'United States v Shi' (2009) 103(4) *American Journal of International Law* 734, 735.

as noting the signatories' deep concern 'about the world-wide escalation of acts of terrorism in all its forms, which endanger or take innocent human lives'. More pithily, the Hostages Convention simply refers to the signatories' conviction that 'it is urgently necessary to develop international co-operation between states in devising and adopting effective measures for the prevention, prosecution and punishment of all acts of taking of hostages as manifestations of international terrorism'. The argument based on theses preambular references has both a general problem and a further problem specific to the SUA Convention. The general problem is that one ordinarily applies a principle of strict construction in criminal law.[73] This demands certainty in the drafting of criminal law so that persons can know in advance if their behaviour accords with law. Neither the principle nor its objective is respected if one construes new substantive elements of a crime—which are simply not contained in the plain text of the operative provisions—out of ambiguous language in the preamble. Unsurprisingly, at least one domestic court has rejected arguments that a person should not be convicted under a national law implementing the SUA Convention unless they have a terrorist motive because to do so would exceed the intention of the treaty's drafters.[74] The argument further confuses the nature of the intent involved. Certainly many or all of the individuals involved in drafting the SUA and Hostages conventions probably believed they were present to negotiate a 'terrorism' convention. However, lawyers are not concerned with the subjective intention of individuals when engaged in treaty interpretation. The job of those interpreting treaties is to give effect to the legislative intention of the drafters as expressed in what they mutually agreed. This is generally an objective exercise (discerning the will of the legislature), the principal guide to which is the text itself.[75] The simple fact that the drafters did not (and could not) reduce to writing any collective agreement on a 'special intent' for terrorism is far more important than preambular references to terrorism. One cannot argue that the conventions were limited by a commonly shared concept of terrorism for the simple reason that there was no such shared conception.

More specifically in the case of the SUA Convention, the Security Council has suggested on numerous occasions that it is an instrument which could be used to combat Somali piracy.[76] This authoritative contemporary international practice should weigh strongly against the argument that a special (yet undefined) terrorist intent requirement must be read into all the suppression conventions because that is what the drafters allegedly intended (despite their inability to reduce that intention to writing).

---

[73] A Cassese, *International Criminal Law*, 2nd edn (Oxford, Oxford University Press, 2008) 41–43, 47–51.

[74] See the references to *United States v Shi*, n 72 above.

[75] See R Gardiner, *Treaty Interpretation* (Oxford, Oxford University Press, 2008) 6 and 9; P Allott, 'Power Sharing in the Law of the Sea' (1983) 77 *American Journal of International Law* 1, 5; compare W Twining and D Miers, *How to Do Things With Rules*, 4th edn (London, Butterworths, 1999) 187–90.

[76] UNSC Resolution 1846 (2008), UN Doc S/RES/1846, para 15; UNSC Resolution 1851 (2008), UN Doc S/RES/1851, preamble; UNSC Resolution 1897 (2009), UN Doc S/RES/1897, preamble; UNSC Resolution 1950 (2010), UN Doc S/RES/1950, preamble; UNSC Resolution 2020 (2011), UN Doc S/RES/2020, preamble; UNSC Resolution 2077 (2012), UN Doc S/RES/2077, preamble.

IV. THE PIRACY/TERRORISM DEBATE AFTER 9/11

Despite the large-scale international naval deployments off Somalia to counter piracy in the region, there have been few efforts to deploy either a 'laws of war' or 'war on terror' paradigm against Somali pirates. The international response to Somali piracy has occurred very much within a law-enforcement paradigm and has been peculiarly resistant to 'securitisation' and the invocation of exceptional counter-terrorism powers.[77] As Major General Buster Howes, Operation Commander of EU NAVFOR, has put it: 'We are engaged in a constabulary task, and that is the fundamental guiding principle that constrains what we can do'.[78]

This has not stopped John Bolton, for example, suggesting that invocation of the rights the US has arrogated to itself in the course of the 'war on terror' would be useful, allowing the extrajudicial execution of suspect pirates on sight:

> Somali piracy fits far better (although admittedly imperfectly) into the war-against-terror paradigm than into law enforcement . . . It is nonsensical to engage in legal contortions, cramming piracy or terrorism into inappropriate criminal-justice models suitable within civil societies but not the state of nature prevailing in Somalia.[79]

Most states, obviously, have rejected the US conception of a global armed conflict with a non-state actor that would allow individuals to be targeted and killed anywhere on the planet.[80] Further, it would be very difficult to characterise Somali piracy as meeting the requirements of 'protracted armed violence between governmental authorities and organized armed groups' for an armed conflict to exist between navies and pirates.[81] For a start, 'Somali pirates' are not organised in anything approaching 'armed groups' in the armed conflict sense; the state interests they attack are diffuse (making it harder to say there are specifically engaged state parties to a conflict); and it would strain credulity if the sporadic use of assault rifles and rocket-propelled grenades against randomly selected vessels could be held to rise to 'protracted armed violence' in the technical sense under the law of armed conflict.[82] Naval operators, as opposed to armchair commentators, are thus very clear that they are operating in a law enforcement, rather than a laws of war, paradigm.

This does not mean, however, that the other alternative—a conventional counter-terrorism framework outside the 'war on terror'—does not raise a number of awkward possibilities. First, there is the question of whether payment of ransom to pirates constitutes the financing of terrorism. There is actually little or no evidence—despite

---

[77] See generally D Guilfoyle, 'International Law and Counter-piracy in the Indian Ocean' (2012) 8 *Journal of the Indian Ocean Region* 202.

[78] House of Commons Foreign Affairs Committee (UK), n 10 above, Evidence Annexe, 14.

[79] JR Bolton, 'Treat Somali Pirates Like Terrorists', *The Washington Times*, 14 October 2011, available at www.washingtontimes.com/news/2011/oct/14/treat-somali-pirates-like-terrorists/.

[80] C Gray, *International Law and the Use of Force*, 3rd edn (Oxford, Oxford University Press, 2008) 227–53, especially 253; D Turns, 'The Law of Armed Conflict (International Humanitarian Law)' in M Evans (ed), *International Law*, 3rd edn (Oxford, Oxford University Press, 2010) 814, 824.

[81] *Prosecutor v Tadić* (Decision on the Defence Motion for Interlocutory Appeal on Jurisdiction), International Criminal Tribunal for the Former Yugoslavia, Appeals Chamber Case No IT-94-1-AR72, 2 October 1995, para 70.

[82] See generally D Guilfoyle, 'The Laws of War and the Fight against Somali Piracy: Combatants or Criminals' (2010) 11 *Melbourne Journal of International Law* 14. See also N Lubell, *Extraterritorial Use of Force Against Non-state Actors* (Oxford, Oxford University Press, 2010) 73–74, 107–08, 225–26.

constant press, policy-maker and academic speculation—of any significant links between pirates and designated 'terrorist' groups, such as the Al-Shabaab insurgency in Somalia.[83] This does not mean that some money raised by piracy may not find its way indirectly to designated terrorist groups; again, to take the Somali example, Al-Shabaab's control of certain strategic ports and areas may place it in a position to 'tax' some pirate activities.[84] However, there is also evidence that Al-Shabaab 'seems to regard the buccaneering and this manner of raising money as an improper activity that goes against the moralistic and strict version of Islam that it follows'.[85]

Nonetheless, even without such links, this chapter has repeatedly made the point that one can commit 'terrorist' offences under some of the suppression conventions without having a terrorist motive. Article 2(1)(a) of the Terrorist Financing Convention makes it an offence to

> by any means, directly or indirectly, unlawfully and wilfully, provide[] or collect[] funds with the intention that they should be used or in the knowledge that they are to be used, in full or in part, in order to carry out . . . [a]n act which constitutes an offence . . . as defined in one of the treaties listed in the annex.

The listed treaties include the SUA and Hostages conventions. Thus Somali pirates could be considered 'terrorists' for the purposes of the Financing Convention. Arguably, then, paying pirate ransoms is providing funds in the knowledge that they will be used (at least in part) to finance future SUA Convention offences or crimes of hostage taking. Does this mean that paying pirate ransoms is an offence under the Convention? The words of comfort to those paying such ransoms must be 'unlawfully and wilfully'. A payment made under duress cannot be 'wilful', and in jurisdictions such as the UK paying ransoms is not inherently 'unlawful'.[86] The UN Security Council has not taken steps to extend its regime targeting the assets of designated terrorists to pirates, although it does not need to as there is a separate regime of targeted economic sanctions under UNSCR 1844 which can be applied to persons designated as threatening 'the peace, security or stability of Somalia'. Interestingly,

> Despite its stance discouraging the payment of ransoms, the UK has taken steps at the UN to ensure that such payments remain legal. The UK placed a technical hold on a US proposal last year to add two known pirate 'kingpins' . . . to the list of people subject to sanctions under UN Security Council Resolution 1844.[87]

Nonetheless, other 'terrorism' conventions may still have an impact on state behaviour, if considered applicable. The SUA Convention Article 7 provides that a state finding a suspect on its territory is required to commence a preliminary investigation and, if the circumstances so warrant, take that suspect into custody. Further, the SUA Convention then contains an obligation upon state parties to either extradite that suspect to a state party having jurisdiction or to submit the case for consideration by prosecutorial

---

[83] House of Commons Foreign Affairs Committee (UK), n 10 above, para 16 and Evidence Annexe at 20, 27, 33, 59 and 63.

[84] Ibid, paras 16 and 116.

[85] Ibid, para 137 (evidence of Sally Healy, a Somalia specialist at Chatham House).

[86] On the question of whether paying ransoms is contrary to 'public policy' at common law, see *Masefield AG v Amlin Corporate Member Ltd* [2010] EWHC 280 (Comm), [2011] EWCA Civ 24 (holding it is not).

[87] House of Commons Foreign Affairs Committee (UK), n 10 above, para 114.

authorities (commonly called an 'extradite or prosecute' obligation).[88] To this end, every state party must have a national law allowing it to prosecute 'in cases where the alleged offender is present in its territory and it does not extradite him', even in the absence of any connection between the crime and the prosecuting state. Put simply, the test for state A is: (i) is the suspect within the territory of state A; (ii) has another state party established jurisdiction in accordance with SUA Convention Article 6 over the offence committed by the suspect; and (3) has state A extradited the suspect to one of these states? If not, state A is obliged to submit the suspect to its prosecutorial authorities.

States may be reluctant, however, to invoke the Convention precisely because it creates a mandatory extradite or prosecute obligation applying to state territory. This could be awkward if Article 7 was found to apply to pirates aboard warships. While a warship is not 'territory' in the sense of being a 'floating island',[89] it is an object (or space) with a special status in international law. On the high seas all vessels are subject to the jurisdiction of their flag state, a status which the Permanent Court of International Justice 'assimilated to' a flag state's jurisdiction over its territory.[90] Human rights bodies and courts have found that vessels under the effective control of a state may fall within its 'jurisdiction' under treaties having principally territorial application.[91] A state's sovereign control over a warship is much stronger than in the case of other vessels: warships on the high seas enjoy complete immunity from the jurisdiction of other states.[92] It should therefore be uncontroversial that—on the high seas—a warship may form part of the flag state's 'jurisdiction' on a basis similar to 'territory'. However, under the SUA Convention, extradite or prosecute obligations apply only within a state's 'territory' and do not seemingly extend to areas under a state's 'jurisdiction'. One could thus argue that the mere presence of persons suspected of SUA Convention offences aboard a warship does not trigger extradite or prosecute obligations. Conversely, one could argue such a result would undermine the object and purpose of the treaty: to see that such suspects do not go unpunished when they come within the effective control of a state party.[93] The point, however, remains unresolved.

V. CONCLUSIONS: ACTS OF TERRORISM AND ACTS OF PIRACY—MUTUALLY EXCLUSIVE OR OVERLAPPING CATEGORIES?

This chapter has attempted to review the debate over the lines of demarcation between acts of piracy and acts of war and terrorism. The terms 'pirate' and 'terrorist' have always been stretched in meaning by their colloquial use as terms of condemnation

---

[88] See Art 10(1), SUA Convention. For a more extended version of this discussion see Guilfoyle, n 77 above, 210–12.

[89] O'Connell, n 39 above, 736–37.

[90] *Lotus Case* [1927] Permanent Court of International Justice, Ser A, No 10, 25.

[91] Eg *PK et al v Spain*, Committee against Torture, Decision, 21 November 2008, UN Doc CAT/C/41/D/323/2007, para 8.2; ECtHR, *Medvedyev v France*, Application No 3394/03, Judgment of the Grand Chamber, 29 March 2010, paras 65–67, 81; ECtHR, *Hirsi v Italy*, Application No 27765/09, Judgment of the Grand Chamber, 23 February 2012, para 180.

[92] UNCLOS, n 2 above, Art 95.

[93] R Geiss and A Petrig, *The Legal Framework for Counter-piracy Operations in Somalia and the Gulf of Aden* (Oxford, Oxford University Press, 2011) 163–64.

rather than terms of legal art. One particular focus has been the peculiar insistence of twentieth- and twenty-first-century authors that the words 'for private ends' constitute piracy and terrorism as mutually exclusive categories. The historical drafting reveals no such necessary outcome. The words themselves have no roots in historical case law, and seem simply to have first been used by a US textbook author in 1892. Their use, albeit with different emphases, by the legal experts of the League of Nations, the authors of the Harvard Research and the ILC rapporteur on the subject seems intended in each case to distinguish not a class of acts of terrorism from piracy, but a class of acts of war, and, in particular, the peculiar nineteenth-century law surrounding the laws of naval warfare applicable to unrecognised civil war insurgencies. While certainly raising the question of subjective motives, the underlying approach of the historical codification efforts was essentially functional.

The chapter has also argued that, as a matter of textual analysis, there is no reason why many acts of piracy could not be prosecuted under the SUA Convention or the Hostage Taking Convention. These conventions, due to the historic debate over the boundary between freedom fighters and terrorists, do not contain a requirement that the offences they define must be committed with a political motive. Thus, a pirate could be prosecuted under a 'terrorism' suppression convention. The chapter has also briefly noted the lack of appetite for assimilating the fight against piracy off the coast of Somalia to the 'war on terror' or any more conventional form of armed conflict. On the latter, there are serious doubts that Somali pirates could qualify as actors in a non-international armed conflict in any event.

Finally, we are left with the question of how best to interpret the words in the treaty law that have caused so much trouble over the years: 'violence . . . for private ends'. This chapter has argued that the preferable approach to defining piracy would have been the functional approach of Lauterpacht, focusing on the unauthorised character of the violence. Indeed, it is possible to argue that the correct interpretation of the words 'violence . . . for private ends' is that they should be read not as opposed to 'politically motivated violence' but as opposed to 'public violence'. That is, violence lacking state sanction may be considered violence 'for private ends'. The correct dichotomy would thus be considered as private/public, not private/political. On this reading, an act of piracy would remain piracy, even if committed for political motives.[94] A growing number of scholars now support this idea.[95] It is, in my view, not only the preferable approach, but one that is as consistent with the confused legal history behind the words 'for private ends' as any other interpretation.

In the final analysis, treating 'pirate' and 'terrorist' as reified categories is unhelpful. We have a criminal law of piracy and a criminal law of terrorism. It is a truism in national law that a wrongful course of conduct may be characterised as more than one offence. On this point, international law is no different.

---

[94] For a strong argument that some categories of politically motivated violence should not be classed as piracy, see Churchill, Chapter 1 above.

[95] Guilfoyle, n 45 above, 37; Halberstam, n 43 above, 290; Geiss and Petrig, n 93 above, 61; Shubber, n 55 above, 200; compare J Kraska, *Contemporary Maritime Piracy: International Law, Strategy, and Diplomacy at Sea* (Santa Barbara CA, ABC-CLIO, 2011) 210.

3

Piracy and the Use of Force

ALEXANDER PROELSS

I. INTRODUCTION

This chapter addresses international legal aspects concerning the use of force against pirates. The general prohibition of the use of force is codified in Article 2(4) of the Charter of the United Nations (UN Charter)[1] and is, notwithstanding all challenges it has faced over the decades,[2] regarded as being valid under customary international law.[3] Traditionally, Article 2(4) UN Charter, or the prohibition of the use of force under customary international law, is considered to exclusively cover force exercised by one or more state(s), not by private individuals.[4] Correspondingly, the right to self-defence as the primary exception to the prohibition of the use of force is usually restricted to measures taken in response to an armed attack by another state.[5] It is beyond controversy that the acts of pirates, eg off the coast of Somalia are not attributable to the (failed) state of Somalia under the principles of attribution accepted under customary international law.[6] Based on a traditional reading, the prohibition of the use of force and its possible exceptions would thus not seem to be applicable in the relationship between pirates and the states involved in anti-piratical actions.

---

[1] Charter of the United Nations of 24 October 1945, 1 *UNTS* XV.

[2] See, eg T Franck, 'Who Killed Article 2(4)?' (1970) 64 *American Journal of International Law* 809; T Franck, 'The United Nations after Iraq' (2003) 97 *American Journal of International Law* 607, 620.

[3] *Military and Paramilitary Activities in and against Nicaragua (Nicaragua v USA)*, Judgment of 27 June 1986, [1986] ICJ Reports 14, 97ff; see also O Dörr, 'Use of Force, Prohibition of' in R Wolfrum (ed), *Max Planck Encyclopedia of Public International Law*, vol X (Oxford, Oxford University Press, 2012) 607, 609; S Kadelbach, *Zwingendes Völkerrecht* (Berlin, Duncker & Humblot, 1992) 228ff.

[4] See J Delbrück, 'The Fight against Global Terrorism' (2001) 44 *German Yearbook of International Law* 9, 15; M Bothe, 'Friedenssicherung und Kriegsrecht' in W Graf Vitzthum and A Proelss (eds), *Völkerrecht*, 6th edn (Berlin et al, De Gruyter, 2013) ch 8, para 8. Note that Art 2(4) UN Charter only obliges the Member States of the UN to 'refrain *in their international relations* from the threat or use of force against the territorial integrity or political independence of any state, or in any other manner inconsistent with the Purposes of the United Nations' (emphasis added).

[5] *Legal Consequences of the Construction of a Wall in the Occupied Palestinian Territories*, Advisory Opinion of 9 July 2004, [2004] ICJ Reports 136, 194; *Armed Activities on the Territory of the Congo (Democratic Republic of Congo v Uganda)*, Judgment of 19 December 2005, [2005] ICJ Reports 168, 221ff. Note that the wording of Art 51 UN Charter does not contain any restriction to armed attacks by another state.

[6] Arts 4–11 of the Articles on Responsibility of States for Internationally Wrongful Acts (cf Annex to UN Doc A/RES/56/83 of 12 December 2001) dealing with the issue of attribution are predominantly held to reflect customary international law.

At the same time, however, it is a matter of fact that both pirates and the states involved in the fight against piracy off the coast of Somalia and elsewhere have resorted to military force, and, as far as anti-piratical actions are concerned, the prevailing view is that recourse to force against pirates is generally justified. Calls for using military might against pirate vessels and mother ships are frequent not only within the sphere of security policy, and it is interesting to note that the international legal requirements for using force against pirates are analysed in detail only at rare occasions. This is why the present chapter attempts to clarify the relationship between the fight against piracy, on the one hand, and the prohibition of the use of force, on the other. The central questions to be answered are whether anti-piratical measures are subject to the standards of the *jus ad bellum* (which would render them in need of justification by reference to the right of self-defence or an authorisation by the UN Security Council) and, if not, how the use of force against pirates can then be justified.

Against this background, it will first be demonstrated that international treaty law as well as the practice of the UN Security Council and the EU are based on the assumption that the use of military force against pirates is indeed covered by international law. The next section is then dedicated to the legal foundation of the use of force against pirates. It refers to the pertinent resolutions of the Security Council, which were adopted on the basis of Chapter VII UN Charter, as potential indications for the relevance of the prohibition of the use of force. The hypothesis that the resolutions may provide legal justification for the violation of that prohibition will be put to the test by analysing whether the Security Council has constitutively authorised (in terms of Article 42 UN Charter) the addressees of its resolutions. It will be shown that no such authorisation exists, which, taking further into account that no state engaged in anti-piratical operations has invoked its right of self-defence under Article 51 UN Charter, indirectly confirms that Article 2(4) UN Charter is not applicable with regard to force used against pirates. In light of this conclusion, the final section addresses potential legal basis outside of the scope of the *jus ad bellum*.

II. USE OF FORCE AGAINST PIRATES

When approaching the issue relevant here, it should be noted that, under the classic law of nations, pirates were considered as being simultaneously criminals and military enemies, without being entitled to rely on the immunities of either of the two groups of persons.[7] Building on the notion that pirates are enemies of all mankind (*hostis humani generis*),[8] Eugene Kontorovich has summarised the legal status of pirates in the nineteenth century in the following terms: 'In short, pirates had a status much like unlawful combatants: they could be dealt with either militarily or criminally at the enforcing state's convenience'.[9]

---

[7] Cf DR Burgess, 'Hostis Humani Generi: Piracy, Terrorism and a New International Law' (2006) 13 *University of Miami International and Comparative Law Review* 293, 299; E Kontorovich, 'A Guantanamo on the Sea: The Difficulty of Prosecuting Pirates and Terrorists' (2010) 98 *California Law Review* 243, 257.

[8] The historic origins of this notion are not completely clear. The term may have first been used by the Roman statesman Cicero. In 1644, Justice Sir Edward Cook stated 'Pirata est hostis humani generis': E Cook, *The Third Part of the Institutes of the Law of England* (London, Lee & Pakeman, 1644) 113.

[9] Kontorovich, n 7 above, 257.

Keeping in mind the significant increase of piratical attacks in the last two decades or so, this description has provoked the question whether the anti-piracy operations undertaken off the coast of Somalia ought to be considered as part of a 'global war on piracy', akin to the 'global war on terror'.[10] Prima facie, the references to the concepts of 'combatant' and 'war' seem to suggest that anti-piracy operations do indeed affect the scope of both the *jus ad bellum* and *jus in bello*.[11] In order to verify this hypothesis, it is first mandatory to demonstrate that international treaty law and practice assume that military force can be used against pirates.

A. International Treaty Law

As far as international treaty law is concerned, the UN Convention on the Law of the Sea (UNCLOS)[12] deserves particular attention. In its part VII, section 1, this 'constitution for the oceans'[13] contains a set of nine articles that repeat almost literally the pertinent provisions of the Geneva Convention on the High Seas,[14] and thus state the international law of piracy as valid today. Article 100 UNCLOS obliges its parties to 'cooperate to the fullest possible extent in the repression of piracy on the high seas or in any other place outside the jurisdiction of any state'. Furthermore, Article 105 UNCLOS entitles every state to 'seize a pirate ship or aircraft, or a ship or aircraft taken by piracy, and under the control of pirates, and arrest the persons and seize the property on board' on the high seas or in any place outside the jurisdiction of any state. Finally, Article 110(1) UNCLOS authorises warships to board a ship on the high seas if there is reasonable grounds for suspecting that that ship is engaged in piracy. While UNCLOS does not contain any express authorisation for states to use force against pirates, the right to stop, board, inspect and seize pirate ships on the high seas in accordance with the aforementioned provisions necessarily implies that force may be used in order to meet the objectives contained therein.[15] Having said that, no indication exists in UNCLOS or any other international agreement that a warship is entitled to sink a vessel under mere suspicion of being engaged in piratical operations,

---

[10] EA Heinze, 'A 'Global War on Piracy'? International Law and the Use of Force Against Sea Pirates,' APSA 2011 Annual Meeting Paper, 2, available at SSRN: http://ssrn.com/abstract=1900413 2. See also D Guilfoyle, Chapter 2 above.

[11] But note that the concept of the 'unlawful combatant' was introduced just in order to circumvent the 'combatant privilege' arising out of international humanitarian law. See K Dörmann, 'Combatants, Unlawful', in Wolfrum, n 3 above, vol II, 360–69. According to the 'combatant privilege', combatants shall not be held responsible for their participation in armed conflict, if and to the extent to which they adhere to the rules and principles of international humanitarian law. The most important legal feature of the combatant privilege is the status as prisoner of war according to the Third Geneva Convention relative to the Treatment of Prisoners of War of 12 August 1949 (75 *UNTS* 135).

[12] United Nations Convention on the Law of the Sea of 10 December 1982 (1833 UNTS 3).

[13] Statement made by the President of the Third United Nations Conference on the Law of the Sea (UNCLOS III), TTB Koh, at the occasion of the adoption of the Convention, available at http://www.un.org/Depts/los/convention_agreements/texts/koh_english.pdf.

[14] Cf Arts 14–22 of the Convention on the High Seas of 29 April 1958 (450 UNTS 11).

[15] See also W Heintschel von Heinegg, 'Repressing Piracy and Armed Robbery at Sea—Towards a New International Regime?' (2010) 40 *Israel Yearbook of Human Rights* 219, 227; T Treves, 'Piracy, Law of the Sea, and Use of Force: Developments Off the Coast of Somalia' (2009) 20 *European Journal of International Law* 399, 412ff; D Guilfoyle, 'Human Rights Issues and Non-Flag State Boarding of Suspect Ships' in C Symmons (ed), *Selected Contemporary Issues in the Law of the Sea* (Leiden, Martinus Nijhoff, 2011) 83, 85; A von Arnauld, 'Die moderne Piraterie und das Völkerrecht' (2009) 47 *Archiv des Völkerrechts* 454, 466.

or to call individual suspects to account for such operations irrespective of internationally agreed standards for the treatment of individuals.

B. Decisions of the UN Security Council

The content of the resolutions that were adopted with particular regard to the situation off the coast of Somalia confirms that the UN Security Council acts on the assumption that states are entitled to use force against pirates. In 2008, it decided that states cooperating with the Transitional Federal Government of Somalia (TFG) in the fight against piracy and armed robbery at sea off the coast of Somalia may, for an initial period of six months:

> (a) enter the territorial waters of Somalia for the purpose of repressing acts of piracy and armed robbery at sea, in a manner consistent with such action permitted on the high seas with respect to piracy under relevant international law; and
> (b) use, within the territorial waters of Somalia, in a manner consistent with action permitted on the high seas with respect to piracy under relevant international law, all necessary means to repress acts of piracy and armed robbery.[16]

This decision was prolonged for another 12 months with Resolution 1846.[17] In the same year, the Security Council even went so far as to decide that the states cooperating with the TFG may

> undertake all necessary measures that are appropriate in Somalia, for the purpose of suppressing acts of piracy and armed robbery at sea . . . provided, however, that any measures undertaken pursuant to the authority of this paragraph shall be undertaken consistent with applicable international humanitarian and human rights law.[18]

The wording of this resolution, which refers not to the 'territorial waters of Somalia' but rather to 'measures that are appropriate in Somalia', as well as the fact that Resolution 1846 (2008) already covered maritime anti-piracy measures, clarify that Resolution 1846 related to anti-piracy operations on land.[19] Since 2008, both decisions have been renewed annually until today.[20] While the entitlement contained therein to take 'all necessary measures' (respectively 'all necessary means') does not refer to the use of force in express terms, it is usually considered today to include a delegation in favour of one or more state(s) to decide upon the use of military means. Notwithstanding the fact that the UN Charter does not envisage any such delegation of the decision to

---

[16] UN Doc S/RES/1838 (2008) of 7 October 2008, para 7. The notion of 'armed robbery at sea' refers to unlawful acts of violence or detention or acts of depredation, or threat thereof, other than acts of piracy (which is by definition (cf Art 101 UNCLOS) spatially limited to the high seas); cf IMO Doc A 22/Res.922 of 22 January 2002, Annex, para 2.2. Thus, the difference between piracy on the one hand and armed robbery at sea on the other is that armed robbery at sea covers piratical activities in waters under the jurisdiction of the coastal state. Critically JA Roach, 'General Problematic Issues on Exercise of Jurisdiction' in Symmons, ibid, 119, 125ff.

[17] UN Doc S/RES/1846 (2008) of 2 December 2008, para 10.

[18] UN Doc S/RES/1851 (2008) of 16 December 2008, para 6.

[19] See Treves, n 15 above, 404.

[20] Cf UN Docs S/RES/1897 (2009) of 30 November 2009, para 7; S/RES/1950 (2010) of 27 November 2010, para 7; S/RES/2020 (2011) of 22 November 2011, para 9; S/RES/2077 (2012) of 22 November 2012, para 12.

use force to individual states or groups of states, the Security Council has regularly applied this 'delegation approach' since the adoption of Resolution 678[21] concerning the 1990 attempt of Iraq to annex Kuwait.[22] In light of this practice, the legal validity of the 'delegation approach' is beyond all question.

Leaving aside here the question whether the aforementioned decisions of the Security Council contain constitutive authorisations of the addressed states to use force against pirates (which will be addressed in the next section), they undoubtedly presume that the undertaking of counter-piracy operations may, depending on the circumstances, involve the use of military force.[23] The same conclusion can be drawn from the EU's anti-piracy operation 'Atalanta',[24] the mandate of which entitles EU Member States to 'take the necessary measures, including the use of force, to deter, prevent and intervene in order to bring to an end acts of piracy and armed robbery which may be committed in the areas where it is present'.[25]

However, the fact that the Security Council and the EU have acted on the assumption that the use of force against pirates is generally admissible does not, in principle, make the need for a legal ground of justification for the use of force irrelevant. A rule expressly permitting the exercise of military force would be superfluous at most if the use of force against pirates were not generally prohibited by Article 2(4) UN Charter or customary international law. This question arguably cannot be answered by way of an isolated analysis of the scope of the prohibition of the use of force. Rather, it is particularly significant in this respect whether indications exist suggesting that the use of force against pirates is held to be in need of justification by the international community. As stated above, the provisions of UNCLOS, though obviously presuming that states may have recourse to military force vis-à-vis pirates, do not provide any express authorisation to use military force against pirates. It is important to determine whether such an authorisation, which would have to be considered as a strong indication for the relevance of Article 2(4) UN Charter, arises from the pertinent resolutions of the Security Council.

III. RESOLUTIONS OF THE UN SECURITY COUNCIL CONCERNING SOMALIA

A. Do the Security Council Resolutions Contain Constitutive Authorisations to Use Force?

Prima facie, the fact that the Security Council has invoked its competences under

---

[21] UN Doc S/RES/678 (1990) of 29 November 1990, para 2: 'Authorizes Member States co-operating with the Government of Kuwait, unless Iraq on or before 15 January 1991 fully implements, as set forth in paragraph 1 above, the above-mentioned resolutions, to use all necessary means to uphold and implement resolution 660 (1990) and all subsequent relevant resolutions and to restore international peace and security in the area'. Critical vis-à-vis the scope of the delegation contained in that resolution is Bothe, n 4 above, para 24.

[22] Cf UN Docs S/RES/794 of 3 December 1992, para 10 (Somalia); S/RES/929 of 22 June 1994, para 3 (Rwanda); S/RES/940 of 31 July 1994, para 4 (Haiti); S/RES/1386 of 20 December 2001, para 3 (Afghanistan); S/RES/1484 of 30 May 2003, para 4 (Congo); S/RES/1973 of 17 March 2011, para 4 (Libya).

[23] Heintschel von Heinegg, n 15 above, 236ff.

[24] Council Joint Action 2008/851/CSPP of 10 November 2008 on a European Union Military Operation to Contribute to the Deterrence, Prevention and Repression of Acts of Piracy and Armed Robbery off the Somali Coast, [2008] OJ L301/33.

[25] Ibid, Art 2(d).

Chapter VII UN Charter seems to suggest that piratical activities infringe the prohibition of the use of force, otherwise an authorisation would generally not be necessary. Indeed, all pertinent resolutions, starting with Resolution 1816,[26] were taken on the basis of Chapter VII UN Charter, which, according to Article 39 UN Charter, requires a determination of the existence of a threat to the peace, a breach of the peace or an act of aggression by the Security Council. Since the attacks of 11 September 2001, the Security Council has regarded acts of international terrorism as a threat to the peace[27] irrespective of whether such acts can be attributed to another state or not. In contrast, in relation to the situation off the coast of Somalia, it did not qualify piracy as a threat to the international peace but rather determined that:

> the incidents of piracy and armed robbery against vessels in the territorial waters of Somalia and the high seas off the coast of Somalia exacerbate the situation in Somalia which continues to constitute a threat to international peace and security in the region.[28]

This formula, which was used in all subsequent resolutions,[29] implies that the Security Council does not regard piracy itself as a threat to or even breach of the international peace.[30] But even if the Security Council had qualified piracy as a threat to the international peace and security, as it had done with international terrorism and with the proliferation of weapons of mass destruction,[31] this would not have automatically implied that piracy would constitute a violation of the prohibition of the use of force, as the scope of this prohibition and that of Article 39 UN Charter are not identical.[32]

In this respect, it should also be noted that no state participating in anti-piracy operations off the coast of Somalia has ever relied on its right of self-defence in terms of Article 51 UN Charter or under customary international law, and that that right has not been mentioned once in the pertinent resolutions of the Security Council. Even if it were accepted, for the sake of argument, that developments concerning the right of self-defence against terrorist attacks have given rise to a customary right of self-defence against non-state actors,[33] it seems difficult to state that the scale and

---

[26] UN Doc S/RES/1816 (2008) of 2 June 2008.

[27] Cf UN Docs S/RES/1368 (2001) of 12 September 2001, para 1; S/RES/1373 (2001) of 28 September 2001, 3rd recital.

[28] UN Doc S/RES/1816 (2008) of 2 June 2008, 12th recital.

[29] UN Docs S/RES/1838 (2008) of 7 October 2008, 12th recital; S/RES/1846 (2008) of 2 December 2008, 14th recital; S/RES/1851 (2008) of 16 December 2008, 11th recital; S/RES/1897 (2009) of 30 November 2009, 14th recital; S/RES/1950 (2010) of 23 November 2010, 20th recital; S/RES/1976 (2011) of 11 April 2011, 18th recital; S/RES/2015 (2011) of 24 October 2011, 17th recital; S/RES/2020 (2011) of 22 November 2011, 27th recital; S/RES/2077 (2012) of 22 November 2012, 29th recital.

[30] The cautious approach of the Security Council is criticised by M Vœlckel, 'La piraterie entre Chartre et Convention: A propos de la Résolution 1816 du Conseil de Sécurité' (2007) 12 *Annuaire du droit de la mer* 479, 485; M Trésoret, *Seepiraterie* (Baden-Baden, Nomos, 2011) 291ff. See also UN Docs S/RES/2018 (2011) of 31 October 2011, 1st and 3rd recitals; S/RES/2039 (2012) of 29 February 2012, recitals 2–4. These resolutions, which concern piracy in the Gulf of Guinea, were not even based on Chapter VII UN Charter.

[31] Cf UN Doc S/RES/1540 (2004) of 28 April 2004, 1st recital.

[32] Bothe, n 4 above, para 11.

[33] It has been argued that, even if Art 51 UN Charter would require an armed attack by another state, the reaction of the international community to the attacks of 11 September 2001 ought to be read as expressing *opinio juris* that the customary right of self-defence can now be lawfully exercised against private actors. See, eg S Talmon, 'Grenzen der "grenzenlosen Gerechtigkeit"' in W März (ed), *An den Grenzen des Rechts* (Berlin, Duncker & Humblot, 2003) 101, 143ff; MN Schmitt, '"Change Direction" 2006: Israeli Operations in Lebanon and the International Law of Self-defense' (2007–08) 29 *Michigan Journal of International*

effects of piratical attacks off the coast of Somalia have reached a degree that would qualify them as 'armed attacks'. Thus, the parallels between the legal status of terrorism and that of piracy are limited, even though both forms of conduct are typically undertaken by private individuals whose acts only involve the responsibility of one or more state(s) if and to the extent to which they can be attributed to them under the principles of attribution accepted under customary international law.[34] As Chapter VII UN Charter has therefore been uncoupled from the prohibition of the use of force and the right of self-defence in the practice of the Security Council, the mere fact that the pertinent resolutions were based on Chapter VII UN Charter does not have any impact on the legal classification of piratical attacks.

More importantly, a closer examination of the aforementioned resolutions reveals that they do not contain any 'constitutive' authorisation to use force.[35] Even though the Security Council resorted to a terminology in its Somalia resolutions that in other instances embodied authorisations *sensu stricto* ('all necessary measures', respectively 'all necessary means'),[36] it is important to note that the situation concerning piracy off the coast of Somalia differs from those on which the 'real' authorisations were based as the TFG, which was generally recognised as the legitimate government of Somalia until 20 August 2012, when the Federal Government of Somalia was inaugurated, had several times requested and thus consented to the anti-piratical operations in its territorial sea. In Resolution 1846, the Security Council expressly affirmed that the authorisations contained therein 'have been provided only following the receipt of the 20 November letter conveying the consent of the TFG'.[37] This statement was included in Resolution 1851, by which the Security Council 'authorised' the states cooperating with the TFG to take anti-piratical measures 'in Somalia', ie on land,[38] and in all resolutions by which the original 'authorisations' were renewed.[39] It is generally accepted today that the use of force by one state on the territory of another state upon the latter state's invitation ('intervention on invitation') serves as sufficient justification for the use of force and, therefore, renders an authorisation by the UN Security Council superfluous, provided that the invitation is extended on a voluntary basis by the generally recognised government of that state.[40] No reason

---

Law 127, 145ff. That Art 51 UN Charter does not subsume and supervene the right of self-defence under customary international law becomes manifest in the phrase 'inherent right of individual or collective self-defence' included in that provision, and has been expressly confirmed by the ICJ in *Nicaragua v USA*, n 3 above.

[34] For references see n 6 above.

[35] The term 'constitutive' is used here to refer to situations in which the Security Council not only confirms in declaratory terms the existence of an exception to the prohibition of the use of force, but also expressly authorises a group of states or the international community to use force. 'Non-constitutive' (ie declaratory) authorisations are by no means invalid, but are to be considered as lacking direct legal effects with regard to the lawfulness of the use of force concerned.

[36] For references see nn 21 and 22.

[37] UN Doc S/RES/1846 (2008) of 2 December 2008, para 11; see also ibid, 6th recital.

[38] UN Doc S/RES/1851 (2008) of 16 December 2008, para 10.

[39] UN Docs S/RES/1897 (2009) of 30 November 2009, para 8; S/RES/1950 (2010) of 23 November 2010, para 8; S/RES/2020 (2011) of 22 November 2011, para 10; S/RES/2077 (2012) of 22 November 2012, para 13 (referring to the consent of 'Somali authorities').

[40] See generally L Doswald-Beck, 'The Legal Validity of Military Intervention by Invitation of the Government' (1985) 56 *British Year Book of International Law* 189; G Nolte, *Eingreifen auf Einladung* (Berlin, Springer, 1999) 602–05. The US-led intervention in Afghanistan following the attacks of Al-Qaeda on 11 September 2001 (Operation Enduring Freedom, OEF) was initially held to be covered by the right

exists why different standards should apply vis-à-vis the use of force on land and in the territorial sea (over which, according to Article 2(1) LOS Convention, the coastal state's sovereignty extends).[41] The fact that the Security Council has at the same time relied on its Chapter VII powers and on the consent of the states concerned at different occasions in the past[42] does not suffice to challenge the concept of consent as sufficient legal ground of justification for the use of force in another state's territory. While this does not lead to the conclusion that the resolutions would have to be considered as being without any legal effect (see Section B below), their relevance concerning the entitlement to use force (and only in that respect) is limited to a declaratory statement of the law.

The Security Council further emphasised the 'primary role of the TFG [respectively Somali authorities] in the fight against piracy and armed robbery at sea off the coast of Somalia'[43] and clarified that the anti-piratical operations were to be undertaken in a manner consistent 'with such action on the high seas with respect to piracy under relevant international law'.[44] Moreover, all pertinent resolutions emphasised that 'international law, as reflected in the United Nations Convention on the Law of the Sea of 10 December 1982 . . . sets out the legal framework applicable to combating piracy and armed robbery at sea, as well as other ocean activities'.[45]

Against this background, it seems difficult to conclude that the resolutions of the Security Council contained real authorisations in terms of Articles 39 and 42 UN Charter. The Security Council referred to international law as its stands today and indicated that the 'authorisations' would not have been granted without the consent of the TFG. No evidence exists that the Security Council intended to widen the scope of powers of the states participating in anti-piratical operations in relation to what is already recognised under the LOS Convention and general international law.[46]

of self-defence. Since the inauguration of the interim administration chaired by today's president Hamid Karzai, the use of force exercised within OEF (which has, in contrast to the International Security Assistance Force, never been authorised by the Security Council) is considered as being legally justified due to the continuous consent of the Afghan government. Concerning the situation off the coast of Somalia, R Geiß and A Petrig, *Piracy and Armed Robbery at Sea: The Legal Framework for Counter-piracy* (Oxford, Oxford University Press, 2009) 76, 78, 84ff, seem to assign only supplementary relevance to the consent of the TFG.

[41] Concerning the territorial sea, Treves, n 15 above, 406, refers to the precedent of an exchange of notes between Albania and Italy of 1997, in which Albania consented to Italian interdiction waters within its territorial sea for a limited period of time.

[42] See the references provided by Geiß and Petrig, n 40 above, 84.

[43] UN Docs S/RES/1851 (2008) of 16 December 2008, para 6; S/RES/1897 (2009) of 30 November 2009, para 7; S/RES/1950 (2010) of 23 November 2010, para 7; S/RES/2020 (2011) of 22 November 2011, para 9; S/RES/2077 (2012) of 22 November 2012, para 12.

[44] UN Doc S/RES/1846 (2008) of 2 December 2008, para 10.

[45] UN Docs S/RES/1838 (2008) of 7 October 2008, 4th recital; S/RES/1846 (2008) of 2 December 2008, 4th recital; S/RES/1851 (2008) of 16 December 2008, 4th recital; S/RES/1897 (2009) of 30 November 2009, 4th recital; S/RES/1950 (2010) of 23 November 2010, 6th recital; S/RES/2020 (2011) of 22 November 2011, 7th recital; S/RES/2077 (2012) of 22 November 2012, 7th recital.

[46] See also D Guilfoyle, 'Counter-piracy Law Enforcement and Human Rights' (2010) 59 *International Comparative Law Quarterly* 141, 145; N Brown, 'Jurisdictional Problems Relating to Non-Flag State Boarding of Suspect Ships in International Waters' in Symmons, n 15 above, 69, 75; Trésoret, n 30 above, 294; Treves, n 15 above, 407; von Arnauld, n 15 above, 467; with regard to the types of enforcement measures see also Geiß and Petrig, n 40 above, 77.

B. Persisting Relevance of the Security Council Resolutions

The conclusion drawn here that the pertinent resolutions cannot be interpreted as containing 'real'—or, to be more precise, constitutive—authorisations does not mean that the resolutions were entirely superfluous. On the contrary, the Security Council pursued a variety of both political and legal aims with its chosen course of action. Its confirmation that the authorisations 'apply only with respect to the situation in Somalia and shall not affect the rights or obligations or responsibilities of Member states under international law, including any rights or obligations, under the Convention, with respect to any other situation' and that they 'shall not be considered as establishing customary international law'[47] first and foremost served to meet concerns by other states that the resolutions might be (mis-)understood as creating new law, eg by making the provisions of UNCLOS on piracy generally applicable in a state's territorial sea.[48] Thus, one of the central purposes of the resolutions was to 'pay homage to state sovereignty'.[49] Secondly, keeping in mind that not all of the states of the world had recognised the TFG as the legitimate government of Somalia, the Security Council strengthened the legal status of the TFG,[50] thereby attempting to address the more general problem of Somalia's status as a failed state. The example of the TFG furthermore shows that recognition of a government by the Security Council as the legitimate representation of a state may, depending on the circumstances, have a quasi-constitutive effect.[51] Thirdly, it has been convincingly pointed out that the course of action followed by the Security Council helped to draw the attention of the international community to the problem of piracy off the coast of Somalia, and thereby galvanised international efforts to address that problem.[52] Some authorities have also referred to the fact that the supplementary authorisation by the Security Council has the benefit of avoiding discussions on the width of the territorial sea of Somalia.[53] Indeed, by the Law on the Territorial Sea and Ports of 10 December 1972,[54] Somalia, acting in clear violation of the international law of the sea, extended its territorial sea to 200 nautical miles, and no indication exists that this law has ever been repealed. Notwithstanding this, it is submitted that the resolutions of the Security Council do not produce any constitutive legal effect in this respect, as they merely refer to the 'territorial waters of Somalia' without any spatial substantiation. The uncertainty concerning the expansion of the territorial sea is thus imported into the resolutions.

---

[47] UN Docs S/RES/1838 (2008) of 7 October 2008, para 8; S/RES/1846 (2008) of 2 December 2008, para 11; S/RES/1851 (2008) of 16 December 2008, para 10; S/RES/1897 (2009) of 30 November 2009, para 8; S/RES/1950 (2010) of 23 November 2010, para 8; S/RES/2020 (2011) of 22 November 2011, para 10; S/RES/2077 (2012) of 22 November 2012, para 13.

[48] See the references cited by Treves, n 15 above, 405; see also Vœlckel, n 30 above, 486; Trésoret, n 30 above, 292ff, 295.

[49] Treves, n 15 above, 407.

[50] Geiß and Petrig, n 40 above, 84; Trésoret, n 30 above, 295.

[51] But see the position of the UK as reflected in *Republic of Somalia v Woodhouse Drake & Carey (Suisse) SA*, High Court, Queen's Bench Division, 13 March 1992, 75 ILR 675, where it was held that recognition of an interim government by the UN would not automatically imply the duty to treat that government as official representation of that state in domestic court cases.

[52] A Murdoch, 'Recent Legal Issues and Problems Relating to Acts of Piracy off Somalia' in Symmons, n 15 above, 139, 143.

[53] Treves, n 15 above, 407; Geiß and Petrig, n 40 above, 85; Trésoret, n 30 above, 295.

[54] Available at http://www.un.org/Depts/los/LEGISLATIONANDTREATIES/PDFFILES/SOM_1972_Law.pdf.

It should also be noted that the 'authorisation' of the Security Council only extends to those states and regional organisations that cooperate with the Somali authorities, and for which advance notification has been provided by these authorities to the UN Secretary-General. Therefore, the primary legal justification for anti-piracy operations is to be found either in UNCLOS or other rules of customary international law (in relation to the high seas), or in the consent given by Somalia (concerning the territorial sea, no matter how wide it is).

The fact that the repeatedly renewed Resolution 1851 obliges states engaged in operations on land ('in Somalia') for the purpose of suppressing acts of piracy and armed robbery at sea to do this in a manner compatible with 'applicable international humanitarian and human rights law'[55] provokes the question whether the Security Council has thereby substantiated the nature of the conflict between the states concerned and the pirates. It is submitted that this question ought to be answered in the negative. While the assessment of the nature of a situation involving the use of armed force by the Security Council may generally provide strong evidence for the existence of an armed conflict, one must note that in a formal sense the Security Council does not have the competence to make binding determinations on the scope of international humanitarian law or on the nature of an armed conflict. In light of the careful approach embodied in the pertinent resolutions, it seems highly unlikely that the Security Council had the intention of making such a far-reaching statement of the law.[56] The use of the term 'applicable' only indicates that the rules of international humanitarian law naturally will have to apply in case the situation should develop one day into an armed conflict in terms of Common Article 3 of the 1949 Geneva Conventions,[57] or even in terms of Article 1(1) of the Second Additional Protocol to the Geneva Conventions.[58] What has been expressed by Resolution 1851 is that states engaged in anti-piratical operations in all cases must respect the human rights of individuals that are potentially affected by measures on land as well as those of the pirates. The Security Council has thus confirmed that, notwithstanding their status as 'enemies of mankind', pirates are entitled to rely on their human rights. Indeed, human rights law does not permit that its protection standards be denied to specific groups of persons, such as pirates or terrorists. Against this background, and taking into account the declaratory nature of the Security Council's appeal contained in Resolution 1851 that states engaged in anti-piratical measures ought to respect human rights law, it is without legal relevance that the reference to international human rights law has not been included in the resolutions dealing with piracy off the coast of Somalia.

In summary, while the resolutions of the Security Council concerning the situation off the coast of and within Somalia have produced important political effects, their impact in terms of international law is essentially limited to safeguarding the scope of the relevant rules and principles as they stand today, to integrating the anti-piratical operations into the frameworks of collective security and human rights law, and to

---

[55] UN Doc S/RES/1851 (2008) of 16 December 2008, para 6.

[56] See also Trésoret, n 30 above, 371.

[57] See n 11 above for reference to the Third Geneva Convention.

[58] Protocol Additional to the Geneva Conventions of 12 August 1949, relating to the Protection of Victims of Non-International Armed Conflicts (Protocol II) of 8 June 1977 (1125 UNTS 609). That the situation in and off the coast of Somalia cannot, as far as anti-piratical activities are concerned, be considered as an armed conflict so far is demonstrated by Trésoret, n 30 above, 369ff.

fostering legal certainty by way of declaratory statements. They do not contain constitutive authorisations to use force against pirates and could not provide a sufficient legal ground of justification. Since states have also not relied on their right of self-defence in terms of Article 51 UN Charter, and taking into account that Article 2(4) UN Charter has, as indicated by its wording, always been understood as excluding force exercised vis-à-vis private actors, none of the reactions of the international community to the phenomenon of piracy in and off the coast of Somalia justifies the conclusion that the *jus ad bellum* would be applicable to piracy.

C. Legitimacy of Using Force against Pirates

The conclusion drawn in the preceding section gives rise to the question whether other international rules exist that may serve as a legal ground of justification for the use of military force against pirates. Historically, the exercise of military force has always been considered as legitimate in order to safeguard the freedom of commerce on the high seas. Clear indications exist also in modern public international law that the use of force in international relations is not exclusively governed by Article 2(4) UN Charter, but can be legally justified beyond the scope of the prohibition contained therein.[59] For example, Article 22(1)(f) of the UN Fish Stocks Agreement,[60] which deals with basic procedures for boarding and inspection of fishing vessels in order to ensure compliance with and enforcement of subregional and regional conservation and management measures for straddling fish stocks and highly migratory fish stocks, states that:

> the inspecting state shall ensure that its duly authorized inspectors . . . shall avoid the use of force except when and to the degree necessary to ensure the safety of the inspectors and where the inspectors are obstructed in the execution of their duties.

Similarly, the International Tribunal for the Law of the Sea (ITLOS) confirmed in the *M/V Saiga* Case that 'international law . . . requires that the use of force must be avoided as far as possible and, where force is inevitable, it must not go beyond what is reasonable and necessary in the circumstances'.[61]

On 17 September 2007 the arbitral tribunal constituted pursuant to Article 287 UNCLOS in the case of *Guyana v Suriname* acknowledged that '[t]he Tribunal accepts the argument that in international law force may be used in law enforcement activities provided that such force is unavoidable, reasonable and necessary'.[62]

Finally, Article 8*bis*(9) of the 2005 Protocol to the SUA Convention (which is, in principle, also applicable to piracy) reads:

> When carrying out the authorized actions under this article, the use of force shall be avoided except when necessary to ensure the safety of its officials and persons on board, or where

---

[59] Cf Treves, n 15 above, 412ff; Guilfoyle, n 15 above, 92ff; Murdoch, n 52 above, 147.

[60] Agreement for the Implementation of the Provisions of the United Nations Convention on the Law of the Sea of 10 December 1982 relating to the Conservation and Management of Straddling Fish Stocks and Highly Migratory Fish Stocks of 4 December 1995 (2167 UNTS 3).

[61] *M/V 'Saiga' No 2 Case (St Vincent and the Grenadines v Guinea)*, Judgment of 1 July 1999, [1999] ITLOS Reports 10, para 155.

[62] (2008) 47 ILM 66, para 445.

the officials are obstructed in the execution of the authorized actions. Any use of force pursuant to this article shall not exceed the minimum degree of force which is necessary and reasonable in the circumstances.[63]

All the aforementioned statements deal with law enforcement measures against private actors (respectively ships) in areas within or beyond the limits of national jurisdiction. They emphasise that force may in principle be used to enforce national or regional binding standards, provided that these standards have been enacted in accordance with international law. Neither the UN Fish Stocks Agreement nor ITLOS referred to the prohibition of the use of force or the right of self-defence, and the arbitral tribunal in the *Guyana v Suriname* case expressly distinguished the force used within the context of law enforcement activities from military actions that affect the *jus ad bellum*.[64] Thus, even aside from the undisputed general principle of law that an individual (or a vessel etc) may act in self-defence in order to protect his/her own life or the lives of others (provided that the exercise of force is not disproportional),[65] international law does not prohibit recourse to military force in an absolute manner. Rather, enforcement measures against private actors that are a priori not covered by the *jus ad bellum*[66] may lawfully involve the exercise of force, subject to the legal limits expressed by the arbitral tribunal in the *Guyana v Suriname* case (unavoidability, reasonability and necessity) that ultimately result from the requirements of international human rights law.[67] Arguably, these limits become manifest in the generally cautious practice of states involved in anti-piracy operations off the coast of Somalia. It is important to note, though, that military force can only be lawfully used in order to allow for the exercise of the enforcement measures concerned. This is why the sinking of a suspect pirate vessel independent of specific enforcement measures such as those codified in Articles 105 and 110 UNCLOS violates international law from the perspectives of both the law of the sea and human rights law.

The aforementioned remarks raise the question whether anti-piratical operations on land involving the use of force may still be qualified as law enforcement operations, or whether they ought to be considered as unique instances of armed conflict. For example, on 9 March 2012 European anti-piracy troops carried out their first air attack on mainland Somalia, with a low-flying helicopter firing at targets on the beach and destroying pirate vessels, fuel supplies and arms. As stated above, the fact that

---

[63] IMO Doc LEG/CONF.15/21, Protocol of 14 October 2005 to the Convention for the Suppression of Unlawful Acts of Violence against the Safety of Maritime Navigation (SUA Convention). The Protocol has entered into force on 28 July 2010.

[64] Above n 62.

[65] Heintschel von Heinegg, n 15 above, 228; Murdoch, n 52 above, 148; Treves, n 15 above, 412ff. Note that this individual right of self-defence ought to be distinguished from the right of self-defence of states in terms of Art 51 UN Charter or corresponding customary international law, respectively.

[66] Cf Bothe, n 4 above, para 11. But see S Schmahl 'Die Bekämpfung der Seepiraterie im Spiegel des Völkerrechts, des Europarechts und der deutschen Rechtsordnung' (2011) 136 *Archiv des öffentlichen Rechts* 44, 71; Y Dinstein, *War, Aggression and Self-Defence*, 5th edn (Cambridge, Cambridge University Press, 2011) 247, who considers extraterritorial law enforcement as a form of self-defence that can be undertaken only in response to an armed attack by private actors unleashed from another state's territory. Note, however, that Dinstein's conclusion seems to exclusively focus on terrorists attacks with regard to which the scope of application of the *jus ad bellum* has, according to many scholars, been modified. For references see n 33 above.

[67] In this respect, ITLOS referred to 'considerations of humanity'; see *M/V 'Saiga' No 2*, n 61 above, para 155.

the repeatedly renewed Resolution 1851 obliges states engaged in operations on land for the purpose of suppressing acts of piracy and armed robbery at sea to do this in a manner compatible with 'applicable international humanitarian and human rights law' only confirms that the rules of international humanitarian law will apply in cases of armed conflict. Thus, while it is impossible to give a general answer to the above question about anti-piratical operations on land, it cannot be excluded that, depending on the nature and intensity of the measures taken, they may amount to an armed conflict in terms of the *jus in bello*. It would be indefensible to conclude that, as a matter of principle and taking into account the 'private' aims pursued by pirates, anti-piratical operations cannot fall within the scope of international humanitarian law. That said, it is submitted that a singular incident such as the one on 9 March 2012, which involved only one helicopter and did not lead to human casualties, does not exceed the threshold of minimum level of intensity which is needed in order to distinguish an armed conflict, in the meaning of Common Article 3 of the Geneva Conventions, from less serious forms of violence such as internal disturbances and tensions, riots or acts of banditry.[68] It would seem difficult to justify a different legal classification of such a situation in relation to measures taken against pirate vessels only because the measures concerned are taken on land and not at sea. At the same time, it is a subject for debate whether the operation concerned fully complied with the legal requirements applicable to the law enforcement measures identified above.

IV. OUTLOOK: IS THERE A NEED FOR A LEGAL BASIS FOR USING FORCE AGAINST PIRATES?

The fact that international treaty practice and case law consider the use of force against pirates as generally lawful does not provide a definite answer as to the legal basis for such action. In light of the aforementioned documents and judgments, it is frequently held that the use of force in the context of enforcement measures is covered by a corresponding rule of customary international law.[69] ITLOS seems to have followed that approach in the *M/V 'Saiga'* case (No 2) by stating that:

> These principles have been followed over the years in law enforcement operations at sea. The normal practice used to stop a ship at sea is first to give an auditory or visual signal to stop, using internationally recognized signals. Where this does not succeed, a variety of actions may be taken, including the firing of shots across the bows of the ship. It is only after the appropriate actions fail that the pursuing vessel may, as a last resort, use force. Even then, appropriate warning must be issued to the ship and all efforts should be made to ensure that life is not endangered . . .[70]

It is submitted that this position is particularly justifiable in light of the fact that it insists on the requirement of a constitutive authorisation to use force also in situations of criminal enforcement not covered by the general prohibition of the use of force. On the other hand, accepting that it is sufficient that international law simply does not prohibit the exercise of military force would seem to be perfectly in line with the

---

[68] See, eg ICTY, *The Prosecutor v Fatmir Limaj*, Judgment, IT-03-66-T, 30 November 2005, para 84.
[69] See, eg Trésoret, n 30 above, 352ff.
[70] *M/V 'Saiga' No 2*, n 61 above, para 156.

so-called 'Lotus approach', under which every course of action that is not expressly prohibited by international law ought to be considered as generally lawful.[71] Viewed from that perspective, international law would have to be interpreted as only setting limits (deriving from customary international law of the sea and human rights law) to the use of force in the context of enforcement measures against pirates. In contrast, Judge Simma has convincingly argued that such a sovereignty-oriented approach does not enable the practitioner of modern international law and international courts to 'enquire into the precise status'[72] of the concepts in question, and has concluded that it should be considered in such situations that 'international law can be neutral or deliberately silent on the international lawfulness of certain acts'.[73] This proposal cannot be assessed here in detail. Suffice it to say that it undoubtedly has the potential to lead to adequate results in many instances, and to foster a better understanding of how the rules and principles of today's multi-dimensional international legal order interact. Having said this, it seems questionable whether it can be applied to the present issue of combating piracy. That international law subordinates the exercise of military force in the context of criminal law enforcement to certain legal limits a priori indicates that the use of force against pirates cannot be considered as an act with regard to which international law would be neutral. Classifying the exercise of force as a 'tolerable' (not lawful!) tool to support criminal enforcement measures would make it impossible to challenge abusive conduct (as a right that could be abused would not exist), and would thereby significantly decrease legal certainty. Finally, no evidence has ever been brought forward that the authority to use force in the context of law enforcement measures against private actors is not supported by sufficiently uniform state practice and *opinio juris*. Against this background, the right to resort to military force against pirates and other private actors in the context of extraterritorial law enforcement ought to be considered as being valid under customary international law.

---

[71] *Case of the SS Lotus (France v Turkey)*, Judgment of 7 September 1927, Permanent Court of International Justice, Ser A, No 10, 5, 18ff. Note that the ICJ arguably based its recent advisory opinion on the unilateral declaration of independence on that approach: see *Accordance with International Law of the Unilateral Declaration of Independence in Respect of Kosovo*, Advisory Opinion of 22 July 2010, [2010] ICJ Reports 403, para 84.

[72] *Accordance with International Law of the Unilateral Declaration of Independence in Respect of Kosovo*, Decl Simma, [2010] ICJ Reports 478, para 9.

[73] Ibid, para 3; see also ibid, para 9: 'and whether it allows for the concept of *toleration*, something which breaks from the binary understanding of permission/prohibition and which allows for a range of non-prohibited options' (original emphasis).

4

Counter-piracy Operations and the Limits of International Humanitarian Law

THILO MARAUHN

I. INTRODUCTION

COUNTER-PIRACY OPERATIONS HAVE recently become integrated into efforts pursued by individual states, groups of states and the international community at large, to maintain international peace and security.[1] To this end, national and multinational naval forces are today patrolling, among others, the Gulf of Aden and off Somalia's east coast.[2] The UN Security Council, which bears 'primary responsibility for the maintenance of international peace and security',[3] has authorised states to use 'all necessary means'[4] or 'all necessary measures'[5] at sea and

---

[1] Reference to 'international peace and security' points towards the involvement of the UN Security Council and Chapter VII of the UN Charter, but it also illustrates that counter-piracy is a matter of security policy in a much broader sense. For a discussion see, among others, M Gill, 'Security at sea: fraud, piracy and the failure of police cooperation internationally' (1996) 13 *International Relations* 3, 43–58; D Guilfoyle, 'Piracy off Somalia. UN Security Council Resolution 1816 and IMO Regional Counter-piracy Efforts' (2008) 57 *International & Comparative Law Quarterly* 57 690; MC Houghton, 'Walking the Plank: How United Nations Security Council Resolution 1816, While Progressive, Fails to Provide a Comprehensive Solution to Somali Piracy' (2009) 16 *Tulsa Journal of Comparative & International Law* 253; C Massarella, 'UN Security Council Resolution 1976 (2011) and Efforts to Support Piracy Prosecutions' (2011) 26 *International Journal of Marine and Coastal Law* 679; RJ Baird, 'Transnational Security Issues in the Asian Maritime Environment' (2012) 66 *Australian Journal of International Affairs* 501.

[2] See, among others, Chapters 11 and 12 below, by E Egede and DM Ong, respectively, as well as J Kraska and B Wilson, 'The Pirates of the Gulf of Aden. The Coalition is the Strategy' (2009) 45 *Stanford Journal of International Law* 243. For a comprehensive review of the legal regime pertaining to piracy underway in Somalia and the Gulf of Aden see R Geiss and A Petrig, *Piracy and Armed Robbery at Sea. The Legal Framework for Counter-piracy Operations in Somalia and the Gulf of Aden* (Oxford, Oxford University Press, 2011) *passim*.

[3] Art 24 UN Charter.

[4] UN SC Resolution 1846 (2008), para 10, lit b: 'Decides that for a period of 12 months from the date of this resolution states and regional organizations cooperating with the TFG in the fight against piracy and armed robbery at sea off the coast of Somalia . . . may: . . . Use, within the territorial waters of Somalia, in a manner consistent with such action permitted on the high seas with respect to piracy under relevant international law, *all necessary means* to repress acts of piracy and armed robbery at sea' (emphasis added).

[5] UN SC Resolution 1851 (2008), preamble: 'Noting . . . requests from the TFG . . . to assist the TFG in taking *all necessary measures* to interdict those who use Somali territory and airspace to plan, facilitate or undertake acts of piracy and armed robbery at sea' (emphasis added) and UN SC Resolution 1851 (2008), para 6: 'decides that . . . states and regional organizations . . . may *undertake all necessary measures*' (emphasis added).

on land[6] to suppress piracy off the Somali coast. It is this use of military force in the context of counter-piracy operations that has given rise to the question whether the laws of war, and in particular international humanitarian law,[7] have any role to play in these operations.

In providing a simple answer[8] to this question, this chapter can simply state: no—there is, as a matter of principle, no role to play for the laws of war in counter-piracy operations. Instead, counter-piracy operations are to be understood as law enforcement activities,[9] to the exercise of which a different set of rules applies.

It is, however, useful to elaborate on the applicability of international humanitarian law (Section II), on the distinction between armed conflict and law enforcement operations (Section III), on the effects of applying either body of law to counter-piracy operations (Section IV) and on some conclusions from the perspective of maintaining international peace and security on the one hand and global order on the other (Section V).

II. THE INTERNATIONAL USE OF MILITARY FORCE AND THE LAW OF ARMED CONFLICT

One of the initial and misleading assumptions sometimes made is that the use of military force per se triggers the application of international humanitarian law.[10] Nor does the traditional denunciation of pirates as *hostis humani generis* (enemies of

---

[6] UN SC Resolution 1851 (2008), para 6, authorises 'all necessary measures that are appropriate *in Somalia*' (emphasis added). In the debate leading to the adoption of UN SC Resolution 1851 (2008), the Secretary of State for Foreign and Commonwealth Affairs of the United Kingdom pointed out that land-based counter-piracy operations were 'an important additional tool to combat piracy'. The US Secretary of State, in that same debate, underlined that 'pursuing pirates on land would have a significant impact. Maritime operations alone were insufficient for combating piracy.' The South African representative 'expressed concern over the provision in the resolution that allowed for states to conduct land-based operations against piracy, saying there was a danger that innocent Somalis could fall victim to those operations'. All quotations are taken from http://www.un.org/News/Press/docs/2008/sc9541.doc.htm (accessed on 21 October 2013), summarising the SC debate of 16 December 2008 (UN Doc SC/9541).

[7] According to H-P Gasser and D Thürer, 'Humanitarian Law, International' in R Wolfrum (ed), *Max Planck Encyclopedia of Public International Law*, online edition (Oxford, Oxford University Press, 2011) para 3, available at http://opil.ouplaw.com/home/epil (accessed on 14 October 2013), 'International humanitarian law, [is] also called "law of armed conflict" or, more traditionally, "laws of war"'. Others apply a more restrictive terminology and consider only 'rules protecting individuals from being attacked' as humanitarian law, and as such as 'part of the rules of methods of warfare': I Detter, *The Law of War*, 2nd edn (Cambridge, Cambridge University Press, 2000) 160. GD Solis, *The Law of Armed Conflict* (Cambridge, Cambridge University Press 2010) 22, characterises international humanitarian law as 'an umbrella term for laws that aim to humanize armed conflict'. Since such parts of the laws of armed conflict as the law of neutrality are not at the heart of this contribution, it follows the broader approach taken by Gasser and Thürer.

[8] D Guilfoyle, 'The Laws of War and the Fight against Somali Piracy. Combatants or Criminals?' (2010) 11 *Melbourne Journal of International Law* 141, 142, poses the question 'of whether the laws of war have any role to play in combating piracy' and replies: 'The simple answer is "no"'. However, he also goes on to explain the differences between armed conflict and law enforcement in the following.

[9] This is the common view adopted by all governments involved in counter-piracy operations; see, among others, Guilfoyle, ibid, 142–43.

[10] This background is illustrated, but obviously not shared, by Guilfoyle, ibid, 142.

humankind)[11] place them outside the law of peace[12] or the law in general.[13] What is essential and decisive in the determination of whether or not international humanitarian law is applicable in a particular situation or to a particular course of action is the existence of an armed conflict. As can be taken from Common Articles 2[14] and 3 of the Geneva Conventions of 1949,[15] the laws of war only apply during an armed conflict. Nothing else emerges from the Additional Protocols of 1977,[16] further treaty law[17] or international customary law.[18]

Since there is no treaty-based definition of the notion of 'armed conflict', pertinent treaty provisions must be interpreted according to the accepted rules of treaty interpretation,[19] taking into account state practice (if available); jurisprudence and doctrine must be looked at.

A. The Absence of an 'International Armed Conflict' in Counter-piracy Operations

Common Article 2 of the Geneva Conventions of 1949 requires a 'declared war

[11] The term has recently even been used to phrase the title of journal articles, see eg DR Burgess, 'Hostis humani generi. Piracy, Terrorism and a New International Law' (2006) 13 *University of Miami International and Comparative Law Review* 293.

[12] This refers to the differences between human rights law and the law of armed conflict. International human rights law is, however, not limited to times of peace, unless derogation clauses apply. On the differences between these two bodies of law see C Dröge, 'Elective Affinities? Human Rights and Humanitarian Law' (2008) 90 *ICRC Review* 501.

[13] This refers to the doctrine of 'enemy criminal law' (*Feindstrafrecht*), developed as an analytical category by G Jakobs, 'Kriminalisierung im Vorfeld einer Rechtsgutsverletzung' (1985) 97 *Zeitschrift für die gesamte Strafrechtswissenschaft* 751; see also G Jakobs, 'On the Theory of Enemy Criminal Law', available at http://www.law-lib.utoronto.ca/bclc/crimweb/foundation/Jakobs%20current.pdf (accessed on 21 October 2013). For a commentary in light of the debate about the (inacceptable) concept of so-called enemy combatants see C Gómez-Jara Díez, 'Enemy Combatants versus Enemy Criminal Law: An Introduction to the European Debate Regarding Enemy Criminal Law and its Relevance to the Anglo-American Discussion on the Legal Status of Unlawful Enemy Combatants' (2008) 11 *New Criminal Law Review* 529. For its application in the context of counter-terrorist operations see A Goppel, *Killing Terrorists: A Moral and Legal Analysis* (Berlin, Walter de Gruyter, 2013) 249–57.

[14] Geneva Convention for the Amelioration of the Condition of the Wounded and Sick in Armed Forces in the Field, 75 UNTS 31 (Geneva Convention (GC) I); Geneva Convention for the Amelioration of the Condition of Wounded, Sick and Shipwrecked Members of Armed Forces at Sea, 75 UNTS 85 (GC II); Geneva Convention relative to the Treatment of Prisoners of War, 75 UNTS 135 (GC III); Geneva Convention relative to the Protection of Civilian Persons in Time of War, 75 UNTS 287 (GC IV). Common Art 2, among others, stipulates that 'the present Convention shall apply to all cases of declared war or of any other armed conflict which may arise between two or more of the High Contracting Parties, even if the state of war is not recognized by one of them'.

[15] Common Art 3 GC refers to an 'armed conflict not of an international character occurring in the territory of one of the High Contracting Parties'.

[16] Protocol Additional to the Geneva Conventions of 12 August 1949, and relating to the Protection of Victims of International Armed Conflicts (Protocol I), 1125 UNTS 3; Protocol Additional to the Geneva Conventions of 12 August 1949, and relating to the Protection of Victims of Non-International Armed Conflicts (Protocol II), 1125 UNTS 609.

[17] For a summary and further references see Gasser and Thürer, n 7 above, paras 21–23.

[18] Most relevant is the customary international law study done under the auspices of the ICRC; see JM Henckaerts and L Doswald-Beck (eds), *Customary International Humanitarian Law* (Cambridge, Cambridge University Press, 2005) *passim*.

[19] The rules on treaty interpretation are included in Art 31(1) of the Vienna Convention on the Law of Treaties and are considered to be customary international law; see generally O Doerr, 'Article 31. General Rule on Interpretation' in O Doerr and K Schmalenbach (eds), *Vienna Convention on the Law of Treaties. A Commentary* (Berlin, Springer, 2012) 521–70.

or . . . any other armed conflict which may arise between two or more of the High Contracting Parties'. This necessitates a conflict between two or more states, ie 'the High Contracting Parties'. A declaration of war or recognition of the situation is not required; rather, the existence of an armed conflict is a question of fact.[20] As can be taken from the Commentary on the Geneva Conventions of 1949, there is an armed conflict in the case of an 'intervention of armed forces', irrespective of duration and intensity.[21]

This reading has been confirmed by the International Criminal Tribunal for the former Yugoslavia (ICTY) in the *Tadić* case, with the Tribunal stating that 'an armed conflict exists whenever there is a resort to armed force between States'.[22] The only extension beyond this definition is included in Article 1, para 4 of Additional Protocol I, which ensures applicability of pertinent law to wars of national liberation.[23]

Since pirates are neither part of a state's armed forces[24] nor agents of a state,[25] counter-piracy operations will not amount to an international armed conflict. As a consequence, the rules on international armed conflicts are not applicable to counter-piracy operations.

B. The Absence of a 'Non-international Armed Conflict' in Counter-piracy Operations

When considering the existence of a 'non-international armed conflict', the starting point is Common Article 3 of the Geneva Conventions of 1949 (GC), which applies to 'armed conflicts not of an international character occurring in the territory of one of the High Contracting Parties'. Again, Common Article 3 GC does not offer a defini-

---

[20] ICRC, 'How is the Term "Armed Conflict" Defined in International Humanitarian Law?', Opinion Paper (March 2008) 3, available at http://www.icrc.org/eng/assets/files/other/opinion-paper-armed-conflict.pdf (accessed on 21 October 2013).

[21] JS Pictet, *Commentary on the Geneva Convention for the Amelioration of the Condition of the Wounded and Sick in Armed Forces in the Field* (Geneva, ICRC, 1952) 32.

[22] ICTY, *The Prosecutor v Dusko Tadić*, Decision on the Defence Motion for Interlocutory Appeal on Jurisdiction, IT-94-1-A, 2 October 1995, para 70.

[23] Art 1, para 4 of the Additional Protocol I extends the application of the rules applicable to international armed conflicts to 'armed conflicts in which peoples are fighting against colonial domination and alien occupation and against racist regimes in the exercise of their right of self-determination, as enshrined in the Charter of the United Nations and the Declaration on Principles of International Law concerning Friendly Relations and Co-operation among states in accordance with the Charter of the United Nations'.

[24] For a definition of armed forces in the context of the rules on international armed conflicts see Art 43, para 1, Additional Protocol I: 'The armed forces of a Party to a conflict consist of all organized armed forces, groups and units which are under a command responsible to that Party for the conduct of its subordinates, even if that Party is represented by a government or an authority not recognized by an adverse Party. Such armed forces shall be subject to an internal disciplinary system which, inter alia, shall enforce compliance with the rules of international law applicable in armed conflict.' For a comprehensive analysis of pertinent treaty and customary law see J-M Henckaerts, 'Armed Forces' in Wolfrum, n 7 above, *passim*.

[25] The Articles on State Responsibility as adopted by the International Law Commission in 2001 (Report of the International Law Commission on the work of its Fifty-third Session, Official Records of the General Assembly, Fifty-sixth Session, Supplement No 10 (UN Doc A/56/10), ch IV.E.1) only establishes responsibility for organs of the state (Art 4), for persons or entities 'empowered by the law of that state to exercise elements of the governmental authority' (Art 5), and for organs 'placed at the disposal of a state by another state' (Art 6). None of these apply to pirates.

tion of a non-international armed conflict.[26] There is, however, agreement that the situation covered by Common Article 3 GC must reach a certain threshold of confrontation.[27] Collective hostilities as well as the need to apply military force rather than mere police force are indicators that the threshold has been reached.[28] Relying upon the phrase 'parties to the conflict', it is argued that non-governmental groups must possess organised armed force. This not only requires a command structure but also the capacity to sustain military operations,[29] and—according to some writers—the ability to secure respect for the laws of war.[30]

Recent international case law has confirmed the threshold requirement and the need for organisational capabilities of non-governmental armed groups, and further specified these criteria.[31] In the ICTY Appeals Chamber's *Tadić* decision, the Tribunal introduced the notion of 'protracted armed violence',[32] which a number of prominent commentators perceive as a mere reformulation of the threshold requirement.[33] In the *Kordić and Cerkez* decision, the ICTY Appeals Chamber stated that the phrase 'protracted armed violence' serves to exclude mere cases of civil unrest.[34] The *Tadić* Trial Chamber explicitly referred to the intensity of the conflict and the organisation of the parties to the conflict.[35] This has subsequently developed into firm jurisprudence of the ICTY.[36] The International Tribunal on Rwanda (ICTR) relied on the *Tadić* decision in the *Akayesu* case[37] and made it clear that intensity had to be determined in an objective way, not depending on the assessment of the parties to the conflict.[38] Subsequent case law of the ICTR followed this approach.[39]

---

[26] C Gray, 'The Meaning of Armed Conflict: Non-international Armed Conflict' in ME O'Connell (ed), *What is War? An Investigation in the Wake of 9/11* (Leiden, Martinis Nijhoff Publishers, 2012) 69, 70; E La Haye, *War Crimes in Internal Armed Conflicts* (Cambridge, Cambridge University Press, 2008) 20.

[27] L Moir, *The Law of Internal Armed Conflict* (Cambridge, Cambridge University Press, 2002) 46–52.

[28] ICTY, *The Prosecutor v Fatmir Limaj*, Judgment, IT-03-66-T, 30 November 2005, para 170, referring to the fact that the two forces 'were substantially engaged in their mutual military struggle'.

[29] ICRC (n 20 above) 3.

[30] La Haye, n 26 above, 6; see also Guilfoyle, n 8 above, 145.

[31] See *The Prosecutor v Fatmir Limaj* Judgment n 28 above, note 294.

[32] *The Prosecutor v Dusko Tadić* Decision, n 22 above, para 70. The notion has been included in Art 8(2)(f) Rome Statute of the International Criminal Court: 'when there is protracted armed conflict between governmental authorities and organized armed groups'. On the interpretation of this clause see A Cullen, 'The Definition of Non-international Armed Conflict in the Rome Statute of the International Criminal Court' (2007) 12 *Journal of Conflict and Security Law* 419, 435–45, arguing in favour of an interpretation of the threshold contained in Art 8(2)(f) Rome Statute identical to that of Common Art 3 GC.

[33] T Meron, 'The Humanization of Humanitarian Law' (2009) 94 *American Journal of International Law* 239, 260; M Bothe, 'War Crimes' in A Cassese, P Gaeta, JRWD Jones (eds), *The Rome Statute of the International Criminal Court. A Commentary* (Oxford, Oxford University Press, 2002) 423; C Kress, 'War Crimes Committed in Non-international Armed Conflict and the Emerging System of International Criminal Justice' (2001) 30 *Israel Yearbook on Human Rights* 103, 118.

[34] ICTY, *The Prosecutor v Dario Kordić, Mario Cerkez*, IT-95-14/2-A, 17 December 2004, para 341.

[35] ICTY, *The Prosecutor v Dusko Tadić*, IT-94-1-T, 7 May 1997, para 562.

[36] Apart from the already mentioned case law, the following may be considered: ICTY, *The Prosecutor v Blagojević and Jokić*, IT-02-60-T, 17 January 2005, para 536; ICTY, *The Prosecutor v Halilović*, IT-01-48-T, 16 November 2005, para 24; ICTY, *The Prosecutor v Galić*, IT-98-29-T, 5 December 2003, para 9; ICTY, *The Prosecutor v Stakić*, IT-97-24-T, 31 July 2003, para 560.

[37] ICTR, *The Prosecutor v Jean-Paul Akayesu*, ICTR 96-4-T, 2 September 1998, paras 619–27.

[38] Ibid, para 603.

[39] For further references see Gray, n 26 above, 76–77.

The definition based upon Common Article 3 GC and elaborated upon by the ICTY and the ICTR is now part of customary international law.[40]

In the light of the criteria set out in the preceding three paragraphs, an argument can be made against the qualification of counter-piracy operations as non-international armed conflicts. Pirates do not normally satisfy the definition of an armed group engaged in a non-international armed conflict. First, they have as their principal targets private merchant vessels and crews, ie their attacks are not directed against other armed groups or government forces.[41] Secondly, while pirates may have a degree of organisation, the organisation 'along clan lines or upon business models . . . is insufficient of itself';[42] bosses of pirate gangs normally lack the 'command', which is 'responsible to that party (to the conflict) for the conduct of its subordinates'.[43] Thirdly, compliance with the laws and customs of war is not on the minds of pirates.[44] Fourthly, it may be argued that pirates exercise 'isolated and sporadic acts of violence',[45] which can even be confirmed by the fact that most of the shipping remains unhampered by piracy.[46]

The definition of a non-international armed conflict in Article 1 of the 1977 Protocol Additional to the Geneva Conventions of 12 August 1949, and relating to the Protection of Victims of Non-international Armed Conflicts (AP II),[47] sets a higher threshold by requiring some degree of territorial control by the non-governmental armed groups.[48] Pirates do not necessarily control territory, even though this has occasionally been the case.[49] But even if they do, this is not normally a (former) part of the territory of the other party to the conflict.[50]

This eventually leads to the question where the conflict occurs, sometimes referred to as the combat zone.[51] Both Common Article 3 GC and Article 1 of AP II require a conflict to occur 'in the territory of one of the High Contracting Parties'. It is noteworthy that the two provisions do not use the term 'jurisdiction' but the term 'territory'. The question arising is whether this reference to 'territory' is essential in

---

[40] A Cullen, *The Concept of Non-international Armed Conflict in International Humanitarian Law* (Cambridge, Cambridge University Press, 2010) 156, with further references.

[41] Guilfoyle, n 8 above, 144–45.

[42] Ibid, 145, referring, among others, to the International Expert Group on Piracy off the Somali Coast, 'Final Report: Assessments and Recommendations', Workshop Commissioned by the Special Representative of the Secretary General of the United Nations to Somalia Ambassador Ahmadeou Ould-Abdallah (21 November 2008), 17, available at http://www.imcsnet.org/imcs/docs/somalia_piracy_intl_experts_report_consolidated.pdf (accessed on 21 October 2013).

[43] Guilfoyle, n 8 above, 145, referring to the customary international law study commissioned by the ICRC (Henckaerts and Doswald-Beck, n 18 above, 14 and 15–17).

[44] Guilfoyle, ibid, 145–46.

[45] Ibid, 146.

[46] Ibid, 146, pointing out that 'close to 99 per cent of all vessels that transit the Gulf of Aden do so without coming under pirate attack and only a minority of such attacks result in hostage-taking'.

[47] Gray, n 26 above, 71; La Haye, n 26 above, 8–9.

[48] Moir, n 27 above, 99–108.

[49] Guilfoyle, n 8 above, 144.

[50] On the notion of territorial control in this context see Moir, n 27 above, 103–05.

[51] See, among others, LR Blank, 'Defining the Battlefield in Contemporary Conflict and Counterterrorism—Understanding the Parameters of the Zone of Combat' (2010) 39 *Georgia Journal of International & Comparative Law* 1; R Heinsch, 'Unmanned Aerial Vehicles and the Scope of the "Combat Zone"— Some Thoughts on the Geographical Scope of Application of International Humanitarian Law' (2012) 25 *Humanitäres Völkerrecht* 184.

determining the existence of a non-international armed conflict[52] or whether this rather concerns the question of the applicability of Common Article 3 GC and Article 1 of AP II, respectively.[53] Even though it is technically feasible to keep the two questions separate, the relatively recent debate on the geographical scope of non-international armed conflicts has an impact on the definition of this type of armed conflict.[54] In respect of counter-piracy operations, there is thus a need to consider whether the applicability of international humanitarian law to these operations depends on them taking place 'in the territory of one of the High Contracting Parties' and possibly also on pirates exercising a degree of territorial control. In other words: does territory matter in deciding on the applicability of international humanitarian law to counter-piracy operations?

The debate about the geographical scope of non-international armed conflicts has arisen around so-called 'transnational' armed conflicts[55] (in the aftermath the ter-rorist attacks of 11 September 2009) and also around the classification of 'spill-over' conflicts,[56] ie non-international armed conflicts affecting neighbouring states. In the *Tadić* case, the ICTY distinctly addressed the prerequisites of a non-international armed conflict on the basis of a more or less abstract definition.[57] In contrast, the US Supreme Court in its *Hamdan* ruling simply determined the broad scope of Common Article 3 GC by contrasting it with Common Article 2 GC.[58] Basically, the US Supreme Court held that all armed conflicts not covered by Common Article 2 GC are auto-matically included in Common Article 3 GC, irrespective of their geographical scope. Whereas the ICTY can point towards the ordinary meaning of 'territory' and to the drafting process,[59] the counter-argument is that the reference to 'territory' only estab-lishes a link between a party to the Geneva Conventions and the non-state parties subjected to the obligations of Common Article 3 GC.[60] Both lines of argument are

---

[52] Moir, n 27 above, 103–05.

[53] T Marauhn and FZ Ntoubandi, 'Armed Conflict, Non-International' in Wolfrum, n 7 above, paras 14, 19 and 23.

[54] See, in particular, K Schöberl, 'Konfliktpartei und Kriegsgebiet in bewaffneten Auseinandersetzungen. Zur Debatte um den Anwendungsbereich des Rechts internationaler und nicht-internationaler bewaffneter Konflikte' (2012) 25 *Humanitäres Völkerrecht* 128.

[55] On the notion of transnational armed conflicts see, among others, GS Corn and ET Jensen, 'Transna-tional Armed Conflict. A "Principled" Approach to the Regulation of Counter-Terror Combat Operations' (2009) 42 *Israel Law Review* 46; C Kreß, 'Some Reflections on the International Legal Framework Governing Transnational Armed Conflicts' (2010) 15 *Journal of Conflict and Security Law* 245.

[56] R Geiß, 'Armed Violence in Fragile States: Low-Intensity Conflicts, Spillover Conflicts, and Sporadic Law Enforcement Operations by Third Parties' (2009) 91 *ICRC Review* 127.

[57] *The Prosecutor v Dusko Tadić* Decision, n 22 above, para 70.

[58] Supreme Court of the United States, *Salim Ahmed Hamdan (Petitioner) v Donald H Rumsfeld (Sec-retary of Defense) et al*, On Writ of Certiorari to the Unites States Court of Appeals for the District of Columbia Circuit, 548 US 557 (2006), no 05.184, 29 June 2006, para 4.d.ii.: 'The DC Circuit ruled Common Article 3 inapplicable to Hamdan because the conflict with al Qaeda is international in scope and thus not a 'conflict not of an international character'. That reasoning is erroneous. That the quoted phrase bears its literal meaning and is used here in contradistinction to a conflict between nations is demonstrated by Common Art 2, which limits its own application to any armed conflict between signatories and provides that signatories must abide by all terms of the Conventions even if another party to the conflict is a non-signatory, so long as the nonsignatory 'accepts and applies' those terms. See http://caselaw.lp.findlaw.com/scripts/getcase.pl?court=us&vol=000&invol=05-184 (accessed on 21 October 2013).

[59] See Schöberl, n 54 above, 136.

[60] Ibid, 136, referring to N Melzer, *Targeted Killing in International Law* (Oxford, Oxford University Press, 2008) 258: 'In fact, as the applicability of Article 3 GC I to IV, contrary to Article 2 GC I to IV, does not require the involvement of a contracting state as a party to the conflict, it is only logical that this

debatable, and in that sense the debate about the territorial link included in Common Article 3 GC may be considered to be relatively open in terms of its outcome.[61] As Common Article 3 GC today is universally applicable, however, the debate has lost some of its relevance.[62]

In contrast, the wording of Article 1 AP II in the views of the majority of commentators precludes an application of the provision to 'transnational' armed conflicts, while its applicability to 'spill-over' conflicts may at least be considered feasible in light of the provision's object and purpose.[63]

It follows that the reference to 'territory' thus does not play a role in determining whether or not counter-piracy operations are subject to the law of armed conflict since no additional argument against the application of the law of armed conflict can be derived from the notion 'territory'.

As a rule, then, counter-piracy operations do not amount to an armed conflict. This will become even more obvious when looking at the distinction between armed conflict and law enforcement operations, and the effects of applying either body of law to counter-piracy operations.

III. DISTINGUISHING NON-INTERNATIONAL ARMED CONFLICT AND INTERNATIONL LAW ENFORCEMENT OPERATIONS

Given that the law of armed conflict normally will not be applicable to counter-piracy operations, the law enforcement paradigm can be taken up. Indeed, most commentators rightly consider counter-piracy operations as law enforcement operations.[64] Pursuant to the Handbook of the International Law of Military Operations,[65] the

> generic concept of law enforcement comprises all territorial and extraterritorial measures taken by a state or other collective entity to maintain or restore public security, law and order or to otherwise exercise its authority or power over individuals, objects, or territory.[66]

While it has rightly been pointed out that the 'concept of law enforcement is not defined in international law' as such, reference can be made, among others, to the UN

---

criterion was replaced by the prerequisite of a territorial link to a contracting state. The legislative novelty of Art 3 GC I to IV was that each contracting state established binding rules not only for its own conduct, but also for that of the involved non-state parties.'

[61] Schöberl, n 54 above, 136.

[62] The Conventions first became universal in 2006, with accessions by the Republic of Nauru and the Republic of Montenegro (the latter effective from 2 February 2007s). See ICRC Press Release 06/96, 'Geneva Conventions of 1949 Achieve Universal Acceptance' (21 August 2006), available at http://www.icrc.org/eng/resources/documents/news-release/2009-and-earlier/geneva-conventions-news-210806.htm (accessed on 21 October 2013). After the Republic of South Sudan became independent on 9 July 2011, the Conventions again became universal with the country's accession to the Conventions in July 2012. See ICRC Press Release 12/154, 'South Sudan: World's Newest Country Signs Up to the Geneva Conventions' (19 July 2012), available at http://www.icrc.org/eng/resources/documents/news-release/2012/south-sudan-news-2012-07-09.htm (accessed on 21 October 2013).

[63] See, among others, Schöberl, n 54 above, 136.

[64] D Guilfoyle, 'Counter-piracy Law Enforcement and Human Rights' (2010) 59 *International & Comparative Law Quarterly* 141 (with further references).

[65] TD Gill and D Fleck (eds), *The Handbook of the International Law of Military Operations* (Oxford, Oxford University Press, 2010).

[66] Ibid, rule 3.02, 33.

Code of Conduct for Law Enforcement Officials[67] and to the UN Basic Principles on the Use of Force and Firearms.[68] Based on these documents, the term law enforcement can best be understood as 'the exercise by state agents of police powers, especially the powers of arrest or detention'.[69] Normally law enforcement only necessitates 'an authority stable and strong enough to impose public security, law and order',[70] the operations of which are largely governed by human rights law,[71] and—should it be applicable—international humanitarian law.[72] At issue are normally habeas corpus rights, the right to life and due process rights. As to the application of potentially lethal force, reference may be made to the notions of precaution, proportionality and necessity,[73] the latter making it clear that lethal force can only be applied 'when less extreme means are insufficient to achieve (the operation's) objectives'.[74]

While pirates normally will not qualify as organised armed groups according to Common Article 3 GC or according to Article 1 of AP II, it cannot be excluded that under exceptional circumstances they may nevertheless meet all the requirements included in these provisions. In light of a resulting possible overlap of human rights law and international humanitarian law in counter-terrorist and counter-piracy operations, it is important to carefully distinguish between the conduct of hostilities and the conduct of law enforcement operations. Debates on so-called unified use of force rules[75] are not very helpful in this particular context, since they tend to push aside the differences and distinctions arising from the two different bodies of law.

Generally, it is desirable to further develop the concept and the rules applicable to international or transnational law enforcement. The exercise of police powers beyond areas of national jurisdiction or in areas of limited statehood has become more important in light of the fact that the security of states and human security have increasingly come under pressure from non-traditional threats.[76]

IV. THE EFFECTS OF APPLYING EITHER BODY OF LAW TO COUNTER-PIRACY OPERATIONS

Among the arguable advantages of the law of armed conflict and the interest of the armed forces to resort to these standards are the degree of detail and its presumed

---

[67] UN GA 34/169 of 17 December 1979.

[68] 'Basic Principles on the Use of Force and Firearms by Law Enforcement Officials, Eighth United Nations Congress on the Prevention of Crime and the Treatment of Offenders, Havana, 27 August to 7 September 1990', UN Doc A/CONF.144/28/Rev.1, 112 (1990), available at http://www1.umn.edu/humanrts/instree/i2bpuff.htm (accessed on 21 October 2013).

[69] N Melzer, 'Conceptual Distinction and Overlaps between Law Enforcement and the Conduct of Hostilities' in Gill and Fleck, n 65 above, 33, 34.

[70] Ibid, 35.

[71] Ibid, 36.

[72] Melzer rightly calls for a careful distinction of which part of the law is applicable, ibid, 36.

[73] Ibid, 37.

[74] Ibid, 37.

[75] For a carefully balanced analysis see D Fleck, 'Law Enforcement and the Conduct of Hostilities—Two Supplementing or Mutually Excluding Legal Paradigms?' in A Fischer-Lescano, H-P Gasser, T Marauhn and, N. Ronzitti (eds), *Frieden in Freiheit. Festschrift für Michael Bothe zum 70. Geburtstag* (Baden-Baden, Nomos, 2008) 391.

[76] These include threats arising from inter- and transnational terrorism, but also from inter- and transnational organised crime and from piracy, to name but a few.

clarity. Indeed, compared with international human rights law and the soft law standards that have been adopted by international organisations for the purpose of avoiding the abuse of law enforcement powers, the law of armed conflict seems to provide more legal certainty.

However, it would be a false perception of the object and purpose of the law to select it according to whether or not it can be easily applied, whether its steering effects are straightforward, or whether its governance capacities are meaningful. The law, and international law in particular, addresses real and potential conflicts, and seeks to manage these conflicts in the interest of specified objectives which particular areas of the law address.

In the case of counter-piracy operations and the distinction between human rights law and international humanitarian law, it is useful to consider some background. Historically, international human rights law and international humanitarian law have been strictly separated.[77] In contrast to this separation doctrine, new approaches have been developed over the last few decades which focus on the overlap between these two bodies of law.[78] In this respect, it is worth noting the recognition that universal and regional human rights law have limited the power of state parties to derogate from human rights in times of emergency, including international and non-international armed conflict.[79]

With these in mind, the ICJ, in its 1996 advisory opinion on nuclear arms, observed that 'the protection of the International Covenant on Civil and Political Rights (ICCPR) does not cease in times of war',[80] and stated that

> whether a particular loss of life, through the use of a certain weapon in warfare, is to be considered an arbitrary deprivation of life contrary to Article 6 of the ICCPR, can only be decided by reference to the law applicable in armed conflict and not deduced from the terms of the (ICCPR) itself.[81]

This approach, based upon the idea of *lex specialis*,[82] might also be read as overlap instead of placing the final say on the legality of certain killings in the hands of international humanitarian law.

In its 2004 assessment of the lawfulness of the construction of a wall in the occupied Palestinian territory, the ICJ did not refine its approach but more generally distinguished three modes of coexistence between human rights law and international humanitarian law:

> As regards the relationship between international humanitarian law and human rights law, there are thus three possible situations: some rights may be exclusively matters of

---

[77] See Dröge, n 12 above, 501: 'Traditionally, international human rights law (IHRL) and international humanitarian law (IHL) are two distinct bodies of law with different subject matters and different roots, and for a long time they evolved without much mutual influence.'

[78] For a discussion of these approaches, see, eg, C Tomuschat, 'Human rights and international humanitarian law' (2010) 21 EJIL 15 and R Cryer, 'The interplay of human rights and humanitarian law—the approach of the ICTY' (2009) 14 *Journal of Conflict and Security Law* 511.

[79] Dröge, n 12 above, 507.

[80] *Legality of the Use by a State of Nuclear Weapons in Armed Conflict* (Advisory Opinion) [1996] ICJ Rep 66, para 25.

[81] Ibid, para 25.

[82] For further details on the application of the *lex specialis* doctrine to the relationship between international human rights law and the law of armed conflict see Dröge, n 12 above, 522–24.

international humanitarian law; others may be exclusively matters of human rights law; yet others may be matters of both these branches of international law.[83]

This approach was confirmed by the ICJ in its 2005 judgment on the dispute between the Democratic Republic of the Congo and Uganda[84] and, to a certain extent, in its decisions regarding the dispute between Georgia and Russia.[85] Human rights courts have gone even further in this regard, albeit not without problems.[86]

Notwithstanding the perceived weaknesses of international human rights law and the perceived strengths of the law of armed conflict, blurring the lines between the two will weaken both bodies of law.[87] It is thus in the interests of all those affected by counter-piracy operations to apply each body of law according to its merits, and not according to convenience.

V. CONCLUSION: MAINTAINING INTERNATIONAL PEACE OR MAINTAINING PUBLIC ORDER?

Overall, it is important to reflect upon the growing importance of international law enforcement operations. It cannot be disputed that traditional security threats have not fully disappeared, but they have at least in practice been superseded by threats to international public order. If individual states and the international community aim to provide adequate security for states and to ensure human security generally, then appropriate bodies of law must be at their disposal. While the law of armed conflict still seems to be appropriate to address challenges arising out of the conduct of hostilities, be it at the international or non-international level, transboundary and international police operations call for more detailed and more refined rules in the context of maintaining public order. The traditional approach towards maintaining the peace may still provide some institutional framework that the international community can rely upon, in particular as far as the question whether military or police force can be applied at all is concerned. However, the question of how law enforcement operations are to be conducted necessitates specification and application of international human rights law to an extent that has so far not been coherently developed. Rather than applying international humanitarian law to counter-piracy operations, it is thus necessary to be clear about which human rights standards are applicable. This, however, is not the object and purpose of this chapter, which has been confined to demonstrating the limitations of international humanitarian law in the context of counter-piracy operations.

---

[83] *Legal Consequences of the Construction of a Wall in the Occupied Palestinian Territories* (Advisory Opinion) [2004] ICJ Rep 136, para 106.

[84] *Armed Activities on the Territory of the Congo (Democratic Republic of the Congo v Uganda)* [2005] ICJ Rep 111, para 216.

[85] *Application of the International Convention on the Elimination of All Forms of Racial Discrimination (Georgia v Russia)* [2008] ICJ Rep 140, para 112.

[86] See Dröge, n 12 above, 510–18.

[87] See T Marauhn, 'Sailing Close to the Wind: Human Rights Council Fact-Finding in Situations of Armed Conflict—The Case of Syria' (2013) 43 *California Western International Law Journal* 401, 448–51.

Part II

National, Regional and International Approaches

5

The European Union's Comprehensive Approach to Combating Piracy at Sea: Legal Aspects

RICARDO GOSALBO-BONO AND SONJA BOELAERT*

I. INTRODUCTION

PIRACY HAS EXISTED throughout history. In ancient times, piracy was a well-known phenomenon in the Mediterranean sea, a place where there was close contact between different cultures and civilisations, the waters of which were infested with robbers of the sea, called 'pirates' (a term that originates from the ancient Greek word 'πειρατής' (*peiratēs*) for 'brigand' or 'assailant', which passed on to Latin as 'pirata') who, in the course of history, have been successively named 'buccaneers', 'filibusters', 'corsairs' and 'privateers'.[1] During the twentieth century, a belief

---

* The contents of this paper reflects the personal views of the authors and does not in any way engage the responsibility of the Council or its Secretariat General.

[1] The terms describe different historical and geographical situations. The 'buccaneers', whose denomination derives from the Caribbean Arawak word *buccan* (*boucane* in French), a wooden frame for smoking meat, were French hunters who used such frames to smoke meat from feral cattle and pigs on the island of Hispaniola (now Haiti and the Dominican Republic). They were driven away from the island by the Spaniards and, helped by the Dutch and the English, turned for that reason to piracy against Spanish shipping. The 'filibusters', a term which derives from the Spanish *filibustero* itself deriving originally from the Dutch *vrijbuiter* (English 'freebooter') meaning 'privateer, pirate, robber', were military adventurers from the US who operated in Central America and the Spanish West Indies. The 'corsairs', whose denomination derives from Medieval Latin *cursārius*, derived from *cursus* (course or a running) and passed on to old French as *corsaire* for pirate, were the plunderers, pirates and privateers operating originally in the so-called Barbary Coast, the coast of the Berber inhabitants of the ports of Tunis, Tripoli and Algiers throughout the Mediterranean, who, in addition to seizing ships, engaged in *Razzias* (raids) on European coastal towns and villages, mainly in Italy, France, Spain and Portugal, with the purpose of capturing Christian slaves for the Islamic market in North Africa and the Middle East. The 'Privateers' were the private owners of armed vessels which had been commissioned by a hostile nation (usually by means of a licence called a 'Letter of Marque and Reprisal') to carry out naval warfare on behalf of this nation against ships of another nation in exchange for authorisations to share any booty captured by way of compensation. See P Gosse, *The History of Piracy* (Mineola, Dover Pubus, 2007); R Steenhard, 'Pirates, Buccaneers and Privateers: Concepts of International Law' (Peace Palace Library, 2012), available at www.peacepalacelibrary.nl/2012/01/pirates-buccaneers-and-privateers-concepts-of-international-law/; F Pellegrino, 'Historical and Legal Aspects of Piracy and Armed Robbery against Shipping' (2012) 43 *Journal of Maritime Law and Commerce*

prevailed that piracy had entered a period of terminal decline. However, this belief has proven to be incorrect.[2] Indeed, since 2007, piracy has returned to the forefront of history owing to the meteoric rise in pirate attacks in the Gulf of Aden, which is a key shipping route. This phenomenon has drawn the world's attention to the security issues of the Horn of Africa and, increasingly, of the Gulf of Guinea.

In particular, Somalia and its coast, the longest coastline on the African continent (2300 miles), have become the linchpin of piracy for several reasons: Somalia is a failed state, with a population of nearly 10 million, immersed in a civil war since 1991 which has caused a breakdown of law and order; it does not possess fully functioning state institutions; it is divided between a few autonomous regions, such as Somaliland and Puntland, and, since the Jubbaland Conference of 28 February 2013, a semi-autonomous administration for the regions of Gedo and Jubbas; and therer are local forms of conflict resolution, consisting of civil law, religious law and customary law. It also faces a variety of challenges, including: an adult literacy rate of under 40 per cent; massive unemployment; no viable economic infrastructure or development opportunities; and poor or nonexistent electricity, communication, transport and health services.[3]

Pirates have thrived in such an environment of violence and poverty, where there is no effective controlling government nor stable and functioning institutions. Pirates operate from coastal Somali towns, where they are able to dock their own skiffs freely, and where they haul back their hijacked property and hostages, the proceeds of which bring economic benefit to those coastal towns. Consequently, such towns are the source of an unlimited supply of potential recruits for piracy and are reluctant to participate or collaborate in counter-piracy operations.

The modus operandi of the pirates has so far been relatively simple: they operate from simple fishing boats, dhows or hijacked vessels known as 'mother ships', and launch their attacks from there using small skiffs; they lack sophisticated equipment and normally do not possess large or varied weapons (they generally carry assault rifles—normally the Avtomat Kalashnikova, or AK-47, first developed in the USSR by Mikhail Kalashnikov)—grenades and even small guns and knives; they hijack the victim vessels, sailing them back to Somali ports. At the height of the phenomenon, pirates held thousands of hostages, and they have carried out hundreds of hijackings;[4] they demand from the shipping companies which own the vessels and even from the nation states of the hostages millions of euros for the release of the hostages.[5] Initially perceived to be a desperate response by the impoverished Somali fishermen

---

429. For an evolution of the legal rules on piracy see I Shearer, 'Piracy', *Max Planck Encyclopedia of Public International Law* (2009), available at http://opil.ouplaw.com/view/10.1093/law:epil/9780199231690/law-9780199231690-e1206.

[2] See also A Priddy and S Casey-Maslen, 'Counterpiracy under International Law', Geneva Academy of International Humanitarian Law and Human Rights Briefing No 1, 2012, 7.

[3] See also M Sahnoun, *Somalia: the Missed Opportunities* (Washington DC, United States Institute of Peace Press, 1994), 18.

[4] See in particular J Lang, 'Report of the Special Adviser to the Secretary-General on Legal Issues Related to Piracy off the Coast of Somalia', UN Doc S:2011/30 (25 January 2011).

[5] Report of the UN Monitoring Group on Somalia, UN Doc S/2010/91 (10 March 2010) 36. See also M Sterio, 'Piracy off the Coast of Somalia' (2012) 4 *Amsterdam Law Forum* 104, 106–07. For examples see D Rothwell, 'Maritime Piracy and International Law' (The Beacon, 2009), available at http://the-beacon.info/countries/africa/maritime-piracy-and-international-law/.

whose livelihood was threatened by the exploitation of Somali fishing waters, piracy has become a well-organised 'business' (in 2011 there were 31 ransoms valued at 150 million euros), and is now considered to be a form of transnational organised crime (with around 50 leaders, 300 chiefs of attack groups and approximately 2,300 local foot soldiers, known as 'lang'),[6] holding hostage, on 6 March 2013, four vessels and a total of 108 crew members.

Piracy disrupts trade and the security of maritime routes: 80 per cent of world trade is reliant on maritime transport (around 17,000 ships annually navigate the Suez Canal through the Gulf of Aden, and around 16,000 other ships navigate the area for other purposes[7]), whereas more than 40 per cent of the world's merchant fleet is controlled by companies from the EU Member States. Piracy costs more than six billion euros to the global economy and inflicts a high price in human suffering on seafarers and all persons taken hostage, thus contributing to regional insecurity. Piracy has become one of the many obstacles to the much-needed economic and social development of Somalia and the other countries in the region affected by it, as well as taking a heavy human toll.

The international community has recently taken some encouraging steps to counter such piracy. Within Somalia, these steps have taken shape with the establishment of the Transitional National Government in 2000, followed by the Transitional Federal Government (TFG) in 2004 (which re-established national institutions) and, with the 2012 election of President Mohamud, the formation of the Federal Government of Somalia (FGS), together with the establishment of a new Federal Parliament operating within the framework of a new provisional constitution. However, these encouraging steps remain insufficient, as the process of state building remains incomplete and the challenge of radical groups such as Al-Shabaab, which has been designated by several states as a terrorist organisation,[8] persists.

From a legal perspective, the upsurge of piracy has generated a significant number of new legal instruments, a rich state practice and a wealth of academic studies in a short period of time.[9] One of the major criticisms of the EU as a global actor has

---

[6] Report of the UN Secretary-General, UN Doc S/2011/360 (15 June 2011) Annex 1–3.

[7] B Wilson, 'The Somali Piracy Challenge: Operational Partnership, The Rule of Law and Capacity Building' (2012) 9 *Loyola University University of Chicago International Law Review* 47.

[8] Lang, n 4 above, para 24.

[9] See generally the extensive Information Resources on Piracy and Armed Robbery at Sea against Ships of the International Maritime Organization (IMO), updated on 9 August 2013. See also R Geiss and A Petrig, *Piracy and Armed Robbery at Sea. The Legal Framework for Counter-piracy Operations in Somalia and the Gulf of Aden* (Oxford, Oxford University Press, 2011), which contains an interesting appendix with the texts of the relevant International Conventions, Security Council Resolutions, EU decisions and international agreements, and Regional and National Instruments; the book also contains a selected bibliography. MJ Struett, JD Carlson, and MT Nance (eds), *Maritime Piracy and the Construction of Global Governance* (London, Routledge, 2013); T Obokata, 'Maritime Piracy as a Violation of Human Rights: A Way Forward for Its Effective Prevention and Suppression?' (2013) 17 *The International Journal of Human Rights* 18; CH Norchi and G Proutrière-Maulion (eds), *Piracy in Comparative Perspective: Problems, Strategies, Law* (Paris, A Pedone, 2012); M Sterio, 'Piracy off the Coast of Somalia' (2012) 4 *Amsterdam Law Forum* 104; B Wilson, 'The Somali Piracy Challenge', n 7 above; RC Beckman and J Ashley Roach (eds), *Piracy and International Maritime Crimes in ASEAN: Prospects for Cooperation* (Cheltenham, Edward Elgar Publishing, 2012); including Symposium, 'Testing the Waters: Assessing International Responses to Somali Piracy' (2012) 10 *Journal of International Criminal Justice* 717; R Haywood and R Spivak, *Maritime Piracy* (London, Routledge, 2012); 'Special Issue: Contemporary Global Maritime Piracy: Location, Trends, Issues and Countermeasures' (2012) 35 *Studies in Conflict and Terrorism* 497; JF Leclercq, 'La répression en droit belge des actes de piraterie moderne extravant le tranport maritime, exemple d'une Union fédérale réussie' (2012) 89

been 'its inability to coordinate its various resources—which in fact are quite vast—in the service of its common political or security interests'.[10] In the face of this criticism, the EU has considered that maritime piracy can only be addressed effectively through a 'comprehensive approach' which not only seeks to tackle its acute symptoms but also attempts to address some of its root causes. In its approach to combating maritime piracy, the EU seeks to combine its military and civilian operations with political, diplomatic and economic tools concerning sanctions, trade, development coopera- tion assistance, humanitarian aid, civil protection, judicial cooperation in criminal matters, police cooperation, fisheries, maritime transport and international coordina- tion with all the actors involved (the UN, the International Maritime Organization (IMO), North Atlantic Treaty Organization (NATO),[11] the African Union, the US, China, India and Russia, and of course the Federal Government of Somalia).[12] The key

---

Revue de droit international et de droit comparé 241; M Sawyer, 'International Conference on Piracy at Sea' (2012) 11 *WMU Journal of Maritime Affairs* 143; D Guilfoyle, 'Prosecuting Somali Pirates: A Critical Evalu- ation of the Options' (2012) 10 *Journal of International Criminal Justice* 767; DF Marley, *Modern Piracy: A Reference Handbook* (California, ABC-CLIO, 2011); F Naert and G-J van Hegelsom, 'Of Green Grass and Blue Waters: A Few Words on the Legal Instruments in the EU's Counter-piracy Operation Atalanta' (2011) 25 *NATO Legal Gazette* 2, available at http://www.ismllw.org/Nato%20Legal%20Gazette.php; KU Leuven Institute for International Law, Working Paper No 149, October 2011, available at http://www.law. kuleuven.be/iir/nl/onderzoek/WP.html; JK Leclercq, 'La lutte contre la piraterie moderne entravant la cir- culation maritime et le droit fondamental des Nations Unies' (2011) 88 *Revue de droit international et de droit comparé* 7; JK Leclercq, 'The Fight against Modern Piracy Impeding Maritime Traffic and Hampering UN Fundamental Rights' (2011) 46 *European Transport Law* 359; S Piedimonte Bodini, 'Fighting Maritime Piracy Under the European Convention on Human Rights' (2011) 22 *European Journal of International Law* 829; D Guilfoyle, 'Combating Piracy: Executive Measures on the High Seas' (2011) 53 *The Japanese Yearbook of International Law* 149; F Naert, A Vanheusden and M Benatar, 'The Belgian Approach to Maritime Piracy in an International Context' (2010) 22 *NATO Legal Gazette* 2, available at http://www. ismllw.org/Nato%20Legal%20Gazette.php; B van Ginkel and F-P van der Putten (eds), *The International Response to Somali Piracy: Challenges and Opportunities* (Leiden, Nijhoff, 2010); D Guilfoyle, 'Counter- piracy Law Enforcement and Human Rights' (2010) 59 *International & Comparative Law Quarterly* 141; D Guilfoyle, *Shipping Interdiction and the Law of the Sea* (Cambridge, Cambridge University Press, 2009); A Fischer-Lescano and L Kreck, 'Piracy and Human Rights: Legal Issues in the Fight against Piracy Within the Context of the European "Operation Atalanta"' (2009) 52 *German Yearbook of International Law* 525; T Treves, 'Piracy, Law of the Sea, and Use of Force: Developments off the Coast of Somalia' (2009) 20 *European Journal of International Law* 399; MD Fink and RJ Galvin, 'Combating Pirates off the Coast of Somalia: Current Legal Challenges' (2009) 56 *Netherlands International Law Review* 367; F Naert, *Inter- national Law Aspects of the EU's Security and Defence Policy, with a Particular Focus on the Law of Armed Conflict and Human Rights* (Antwerp, Intersentia, 2009) 179; T Heinicke, 'Piratenjagd vor der Küste Somalias: Überlegungen zu den rechtlichen Rahmenbedingungen der EU NAVFOR Somalia/ATALANTA- Operation' (2009) 42 *Kritische Justiz* 178; D Guilfoyle, 'Piracy off Somalia: UN Security Council Resolution 1816 and IMO Regional Counter-piracy Efforts' (2008) 57 *International & Comparative Law Quarterly* 690; G Breda and JP Pierini, 'Legal Issues Surrounding Maritime Counterdrug Operations and the Related Question of Detention as Highlighted in the Medvedyev and Others v France Decision of the European Court of Human Rights' (2008) 47 *Military Law & the Law of War Review* 167.

[10] B Germond and M Smith, 'Re-thinking European Security Interests and the ESDP: Explaining the EU's Anti-piracy Operation' (2009) 30 *Contemporary Security Policy* 573, 574.

[11] See also PM Olson, Chapter 7 below.

[12] 'The EU Strategic Framework for the Horn of Africa', Council Conclusions of 14 November 2011, Doc No 16858/11, available at http://eeas.europa.eu/agenda/2012/200212_factsheet_piracy.pdf. A non-legal approach of the EU comprehensive approach may be found in H Ehrhart and K Petretto, 'The EU, the Somalia Challenge, and Counter-piracy. Towards a Comprehensive Approach?' (2012) 2 *European Foreign Affairs Review* 261. Similarly to the EU, the 2007 USA 'Cooperative Strategy' abandoned the concept of 'naval power', focusing on the use of warships and aircraft in favour of the more comprehensive concept of 'maritime power' applicable to all components of diplomatic, informational, military and economic aspects of national power in the maritime field under international law. See J Kraska, 'Grasping the Influence of Law on Sea Power' (2009) 62 *Naval War College Review* 113, 121.

strategic document is the EU's Strategic Framework for the Horn of Africa,[13] which applies to the countries belonging to the Intergovernmental Authority for Development (IGAD), such as Djibouti, Eritrea, Ethiopia, Kenya, Somalia, Sudan, South Sudan and Uganda. The EU's decision to concentrate on the Horn of Africa[14] has been based on a number of considerations: the region's geostrategic importance; the EU's long-standing engagement with countries of the region, in particular through the Cotonou Agreement with the ACP (African, Caribbean and Pacific countries); the EU's desire to help lift people from poverty into self-sustaining economic growth; and the need for the EU to protect its own citizens from security threats.[15] The EU's commitment in the region is underlined by the appointment of a Special Representative for the Horn of Africa. The Special Representative, Alexander Rondos, has the 'comprehensive' mandate to contribute to the development and implementation of a coherent, effective and balanced Union approach to piracy originating in Somalia, encompassing all aspects of Union action, particularly in the political, security and development areas, and to be the Union's key interlocutor on piracy for the international community.[16]

The legal parameters of EU policies are set out in the two main Union Treaties recently amended by the Lisbon Treaty, namely the Treaty on European Union (TEU) and the Treaty on the Functioning of the European Union (TFEU).[17] As will be seen below, to the extent that the EU's counter-piracy efforts encompass both common foreign and security policy (CFSP) and non-CFSP areas, the decision-making, programming and budgeting of the various actions continue to follow—at least from an internal EU perspective—different paths. The legal aspects of the EU's comprehensive approach to combating piracy include a panoply of legal instruments, which are the subjects of analysis of this paper. The paper is divided into two parts, dealing, respectively, with the fight against piracy within the CFSP and measures on institution building and other measures taken within the scope of other EU policies.

II. THE FIGHT AGAINST PIRACY UNDER THE EU COMMON FOREIGN AND SECURITY POLICY

The EU's action on the international scene is guided by, and conducted in conformity with, the democratic principles which have inspired the creation of the Union: democracy, the rule of law, the universality and indivisibility of human rights and fundamental freedoms, respect for human dignity, the principles of equality and solidarity, and respect for the principles of the UN Charter and international law (Article

---

[13] Council Conclusions of 14 November 2011, ibid.

[14] In EU documents the 'Horn of Africa' is used mainly to refer to the countries belonging to IGAD.

[15] Council Conclusions of 14 November 2011, n 12 above.

[16] Mr Alexander Rondos was appointed European Union Special Representative for the Horn of Africa on 1 January 2012. His mandate was extended up to 31 October 2014. See Council Decision 2011/819/CFSP of 8 December 2011 appointing the European Union Special Representative for the Horn of Africa, [2011] OJ L327/62; Council Decision 2012/329/CFSP of 25 June 2012 extending the mandate of the European Union Special Representative or the Horn of Africa, [2012] OJ L165/62; Council Decision 2013/527/CFSP of 24 October 2013 on ending and extending the mandate of the European Union Special Representative for the Horn of Africa, [2013] OJ L284/23.

[17] For the latest version see Consolidated Versions of the Treaty on European Union and the Treaty on the Functioning of the European Union, [2012] OJ C326/1.

21(1) TEU). The Union's competence in CFSP matters is very wide, since it covers 'all areas of foreign policy and all questions relating to the Union's security, including the progressive framing of a common defence policy that might lead to a common defence' (Article 24(1) TEU). In particular, where the international situation requires operational action by the Union, the operational capacity of the Union is drawn from civilian and military assets provided by the Member States. The Union uses these operational assets on missions and crisis management operations outside the Union for peace-keeping, conflict prevention and the strengthening of international security in accordance with the principles of the UN Charter (Article 42 TEU). Decisions relating to the Union's missions and operations are taken by the Council of the EU acting unanimously on a proposal from the High Representative for Foreign Affairs and Security Policy (the High Representative) or an initiative from a Member State (Articles 31 and 42(4) TEU). These crisis management operations using civilian and/ or military means include the following tasks: humanitarian and recue tasks, military advice and assistance tasks, conflict prevention and peace-keeping tasks, tasks of combat forces in crisis management (including peace-keeping and post-conflict stabili-sation) and joint disarmament operations. All these tasks 'may contribute to the fight against terrorism, including by supporting third countries in combating terrorism in their territories' (Article 43(1) TEU). Clearly, the Union acts in accordance with inter-national law with the prior autorisation of the third countries concerned or with the autorisation of the UN, or as otherwise permitted by international law (eg under the law of the sea).

The establishment by the Council of the EU of crisis management operations and missions takes place after the completion of a series of procedures, referred to as 'crisis management procedures', which relate to the planning and launch of the operation.[18] The relevant planning documents include a Crisis Management Concept, comprising the general political assessment and a comprehensive course of action with its different elements, a Concept of Operations, containing the military planning elements of the operations, the Operation Plan and, with regard to military operations, a set of Rules of Engagement prepared by the Operation Commander, who also conducts a Force Generation Process in order to ensure that EU operations have the required manpower and materials to achieve their objectives.

These procedures are steered and monitored by the EU's Political and Security Committee (PSC), which, composed of Member States officials at ambassadorial level, operates under the responsibility of the Council of the EU and of the High Repre-sentative, exercises the political control and strategic direction of operations (Article 38 TEU), and is at the centre of the elaboration and approval of all the planning documents.

With regard to military operations, the PSC is assisted by the EU Military Com-mittee (which represents the Chiefs of Defence of the Member States at the level of permanent military representatives and provides the PSC with advice and recom-mendations on all military matters within the EU[19]), the Crisis Management and

---

[18] See in general A Björkdahl and M Strömvik, *EU Crisis Management Operations: ESDP Bodies and Decision-Making Procedures* (Copenhagen, Danish Institute for International Studies, 2008).

[19] Council Decision of 22 January 2001 setting up the Military Committee of the European Union, [2001] OJ L27/4.

Planning Directorate (which, within the EU External Action Service (EEAS), ensures the coherence and effectiveness of the operations and develops policies, concepts and capabilities) and the EU Military Staff (which, under the authority of the High Representative, provides, inter alia, early warning, situation assessment, strategic planning and training).

With regard to civilian operations (which usually develop the four priority areas defined by the Feira European Council in June 2000, ie police, strengthening of the rule of law, strengthening civilian administration and civil protection), the PSC is assisted by the Committee for Civilian Aspects of Crisis Management, composed of Member State experts on these issues, and by the Civilian Planning and Conduct Capability (CPCC), which, within the EEAS, has a mandate to plan and conduct civilian operations under the political control and strategic direction of the PSC, to provide assistance and advice to the High Representative, the Presidency and the relevant bodies of the Council of the EU, and to direct, coordinate, advise, support, supervise and review civilian CSDP operations. The CPCC works in close cooperation with the other crisis management structures within the EEAS and the European Commission.

A Council decision establishing an EU operation will typically define the political context in which the decision is to be carried out and will include an authorisation to the PSC to take all relevant decisions concerning the political control and strategic direction of the operation (including, if need be, the establishment of a Committee of Contributors), and an invitation to the European Commission to direct, within its sphere of competence, its actions in a manner consistent with the Council decision. The decision will also specify the role of the High Representative, and appoint the Operation Commander and, where relevant, an EU Special Representative. The Special Representative acts under the authority of the High Representative and the strategic guidance and political direction of the PSC, working in close coordination with the EEAS and its relevant departments. He regularly provides the High Representative and the PSC with reports.

With regard to the fight against piracy off the coast of Somalia, the EU has established the following military and civilian operations.

A. The European Naval Force Somalia (EU NAVFOR Somalia or Operation Atalanta)

Operation Atalanta (named after the virgin huntress ταλάντη, Atalantē, of Greek mythology) also known as EU Naval Force Somalia (EU NAVFOR Somalia), is the first naval mission of the EU within the framework of the CFSP. It is based on Joint Action 2008/851/CFSP adopted on 10 November 2008 by the Council of the EU, which establishes a EU military operation 'to contribute to the deterrence, prevention and repression of acts of piracy and armed robbery off the Somali coast'.[20] That Joint Action was adopted in explicit support of successive UN Security Council

---

[20] Council Joint Action 2008/851/CFSP of 10 November 2008 on a European Union military operation to contribute to the deterrence, prevention and repression of acts of piracy and armed robbery off the Somali coast, [2008] OJ L301/33.

(UNSC) Resolutions 1814 (2008),[21] 1816 (2008),[22] 1838 (2008),[23] 1846 (2008).[24] It was also subsequently adopted in support of UNSCRs 1851 (2008),[25] 1950 (2010),[26] 1976

[21] In its Resolution 1814 (2008) on the situation in Somalia, adopted on 15 May 2008, the UNSC requested the Secretary-General to continue and intensify his efforts, working together with the international community, to promote an ongoing political process in Somalia (operational para 1) and called on states and regional organisations, in close coordination with one another, to take action to protect shipping involved in the transport and delivery of humanitarian aid to Somalia and in activities authorised by the UN (operational para 2).

[22] In Resolution 1816 (2008) the Security Council expresses its concern at the threat that acts of piracy and armed robbery pose to the delivery of humanitarian aid to Somalia, the safety of commercial maritime routes and international navigation. The UNSC also welcomes the initiatives by NATO to counter piracy off the Somalia coast, including by escorting vessels of the World Food Programme (WFP) and, in particular, the decision by the EU on 10 November 2008 to launch a naval operation to protect WFP maritime convoys bringing humanitarian assistance to Somalia and other vulnerable ships, and to repress acts of piracy and armed robbery at sea off the coast of Somalia (operational para 6). In addition, the Security Council called upon states and regional organisations that had the capacity to do so to take part actively in the fight against piracy and armed robbery at sea off the coast of Somalia—in particular, consistent with that resolution and relevant international law, by deploying naval vessels and military aircraft, and by seizing and disposing of boats, vessels, arms and other related equipment used in the commission of piracy and armed robbery off the coast of Somalia, or for which there is reasonable ground for suspecting such use (operational para 7). In particular, the Security Council, prompted by the lack of capacity of the TFG to interdict pirates or patrol and secure either the international sea lanes off the coast of Somalia or Somalia's territorial waters, decided to authorise states cooperating with the TFG, of which advanced notification had been given by the TFG to the UN Secretary-General, to enter the territorial waters of Somalia for the purpose of repressing acts of piracy and armed robbery at sea, and use within the territorial waters of Somalia, in a manner consistent with action permitted on the high seas with respect to piracy under relevant international law, all necessary means to repress acts of piracy and armed robbery (operational para 7). The same resolution urges UN Member States to cooperate with interested international organisations, including the IMO, to ensure that vessels entitled to fly their flag receive appropriate guidance and training on avoidance, evasion and defensive techniques, and to avoid the area whenever possible (operational para 4).

[23] In its Resolution 1838 (2008) on the situation in Somalia, adopted on 7 October 2008, the UNSC commended the contribution made by some states since November 2007 to protect WFP maritime convoys, and the establishment by the European Union of a coordination unit with the task of supporting the surveillance and protection activities carried out by some Member States of the EU off the coast of Somalia. In particular, the UNSC commended the ongoing planning process towards a possible EU naval operation, as well as other international or national initiatives taken with a view to implementing Resolutions 1814 (2008) and 1816 (2008), and urged states that had the capacity to do so to cooperate with the TFG in the fight against piracy and armed robbery at sea in conformity with Resolution 1816 (2008). The UNSC also urged states and regional organisations, in conformity with Resolution 1814 (2008), to continue to take action to protect WFP maritime convoys, which are vital in bringing humanitarian assistance to the affected populations in Somalia.

[24] In its Resolution 1846 (2008) the UNSC decided that states and Regional Organisations are able to use 'all necessary means' (ie the use of force) to fight piracy off Somalia coast after having obtained the consent from the TFG.

[25] In Resolution 1851 (2008), the UNSC invited all states and regional organisations fighting piracy off the coast of Somalia to conclude transfer agreements with countries willing to take custody of pirates and continued to authorise all necessary measures for the purpose of suppressing acts of piracy and armed robbery at sea (operational para 6). In addition, operational para 6 of UNSC Resolution 1851 authorises 'all necessary measures that are appropriate in Somalia, for the purpose of suppressing acts of piracy and armed robbery at sea, pursuant to the request of the TFG, provided, however, that any measures undertaken pursuant to the authority of this paragraph shall be undertaken consistent with applicable international humanitarian and human rights law'. On 1 March 2012, the TFG notified the UN Secretary-General that the EU could apply operational para 6 and conduct actions destroying paraphernalia found at logistics dumps on Somali Coastal territory.

[26] In Resolution 1950, adopted in 2010, the UNSC called upon all states to criminalise piracy under their domestic law and to favourably consider the prosecution of suspected, and the imprisonment of convicted, pirates apprehended off the coast of Somalia, consistent with applicable international law including international human rights law; to take appropriate actions under their existing domestic law to prevent the illicit financing of acts of piracy and the laundering of its proceeds, and, in cooperation with INTERPOL and

(2011),[27] 2020 (2011)[28] and 2077 (2012),[29] on the situation in Somalia, adopted under Chapter VII of the UN Charter, which, although drafted very cautiously, link the activities of pirates off the coast of Somalia with the notion of a threat to international peace and security. The Joint Action has been amended several times—on 8 December 2009,[30] on 30 July 2010,[31] on 7 December 2010[32] and on 23 March 2012[33]—in particular to take account of the evolution of the situation of Somalia, as laid down in the successive mandates contained in the UNSC resolutions and the changing modus operandi of pirates.

(i) The Political Control and Strategic Direction of the Operation

The political control and strategic direction of the Atalanta operation is exercised by the PSC under the responsibility of the Council of the EU.[34] The PSC also takes the relevant decisions in accordance with Article 38 TEU to amend the planning documents, including the Operation Plan, the Chain of Command and the Rules of Engagement.

The proper conduct and execution of the military operation falls under the responsibility of the Operation Commander, Rear Admiral Robert Tarrant,[35] from the Operational Headquarters (OHQ) at Northwood, UK. There is a Deputy Operation Commander (at present Rear Admiral Eric Dupont) and, since 2 July 2013, an EU Force Commander, Commodore Peter Lenselink,[36] who exercises command and control of all of the operation's military forces in the 'joint operation area' (the area of land, sea and airspace in which military operations are conducted to accomplish a specific mission).[37] The proper conduct and execution of the operation is regularly

---

Europol, to further investigate international criminal networks involved in piracy off the coast of Somalia, including those responsible for illicit financing and facilitation (operational paras 13, 15 and 16).

[27] In Resolution 1976, adopted in 2011, the UNSC recognised that piracy is a crime subject to universal jurisdiction and reiterated its call on states to favourably consider the prosecution of suspected, and the imprisonment of convicted, pirates apprehended off the coast of Somalia (operational para 14), underlining the need to investigate and prosecute those who finance, plan, organise or unlawfully profit from piracy (operational para 15).

[28] In Resolution 2020 of 2011, the UNSC welcomed the recommendations and guidance of the IMO on preventing and suppressing piracy and armed robbery against ships (operational para 25). Furthermore, in 2012 the Security Council adopted Resolution 2036 relating to the mandate reinforcement of the African Union Mission to Somalia (AMISOM). Mention should also be made of Resolution 2039 (2012), in which the Security Council, expressing its concern over the threat of piracy and armed robbery at sea in the Gulf of Guinea, urged states to work through regional organisations, including the Economic Community of Central African States (ECCAS), the Economic Community of West African States (ECOWAS), the Gulf Cooperation Council (GCC) and the African Union (AU), to develop a regional anti-piracy strategy.

[29] In Resolution 2077, adopted in 2012, the UNSC renewed until November 2013 the authorisations and mandates contained in its previous resolutions relating to the international action to fight 'unremitting' piracy off the Somali coast. In Resolution 2125, adopted in 2013, the authorisations and mandates were renewed for a further period of 12 months.

[30] [2009] OJ L322/27.

[31] [2010] OJ L201/33.

[32] [2010] OJ L327/49.

[33] [2012] OJ L89/69.

[34] The role of the PSC in crisis management operations is set out in Art 38 TEU.

[35] Appointed by PSC Decision (2013/356/CFSP) of 18 December 2012, [2012] OJ L352/46.

[36] PSC Decision of 2 July 2013, [2013] OJ L187/8.

[37] PSC Decision Atalanta/3/2012 of 27 November 2012 on the appointment of an EU Force Commander for the European Union military operation to contribute to the deterrence, prevention and repression of acts of piracy and armed robbery off the Somali coast (Atalanta), [2012] OJ L332/20.

monitored by the EU Military Committee, which may invite the EU Operation Commander and/or the Force Commander, as appropriate, to its meetings. The Chairman of the Military Committee acts as primary point of contact with the Operation Commander and reports, at regular intervals, to the PSC.[38]

The High Representative (who is also President of the Foreign Affairs Council) implements the Joint Action, and coordinates her activities with the EU Operation Commander and the EU Force Commander. The High Representative acts as primary point of contact with the UN, the Somali authorities, the authorities of neighbouring countries and other relevant actors. The High Representative is assisted by the EU Special Representative for the Horn of Africa, Alexander Rondos.

Staff and assets are provided by the EU Member States and contributing non-EU Member States.[39] Operation Atalanta reached its initial operational capability on 13 December 2008 and full operational capability in February 2009. At present it comprises six ships patrolling the seas around Somalia: two from Spain and one each from Italy, Germany, France and Romania; there are also four aircraft currently active, performing reconnaissance and transport roles. Including land-based personnel, EU NAVFOR Somalia consists of around 1,500 military personnel. The common costs of Operation Atalanta amounted to €8.4 million for 2010, €8.05 million for 2011 and €8.3 million for 2012, and a budget of €14.9 million has been provided for the common costs until December 2014.[40] The cost of supplying other military assets and personnel is shared by the contributing states according to their involvement in the operation, with each participating state essentially bearing the cost of the resources it deploys.

Most Member States of the EU participate in Operation Atalanta, the exceptions being Austria, Estonia, Slovakia and Denmark, the latter by virtue of Article 5 of Protocol 22 annexed to the TEU and TFEU, according to which Denmark does not participate in any EU operations having military implications. In addition, Operation Atalanta is supported by a number of non-Member State countries, including Croatia, Montenegro, Norway, Switzerland and Ukraine.

The area of operation of the EU forces includes the Somali coastal territory and internal waters, and the maritime areas off the coasts of Somalia and neighbouring countries within the region of the Indian Ocean. This conforms to the political objective of an EU maritime operation, as decided by the Council of the EU in Joint Action 2008/851/CFSP, as subsequently amended, to international law and to the mandate set out in the relevant UNSC resolutions, which together provide the legal bases upon which Operation Atalanta can operate legally on the high seas, in Somali coastal areas as well as in Somalia's internal and territorial waters.[41] Thus Operation Atalanta covers an area of 2,000,000 square nautical miles from the south of the Red Sea, the

---

[38] Arts 6 and 7 of Joint Action 2008/851/CFSP, n 20 above, as amended.

[39] Norway was the first non-EU country to contribute to the operation with one warship, in 2009. Furthermore, Croatia and Ukraine have provided staff officers to the Operational Headquarters. Additionally, offers by Montenegro and Serbia to contribute have been accepted and a Participation Agreement has been concluded to this effect, allowing the contribution of naval officers. See EU NAVFOR, available at http://eunavfor.eu/about-us/mission/.

[40] EU NAVFOR, ibid.

[41] Council Decision 2012/174/CFSP of 23 March 2012 amending Joint Action 2008/851/CFSP on a European Union military operation to contribute to the deterrence, prevention and repression of acts of piracy and armed robbery off the Somali coast, [2012] OJ L89/69.

Gulf of Aden and the western part of the Indian Ocean, including Seychelles. The current mandate of the mission will expire in December 2014.[42]

Pursuant to Article 1 of Joint Action 2008/851/CFSP, as amended most recently by Council Decision 2012/174/CFSP, Operation Atalanta contributes 'in a manner consistent with action permitted with respect to piracy under Article 100 et seq of the UN Convention on the Law of the Sea signed in Montego Bay on 10 December 1982' to the protection of vessels of the World Food Programme (WFP)[43] delivering food aid to displaced persons in Somalia, in accordance with the mandate laid down in UNSC Resolution 1814 (2008). Operation Atalanta also contributes to the protection of vulnerable vessels cruising off the Somali coast; the deterrence, prevention and repression of acts of piracy and armed robbery off the Somali coast, in accordance with the mandate laid down in UNSC Resolutions 1846 (2008) and 1851 (2008); and the monitoring of fishing activities off the Somali coast.

In paragraph 11 of Resolution 1814 (2008), the UNSC, reiterating its support for the contribution made by some states to protect the maritime convoys of the WFP, had called

> upon states and regional organizations, in close coordination with each other and as notified in advance to the Secretary-General, and at the request of the (Somali) Transitional Federal Government, to take action to protect shipping involved with the transportation and delivery of humanitarian aid to Somalia and United Nations-authorized activities.

With regard to Somalia, the WFP aims to address basic food needs, strengthen coping mechanisms and support the efforts to achieve food security of vulnerable Somalis so they can cope more effectively with hardships. Its activities range from relief, which is provided during emergencies, to activities designed to strengthen the resilience of households against future shocks, such as droughts and floods. It uses a targeted approach to provide relief assistance for people and communities in crisis, including social safety nets and livelihood support projects, some of which are provided on a seasonal basis when needs are greatest, such as between harvests. It also concentrates on nutritional programming. UNSC Resolution 1814 (2008), requesting protection for ships chartered by WFP and carrying humanitarian aid to Somalia, was the result of the hijacking of two WFP ships in 2005, and the subsequent attempts to hijack more of its ships throughout the following years.

In order to address the concerns regarding illegal fishing off the Somali coast by large transnational fishing companies using trawlers, which is reportedly one of the main reasons for Somalis turning to piracy,[44] UNSC Resolution 1897 (2009) reaffirmed 'its respect for the sovereignty, territorial integrity, political independence and unity of Somalia, including Somalia's rights with respect to offshore natural resources, including fisheries, in accordance with international law'; acknowledged 'Somalia's

---

[42] Art 16(3) of Joint Action 2008/851/CFSP as amended by Council Decision 2012/174/CFSP, [2012] OJ L89/70.

[43] The WFP was established in 1961 as part of the UN system and is voluntarily funded; it is devoted to fighting hunger worldwide, promoting a world in which every man, woman and child has access at all times to the food needed for an active and healthy life. It has five objectives: to save lives and protect livelihoods in emergencies; to prepare for emergencies; to restore and rebuild lives after emergencies; to reduce chronic hunger and undernutrition everywhere; and to strengthen the capacity of countries to reduce hunger.

[44] J Bahadur, *Deadly Waters; Inside the Hidden World of Somali Pirates* (London, Profile Books, 2011) 57ff.

rights with respect to offshore natural resources, including fisheries, in accordance with international law'; and called upon

> states and interested organizations, including the IMO [the International Maritime Organisation], to provide technical assistance to Somalia, including regional authorities, and nearby coastal states upon their request to enhance their capacity to ensure coastal and maritime security, including combating piracy and armed robbery at sea off the Somali and nearby coastlines, and stresses the importance of coordination in this regard through the CGPCS [the Contact Group on Piracy off the Coast of Somalia].[45]

This is the justification for the adoption by Council of the EU of Decision 2009/907/CFSP of 8 December 2009, which amends Article 1 of Council Joint Action 2008/851/CFSP to add 'the monitoring of fishing activities off the coast of Somalia' as a new mission of Operation Atalanta.[46]

The tasks which Operation Atalanta is to perform and their modalities and geographical location are laid down in Article 2 of Joint Action 2008/851/CFSP, as amended by Council Decisions 2012/174/CFSP of 23 March 2012, 2010/766/CFSP of 7 December 2010 and 2009/907/CFSP of 8 December 2009, which provides that Atalanta shall, as far as available capabilities allow:

> (a) provide protection to vessels chartered by the WFP, including by means of the presence on board those vessels of armed units of Atalanta, including when sailing in Somalia's territorial and internal waters; (b) provide protection, based on a case-by-case evaluation of needs, to merchant vessels cruising in the areas where it is deployed; (c) keep watch over areas off the Somali coast, including Somalia's territorial and internal waters, in which there are dangers to maritime activities, in particular to maritime traffic; (d) take the necessary measures, including the use of force, to deter, prevent and intervene in order to bring to an end acts of piracy and armed robbery which may be committed in the areas where it is present; (e) in view of prosecutions potentially being brought by the relevant states under the conditions in Article 12, arrest, detain and transfer persons who have committed, or are suspected of having committed, acts of piracy or armed robbery in the areas where it is present and seize the vessels of the pirates or armed robbers or the vessels caught following an act of piracy or an armed robbery and which are in the hands of the pirates, as well as the goods on board; (f) liaise with organisations and entities, as well as states, working in the region to combat acts of piracy and armed robbery off the Somali coast, in particular the 'Combined Task Force 151' maritime force which operates within the framework of 'Operation Enduring Freedom'; (g) once sufficient progress has been made ashore in the area of maritime capacity building, including security measures for the exchange of information, assist Somali authorities by making available data relating to fishing activities compiled in the course of the operation; (h) collect, in accordance with applicable law, data concerning persons referred to in point (e) related to characteristics likely to assist in their identification, including fingerprints; (i) for the purpose of circulating the data via INTERPOL's channels and checking it against INTERPOL's databases, transmit to the National Central Bureau ('NCB') of the International Criminal Police Organisation—INTERPOL located in the Member State where the Operational Headquarters is stationed, in accordance with arrangements to be concluded between the EU Operation Commander and the Head of the NCB, the following data: personal data concerning persons referred to in point (e) related

---

[45] UNSC Resolution 1897 (2009), preamble and operative para 5.
[46] Council Decision 2009/907/CFSP of 8 December 2009 amending Joint Action 2008/851/CFSP, [2009] OJ L322/27.

to characteristics likely to assist in their identification, including fingerprints, as well as the following particulars, with the exclusion of other personal data: surname, maiden name, given names and any alias or assumed name; date and place of birth, nationality, sex; place of residence, profession and whereabouts; driving licenses, identification documents and passport data. This personal data shall not be stored by Atalanta after its transmission to INTERPOL; and data related to the equipment used by such persons.

These sweeping and wide powers of Operation Atalanta correspond to the relevant mandates and authorisations contained, in particular, in the UN Convention on the Law of the Sea of 10 December 1982 (UNCLOS)[47] and the relevant UNSC resolutions, examined below.

Indeed, in its Resolution 1846 (2008), the UNSC, acting under Chapter VII of the UN Charter in accordance with its mission to maintain peace and security worldwide, welcomed the initiatives by Canada, Denmark, France, India, the Netherlands, the Russian Federation, Spain, the UK, the US, and regional and international organisations (in particular, NATO, the African Mission in Somalia (AMISOM), the IMO and the EU) to counter piracy off the coast of Somalia pursuant to its previous resolutions. The UNSC also called upon states and regional organisations 'that have the capacity to do so, to take part actively in the fight against piracy and armed robbery at sea off the coast of Somalia, in particular, consistent with this resolution and relevant international law', by deploying naval vessels and military aircraft, and through the seizure and disposition of boats, vessels, arms and other related equipment used in the commission of piracy and armed robbery off the coast of Somalia, or for which there is reasonable ground for suspecting such use. As a consequence of UNSC Resolution 1846 (2008), Operation Atalanta is also engaged in the protection of vessels from AMISOM and the protection of vulnerable shipping off the Somali coast on a case-by-case basis.[48] Furthermore, Operation Atalanta complements another EU initiative, the Maritime Security Centre—Horn of Africa, set up in 2008 as a command centre from which vessels transiting through the region are monitored 24 hours a day, whereby group transit systems are arranged for transport through the Gulf of Aden and up-to-date information is relayed to captains and naval forces through an interactive website.

UNSC Resolution 1846 (2008) is also important for containing two fundamental principles. On the one hand, beyond general international law, it authorises the international actors involved in the fight against piracy to enter the territorial waters of Somalia and to use all necessary means to repress piracy in such waters under the following conditions:

> states and regional organizations cooperating with the TFG in the fight against piracy and armed robbery at sea off the coast of Somalia, for which advance notification has been provided by the TFG to the Secretary-General, may: (a) Enter into the territorial waters of Somalia for the purpose of repressing acts of piracy and armed robbery at sea, in a manner consistent with such action permitted on the high seas with respect to piracy under relevant international law;

---

[47] 1833 UNTS 397.
[48] Council Joint Action 2008/851/CFSP, n 20 above; Council Decision 2010/766/CFSP of 7 December 2010 amending Joint Action 2008/851/CFSP on a European Union military operation to contribute to the deterrence, prevention and repression of acts of piracy and armed robbery off the Somali coast, [2010] OJ L327/49.

and (b) Use, within the territorial waters of Somalia, in a manner consistent with such action permitted on the high seas with respect to piracy under relevant international law, all necessary means to repress acts of piracy and armed robbery at sea.[49]

On the other hand, it relaxes the general principle of the law of the flag for the purpose of the prosecution of pirates seized, by calling upon

all states, and in particular flag, port and coastal states, states of the nationality of victims and perpetrators of piracy and armed robbery, and other states with relevant jurisdiction under international law and national legislation, to cooperate in determining jurisdiction, and in the investigation and prosecution of persons responsible for acts of piracy and armed robbery off the coast of Somalia, consistent with applicable international law including international human rights law, and to render assistance by, among other actions, providing disposition and logistics assistance with respect to persons under their jurisdiction and control, such victims and witnesses and persons detained as a result of operations conducted under this resolution.[50]

The principles adopted in UNSC Resolution 1846 (2008) were expanded and reinforced by the UNSC in its Resolution 1851 (2008), according to the fourth preambular paragraph of which the UNSC, acting under Chapter VII of the UN Charter, further reaffirms that 'international law, as reflected in the UN Convention on the Law of the Sea of 10 December 1982 (UNCLOS), sets out the legal framework applicable to combating piracy and armed robbery at sea, as well as other ocean activities'. In response to the invitation by the Somali TFG, the UNSC decided that

states and regional organizations cooperating in the fight against piracy and armed robbery at sea off the coast of Somalia for which advance notification has been provided by the TFG to the Secretary-General may undertake all necessary measures that are appropriate in Somalia, for the purpose of suppressing acts of piracy and armed robbery at sea, pursuant to the request of the TFG, provided, however, that any measures undertaken pursuant to the authority of this paragraph shall be undertaken consistent with applicable international humanitarian and human rights law.[51]

Thus, the UNSC authorised the use of force 'in Somalia' to interdict those using Somali territory to plan, facilitate or undertake acts of piracy and armed robbery,

by deploying naval vessels and military aircraft and through seizure and disposition of boats, vessels, arms and other related equipment used in the commission of piracy and armed robbery at sea off the coast of Somalia, or for which there are reasonable grounds for suspecting such use[52]

consistent with that Resolution, Resolution 1846 (2008), and international law. In addition, the UNSC

affirms that the authorization provided in this resolution applies only with respect to the situation in Somalia and shall not affect the rights or obligations or responsibilities of Member States under international law, including any rights or obligations under UNCLOS, with respect to any other situation, and underscores in particular that this resolution shall

---

[49] UNSC Resolution 1846 (2008), operative para 10.
[50] Ibid, operative para 14.
[51] Resolution 1851 (2008), operative para 6.
[52] Ibid, operative para 2.

not be considered as establishing customary international law, and affirms further that such authorizations have been provided only following the receipt of the 9 December 2008 letter conveying the consent of the TFG.[53]

All states and regional organisations fighting piracy off the coast of Somalia were invited

> to conclude special agreements or arrangements with countries willing to take custody of pirates in order to embark law enforcement officials ('shipriders') from the latter countries, in particular countries in the region, to facilitate the investigation and prosecution of persons detained as a result of operations conducted under this resolution for acts of piracy and armed robbery at sea off the coast of Somalia, provided that the advance consent of the TFG is obtained for the exercise of third state jurisdiction by shipriders in Somali territorial waters and that such agreements or arrangements do not prejudice the effective implementation of

the 1988 Convention for the Suppression of Unlawful Acts against the Safety of Maritime Navigation (the SUA Convention[54]), which provides for parties to create criminal offences, establish jurisdiction and accept delivery of persons responsible for, or suspected of, seizing or exercising control of a ship by force or threat thereof, or any other form of intimidation.[55]

The application by Operation Atalanta of Article 2 of Joint Action 2008/851/CFSP, as amended, has given rise to many legal questions concerning the definition of piracy and armed robbery at sea, the seizure of vessels and the use of force, the prosecution and/or transfer of persons arrested and detained with a view to their prosecution, and the respect for human rights and, in particular, of the principle of non-refoulement. These legal questions are analysed in the following pages.

(ii) The EU Definition of Piracy and Armed Robbery

Questions inevitably arise concerning the legal meaning and scope of the terms 'piracy' and 'armed robbery' with regard to EU law. These definitions are relevant because any confusion in terminology invariably leads to conflicting debates about upholding the principle of state sovereignty, on the one hand, and supporting the universal jurisdiction over crimes at sea, on the other.

There are numerous meanings of the word 'piracy'—most with no direct legal implications—and the establishment of an authoritative definition of piracy in law has always been rather problematic. The EU Joint Action 2008/851/CFSP and its amending decisions relating to Operation Atalanta do not contain any definition of piracy and therefore there is no conception of piracy which is autonomous and proper to the law of the EU. However, the EU Joint Action, as amended successively, makes a cross-reference to piracy as understood by international law[56] (which includes customary international law, international treaty law and UNSC resolutions adopted under Chapter VII of the UN Charter, relating to the specific situation of piracy off the

---

[53] Ibid, operative para 10.
[54] Convention for the Suppression of Unlawful Acts against the Safety of Maritime Navigation (Rome, 10 March 1988) 1678 UNTS 201.
[55] Ibid, operative para 3.
[56] On the subject of piracy and the development of international law see also MD Evans and S Galani, Chapter 15 below.

coast of Somalia), municipal law and state practice. The same applies to the concept of 'armed robbery'.

First of all, customary international law developed a definition of piracy in response to the threat it posed to trade routes during the seventeenth, eighteenth and nineteenth centuries. Customary international law binds all subjects of international law—thus also the EU.[57] Originally, as is well known, the law on piracy was related to the *ius fetiale*, the set of rules regulating treaties as well as oaths within the context of war and related transactions. Two thousand years ago, Marcus Tullius Cicero is said to have described pirates as not forming part of the lawful enemies which Romans were bound to recognise by means of an oath. Instead, pirates were regarded as 'the common enemies of all' (*communis hostis omnium*;[58] the better known phrase *hostis humani generis* appears to derive from medieval paraphrasing by the English barrister, judge and politician Edward Coke). The vehemence of the denunciation by Cicero was prompted not only by the nature of the acts committed by pirates, which were equally committed by other types of criminals such as brigands and thieves, but also by the fact that those acts were committed at sea, an element of nature that is not the natural locus for human beings.[59] Ever since, pirates have always been considered outlaws and piracy an international crime under the *ius gentium*, which acknowledged it as covering any unauthorised act of violence committed by a private vessel on the 'open sea' (high seas) against another vessel (public or private) with the intent to plunder (*animo furandi*).[60] Whilst a pirate is considered to be the enemy of every state, a ship or aircraft may retain its nationality although it has become a pirate ship or aircraft.[61] The retention or loss of nationality is determined by the state from which such nationality was derived. Piracy is an 'international crime' but, since international law has no means of trying and punishing pirates, 'such crimes are left to the municipal laws of each country';[62] and a pirate can be brought to justice by 'any nation into whose jurisdiction he may come'.[63] As Judge Guillaume at the International Court of Justice indicated, 'international law knows only one true case of universal jurisdiction: piracy'—probably meaning that piracy is the only case of truly universal jurisdiction

---

[57] Art 3(5) TEU and consistent case law of the Court of Justice, as recently confirmed in Case C-366/10 *Air Transport Association of America and Others v Secretary of State for Energy and Climate Change*, Judgment of 21 December 2011, nyr, points 101–02.

[58] Cicero's full statement concerning pirates, which embodies the essence of this phrase, is: 'Nam pirata non est ex perduellium numero definitus, sed communis hostis omnium; hoc nec fides debet nec ius iurandum esse commune'. MT Cicero, *De Officiis*, book II, ch XXIX, 107 (transl 'For a pirate is not included in the list of lawful enemies, but is the common enemy of all; among pirates and other men there ought be neither mutual faith nor binding oath'), cited in T Stadnik, 'Pirates—The Common Enemies of All, the Enemies of the Human Race, the Law of War and The Rule of Law', LexisNexis International Law Blog, 5 May 2009, available at http://www.lexisnexis.com/legalnewsroom/international-law/b/international-law-blog/archive/2009/05/05/pirates-_2d00_-the-common-enemies-of-all_2c00_-the-enemies-of-the-human-race_2c00_-the-law-of-war-and-the-rule-of-law.aspx.

[59] Stadnik, ibid.

[60] In *The Republic of Bolivia v The Indemnity Mutual Marine Assurance Co* (1909) 1 KB 785. See R Jennings and A Watts, *Oppenheim's International Law*, 9th edn (London, Longman, 1996), 747.

[61] Art 18 of the Geneva Convention of 1958 on the High Seas Convention and Art 104 UNCLOS.

[62] Viscount Sankey LC, *In re Piracy Jure Gentium* [1934] AC 586, Special Reference before the Privy Council.

[63] Judge Moore, *Lotus Case (France v Turkey)* (1927) PCIJ, Series A, No 10, 70.

under customary international law, the other cases deriving from international conventions.[64] Indeed, as Judge Moore stated,

> Piracy by the law of nations, in its jurisdictional aspects, is sui generis. Though statutes may provide for its punishment, it is an offence against the law of nations; and as the scenes of the pirate's operations is the high seas, which is not the right or the duty of any nation to police, he is denied the protection of the flag he may carry and is treated as an outlaw, an enemy of mankind whom any nation may in the interest of all capture and punish.[65]

Under customary international law, piracy is conceived as a crime against the safety of traffic on the open sea and cannot be committed anywhere else than on the open sea, ie on the high seas only,[66] the natural scope of operation of international law. Since the eighteenth century, the ship and goods seized by pirate vessels must be restored to their owners by virtue of the principle *pirata non mutat dominium* (an obligation to give the goods back to the original owner). Hence, after recapture, the pirate vessel must be restored to its original owner. Under customary international law, pirates were both criminals and military enemies: unlike prisoners of war, pirates could be captured and tried; if encountered on the high seas, they could be attacked or killed; and there was no obligation to return the captured pirates to a port, for trial for summary proceedings could be held on board ships. These characteristics assimilated the status of pirates to that of unlawful combatants.

Article 1 of EU Joint Action 2008/851/CFSP, as amended,[67] makes explicitly applicable the definition of piracy contained in Article 100 and following UNCLOS,[68] which is based on the work of the International Law Commission (ILC)[69] and on the definition of piracy inserted in several international conventions.[70] More particularly, Article 101 of the UNCLOS provides that piracy[71] consists of

> any of the following acts: (a) any illegal acts of violence or detention, or any act of depredation, committed for private ends by the crew or the passengers of a private ship or a private aircraft, and directed on the high seas, against another ship or aircraft, or against persons or property on board such ship or aircraft; (or) against a ship, aircraft, persons or property in a place outside the jurisdiction of any state; (b) any act of voluntary participation in the operation of a ship or of an aircraft with knowledge of facts making it a pirate ship or aircraft; (c) any act of inciting or of intentionally facilitating an act described in subparagraph (a) or (b).[72]

It is generally accepted that the UNCLOS definition of piracy must be regarded as

---

[64] ICJ Arrest Warrant Case (*Democratic Republic of the Congo v Belgium*, 2002, ICJ Rep 3 per President Guillaume).

[65] Judge Moore.

[66] As a result of Art 58(2) UNCLOS the UNCLOS high seas provisions apply *mutatis mutandis* to the EEZ.

[67] Art 1(1) of Council Joint Action 2008/851/CFSP, n 20 above.

[68] Above n 47.

[69] In 1956 the ILC adopted a report containing Arts concerning the Law of the Sea. In particular, Art 39 defines piracy. The report also contains commentaries on the draft articles and appears in (1956) II *Yearbook of the International Law Commission*.

[70] Art 39 of the ILC's articles defining piracy is incorporated into Art 15 of the 1958 Geneva Convention on the High Seas (13 UST 2312, 450 UNTS 11).

[71] See also R Churchill, Chapter 1 above.

[72] UNCLOS, n 47 above.

'having great authority',[73] as it reflects modern customary law. However, a few remarks are in order. First, the UNCLOS definition of piracy requires that there be two vessels involved, which excludes the so-called 'internal seizure' within a vessel.

Secondly, it is important to stress that only private vessels can commit piracy—public vessels (warships or public aircraft) which commit unjustified acts of violence are not pirate vessels and redress for such acts needs to be sought from the flag state.[74] In addition, as it is now accepted that the motive, ie the intent to plunder (*animo furandi*), is not a constitutive element, a private neutral vessel that attacks a belligerent vessel is also a pirate ship; another example of piracy is that mutinous crew and passengers of a ship or aircraft on the open sea, even if it is a government craft, are considered to commit piracy (as set out in Article 40 of the articles of the International Law Commission, Article 17 of the Geneva Convention on the High Seas and Articles 102 and 103 UNCLOS) if they attack 'for private ends' (Article 15 UNCLOS).

Thirdly, insofar as the object of piracy is concerned, the act of piracy can be directed against any public or private aircraft or vessel, or the persons or goods thereon; the motive is no longer relevant: it can be prompted by private gain, revenge or hatred; furthermore, there is no requirement that the act be committed, a mere attempt is enough.

Fourthly, whereas initially piracy could only be committed on the high seas, this limitation was broadened by Article 15 of the 1958 High Seas Convention to any place outside the jurisdiction of any state and remains unchanged in Article 101(a)(ii) UNCLOS; in addition, as a result of Article 58(2) UNCLOS, similar acts committed in the exclusive economic zones also qualify as acts of piracy. Violence conducted in the territorial sea (which in the case of the Somali Coast is recurrent) or without involvement of two ships (as in the violent taking of control of a ship by members of its crew) do not fall within the UNCLOS definition of 'piracy', as was rightly held in the famous cases of the incidents on the Portuguese merchant ship *Santa Maria* in 1961[75] (which did not involve an attack of one vessel on another for private ends) and the Italian cruise ship *Achille Lauro* in 1985[76] (which took place off the coast of Egypt).

Fifthly, as regards the action which may be taken against a pirate ship, military

---

[73] Jennings and Watts, n 60 above, 747.

[74] Some doubt has been cast on this rule as a result of certain treaties, including the Nyon Arrangement of 14 September 1937 (The Nyon Agreement, 181 LNTS 137), which addressed the question of attacks on international shipping in the Mediterranean sea during the Spanish Civil War and which branded the sinking of merchant ships by submarines as piratical acts against the dictates of humanity. However, in adopting its articles and commentaries on the law of the sea, the ILC took the view that questions arising in connection with acts committed by warships in the service of rival governments engaged in civil war were too complex. It remained of the view that such treaties did not invalidate the principle that piracy can only be committed by private ships. Art 15 of the 1958 Geneva Convention and Art 101 of UNCLOS confirm this view. Conversely, where the non-governmental nature of a ship is clear, the qualification of piracy follows. For example, during the insurrection war of 1873 in Spain (in which Great Britain, France and Germany participated), Spanish warships that did not recognise the Spanish government were classified as pirates.

[75] In that incident a group of Portuguese and Spanish members of the opposition to the Portuguese and Spanish dictatorships disguised as passengers boarded the Santa Maria in Guaira (Venezuela), then seized the ship and forced it to take a different course until it was intercepted by US naval vessels and was liberated following negotiations (the incident is also known as *Operation Dulcinea*).

[76] As the Italian cruiser was sailing from Alexandria to Port Said off the coast of Egypt, she was hijacked by four male members of the Palestine Liberation Front. The hijackers directed the cruiser to Tartus in Syria but, as the US had placed several navy vessels in the sorroundings, they were denied permission to dock at Tartus and returned to Port Said, where the ship was liberated and the hostages released.

personnel on the warships have a right to visit another vessel to ascertain whether it is engaged in piracy and, in exercising this so-called 'right of visit' (pursuant to Article 110(1) UNCLOS), such personnel have a right to be armed. In addition (Article 105 UNCLOS):

> On the high seas, or in any other place outside the jurisdiction of any state, every state may seize a pirate ship or aircraft, or a ship or aircraft taken by piracy and under the control of pirates, and arrest the persons and seize the property on board. The courts of the state which carried out the seizure may decide upon the penalties to be imposed, and may also determine the action to be taken with regard to the ships, aircraft or property, subject to the rights of third parties acting in good faith.

Article 105 confers very wide powers on the flag state of the seizing ship: namely, the right to arrest persons and to seize property, including the right to decide upon penalties and to decide upon action with regard to the captured ship or property, and the right to submit the persons arrested and the property to judicial proceedings. Thus, Article 105 reflects the rule of customary international law relating to the universal jurisdiction of the courts of the seizing states (although the wording of Article 105 ('may') seems to provide an option for the exercise of universal jurisdiction and does not lay down a duty to do so), but does not establish an exclusive jurisdiction by the courts of the seizing states. The courts of other states remain free to exercise jurisdiction under the conditions provided for by their national law. However, they will need to limit themselves to punishing suspected pirates for acts of piracy within the meaning of the term as established by *jure gentium*. This does not mean that states cannot punish pirates for a much wider range of acts; rather, these will fall outside the legal qualification of piracy. For example, the *Achille Lauro* incident of 1985 would now qualify not only as an act of piracy, but also as an act of terrorism falling under the SUA Convention.

Sixthly, UNCLOS establishes a duty to cooperate in the repression of piracy (Article 100 UNCLOS).[77]

Seventhly, for the purpose of UNCLOS, pirates are civilians in private vessels.

In addition to customary international law and the treaty provisions of UNCLOS, the concept and scope of counter-piracy actions off the coast of Somalia have been completed by UNSC resolutions adopted under Chapter VII of the UN Charter, which, as has been suggested, extend the limited scope of the rules of general international law relating to piracy on three grounds: *ratione materiae*, *ratione loci* and *ratione temporis*.[78]

With regard to the grounds *ratione materiae*, the UNSC resolutions do not define piracy but refer to the provisions of UNCLOS. However, the UNSC resolutions include 'armed robbery at sea' as an act of piracy. Neither the law of the EU (in particular, EU Joint Action 2008/851/CFSP) nor international law has an established definition or an international crime of 'armed robbery at sea', but it is a term used by the IMO to cover all acts of violence 'the purposes of which are identical or similar to those of piracy but are not covered by the conventional definition of it',[79] in particular those

---

[77] See also A Norris, 'The "Other" Law of the Sea' (2011) 64 *Naval War College Review* 78; J Kraska and B Wilson, 'Piracy, Policy, and Law' (2008) 134 *US Naval Institute Proceedings* 52.

[78] Treves, n 9 above, 403ff.

[79] Ibid, 403.

acts of violence that may be perpetrated without using a ship against the targeted ship.[80] The IMO definition of 'armed robbery at sea' applies only to activities in waters under the jurisdiction of a state, not to acts of piracy on the high seas. Instead, this lacuna is filled by UNSC Resolutions 1816 (2008) (penultimate preambular paragraph) and 1846 (2008) (penultimate preambular paragraph), which use the expression 'piracy and armed robbery against vessels in the territorial waters of Somalia and the high seas off the coast of Somalia'.

There are a number of international conventions which do not contain the UNCLOS geographical limitations, which provide for offences which partially cover the conduct referred to as 'armed robbery at sea' in EU Joint Action 2008/851/CFSP and the UN resolutions. In particular, unlike Article 101 UNCLOS in respect of pirates, acts referred to as 'armed robbery at sea' may fall within the scope of the 1992 SUA Convention, adopted following the incident of the Italian cruiser *Achille Lauro*. Article 3 of the SUA Convention contains a long list of unlawful acts threatening the safety of maritime navigation, mostly relating to terrorist acts, but it also lists acts which are relevant for the prosecution of armed robbers at sea, such as the seizure and exercise of control over a ship by force or intimidation (Article C.3(1)(a)), or the prohibition to perform an act of violence against a person on board of a ship (Article C.3(1)(b)). Again, unlike UNCLOS, the SUA Convention does not contain a geographical limitation to the high seas but also applies to the territorial sea.[81] Finally, state parties to the SUA Convention are either obliged to establish jurisdiction whenever there is a specific connection between the state and either the offence or the offender (the so-called mandatory 'primary jurisdiction') or, irrespective of whether such a connection exists, to establish jurisdiction in cases where the alleged offender is present on its territory and is not extradited (the so-called 'secondary jurisdiction') (Article C.6(1), (2) and (4)).

There is, in addition, the UN Convention against Transnational Organized Crime (UNTOC), in force with its three Protocols since 2003. Under UNTOC state parties commit themselves to taking measures against organised crime including the creation of domestic criminal offences, efficient frameworks for extradition, law enforcement cooperation and mutual legal assistance.[82] There is no doubt that piracy and armed robbery also can—and must—be understood as a form of organised crime that takes place on land and at sea, with kidnapping of crews and ships for ransom as the business model. The network leaders, financiers and instigators go largely unpunished even if some of the 'foot soldiers' (ie locals recruited as common soldiers for the purpose of committing acts of piracy) are less lucky and end up in prison. It is therefore vital to increase the risk/reward ratio for those who benefit most from piracy and to damage the underlying business model. The payment of cash or other benefits by private shipowners for the support of foreign governments in protecting the ships through maritime routes threatened by piracy does not comply with national law (eg the US Foreign Corrupt Practices Act and anti-terrorist laws) or the UNTOC Convention. Therefore, it is paramount to ensure the ability of international actors to identify,

---

[80] See IMO Resolution A.922 (22) of 29 November 2001 adopting the Code of Pratice for the Investigation of the Crimes of Piracy and Armed Robbery against ships. See Art 1(2) of the IMO-sponsored 'Code of Conduct Concerning the Repression of Piracy and Armed Robbery against Ships in the Western Indian Ocean and the Gulf of Aden', available at www.imo.org/newsroom/mainframe.asp?topicid=1773xdoc-id=10933.

[81] Treves, n 9 above, 410.

[82] UN General Assembly Resolution 55/25, Doc A/RES/55/25 of 15 November 2000.

trace, seize and confiscate those criminal assets. For that purpose, Operation Atalanta has been authorised to collect, 'in accordance with applicable law', data of the persons concerned which is likely to assist in their identification, including fingerprints, and to circulate such data via channels of the International Criminal Police Organization (INTERPOL) and check it against the latter's databases. Such data, which includes personal data and data related to the equipment used, is to be transmitted to the National Central Bureau (NCB) of INTERPOL located in the Member State where the operational headquarters is stationed, in accordance with arrangements to be concluded between the EU Operation Commander and the Head of the NCB. In particular, the data includes the following:

> personal data concerning persons related to characteristics likely to assist in their identification, including fingerprints, as well as the following particulars, with the exclusion of other personal data: surname, maiden name, given names and any alias or assumed name; date and place of birth, nationality, sex; place of residence, profession and whereabouts; driving licenses, identification documents and passport data. This personal data shall not be stored by Atalanta after its transmission to INTERPOL . . . [and] data related to the equipment used by such persons.[83]

Furthermore, in the context of the EU, a cooperation mechanism among prosecutors of the countries concerned in order to bring together admissible evidence for legal action against major piracy financiers, negotiators and organisers is in the process of being established and a Dutch–German joint investigation team started its work in January 2012 under the legal framework of Eurojust, the EU agency dealing with judicial cooperation in criminal matters. The High Representative has been authorised to release, on the basis of reciprocity, classified EU information and documents, at the level of EU restricted, generated for the purposes of Operation Atalanta to the US-led Coalition Maritime Force, as well as to relevant third states and international organisations. It is also worth mentioning that the UN Office on Drugs and Crime (UNODC) has developed a counter-piracy programme which assists with judicial, prosecutorial and police capacity building programmes, as well as data and logistical assistance, for the benefit of Somalia and the surrounding regional states.

Finally, under the International Convention against the Taking of Hostages (the Hostages Convention) in force since 1983, the state parties are obliged to establish jurisdiction over the offence of 'hostage-taking', as defined in Article 1 of the Hostages Convention to include hostage-taking properly, attempts to commit an act of hostage-taking and participation as an accomplice in an act of hostage-taking. The Hostages Convention 'does not exclude any criminal jurisdiction exercised in accordance with internal law' (Article 5(3)) and distinguishes, on the one hand, between 'primary jurisdiction'(Article 5(1)) in the cases of offences under the Convention committed in the territory of a state (the principle of territoriality), on board a ship holding the flag of the state (the flag state principle), by one of their nationals (the personality principle), and on the one hand, 'secondary jurisdiction' (Article 5(2)) in other cases under the rule *aut dedere aut judicare* (ie 'prosecute or extradite'),[84] which is also laid down in the SUA Convention for that purpose, according to which the obligation to

---

[83] Art 2(h) and (i) of Joint Action 2008/851/CFSP, as amended by Council Decision 2010/766/CFSP of 7 December 2010, [2010] OJ L327/49.

[84] UN General Assembly Resolution 146/34, Doc A/34/46 of 17 December 1979.

prosecute is not dependent on a prior extradition request and its denial; rather, the obligation to prosecute applies in all cases of non-extradition.

As has already been pointed out, the limited geographical scope of rules of international law on piracy has also been broadened *ratione loci* in the case of Somalia by a number of UNSC resolutions, in particular Resolutions 1816 (2008), 1846 (2008) and 1851 (2008), which authorise certain states to enter Somali territorial waters in a manner which is compatible with action permitted on the high seas. This *mutatis mutandis* equivalence of application of the rules of international law concerning piracy on the high seas also to Somali territorial waters permits the pursuit of pirates from the high seas into Somali territorial waters and the use of 'all necessary means' in such territorial waters (paragraph 7 of Resolution 1816). Finally, following the incident of the French cruise ship *Le Ponant*, in which French troops pursued pirates onto the mainland,[85] paragraph 6 of UNSC Resolution 1851 (2008) authorises the taking of 'all necessary measures that are appropriate in *Somalia*, for the purpose of suppressing acts of piracy and armed robbery at sea' (emphasis added). These authorisations of the use of force, which permit action beyond the limits of customary international law, gave rise to some apprehension on the part of states with a history of incidents of piracy, which feared the setting of a precedent for the erosion of national territorial sovereignty. For that reason, the text of the resolutions and the statements by the members of the UN Security Council accompanying them stress that the resolutions apply exclusively to the situation of Somalia and cannot be considered 'as establishing customary law'. Indeed, the measures were sought and welcomed by the Somali TFG/FGS, which considered itself unable to deal with the problem of piracy and wanted to avoid discussions concerning the extension of the Somali territorial sea.[86] Moreover, the UNSC resolutions require that any action in the territory of Somalia has to receive the prior authorisation of the Somali TFG/FGS. This is made explicit in the text of the UNSC resolutions themselves, which expressly 'affirm' that authorisation is secured 'only following receipt of the letter from the Permanent Representative of the Somalia Republic to the United Nationals to the President of the Security Council . . . conveying the consent of the TFG'.[87] Consequently, the content of the UNSC resolutions is not at all 'revolutionary' since, under international law, any coastal state is entitled to provide such authorisations with regard to its territorial jurisdiction irrespective of the existence of a resolution of the UNSC under Chapter VII, as expressly recognised in Article 13(1) of EU Joint Action 2008/851/CFSP. This provision for the consent of the coastal state ensures respect for national sovereignty, support for the TFG/FGS, a margin of discretion for the TFG/FGS with regard to which states it authorises and

---

[85] The French cruise ship *Le Ponant* and its passengers were taken for ransom by Somali pirates. They were freed at sea by the French forces which, on 11 April 2008, pursued the pirates into Somali territory and succeeded in capturing six of them in Somali land. On 20 April 2008, the Somali Prime Minister, Nur Hassan Hussein, declared to international media that 'The French forces arrested six Somali pirates and took them to France to face justice. We encourage such steps by the French. The Somali government asks the international community to take action against piracy.' The uncertainty about the real meaning and scope of this declaration led France to propose the draft of what became SC Resolution 1851. See the facts and comments in *Sentinelle* No 145 of 20 April 2008, available at http://www.sentinelle-droit-international.fr/bulletins/a2008/20080420_bull_145/sentinelle_145.htm.

[86] For a detailed analysis of these aspects of the UNSC resolutions see Treves, n 9 above, 402–05.

[87] Preamble and para 9 of Resolution 1816 (2008), para 11 of Resolution 1846 (2008) and para 10 of Resolution 1851 (2008).

avoidance of conflict with the Somali Law of 1972 that established that the territorial sea of Somalia extended to 200 miles from the coast into the sea,[88] which is not compatible with the provisions of UNCLOS on the matter. It should be noted that, as examined below, the reference to the use of force to conform with applicable international human rights and humanitarian law limits the scope of the UNSC resolutions since pirates are not combatants but civilians and, under international humanitarian law, in principle, when applicable, civilians may not be specifically targeted except in self-defence.[89] Finally, as explained below, UNSC Resolution 1851 (2008) widens the scope of permissible 'hot pursuit' from the high seas into the territorial waters of Somalia and the land of Somalia; it is understood that the activities undertaken 'do not have the practical effect of denying or impairing the right of innocent passage to the ships of any third state' (UNSC Resolution 1816 (2008), paragraph 8 and UNSC Revolution 1846 (2008), paragraph 13), and the contents of the geographical extensions do 'not affect the rights, obligations or responsibilities of member states under international law, including under UNCLOS nor can they be considered as establishing customary international law' (UNSC Resolution 1816 (2008), paragraph 9 and UNSC Resolution 1846 (2008), paragraph 11).

Moreover, the above *ratione materiae* and *ratione loci* extensions of the scope of the rules of international law relating to piracy off the Somali coast are conditioned by several elements, including the *ratione temporis* condition, according to which the contents of the UNSC resolutions are valid only while they remain in force (until November 2014, as last decided in UNSC Resolution 2125 (2013)).

Finally, there exist various and diverging definitions of 'piracy' and 'armed robbery' in municipal law, in particular in the domestic law of the EU Member States and of the regional states, for it is clear that, within the scope of its own jurisdiction, a sovereign state has the power to enact offences which can be categorised as 'acts of piracy' even if they are not recognised as such under international law. Under the domestic law of certain states, these terms have been extended to cover crimes other than those defined above, such as slave trading. Other states have not enacted any legislation on piracy and experience difficulties in bringing pirates to justice. In any case, the experience associated with the criminalisation and prosecution of pirates is excessive for certain states. However, it is clear that the failure to prosecute persons responsible for acts of piracy and armed robbery at sea off the coast of Somalia undermines the international anti-piracy efforts of the international community. For that reason, the UNSC has expressed its concern over cases when persons suspected of piracy are released without facing justice (a practice described as 'catch and release') and has declared its determination to create conditions to ensure that pirates are held accountable. It has taken certain measures to improve the situation by creating for example the International Trust Fund supporting initiatives of the Contact Group on Piracy off the Coast of Somalia, which, administered by UNODC, defrays the expenses associated with the prosecution of suspected pirates and supports other counter-piracy initiatives. The UNSC also welcomed and encouraged the contributions of participating states and encouraged other potential donors to contribute to the fund. More particularly, in its

---

[88] See www.un.org/Depts/?/legislationandtreaties/statesfiles/S. See also Treves, ibid.

[89] See E Kontorovich, 'International Legal Responses to piracy off the Coast of Somalia' (2009) 13:2 *The American Society of International Law Insights* 3, available at http://www.asil.org/insights090206.cfm.

Resolution 1918 (2010), the UNSC has, inter alia, called on 'all states, including states in the region, to criminalize piracy under their domestic law and favourably consider the prosecution of suspected, and imprisonment of convicted, pirates apprehended off the coast of Somalia, consistent with applicable international human rights law',[90] and requested the UN Secretary-General

> to present to the Security Council a report on possible options to further the aim of prosecuting and imprisoning persons responsible for acts of piracy and armed robbery at sea off the coast of Somalia, including, in particular, options for creating special domestic chambers possibly with international components, a regional tribunal or an international tribunal and corresponding imprisonment arrangements, taking into account the work of the CGPCS, the existing practice in establishing international and mixed tribunals, and the time and the resources necessary to achieve and sustain substantive results.[91]

A number of issues related to the above are examined in detail in the following pages. The first issue tackled is the seizure of vessels by the EU in its fight against piracy.

(iii) The Seizure of Vessels and the Use of Force by the EU

Article 2(d) of Joint Action 2008/851/CFSP authorises the EU to: 'take the necessary measures . . . to deter, prevent and intervene in order to bring to an end acts of piracy and armed robbery which may be committed in the areas where it is present'.[92]

This provision governs two situations—namely, the seizure of vessels and the use of force by the EU. Again, the implementation of the provision by the EU must be in accordance with international law.

The applicable international law which authorises states and the EU to capture a suspected pirate vessel derives from both customary international law and international treaty law.

In principle, customary international law imposes the principle of territorial jurisdiction according to which, as held by the Permanent Court of International Justice in the case of the SS *Lotus*

> the first and foremost restriction imposed by international law upon a state is that—failing the existence of a permissive rule to the contrary—it may not exercise its power in any form in the territory of another state. In this sense jurisdiction is certainly territorial; it cannot be exercised by a state outside its territory except by virtue of a permissive rule derived from international custom or from a convention.[93]

However, this principle does not apply to the case of pirates since, as has been explained above, pirates are *hostes humani generis* ('enemies of all humankind') because they endanger the safety of navigation and restrict the freedom of the high seas—a fundamental principle of international law. For that reason, customary international law has historically considered that any state may seize a pirate vessel and arrest the persons on board even outside its territory and any state may bring pirates back to its territory

---

[90] Operative para 2.
[91] Operative para 4.
[92] Art 2, para d of the Joint Action 2008/851/CFSP, n 20 above.
[93] Collection of Judgments, Series A-No 10, 1927, para 45.

for them to be tried by its own courts. Some have recently contested this traditional reasoning and consider that, since customary international law on piracy

> only applies to events on the high seas, factually piratical acts committed in territorial waters are not, at international law, piracy and special common jurisdiction does not apply. A theory predicated on pirates as hostes humani generis, would surely not draw such arbitrary geographical distinctions. Being an 'enemy of all mankind' is thus not a substantive element or consequence of the offence, but purely a rhetorical phrase reflecting its seriousness.[94]

Instead, some suggest that the universal jurisdiction over acts of piracy is not founded on the principle of *hostes humani generis* but is instead based on the 'common interest', whereby states, 'through customary or conventional rule, have given comprehensive permission in advance to foreign states' assertion of law enforcement jurisdiction over their vessels, resulting in the absence of any flag state immunity from boarding'.[95] It is submitted that, at present, customary international law on piracy, which has been incorporated into international treaty law, upholds the principle of universal jurisdiction over acts of piracy committed on the high seas while the same acts committed in territorial waters are governed by the principle of territorial jurisdiction.[96]

Indeed, Article 105 UNCLOS provides that

> On the high seas, or in any other place outside the jurisdiction of any state, every state may seize a pirate ship or aircraft, or a ship or aircraft taken by piracy and under the control of pirates, and arrest the persons and seize the property on board. The courts of the state which carried out the seizure may decide upon the penalties to be imposed, and may also determine the action to be taken with regard to the ships, aircraft or property, subject to the rights of third parties acting in good faith.

A seizure on account of piracy may be carried out 'only by warships or military aircraft, or other ships or aircraft clearly marked and identifiable as being on government service and authorized to that effect' (Article 107). The seizure can only be effected on 'adequate grounds' since otherwise 'the state making the seizure shall be liable to the state the nationality of which is possessed by the ship or aircraft for any loss or damage caused by the seizure' (Article 106). All states are required to 'cooperate to the fullest possible extent in the repression of piracy on the high seas or in any other place outside the jurisdiction of any state' (Article 100 UNCLOS, which incorporates Article 19 of the High Seas Convention). These principles constitute an exception to the general principle governing the law of the sea according to which 'The high seas are open to all states, whether coastal or land-locked' (Article 87 UNCLOS).

In particular, the right of 'hot pursuit' deserves special consideration. Customary international law authorises a coastal state to pursue and seize a non-national vessel suspected of being a pirate vessel having committed act of piracy within the state's maritime jurisdictional zones where the pirate vessel flees to the high seas to avoid arrest;[97] the right of hot pursuit can only be exercised by means of warships or military aircraft, or other ships or aircraft clearly marked and identifiable as being on

---

[94] See Guilfoyle, *Shipping Interdiction*, n 9 above, 28–29.
[95] Ibid.
[96] On this point see Priddy and Casey-Maslen, n 2 above, 23–24.
[97] *The King v The Ship North*, 37 SCR 385 (1905–06). For a study of the rules of customary international law relating to hot pursuit see N Poulantzas, *The Right of Hot Pursuit in International Law*, 2nd edn (The Hague, Martinus Nijhoff Publishing, 2002), which also includes a brief analysis of UNCLOS. See also

government service and authorised to that effect. Similarly, according to Article 111 UNCLOS, the hot pursuit of a foreign ship may be undertaken when the competent authorities of the coastal state 'have good reason to believe that the ship has violated the laws and regulations of that state' and the foreign ship or one of its boats is within the internal waters, the archipelagic waters, the territorial sea or the contiguous zone of the pursuing state. The hot pursuit may only be continued outside the territorial sea or the contiguous zone if the pursuit has not been interrupted.[98] The right of hot pursuit ceases as soon as the pursued ship enters the territorial sea of its own state or of a third state.[99] Notwithstanding, UNSC Resolution 1851 (2008), as discussed, has broadened the hot pursuit under international law from the high seas into the territorial waters of Somalia and the land of Somalia. In any case, as was held in the *I'm alone* case, the right of hot pursuit does not include the right to sink the pursued vessel deliberately but accidental sinking in the course of arrest may be lawful.[100]

Article 2(d) of Joint Action 2008/851/CFSP authorises the EU to 'take the necessary measures, including the use of force', to combat piracy and armed robbery at sea.

The question arises whether this provision complies with general international law,[101] which considers that the use of force from the perspective of the *ius ad bellum* is only lawful in three situations: (i) when it is in accordance with authority granted under the international law of the sea; (ii) when it is explicitly authorised under Chapter VII of the UN Charter; or (iii) when it is a lawful act of self-defence against an attack by pirates or is conducted for the defence of others.[102] Furthermore, the use of force has in any case to comply with applicable human rights or international humanitarian law (*ius in bello*).

Under the modern general international law of the sea, UNCLOS does not expressly authorise the use of force on the high seas, but it is accepted that, since Article 105 authorises the seizing of pirate vessels and the arrest of suspected pirates, it must implicitly include an authorisation to use force when it is absolutely necessary, because

---

W Gilmore, 'Hot Pursuit, the Case *R v Mills and Others*' (1995) 44 *International & Comparative Law Quarterly* 949.

[98] It is not necessary that, at the time when the foreign ship within the territorial sea or the contiguous zone receives the order to stop, the ship giving the order should likewise be within the territorial sea or the contiguous zone. If the foreign ship is within a contiguous zone, as defined in Art 33, the pursuit may only be undertaken if there has been a violation of the rights for the protection of which the zone was established. The right of hot pursuit shall apply *mutatis mutandis* to violations in the exclusive economic zone or on the continental shelf, including safety zones around continental shelf installations, of the laws and regulations of the coastal state applicable in accordance with the UNCLOS Convention to the exclusive economic zone or the continental shelf, including such safety zones. Hot pursuit is not deemed to have begun unless the pursuing ship has satisfied itself by such practicable means as may be available that the ship pursued or one of its boats or other craft working as a team and using the ship pursued as a mother ship is within the limits of the territorial sea or, as the case may be, within the contiguous zone or the exclusive economic zone or above the continental shelf. The pursuit may only be commenced after a visual or auditory signal to stop has been given at a distance which enables it to be seen or heard by the foreign ship.

[99] Where a ship has been stopped or arrested outside the territorial sea in circumstances which do not justify the exercise of the right of hot pursuit, it has the right to be compensated for any loss or damage that may have been sustained.

[100] See Reports of International Arbitral Awards, vol III, 1609, 1615.

[101] See too A Proelss, Chapter 3 above.

[102] Priddy and Casey-Maslen, n 2 above, 24.

otherwise the seizure or arrest would be impossible.[103] The same conclusion applies in the case of Article 110 and 111 UNCLOS, which authorise, respectively, the stopping and boarding of ships for the purpose of the 'right of visit'[104] and the engaging in 'hot pursuit'.

As has been suggested above, the use of force authorised in the context of piracy is not, in our view, that envisaged in the situations of armed conflict, since the situation of piracy is not the one of armed conflict governed by international humanitarian law. Pirates are not 'combatants' and, if considered 'civilians', are not specifically targeted by international humanitarian law, except in cases of immediate self-defence:[105] indeed, the practice of warships in Somali waters indicates that force is only used in response to the pirates' use of weapons.[106]

It is a general principle of law that reasonable force may be used in self-defence, to defend others or to prevent a crime that poses a threat to human life. It has been suggested that this is the most common legal justification for killing or injuring suspected pirates.[107] There are several examples proving the case, the most commonly reported being that which took place on 19 November 2008, when the Indian navy reported that the *INS Tabar* had come under attack from pirates: the *INS Tabar* crew requested the pirate vessel to stop in order to allow a search, but the pirates responded with a threat to sink the *INS Tabar* if it came any closer, then opened fire on it, prompting the Indian navy to respond by returning fire. After this immediate armed response, it was reported that the attack continued for about three to four hours, finally resulting in the sinking of the pirate's 'mother ship' and the pirates abandoning another pirate vessel, although several of them managed to escape in the dark by means of a speedboat. An Indian navy spokesman reported that 'We fired in self-defence and in response to firing upon our vessel. It was a pirate vessel in international waters and its stance was aggressive.'[108] It is obvious that, under international law, even the right to use force in self-defence is not unrestricted, since the nature and degree of force used must not exceed what is proportionate and necessary in the circumstances.[109]

---

[103] D Guilfoyle, 'The Laws of War and the Fight against Somali Piracy: Combats or Criminals?' (2010) 11 *Melbourne Journal of International Law* 10.

[104] It should be recalled that Art 110 UNCLOS provides that '1. Except where acts of interference derive from powers conferred by treaty, a warship which encounters on the high seas a foreign ship, other than a ship entitled to complete immunity in accordance with articles 95 and 96, is not justified in boarding it unless there is reasonable ground for suspecting that:(a) the ship is engaged in piracy;(b) the ship is engaged in the slave trade;(c) the ship is engaged in unauthorized broadcasting and the flag state of the warship has jurisdiction under article 109;(d) the ship is without nationality; or(e) though flying a foreign flag or refusing to show its flag, the ship is, in reality, of the same nationality as the warship. 2. In the cases provided for in para 1, the warship may proceed to verify the ship's right to fly its flag. To this end, it may send a boat under the command of an officer to the suspected ship. If suspicion remains after the documents have been checked, it may proceed to a further examination on board the ship, which must be carried out with all possible consideration. 3. If the suspicions prove to be unfounded, and provided that the ship boarded has not committed any act justifying them, it shall be compensated for any loss or damage that may have been sustained. 4. These provisions apply mutatis mutandis to military aircraft. 5. These provisions also apply to any other duly authorized ships or aircraft clearly marked and identifiable as being on government service.'

[105] Treves, n 9 above, 412–15.

[106] For a description of several examples, see ibid.

[107] Guilfoyle, n 100 above, 10.

[108] 'Indian Navy "Sank Thai Trawler"', *BBC News*, 25 November 2008, available at http://news.bbc.co.uk/1/hi/world/south_asia/7749245.stm.

[109] See also Priddy and Casey-Maslen, n 2 above, 28.

The question arises whether the use of force against pirates is legitimate in situations other than of self-defence. It has been suggested that an affirmative answer may be based on considerations similar to those envisaged, for example, in Article 22(1)(f) of the 1995 UN Fish Stocks Agreement, which provides for non-flag states to board and inspect fishing vessels on the high seas and permits the use of force on an exceptional basis 'when and to the degree necessary to ensure the safety of the inspectors and where the inspectors are obstructed in the execution of their duties'.[110] The question of the proportionality or degree of intensity in the use of force, however, remains open.[111]

In this regard, in *The 'M/V Saiga' (No 2) Case (Saint Vincent and The Grenadines v Guinea)*, the International Tribunal for the Law of the Sea has ruled that international law requires that the use of force in the arrest of ships

> must be avoided as far as possible and, where force is unavoidable, it must not go beyond what considerations of humanity must apply in the law of the sea, as they do in other areas of international law. These principles have been followed over the years in law enforcement operations at sea. The normal practice used to stop a ship at sea is first to give an auditory or visual signal to stop, using internationally recognized signals. Where this does not succeed, a variety of actions may be taken, including the firing of shots across the bows of the ship. It is only after the appropriate actions fail that the pursuing vessel may, as a last resort, use force. Even then, appropriate warning must be issued to the ship and all efforts should be made to ensure that life is not endangered . . .[112]

These principles are incorporated into several legal texts, some of them only having a soft-law nature, such as Article 3 of the 1979 UN Code of Conduct for Law Enforcement Officials, which provides that 'Law enforcement officials may use force only when strictly necessary and to the extent required for the performance of their duty',[113] Principle 4 of the 1990 Basic Principles on the Use of Force and Firearms by Law Enforcement Officials, according to which

> Law enforcement officials, in carrying out their duty, shall, as far as possible, apply non-violent means before resorting to the use of force and firearms. They may use force and firearms only if other means remain ineffective or without any promise of achieving the intended result

and Principle 5 of the same Basic Principles, which provides that 'Whenever the lawful use of force and firearms is unavoidable, law enforcement officials shall: . . . (a) Exercise restraint in such use and act in proportion to the seriousness of the offence and the legitimate objective to be achieved'.[114]

These texts indicate that, whenever it is necessary to use force, such force must be proportionate to the seriousness of the threat, and that the intentional use of lethal force is only permitted when it is strictly unavoidable to protect life. Consequently,

---

[110] UNGA, Doc A/CONF. 164/37 of 8 September 1995.

[111] Treves, n 9 above, 412.

[112] See *The 'M/V Saiga' (No 2) Case (Saint Vincent and The Grenadines v Guinea)* [1999] ITLOS, Rep 10, para 155.

[113] Code of Conduct for Law Enforcement Officials, GA Resolution 34/169, annex, 34 UN GAOR Supp (No 46), 186.

[114] Basic Principles on the Use of Force and Firearms by Law Enforcement Officials, Eighth UN Congress on the Prevention of Crime and the Treatment of Offenders, Havana, 27 August to 7 September 1990, UN Doc A/CONF.144/28/Rev.1 (1990) 112.

targeted killings in response to piracy on the high seas are unlawful.[115] Finally, Article 8bis of the 2005 Protocol to the SUA Convention for the Suppression of Unlawful Acts of Violence against the Safety of Maritime Navigation provides that:

> The use of force shall be avoided except when necessary to ensure the safety of its [government] officials and persons on board, or where the officials are obstructed in the execution of the authorized actions. Any use of force pursuant to this article shall not exceed the minimum degree of force which is necessary and reasonable in the circumstances.

This provision applies only to situations between two state parties to the Protocol. The Protocol has so far been ratified by 11 states.

It follows from the above that the general international law of the sea requires that the use of force be avoided as far as possible and, where force is inevitable, it must not go beyond what is reasonable and necessary in the circumstances. Considerations of humanity must apply in the law of the sea, as they do in other areas of international law.[116] These principles of general international law are also applicable *mutatis mutandis* to the use of force against pirates.[117]

In addition to the principles of general international law, the UNSC has concluded that piracy off the coast of Somalia constitutes 'a threat to international peace and security in the region' (preamble of UNSC Resolution 1846 (2008)) and, acting under Chapter VII of the UN Charter, has explicitly authorised, in particular in its Resolutions 1846 (2008) and 1851 (2008), the use of 'all necessary means for repressing acts of piracy and armed robbery', which, in the vocabulary of the UN, means the

---

[115] As an illustration, the French legislation governing the use of force at sea is governed by Decree No 95-411 of 19 April 1995 governing recourse to coercion and the use of force at sea, modified by Decree No 2005-1514 of 6 December 2005. Art 1of the Decree provides that the coercion measures foreseen under Art 7 of the Law of 15 July 1994 (Law No 94–589 of 15 July 1994 governing the exercise by the state of its enforcement powers at sea) 'includes, on the one hand, the firing of warning shots, and, on the other, the use of force which consists of live firing and aimed shots'. Art 2 provides that 'Warning shots are authorized by the Maritime Prefect or the representative of the Government overseas as foreseen by the decree of 6 December 2005. These individuals shall immediately inform the relevant ministers of the authorities they give. Warning shots comprise a single shot followed by three shots across the bow. This sequence is preceded by warnings to the ship to stop or reroute that are transmitted by any visual, radio, or acoustic means.' Art 3 provides that 'In the event the Master fails to comply with the challenges, which may be followed by warning shots, the Maritime Prefect or representative of the Government overseas may order live firing to exert pressure on the Master [of the other vessel]. The use of force may lead to taking control of the other vessel. A report is to be made immediately to the Prime Minister, the Minister responsible for the resources and staff used, and other relevant ministers.' Art 4 provides that 'In the event that the warning shots and, if conducted, live firing, have had no effect, the Maritime Prefect or representative of the Government overseas may request the Prime Minister to authorise the opening of live firing against the vessel. This authorisation is given after reasonable efforts have been made to obtain the views of the Minister for Foreign Affairs. Live firing is preceded by renewed challenges. This is reported in the ship's logbook. In no case may it be directed against individuals. Explosive projectiles may not be used. A report is made in the same manner as under Article 3.' And Art 5 provides that 'The provisions of this decree shall be without prejudice to the exercise of self-defence and do not prevent the exercise of specific competences of government officials given specific powers to use force'.

[116] '*M/V Saiga*' (*No 2*), n 112 above, para 155. See also the arbitral awards in the 'I'm Alone' (Canada, United States) (1935) 3 *Reports of International Arbitral Awards* 1609, and in the case of the *Red Crusader*, in the same Reports, vol XXIX (1962), 521. See also the judgment by the International Court of Justice in 1986 in the case *Military and Paramilitary Activities in and against Nicaragua* [1986] ICJ Rep 14. See also the Guyana v Suriname arbitral award, which held that 'activities permitted by international law for the enforcement of rights may include the use of force, provided such force is unavoidable, reasonable, and necessary.' (Award of the Hague Arbitral Tribunal of 17 September 2007, para 445, p 147).

[117] Treves, n 9 above, 414.

use of force, including in the territorial sea of Somalia and on Somali land. Both resolutions therefore go further than UNCLOS not only in respect of the *ratione loci* but also the *ratione materiae* of the rules relating to piracy. As it has been indicated above, in its Resolution 1846 (2008), the UN Security Council authorised states and regional organisations cooperating with the TFG (FGS) in the fight against piracy and armed robbery at sea off the coast of Somalia, for which advance notification has been provided by the TFG (FGS) to the Secretary-General, to

> (b) Use, within the territorial waters of Somalia, in a manner consistent with such action permitted on the high seas with respect to piracy under relevant international law, all necessary means to repress acts of piracy and armed robbery at sea.[118]

In addition, it called upon states and regional organisations 'that have the capacity to do so' to take part actively in the fight against piracy and armed robbery at sea off the coast of Somalia,

> by deploying naval vessels and military aircraft, and through seizure and disposition of boats, vessels, arms and other related equipment used in the commission of piracy and armed robbery off the coast of Somalia, or for which there is reasonable ground for suspecting such use.[119]

In UNSC Resolution 1851 (2008), which applies under the same general conditions of UNSC Resolution 1846 (2008), the UN Security Council noting the primary role of the TFG in rooting out piracy and armed robbery at sea, decided that

> states and regional organizations cooperating in the fight against piracy and armed robbery at sea off the coast of Somalia may undertake all necessary measures that are appropriate in Somalia, for the purpose of suppressing acts of piracy and armed robbery at sea . . . provided, however, that any measures undertaken pursuant to the authority of this paragraph shall be undertaken consistent with applicable international humanitarian and human rights law.[120]

As mentioned above, the TFG (FGS) has notified the UN Secretary-General that the EU is authorised to undertake all necessary measures in the fight against piracy and armed robbery both in Somali territorial sea and in the land of Somalia.

Attention should also be drawn to a practice that has developed which consists in using armed convoys or escort ships to accompany private vessels, or to bring military personnel on board vessels flying certain flags (the so-called vessel protection detachments). In particular, Danish, Israeli, German and Russian marines and commandos have been reported to have been present on board domestic registered vessels as a military escort/guard.

Furthermore, as the last resort to avert the threat of pirate attacks, shipowners increasingly have recourse to private armed guards,[121] usually defined as privately con-

---

[118] Resolution 1846 (2008), operative para 10.

[119] Ibid, operative para 9.

[120] UNSC Resolution 1851 (2008), operative para 6.

[121] The 1977 Protocol I to the Geneva Conventions adopts a number of criteria to which a 'mercenary' or armed guard needs to adhere. For further reading on the issue see ICRC, Protocol Additional to the Geneva Conventions of 12 August 1949, and relating to the Protection of Victims of International Armed Conflicts (Protocol I), Protocols additional to the Geneva Conventions, International Committee of the Red Cross, Diplomatic Conference of Geneva of 1974–1977, 1977, Art 47. For a critique of this Convention, and its alleged inapplicability on the modern-day PSCs, see TS Millard, 'Overcoming Post-Colonial Myopia: A

tracted armed security personnel (PCASP),[122] provided by maritime private military and security companies (PMSCs). There are more than 22 major PMSCs in operation, mostly based in the UK, and they deploy armed escort vessels that are contracted privately. These companies provide professional protection to private ships, tailored to the requirements of their customers, and their services typically include security audits, training courses for crew on how to respond to an attack, aiding with the recovery of hijacked ships, deploying guards (armed and unarmed) and occasionally escorting boats to accompany freighters when transiting through high-risks areas.[123] With regard to the PCASPs, the personnel sometimes operate on behalf of states on board their own ships, while other times they operate on board private ships. There is, however, controversy over the legality of these actors (one of the oft-repeated arguments against the employment of PCASP is the fear of violence escalating), but the position of the international community, including the EU, is shifting towards its acceptance as a fait accompli. It is interesting to note the evolution of the IMO, which was initially strongly opposed to PCASPs[124] but has now come to develop interim guidance on PCASPs for states.[125] There is, however, no international guidance on private vessels endorsed by states, and at present national legislation on this issue, 'if (it) exists, may prove to be either unenforced or unenforceable'.[126]

Actually, the legal issues which arise from the activities of PMSCs (such as status, employment capacity, insurance coverage) and from the use of PCASPs, (including their chain of command when on board), still remain largely unanswered owing inter alia to the fact that the nature of their services usually remains confidential.[127] In prin-

---

Call to Recognize and Regulate Private Military Companies' (2003) 176 *Military Law Review* 1. Another important international source is the 'Mercenaries Convention': see UN, International Convention against the Recruitment, Use, Financing and Training of Mercenaries, 2163 UNTS 1989. See also I Österdahl, 'The Public-Private in Armed Conflict: The Accountability of Private Security Companies', Uppsala Faculty of Law Working Paper 2010:3 (Uppsala, Uppsala Faculty of Law, 2010).

[122] IMO, 'Interim Recommendations for Flag States Regarding the Use of Privately Contracted Armed Security Personnel On Board Ships in the High Risk Area', MSC.1/Circ 1406 (International Maritime Organization, 2011), 1.

[123] P Chalk, 'Private Maritime Security Companies (PMSCS) and Counter-piracy' (Counterpiracy Briefing Papers, 2012), available at www.counterpiracy.ae/upload/briefing Peter%20Chalk-Essay-Eng.pdf.

[124] For example, the position of the IMO towards the employment of armed guards has gradually shifted from a strong opposition to moderate disagreement but, at the same time, recognition of the de facto practice of employment of PCASPs. Two recent documents address this issue: 'Interim Recommendations Regarding the Use of Privately Contracted Armed Security Personnel On Board Ships', n 122 above, which is addressed to the flag states and provides for basic guideliness regarding the adoption of a standpoint regarding the PCASPs (which should lead to the adoption of national legislation/acts regarding the issue of PCASPs), and 'Interim Guidance to Shipowners, Ship Operators, and Shipmasters on the Use of Privately Contracted Armed Security Personnel On Board Ships in the High Risk Area', MSC.1/Circ 1405 (International Maritime Organization, 2011). According to the latter document, the issue of PCASPs is no longer focused on whether such services should or should not be adopted, but what criteria should be used in order to secure quality services. Thus, the IMO has recognised that the PCASPs are often employed in practice. A new report by L Pingeot, entitled *Dangerous Partnership. Private Military & Security Companies and the UN* (New York, Global Policy Forum, 2012), finds that the UN is increasingly contracting PMSCs for security services—armed and unarmed—and that contracting is 'unaccountable and out of control'. See M Mudric 'Armed Guards on Vessels' (2011) 50:165 *Comparative Maritime Law* 217.

[125] See in particular 'Interim Guidance Agreed by IMO Maritime Safety Meeting' (IMO, 20 May 2011).

[126] Report of the Monitoring Group on Somalia and Eritrea, UNSC Resolution 1916 (2010), UN Doc S/2011/433 (18 July 2011), 181.

[127] One such issue is the question whether the armed guards could potentially be treated as pirates. The PCASPs may offer to escort vessels boarded with a team of highly specialised armed guards capable of engaging in both defensive and offensive actions. In cases of engagement, it is conceivable that such escort

ciple the PCASPs are authorised to use force and their actions are governed by the national law which is applicable, which, depending on the circumstances, may be the law of the state of the flag of the vessel, the law of the nationality of the PCASPs, the law of the state where the PMSC is registered or, when in territorial waters, the law of the local state. Even if the national law which is applicable allows the use of firearms on board vessels, it is necessary to ensure the legal (dis)embarkation of PCASPs since not all coastal states are willing to allow the passage of armed personnel through their maritime zone of control. Should the PCASPs need to resort to the use of force, the IMO recommends that 'in no case should the use of force exceed what is strictly necessary, and in all cases should be proportionate to the threat and appropriate to the situation',[128] though further clarification is needed from the professional practice and the case law of the courts. In principle, the right of the PCASPs to use force is restricted to self-defence or to the defence of others. If they use force beyond the scope of these two cases, they will most likely become liable to criminal prosecution.

On this topic, there is also the 2008 Montreux Document on PMSCs during armed conflict, which was elaborated by the International Committee of the Red Cross and, as such, is not a maritime instrument, but addresses all legal issues relating to individual accountability for misconduct in different jurisdictions and the duty of the authorities to oversee and screen the actions of firms in order to avoid potential misconduct.[129]

Finally, since individual PMSCs submit their Rules for the Use of Force to flag states as a part of the flag state approval process, regard should also be had to the set of 100 Series Rules, discussed recently in an international legal conference entitled 'Counter Piracy: Rules for the Use of Force', which took place under the auspices of the Security Association for Maritime Industry in London in February 2013. The set of 100 Series Rules is said to be designed to 'alleviate uncertainty' and provide a 'clear legal basis for acts of self-defence', and is being developed for the benefit of the entire maritime industry. The set is underpinned by a thorough public international and criminal law legal review using an objective international law test of what force is 'reasonable and necessary' and 'proportionate' when used, as a lawful last resort, in

---

vessels can attempt to board alleged pirate vessels. This could possibly be interpreted as an act of piracy, according to UNCLOS Art 101, and could also stand in contrast to Art 19, where the concept of free passage is disturbed by the introduction of weapons. For this reason, one solution presented to the PCASPs is to formulate contracts in such a manner that the PCASP become supernumeraries to the crew of the protected vessel (according to which, arguably, such an offensive measure could be interpreted as a defensive). See Mudric, n 119 above.

[128] 'Interim Guidance to Shipowners, Ship Operators, and Shipmasters on the Use of Privately Contracted Armed Security Personnel On Board Ships in the High Risk Area', MSC.1/Circ 1405 (International Maritime Organization, 2011) point 3.5, Annex, 7; 'Interim Guidance to Private Maritime Security Companies Providing Contracted Armed Security Personnel On Board Ships in the High Risk Area', MSC.1/Circ 1443; 'Interim Recommendations for Port and Coastal States Regarding the Use of Privately Contracted Armed Security Personnel On Board Ships in the High Risk Area', MSC.1/Circ 1408; 'Revised Interim Recommendations for Flag States Regarding the Use of Privately Contracted Armed Security Personnel On Board Ships in the High Risk Area', MSC.1/Circ 1406/Rev.1; 'Revised Interim Guidance to Shipowners, Ship Operators and Shipmasters on the Use of Privately Contracted Armed Security Personnel On Board Ships in the High Risk Area', MSC.1/Circ 1405/Rev.2; and a joint MSC and Facilitation Committee circular, 'Questionnaire on Information on Port and Coastal State Requirements Related to Privately Contracted Armed Security Personnel On Board Ships', which is aimed at gathering information on current requirements.

[129] International Committee of the Red Cross, 'The Montreux Document on Pertinent International Obligations and Good Practices for states Related to Operations of Private Military and Security Companies during Armed Conflict' (2008), available at http://www.icrc.org/eng/assets/files/other/icrc_002_0996.pdf.

self-defence. The aim of the 100 Series Rules is to set an international standard against which PCASP may be professionally trained, PMSCs may be audited and actions may be both measured and judged by competent authorities. The set will complement the existing guidance provided by the industry on the drafting of the Rules for the Use of Force. The set will also, in addition to supporting the requirement of the International Organization for Standardization, which has developed the specification ISO/PAS 28007—an international regulatory document which is publicly available and which includes the Guidelines for Private Maritime Security Companies (PMSC) providing privately contracted armed security personnel (PCASP) on board ships (and pro forma contract)—be the only published international standard dealing with armed guards on ships. The 100 Series Rules will not bind flag states as to their use, but will instead provide an option for their potential incorporation into national guidance, as determined by national law. The set of 100 Series Rules does not, however, cover the issue of indemnity or immunity arising from the civil or criminal liability which is incurred when force has been used unlawfully.

Since the use of force can only be restrictive, the question arises as to the status of persons captured as suspected pirates and the conditions under which such persons can be held by the seizing ship for the purpose of their prosecution.

(iv) The Prosecution and/or Transfer of Persons Arrested and Detained with a View to Their Prosecution

Article 12 of Joint Action 2008/851/CFSP, as amended by Decision 2012/174/CFSP of 23 March 2012,[130] provides that, 'on the basis of Somalia's acceptance of the exercise of jurisdiction by EU Member States or by third states (participating in Operation Atalanta) and Article(s) 105' and 101 and 103 of UNCLOS, persons suspected of intending to commit, committing or having committed acts of piracy or armed robbery in Somali 'territorial or internal waters or on the high seas' who are arrested and detained, with a view to their prosecution, and property used to carry out such acts

> shall be transferred . . . to the competent authorities of the Member State or of the third state participating in the operation, of which the vessel which took them captive flies the flag; or if that state cannot, or does not wish to, exercise its jurisdiction, to a Member State or any third state which wishes to exercise its jurisdiction over the aforementioned persons and property.

Equally, persons suspected of intending to commit, committing or having committed acts of piracy or armed robbery who are arrested and detained by Operation Atalanta with a view to their prosecution, 'in the territorial waters, the internal waters or the archipelagic waters of other states in the region' in agreement with these states, and property used to carry out such acts, 'may be transferred to the competent authorities of the state concerned, or, with the consent of the state concerned, to the competent authorities of another state'. No such persons

> may be transferred to a third state unless the conditions for the transfer have been agreed with that third state in a manner consistent with relevant international law, notably international

---

[130] [2012] OJ L89/70.

law on human rights, in order to guarantee in particular that no one shall be subjected to the death penalty, to torture or to any cruel, inhuman or degrading treatment.[131]

The wording of Article 12 reflects the challenging legal evolution of the question of the prosecution of pirates.

The first difficulty arises from the unsatisfactory regulatory situation of piracy under the national law of the state whose flag the seizing ship is entitled to fly, ie the 'flag state'. As has been submitted, UNCLOS does not impose a duty on states or international organisations to combat piracy, nor does it require states to criminalise acts of piracy under their internal law. Instead, the Convention builds on laws laid out elsewhere: on the one hand, under Article 92 UNCLOS, a state has exclusive jurisdiction on the high seas; on the other hand, under Article 105 UNCLOS, the exercise of such universal jurisdiction by the flag state is optional. The situation is different with regard to the SUA Convention, which specifies the rights of individuals and the obligations of states on the issue of 'maritime crimes', and requires them to take all necessary steps under their domestic laws to fight those crimes and, in particular, to establish jurisdiction over the offences listed, including the collection of evidence and the prosecution, whenever an offence is committed: (i) against or on board a ship flying the flag of the state in question; (ii) in the territory of that state; or (iii) by a national of that state. Therefore, as piracy and armed robbery at sea are both covered by the SUA Convention and hence perceived as maritime crimes, the SUA Convention establishes an obligation both to criminalise offences by pirates or armed robbers and to establish jurisdiction (Articles 3 and 6 of the SUA Convention), and UNSC Resolution 1846 (2008) urges state parties 'to fully implement' those obligations. As a result, some states approach piracy cases by condemning the act of piracy as a crime; other states condemn certain criminal acts but do not fully address them as piracy; while still other states have initiated a practice of arranging for the coastal states to take responsibility for the prosecution of pirates by virtue of the principle *lex loci delicti commissi*, according to which the prosecution must take place where the delict has been committed and according to the law of that coastal state concerned.

In order to remedy this uncertain legal situation, the UNSC, noting that the Somali TFG (FGS) did not have the capacity to deal with the issue, has taken several steps: on the one hand, UNSC Resolution 1851 (2008) set the foundations for the development of an international framework for prosecuting pirates by obliging coastal states that had signed up to the SUA Convention to accept jurisdiction for cases of the maritime crime of piracy unless they could prove that the SUA Convention did not apply; on the other hand, the same UNSC Resolution called on all states and organisations to establish a mechanism for international cooperation in combating piracy off the coast of Somalia and to work to enhance the capacity of relevant states in the region to combat piracy through legal action, including by concluding special agreements or arrangements with those countries willing to take custody of pirates in order to embark law enforcement officials (called 'shipriders') from those countries to facilitate the investigation and prosecution of persons detained during operations; finally, UNSC Resolutions 1897 of November 2009 and Resolution 1918 (April 2010) call on all states

---

[131] Art 2, point e of Joint Action 2008/851/CFSP as amended by Council Decision 2010/766/CFSP of 7 December 2010, [2010] OJ L327/49.

to criminalise piracy under their domestic laws and urge them to consider the prosecution and imprisonment of captured pirates.

So far, the practice and attitude of the EU Member States with regard to the custody and prosecution of suspected pirates and armed robbers is varied: while some of them have agreed to exercise jurisdiction when certain conditions are met (eg France, Italy, Spain, the Netherlands, Belgium), others are more reluctant (eg UK, Germany).[132]

In France, acts of piracy fall within the scope of Chapter IV, Articles 224-1 to 224-8-1 of the French Penal Code of the French penal code, which apply to all offences committed within the territory of the French Republic, or on board ships flying the French flag or committed against such ships, wherever they may be, and these provisions have been tested in such piracy cases as that involving the luxury yacht *Le Carré d'As IV*.[133]

The Netherlands agreed to exercise jurisdiction over the five men captured in the Gulf of Aden by the Royal Danish Navy Vessel, *HDMS Absalon*, after an extradition agreement was concluded between Denmark and The Netherlands.[134] The Rotterdam District Court held that the period of detention of 40 days that had elapsed before the captured men were brought to justice was too long and consequently breached Article 5 of the European Convention of Human Rights, which requires that detainees be brought 'promptly before a judge'. However, the Court did not dismiss the conviction.[135]

The UK has operated under the conditions laid down in a legal opinion of the Legal Service of the Foreign Office, widely reported in the press, advising that suspected pirates should not be returned to Somalia owing to their exposure to harsh treatment and the infringement of their rights under the UK Human Rights Act 1998. The UK Foreign Office also warned of the risk that captured pirates might claim asylum in Britain on human rights grounds if detained by the Royal Navy. For the above reasons, the UK and Kenya formalised an agreement on 11 December 2008 to hand over any suspected pirates captured by the British Navy on the high seas to Kenya.[136]

In Germany, the German Parliament authorised the navy frigate *Karslruhe* to take preventive measures as well as to provide assistance to free captured ships, even by the boarding of special forces. Since the German authorisation is mainly for preventive purposes, Germany is reluctant to prosecute detained pirates in Germany and hands them over to other states. However, in 2010, 10 suspected Somali pirates captured during the hijacking of a German cargo ship, *MV Taipan*, went on trial in Hamburg, in Germany's first modern-day piracy trial, 609 years after the famous German pirate

---

[132] Lang, n 4 above, 42.

[133] On 16 September 2008, the 50-foot *Carré d'As IV* was sailing from Australia to the Suez Canal when it was attacked by pirates and captured, with its two crew held for ransom. Four days later, the French frigate *Courbet* (F 712) arrived on the scene and began shadowing the captured yacht, finally assaulting and recovering it. The French authorities then took the pirates to Djibouti, where they were flown to France to stand trial.

[134] See the collective article by members of the law firm K&L/Gates, 'The Pirates of Puntland: Practical, Legal and Policy Issues in the Fight against Somali Piracy' (K&L/Gates, March 2009), available at http://www.klgates.com/files/Publication/ac22f46f-de64-41d5-a99c-8566b961c41e/Presentation/PublicationAttachment/fbdacf5a-55e1-408d-833b-a4bc8a15dc70/3_09_The_Pirates_of_Puntland.pdf, 8–9.

[135] *Case of the Somali Pirates*, De Rechtspraak, 17 June 2010.

[136] K&L/Gates, n 129 above, 9. See G Gauci, 'Piracy and its Legal Problems with Specific Reference to the English Law of Maritime Insurance' (2012) 41 *Journal of Maritime Law and Commerce* 541.

Klaus Störtebeker, who lived from 1360 to 1401, and who had plagued the Baltic, was tried in the very same city.

The Italian Navigation Code criminalises piracy in its Articles 1135 and 1136 when the two following conditions are satisfied: (i) there is *animus furandi*, ie the conscious intent to plunder and rob—an element which is no longer required under international law—and (ii) there is the involvement of two ships. The Code applies to crimes committed both on the high seas and in territorial seas. The Code has been supplemented by Law No 12/2009, which, inter alia, establishes the Ordinary Tribunal of Rome as the competent jurisdiction to judge on piracy issues, and by Decree-Law No 107 of 12 July 2011 (Law No 130/2011), which authorises the presence of armed guards on board Italian vessels.[137]

Spain has reintroduced the crime of maritime piracy in its Criminal Code (Articles 616ter and 616quater) by means of the Organic Law 5/2010, which has laid down a very wide definition of the crime: it does not include the requirement of an *animus furandi* and does not limit the crime of piracy to acts on the high seas, but it does require that, for the jurisdiction of the Spanish courts to be triggered, the crime has to have certain connecting factors with Spain, such as the involvement of Spanish nationals.[138]

However, practice has revealed that in general the seizing states are reluctant to exercise universal jurisdiction[139] owing to a series of factors such as financial costs, legal complexities, human rights concerns,[140] the difficulty of prosecutions and, in the words of the preambular paragraph of UNSC Resolution 1846 (2008), 'the lack of capacity, domestic legislation, and clarity about how to dispose of pirates after their capture' by certain states. Such factors are an important underlying cause of the lack of robust international action against pirates.

One alternative, which was the dominant approach during a certain period, has been to avoid capturing pirates in the first place, or, if captured, to release them without charging them. In the light of this situation, operative paragraph 11 of UNSC Resolution 1816 and operative paragraph 14 of UNSC Resolution 1846 (2008) called upon

---

[137] For a comment see F Pellegrino, 'Historical and Legal Aspects of Piracy and Armed Robbery against Shipping' (2012) 43 *Journal of Marinr Law and Commerce* 429.

[138] See JL Rodriguez-Villasante, 'Problemas juridico-penales e internacionales del crimen de la piratería' (2009) 93 *Revista Española de Derecho Militar* 187. See also M Gardner, 'Piracy Prosecutions in National Courts' (2012) 10 *Journal of International Criminal Justice* 797.

[139] So far, the following countries have prosecuted pirates: Somalia, Yemen, Kenya, Seychelles, Oman, Tanzania, Maldives, France, Germany, The Netherlands, Spain, Belgium, US, South Korea, India, Malaysia, Madagascar and Japan.

[140] The incident concerning the Danish Navy ship *Absalon* is a case in point: after having captured 10 pirates in the waters of Somalia, detained them for six days and confiscated their weapons, the *Absalon* released them instead of transferring them to the Somalian authorities on the basis of concerns for the respect for human rights with regard to the right to a fair trial, breach of the prohibition of torture or inhuman and degrading treatment, or breach of the prohibition of the death penalty if judged in Denmark and deported to Somalia. Member States of the EU have been brought to the European Court of Human Rights on the grounds that their conduct and the length of detention of captured criminals at sea had been in breach of Art 5 ECHR (which provides that any arrested or detained person had to be brought promptly before a judge) and Art 5(2) ECHR (deprivation of liberty). See *Rigopoulos v Spain*, no 37388/97, ECHR (1999) and *Medveyev and others v France*, no 3394/03, ECHR (2008).

all states, and in particular flag, port and coastal states, states of the nationality of victims and perpetrators of piracy and armed robbery, and other states with relevant jurisdiction under international law and national legislation, to cooperate in determining jurisdiction, and in the investigation and prosecution of persons responsible for acts of piracy and armed robbery off the coast of Somalia, consistent with applicable international law including international human rights law, and to render assistance by, among other actions, providing disposition and logistics assistance with respect to persons under their jurisdiction and control, such victims and witnesses and persons detained as a result of operations conducted under this resolution.

Another alternative that is used less frequently is to return the suspected pirates or armed robbers to the country of their nationality, ie to Somalia, for their prosecution. However, the lack of a functioning government in Somalia and the likelihood that, if returned to Somalia, the suspected pirates would be subject to cruel treatment and/or unfair trials has discouraged the EU and its Member States from pursuing the practice. Above all, the application of Somali law poses particular problems, for, as described in the report of Jack Lang, the Special Adviser to the UN Secretary-General on Legal Issues Related to Piracy off the Coast of Somalia, there are three levels of applicable municipal law in Somalia: first, customary law (the *xeer*, the polycentric Somali legal system whereby elders serve as judges in a *guurti* or court traditionally formed beneath an acacia tree where they arbitrate a dispute using precedents based on local principles, which resemble those of natural law, until both parties are satisfied), which is valued by the population because it is flexible and consensual; secondly, Sharia law, traditionally applied primarily in civil matters—in particular, family matters—but which, pursuant to the Somali 2012 Constitution has become the main source of legislation; and thirdly, the law that is a vestige of colonisation by the British in Somaliland and the Italians in Puntland and in central and southern Somalia. It remains to be seen whether criminal law falls within the latter category or is governed by Sharia. However, as pointed out by the Special Adviser to the UN Secretary-General, since few judges and prosecutors in Somalia have had legal training and thus many are ignorant about statutory law, they feel inclined to apply customary law primarily, including Sharia law. Furthermore, at the time of the elaboration of the UN Special Adviser's report, the Somali Criminal Code made no provision for the offence of piracy, even though efforts to introduce these were under way.[141] So far, these efforts have not yet resulted in a comprehensive set of counter-piracy laws for the whole of Somalia, despite Somaliland having enacted laws to combat piracy (Law No 52/2012) and even to regulate the transfer of prisoners (Law No 53/2012), a lacuna that the UNSC has recently requested be filled promptly (UNSC Resolution 2077 (2012) of 21 November 2012).

A third alternative has been to transfer the suspected pirates to regional coastal states for their prosecution. However, the question of the legality of such transfers has been raised. Indeed, the doctrine is divided on the question as to whether this transfer is compatible with the wording of Article 105 UNCLOS, which provides that

---

[141] UNSC S/2011/30, 25 January 2011, Annex to the letter dated 24 January 2011 from the Secretary-General to the President of the Security Council Report of the Special Adviser to the Secretary-General on Legal Issues Related to Piracy off the Coast of Somalia, paras 102, 104 and 116.

The courts of the state which carried out the seizure may decide upon the penalties to be imposed, and may also determine the action to be taken with regard to the ships, aircraft or property, subject to the rights of third parties acting in good faith.[142]

While some authors consider that Article 105 UNCLOS limits the competence to prosecute to the *forum deprehensionis* (the jurisdiction of the seizing state) and that it cannot be interpreted as allowing the transfer of suspected pirates to any other state,[143] other authors are of the view that, by not expressly prohibiting such transfers, the wording of Article 105 UNCLOS, reflects 'the application to piracy of the universality principle of criminal jurisdiction' and that such transfers are thus compatible with the provisions of UNCLOS.[144] Indeed, the practice of states and international organisations participating in the counter-piracy missions in the Gulf of Aden is to interpret Article 105 UNCLOS as permitting such transfers. This is also the legal position taken by the EU in Article 12 of the EU Joint Action 2008/851/ CFSP. This legal position appears to conform to the call by the UN Security Council to cooperate in determining a jurisdiction where the suspects of piracy and armed robbers can be prosecuted (UNSC Resolutions 1816 and 1846 (2008)). It is also consistent with piracy attacks which take place in the territorial waters of a state which do not fall within the scope of Article 105 UNCLOS since the latter only applies on the high seas. Furthermore, both the SUA Convention and the Hostages Convention, which also apply in territorial waters, contain *aut dedere–aut iudicare* ('extradite or prosecute') provisions. Finally, it should be noted that general international law does not contain any rule prohibiting the transfer of suspects for the purpose of being prosecuted in the jurisdiction of third states. Rather, it regulates the conditions and limits under which such transfers have to take place, namely respect for human rights and compliance with the principle of non-refoulement.[145] Thus, the practice of the EU and its Member States when the seizing state cannot or does not wish to exercise jurisdiction has been to transfer suspected pirates and armed robbers to any third state which wishes to exercise jurisdiction, provided that the conditions for transfer have been agreed with that third state in a manner which complies with the relevant international law.[146]

The exercise of jurisdiction by coastal states is facilitated whenever the so-called 'shiprider agreements' have been entered into with regional states. Under such agreements, the law enforcement officials from the countries of the region are authorised to embark on the vessels of the states which patrol the area for the purpose of repressing piracy. The 'shiprider agreements' overcome the legal hurdles posed by transfers and extraditions since officials embarked on vessels pursuant to the agreement may legitimately take action in the territorial waters of their home coastal state even if the vessel on which they are embarked does not fly the flag of that state.

---

[142] For an explanation of the wording of Art 105 UNCLOS see A Rubin, *The Law of Piracy*, 2nd edn (New York, Transnational Publishers, 1998) 359–60.

[143] For the view, based on a strict reading of Art 105, that UNCLOS prohibits the transfer of pirates by the seizing state to third states see Kontorovich, n 89 above; see also R Lagoni, 'Piraterie und widerrechtliche Handlungen gegen die Sicherheit der Seeschiffahrt' in J Ipsen and E Schmidt-Jortzig (eds), *Recht-Staat-Gemeinwohl, Festschrift fur Dietrich Rauschning* (Koln, Carl Heymanns Verlag KG, 2001) 501.

[144] See Shearer, n 1 above; see also JA Roach, 'Countering Piracy off Somalia/International Law and International Institutions' (2010) 104 *American Journal of International Law* 404.

[145] See Geiss and Petrig, n 9 above, 197. See further below.

[146] Art 12, para 2 of the Joint Action.

In this way, pirates and armed robbers at sea can be brought directly within the jurisdiction of the shiprider's home state, and the questions of transfer or extradition can be avoided.[147]

The EU has concluded a series of international agreements on the transfer of suspected pirates with several states in the African region. A first such agreement was concluded with Kenya,[148] a second with Seychelles[149] and a third with Mauritius.[150] The EU has additionally negotiated a transfer agreement with Tanzania. Each of these agreements contains explicit obligations on the contracting parties to treat the suspects concerned humanely and in accordance with human rights obligations, including the prohibition of torture and degrading treatment or punishment, the prohibition of arbitrary detention and fair trial rights.[151] No death penalty can be applied.[152]

Ever since 2006, Kenya has resorted to universal jurisdiction to prosecute pirates and combat the increase in piracy in the Western Indian Ocean. It has done so on the basis of agreements concerning the transfer of piracy suspects for criminal prosecution, which have been concluded with the UK, the US, Canada, China and Denmark, the contents of which have not yet been disclosed to the public. The secret nature of such agreements has prompted the suggestion that the Kenyan government is therefore allowed to act 'without any control'.[153]

By contrast, the Exchange of Letters between the EU and Kenya has been made public and contains two definitions that delimit their scope of application *ratione personae* and *ratione loci*: on the one hand, the term 'piracy' is defined as in Article 101 UNCLOS, which means that incidents taking place in the territorial waters of Somalia do not fall within the scope of the agreement, notwithstanding the extensions adopted by the UNSC resolutions; on the other hand, the term 'transferred person' includes any person suspected of intending to commit, committing or having committed acts of piracy. Thus, having the necessary *mens rea*, even if there is no *actus reus* element of actually committing an act of piracy, suffices to fall under the scope of the agreement.

In addition, the following principles and conditions are incorporated into the agreement.

First, Kenya will accept, upon the request of EU NAVFOR, the transfer of persons detained by EU NAVFOR in connection with piracy and associated seized property by

---

[147] Above n 126, 54.

[148] Exchange of Letters between the European Union and the Government of Kenya on the conditions and modalities for the transfer of persons suspected of having committed acts of piracy and detained by the European-Union led naval force (EUNACFOR), and seized property in the possession of EU NAVFOR, from EU NAVFOR to Kenya and for their treatment after such transfer, [2009] OJ L79/49.

[149] Exchange of Letters between the European Union and the Republic of Seychelles on the Conditions and Modalities for the Transfer Suspected Pirates and Armed Robbers from EU NAVFOR to the Republic of Seychelles and for their Treatment after such transfer, [2009 OJ L315/37.

[150] Agreement between the European Union and the Republic of Mauritius on the conditions of transfer of suspected pirates and associated property from the European-Union-led naval force to the Republic of Mauritius and on the conditions of suspected pirates after their transfer, [2011] OJ L254/3.

[151] Mauritius Agreement, Art 3(5); similar provisions are set out in the other two transfer agreements.

[152] Mauritius Agreement, Art 5; Kenya Agreement, point 4. The death penalty issue is not mentioned in the agreement with Seychelles, but it should be noted that Seychelles municipal law does not provide for the death penalty for any crime.

[153] M Taussig-Rubbo, 'Pirate Trials, the International Criminal Court, and Mob Justice: Reflections on Postcolonial Sovereignty in Kenya' (2010) 1 *International Journal of Human Rights, Humanitarianism and Development* 56.

EU NAVFOR, and will submit such persons and property to its competent authorities for the purpose of investigation and prosecution; EU NAVFOR will, when acting under the Exchange of Letters, transfer persons or property only to competent Kenyan law enforcement authorities.

Secondly, the Exchange of Letters contains several provisions ensuring respect for human rights and due process: both prior to and following transfer, persons will be treated humanely and in accordance with international human rights obligations, including the prohibition against torture and cruel, inhumane and degrading treatment or punishment, the prohibition of arbitrary detention and in accordance with the requirement to have a fair trial. In particular, any transferred person will be brought promptly before a judge or other officer authorised by law to exercise judicial power, who will decide without delay on the lawfulness of the transferred person's detention and will order that person's release if the detention is not lawful. Any transferred person will be entitled to trial within a reasonable time or to release and be entitled to a fair and public hearing by a competent, independent and impartial tribunal established by law. In addition, any transferred person charged with a criminal offence will be presumed innocent until proved guilty according to law and not compelled to testify against himself/herself or to confess guilt.

Thirdly, any transferred person convicted of a crime will have the right to his or her conviction and sentence reviewed by, or appealed to, a higher tribunal in accordance with the law of Kenya.

Fourthly, Kenya will not transfer any transferred person to any other state for the purposes of investigation or prosecution without prior written consent from EU NAVFOR.

Fifthly, no transferred person will be liable to suffer the death penalty. Kenya will, in accordance with applicable laws, take steps to ensure that any death sentence is commuted to a sentence of imprisonment: EU NAVFOR will provide detention records to Kenya with regard to any transferred person, and these records will include, so far as possible, the physical condition of the transferred person while in detention, the time of transfer to the Kenyan authorities, the reason for detention, the time and place of the commencement of detention, and any decisions taken with regard to the detention.

Sixthly, Kenya will be responsible for keeping an accurate account of all transferred persons, including, but not limited to, keeping records of any seized property, their physical condition, their place of detention, any charges against them and any significant decisions taken in the course of their prosecution and trial. These records will be available to representatives of the EU and EU NAVFOR upon request in writing to the Kenyan Ministry of Foreign Affairs.

Seventhly, Kenya will notify EU NAVFOR of the place of detention of any person transferred, any deterioration of the person's physical condition and any allegations of alleged improper treatment. Representatives of the EU and EU NAVFOR will have access to any persons transferred as long as such persons are in custody and will be entitled to question them. National and international humanitarian agencies will also, upon request, be allowed to visit transferred persons.

The Exchange of Letters between the EU and Kenya contain an important clause providing that EU NAVFOR, 'within its means and capabilities', will provide all assistance to Kenya with a view to investigating and prosecuting transferred persons.

All issues arising in connection with the application of those provisions are to be examined jointly by Kenyan and EU competent authorities. Failing any prior settlement, disputes concerning the interpretation or application of those provisions are to be settled exclusively by diplomatic means between Kenyan and EU representatives.

In practice, the application of the EU/Kenya agreement and prosecutions in Kenya have not been smooth. To start with, the High Court of Kenya held that Kenyan courts were 'bound to apply international norms and instruments since Kenya is a member of the civilized world and not expected to act in contradiction to expectations of member states of the UN',[154] but that Kenya did not have jurisdiction over piracy offences unless they took place in its territorial waters.[155] These limitations were corrected with the enactment of a new (2009) Merchant Shipping Act, section 369 of which defines the crime of piracy comprehensively.[156] As a result, Kenya has become an important jurisdiction for the trial of suspected pirates and armed robbers. Kenyan courts have given prison sentences to several captured Somali pirates and have accepted suspected pirates from Germany and India. Kenya has played a leading role in developing the first regional prosecution centre that has assisted the trials of many suspected Somali pirates. Indeed, UNODC and other members of the international community have praised Kenya for playing a pivotal role in combating piracy off the Horn of Africa through its support of prosecutions. However, it has been proven doubtful whether Kenya, itself a developing state, is able to take on the costly and complicated task of handling the majority of piracy cases, including their incarceration post-conviction. Kenyan officials have claimed that international financial support is necessary in order to deal with the influx of prisoners and to improve its strained justice system. The international community, and in particular the EU, has provided support for the creation of a court that would hear maritime piracy cases in Mombasa. Additional funding was also provided from UNODC and donors from Germany, France, Australia and Canada. Furthermore, efforts have been underway to improve the standards at Shimola Tewa Prison in Mombasa, and other major improvements have reportedly been made to Kenya's judicial system as a result of the joint EU–UNODC programme that was launched to support the judicial systems of Kenya with €1.7 million. However, as a result of the concern expressed by the international community with the Kenyan judicial system, with the Kenyan Evidence Act and with the treatment of pirates in Kenyan courts and prisons, and as a result of the investigation being carried out by the International Criminal Court on violence which arose after the 2007 elections, Kenya halted piracy trials and, in April 2010, General Wako, the Kenyan Attorney General, announced the end of the Kenya's pirate programme. Kenya thus denounced and terminated its transfer agreement with the EU. These moves, however, have been partially reversed, in part in exchange for continued financial contributions from the EU and the international community. Therefore, at present, transfers to Kenya remain possible, albeit only on a case-by-case basis.[157]

---

[154] *Hassan M Ahmed v Republic*, Crim Application No 198, 12 May 2009.

[155] *MM Dashi et al*, High Court of Kenya at Mombasa (2009).

[156] The text of this provision may be found in Geiss and Petrig, n 9 above, 293.

[157] Council Decision 2009/293/CFS of 26 February 2009 concerning the Exchange of Letters between the European Union and the Government of Kenya on the conditions and modalities for the transfer of persons suspected of having committed acts of piracy and detained by the European Union-led naval force (EU NAVFOR), and seized property in the possession of EU NAVFOR, from EU NAVFOR to Kenya and for

In comparison with the EU–Kenya agreement, the Exchange of Letters between the EU and Seychelles, which applies on a transitional basis pending the conclusion of a full-fledged transfer agreement, has a different scope *ratione personae* and *ratione loci*. While the Kenya agreement includes the transfer of any person detained by EU NAVFOR in connection with piracy, the agreement between the EU and Seychelles applies only where there is a connecting factor with Seychelles since it applies to those

> captured in the course of its operations in the exclusive economic zone, territorial sea, archipelagic waters and internal waters of the Republic of Seychelles . . . [and the authorisation is] extended to the protection of Seychelles flagged vessels and Seychellois Citizens on a non-Seychelles flagged vessel beyond the limit aforementioned and in other circumstances on the high seas at the discretion of the Republic of the Seychelles.

These restrictions appear justified inter alia by the limited capacities of the Republic of Seychelles 'to accept, try, detain and incarcerate suspected pirates and armed robbers'. In addition, the EU–Seychelles transfer agreement ensures that, in consideration of the acceptance by Seychelles of the transfer of any suspected pirate or armed robber to its territory, the EU provides the Republic of Seychelles 'with such full financial, human resource, material, logistical and infrastructural assistance for the detention, incarceration maintenance, investigation, prosecution, trial and repatriation of the suspected or convicted pirates and armed robbers'. Furthermore, in the event of the Attorney General of Seychelles deciding that there is insufficient evidence to prosecute, EU NAVFOR undertakes to take the full responsibility, including the financial costs, of transferring the suspected pirates and armed robbers back to their country of origin within 10 days of EU NAVFOR having been notified of such a decision. The actual transfer of suspected pirates and armed robbers is to be carried out 'as far as possible' in accordance with the 'Guidance for the Transfer of Suspected pirates, armed robbers and seized property to Seychelles', which has been elaborated by the Attorney-General of the Republic of Seychelles. On its part, the Government of the Republic of Seychelles has confirmed that

> any transferred person will be treated humanely and will not be subjected to torture or cruel, inhuman or degrading treatment or punishment; will receive adequate accommodation and nourishment, access to medical treatment and will be able to carry out religious observance.

Finally, the EU–Seychelles Exchange of Letters contains the familiar conditions with regard to respect of human rights and due process, save that, as a result of the abolition of the death penalty by Seychelles, the Exchange of Letters does not contain any clause with regard to the death penalty.[158]

In practice, Seychelles, along with Kenya, is among the few regional countries willing and able to actively take on piracy prosecutions, with 64 prosecutions to date. Seychelles opened a regional prosecution centre for dealing with piracy cases in 2010, becoming the second regional nation to actively pursue piracy prosecutions or at least the incarceration of convicted pirates. This was made possible as a result of the 2010 amendment to the Criminal Code, which allowed the island nation to try pirate cases

---

their treatment after such transfer, [2009] OJ L79/47. The agreement was provisionally applied as from the date of signature but terminated by Kenya as from 30 September 2010.

[158] Above n 149.

under universal jurisdiction. The new Articles 65(4) and (5) of the Criminal Code are modelled closely on UNCLOS and also allow persons to be prosecuted for conspiracy to commit piracy where there is a common intention to perpetrate the crime. Seychelles has also benefited from international and EU financial support: since January 2010, Seychelles has benefited from a joint EU–UNODC counter-piracy programme which aims to assist the nation with €0.78 million in its efforts of improving its police, coastguard, courts and prisons. The programme provides for training and equipment, as well as the construction of judicial facilities. However, the prison capacity in this small island nation is limited, making it increasingly important for other regional states to begin taking on piracy prosecutions. In particular, Seychelles has offered to serve as a temporary regional prosecution centre until a system is established for the prisoners to be transferred back to Somalia after sentencing. In 2009, Somalia and Seychelles signed an agreement that allows for the transfer of sentenced persons between the two republics under certain conditions. Similar memoranda of understanding were signed with both Puntland and Somaliland in April 2011.

The EU has also concluded a formal agreement on the conditions of transfer of suspected pirates and associated seized property with the Republic of Mauritius.[159] Article 1 of the agreement defines the conditions and modalities for

> (a) the transfer of persons suspected of attempting to commit, committing or having committed acts of piracy within the area of operation of EU NAVFOR, on the high seas off the territorial seas of Mauritius, Madagascar, the Comoros Islands, Seychelles and Réunion Island, and detained by EU NAVFOR; (b) the transfer of associated property seized by EU NAVFOR from EU NAVFOR to Mauritius; and (c) the treatment of transferred persons.

Piracy is understood as defined in Article 101 UNCLOS (Article 2(e)) and, for that purpose, Mauritius has revised its Criminal Code by means of the Piracy and Maritime Violence Act 2011 in order to allow for the prosecution of pirates on the basis of UNCLOS and in the case of a 'maritime attack' in Mauritian territorial waters. The transfer is governed by the following principles: first, Mauritius will accept a transfer 'on a case to case basis by Mauritius, taking into account all relevant circumstances including the location of the incident' and in particular 'receipt of evidence as forwarded by EU NAVFOR that there are reasonable prospects of securing a conviction of persons detained by EU NAVFOR'; secondly, EU NAVFOR 'shall only transfer persons to the competent law enforcement authorities of Mauritius'; thirdly, any transferred person

> shall be treated humanely and in accordance with international human rights obligations, embodied in the Constitution of Mauritius, including the prohibition of torture and cruel, inhumane and degrading treatment or punishment, the prohibition of arbitrary detention and in accordance with the requirement to have a fair trial.

In particular, Article 5 explicitly provides that 'No transferred person shall, in accordance with Mauritius Abolition of Death Penalty Act, be charged with an offence that carries the death penalty, be sentenced to death or be the subject of an application of the death penalty'. A joint EU–UNODC programme has been launched and €1.08 million have been provided to support Mauritius's judicial system.

---

[159] Council Decision 2011/640/CFSP of 12 July 2011, [2011] OJ L254/1.

At present, the EU is engaged in negotiations regarding the conclusion of transfer agreements with Mozambique, South Africa, Tanzania and Uganda.[160] On the whole, over 1000 pirates are currently being prosecuted in some 20 countries. An essential step towards creating a successful regional approach is by providing prosecuting states with the opportunity to transfer convicted pirates back to prisons in Somalia. This would involve the prosecuting state entering into prison transfer agreements with officials in Somalia and there being sufficient evidence that Somalia's prisons meet international standards. The EU has not so far concluded a transfer agreement with Somalia for several reasons, namely, the absence of a functioning judicial system; the limited availability of prisons that meet international standards; the lack of the capacity required to take on prosecutions by the semi-autonomous state of Puntland, despite Puntland's authorities having reported that they have initiated counter-piracy policies, that security forces have cracked down on pirate hideouts, that a substantial number of pirates has been arrested and tried, and that an estimated 250 pirates were reportedly being held in a prison in Puntland's capital city, Bossaso, in 2010;[161] and the absence of a comprehensive set of legislation against piracy in Somalia. Meanwhile, the joint EU–UNODC counter-piracy programme has undertaken a number of capacity building efforts within Somalia to increase its ability to meet international standards for the treatment of prisoners and support Somalia's long-term goal of one day taking on piracy prosecutions.

Overall, the situation remains one where 'there are no uniform procedural standards across the national contexts where prosecution might occur and domestic legal systems may lack the necessary legislation to prosecute fairly and effectively'.[162] In addition, the emphasis placed on dealing with Somali piracy cases in the courts of the coastal states of the region puts a substantial financial burden on the East African countries, a burden that adds to their existent limited resources. There have been several steps taken in order to remedy the situation. On the one hand, as has been already indicated, the EU and UNODC have initiated a counter-piracy programme that seeks to support the trial and treatment of piracy suspects in regional states, to enhance criminal justice capacity among Somalia's neighbours, and to ensure that trials and imprisonment in those countries are humane and efficient and take place within a sound rule-of-law framework; in particular, a piracy prisoner transfer programme was established by UNODC in June 2010 in response to calls from prosecuting states for a long-term imprisonment solution for pirates convicted in their courts. On the other hand, as will be explained below, the EU has taken measures to restore the rule of law in Somalia. Finally, as requested by UNSC Resolution 1918 (2010), the UN Secretary-General has put forward seven options in order to raise the judicial standards and ensure that suspected pirates are prosecuted in accordance with international standards either at the regional or international level. Options at the regional level include, for instance, pros-

---

[160] For further details regarding the transfer agreements concluded by the EU see the next Chapter by Thym in this volume.

[161] For an examination of the laws of Somalia, Kenya and Djibouti, see A Petrig (ed), *Sea Piracy Law, Selected National Legal Frameworks and Regional Legislative Approaches* (Berlin, Duncker & Humbolt, 2010).

[162] E Andersen, B Brockman-Hawe and P Goff, 'Supressing Maritime Piracy: Exploring the options in Internaitonal Law', Workshop Report (American Society of International Law et al, 2009), available at http://acuns.org/wp-content/uploads/2012/06/SuppressingMaritimePiracyExploringOptionsIntlLaw.pdf.

ecution in the regular domestic courts of regional states; the establishment of a Somali Court sitting in the territory of a third state based on the 'Lockerbie model';[163] and the establishment of specialised piracy chambers in the domestic courts of regional states, as recommended by UN Special Adviser Jack Lang, who advocated for the establishment of specialised piracy courts that would comprise a specialised court in Puntland and another in Somaliland, as well as an extraterritorial Somali specialised court. At the international level, the possible options for improving piracy prosecutions include the establishment of an international tribunal by means of a UNSG Resolution under Chapter VII UN Charter; the setting up of a regional piracy tribunal on the basis of a multilateral agreement among regional states under the auspices of the UN; the setting up of an international tribunal on the basis of an agreement between a state in the region and the UN;[164] and the possibility of prosecuting in existing international fora, such as the International Criminal Court or the International Tribunal for the Law of the Sea.[165] So far the recommendations of the UN Secretary-General (all of which have dire financial implications or require the provision of financial support to the countries concerned) have not come to fruition.

On the whole, since the beginning of Operation Atalanta, EU NAVFOR have transferred 79 suspected pirates to Kenya, 42 to Seychelles, 12 to Mauritius and 16 to the Member States of the EU. Seychelles has had recourse to the so-called 'post-trial transfers' of 12 convicted pirates to Puntland. So far, 91 pirates have been convicted, and 49 suspected pirates are awaiting trial.

The issue of the compliance by Operation Atalanta of humanitarian and human rights standards has given rise to particular legal difficulties, given the requirement of the UNSC that the enforcement measures in the fight against piracy have to 'be undertaken consistent with applicable international humanitarian and human rights law' (paragraph 6 of UNSC Resolution 1851 (2008)), and the TEU's own requirements on human rights derived from Articles 2 and 6 TEU as well as the duty that the external action of the EU has to be defined and implemented in order to 'consolidate and support democracy, the rule of law, human rights and the principles of international law', as set out in Article 21(2)(b) TEU.

(v) The EU's Respect for International Humanitarian Law, Refugee Law and Human Rights: The Principle of 'Non-refoulement'

The duties of the EU and its Member States in Operation Atalanta vary depending on whether consideration is given to international humanitarian law, refugee law or international human rights law, together with respect for the principle of non-refoulement.

With regard to international humanitarian law,[166] it has been pointed out that, under modern international law (treaty law and UNSC resolutions), the status of

---

[163] It was a special sitting of the Scottish High Court of Justiciary set up under Scots Law in Utrecht, in the Netherlands, for the trial of two Libyans charged with murder in connection with bombing of PanAm Flight 103 over Lockerbie in Scotland on 21 December 1988. See the High Court of Justiciary, Statutory Instrument 1988 No 2251.

[164] See in particlar the Report of the UN Secretary-General pursuant to UNSC Resolution 1918, 26 July 2010, where the UN Secretary-General discusses seven options.

[165] For an analysis of these options see Greiss and Petrig, n 9 above, 168–84.

[166] See too T Marauhn, Chapter 4 above.

pirates is different from that under customary international law, which in the Age of
Sail (ie the era spanning from the sixteenth to the nineteenth centuries throughout
which sailing ships were an important means of transport) allowed for the summary
execution of captured pirates. The modern law of the sea reserves the high seas for
'peaceful purposes' and, save for situations of immediate self-defence, naval forces
cannot use war-like force against pirates but only seek to apprehend them. This begs
the question whether the suspected pirates detained by armed forces and held aboard
naval ships benefit from the protection afforded by international humanitarian law and
the Geneva Conventions, whether there is a presumption that they have to be treated
and protected as prisoners of war, and whether the campaign against piracy within
the territorial waters of Somalia could potentially qualify as an 'armed conflict not of
an international character' under international humanitarian law. The docrine agrees
that pirates cannot be categorised as 'belligerents' under the laws of war nor as 'illegal
combatants', nor are they 'true civilians' on board of private vessels because they are
armed, even if this is not per se an international crime. Indeed, Rubin pointed out
that, historically, piracy was not a

> war crime . . . or by any known definition applied in diplomatic practice or court cases.
> Indeed, the term piracy was historically used to distinguish those who fought as privateers
> under the laws of war and those who had no valid commissions or sailed under the
> commissions of unrecognized powers and thus were subject not at all to the laws of war
> but to the normal criminal law of some state with the necessary legal interest to try them.[167]

Thus, to some authors pirates are unique in that they are not a 'true criminals' but
'arguably a hybrid between criminals and combatants',[168] and unless they are stopped
in the narrow space of time between their speeding towards a vessel and their boarding
it, the anti-piracy situation becomes a hostage situation. For other authors, the attack
of a pirate vessel on the high seas could theoretically lead to accusations of 'targeted
killing' of protected targets.[169]

   In the light of these hypotheses, the question arises whether captured pirates benefit
from any protection afforded by the Geneva Conventions. On first inspection, captured
pirates do not appear to fall under the common Article 2, common to both the Third
(Convention Relative to the Treatment of Prisoners of War) and Fourth (Convention
Relative to the Protection of Civilian Persons in Time of War) Geneva Conventions,
because they apply either to 'all cases of declared war or of any other armed conflict
which may arise between two or more of the High Contracting Parties, even if the
state of war is not recognized by one of them', or to 'cases of partial or total occupation of the territory of a High Contracting Party, even if the said occupation meets
with no armed resistance', and to conflicts where one of the 'powers' is not a party to
the Conventions. It has been suggested, however, that in certain circumstances, Articles
4 and 5 of the (Third) 1949 Geneva Convention Relative to the Treatment of Prisoners
of War[170] may afford captured pirates the same protection as that afforded to prisoners
of war, provided that they are in a situation in which they are 'members of the armed

---

[167] See also Rubin, n 13 above 6, 316.
[168] See also Guilfoyle, n 100 above, 10.
[169] See also E Kontorovich, *Piracy and International Law* (Global Law Issues, 2009), available at http://
jcpa.org/article/piracy-and-international-law/, point III, A.
[170] 6 UST 3316, 75 UNTS 135.

forces of a state but are pursuing piratical attacks for private ends', or are not actually pirates but 'rather a legitimate naval *levée en masse* rising up to repel invasion who are mistaken for pirates'.[171] In any case, if there is a doubt as to the status of a captured person, that person is entitled to be treated as a prisoner of war until a competent tribunal has determined his or her status. Conversely, captured pirates do not qualify as 'protected persons' under the (Fourth) Geneva Convention Relative to the Protection of Civilian Persons in Time of War since Article 4 defines 'protected persons' as only 'those who, at a given moment and in any manner whatsoever, find themselves, in case of a conflict or occupation, in the hands of a Party to the conflict or Occupying Power of which they are not nationals'.[172]

It is submitted that, even if captured pirates are not afforded the protection granted to 'prisoners of war', it appears evident that they can benefit from the minimal protection afforded by the common Article 3 of the Geneva Conventions,[173] which applies within a signatory's territory during an armed conflict not of an international character (regardless of citizenship or lack thereof), even if they are not classified as prisoners of war. Such protection is offered to non-combatants, combatants who have laid down their arms and combatants who are *hors de combat* (out of the fight) owing to wounds, detention or any other cause. In accordance with this provision, those persons are 'in all circumstances [to] be treated humanely'. Such treatment includes the prohibition of 'outrages upon personal dignity, in particular humiliating and degrading treatment' and the requirement that the passing of sentences be 'pronounced by a regularly constituted court, affording all the judicial guarantees which are recognized as indispensable by civilized peoples'.

With regard to respect for human rights, the first question which arises is whether EU Member States may be held accountable for a breach of the European Convention on Human Rights and Fundamental Freedoms resulting from the actions of their military personnel deployed in the context of Operation Atalanta.

On the one hand, in *Behrami and Behrami v France* and *Saramati v France, Germany and Norway*,[174] the European Court of Human Rights held that the complaints by the applicants for alleged violations of the Convention resulting from the actions of French, German, and Norwegian military personnel belonging to The NATO Kosovo Force (KFOR) and to the forces of the United Nation Interim Administration Mission in Kosovo (UNMIK) operating in Kosovo, were inadmissible *ratione personae* with the Convention because that personnel was not acting on behalf of its respective states, but as agents of the international organisation responsible for the operation. The acts in question were therefore, in principle, attributable to the international organisation, ie the UN acting under Chapter VII of the UN Charter. So far, the Court of Human Rights has not yet examined the question of military operations conducted by the armed forces of Council of Europe Member States under some EU command, as in Operation Atalanta. But it is reasonable to believe that the European Court of Human Rights will follow *Behrami* and *Saramati* not only in a situation whereby the operation is conducted by the EU (and not by individual EU Member States), but also where it is

---

[171] M Passman, 'Protection Afforded to Captured Pirates Under the Law of War and International Law' (2008) 33 *Tulaine Maritime Law Journal* 1, 16.
[172] 6 UST 3516, 75 UNTS 287.
[173] See generally Kontorovich, n 169 above.
[174] Application Nos 71412/01 and 78166/01 (Joined Cases), ECHR 2007.

conducted by the EU pursuant to a series of UNSC resolutions adopted under Chapter VII of the UN Charter.

However, the Grand Chamber of the Court of Human Rights in *Bosphorus v Ireland*[175] introduced an important nuance which was confirmed and explained in detail in a more recent German case, *Rambus Inc. v Germany:*[176] if the authorities of the states intervene at some point, either directly or indirectly, in the acts which result in the alleged violations of the Convention, the Court can, if we use corporate law terminology, '*pierce the corporate veil*'and hold responsible the EU Member States rather than the EU itself.[177]

This was the solution retained by the European Court of Human Rights, in *Al-Skeini and Others v UK*[178] and *Al-Jedda v UK,*[179] both cases relating to British military operations in Iraq involving the killing or detention of individuals. In both cases, the Court of Human Rights found that the UK was responsible for securing to everyone within its jurisdiction the rights and freedoms defined in the Convention, as laid down in Article 1 thereof. In *Al-Skeini*, the Court confirmed the exceptional, restrictive nature of extraterritorial jurisdiction: on the one hand, it extended the notion of '*full and effective control*' of state agents considering that state jurisdiction does not arise solely from the control exercised by state agents over a physical space (buildings, ships, etc.) but requires the '*exercise of physical power and control over the person in question*'; on the other hand, the Court acknowledged the extraterritorial jurisdiction of the UK only in the light of the '*exceptional circumstances*' arising from the fact that, following the fall of the previous Iraqi regime, the UK had 'assumed in Iraq the exercise of some of the public powers normally to be exercised by a sovereign government'. and in particular, it had assumed 'authority and responsibility for the maintenance of security in South East Iraq'. Both these conditions—exercise of physical power and control on individuals, and assumption of authority and responsibility for the maintenance of security—might prove problematic for the establishment of extraterritorial jurisdiction when firing at a pirate vessel on the high seas. In *Al-Jedda*, the Court found that the detention of the applicant in Iraq was attributable to the UK, despite the argument of the British Government that British troops had been acting under UNSC resolutions. The Court considered that, at the time, the UN was merely providing humanitarian relief, supporting the reconstruction of Iraq and helping the formation of an Iraqi interim government. In the Court's view, the UN therefore had neither effective control nor ultimate authority and control over security operations carried out by British troops present in Iraq.

This gives rise to the question, whether the legal reasoning in the rulings *Bosphorus v Ireland, Al-Skeini and Others v UK* and *Al-Jedda v UK* could be applicable in the case of Operation Atalanta, considering that, pursuant to Article 42 TEU, the EU uses

---

[175] Application No 45036/98, *Bosphorus Hava Yolları Turizm ve Ticaret Anonim Şirketi v Ireland* [GC], ECHR 2005-VI.

[176] Application No 40382/04 (decision on admissibility), 16 June 2009.

[177] A decision to 'pierce the veil' is applied by common law courts in exceptional situations (such as fraud) whereby the rights or duties of a corporation (which is usually treated as a separate legal person, solely responsible for the liabilities it incurs and the sole beneficiary of the assets it holds) are treated as the rights or liabilities of its shareholders, with the result that the principle of separate personhood is not upheld and the court can thus 'pierce' or 'lift' the corporate veil. See Piedimonte Bodini, n 9 above.

[178] Application No 55721/07, 7 July 2011, paras 136 and 149.

[179] Application No 27021/08, 7 July 2011.

the military capabilities of the Member States '*provided*' or made '*available*' by the Member States. Some practical examples of complex questions which that might arise in the course of Operation Atalanta include:

> what would be the consequence of a pirate captured in the context of Operation Atalanta dying while being transferred on board an Italian warship? Would the death be imputable to the EU, which had overall responsibility for the operation, or would the death be imputable to Italy to which the warship belonged? Would the responsibility of the EU be engaged? Or that of Italy? Or, rather, of both?[180]

It is submitted that the EU system has been conceived in order for Member States to assume the responsibility for these kinds of situations. It cannot be excluded that, in very specific cases, the responsibility of the EU as such is engaged. This is the approach taken by the EU in the context of the EU's accession to the European Convention of Human Rights and Fundamental Freedoms. In particular, where persons employed or appointed by a Member State act within the framework of an EU operation, their acts, measures or omissions are attributed to the Member State. However, this principle of the responsibility of the Member States does no preclude that the EU may be held responsible as a co-respondent. In addition, the EU is responsible, under EU law, for the acts, measures and omissions of the EU institutions, bodies, officers and personnel employed by them when performing their official functions.

Finally, further consideration must be given to the question as to whether pirates benefit from the prohibition under international law to expel or return persons to places where their life or freedom could be threatened (the principle of non-refoulement). It should be noted that the scope of the principle differs depending on the branch of the law within which the principle is applied. In particular, it differs with respect to the category of persons protected by the prohibition, the nature of the threat faced by such persons and the content of the protection available under the different instruments, such as the Convention against Torture, the European Convention of Human Rights, the International Covenant of Civilian and Political Rights, the Refugee Convention and other instruments including on international humanitarian law.[181]

Pursuant to Article 33(1) of the Convention relating to the Status of Refugees

> No Contracting state shall expel or return ('refouler') a refugee in any manner whatsoever to the frontiers of territories where his life or freedom would be threatened on account of his race, religion, nationality, membership of a particular social group or political opinion.

However, a pirate in principle does not qualify as a 'refugee' under the Convention (Article 1.A.2), which defined the terms as

> any person who owing to well-founded fear of being persecuted for reasons of race, religion, nationality, membership of a particular social group or political opinion, is outside the country of his nationality and is unable, or owing to such fear, is unwilling to avail himself of the protection of that country; or who, not having a nationality and being outside the country of his former habitual residence as a result of such events, is unable or, owing to such fear, is unwilling to return to it.

---

[180] Piedimonte Bodini, n 9 above, 829–48.
[181] See Geiss and Petrig, n 9 above, 207ff.

Thus, any defence based on Article 1.A.2 of the Convention raised by a pirate in the course of a prosecution appears likely to fail.[182]

Equally, the protection afforded by the principle of non-refoulement under international humanitarian law is likely to be discarded in the case of captured pirates if, outside the scope of our suggestions above, counter-piracy operations, as opposed to the non-international armed conflict on Somali main land, are categorised as law enforcement operations rather than the conduct of hostilities in the context of an armed conflict.[183]

The question of the application of the principle of non-refoulement, as embodied in international human rights law, could also arise whenever a specific transfer of pirates risks certain human rights violations in the receiving state. First, the prohibition of refoulement contained in Article 3 of the Convention of Torture can only be applied where 'there are substantial grounds for believing' that the pirates would be in danger of being subjected to torture, as defined in Article 1 of the Convention, which requires that the pain or suffering inflicted reaches the level of being 'severe'.[184] In addition, the Convention requires a state party to assess its non-refoulement obligation on an individual basis and provide all procedural guarantees to the person expelled, returned or extradited. Under these conditions, the principle of non-refoulement would apply to pirates. Secondly, the International Covenant on civilian and Political Rights derives the principle of non-refoulement from Article 7 (prohibition of torture) and Article 6 (right to life); in particular, the application of the latter provision differs depending on whether a state has abolished or retained the death penalty: in the case *Judge v Canada*, the Human Rights Committee ruled that abolitionist states are always prevented by the Covenant from deporting or extraditing a person to a retentionist state where that person faces a real risk of being subjected to the death penalty.[185] Thirdly, the non-refoulement principle derives from Article 3 of the European Convention on Human Rights (risk of being subjected to torture or inhuman or degrading treatment or punishment) and from Article 13 of the same convention (availability of effective remedy) and, according to the European Court of Human Rights, does not necessarily have to be raised before a judicial authority but before any body affording the procedural guarantees and powers ensured by the Convention.[186]

It is recalled that, as indicated above, the EU and its Member States have taken measures in their transfer agreements with Kenya, Seychelles and Mauritius to ensure that transfer practices are in conformity with the principle of non-refoulement deriving from human rights instruments. Critics have questioned whether these diplomatic assurances constitute adequate safeguards or, rather, as has been alleged,[187] are a means to circumvent the absolute nature of the principle of non-refoulement.

---

[182] For the text of the 1951 Convention relating to the status of refugees, see 189 UNTS 137.

[183] See C Droege, 'Transfer of Detainees: Legal Framework, Non-refoulement, and Contemporary Challenges' (2008) 90 *International Review of the Red Cross* 674.

[184] M Nowak and E McArthur, *The UN Convention against Torture: A Commentary* (Oxford, Oxford University Press 2008) 148–49, 127, 165, 195–96 and 218–19.

[185] Ibid, 188, para 50.

[186] F van Dijk, F van Hoof, A van Rijn and L Zwaak (eds), *Theory and Practice of the European Convention on Human Rights*, 4th edn (Antwerp, Intersentia Publishers 2006) 1006.

[187] See, eg International Commission of Jurists, *Report on Terrorism, Counter-Terrorism and Human Rights* (Geneva, International Commission of Jurists, 2009), available at http://news.bbc.co.uk/1/shared/bsp/hi/pdfs/16_02_09_ejp_report.pdf; Amnesty International *Dangerous Deals—Europe Reliance on Diplomatic*

The European Court of Human Rights has ruled on this issue in a number of cases (*Saadi v Italy*,[188] *Ismoilov v Russia*,[189] *Ryabikin v Russia*,[190] *Ben Khemais v Italy*[191] and *Klein v Russia*[192]). It has held that the diplomatic assurances received by the sending states were insufficient to safeguard against abuse upon return to the receiving country, in particular in the case of diplomatic assurances against torture 'from a state where torture is endemic or persistent'.[193] In *Medvedyed and Others v France*,[194] a case decided by the Grand Chamber of the Court of Human Rights, the applicants were crew-members of the *Winner*, a cargo vessel registered in Cambodia. As the French authorities suspected that the vessel was carrying significant quantities of narcotics to be distributed in Europe, the French Navy apprehended it on the high seas off the shores of Cape Verde and confined the crew to their quarters on board under French military guard. The applicants complained that they had been unlawfully deprived of their liberty, particularly as the French authorities had not had jurisdiction; the Court held that France had exercised full and exclusive control over the Cambodian vessel and its crew, at least de facto, from the time of its interception, in a continuous and uninterrupted manner. Besides the interception of the vessel, its rerouting had been ordered by the French authorities and the crew had remained under the control of the French military throughout the journey to Brest in France. Accordingly, the Court found that, with regard to the events, from the stopping of the *Winner* on the high seas and throughout the 13 days of alleged deprivation of liberty until the ship reached Brest, the applicants were under the jurisdiction of France for the purposes of Article 1 of the Convention (according to which 'The High Contracting Parties shall secure to everyone within their jurisdiction the rights and freedoms defined in Section I of [the] Convention'). It also found that the deprivation of liberty to which the applicants were subjected between the boarding of their ship and its arrival in Brest was not 'lawful' within the meaning of Article 5 § 1, for lack of a legal basis of the requisite quality to satisfy the general principle of legal certainty. For that reason, the Court ruled that there had been a violation of Article 5(1) of the Convention. Moreover, the Court rejected the applicants' plea that they had not been brought 'promptly' before a judge or other officer authorised by law to exercise judicial power after their ship was intercepted, as required by Article 5(3) of the Convention, according to which

> Everyone arrested or detained in accordance with the provisions . . . of this Article shall be brought promptly before a judge or other officer authorised by law to exercise judicial power and shall be entitled to trial within a reasonable time or to release pending trial. Release may be conditioned by guarantees to appear for trial.

The Court found that a period of eight or nine hours was perfectly compatible

---

Assurances against Torture (London, Amnesty International Publications, 2010), available at www.amnesty.org/en/library/info/EUR01/012/2010.

[188] Application No 2947/06, ECHR, 24 April 2008.
[189] Application No 37201/06, ECHR, 28 February 2009.
[190] Application No 8320/04, ECHR, 19 June 2008.
[191] Application No 246/07, ECHR, 24 February 2009.
[192] Application No 24268/08, ECHR, 1 April 2010.
[193] Application No 2947/06, ECHR, 24 April 2008, para 127.
[194] See Application No 3394/03, ECHR, 29 March 2010; for a comment see Piedimonte Bodini, n 9 above, 829–48.

with the concept of 'brought promptly' enshrined in Article 5(3) of the Convention and in the Court's case law. Accordingly, there had been no violation of Article 5(3).[195]

The case law analysed above appears to confirm that the guarantees or 'diplomatic assurances' relating to human rights in transfer agreements do not violate particular provisions of the European Convention per se. Rather, the European Court of Human Rights appears to opt for a case-by-case assessment of whether the 'practical application' of such diplomatic assurances provide sufficient protection for the purpose of the European Convention.[196]

Two issues remain to be considered with regard Operation Atalanta, namely, the participation of third countries in the operation and the question of the status of the forces used in the operation.

(vi) Participation by Third Countries in Operation Atalanta

The EU has invited third states to participate in the operation. Norway was the first non-EU country to contribute to the operation, with one warship in 2009. Furthermore, Croatia and Ukraine have provided staff officers to the OHQ. Additionally, offers by Montenegro and Serbia to contribute to the operation have been accepted. The operational contribution to Operation Atalanta includes navy vessels (surface combat vessels and auxiliary ships), maritime patrol and reconnaissance aircrafts and vessel protection detachment teams.

Third states that make significant military contributions to Operation Atalanta are granted the same rights and are subject to the same obligations, in terms of day-to-day management of the operation, as Member States taking part in the operation. For that purpose a Committee of Contributors has been established (Article 10 of the Joint Action 2008/851/CFSP). The participation of third states is subject to the decision-making autonomy of the EU and to its single institutional framework.

The contributions and detailed arrangements for the participation of third states are the subject of international agreements concluded in accordance with Article 37 TEU. So far, the EU has concluded agreements with the Republic of Croatia on 27 July 2009[197] and with Montenegro on 22 March 2010.[198]

A participation agreement typically contains provisions which ensure that the participating forces and personnel of third states undertake their mission in accordance with the EU Joint Action 2008/851/CFSP, all relevant EU decisions, the Operation Plan and any implementing measures. It will also ensure that the forces and personnel seconded to the EU operation carry out conduct and duties solely in the interest of the EU operation. All forces and personnel of participating third states remain under the full command of their national authorities, but the national authorities of the participating third state transfer the operational and tactical command and/or control of their forces and personnel to the EU Operation Commander, who may, following

---

[195] As explained above, in more recent judgments relating to British military operations in Irak involving the detention and killing of individuals, the European Court of Human Rights held that the UK was responsible under Art 1 of the ECHR; eg Application No 55721/07, *Al-Skeini and Others v UK*, ECHR, 7 July 2011; Application No 27021/08, *Al-Jedda v UK*, ECHR, 7 July 2011.

[196] See also Geiss and Petrig, n 9 above, 217–20; Naert and van Hegelsom, n 9 above.

[197] [2009] OJ L202/83.

[198] [2010] OJ L88/83.

consultations with the participating third state, request that state's withdrawal from the operation at any time. The financial costs associated with participation in the operation are assured by the participating third state (unless the costs are subject to common funding).[199] The participation agreement will also ensure that the contributing third state is responsible for answering any claims linked to its forces or personnel, and will waive any claim against any state participating in the operation. Where the liability of the contributing state is established, that state is to pay compensation in the event of death, injury, loss or damage to natural or legal persons from the state in which the operation is conducted. Failure by any party to comply with the obligations laid down in the participation agreement entitles the other party to terminate the agreement, and any dispute concerning the interpretation or application of the agreement is settled by diplomatic means.

The participation agreements are implemented by any necessary technical and administrative arrangement concluded between the HR or the Operation Commander and the appropriate authorities of the participating third state. In particular, the exchange of classified information between the EU and third states is the subject of special agreements on security procedures between third states and the EU.[200]

The status of the contributing forces and personnel is governed by the agreed EU status of forces agreements with countries in the region. However, this issue requires further consideration.

(vii) The Status of Forces Used in Operation Atalanta

The fulfilment and smooth functiong of Operation Atalanta requires that the EU-led forces and their personnel that are stationed on the land territory of such third states and who operate in the territorial and internal waters of such third states benefit from the usual priviliges and immunities, and further guarantees required by Article 11 of Joint Action 2008/851/CFSP.

The modalities relating to the status of EU forces have been the subject of agreements with third states on the basis of Article 37 TEU, which empowers the EU to conclude agreements with one or more states or international organisations in this field. To date, the EU has concluded three such agreements—with the Republic of Somalia,[201] the Republic of Djibouti[202] and Seychelles.[203] A typical agreement on the status of the EU-led naval force will apply within the territory of the host state, including its internal waters, territorial sea and airspace, and will provide for the obligation by EU NAVFOR and its personnel to respect the laws and regulation of the host state, to inform national authorities of the calls to the host state's ports by EU

---

[199] See, eg [2008] OJ L345/96.

[200] See, eg [2006] OJ L116/74.

[201] Agreement between the European Union and the Somali Republic on the status of the European Union-led naval force in the Somali Republic in the framework of the EU military Operation Atalanta, [2009] OJ L10/29.

[202] Agreement between the European Union and the Republic of Djibouti on the status of the European Union-led naval force in the Republic of Djibouti in the framework of the EU military Operation Atalanta, [2009] OJ L33/43.

[203] Agreement between the European Union and the Republic of Seychelles on the status of the European Union-led naval force in the Republic of Seychelles in the framework of the EU military Operation Atalanta, [2009] OJ L323/14.

NAVFOR vessels and to carry passport and military identity cards, EU flags and other distinctive identification at all times. In exchange, the host state grants EU NAVFOR and its personnel freedom of movement and freedom to travel within its territory, including its waters and airspace. They are also authorised to exercise or practise with weapons, aircraft or military means.

As a result, EU NAVFOR vessels and aircraft are inviolable and immune from search, requisition, attachment or exemption, and from every form of legal process; its personnel is not liable to any form of arrest or detention, and enjoys immunity from the criminal, civil and administrative jurisdiction of the host country under all circumstances, although immunity from prosecution may be waived by the sending state or the EU institution. Such immunity, however, provides no exemption from the jurisdiction of the sending state. In particular, the competent authorities of the sending state have the right to exercise on the territory of the host state all the criminal jurisdiction and disciplinary powers conferred upon them by the law of the sending state. In addition, EU NAVFOR and its personnel enjoy the right of unrestricted communication and are not liable for any damage or loss of civilian or government property related to operational necessities; archives, documents and official correspondence of EU NAVFOR are inviolable; and EU NAVFOR and its personnel are exempt from paying duties, fees, tolls, taxes and similar charges. Contracts concluded by EU NAVFOR in the host state are governed by the proper law of the contract (the law chosen by the parties). The EU force commander is authorised to take charge of the repatriation of deceased personnel and, lastly, any dispute between the parties is to be settled by diplomatic means.

In addition to Operation Atalanta, the Council of the EU established, within the framework of the EU comprehensive approach towards Somalia, the EU Training Mission for Somalia (EUTM Somalia) with a view to responding to the priority needs of the Somali people and its new government, and to stabilising the country.

B. The EU Training Mission for Somalia

The EUTM Somalia mission was established by the Council of the EU on 15 February 2010 in order to contribute to the training of Somali security forces.[204] The mission was launched on 7 April 2010.[205]

The EUTM Somalia operation takes place with the consent of the Somali government and is based, on the one hand, on UNSC Resolution 1872 (2009), which stresses the importance of re-establishing, training, equipping and retaining Somali security forces, and which urges Member States and regional and international organisations to offer technical assistance to the Somali Security Forces. On the other hand, EUTM Somalia is based on UNSC Resolutions 1897 (2009), which recalls the resolutions on Somalia and reaffirms the UN's respect for the sovereignty, territorial integrity, political independence and unity of Somalia.

---

[204] Council Decision 2010/96/CFSP, [2010] OJ L44/16, amended and extended by Council Decision 2011/483/CFSP of 28 July 2011, [2011] OJ L198/37, and extended further on 21 December 2012 by Council Decision 2012/835/CFSP, [2012] OJ L357/13.
[205] Council Decision 2010/197/CFSP, [2010] OJ L87/33.

The EU military training is focused on developing the command and control of the Somali National Security Forces, with a view of transferring EU training expertise to local actors, as defined in the Crisis Management Concept approved by the Council of the EU on 17 November 2009. Since 9 August 2011, the EU mission Commander is Colonel Michael Beary. By the end of 2012, more than 3000 Somali soldiers and officers had been trained.

The EU military training is carried out mainly in Uganda, with an element based in Nairobi. Since 8 January 2013, EUTM Somalia has also had a presence in Mogadishu. This presence includes the deployment of an initial preparatory planning team and other personnel from the mission headquarters. In particular, the plan is to have mentors, trainers and advisors deployed in Somalia as soon as possible.

As is always the case, the implementation of the mission is monitored politically by the PSC and militarily by the European Military Committee, while the High Representative ensures that the mission is implemented in accordance with the Union's external action as a whole, including the Union's development programmes. Participation in EUTM Somalia is open to third states. The EU shares its classified information in relation to the operation with the third states concerned and with the UN, the African Union (AU) and, in particular, AMISON, whose mandate is to support transitional governmental structures, train the Somali security forces and support Somalia in its battle against Al-Shabaab militants.

In addition to the two military operations (Operation Atalanta and EUTM Somalia), the EU has established a civilian mission, called the EU Civilian Mission on Regional Maritime Capacity building in the Horn of Africa (EUCAP Nestor).

C. The EU Civilian Mission on Regional Maritime Capacity Building in the Horn of Africa

EUCAP Nestor was established by Council Decision 2012/389/CFSP of 16 July 2012,[206] in order to achieve the dual objective of, on the one hand, strengthening the rule of law in Somalia by focusing primarily on the new federal government, on the regions of Putland and Somaliland, and on supporting the development of a coastal police force and the judiciary; and, on the other hand, strengthening the sea-going maritime capacity of Djibouti, Kenya, Seychelles and Somalia. Following an invitation from the Tanzanian authorities, EUCAP Nestor is also to be deployed in Tanzania.

EUCAP Nestor has a unified chain of command. Its mission headquarters are in Djibouti. It has a project cell for identifying and implementing projects. The Director of the Civilian Planning and Conduct Capability (CPCC) within the EEAS acts as the Civilian Operation Commander for the mission. The responsibility for, and the exercise command and control at the theatre level of, EUCAP Nestor is assured by a Head of Mission, who at present is Mr Jacques Launay.[207] As with other EU missions, the PSC, under the responsibility of the Council of the EU and of the High Representative, exercises political control and determines the strategic direction of the mission. EUCAP Nestor is also open to the participation of third states.

---

[206] Council Decision 2012/389/CFSP of 16 July 2012, [2012] OJ L187/40.
[207] 'Political and Security Committee Decision of 17 July 2012 (2012/426/CSFP), [2012] OJ L198/16.

The tasks of EUCAP Nestor do not include any executive function, but the mission does contribute, among other things, to providing assistance to the authorities in the region in effectively organising the coastguard function, delivering training courses, assisting Somalia in developing its own land-based coastal policy capability, identifying priority equipment capability gaps, assisting in strengthening national legislation and the rule of law, and promoting and strengthening regional cooperation in the field of maritime capacity building.[208]

EUCAP Nestor constitutes an important element in the fight against piracy as a particular form of organised crime in that it maximises synergies between the civilian and the military aspects of the fight against piracy and armed robbery. It also reinforces the ability of countries such as Djibuti, Kenya, Seychelles and Tanzania to fight piracy and face other challenges, such as illegal fishing and trafficking. Furthermore, it works in an integrated and complementary manner with other instruments of the EU, in particular in the fields of humanitarian aid and development cooperation, and within the framework of the EU Strategic Framework for the Horn of Africa.

Therefore, EUCAP Nestor is fully complementary to the two EU military missions, and together they form a coherent and integrated CSDP package supporting the EU's comprehensive approach to fighting piracy and the EU Strategic Framework for the Horn of Africa.[209]

As part of the EU comprehensive approach, special consideration should be given to the sanctions and restrictive measures that the EU has imposed on Somalia in order to stabilise the country.

D. The EU Sanctions and Restrictive Measures against Somalia

The EU has the power to impose restrictive measures and sanctions (the two terms are interchangeable) in pursuit of the specific objectives set out in the TEU. CFSP decisions imposing sanctions are adopted on the basis of Article 29 of the TEU either autonomously or on the basis of UNSC resolutions. The EU CFSP sanctions and restrictive measures may be of a diplomatic nature and target governments of third countries, or non-state entities and individuals (such as terrorists). Such measures may include arms embargoes, trade restrictions (import and export bans), financial restrictions, restrictions on admission of persons (visa or travel bans) or other measures, as appropriate. Where the CFSP decision provides for the interruption or reduction, in part or completely, of economic and financial relations with one or more third countries, the Council adopts the necessary measures on the basis of Article 215 TFEU.[210]

For the purpose of establishing peace and stability in Somalia, the EU has adopted an array of restrictive measures against Somalia and certain Somali entities and individuals. As early as 2002, the EU imposed an arms delivery embargo on Somalia (Common Position 2002/960/CFSP of 10 December 2002)[211] following the adoption

---

[208] Art 3 of Council Decision 2012/389/CFSP of 16 July 2012, [2012] OJ L187/40.

[209] Council Conclusions of 14 November 2011, n 12 above.

[210] For the history of EU Policy on sanctions see J Kreutz, 'Hard Measures by a Soft Power? Sanctions Policy of the European Union' (Bonn, Bonn International Center for Conversion 2006), available at http://www.bicc.de/uploads/tx_bicctools/paper45.pdf.

[211] [2002] OJ L334/1.

of UNSC Resolutions 733 (1992), 1356 (2001) and 1425 (2002) relating to an arms embargo against Somalia. The EU arms delivery embargo included a prohibition of

> the supply or sale of arms and related material of all types, including weapons and ammunition, military vehicles and equipment, paramilitary equipment and spare parts for the aforementioned to Somalia by nationals of Member States or from the territories of Member States

irrespective of whether they originated in their territories (Article 1(1) Common Position 2002/960/CFSP of 10 December 2002). In addition, the EU prohibited (in Article 1(2) of Common Position 2002/960/CFSP)

> The direct or indirect supply to Somalia of technical advice, financial and other assistance and training related to military activities, including in particular technical training and assistance related to the provision, manufacture, maintenance or use of the items mentioned in paragraph 1, by nationals of Member States or from the territories of the Member States.

On 16 February 2009, the Council of the EU adopted Common Position 2009/138/CFSP which, in implementation of UNSC Resolution 1844 (2008), repealed Common Position 2002/960/CFSP and introduced exceptions to the arms embargo whenever the supply or sale of arms or related material was

> intended solely for the support of or use by the AMISOM mission . . . or for the sole use of states and regional organisations undertaking measures in accordance with paragraph 6 of UNSCR 1851 (2008) and paragraph 10 of UNSCR 1846 (2008)

or was intended 'solely for the purpose of helping to develop security sector institutions, . . . and in the absence of a negative decision by the Committee established by paragraph 11 of UNSCR 751 (1992)' or concerned the supply of

> non-lethal military equipment intended solely forhumanitarian or protective use, or of material intended for institution building programmes of the Union, or Member States, including in the field of security, carried out within the framework of the Peace and Reconciliation Process, as approved in advance by the Sanctions Committee, and to protective clothing, including flak jackets and military helmets, temporarily exported to Somalia by UN personnel, representatives of the media and humanitarian and development workers and associated personnel for their personal use only.[212]

In addition, the Common Position 2009/138/CFSP introduced certain restrictive measures such as a travel ban and a freezing of the assets of the persons and entities designated by the UN Sanctions Committee (listed in the Annex to the Common Position) as

> engaging in or providing support for acts that threaten the peace, security or stability of Somalia, including acts that threaten the Djibouti Agreement of 18 August 2008 or the political process, or threaten the TFIs (ie the Transitional Federal Institutions of Somalia) or AMISOM by force,

as 'having acted in violation of the arms embargo and related measures' or as having obstructed the delivery of humanitarian assistance to Somalia, or access to or distribu-

---

[212] Art 1(3) of 2009/138/CFSP.

tion of humanitarian assistance in Somalia (Article 2 of Common Position 2009/138/CFSP).[213]

On 1 March 2010, the Council of the EU adopted Decision 2010/126/CFSP implementing UNSC Resolution 1907 (2009), which called upon all states to inspect, in accordance with their national law and with international law, all cargoes to and from Somalia in their territory, including seaports and airports, if they had reasonable grounds to believe that the cargo contained items the supply, sale, transfer or export of which was prohibited under the general and complete arms embargo to Somalia pursuant to paragraph 5 of UNSC Resolution 733 (1992), as amended by subsequent resolutions.[214]

On 26 April 2010, the Council of the EU adopted Decision 2010/231/CFSP consolidating into a single legal document its previous decisions and instruments and implementing UNSC Resolution 1916 (2010), which, on the one hand, eased some restrictions to enable the delivery of supplies and technical assistance by international, regional and subregional organisations, and ensured delivery of urgently needed humanitarian assistance by the UN, while, on the other hand, incorporating the list of persons and entities which were subject to restrictive measures adopted by the UN Sanctions Committee (established in paragraph 11 of UNSC Resolutions 751, 1992) on 12 April 2010.[215]

On 15 October 2012, the Council of the EU adopted Decision 2012/633/CFSP implementing UNSC Resolution 2060 (2012), which amended the arms embargo in order to ease the supply, sale or transfer of weapons and military equipment, and the supply of direct or indirect technical advice, financial and other assistance and training related to military activities, solely for the support of or use by the UN Political Office for Somalia, and which also updated the list of persons and entities subject to restrictive measures as decided by the UN Sanctions Committee (decisions of 11 July 2012, 25 July 2012 and 23 August 2012).[216]

Finally, it should be noted that on 6 March 2013 the UNSC Resolution 2093 approved the suspension of the arms embargo relating to the purchase of light weapons by the Somali government for the period of one year, but retained certain restrictions on the procurement of heavy arms. The UNSC also exempted from the embargo the delivery of weapons and military equipment intended for the development of the security forces of the Federal Government of Somalia and for the security of the Somali people.

Asset freeze and export bans require EU implementing legislation, and the EU has adopted a series of regulations, on the basis of Article 215 TFEU, which provide for the freezing of funds and economic resources of the persons and entities subject to the restrictive measures, and for a ban on the provision of certain services to those persons and entities.

The aforementioned EU measures bind the Member States and are directly implemented by them. Indeed, although EU sanctions are designed to have political effect in Somalia, restrictive measures only apply within the territories of the EU that are within the territory of the EU Member States, including their airspace. In addition,

---

[213] [2009] OJ L46/73.
[214] [2010] OJ L51/18.
[215] [2010] OJ L105/17.
[216] [2012] OJ L182/47. See also Council Decision 2012/388/CFSP ([2012] OJ L187/38) and Council Decision 2011/635/CFSP ([2011] OJ L249/12).

they apply to EU citizens and nationals of the EU Member States, whether or not they are in the EU, to companies and organisations and their branches, incorporated under the law of a Member State, irrespective of whether they are in the EU, to any business done in whole or in part in the EU, and on board aircraft or vessels under the jurisdiction of a Member State. In short, these EU sanctions do not apply extraterritorially.

The EU targeted sanctions ('restrictive measures' in EU terminology) against Somalia have to comply with the requirements of due process and the rule of law. For that purpose, the Council of the EU notifies persons and entities targeted by an asset freeze or travel ban of the measures taken against them. At the same time, it brings to their attention the legal remedies available: they can ask the Council to reconsider its decision by providing observations on the listing and they can challenge the measures before the General Court of the EU.[217] In addition, EU sanctions must respect international law, human rights and fundamental freedoms, and the international obligations of the EU and its Member States, in particular the World Trade Organization Agreement.[218]

The EU's targeted sanctions contain an expiry or review clause in order to ensure that they are repealed or adapted in response to developments in Somalia.

The EU is not alone in its efforts to fight piracy in the Horn of Africa and its comprehensive approach includes cooperation with other international actors present in the region.

E. EU Cooperation with Other International Actors

The EU has taken initiatives to align its counter-piracy action with that of other international actors, as well as, in the absence of a unique international chain of command, to unify effort by means of international cooperation. Among the many actors and modalities of cooperation, the following are worthy of note.

The EU has established a very close cooperation with the UN and has been a major actor in the implementation of the UNSC resolutions dealing with counter-piracy. In particular, the EU welcomed the establishment of the UN Assistance Mission in Somalia in June 2013, which, according to UNSC Resolution 2102 (2013), supports the Federal Governement of Somalia in the process of peace and reconciliation. The EU is also actively engaged in various international initiatives within the UN framework, in particular within the framework of the Contact Group on Piracy off the Coast of Somalia, established in 2009 following the adoption of UNSC Resolution 1851 (2008). The Contact Group is an international cooperation mechanism, which serves as a point of contact among affected and contributing states, international organisations and industries concerned, for all aspects which are relevant in combating piracy. It deals with all aspects of the fight against piracy (paragraph 4 of UNSC Resolution 1851 (2008)). The Contact Group is assisted by the UN Secretariat and the IMO, and by four working groups dealing respectively with operational coordination (WG1),

---

[217] 'Guidelines on Implementation and Evaluation of Restrictive Measures', Council Document 15579/03 of 8 December 2003. See also 'EU Best Practices', Council Document 13851/4/04 REV4 of 29 December 2004, 15115/05 of 29 November 2005 and 10533/06 of 14 June 2006.

[218] 'Basic Principles on the use of Restrictives Measures', Council Document 10198/1/04 REV1 of 7 June 2004.

legal issues (WG2), interrelations with shipping industry (WG3) and communication activity (WG4).[219] On 1 January 2014 the EU assumed the chairmanship of the contact group for one year.

The EU also cooperates with the IMO, which has made the issue of combating piracy an important part of its work. It is worth recalling 2001 IMO Assembly Resolution No 50, entitled Code of Practice for the Investigation of the Crimes of Piracy and Armed Robbery against Ships,[220] 2005 IMO Assembly Resolution No 51, entitled Piracy and Armed Robbery against Ships in Waters off the Coast of Somalia,[221] and the several pertinent circulars of the IMO Maritime Safety Committee containing recommendations to governments to prevent and suppress piracy.[222] These instruments contain non-binding guidelines for owners, operators, masters and crews of ships and are. In addition, IMO Document No 56, 'Best Management Practices to Deter Piracy in the Gulf of Aden and Off the Coast of Somalia', contains useful operational measures such as recommended routes, transit corridors, procedures and controls.

Above all, there is the 2009 IMO (Djibouti) Code of Conduct concerning the Repression of Piracy and Armed Robbery against Ships in the Western Indian Ocean and the Gulf of Aden, which has been signed by the representatives of Djibouti, Ethiopia, Kenya, Madagascar, Maldives, Seychelles, Somalia, the United Republic of Tanzania and Yemen, Comoros, Egypt, Eritrea, Jordan, Mauritius, Oman, Saudi Arabia, Sudan and the UAE—a total 18 countries from the 21 eligible. The Code of Conduct takes into account and promotes the implementation of those aspects of UNSC Resolutions 1816 (2008), 1838 (2008), 1846 (2008) and 1851 (2008) and of UN General Assembly Resolution 63/111, which fall within the competence of IMO.

In particular, the signatories to the Code of Conduct have agreed to cooperate, in a manner compatible with international law, in: (i) the investigation, arrest and prosecution of persons who are reasonably suspected of having committed acts of piracy and armed robbery against ships, including those inciting or intentionally facilitating such acts; (ii) the interdiction and seizure of suspect ships and property on board such ships; (iii) the rescue of ships, persons and property subject to piracy and armed robbery, and the facilitation of proper care, treatment and repatriation of seafarers, fishermen, other shipboard personnel and passengers subject to such acts, particularly those who have been subjected to violence; and (iv) the conduct of shared operations—both among signatory states and with navies from countries outside the region—such as nominating law enforcement or other authorised officials to embark on patrol ships or aircraft of another signatory.

In addition, the Code of Conduct provides for the sharing of related information, through a number of centres and national focal points using existing infrastructures and arrangements for ship-to-shore-to-ship communications (ie the Regional Maritime Rescue Coordination Centre in Mombasa, Kenya and the Rescue Coordination Sub-Centre in Dar es Salaam, Tanzania) and the regional maritime information centre, which is being established in Sana'a, Yemen. The signatories also undertook to review their national legislation with a view to ensuring that there are laws in place to

---

[219] Contact Group website: http://www.thecgpcs.org/main.do?action=main.
[220] IMO Assembly Resolution A.922(22) No 50.
[221] IMO Assembly Resolution A.1002(25) No 51.
[222] MSC/Circ 622/Rev.1 No 52, 622/rev.2, 623/rev.3 No 53, 623/rev.4 No 54 and MSC 1/Circ 1334 No 55.

criminalise piracy and armed robbery against ships, and to make adequate provision for the exercise of jurisdiction, conduct of investigations and prosecution of alleged offenders.[223]

IMO contracting governments also make use of the valuable Long-Range Identification and Tracking (LRIT) system, a secure satellite-based system for tracking ships. In order to facilitate the efforts of EU NAVFOR and NATO, the IMO has established the Information Distribution Facility, which provides the LRIT information of ships off the coast of Somalia and the wider Indian Ocean to naval forces.

In order to implement the EUCAP Nestor mission, the EU has formed strategic partnerships, in addition to that formed with the IMO, UNODC and the United National Development Programme (UNDP). EUCAP Nestor also complements other EU projects relating to maritime security, such as the Critical Maritime Routes Programme, which reinforces maritime governance under the Instrument of Stability, and provides financial support to the implementation of the Eastern and Southern African-Indian Ocean Regional Strategy and Action Plan against Piracy under the European Development Fund (EDF). In particular, the EU is heavily engaged in follow-up actions and was instrumental in the adoption of the Eastern and Southern Africa–Indian Ocean (ESA-IO) regional strategy, which provides for a regional framework to prevent and combat piracy and to promote maritime security through a three-pillar approach, consisting of: the development and implementation of a Somalia Inland Action Plan to counter and prevent piracy; the encouragement of states in the region to prosecute pirates, with the financial and technical support of the international community; and the strengthening of regional states' capacities to secure their maritime zones. The Somalia Inland Action Plan underpins the ESA-IO Regional Strategy and includes provisions on information exchange, cooperation, joint action and capacity building measures.[224]

The EU is supporting AMISOM significantly, with financial support of more than €325 million having been disbursed between 2007 and 2012, with the aims of creating the security conditions necessary for peace and stability, and providing protection to key infrastructures to enable the Somali Transitional Federal Institutions to carry out their functions. The EU has supported the recent UNSC Resolution authorising the increase of AMISOM's strength to more than 17,000 persons.[225]

The EU has taken the initiative to establish the Operation Atalanta Maritime Security Centre—Horn of Africa (MSCHOA), a civil–military coordination centre with the task of safeguarding merchant ships operating in the region from acts of piracy. MSCHOA possesses an internet portal enabling all those involved in the region to liaise and communicate. The EU supports other programmes such as the

---

[223] Information provided by IMO: http://www.imo.org/OurWork/Security/PIU/Pages/DCoC.aspx.

[224] 'Joint Communiqué from the Eastern and Southern Africa—Indian Ocean Ministers and European Union High Representative at the 2nd Regional Ministerial Meeting on Piracy and Maritime Security in the Eastern and Southern Africa and Indian Ocean Region, October 2010, Grand Bay, Republic of Mauritius', available at http://www.consilium.europa.eu/uedocs/cms_data/docs/pressdata/EN/foraff/116942.pdf.

[225] But see the latest AU report to the UNSC on AMISOM setting out continuing challenges for the mission, including in particular resource limitations, whilst stressing the overall positive direction in which Somalia is evolving: Letter dated 21 June 2013 from the UN Secretary-General to the President of the Security Council transmitting the Report of the Chairperson of the African Union Commission on the implementation of the African Union Mission in Somalia, submitted in pursuance of paragraph 8 of Security Council resolution 2093 (2013).

Regional Maritime Security Programme (MASE), which tackles piracy on land, and the Progamme Enhancing Maritime Safety and Security through Information Sharing and Capacity Building (MARSIC), a European Maritime Cooperation project in the Gulf of Aden and the Indian Ocean, covering a period of implementation of 5 years (2010–15) with a budget of €6 million, which aims to enhance maritime capacity building in countries party to the IMO (Djibouti) Code of Conduct, with the goals of information sharing, education and training, improvement of the legal framework and capacity building for public bodies in partner countries. For operational issues, the Shared Awareness and Deconfliction (SHADE) mechanism has emerged as a military forum which includes other international actors in order to discuss 'their successes and challenges, share best practices and coordinate forthcoming activities'[226] with regard to their fight against piracy.

The efforts of the EU to counter piracy in the Gulf of Aden have been rendered more effective by means of cooperation with other multinational missions in the region, in particular with Operation Ocean Shield, led by NATO, and with Combined Task Force 151, led by the US. The EU also coordinates its action with several states which are operating independly in the region under different structures, which share the common objective of combating piracy as laid down in the UNSC resolutions, and which benefit from the enforcement powers under those resolutions, as well as from the acceptance of the Somali Transition Federal Government. States which have deployed naval ships and/or aircraft include Japan, China, the Russian Federation, India, Malaysia, the Republic of Korea, Saudi Arabia, the Islamic Republic of Iran and Yemen.[227] The EU's Operation Atalanta, together with the Combined Task Force, NATO, China, Japan and the Republic of Korea, supports the so-called 'Internationally Recommended Transit Corridor' (IRTC), which has been endorsed by the IMO, according to which commercial ships which have been registered in advance using MSCHOA are enabled to transit 'high risk' seas at agreed times, protected by the naval forces patrolling the area, with a high degree of success.[228]

Other relevant cooperative frameworks include the UK Maritime Trade Organization Office in Dubai, which also acts as a point of contact for merchant vessels, putting them in contact with military forces in the region, and the Maritime Liaison Office, which facilitates the exchange of information between the US Navy, the Combined Maritime Forces (a multinational naval partnership of 27 nations which aims to promote security and stability in the most important shipping lanes of the world) and the commercial maritime community within the United States Central Command's area of responsibility.

It is pertinent now to assess the CFSP aspects of the EU action against piracy and armed robbery off the Somali Coast.

[226] '18th SHADE Meets to Discuss Counter-Piracy", communication posted by Combined Maritime Forces on 11 January 2011.
[227] Geiss and Petrig, n 9 above, 17 and 49.
[228] Report by the UN Secretary-General on UNSC Resolution 1846, 13 November 2009, para 37.

F. Assessment

EU law does not provide an autonomous definition of piracy, nor does it have an autonomous delimitation of EU jurisdiction with regard to its punishment either *ratione materia* or *ratione loci*. These elements of piracy are borrowed by the EU from international law. As discussed above, general international law, as reflected in UNCLOS, deals only with piracy on the high seas (and the EEZ) but does not categorise piracy as an international crime on which criminal prosecution can be based, nor does it vest states with the necessary jurisdiction to enforce it or adjudicate on it. UNCLOS's main concern is to ensure freedom of the high seas, and the enforcement powers laid down in Articles 110 and 105 are addressed against pirate ships and their entire crew, rather than against individual persons (pirates) or the underlying criminal structures.

In the case of piracy off the coast of Somalia, the UNCLOS deficiencies—in particular, its narrow scope in targeting different forms of maritime violence, the geographical limitations of its enforcement regime to the high seas and its lack of application to Somali territorial waters, including inland Somalia—have been remedied by the UNSC in Resolutions 1816, 1846, 1851, 1897 and 1918, which expand the range of enforcement competences, including the notion of armed robbery at sea, acting under Chapter VII of the UN Charter, ie justifying its intervention as a question of threat to world peace rather than a specific question of piracy and armed robbery per se on which states remain competent. These resolutions, the scope of which has been endorsed by the Transitional Federal Government of Somalia, do not have the effect of modifying the rules of general international law or international treaty law but constitute a *lex specialis* for addressing the particular situation created by the upsurge of piracy off the coast of Somalia, justified by its threat to peace and security in the world. In addition, the UNSC has invoked in its resolutions a number of counter-terrorist conventions (the SUA and the Hostage Conventions) in order to cover the acts of violence and armed robbery in the Gulf of Aden as comprehensively as possible.

Therefore, the EU CFSP legal framework for its Atalanta, EUTM Somalia and EUCAP Nestor operations and for the accompanying CFSP sanctions regime is governed by several legal regimes depending on whether pirates are pursued on the high seas (governed exclusively by UNCLOS), in Somalia's territorial waters (governed by UNSC Resolutions 1816, 1846 and 1897) or on Somalia mainland (in conformity with Resolution 1851 paragraph 6, which authorises the taking of 'all necessary measures that are appropriate in Somalia, for the purpose of suppressing acts of piracy and armed robbery at sea' and therefore implies the exercise of a wide margin of discretion in pursuit of their objective to eradicate piracy and armed robbery at sea off the coast of Somalia), and depending of the type of act of violence (the SUA and the Hostage Conventions).

Since its launch, Operation Atalanta has had a success rate of 100% in providing escorts to vessels of the WFP delivering humanitarian aid to the Somali people; it has also been succesful in providing protection to AMISOM shipments, which are critical to the success of the AU operation in Somalia; and has ensured the protection of other vulnerable shipping within the IRTC, as well as providing other assistance. Confrontation with pirates very rarely ends in death, although this has happened under the command of the forces of individual states (eg by the French Special Forces).

Experience has shown that the identification and consideration of the development and execution of a pirate attack is key in order for the counter-piracy strategy to succeed. So far, a well-developed organisation has been identified as the key element that sustains Somali pirates:[229] they continue to have 'well-defined networks and hierarchies of financiers, senior leaders and seagoing pirate crews',[230] and some private organisations even have 'chain of command' structures and provide training for new recruits. In addition, the pirates plan the attack on shore and take account of the operating environment in order to make the attack more effective. The use of 'mother ships' is also an important element in the success of the attack. Finally, pirates have access to GPS coordinates via informants with access to the tracking data of ships, and this allows them to locate target vessels in vast expanses of sea.[231]

Operation Atalanta has had to face important legal difficulties which stem from the plurality of the applicable legal regimes and the requirements of international human rights law, including the principle of non-refoulement. Owing to lacunae and deficiencies in both international and national law with regard to the treatment of suspected pirates and armed robbers, particular problems arise relating to jurisdiction and respect for legal requirements relating to domestic law, international humanitarian law, refugee law, international human rights law and the principle of non-refoulement when suspected pirates and armed robbers are captured, detained and prosecuted. For those reasons in particular, the Member States of the EU show a certain degree of reluctance to prosecute in their domestic jurisdictions. In order to resolve this issue, the EU and some of its Member States have concluded agreements in order to have suspected pirates and armed robbers transferred and prosecuted in the coastal states in the region of the Horn of Africa. In such agreements the EU has sought to ensure compliance with the requirements of international law, including human rights law and EU law.

Since the establishment of EUTM Somalia, considerable progress has been made in the development of the Somali National Security Forces, which have contributed significantly to improving security and living conditions in Somalia. However, the Somali National Security Forces are not yet fully capable of fulfilling their mission without external support. EUTM Somalia has been requested to continue its support on capacity building, encompassing not only training but also the deployment of EU advisers to the Somali Ministry of Defence and support the Somali Security Sector Development.

So far, EUCAP Nestor has accomplished three main objectives. First, it has managed to overcome logistical difficulties relating to the opening of its mission headquarters in Djibouti. Secondly, in Seychelles, the mission has been able to deliver monitoring, advice and training. Thirdly, the mission has established relations with key Somali interlocutors and has held a first seminar with participants from both federal and Puntland authorities in Djibouti.

However, the mission remains only partially operational owing, inter alia, on the one hand, to the absence of legal agreements with Kenya and Tanzania which have

---

[229] See in particular the Lang Report, n 4 above.
[230] Testimony of St Caldwell and J Pendleton before the Subcommittee on Coast Guard and Maritime Transportation, USA House of Representatives, GAO 11-449T.
[231] Wilson, n 7 above.

prevented the mission from achieving the wider political presence it was intended to have and, on the other hand, the need to adapt to the request by the new Somali government to assist in addressing maritime security more broadly, a request that would require an adaptation of the mandate of the mission.

With little international assistance, the newly created Puntland Maritime Police Force (PMPF) has cleared pirate gangs from their stronghold in Eyl and a number of other coastal towns. Local understanding and intelligence has reportedly endeared the PMPF, who also engage in fisheries protection and humanitarian assistance, to the communities in which they operate. While it has been successful, the PMPF lacks the resources to confront pirate gangs across the wide expanse of the region's coast. Puntland's annual state budget was a reported $20 million in 2010, while the pirates took in an estimated $160 million in ransoms.

A lasting solution to the piracy problem requires the international community to begin shifting resources away from the military-centric strategy towards a programme for regional maritime security capacity building. In particular, the EU, NATO and other counter-piracy actors must deepen their engagement with, and support for, authorities in Somalia's pirate-prone areas, primarily the autonomous states of Puntland and Galmudug. A similar problem exists in neighbouring Galmudug, where authorities have expressed plans to launch operations in the pirate hub of Hobyo, but lament the lack of sponsoring by international organisations.There are numerous ways that the international community can support local counter-piracy initiatives. Coastal infrastructure, such as roads, docks, and radar stations, need to be developed, while maritime police forces require training, vessels and (most importantly) payment. Investing in maritime security capacity building, stabilisation, the rule of law, the eradication of poverty, trade preferences and development, and humanitarian aid are the necessary strategic elements that complement the EU's comprehensive approach, as analysed in the following pages.

III. THE NON-CFSP EXTERNAL ACTION INSTRUMENTS TO COMBAT PIRACY

The EU comprehensive approach towards Somalia comforms to the 'whole of government approach' developed by the Organisation for Economic Cooperation and Development in 2006, and includes all EU services responsible for improving governance, strengthening security, providing humanitarian aid, as well as working towards better education and economic development. In particular, the EU has taken action in the fields of development cooperation, trade preferences and humanitarian aid, together with specific action under the Cotonou agreement.

A. The EU Development Programme for Somalia

The EU policy in the field of development cooperation with Somalia has as its primary objective the reduction and, in the long-term, the eradication, of poverty (as envisaged in Article 208 TFEU, The European Consensus on the EU Development Policy), which is implemented in a manner which is compatible with the development action by the EU Member States; action in this field is mutually complementary and reinforcing.

Under the TEU, the EU has the power to adopt multiannual cooperation programmes or programmes with a thematic approach and conclude agreements with third countries and international organisations (Article 209).

The general financial framework for development cooperation in Somalia is based on the Development Cooperation Instrument (DCI), established by Regulation No 1905/2006, which covers the period between 2007 and 2013, the primary and over-arching objective of which is the eradication of poverty in partner countries and regions by means of three categories of programmes: (i) bilateral and regional geographic programmes covering cooperation with Asia, Latin America, Central Asia, the Middle East and South Africa; (ii) thematic programmes covering the following issues: investing in people, environment and sustainable management of natural resources, including energy, non-state actors, local authorities, food security, and migration and asylum; and (iii) accompanying measures for sugar-producing countries.[232]

The EU financial contribution, which amounted to 158 million in 2012, aims at developing and bringing forward the Somali peace process and preventing failed states such as Somalia from becoming safe heavens for international terrorists. The strategic framework for the EU's development cooperation with Somalia appears in the Joint Strategic Paper for Somalia (2008–2013).[233] The main areas of the EU development cooperation are governance, education, economic development and food security. Somalia also benefits from various EU thematic programmes with non-state actors and from human rights programmes. All areas of activity (including gender environment, HIV/AIDS and conflict prevention) are mainstreamed whenever possible, with the overall aim of improving the lives of the poorest and most vulnerable groups.

Somalia is also eligible for EU financial contributions under Regulation No 1889/2006 on establishing a financing instrument for the promotion of democracy and human rights worldwide of 20 December 2006 (the so-called Human Rights Instrument),[234] which aims at (i) enhancing respect for human rights and fundamental freedoms in the countries and regions where they are most threatened; (ii) supporting civil society in its role of promoting human rights and democracy, the peaceful conciliation of particular interests, and its duty of representation and political participation; (iii) supporting actions associated with human rights and democracy in areas covered by the Community guidelines; (iv) strengthening the international and regional framework in the field of the protection of human rights, justice, the rule of law and the promotion of democracy; and (v) building confidence in democratic electoral processes by enhancing their reliability and transparency, in particular through election observation.

EU aid under this instrument is granted in support of actions such as the promotion of participatory and representative democracy, processes of democratisation, mainly through civil society organisations, in particular: promoting the freedoms of association and assembly, opinion and expression; strengthening the rule of law and the independence of the judiciary; promoting political pluralism and democratic political representation; promoting the equal participation of men and women in social, economic and political life; supporting measures to facilitate the peaceful con-

---

[232] [2006] OJ L378/41. The current DCI regulation expires on 31 December 2013.
[233] European Commission, 'Somalia: Joint Strategy Paper for the Period 2008–2013' (Brussels, 2007), available at http://ec.europa.eu/development/icenter/repository/scanned_so_csp10_en.pdf.
[234] [2006] OJ L386/1.

ciliation of group interests; and, in general, protecting, mainly through civil society organisations, human rights and fundamental freedoms proclaimed in the Universal Declaration of Human Rights and other international and regional instruments.

Assistance is implemented through different means: strategy papers (which define priorities, the international situation and the activities of the main partners); annual action programmes based on the strategy papers and their possible amendments; special measures which are not provided for in the strategy papers and which may be adopted by the European Commission; and ad hoc measures so that the Commission can make small grants to human rights defenders responding to urgent protection needs. The instrument has been granted a budget of €1.104 million for the period 2007–13.

Somalia also benefits from Regulation No 1717/2006 Establishing an Instrument for Stability of 15 November 2006,[235] a financial and political instrument at the disposal of the EU. Actions under this instrument are prepared at strategic level by the EEAS and implemented by the European Commission. The instrument for stability has three objectives: (i) to respond to urgent needs due to political instability or a major disaster; (ii) to build the conditions for long-term stability. in particular by addressing some major risks and threats that prevent political security and economic development, such as terrorism, organised crime, illicit trafficking and chemical/biological/nuclear risks, but also new challenges such as pandemics, cybercrime, climate change or the protection of critical infrastructure; and (iii) to participate in the crisis management cycle by supporting EU crisis management operations under the CFSP and by helping to restore stability after a crisis or conflict.

The Instrument for Stability may be deployed for crisis response and crisis preparedness (to prevent or resolve conflict, for situations threatening to escalate into armed conflict or severe destabilisation, or when there is the urgent need to secure the conditions for the delivery of aid by the EU), including in the case of major natural disaster. The Instrument for Stability also addresses transregional risks and threats that are either natural or criminal in nature and may jeopardise the health, environment, economic development or safety conditions of people in the region. The transregional approach provided by the Instrument for Stability complements national measures provided by EU geographical instruments and contributes to strengthening the rule of law, good governance, safety and security at the regional level. In order to operate this transregional approach, regional centers of excellence (so-called Chemical, Biological, Radiological and Nuclear Security (CBRN) Centres of Excellence) are being established in Africa, including Somalia, and four key regions of the world (the Middle East, Southeast Asia, the Caucasus and Central Asia) in order to operate this transregional approach.

The Instrument for Stability can only finance operations where other financial instruments cannot respond within the necessary time frame: it cannot finance EU humanitarian assistance (which is the responsibility of the European Commission Humanitarian Aid and Civil Protection, ECHO) or finance projects lasting longer than 18 months since the latter are eligible for finance under the regular financial instruments.The total budget for the period 2007–13 is €2 billion, of which a maximum of 27% (approximately €550 million) will be spent on longer-term EU response to global

---

[235] [2006] OJ L327/1.

and transregional threats. The remaining 73% is earmarked for rapid initial responses to situations of political crisis and natural disasters.

Financial assistance with regard to the prosecution, courts, police and prison services of Somalia and other countries concerned with the fight aganst piracy[236] is carried out through a cooperation mechanism between the prosecutors of the countries concerned in order to bring together admissible evidence for legal action against major piracy financiers, negotiators and organisers. In particular, the EU lends support to international efforts to combat piracy as a form of organised crime by increasing the risk/reward ratio for those who benefit most from piracy in order to disrupt the underlying 'business model'—including by tracking and disrupting the financial flows.[237]

In addition, the EU provides assistance to the UNDP and UNODC in their work for fair and efficient piracy trials and for incarceration in Somalia. Overall, the EU and its Member States are the largest contributors to the UNODC's counter-piracy programme.[238]

With regard to maritime capacity building for Somalia, the EU has, since 2009, provided substantial funding for the Critical Maritime Routes Programme.[239] The programme is specifically focused on the security and safety of essential maritime routes in areas affected by piracy to help to secure shipping and trading lines of communication. The EU contribution to the programme amounts to €7.6 million. In addition to Somalia, the countries covered by the programme are Djibouti, Yemen, Kenya, Seychelles and Tanzania. The programme will run until 2014. Its long-term goal is to improve maritime governance by the region itself. Among the various projects funded are programmes aimed at improving information sharing in the region, capacity building, the training of maritime officials and coast guards from the region, support for surveillance and security of territorial waters by the region, and training and equipment support for national law enforcement capacities, with specific focus on the financiers and organisers of piracy.

The ongoing Maritime Security and Safety (MARSIC) project, with an budget of €6 million, supports maritime security by enhancing information sharing and training capacities; it contributes to the implementation of the regional Djibuti Code of Conduct targeted at fighting piracy and armed conflict against ships; it focuses on capacity building and training of maritime administrative staff, officials and coast-guards from the region, including assistance to stting up the Djibuti Regional Training Centre for maritime affairs; and it supports the operations of the Regional Information Sharing Centre, which reports on piracy incidents from Sana'a (Yemen), and includes €1.6 million for a police support component implemented by INTERPOL.[240] INTERPOL supports national law enforcement capacities to combat maritime piracy by providing necessary training and equipment to perform effective investigations including on piracy financiers and organisers.

---

[236] Information provided by the EEAS, available at www.eeas.europa.eu/piracy/judicial_cooperation_en.htm.

[237] Ibid.

[238] T Bargfrede, 'The EU Fight against Piracy in the Horn of Africa, Actions under the Common Security and Defence Policy (CSDP) and the Comprehensive Approach' (Brussels, Crisis Management and Planning Directorate, European External Action Service, 28 March 2012), available at http://ec.europa.eu/transport/modes/maritime/events/doc/2012–03–28-piracy/1–1-session1-eeas-bargfrede-csdp.pdf.

[239] Source: EEAS, available at http://www.eeas.europa.eu/piracy/regional_maritime_capacities_en.htm.

[240] Source: EU Instrument for Stability brochure, available at http://ec.europa.eu/europeaid/infopoint/publications/europeaid/documents/207a_en.pdf.

Overall, the EU has indeed become the largest donor of development aid to Somalia, having committed €315.4 million since 2008 for governance, security and economic growth. An additional €200 million has been budgeted for 2011–13, which will allow the EU to strengthen its engagement and to support new activities in these fields. A portion of these new funds will be directed at supporting the fishing industry and helping coastal communities to tackle some of the root causes of piracy. There will also be increased EU support to enable the Somali rule of law and justice sector to deal better with crimes like piracy and armed robbery.[241] The EU is helping Somalia to build democratic structures and strong administrations which will support the implementation of the political transition. This includes strengthening the rule of law and security, a constitutional process based on national reconciliation, effective governance and the enhancement of the capabilities of non-state actors. At present, the EU investment in this field amounts to €113 million. The EU provides funding for Somalia's Transitional Federal Institutions through cooperation activities in the governance sector managed by the UN. Part of the EU's current assistance in this area is implemented in Somalia via the UNDP Rule of Law and Security Programme.[242] The EU supports food security, the development of livestock and infrastructure, livelihoods, and projects for the rural and urban supply of water with a financial aid of €135 million. A new project of €25 million, from the Millenium Development Goals, tackles food security in Puntland, while €85 million has been made available to improve education.

As one of the EU initiatives to counter piracy in the East African and Western Indian Ocean region, the Joint Research Centre of the European Commission is running, at the request of the European Parliament, a Pilot Project on Piracy, Maritime Awareness and Risks (PMAR), which is financed by €1 million from the EU through the Commission's Directorate General for Development and Cooperation—(EuropeAid). The PMAR project examines technologies which increase maritime awareness and which could be used by authorities in regions affected by piracy. An experimental system with state-of-the-art software is under development. The system integrates data from vessel-based reporting systems, such as LRIT, the Automated Identification System and the Vessel Monitory System, and from earth observation systems (eg vessel detections from satellite images) into a single maritime picture. With this system it is possible to indicate the estimated ship positions in real time on a digital map, with an update rate of once every 15 minutes. The system also includes the production of maps on ship traffic density and contains a historic piracy risk occurrence.

Finally, while not directly focused on counter-piracy, actions to support the fisheries sector of the region and to suppress illegal fishing are considered to have indirect positive effects in improving regional maritime security capacities at large. In this regard, there are various technical assistance programmes funded by the EU, the ultimate aim of which is to improve local and regional capacities for the sustainable exploitation of fisheries resources. Thus, the EU assists with surveillance of illegal unregulated and unreported fisheries through the Fisheries Partnership Agreements in the Indian Ocean[243] (including technical assistance through the Cotonou Agreement

---

[241] Source: EEAS, 'The Way Out: Stabilisation in Somalia through Assistance and Dialogue', available at http://www.eeas.europa.eu/piracy/stabilisation_en.htm.

[242] Bargfrede, n 238 above.

[243] Source: EEAS website, n 239 above.

(ACP FISH II) and Environment and Sustainable Management of Natural Resources including Energy programmes). A Regional Surveillance Plan for Fisheries (2007–2011) has been funded with €10 million, and the SmartFish Programme, funded with €21 million, is currently underway with the aim of improving the capacities for the sutainable exploitation of fisheries resources, including support of the Somali fishing industry.

B. Somalia as beneficiary of the Cotonou Agreement

Somalia has not ratified the so-called Cotonou Agreement, the treaty between the EU and the Member States, on the one part, and the 79 ACP countries on the other—which was signed in June 2000 and entered into force in 2003, and was subsequently revised in 2005 and 2010.[244] Nevertheless, in the absence of an internationally recognised national government and of functioning institutions able to ensure signature and ratification, Somalia has been granted access to resources for development finance cooperation (Decision No 2/2008 of the ACP–EC Council of Ministers of 18 November 2008 on the allocation of resources to Somalia from the tenth EDF).[245]

In addition to the reduction and eventual eradication of poverty, the Cotonou Agreement also aims to contribute to the sustainable development and gradual integration of ACP countries into the world economy, and in particular to the fight against impunity and promotion of criminal justice through the International Criminal Court. The Cotonou Agreement is designed to last for a period of 20 years and is based on four main principles: (i) equality of partners and ownership of development strategies, which means that it is up to ACP states to determine how their societies and economies should develop; (ii) open participation, which means that, in addition to the central government as the main actor, partnership under the Cotonou Agreement is open to other actors (eg civil society, the private sector and local governments); (iii) dialogue and mutual obligations, which means that the Cotonou Agreement is not merely a pot of money, and that the signatories have assumed mutual obligations (eg respect for human rights) which will be monitored through continuing dialogue and evaluation; and (iv) differentiation and regionalisation, which means that cooperation agreements vary according to each partner's level of development, needs, performance and long-term development strategy, with special treatment given to countries that are considered the least developed or vulnerable (landlocked or island states).

The financial aid is allocated to ACP countries in five-yearly cycles under the Financial Protocol of the Cotonou Agreement and disbursed from the tenth (2008–13) EDF, an intergovernmental fund financed by the EU Member States outside the framework of the EU budget, which has a budget that has increased significantly from €13.5 billion to €22.7 billion, with €5.6 billion earmarked to support regional programmes, especially investments in regional African infrastructure projects through the EU–Africa Partnership on Infrastructure. Being the main financial instrument for development cooperation in ACP countries, the tenth EDF includes three financial envelopes: a national envelope, covering bilateral cooperation with individual ACP countries; a

---

[244] [2000] OJ L317; [2004] OJ L297; [2005] OJ L209; [2005] OJ L287; [2006] OJ L247; [2010] OJ L287. There is a consolidated version of the Agreement published by the European Commission.
[245] [2008] OJ L338/53.

regional one, covering relations with ACP regions, namely Central Africa, West Africa, Eastern and Southern Africa and Indian Ocean, the Southern African Development Community, the Caribbean and the Pacific; and a third one (intra-ACP) to address the common challenges facing ACP states that transcend geographical criteria.

The tenth EDF supports MASE, which is devoted to the implementation of the Eastern and Southern Africa–Indian Ocean Regional Strategy and Action Plan to fight piracy and promote maritime security, with €37.5 million. In particular, MASE funds a €6 million project aimed mainly at developing a strategy to tackle piracy on land in Somalia, enhancing judicial capabilities to arrest, transfer, detain and prosecute suspected pirates, addressing economic impact and financial flows relating to piracy, and improving national and regional capacities in maritime security functions, including surveillance and coastguard functions.

The intra-ACP envelope funds the African Peace Facility, which, within the Joint Africa–EU Strategy, contributes to, among other initiatives, AMISOM. The tenth EDF provides a total of €2 billion through bilateral support to the Horn countries and through a share of €645 million, available to four regional organizations, including IGAD, and through it Somalia, for regional projects.[246] Also coming under the ACP/development agenda is the political dialogue provided for the Cotonou Agreement, which is conducted by the EU not only with the countries of the Horn but also with IGAD.[247]

Decision No 2/2008 of the ACP–EC Council of Ministers of 18 November 2008 provides that Somalia will benefit from an allocation comparable to that received by countries from the ACP group which have ratified the Cotonou Agreement. This benefit comprises €215.8 million, taken from the tenth EDF reserve for national and regional cooperation for special support in favour of Somalia. From this global amount, €212 million, programmed under a special assistance strategy, is used for institution building and economic and social development activities, taking particular account of the needs of the most vulnerable sections of the population. In addition, an amount of €3.8 million is used to cover unforeseen needs, such as emergency assistance where such support cannot be financed from the EU budget. Finally, the Commission acts 'on behalf of the Somali people' for the time being in assuming the functions of National Authorising Officer for the programming and implementation of this allocation in accordance with the ACP–EC Partnership Agreement.[248]

In 2011, an ad hoc review increased support to Somalia by €175 million, to which another €25 million was added in the course of the process of the Millenium Development Goals initiative. The EU's total allocation for Somalia under the tenth EDF funding amounts to €412 million. In particular, on 23 February 2012, the EU approved the financing of €67 million from the tenth EDF African Peace Facility to support the African Union Mission in Somalia (AMISOM VII).[249]

---

[246] Source: EEAS relations with the ACP, available at http://eeas.europa.eu/acp/index_en.htm.

[247] IGAD was founded in 1996 as a regional development organisation in the Eastern part of Africa. Its headquarters are in Djibouti.

[248] Decision No 2/2008 of the ACP–EC Council of Ministers of 18 November 2008 on the allocation of resources to Somalia from the 10th European Development Fund, Doc ACP/81/083/08 ACP-CE 2119/08. The decisions has been taken pursuant to Art 93(6) of the AC–EU Partnership Agreement and in accordance to the conclusions adopted by the ACP-EU Council of Ministers on 18 November 1998.

[249] European Commission Decision C(2012) 1255 of 23 February 2012.

C. The EU Special Trade Preferences for the Development of Somalia

Somalia also benefits from the EU special trade regimes for developing countries. One such special trade regime is included in the Generalised System of Preferences (GSP), which is an autonomous trade arrangement that was created following UNCTAD recommendations to help developing countries by making it easier for them to export their products to the EU. The GSP is a specific instrument focusing on a single dimension: preferences for trade in goods. It does not have the ambition or the possibility to tackle other problems faced by developing countries. The GSP provides for reduced tariffs for goods when entering the EU market and, through the additional export revenue which is generated, fosters the income growth of developing countries and supports economic growth and job creation.

The GSP is subject to WTO law, in particular to the GATT and its so-called 'enabling clause', which allows for an exception to the WTO 'most-favoured nation' principle (ie equal treatment should be accorded to all WTO Members).

As the needs of developing countries vary widely, a differentiated approach has been taken in GSP: (i) through the so-called Standard GSP the EU provides non-reciprocal preferential access to the EU market to 176 developing countries and territories in the form of reduced tariffs on more than 6,200 tariff lines; (ii) in addition, the GSP Plus is a special incentive arrangement for sustainable development and good governance for 15 beneficiary countries which offers additional tariff reductions to developing countries that are considered to be vulnerable, provided that they have ratified and implemented 27 international conventions, including those on human rights and labour rights; (iii) finally, the Everything but Arms arrangement provides for duty-free and quota-free access for all products for the 49 least developed countries. The present, the EU scheme of generalised tariff preferences is defined by Council Regulation (EC) No 732/2008,[250] as amended by the so-called 'roll-over' Regulation No 512/2011, which extends the application of the present system until 31 December 2013.[251] A new preferential system has been laid down in EU Regulation 978/2012 of 25 October 2012, which will apply as of 1 January 2014.[252]

The EU trade relations with Somalia are governed by the framework provided by the EU trade relations with the countries belonging to IGAD, the regional development organisation in East Africa comprising eight countries which benefit from the GSP provisions under the Everything but Arms initiative, which provides duty-free access to EU markets for all products.[253] In addition, Somalia will also benefit from the trade concessions that the EU is currently negotiating under the Economic Partnership Agreements with the IGAD countries through the East African Community and Eastern and Southern Africa.

---

[250] [2008] OJ L211/1.

[251] [2011] OJ L145/28.

[252] [2012] OJ L303.

[253] In February 2001, the Council of the European Community adopted Regulation (EC) 416/2001, the so-called 'EBA [Everything But Arms] Regulation', granting duty-free access to imports of all products from LDCs except arms and ammunitions, without any quantitative restrictions (with the exception of bananas, sugar and rice for a limited period). The EBA was later incorporated into the GSP Council Regulation (EC) No 2501/2001. The most recent legislative text is Regulation (EU) No 978/2012 of the European Parliament and of the Council of 25 October 2012 applying a scheme of generalised tariff preferences and repealing Council Regulation (EC) No 732/2008, [2012] OJ L303/1.

D. EU Humanitarian Aid and Civil Protection in Somalia

Somalia is a recipient of EU humanitarian aid—the ad hoc assistance, relief and protection for people who are victims of natural or man-made disasters and who are in need of humanitarian assistance arising from different situations. The EU policy in the field of humanitarian aid is 'conducted in compliance with the principles of international law and with the principles of impartiality, neutrality and non-discrimination' (Article 214, paragraphs 1 and 2 of the TFEU). The TFEU envisages the establishment of a European Voluntary Humanitarian Aid Corps as a framework for joint contributions from young Europeans to the humanitarian aid operations of the Union, which is in the process of being set up (Article 214, paragraph 5 of the TFEU). The EU humanitarian aid operations are coordinated and consistent with those of international organisations and bodies, in particular those forming part of the UN system (Article 214, paragraph 6 of the TFEU). The purposes of EU humanitarian aid are to save and preserve life, to reduce or prevent suffering, and to safeguard the integrity and dignity of people.

Humanitarian aid to Somalia is governed by Regulation (EU) No 1257/96 of 20 June 1996 concerning humanitarian aid,[254] as amended by Regulation (EU) No 1882/2003 of 29 September 2003[255] and Regulation (EU) No 219/2009 of 11 March 2009.[256] It is worth noting that, under the EU regime, humanitarian aid covers not only short-term relief but also disaster prevention and reconstruction operations. Such operations last as long as is necessary and are targeted at the immediate requirements arising out of natural disasters (eg flooding, earthquakes), man-made disasters (eg outbreaks of war and fighting) or other exceptional comparable circumstances. By focusing on supplies and services, the EU policy aims to prevent and alleviate suffering. To ensure that the policy is both effective and comprehensive, coordination between the Member States and the European Commission is reinforced by cooperation with non-governmental organisations (NGOs) and international organisations.

As a short-term measure (lasting a maximum of six months), humanitarian aid is primarily intended to: (i) save life during emergencies and their immediate aftermath; (ii) provide the necessary assistance and relief to people affected by longer-lasting crises arising, in particular, from outbreaks of fighting or wars; (iii) carry out short-term rehabilitation and reconstruction work, especially on infrastructure and equipment, in the post-emergency phase; (iv) cope with the consequences of population movements by means of schemes to assist repatriation and resettlement where appropriate; and (v) ensure preparedness for the risks concerned and use a suitable rapid early warning and intervention system. The aid can also be used to finance improvements in its implementation, eg preparatory feasibility studies, project evaluation, campaigns to increase understanding of humanitarian issues, greater coordination between the Union and Member States. Humanitarian aid is grant-financed and non-refundable, and can cover items such as relief distribution, expenditure on external staff and the construction of shelters.

A Union humanitarian aid operation can be initiated at the request of the Com-

---

[254] [1996] OJ L163/1.
[255] [2003] OJ L284/1.
[256] [2009] OJ L87/109.

mission, NGOs, international organisations, Member States or beneficiary countries. The European Commission has three separate decision-making procedures available to it: (i) the *delegation procedure*, according to which, in order to speed up the response to sudden emergencies, the European Commission has delegated powers to the Director of ECHO for primary emergency humanitarian decisions within certain limits (a maximum amount of €3 million, a maximum duration of three months); (ii) the *empowerment procedure*, according to which the Member of the Commission responsible for humanitarian aid is empowered to take decisions relating to emergency operations up to €30 million for a maximum of six months as well as non-urgent decisions up to a maximum of €10 million, provided that a consultation procedure (within cabinets and departments) has been followed and that the emergency decisions exceeding €10 million and non-urgent decisions exceeding €2 million have been approved by the Humanitarian Aid Committee; and (iii) the *written procedure* for all decisions not covered by the delegation or empowerment procedures.

Somalia figures prominently in the EU humanitarian aid priorities since it is experiencing one of the most serious humanitarian crises in the world. Although famine conditions are gradually being brought under control, over three million people are still in need of humanitarian assistance, of whom over 870,000 are in a crisis or emergency situation[257]—a need aggravated by drought, food insecurity and conflict. Translating the commitments of the European Consensus on Humanitarian Aid into practical actions, EU humanitarian action focuses on aid effectiveness, results orientation and impact in order to get the best value for money through development on thematic and cross-cutting issues such as WASH (water, sanitation and hygiene), gender, nutrition, disaster risk reduction, targeted dissemination, training strategies and implementation monitoring.[258] In particular, the EU is providing needs-based humanitarian assistance to the people suffering from drought and conflict, including internally displaced persons and refugees.

The EU humanitarian assistance to Somalia has two primary sources of funds: the general budget of the Union and the European Development Fund. The EU has allocated €243 million in humanitarian aid to Somalia over the period from 2008 to 2012, and this assistance (directed by ECHO) is channelled through various partner organisations, including the International Committee of the Red Cross, UN agencies and NGOs such as the UN High Commissioner for Refugees' Regional Protection Programme in Kenya, Djibouti and Yemen.[259] For 2013, the total humanitarian funding by the EU to Somalia amounts to €60 million.

At this juncture, the question of the consistency of the EU's comprehensive approach towards Somalia needs to be addressed.

---

[257] European Commision Humanitarian Aid and Civil Protection, 'Factsheet Somalia' (September 2013).
[258] European Commission's Resilience Communication, COM(2012) 586 of 3 October 2012.
[259] Council Conclusions adopted on 14 November 2011, Council Doc 16858/11, available at http://register.consilium.europa.eu/pdf/en/11/st16/st16858.en11.pdf.

IV. THE LEGAL DIFFICULTIES OF ENSURING COMPREHENSIVENESS

The Lisbon Treaty has made great strides in laying the basis for ensuring coherence between CFSP and non-CFSP policies. The EU Treaties contain multiple references to the need for consistency between these policies and set out uniform principles and objectives to guide the EU's external action.[260] In addition, the Lisbon Treaty has led to the adoption of an overarching single institutional framework for EU action to ensure the 'consistency, effectiveness and continuity of its policies and actions'.[261]

General political guidance for all aspects of the external action of the EU is given by the European Council, which, following the Lisbon Treaty, became a separate institution and has a permanent president.[262] The Council of the EU is the policy-making body for both CFSP and non-CFSP acts. Overall coordination is provided also by the Committee of Permanent Representatives of the Council, which carries out preparatory work for Council decision-making generally,[263] and the PSC, which advises the Council on CFSP-related matters.[264] The High Representative presides over the Council in its Foreign Affairs configuration and works closely with both the Council and the Commission. The High Representative is served by the EEAS, heads the delegations of the EU abroad and is also one of the Commission's Vice-Presidents.[265]

However, there still remain important differences between the EU's action under CFSP and non-CFSP policies. In particular, there is a legal divide between CFSP and non-CFSP with regard to the distribution of powers between the EU and its Member States. There are also distinct procedures in the decision-making process, in the distribution of power between EU institutions, in the effects of the EU acquis and in the effectiveness of its implementation.[266] All of these differences have had an impact on the effectiveness of the EU's comprehensive approach towards the fight against piracy.

First, under the TFEU, the EU action in non-CFSP matters, including external action based on 'internal' competences, is essentially circumscribed by the scope of the treaty provisions which lay down the precise objectives of the various non-CFSP policy areas.

Secondly, the EU decision-making process in non-CFSP policy areas involves—in greatly simplified terms—three main institutional actors: the Council of the EU, the Commission and the European Parliament. The Council of the EU, jointly with the European Parliament, exercises legislative and budgetary functions.[267]

Legislative acts are the hallmark of non-CFSP policies. The Commission generally[268] has the power of initiative to propose legislative action, after which it is up to the Council and the European Parliament together (under the ordinary legislative

---

[260] See, eg Arts 3(5) and 21(3), 22(1), 23 TEU and Art 205 TFEU, respectively.

[261] Art 13(1) TEU.

[262] Art 15 and 22 TEU.

[263] Art 17(7) TEU.

[264] Art 38 TEU.

[265] Art 18, 22(2) and 30(1) TEU.

[266] There is now a general list of external objectives for non-CFSP policies in the EU Treaty (Art 21 TEU) complemented by policy-specific articles of the TFEU for each of the Union's 'internal policies' (Part 5 TFEU).

[267] Art 16(1) TEU.

[268] Exceptionally, an initiative for legislative action can also come from a quarter of EU Member States. This is the case only in three areas relating to the former third pillar: judicial cooperation in criminal matters, police cooperation and administrative cooperation on these matters (Art 76(b) TFEU).

procedure) or to the Council (under a special legislative procedure) to act upon the proposal. Qualified majority voting in the Council is the default rule.[269] For the negotiation and conclusion of EU agreements on non-CFSP matters, the TFEU procedure starts with a recommendation by the Commission to the Council for the opening of negotiations.[270] The Council needs to authorise the negotiations, it appoints the negotiator, issues negotiating directives, and decides on signature and conclusion of the agreements.[271] Negotiations on non-CFSP matters are generally conducted by the Commission. Once the agreement is negotiated, the Council can decide on signature and provisional application. The European Parliament must be kept informed at all stages of the procedure,[272] but has a formal role only in the procedure for ratification by the Union. For most agreements outside the CFSP, the Council can only decide to conclude an agreement once the European Parliament has given its consent.[273]

Thirdly, all counter-piracy measures based on non-CFSP policies are charged to the general budget of the EU, with the exception of action based on the EDF. The Commission is responsible for executing the EU budget and for the administration of the various EU-funded programmes.[274]

Fourthly, the Commission is generally empowered to represent the Union in non-CFSP fields.[275]

Fifthly, EU acts in non-CFSP areas are subject to the normal direct and indirect reviews by the Court of Justice of the EU (CJEU), although there are two exceptions—a temporary and a permanent one—relating to the former third pillar of the Union (judicial cooperation in criminal matters and police cooperation).[276]

Even after the Lisbon Treaty, EU action under the CFSP/CDSP policy area continues to be different in many respects.

True, the Lisbon Treaty has formally placed the CFSP and non-CFSP limbs on the same legal footing and has removed any lingering doubt about the legal personality of the EU and its legal capacity to conclude international treaties on CFSP matters.[277] In addition, EU action in CFSP matters has been formally included in the systematised list of EU competences in the TFEU.[278] However, 'the common foreign and security

---

[269] Art 16(3) TEU.
[270] Art 218(3) TFEU.
[271] Art 218(2)–(6) TFEU.
[272] Art 218(10) TFEU.
[273] Art 218(6) TFEU.
[274] Art 17(1) TEU.
[275] Ibid.
[276] There is a five-year transitional period (ending 1 November 2014) in which the previous rules regarding jurisdiction of the CJEU over existing former third pillar measures apply; see Protocol 36 to the Lisbon Treaty, on transitional provisions, Title VII. There is also, however, a permanent exception to the judicial coverage. According to Art 276 TFEU, the CJEU has no jurisdiction to review third pillar measures pertaining to the validity or the proportionality of operations carried out by the police or other law-enforcement services of a Member State or the exercise of the responsibilities incumbent upon Member States with regard to the maintenance of law and order and the safeguarding of internal security.
[277] Arts 1(3), 40 and 47 of the TEU.
[278] Even if, post-Lisbon, the CFSP (including CDSP) has been formally included in the list of competences enumerated in Arts 2–6 TFEU, it is clear that such policies continue to form a separate area of Union competence, 'subject to specific rules and procedures' (Art 24(1) TEU). In the articles regulating the division of competences between the Union and its Member States (Arts 2–6 TFEU), the Union's competence in the area of CFSP/CSDP is mentioned separately in Art 2(4) TFEU. CFSP/CSDP falls formally under shared competences (Art 4(1) TFEU *a contrario*). In view of the comprehensive list of competences set out in the

policy is subject to specific rules and procedures'.[279] In particular, in terms of objectives and in the decision-making process, the CFSP remains a separate area of EU action. Substantial differences also remain in respect of the scope of judicial review, financing and the budget.

First, unlike non-CFSP policies, the CFSP is not tied to particular policy objectives: it may extend to 'all areas of foreign policy and all questions relating to the Union's security'.[280] This explains the great range and flexibility of foreign policy objectives pursued by CFSP/CSDP operations in comparison with the circumscribed scope of non-CFSP action.

Secondly, in terms of decision-making, CFSP action retains many features of intergovernmental decision-making. All CFSP acts emanate from the European Council or the Council, with only limited roles for the Commission and the European European Parliament. On matters relating to the CFSP, Member States and the High Representative have a right of initiative.[281] Unanimity in the Council is the main rule. The adoption of legislative acts on CFSP matters is excluded.[282]

Moreover, in respect of the procedure for the negotiation and conclusion of EU agreements that encompass exclusively or principally CFSP matters, there are crucial differences as regards institutional actors as well. The TFEU procedure starts with a recommendation by the High Representative to the Council for the opening of negotiations.[283] The Council authorises the negotiations, appoints the negotiator, issues negotiating directives, and decides on signature and conclusion.[284] Negotiations on CFSP matters are conducted by the High Representative. Once the agreement is negotiated, the Council can decide on signature and provisional application, as well as conclusion of the agreement. The European Parliament must be kept informed at all stages of the procedure,[285] but, unlike for agreements on non-CFSP matters, it has no institutional role at the conclusion stage where agreements relate exclusively to the CFSP.[286] As will be seen below, there is currently disagreement between the EU's institutions as to whether the above-mentioned transfer agreements negotiated by the EU relating to maritime piracy fall under this CFSP exception.

Thirdly, counter-piracy operations that fall under the CFSP/CSDP are charged to the Union budget in accordance with rules specific to the financing of EU crisis management operations[287] Accordingly, administrative expenditure of the institutions arising from the implementation of the CSDP, both for civilian missions and military operations, are charged to the Union's budget. The same applies, as a general rule, to operating expenditure, except for cases in which the Council, acting unanimously, decides otherwise, and for expenditure arising from operations having military or defence implications. Expenditure covering military operations is not charged to the

---

TFEU, a new element has been inserted in the TEU confirming that national security remains a reserved national competence of EU Member States (Art 4(2) TEU).

[279] Art 24(1) TEU.
[280] Ibid.
[281] Arts 24(1), 30(1) and 36 TEU.
[282] Art 31(1) TEU.
[283] Art 218(3) TFEU.
[284] Art 218(2)–(6) TFEU.
[285] Art 218(10) TFEU.
[286] Art 218(6) TFEU.
[287] Art 41 TEU.

Union budget but is generally charged to the Member States in accordance with their gross national product, unless the Council unanimously decides otherwise. If, on a decision to embark on an operation having military or defence implications, a Member State abstains in a vote and makes a formal declaration (qualified abstention), it is not obliged to contribute to the financing of the respective expenditure. There is a special mechanism called 'Athena', which, as has been explained above, manages common expenditure relating to operations with military or defence implications.[288] Overall though, the costs financed by Athena account for less than 10% of the total costs for a typical military CSDP operation, the rest being borne by participating states following the principle 'costs lie where they fall'.

Fourthly, as far as the international representation of the Union is concerned, and in contrast to the rule for non-CFSP policies, the President of the European Council and the High Representative ensure the Union's representation in matters relating to the CFSP/CSDP.[289]

Fifthly, in terms of judicial review, in principle, the Luxembourg-based CJEU has no jurisdiction in CFSP/CSDP matters,[290] with two exceptions: the CJEU has competence to 'police' the boundaries between CFSP and non-CFSP competences of EU action[291] and to review EU restrictive measures ('sanctions') imposed upon natural or legal persons.[292] In the section below, the relevance of these two exceptions for the EU's counter-piracy efforts will be discussed.

A. Incomplete Judicial Coverage

As indicated above, because EU action to counter piracy involves both non-CFSP and CFSP policies, judicial 'coverage' by the Luxembourg-based CJEU is not complete. Action based on the pre-Lisbon first pillar policies[293] is, as a rule, subject to the normal judicial review by the CJEU. In contrast, in adopting the Lisbon Treaty, the EU Member States confirmed the reverse principle with respect to CFSP/CSDP: the general rule is that there is no competence for the CJEU to review CFSP/CDP measures. As will be seen below, there is already litigation between EU institutional actors regarding the correct internal procedures for EU action pertaining to EU counter-piracy efforts. The outcome of this litigation will have consequences not only for the balance of power between the EU institutions regarding CFSP/CSDP operations, but may also

---

[288] Athena has replaced earlier, temporary mechanisms and has existed as a permanent mechanism since 2004. It acts on behalf of the participating Member States (all Member States of the EU except Denmark), and third states when the latter contribute to the financing of the common costs of a specific operation. See Council Decision 2008/975/CFSP of 18 December 2008 establishing a mechanism to administer the financing of the common costs of European Union operations having military or defence implications (Athena), [2008] OJ L345/96.

[289] Art 15(6), subpara 2 TEU and Art 27(2) TEU.

[290] Art 24(1) TEU and 275 TFEU.

[291] Art 40 TEU.

[292] Art 275 TEU. This provision is essentially a reflection of the case law of the Union's courts in regard to restrictive measures (including, in particular, the freezing of assets) imposed on natural and legal persons in the framework of the Union's measures combating terrorism or in the framework of economic sanctions directed at third countries.

[293] That is to say, all EU policies except for the former second pillar (CFSP) and the former third pillar (judicial cooperation in criminal matters and police cooperation).

affect the prospects of private litigants having at least part of the EU's action in matters of counter-piracy reviewed by the CJEU.

As mentioned above, with the amendments introduced by the Lisbon Treaty, judicial 'coverage' by the CJEU with regard to pre-Lisbon first and third pillar matters is practically complete, except for two matters pertaining to police and judicial cooperation in criminal matters. Apart from a temporary exception which expires in 2004, there is also a permanent exception: the CJEU has no competence over measures relating to the validity or proportionality of operations carried out by the police or other law-enforcement services of Member States, or over the exercise of the responsibilities incumbent upon the Member States with regard to the maintenance of law and order and the safeguarding of internal security.[294]

Whether the latter exception has any relevance at all for EU counter-piracy efforts depends on the view one takes of the pertinence of the (former) third pillar in such operations and, more specifically, the question of whether such operations fall mainly or exclusively under the EU's foreign and security policy or whether there is a separate, substantial component based on the EUs competence with regard to police and criminal matters. The latter question may be addressed by the CJEU in a case which has been recently brought by the European Parliament against the Council. The case relates to the above-mentioned transfer agreement concluded between the EU and Mauritius in 2011 pertaining to suspected pirates and associated property caught in the course of Operation Atalanta.[295] The Parliament contends that the transfer agreement in question involves not only elements of CFSP but also judicial cooperation in criminal matters as well as police cooperation (former third pillar), in addition to the EU's competence regarding development cooperation (former first pillar). In the Parliament's view, the transfer agreement therefore does not exclusively relate to CFSP and could, therefore, only have been concluded with the Parliament's consent pursuant to the procedures for conclusion of non-CFSP agreements, discussed above.

This litigation is an illustration of frequent battles between EU institutional actors about the correct 'legal basis' on which to found particular EU action. Whilst undoubtedly slightly obscure to the outside world, the legal basis defines whether the EU has competence to act, sets the limits of that competence, and determines the role of institutions in the elaboration of the act, the voting rules in the Council and the scope of judicial review by the CJEU.[296] Precisely because of the many policy areas that are potentially involved in EU action to counter maritime piracy, the Council's opposition to the Parliament's continuous efforts to push for more say in the EU's foreign and security policy as well as the potential consequences of opening up CFSP/CSDP actions to judicial review by the CJEU, the outcome of this litigation cannot be underestimated.

---

[294] Art 276 TFEU.

[295] CJEU Case C-658/11 *European Parliament against the Council of the European Union*, relating to the Council Decision 2011/640/CFSP of 12 July 2011 on the signing and conclusion of the Agreement between the European Union and the Republic of Mauritius on the conditions of transfer of suspected pirates and associated seized property from the European Union-led naval force to the Republic of Mauritius and on the conditions of suspected pirates after transfer.

[296] The CJEU regards the choice of correct legal basis as an issue of constitutional importance: ECJ Opinion 2/00 *Cartagena Protocol* [2001] ECR I-9713, para 5; ECJ Case C-370/07 *Commission v Council* [2009] ECR I-8917, paras 46–49; ECJ Opinion 1/08 *General Agreement on Trade in Services* [2009] ECR I-11129, para 110.

There have been two earlier notable cases in which the CJEU has ruled on the demarcation between CFSP and non-CFSP action under the EU Treaties. In the first case, brought under the pre-Lisbon version of the Treaties, the Court ruled in favour of the non-CFSP part of the EU policies concerned (in this case, development cooperation). In the second case, brought under the most recent (Lisbon) version of the Treaties, the Court favoured the CFSP part of the Treaties over the former third pillar.

Starting with the first case, under the pre-Lisbon version of the TEU, the Court was empowered to police the division of powers between the second (CFSP) and third (PJCC) pillars of the TEU on the one hand and the (former) Community pillar on the other. However, there was only one dimension to the Court's review: Article 47 TEU provided essentially that the second and third pillars should not encroach on the first (Community) pillar. In the *Small Arms and Light Weapons (SALW)* case of 2008[297] the Commission considered that the Council had unlawfully based a Joint Action on the CFSP pillar and had unlawfully affected the Community pillar in breach of Article 47 TEU. The CFSP Joint Action in question was for the financing of a programme on combating the spread of such weapons. In the Commission's view, this CFSP action 'affected' Community powers in the field of development aid which were largely covered by action taken under the first pillar ACP/Cotonou agreement. The CJEU ruled in favour of the Commission. It held that, on account of both its aim and its content, the CFSP Joint Action pursued a number of objectives falling within the scope of development cooperation which were not merely incidental to the CFSP objectives. Accordingly, the Court found that the CFSP measure 'affected' the (former) Community measure and hence needed to be annulled because it had been adopted in breach of Article 47 TEU.[298]

As indicated above, with the entry into force of the Lisbon Treaty, Article 47 TEU has been replaced by Article 40 TEU. This changes the legal picture substantially, as the new version of the rule provides not only that the CFSP is not to encroach on other policies of the treaties, but also vice versa. This article was indirectly relevant in a recent case brought shortly after the entry into force of the Lisbon Treaty by the European Parliament, which sought to contest the legal basis of an EU measure relating to restrictive measures to combat terrorism perpetrated by Al Qaeda.[299] The Council had adopted the contested measure, choosing as a legal basis the CFSP-related provision, which only provides for a minor role for the Parliament.[300] Convinced that

---

[297] CJEU Case C-91/05 *Commission v Council* [2008] ECR I-651, para 60.

[298] Ibid, paras 79–110.

[299] The measure at issue was the adoption by the Council of revised restrictive measures (Regulation (EU) No 1286/2009) directed against certain persons and entities associated with Usama bin Laden, the Al-Qaeda network and the Taliban. The aim of the revision was to include a due process regime for parties subject to freezing of funds and economic resources, to comply with the Judgment of 3 September 2008 of the CJEU in the Kadi and Al Barakaat cases. CJEU Joined Cases C-402/05 P and C-415/05 P *Yassin Abdullah Kadi and Al Barakaat International Foundation v Council of the European Union and Commission of the European Communities*, Judgment of the Court (Grand Chamber) of 3 September 2008, [2008] ECR I-06351.

[300] The Parliament contended that the Council had unlawfully chosen Art 215 of the TFEU as the legal basis for the revised restrictive measures regime. This article constitutes a bridge between the TFEU and the part of the TEU which deals with CFSP, allowing the adoption of targeted sanctions where a CFSP decision to that effect has been taken. The procedure set out in Art 215 TFEU involves the Council acting by qualified majority on a joint proposal by the High Representative and the Commission, with the Parliament being informed once the measures have been adopted. In the Parliament's view, however, the revised Al Qaeda restrictive measures regime should have been based instead on Art 75 TFEU. The latter is a new

its institutional prerogatives had been unlawfully curtailed, the Parliament contended that the measure should instead have been based on (a former third pillar) provision of the treaties that would have allowed the Parliament to play its full role as co-leg-islator with the Council for the adoption of the measures concerned. In its judgment of 19 July 2012, the CJEU dismissed the Parliament's legal challenge, confirming that the Council had correctly chosen the CFSP-related legal basis for the contested measure. The CJEU accepted that the fight against terrorism and its financing may well be among the objectives of the area of freedom, security and justice, but held that the objective of the fight against international terrorism and its financing in order to preserve international peace and security corresponds, nevertheless, to the objectives of the Treaty provisions on CFSP.[301]

It remains to be seen whether the CJEU will take a similar view in the case regarding the EU–Mauritius transfer agreement. If the CJEU were to follow the Parliament's position that the agreement does not relate exclusively to the CFSP, the consequences would not be limited to the role of the Parliament in the EU decision-making process relating to such agreements (ie the need for the EP's consent in the conclusion phase): at the very least, a part of the content of the transfer agreement itself would then be opened up for judicial review by the CJEU.[302]

B. Judicial Review of EU Counter-piracy Action by Private Litigants?

It seems rather unlikely at this stage that the EU courts in Luxembourg would be successfully seized by private litigants of cases involving former first pillar EU action pertaining to EU counter-piracy efforts. Such litigation regarding non-CFSP policies can never be excluded, but court cases will most probably be confined to contractual and administrative matters relating to (former) first pillar measures.

Insofar as the CFSP aspect is concerned, an important point to note is that legal action regarding the correct demarcation between CFSP and non-CFSP policies is not the preserve of EU institutional actors alone. The EU legal system does not prevent private litigants from contesting the correct legal basis of EU action before the CJEU as well.[303] However, apart from policing the border with non-CFSP action, the CJEU has no competence to review CFSP action itself. A CFSP/non-CFSP demarcation case, whether brought by institutional actors or private litigants, may lead to a judgment by the CJEU on where the line between the various policies needs to be drawn, but will

---

provision introduced by the Lisbon Treaty into the EU's internal policy in the area of 'freedom, security and justice', which provides for the adoption by the Union of a framework of administrative measures including the freezing of funds to prevent and combat terrorism. In contrast to Art 215 TFEU, the procedure of Art 75 TFEU is the ordinary legislative procedure which allows the Parliament to play a full role as co-legislator with the Council for the adoption of such a framework.

[301] CJEU Case C-130/10 *European Parliament v Council of the European Union*, Judgment of the Court (Grand Chamber) of 19 July 2012, nyr.

[302] At the very least for those parts that do not fall under the CFSP: these will no longer be entirely exempted from judicial review pursuant to Art 275 TFEU (the CFSP exception) and to the extent that the exception set out in Art 276 TFEU (the formed third pillar exception) is not judged to be relevant for such agreements in counterpiracy matters (see *supra* on this question).

[303] For a notable example where private litigants contested with some success the legal basis of EU action see CJEU Joined Cases C-402/05 P and C-415/05 P, n 299 above, paras 158–236.

not lead to the Court reviewing the contents of the CFSP measure concerned, once the border has been drawn.

This is notwithstanding the fact that throughout its case law the CJEU has consistently held that, in the exercise of its powers, including in particular legislative powers, the EU needs to abide by the rules of international law that are binding on it, regardless of their source (customary law or treaty law).[304] It is noteworthy that the TEU, as amended by the Lisbon Treaty, includes an explicit commitment that the EU's external action be guided by the rule of law, by the universality and indivisibility of human rights and fundamental freedoms, and that the EU work to achieve a high degree of cooperation in all fields of international relations to consolidate and support the rule of law, human rights, and respect for the principles of the UN Charter and international law.[305]

In addition, the legal instruments adopted by the EU in the context of maritime piracy include an explicit commitment to respect the UN Convention on the Law of the Sea.[306] However, the Court's case law on the status of international law in the Union's legal order is often linked with the extent to which private litigants can rely on rules of general international law before EU courts. Generally speaking, this case law is fairly restrictive as regards the right of non-privileged litigants (ie other than EU institutions and EU Member States) to rely on international law for the purposes of contesting the legality of EU acts.[307] For example, in the *Intertanko* case, the CJEU denied the right of private litigants to have the validity of a (first pillar) EU directive tested against provisions of the 1982 UNCLOS, even though the EU and all its Member States are parties to that Convention.[308] Similarly, the CJEU has recently confirmed its case law denying the right of private litigants to invoke international agreements to contest the validity of EU acts except under strict conditions. The Court is more lenient for customary law: it allows private litigants to invoke basic principles of customary international law to test the legality of EU action.[309] On the other hand, the Court has always made an exception for human rights-based challenges. In particular, the Court has always given strong recognition to certain provisions of the European Convention on Human Rights and Fundamental Freedoms. Article 6(3) of the TEU,

---

[304] Case C-286/90 *Anklagemindigheden v Poulsen and Diva Navigation* [1992] ECR I-6019, para 9; Case C-308/06 *The Queen on the application of: International Association of Independent Tanker Owners (Intertanko), International Association of Dry Cargo Shipowners (Intercargo), Greek Shipping Co-operation Committee, Lloyd's Register, International Salvage Union v Secretary of State for Transport* [2008] ECR I-4057, para 51.

[305] Arts 3(5) and 21, paras 1 and 2(b) TEU.

[306] Council Joint Action 2008/851/CFSP, n 20 above, recital 2 ('relevant international law') and Art 1 (in a manner consistent with action permitted with respect to piracy under Art 100 et seq of the UN Convention on the Law of the Sea signed in Montego Bay on 10 December 1982); Council Decision 2010/766/CFSP, n 48 above, recital 6 (reference to "provisions of the UN Conventions on the Law of the Sea') and Art 1(3) (reference to Arts 101, 103 and 105 of the same convention).

[307] For a thorough discussion of the approach by the CJEU to public international law see S Boelaert, 'European Union Courts' in C Giorgetti, *The Rules, Practice, and Jurisprudence of International Courts and Tribunals* (Leiden, Martinus Nijhoff, 2012) 415, 430–51.

[308] Above n 297.

[309] The cumulative criteria for invoking treaty law by private litigants are threefold: the EU must be bound by the treaty's rules; the nature and the broad logic of the treaty do not preclude review by the Court; and the provisions of the treaty relied upon must be unconditional and sufficiently precise: CJEU, Case C-366/10 *Air Transport Association of America v Secretary of State for Energy and Climate Change*, Judgment (Grand Chamber) of 21 December 2011, nyr, paras 52–54. The Court is, however, more lenient as regards reliance by private litigants on principles of customary law: ibid, paras 101–09.

introduced by the Treaty of Lisbon, essentially codifies this case law and is now complemented by the EU's Charter of Fundamental Rights, which has been given the same legal status by the Lisbon Treaty as the TEU and the TFEU pursuant to Article 6(1) TEU. In addition, the Court's judgment of 2008 in the *Kadi and Al Barakaat* joined cases shows that it will not easily be swayed by foreign policy-related arguments when private litigants seek to challenge EU acts, even those adopted by the EU to give effect to UNSC resolutions, on account of alleged violation of their fundamental rights.[310] The Court termed the protection of fundamental rights an issue of 'constitutional importance'.[311]

A question that could arise in this regard concerns the right for persons to contest before the CJEU 'restrictive measures' imposed upon them in accordance with Article 275, paragraph 2 and Article 263 TFEU. Is this exception at all relevant to the EU's current counter-piracy efforts? In other words, could suspected pirates who are captured in EU-led operations and transferred to third countries, or natural and legal persons who are in any other manner at the 'receiving end' of the EU's maritime counter-piracy action, avail themselves of this exception to contest such EU action before the Union's courts in Luxembourg? It is doubtful that such an interpretation would succeed, as this would mean stretching the notion of 'restrictive measures' beyond its ordinary meaning, as used in EU acts, and would go against the explicit 'carve-out' of CFSP measures from judicial review, which has been set out in EU primary law.[312] However, regardless of whether access to the CJEU is available to private litigants affected by EU counter-piracy operations, applicants continue to have the option of turning to the national courts of EU Member States involved in the operations concerned and may eventually turn to the European Court of Human Rights (ECtHR) in Strasbourg.

In any case, for successful recourse to the latter, a number of obstacles relating to admissibility will need to be overcome.

In particular, there are obstacles regarding the application of the Convention outside the territory of the Contracting Parties. The ECtHR's case law on extraterritorial application of the European Convention is still evolving, even if the recent judgment in *Hirsi Jamaa* certainly lends support for the ECtHR accepting competence

---

[310] CJEU Joined Cases C-402/05 P and C-415/05 P, n 299 above, para 326: 'the Community judicature must, in accordance with the powers conferred on it by the EC Treaty, ensure the review, in principle the full review, of the lawfulness of all Community acts in the light of the fundamental rights forming an integral part of the general principles of Community law, including review of Community measures which, like the contested regulation, are designed to give effect to the resolutions adopted by the Security Council under Chapter VII of the Charter of the UN'.

[311] CJEU Joined Cases C-402/05 P and C-415/05 P, ibid, para 285: 'It follows from all those considerations that the obligations imposed by an international agreement cannot have the effect of prejudicing the constitutional principles of the EC Treaty, which include the principle that all Community acts must respect fundamental rights, that respect constituting a condition of their lawfulness which it is for the Court to review in the framework of the complete system of legal remedies established by the Treaty'.

[312] True, a suspected pirate might be able to demonstrate that his or her capture, arrest and transfer by the EU amount to actions which are pursuant to Art 263, para 4 TFEU 'direct and individual concern'. On the other hand, the adjective 'restrictive' used in Art 275 TFEU, para 2 is a term of art that needs to be given a specific meaning. The notion of 'restrictive measures' refers to measures such as asset freeze and travel bans adopted by the EU in the framework of economic sanctions against third countries and to combat terrorism, not to any other measures. Furthermore, Art 275, para 2 TFEU constitutes an exception to the principle set out in Art 24(1), para 2 TEU and Art 275, para 1 TFEU, according to which the CJEU shall have no jurisdiction with respect to CFSP and acts adopted on that basis. Any exception to this must be interpreted restrictively.

for counter-piracy actions conducted by EU Member States on the high seas outside the Convention area.[313] Another important obstacle is the question of attribution of UN-sanctioned operations. The ECtHR may decide that it is prevented from reviewing actions attributable to the UN under Chapter VII of the UN Charter on account of the generalised immunity of such operations, for the reasons set out in the *Behrami/Saramati* line of cases.[314] In addition, from an EU perspective, any proceedings before the ECtHR relating to counter-piracy operations will raise complex questions as to whether acts occurring, for example, in the course of Operation Atalanta need to be attributed to the EU as such and/or to the contributing EU Member States and/or to the EU Member State whose warship arrested, detained or transferred the suspect.

A final point that needs to be borne in mind is that the EU has recently finalised the negotiations for its accession to the ECHR.[315] One of the provisions that held up finalisation of the negotiations for a long time is the question of attribution of responsibility for CFSP/CSDP acts in relation to which the CJEU itself has no competence. The solution agreed between negotiators is that, for the purposes of challenges before the ECtHR, EU Member States will be attributed legal responsibility for acts or omissions when they implement EU law, including CFSP/CSDP-related measures. This is without prejudice to the EU as an organisation to become co-respondent and eventually be held co-responsbile by the ECtHR for the act or omission at issue.[316]

---

[313] ECtHR Grand Chamber, *Hirsi Jamaa and Others v Italy*, Application No 27765/09, Judgment of 23 February 2012.

[314] ECtHR Grand Chamber, *Behrami and Behrami v France* and *Saramati v France, Germany and Norway*, Decision (Grand Chamber) of 2 May 2007 on the admissibility of Application Nos 71412/01 and 78166/01. The ECtHR confirmed its view concerning the attribution to the UN of conduct by national contingents of peacekeeping operations in the following cases: *Kasumaj v Greece*, Decision of 5 July 2007 on the admissibility of Application No 6974/05; *Gajić v Germany*, Decision of 28 August 2007 on the admissibility of Application No 31446/02; and *Berić and others v Bosnia and Herzegovina*, Decision of 16 October 2007 on the admissibility of Applications Nos 36357/04, 36360/04, 38346/04,41705/04, 45190/04, 45578/04, 45579/04, 45580/04, 91/05, 97/05, 100/05, 1121/05, 1123/05,1125/05, 1129/05, 1132/05, 1133/05, 1169/05, 1172/05, 1175/05, 1177/05, 1180/05, 1185/05,20793/05 and 25496/05.

[315] The draft accession agreement will have to be ratified by all 47 Council of Europe Members, and will require on the EU side a heavy procedure in accordance with Art 218 TFEU (a positive opinion from the CJEU, unanimity within the Council for signature and conclusion, consent of the European Parliament and approval of the conclusion decision by all EU Member States in accordance with their constitutional procedures; and, in addition, it is understood that the EU and its Member States will need to agree on accompanying internal rules).

[316] The provision negotiated reads in substance as follows: 'For the purposes of the Convention, of the protocols thereto and of this Agreement, an act, measure or omission of organs of a member state of the European Union or of persons acting on its behalf shall be attributed to that state, even if such act, measure or omission occurs when the state implements the law of the European Union, including decisions taken under the Treaty on European Union and under the Treaty on the Functioning of the European Union. This shall not preclude the European Union from being responsible as a co-respondent for a violation resulting from such an act, measure or omission, in accordance with Article 36, paragraph 4, of the Convention and Article 3 of this Agreement' (Art 1(4) of the Draft revised agreement on the accession of the European Union to the Convention for the Protection of Human Rights and Fundamental Freedoms', Appendix I to the Final Report to the CDDH, Fifth Negotiation Meeting Between the CDDGH Ad Hoc Negotiation Group and the European Commission on the Accession of the European Union to the European Convention on Human Rights, Council of Europe document 47+1(2013)008rev2, available at http://www.coe.int/t/dghl/standardsetting/hrpolicy/Accession/Meeting_reports/47_1(2013)008rev2_EN.pdf).

V. CONCLUSION

In conclusion, the EU has demonstrated that it aims to secure a 'comprehensive approach' in reaching a solution to the piracy problem. Its comprehensive legal action to counter piracy is anchored in EU law, UNSC resolutions adopted under Chapter VII of the UN Charter, customary international law, multilateral and bilateral treaty law, as well as municipal law. It includes launching crisis management operations, imposing restrictive measures, providing development cooperation, institution building and stabilisation, promoting respect for the rule of law, international law and human rights, granting trade preferences and providing humanitarian aid.

The EU's 'comprehensive approach' towards combating piracy and armed robbery off the coast of Somalia and to the wider Horn of Africa, including the development and stabilisation of the country, has been alleged to constitute an 'uploading of Western and European ideas of how a state should function on to Somalia, with a centralised decision making body and democratic principles',[317] a goal that does not befit a country historically based on decentralised structures, mostly functioning at the local level, and governed by a variety of traditional clans, local customs and laws (including Sharia law). However, it should be noted that the EU support for a centralised solution has been, and continues to be, advocated by the TFG, which considers that it is precisely the absence of functioning centralised structures that have facilitated the thriving of pirates, organised crime and conflict.

With regard to the EU CSDP/CFSP operations off the coast of Somalia, experience shows that the EU efforts to combat piracy and armed robbery, combined with those of other international actors, have led to a downturn in pirate activity in the Western Indian Ocean. Whilst there is general agreement that this positive trend is easily reversible, there can be little doubt that the EU CFSP/CSDP operation has contributed to the observed decline in piracy attacks and the end of impunity for suspected pirates and armed robbers. In January 2013, the number of suspected pirates transferred to competent authorities was close to 130 individuals. A substantial number of them have subsequently been successfully convicted, with the remainder currently waiting trial. In addition, Operation Atalanta has had a 100 per cent success rate in the protection of the maritime logistics operations of the WFP and AMISOM.

With regard to the EU's non-CFSP action, the EU can be seen to be taking the lead on development issues in Somalia, by engaging in concrete action, rather than just rhetoric, on the issue. However, the provision of humanitarian aid to Somalia is difficult as a result of restricted access to, and high insecurity in, the area. The EU's non-CFSP action focuses on emergency response in order to save lives in the South-Central regions of Somalia and in urban areas of Puntland and Somaliland, with particular emphasis on initiatives which aim to reduce the risk of disasters and strengthen the resilience of the most vulnerable communities.[318]

---

[317] The terms are taken from R Paige, 'The EU as a Counter-piracy Actor', *e-International relations*, 7 November 2012, available at http://www.e-ir.info/2012/11/07/the-eu-as-a-counter-piracy-actor/. See also HG Ehrhart and K Petretto, *The EU and Somalia: Counter-piracy and the Question of a Comprehensive Approach* (Hamburg, European Free Alliance, 2012), available at www.greenefa.eu/fileadmin/dam/documents/studies/Ehrhart_Petretto_EUandSomalia_2012_fin.pdf.

[318] See 'General Guidelines on Operational Priorities for Humanitarian Aid in 2013', Commission Staff working document SWD (2012) 405 final (27 November 2012) 11–12.

Despite the EU's overall success, much remains to be done by the EU in Somalia, even if the piracy problem were to be solved. Furthermore, the EU comprehensive approach cannot per se guarantee success, given the very serious and varied issues affecting Somalia. The various EU policies are subjected to a CFSP/non-CFSP policy divide which creates hurdles in terms of procedures, responsibilities, decision-making processes and judicial review. The EU's comprehensive approach to problem-solving renders the EU vulnerable to a lot of criticism about its weaknesses, but the EU should be commended for having shown the commitment to follow through with its promise to try and solve the 'root causes' of piracy on land in Somalia and for contributing to a brighter future for Somalia, a future which remains in the hands of the Somali people.

6

Transfer Agreements for Pirates Concluded by the EU—a Case Study on the Human Rights Accountability of the Common Security and Defence Policy

DANIEL THYM

I. INTRODUCTION

EUROPEAN MEASURES TO fight piracy in the Gulf of Aden have received much political and academic attention. They raise a number of formidable legal and conceptual questions, ranging from the legality of military operations and the apprehension of suspected pirates to cooperation among states and international actors. The EU approach is examined in detail in Chapter 5 in this volume. Within this overall context, this paper focuses on transfer agreements which the EU has concluded with countries in the region, notably Kenya, Seychelles and Mauritius, as a basis for the transfer of alleged pirates for detention and trial abroad. These agreements have been criticised as a potential evasion strategy circumventing human rights obligations incumbent upon the EU and its Member States. While the substantive human rights standards are well established on the basis of European Court of Human Rights (ECtHR) case law, it is less clear how and through which institutional fora their respect may be guaranteed within the broader institutional context of the EU's Common Security and Defence Policy (CSDP). This chapter addresses these questions and explores the fora which may guarantee the human rights accountability of Europe's foreign, security and defence policy.

II. POLITICAL AND LEGAL CONTEXT

It is well known that Somali-based piracy and armed robbery at sea became a matter of international concern in 2008 after a notable increase in the number of attacks on different vessels which threatened the prompt and effective delivery of humanitarian aid to Somalia and endangered the safety of crucial commercial maritime routes off the Horn of Africa. Various international actors were involved in efforts to fight piracy on the High Seas and in the territorial waters of Somalia. Legally, these efforts received authoritative support from the UN Security Council, which, in a number of resolutions, urged the international community to increase and coordinate their efforts to deter acts of piracy and armed robbery at sea.[1] Naval patrols of military ships and aircrafts were the prominent and immediate response to prevent further escalation; NATO, the US and India were among those who deployed military vessels to deter pirates. Within this broader picture, the EU embarked upon one of its most extensive military missions: the European Union Naval Force (EU NAVFOR) Somalia, dubbed as 'Operation Atalanta', which has patrolled the waters off the Horn of Africa since late 2008 and whose mandate has been extended until the end of 2014.[2]

While many European states were quick to send naval vessels to the Horn of Africa, most were undecided as to how to deal with those suspected of having committed or having intended to commit acts of piracy or armed robbery. This uncertainty resulted in cases where European ships released suspected pirates because they did not know how to deal with them.[3] In particular, most European states disliked the option of prosecuting suspected pirates in domestic courts.[4] Multiple reasons explain this lack of enthusiasm for criminal charges back home: national criminal justice systems are not prepared to deal with crimes committed thousands of miles away, investigations might prove problematic to pursue in Somalia and, as a result, it may occasionally be difficult to meet strict standards of proof for criminal charges in domestic courts; economic efficiency also advised against costly trials and detention at home, since the money could be used much more beneficially abroad; finally, public opinion might turn against those bringing pirates to European cities and prisons, especially given that it might prove difficult to deport them at a later stage. In short, most Member States participating in the operation Atalanta were eager to exploit alternative ways to prosecute pirates in the region.

Yet the transfer of suspected pirates to third states for purposes of trial and detention need not be motivated by domestic reasons alone. International division of labour and general principles of international law support inter-state cooperation in prosecuting pirates. The United Nations Convention on the Law of the Sea calls upon all states to cooperate to the fullest possible extent in the repression of piracy and allows

---

[1] See, among the early resolutions, UN Security Council, Resolution No 1816 (2008) of 2 June 2008; Resolution No 1846 (2008) of 2 December 2008; and Resolution No 1897 (2009) of 30 November 2009; for more detail see D Guilfoyle, 'Counter-piracy Law Enforcement and Human Rights' (2010) 59 *International & Comparative Law Quarterly* 141, 145–48.

[2] Council Joint Action 2008/851/CFSP on an EU military operation to contribute to the deterrence, prevention and repression of acts of piracy and armed robbery off the Somali coast of 10 November 2008, [2008] OJ L301/33, and the extension of the mandate through Council Decision 2012/174/CFSP of 23 March 2012, [2012] OJ L89/66.

[3] In April 2011, a Finnish Brigade released 18 suspected pirates after requests to a number of states, who were considered to have an interest, proved to be unsuccessful; see Council of the EU press release, 'Operation Atalanta' (21 April 2011), available at http://eunavfor.eu/ eu-navfor-releases-suspected-pirates-after-prosecution-attempts-prove-unsuccessful/.

[4] The German government assumes that prosecution within Germany should only occur in scenarios where the legal interests of the Federal Republic are at stake; see question No 16 in Antwort der Bundesregierung auf die Kleine Anfrage: Beteiligung deutscher Soldaten am geplanten EU-Einsatz 'Atalanta', Deutscher Bundestag Drucksachen (parliamentary documents) No 16/11352 of 12 December 2008.

states who have seized suspected pirates to decide on the penalties to be imposed.[5] One step further, the Convention for the Suppression of Unlawful Acts against the Safety of Maritime Navigation (SUA Convention) obliges states either to prosecute or extradite alleged pirates and other offenders, as defined by the Convention, and prioritises prosecution by countries of origin, the country in whose territorial waters the act of piracy occurred or by the country that owns the seized ship.[6] Of course, these countries are not available to prosecute those involved in East African piracy: Somalia is in many respects a failed state without a functioning criminal justice system; Liberia or Panama may be eager to serve as flag states, but are less keen to prosecute suspected pirates. The international community therefore has had to identify alternatives routes for the prosecution of Somali pirates.

Building upon these rules, the UN Security Council

> call[ed] upon all States, and in particular flag, port and coastal States, States of the nationality of victims and perpetrators . . . to cooperate in determining jurisdiction, and in the investigation and prosecution of persons responsible for acts of piracy and armed robbery

while adding that these measures should be 'consistent with applicable international law including international human rights law'.[7] Taking up initial debates about how to prosecute piracy, the Security Council invited all states in Resolution 1897 (2009) 'to conclude special agreements or arrangements with countries willing to take custody of pirates . . . in particular countries in the region', with a view to allow for the embarkation law enforcement officials from these countries (so-called shipriders) in order to facilitate investigation and prosecution.[8] While the EU never concluded such 'shiprider agreements', it went some length to negotiate agreements with Kenya, Seychelles and Mauritius on the transfer of suspected pirates.

III. EU TRANSFER AGREEMENTS

In its initial Joint Action authorising the military mission on the deterrence, prevention and repression of acts of piracy and armed robbery off the Somali coast, the EU committed itself to the prosecution of those who committed or intended to commit acts of piracy. In doing so, it assumed that 'the competent authorities of the Member State . . . of which the vessel which took them captive flies the flag' would assume

---

[5] See Art 100 and the second sentence of Art 105 UN Convention on the Law of the Sea of 10 December 1982, [1998] OJ L179/3.

[6] See, on the *aut dedere aut iudicare* obligation, Art 7 and, on jurisdiction, Art 6(1) Convention for the Suppression of Unlawful Acts against the Safety of Maritime Navigation of 10 March 1986, 1678 UNTS 221.

[7] Operative No 11 of UN Security Council Resolution 1816, n 1 above; operative No 14 of UN Security Council Resolution 1846, n 1 above, reiterated the appeal and went on in No 15 to remind state parties to the SUA Convention of their obligations.

[8] Operative No 6 of UN Security Council Resolution 1897, n 1 above, which also took up previous wording on jurisdiction (No 12) and the SUA Convention (No 14).

primary responsibility for prosecution.[9] Only 'if that State cannot, or does not wish to, exercise its jurisdiction' should the suspect be transferred to a third state which 'wishes' to exercise its jurisdiction.[10] In the light of established ECtHR case law, it was evident that such transfer could not be realised ad hoc, but required that

> the conditions for the transfer have been agreed with that third State in a manner consistent with relevant international law, notably international law on human rights, in order to guarantee in particular that no one shall be subjected to the death penalty, to torture or to any cruel, inhuman or degrading treatment.[11]

Negotiating and implementing such transfer agreements with third states proved cumbersome, but the EU used its political clout to convince Kenya,[12] Seychelles[13] and, more recently, Mauritius[14] to consent to transfer arrangement, which, in the case of Kenya and Seychelles, proceeded by way of an exchange of letters.[15] In March 2010, the Council authorised the High Representative to open negotiations with a view to concluding transfer agreements with South Africa, Tanzania and Uganda, which hitherto have not been concluded.[16] Meanwhile, agreements with Kenya, Seychelles and Mauritius did not remain dead letter. By September 2010, 10 groups of suspected pirates comprising 79 persons were transferred to the Kenyan authorities, while another seven individuals have been surrendered to the authorities of Seychelles.[17] Around the same time, Kenya revoked its agreement with the EU (after domestic criticism about neo-colonial behaviour of European powers 'dumping' unwanted aliens to poor African

---

[9] Art 12.1, indent 1 of Council Joint Action 2008/851/CFSP, n 2 above; Council Decision 2012/174/CFSP of 23 March 2012, [2012] OJ L89/66, specifies in a new second paragraph that pirates caught in the territorial waters of a state should be transferred to this state subjected to the human rights requirements discussed below.

[10] Art 12.1, indent 2 of Council Joint Action 2008/851/CFSP, n 2 above.

[11] Art 12.2 of Council Joint Action 2008/851/CFSP, n 2 above, which later became Art 12.3 of Council Decision 2012/174/CFSP, n 9 above.

[12] Exchange of Letters between the European Union and the Government of Kenya on the conditions and modalities for the transfer of persons suspected of having committed acts of piracy and detained by the European Union-led naval force (EU NAVFOR), and seized property in the possession of EU NAVFOR, from EU NAVFOR to Kenya and for their treatment after such transfer, signed on 6 March 2009, [2009] OJ L79/49, adopted by Council Decision 2009/293/CFSP, [2009] OJ L79/47, which has been provisionally applied since the day of signature.

[13] Exchange of Letters between the European Union and the Republic of Seychelles on the Conditions and Modalities for the Transfer of Suspected Pirates and Armed Robbers from EU NAVFOR to the Republic of Seychelles and for their Treatment after such Transfer, signed on 26 October 2009, [2009] OJ L315/37, adopted by Council Decision 2009/877/CFSP, [2009] OJ L315/35, which has been provisionally applied since the day of signature.

[14] Agreement between the European Union and the Republic of Mauritius on the conditions of transfer of suspected pirates and associated seized property from the European Union-led naval force to the Republic of Mauritius and on the conditions of suspected pirates after transfer, signed on 14 July 2011, [2011] OJ L254/3, adopted by Council Decision 2011/640/CFSP, [2011] OJ L254/1, not yet entered into force, but provisional application as from the date of signature.

[15] This form does not diminish that legal value of the agreement; see Art 2.1.a Vienna Convention on the Law of Treaties of 23 May 1969, 1155 UNTS 331.

[16] See the press release of the 3005th Council meeting (Foreign Affairs) on 22 March 2010, Council Doc 7828/1/10 REV 1 (Presse 73), 16; neither Council documents nor the Official Journal indicate that negotiations were successful.

[17] See Council of the European Union, 'EU NAVFOR Will Transfer a Further Four Indicted Pirates to Kenya Authorities', 27 September 2010, available at http://eunavfor.eu/eu-navfor-will-transfer-a-further-four-interdicted-pirates-to-kenya-authorities/.

states).[18] Later press releases demonstrate at least nine further transfers to Seychelles plus 12 surrenders of suspected pirates to Mauritian authorities.[19] In quite a number of cases, these trials have subsequently been concluded and resulted in convictions of many years in prison.[20]

The EU is eager to present its military engagement as part of a broader approach to support nation building in Somalia and enhance economic development in the region. Operation Atalanta is complemented by two CSDP missions to strengthen maritime capacities in the Horn of Africa (EUCAP Nestor),[21] together with a training mission (EUTM Somalia), which contributes to the training of several thousand Somali security forces through EU advisors in Uganda.[22] More importantly, security and defence activities are supplemented by extensive development, humanitarian and economic initiatives which aim at laying the basis for lasting peace through economic and social stability.[23] These measures might not always be successful, but they reflect the political intention to address the fundamental problems of piracy.

In a similar vein, the EU is eager not to present the transfer agreements as isolated attempts in 'burden shifting', which obliges poorer states in the region to assume responsibilities which European states try to avoid. The EU is the single largest donor to the Counter Piracy Programme of the United Nations Office for Drugs and Crime (UNODC), which began in 2009 with a mandate to assist Kenya and which has in the meantime been widened to Seychelles, Mauritius, Tanzania, Maldives and Somalia.[24] It focuses on fair and efficient trials and imprisonment with judicial, prosecutorial and police capacity building programmes, as well as office equipment, law books and specialist coast guard equipment. International support may thus serve as a trigger for the reform of domestic criminal justice systems at large.[25] In March 2013, 17 convicted pirates, who had been arrested by the authorities of Seychelles and tried in the country, volunteered to be transferred to a prison in Somaliland, which was constructed by and is mentored by UNODC.[26]

[18] See BBC, 'Kenya Ends Co-operation in Hosting Somali Pirate Trials', available at http://www.bbc.co.uk/news/world-africa-11454762.

[19] See Council of the European Union, EU NAVFOR press releases of 25 January 2013 and 28 February 2013, available at http://eunavfor.eu/eu-naval-force-transfers-twelve-suspect-pirates-to-mauritius-for-prosecution-after-attack-on-merchant-vessel-off-somalia-2/ and http://eunavfor.eu/nine-suspected-pirates-transferred-to-seychelles-by-dutch-eu-naval-force-frigate-de-ruyter/.

[20] Each verdict is received with fanfare by the press section of Operation Atalanta: http://eunavfor.eu/latest-news/.

[21] See Council Decision 2012/389/CFSP on the European Union Mission on Regional Maritime Capacity Building in the Horn of Africa of 16 July 2012, [2012] OJ L187/40.

[22] Council Decision 2010/96/CFSP on a European Union military mission to contribute to the training of Somali security forces of 15 February 2010, [2010] OJ L44/16.

[23] See the overview by HG Ehrhart and K Petretto, 'The EU, the Somalia Challenge, and Counter-piracy' (2012) 17 *European Foreign Affairs Review* 261.

[24] For more detail, see http://www.unodc.org/easternafrica/en/piracy/index.html.

[25] See JT Gathii, 'Kenya's Piracy Prosecutions' (2010) 104 *American Journal of International Law* 416.

[26] See UNODC, 'Support to the Trial and Related Treatment of Piracy Suspects, Issue Eleven', March 2013, see n 24 above.

IV. HUMAN RIGHTS STANDARDS

For the purposes of this chapter, the substantive human rights standards which EU Member States have to respect are easy to identify. Over the past 20 years, the ECtHR has established a number of criteria for the extraterritorial application of human rights and the relevant degree of protection which the High Contracting Parties must guarantee to citizens and foreigners in cases of extradition or expulsion. These standards shall be briefly described in this section with a view to presenting potential legal challenges to the EU transfer agreements. Since the ECtHR's standards are, generally speaking, more ambitious than other international human rights requirements, including of the International Covenant on Civil and Political Rights and of the UN Convention against Torture,[27] in situations of extradition or deportation, this chapter focuses on the European Convention on Human Rights (ECHR). For practical purposes, the ECtHR's standard presents the main point of reference for EU military missions.

As a starting point of its case law, the ECtHR notes that Article 1 ECHR guarantees that rights and freedoms enshrined in the Convention shall be accorded by the High Contracting Parties to 'everyone within their jurisdiction'. Although jurisdiction in this sense is essentially territorial, the Court maintains that state acts which are performed, or are producing effects, outside their territories can constitute an exercise of jurisdiction within the meaning of Article 1 of the Convention. Such extraterritorial jurisdiction covers situations in which a state exercises effective control of an area outside its national territory in situations of military occupation[28] or whenever the state, through its agents operating outside its territory, exercises control and authority over an individual.[29] While it is not crystal clear which requirements must be met for a state agent to exercise effective control in combat situations[30] or whenever state agents give instructions to shipowners,[31] it is well established that states have jurisdiction over detainees.[32] Since any transfer of alleged pirates for purposes of prosecution will usually occur after prior detention, EU Member States hold jurisdiction within the meaning of Article 1 ECHR.

One step further, the ECtHR argues, controversially, that the High Contracting Parties do not exercise jurisdiction whenever the UN Security Council retains 'ultimate

---

[27] For an overview see K Wouters, *International Legal Standards for the Protection from Refoulement* (Antwerp, Intersentia, 2009) chs 4 and 5, MJ Dennis, 'Application of Human Rights Treaties Extraterritorially in Times of Armed Conflict and Military Occupation' (2005) 99 *American Journal of International Law* 119; A von Arnauld, 'Das (Menschen-)Recht im Auslandseinsatz. Rechtsgrundlagen zum Schutz von Grund- und Menschenrechten' in D Weingärtner (ed), *Streitkräfte und Menschenrechte* (Baden-Baden, Nomos, 2008) 61, 62–66.

[28] See ECtHR, *Loizidou v Turkey*, Application No 15318/89, Judgment of 23 March 1995 (GC), para 62.

[29] See ECtHR, *Al-Skeini et al v the United Kingdom*, Application No 55721/07, Judgment of 7 July 2011 (GC), paras 66–67.

[30] See ECtHR, *Banković et al v Belgium et al*, Application No 52207/99, Decision of 12 December 2001 (GC), paras 75 and 80.

[31] On border controls in relation to migrants' ships see ECtHR, *Hirsi Jamaa et al v Italy*, Application No 27765/09, Judgment of 23 February 2012 (GC), paras 76–82; M Giuffré, 'Watered-Down Rights on the High Seas' (2012) 61 *International & Comparative Law Quarterly* 728.

[32] See, by way of example, ECtHR, *Medvedyev et al v France*, Application No 3394/03, Judgment of 29 March 2008 (GC), paras 62–67.

authority and control over the security mission'[33] by delegating to NATO or other international organisations the power to establish and conduct military operations—a conclusion which has been met with criticism by international commentators, since it is based upon a rather peculiar reading of the rules of general public international law on the attribution of state measures.[34] If the ECtHR upholds this line of reasoning, most EU military missions, including Operation Atalanta, would not be subject to the Court's jurisdiction, since Operation Atalanta, in particular, was explicitly sanctioned by the Security Council acting under Chapter VII of the UN Charter.[35] However, this question does not have to be discussed further for the purposes of this chapter, since it will be demonstrated later that the position of the Strasbourg Court on Article 1 ECHR cannot be extended to the EU Charter of Fundamental Rights and that, therefore, EU human rights apply to military missions irrespective of UN authorisation and public international law rules on attribution of state contributions to international military operations (see Section V below).

Insofar as the High Contracting Parties have jurisdiction within the meaning of Article 1 ECHR, the Strasbourg Court applies a double scrutiny standard, if alleged pirates are transferred to a third state for prosecution and/or detention (plus additional procedural safeguards for prior arrest[36]). This double scrutiny standard flows from Article 3 ECHR, which prohibits inhuman or degrading treatment or punishment, and the fair trial guarantees of Articles 5 and 6 ECHR, which the ECtHR has extended to extradition and expulsion.

First, there is extensive case law on the application of Article 3 ECHR to extradition or expulsion. The Strasbourg Court developed criteria which prohibit extradition or expulsion to a third state if the transferee faces a real risk of torture or inhuman or degrading treatment.[37] In a first step, this line of case law concerns 'classic' situations of ill-treatment by state agents, in particular during detention in the third state after the transfer; in our case, this relates to the treatment of alleged pirates by police or penitentiary officers in Kenya or Seychelles.[38] Further, the Court assumes, controversially, that the lack of material living conditions in the host state may amount to violation of Article 3 ECHR if the transferee has to live in extreme poverty or

---

[33] ECtHR, *Behrami v France & Saramati v France, Germany and Norway*, Application Nos 71412/01 and 78166/01, Decision of 2 May 2007 (GC), para 135.

[34] See M Milanović and T Papić, 'As Bad As It Gets: The European Court of Human Rights' *Behrami and Saramati* Decision and General International Law' (2009) 58 *International & Comparative Law Quarterly* 267; KM Larsen, 'Attribution of Conduct in Peace Operations: The 'Ultimate Authority and Control' Test' (2008) 19 *European Journal of International Law* 509.

[35] See the references in n 1 and S Piedimonte Bodini, 'Fighting Maritime Piracy under the European Convention on Human Rights' (2011) 22 *European Journal of International Law* 829, 844–46.

[36] While the arrest of alleged pirates will regularly be covered by Art 5(1)(c) ECHR, he/she 'shall be brought promptly before a judge or other officer authorised by law to exercise judicial power' in accordance with Art 5(3) ECHR, which may meet practical obstacles, when the persons are not brought back to the mainland; for further comments, see ECtHR, *Medvedyev et al*, n 32 above, paras 117–34, and the comments by on piracy operations by Guilfoyle, n 1 above, 159–60, as well as A Fischer-Lescano and L Kreck, 'Piraterie und Menschenrechte' (2009) 47 *Archiv des Völkerrechts* 481, 496–506.

[37] For an overview of various aspects see P Boeles et al, *European Migration Law* (Antwerp, Intersentia, 2009) 291–314; M Bossuyt, *Strasbourg et les demandeurs d'asile: des juges sur un terrain glissant* (Brussels, Bruylant, 2010), 7–48; A Zimmermann, 'Ausweisungsschutz' in R Grote and T Marauhn (eds), *Konkordanzkommentar* (Tübingen, Mohr Siebeck, 2005), ch 27, paras 29–81.

[38] See the Court's summary of its case law in ECtHR, *MSS v Belgium & Greece*, Application No 30696/09, Judgment of 21 January 2011 (GC), paras 214–21.

may be excluded from mandatory medical treatment (the precise standard remaining elusive).[39] This second aspect is less relevant in our context, since suspected pirates do not primarily complain about living conditions but rather about potential ill-treatment by the host state. In practice, most cases evolve around the standard of proof which applicants and national courts have to meet when assessing complaints with regard to Article 3 ECHR.[40] This applies in particular to diplomatic assurances, which will be discussed in the next section.

Secondly, it is, by now, established ECtHR case law that an issue might exceptionally be raised under Articles 5 and/or 6 ECHR by an expulsion or extradition in circumstances where the applicant risks suffering a flagrant denial of justice in the requesting country. In the Court's case law, the term 'flagrant denial of justice' has been made use of for trials which are manifestly contrary to the principles embodied in Articles 5 and/or 6 ECHR, which the Court defines as follows:

> conviction *in absentia* with no possibility subsequently to obtain a fresh determination of the merits of the charge; a trial which is summary in nature and conducted with a total disregard for the rights of the defence; detention without any access to an independent and impartial tribunal to have the legality the detention reviewed; deliberate and systematic refusal of access to a lawyer, especially for an individual detained in a foreign country.[41]

It should be noted, however, that the Strasbourg Court highlights the exceptional character of these limits, which may only be violated in extreme scenarios. In more than 20 years, it has found only two violations.[42]

V. CONTENTS OF EU TRANSFER AGREEMENTS

EU transfer agreements with Kenya, Seychelles and, most recently, Mauritius have been drafted with the ECtHR case law in mind. They make a notable effort to balance the requirements of practical expediency with the perspective of third states while complying with ECtHR case law. The transfer agreements with both Kenya and Mauritius

---

[39] See ECtHR, *MSS*, ibid; seel also my critical comments in D Thym, 'Menschenrechtliche Feinjustierung des Dublin-Systems zur Asylzuständigkeitsabgrenzung' (2011) *Zeitschrift für Ausländerrecht* 368, 369–71. For the somewhat more lenient, recent approach see ECtHR, *Nacic et al v Sweden*, Application No 16567/10, Judgment of 15 May 2012, para 86; ECtHR, *Mohammed Hussein et al vs the Netherlands and Italy*, Application No 27725/10, Decision of 2 April 2013, paras 70–71.

[40] See T Spijkerboer, 'Subsidiarity and "Arguability": the European Court of Human Rights' Case Law on Judicial Review in Asylum Cases' (2009) 21 *International Journal of Refugee Law* 48; RA Lorz and H Sauer, 'Wann genau steht Art 3 EMRK einer Auslieferung oder Ausweisung entgegen?' (2010) *Europäische Grundrechte-Zeitschrift* 389, 393–402.

[41] ECtHR, *Othman (Abu Qatada) v the United Kingdom*, Application No 8139/09, Judgment of 17 January 2012, para 259; C Michaelsena, 'The Renaissance of *Non-Refoulement*? The *Othman (Abu Qatada)* Decision of the European Court of Human Rights' (2012) 61 *International & Comparative Law Quarterly* 750, 760–65; for a critical comment on earlier case law see K Hailbronner, 'Artikel 6 EMRK als Hindernis der Auslieferung und Abschiebung' in J Bröhmer et al (eds), *Internationale Gemeinschaft und Menschenrechte. Festschrift für Georg Ress* (Cologne, Carl Heymanns, 2005) 997–1010; H Battjes, 'The *Soering* Threshold: Why Only Fundamental Values Prohibit Refoulement in ECHR Case Law' (2009) 11 *European Journal of Migration and Law* 205.

[42] ECtHR, *Othman*, n 41 above; ECtHR, *Soering v United Kingdom*, Application No 14038/88, Judgment of 7 July 1989.

are almost identical in substance (though different in form),[43] while the arrangement with Seychelles consists of mutually agreed standards for the treatment of suspected pirates, together with a unilateral declaration of the EU on monitoring mechanisms for alleged pirates after the transfer.[44] In essence, the arrangements concern three key issues.

First, all transfer agreements go some length to meet the ECtHR's requirements for a fair trial and appropriate detention conditions. They do not limit themselves to stating, in abstract terms, that the transferee shall be treated humanely in accordance with international human rights obligations and that any detainee shall receive adequate accommodation, nourishment and access to medical treatment. Rather, they specify a list of procedural standards mirroring the Court's requirements for a fair trial, including: the presumption of innocence, judicial independence, prompt information in a language which they understand, communication with a counsel of their choice, trial without undue delay, free legal assistance, cross-examination of evidence and witnesses, free assistance of an interpreter and absence of an obligation to testify against themselves.[45] Moreover, Kenya and Mauritius promise not to apply the death penalty[46]—in line with ECtHR case law, which prohibits extradition in the light of Article 3 unless the receiving state commits itself not to charge the transferee with an offence which would carry the death penalty.[47]

Secondly, the EU makes an effort to establish procedures which guarantee that the commitments to which the third states have signed up on paper are put into practice. With broad financial support from the EU, prison facilities for pirates have been upgraded to meet international standards.[48] Moreover, the agreements with Kenya and Mauritius lay down detailed recording and reporting obligations, including detention records and notification to the EU of the place of detention, any deterioration of the physical status and timing of trials.[49] It is intended that, through the implementation of arrangements between EU personnel and Kenyan or Mauritian authorities, points of contact for permanent cooperation may be established.[50] Finally, supervision of detention practices shall not be limited to public authorities, since '[n]ational and

---

[43] The agreement with Kenya, n 12 above, consists of an exchange of letters together with an annex which was meant to be a transitional arrangement pending the conclusion of a permanent agreement but which nonetheless addresses, often verbatim, the same issues as the agreement with Mauritius, n 14 above, which was concluded as a formal treaty with articles and ratification requirements.

[44] A unilateral declaration annexed to the exchange of letters with Seychelles, n 13 above, does not have the same legal value as similar provision in the agreements with Kenya and Seychelles which are an integral part of agreements.

[45] See No 3 annex to the exchange of letters with Kenya, n 12 above; indent 5 of the exchange of letters with Seychelles, n 13 above; Art 4 of the agreement with Mauritius, n 14 above.

[46] No 4 annex to the exchange of letters with Kenya, n 12 above; Art 5 of the agreement with Mauritius, n 14 above. The exchange of letters with Seychelles, n 13 above, does not touch upon the issue, given that the death penalty has been abolished in the country.

[47] See the classic position in ECtHR, *Soering*, n 42 above.

[48] See n 23 and accompanying text.

[49] See No 5 annex to the exchange of letters with Kenya, n 12 above; Art 6 of the agreement with Mauritius, n 14 above.

[50] See No 9 annex to the exchange of letters with Kenya, n 12 above; Art 10 of the agreement with Mauritius, n 14 above.

international humanitarian agencies will, at their request, be allowed to visit persons transferred under this Exchange of Letters'.[51]

These documentation and reporting requirements are no coincidence, but reflect ECtHR case law on diplomatic assurances whenever extradition or expulsion to a third state would involve a violation of Article 3 ECHR unless the receiving state commits itself to respect certain standards.[52] The Court has consistently held that the existence of domestic laws and accession to international human rights treaties are not in themselves sufficient and that, besides written commitments, diplomatic assurances have to provide, in their practical application, sufficient guarantees for actual implementation.[53] In its *Abu Qatada* judgment of January 2012, the ECtHR lists no less than 11 considerations which will guide the case-by-case analysis of whether diplomatic assurances provide a reliable guarantee that the transferee will be treated humanely.[54] It seems to me that the obligations, to which both Kenya and Mauritius have signed up, meet these standards in the context of a stable bilateral relationship with the EU, which counts as one of their most important trading partners and is the largest donor of development aid.[55] If that is correct, the EU transfer agreements with Kenya and Mauritius comply with human rights standards, while arrangements with Seychelles fall short of ECtHR standards, given the lack of monitoring procedures.[56]

Thirdly, transfer agreements are not only concerned with the treatment of suspected pirates in the receiving state, but also consider potential indirect removal to other states for purposes of prosecution and/or detention, which, again, may give rise to an issue under Article 3 ECHR, since the other state would not be bound by the diplomatic assurances to which the receiving state has subscribed. In situations of a real risk of indirect removal, the ECtHR prohibits extradition or deportation from the first receiving state. While the Exchange of Letters with Kenya and Seychelles state explicitly that they 'will not transfer any transferred person to any other State without prior written consent from EU NAVFOR',[57] the agreement with Mauritius is more ambiguous, providing only for the 'consultation' of the EU, while adding that '[i]n case of serious concerns about the human rights situation in that other State, no transfer shall take place before a satisfactory solution will have been found through consultations between the Parties to address the concerns expressed'.[58] Whereas the consent requirement with Kenya and Seychelles meets ECtHR standards, the rule in

---

[51] No 5(f) annex to the exchange of letters with Kenya, n 12 above; Art 6(6) of the agreement with Mauritius, n 14 above.

[52] For an introduction to ECtHR standards for diplomatic assurances see Wouters, n 27 above, 293–304; see also Lorz and Sauer, n 40 above, 402–06.

[53] See ECtHR, *Saadi v Italy*, Application No 37201/06, Judgment of 28 February 2008 (GC), paras 147–48.

[54] See ECtHR, *Othman*, n 41 above, para 189.

[55] For a more critical view see Guilfoyle, n 1 above, 161–65; Fischer-Lescano and Kreck, n 36 above, 517–18. The Administrative Court (VG) Köln, Judgment of 11 November 2011, Case 25 K 4280/09, available at http://www.justiz.nrw.de/nrwe/ovgs/vg_koeln/j2011/25_K_4280_09urteil20111111.html, which is discussed by D König and TR Salomon in Chapter 10 below, concluded that the transfer to Kenya only four days after the exchange of letters between the EU and Kenya was illegal, given that no implementing arrangements had yet been agreed upon; it did not take a firm position on whether the assurances could be adequate in principle; in any case, it is only a decision of first instance, which could have been reversed on appeal

[56] Monitoring mechanisms may, however, be established ad hoc on a case-by-case basis when a suspected pirate is transferred to Seychelles.

[57] Indent 5.8 of the exchange of letters with Seychelles, n 13 above and No 3(h) annex to the exchange of letters with Kenya, n 12 above.

[58] Art 4(8) of the agreement with Mauritius, n 14 above.

the Mauritian agreement would require closer scrutiny, especially considering the reliability of the Mauritian government, domestic human rights records and the stability of bilateral relations with the EU.[59]

VI. EXTENDED GUARANTEES UNDER THE EU CHARTER

With the entry into force of the Lisbon Treaty, the EU's quest for international visibility benefits from a uniform legal framework. The former 'second pillar' on the Common Foreign and Security Policy (CFSP), which includes the CSDP,[60] has been integrated into the Union legal order. This has repercussions for the analysis of EU transfer agreements, since EU law upholds a principled commitment to democracy, the rule of law and human rights. While it is correct that CFSP shall be 'subject to specific rules and procedures',[61] which I have portrayed elsewhere as Treaty rules governing the exercise of intergovernmental executive power,[62] the integration of the CFSP into the uniform Treaty framework implies that many political and legal accountability mechanisms now extend to security and defence—albeit with some caveats. The remainder of this chapter focuses on EU transfer agreements for suspected pirates as a case study for the legal accountability of CSDP operations.[63] It will be demonstrated that the EU legal order offers increased protection and provides for diverse control fora with the power to hold the implementation of transfer agreements to account.

One core difference between the 'constitutional' character of Union law and the 'international' features of classic international law concerns the hierarchy of norms. Within the EU legal order, secondary law must respect the procedural and substantive imperatives of primary law. This 'legal constitutionalism' remains the backbone of the Court's famous description of the EU Treaties as 'a Community based on the rule of law, inasmuch as . . . its institutions can[not] avoid a review of the question whether the measures adopted by them are in conformity with the basic constitutional charter'.[64] This contention does not contradict my conclusion about the intergovernmental character of the CSFP.[65] While the Lisbon Treaty eschews the vertical 'supranationalisation' of the CFSP with regard to domestic legal effects within national legal systems, it proceeds with its horizontal 'constitutionalisation'. Against this background, the most important consequence of the Lisbon Treaty is normative: constitutional control standards, such as human rights, apply to all areas of Union action. Security and defence policies are, as an integral part of Union law, no exception. Primary law guides and restricts CFSP and CSDP in the same way as it controls domestic EU policies.

---

[59] See ECtHR, *Hirsi Jamaa et al*, n 31 above, paras 143–58; on the necessary assessment on a case-by-case basis see ECtHR, *Othman (Abu Qatada)*, n 41 above, paras 187–89.

[60] Chapter 2 of the EU Treaty comprises two sections: 'common provisions' for both CFSP and CSDP (Arts 23–41) and specific CSDP rules (Arts 42–46).

[61] Art 24(1)(2) TEU.

[62] See D Thym, 'The Intergovernmental Constitution of the EU's Foreign, Security & Defence Executive' (2011) 7 *European Constitutional Law Review* 453.

[63] Council Decisions adopting the transfer agreements, nn 12–14 above, all emanate from Union competences for CFSP; the same applies to the Council Decisions establishing and extending Operation Atalanta, n 2 above.

[64] ECJ, Case 294/83 *Les Verts* [1986] ECR 1339, para 23.

[65] See Thym, n 62 above, 466–76; see also the generic statement in Art 24 TEU, n 61 above.

In contemporary constitutionalism, human rights serve as the central point of reference for the substantive control of state action. As a matter of principle, the Lisbon Treaty does not leave any doubt that foreign affairs must respect human rights. Article 51 Charter of Fundamental Rights states paradigmatically: 'The provisions of this Charter are addressed to the institutions, bodies, offices and agencies of the Union'. As a result, the Council or the PSC are not allowed to authorise CFSP actions[66] which violate the Charter of Fundamental Rights. For the purposes of this contribution, this implies that transfer agreements with third states have to respect the ECtHR's principles on Articles 3, 5 and 6 ECHR, since corresponding guarantees in Articles 4, 6 and 47 of the EU Charter have to be interpreted in analogy with ECtHR case law.[67] If transfer agreements and their implementation respect these requirements, they are compatible with the Charter.

An additional twist concerns obligations of the Member States to comply with the Charter when national agents transfer pirates on the basis of the agreements. Since the Union legal order does not embrace the rules of public international law on the attribution of state activities to international organisations,[68] the Charter applies to national contingents within EU military operations 'only when they are *implementing* Union law'.[69] There has been much debate about what precisely represents implementation[70] and the extension of these principles to military action raises additional questions, since Article 51 has been designed for legislative implementation, such as the transposition of directives and not for operative police or military action.[71] This question is far from academic, since the ECtHR's standards for diplomatic assurances emphasise that state practice must comply with the Convention—actual transfers, however, will regularly not be undertaken by EU agents but rather by national contingents within EU NAVFOR Atalanta.[72] The issue was settled in the *Åkerberg Fransson* judgment, in which the EU Court of Justice (ECJ) confirmed that the Charter applies to all Member States action 'within the scope of EU law'.[73] Since military contingents within CSDP missions meet this requirement, the Charter applies not only to the Council and the PSC, but also to national troops participating in CSDP operations.

---

[66] As a subsidiary body of the Council, the Political and Security Committee exercises, in accordance with Art 38 TEU, the day-to-day political control and strategic direction of the EU crisis management operations, including EU NAVFOR Atalanta.

[67] See Art 52(3) of the EU Charter and the Explanations Relating to the Charter of Fundamental Rights, [2007] OJ C303/17. Additional guarantees in Arts 1 and 18 of the Charter are not wider than the protection conferred by Art 3 ECHR: see ECJ, Joined Cases C-411/10 and C-493/10 *NS et al* [2011] ECR I-0000, paras 109–14.

[68] In contrast to Arts 6–7 Draft Articles on the Responsibility of International Organizations, adopted by the International Law Commission at its 63rd session in 2011, EU law assumes for internal purposes that Member States defend their activities on their own behalf, but must respect EU standards in doing so; see C Walter and A von Ungern-Sternberg, 'Piratenbekämpfung vor Somalia—Zum Zusammenspiel europäischer und deutscher Grundrechte' (2012) *Die Öffentliche Verwaltung* 861, 862–63.

[69] Art 51(1) of the Charter (emphasis added).

[70] See P Eeckhout, 'The EU Charter of Fundamental Rights and the Federal Question' (2002) 39 *Common Market Law Review* 945, 969–85.

[71] An application of the Charter to national action within military operations is supported by C Ladenburger in P Tettinger and K Stern (eds), *Europäische Grundrechte-Charta—Kölner Gemeinschafts-Kommentar* (Cologne, CH Beck, 2006) Art 51, para 33.

[72] See the comments in Section IV above.

[73] Case C-617/10 *Åkerberg Fransson* [2013] ECR I-0000, paras 18–22; alternatively, it had been argued that the Charter does not apply whenever Member States have discretion on what to do—a criterion which may have excluded practical aspects of CSDP operation decided by national commanders on the ground.

It has been mentioned earlier that the ECtHR maintains, controversially, that it does not have jurisdiction for military operations which are conducted under the ultimate authority and control of the UN Security Council, including in situations where international organisations, such as NATO or the EU, are mandated with setting up and conducting a mission authorised by the UN.[74] This assumption cannot be extended to the EU Charter for two interrelated reasons:

First, the Charter does not limit its application 'to everyone within the jurisdiction [of the High Contracting Parties]'.[75] Instead, Article 51 determines the scope of the Charter in generic terms which undoubtedly embrace any Council action, including the negotiation and conclusion of transfer agreements.

Secondly, the ECtHR arguably grounds its deference to the UN on the assumption that the primacy of the UN Charter hinders indirect judicial oversight of UN operations.[76] Again, this assumption cannot be extended to the EU Charter, since

> such immunity from jurisdiction for a Community measure . . . as a corollary of the principle of the primacy at the level of international law of obligations under the Charter of the United Nations . . . cannot find a basis in the EC Treaty.[77]

When it comes to human rights, neither CFSP nor UN mandated missions are an exclave. EU military missions must respect the rights set out in the Charter.

VII. CONTROL FORA FOR CFSP/CSDP OPERATIONS

We need to distinguish between normative control standards and the availability of accountability fora. Application of the EU Charter in abstract terms does not automatically provide a forum for institutionalised scrutiny. In particular, the European Court of Justice (ECJ) in Luxembourg is prevented from exercising judicial accountability. Article 275(1) TFEU states unequivocally that the ECJ 'shall not have jurisdiction with respect to the provisions relating to the [CFSP] nor with respect to acts adopted on the basis of those provisions'. It is true that there is an explicit exception for decisions imposing sanctions against individuals, which closes a loophole that became evident in the *Kadi* case.[78] This exception does not, however, unmake the exclusion of ECJ jurisdiction in other CFSP matters, including in situations where Member States transfer suspected pirates on the basis of transfer agreements to third states. This need not be the last word, however. There are alternative channels for legal accountability.

First, the CJEU may be tempted to test the limits of Article 275 TFEU. In earlier cases, it extended its power to access to CFSP documents[79] and effectively controlled

---

[74] See n 33 above and accompanying text.

[75] Art 1 ECHR, described above in Section III, which guides the ECtHR's analysis.

[76] See the (indirect) references to Art 103 UN Charter and the primacy of UN law in public international law in ECtHR, *Behrami & Saramati*, n 33 above, paras 122, 148 and 149.

[77] ECJ, Joined Cases C-402 and 415/05 P *Kadi v Council and Commission* [2008] ECR I-6351, para 299 (see also paras 300–07).

[78] See Art 275(2) TFEU; for a more detailed analysis see A Hinarejos, *Judicial Control in the European Union* (Oxford, Oxford University Press, 2009) ch 3.

[79] See M-G Garbagnati Ketvel, 'The Jurisdiction of the European Court of Justice in Respect of the Common Foreign and Security Policy' (2006) 56 *International & Comparative Law Quarterly* 77, 82–83.

the borderline between the pillars.[80] In future, it may use new rules on the judicial scrutiny of international agreements[81] or ambiguous formulations about non-contractual liability[82] to stretch its control function further. Most importantly, however, the Court of Justice may activate the fundamental right to an effective judicial remedy in Article 47 of the Charter in situations in which CFSP action directly affects the legal position of individuals, such as the transfer of alleged pirates to a third state, and balance this fundamental right with the exclusion of its jurisdiction in Article 275 TFEU, thereby effectively establishing a certain degree of judicial scrutiny. It would not be the first time that the ECJ extends its jurisdiction against explicit Treaty language under recourse to general constitutional principles.[83] In a related scenario, Luxembourg proved its readiness to scrutinise (former) limitations to its jurisdiction in criminal matters[84]—a strategy which might repeat itself in security and defence. The judges will not set aside Article 275 TFEU entirely, but a careful expansion to corollary aspects of foreign, security and defence policies, for instance non-contractual liability, would not come as a surprise.

Secondly, the exclusion of ECJ jurisdiction does not prevent national courts from filling the gap—indeed, they might find themselves obliged to do so under the EU's overarching constitutional rules. In a remarkable follow-up judgment to its first *Kadi* judgment, the General Court (then still the Court of First Instance) held that Member States are obliged to provide judicial protection at national level and that they should set aside national rules which prevent courts from carrying out review of foreign affairs.[85] Additionally, we may nowadays point to the obligation of Member States in the Lisbon Treaty to 'provide remedies sufficient to ensure effective legal protection in the fields covered by Union law'.[86] It is true that there is, at this moment in time, a lot of uncertainty about the conditions of national judicial CFSP oversight, but I would not be surprised if extension of legal and judicial scrutiny within the EU soon reached security and defence—with national courts exercising control of foreign policy in general and military missions in particular.

Thirdly, legal accountability may be enhanced by non-judicial fora. Here, the abolition of the pillar structure has tangible side effects. The new unity of the Union legal order implies that the Ombudsman, the Court of Auditors and Committees of Inquiry

---

[80] See ECJ, Case C-91/05 *Commission vs Council* [2008] ECR I-3651; see also the analysis by P Van Elsuwege, 'EU External Action after the Collapse of the Pillar Structure' (2010) 47 *Common Market Law Review* 987, 1002–08.

[81] Art 218(11) TEU continues the earlier Art 300(8) EC, but is broader insofar as it includes CFSP agreements (it remains unclear how this rules interacts with Art 275 TFEU).

[82] While the extension of liability under Art 340 TFEU to CFSP is beyond doubt, the corresponding rule on ECJ jurisdiction (Art 268 TFEU) will have to be reconciled with the exclusion of ECJ jurisdiction under Art 275 TFEU.

[83] See ECJ, Case 294/83 *Les Verts*, n 64 above, on the extension of active and passive standing rights to the European Parliament which an earlier version of Art 263 TFEU did not provide for.

[84] See CJEU, Joined Cases C-354/04 and C-355/04 P *Gestoras Pro Amnistía & Segi v Council* [2007] ECR I-1579, paras 50–54; D Curtin, *Executive Power of the European Union* (Oxford, Oxford University Press, 2009) 191–93, 202–03; P Eeckhout, 'The EU's Common Foreign and Security Policy after Lisbon: From Pillar Talk to Constitutionalisation?' in A Biondi, D Curtin and S Ripley (eds), *EU Law after Lisbon* (Oxford, Oxford University Press, 2011) 265, 281–82.

[85] See General Court (CFI), Case T-253/02 *Ayadi vs Council* [2006] ECR II-2139, paras 151–52; P Craig, *The Lisbon Treaty* (Oxford, Oxford University Press, 2010) 434–35.

[86] Art 19(1)(2) TEU.

established by the European Parliament may now scrutinise CFSP action.[87] To be sure, these institutions are not courts and may apply other standards than legal requirements alone. That is not to say, however, that such alternative fora for non-judicial accountability may not embrace legal aspects and complement corresponding powers of national accountability fora.

VIII. CONCLUSION

Agreements which the EU has concluded with Kenya, Seychelles and Mauritius on the transfer of suspected pirates for purposes of prosecution and detention illustrate that the European Convention is not limited to intra-European affairs, but embraces transnational cooperation with third states thousands of miles away. In line with established ECtHR case law, military missions conducted by the EU and/or its Member States are bound to respect the European Convention. Once alleged pirates have been arrested, they are within the jurisdiction of the High Contracting Parties within the meaning of Article 1 ECHR. As a result, ECtHR standards for extradition or expulsion on the basis of Articles 3, 5 and 6 ECHR, which prescribe humane detention conditions and fair trials and prohibit other forms of ill-treatment, must be respected. All EU transfer agreements go some length to meet these requirements by listing various procedural and substantive standards with which third states must comply and by establishing reporting and monitoring mechanisms which ensure that the diplomatic assurances are complied with in practice. As a result, it seems that the transfer agreements comply with human rights law and that various transfers which have taken place on their basis in recent years were lawful.

While ECtHR case law on human rights constraints for extradition and expulsion is well established, the impact of the EU Charter of Fundamental Rights on the legal accountability of military missions conducted within the framework of the CFSP presents some novelties. They relate, firstly, to extended substantive guarantees, if the EU Charter does not follow the controversial assumption of the Strasbourg Court that UN-mandate missions are exempt from ECtHR oversight. Any EU military mission has to comply with the EU Charter also when acting within the auspices of the UN Security Council. In spite of this, institutionalised control is hampered by the exclusion of ECJ jurisdiction in CFSP. As a result, national courts and alternative fora for legal accountability, such as parliamentary committees of inquiry at both national and European level, may take centre stage when they scrutinise the legality of EU military missions. Eventually, the Luxembourg court may be tempted to test the exclusion of its jurisdiction in CFSP whenever military missions directly affect the legal position of individuals. This would guarantee effective judicial oversight, even if the judges concluded that EU practice did comply with human rights standards.

---

[87] This follows from the merger of the former pillars, since Art 28 TEU-Nice did not incorporate Arts 193–95 and Art 255 TEC-Nice into the second pillar on security and defence; within the uniform Treaty framework, explicit incorporation is no longer necessary.

7

Countering Piracy off the Coast of Somalia: A NATO Perspective

PETER M OLSON

I. INTRODUCTION

T HE CONTRIBUTION OF the North Atlantic Treaty Organization (NATO, the Alliance) to addressing the problem of piracy off the coast of Somalia is both highly significant and inherently limited. Although NATO's mission focuses on addressing piracy directly through deployment of naval forces and coordination of protective actions, the Alliance has recognised from the beginning that the root causes of the Somali piracy problem relate to the failure of the Somali state and its institutions, and that enduring solutions must be found through political means to which NATO is not structured to contribute.[1] NATO's role is thus largely that of a 'first responder'—addressing immediate symptoms and stabilising the situation in order to buy time for others to address more fundamental issues.

The NATO mission, Operation Ocean Shield, is conducted under a mandate from the North Atlantic Council (the Council), responding to widespread commercial and governmental concern about the growth of piracy in the Somali Basin and nearby waters, and building on a series of UN Security Council Resolutions (UNSCRs) authorising the use, in a manner consistent with the actions permitted on the high seas, of 'all necessary means' to repress piracy and armed robbery at sea in the territorial waters of Somalia. The mission is carried out as a law enforcement action aimed at suppressing criminal activity. Although designed for and conducted by military forces, Ocean Shield is neither conceived nor implemented as a counter-terrorism or combat operation.

Primarily through Ocean Shield, NATO concentrates on actions contributing directly to the physical security of shipping—escort, deterrence, intervention in ongoing attacks on vessels, tracking and monitoring of both merchant vessels and pirates; provision of information to military and commercial vessels; contributing to the development of so-called 'best management practices' (BMPs) to deter pirate attacks; and coordination of

---

* The views expressed in this article do not necessarily reflect official NATO policy.

[1] It should be noted that NATO's contribution to addressing the situation in Somalia also includes the provision of important air- and sealift support for the African Union Mission to Somalia (AMISOM).

military forces from NATO and non-NATO states alike. While existing UNSCRs also envisage the possibility of military action on land against pirates and their support facilities and systems, NATO has to date confined its military operations to the high seas, territorial seas and waters up to the high water mark. Unlike the EU, NATO has not to date considered it necessary to conduct activities on or over Somali land territory, or sought authorisation from the Council or Somali authorities to do so.

The tasks NATO, along with the EU, the US and other states, is conducting are essential ones, and in recent months have met with increasing success. Enduring solutions to the piracy problem, however, require addressing other, more fundamental, issues. Among these are the dysfunctional Somali government and related societal issues, the need to rebuild judicial and other administrative capabilities, and the possible establishment of international mechanisms such as tribunals to try and imprison pirates.

II. INSTITUTIONAL FACTORS

The role just described is a direct consequence of NATO's mandate, structure and working methods.

NATO has a dual political and military character; it was created by a group of like-minded democracies for the purpose of defending and ultimately advancing a clearly defined set of distinct political values. It is thus a context, and the Council a key forum within it, for coordinating the national security policies of its Member States within the broader context of their national foreign policies.

That said, an essential defining characteristic of the Alliance is its military dimension, and the fact that it is a highly effective operational military organisation. NATO's principal operational tool, and its unique contribution to counter-piracy activities off Somalia, is its experience in and history of structuring, deploying and sustaining operationally effective multinational military forces. Multinational military coordination is the Alliance's *raison d'être* and core competence, and it has honed and demonstrated this capacity repeatedly over the last two decades in operations conducted in the Balkans, Afghanistan and Libya, as well as in Ocean Shield. Of particular relevance to this mission, NATO has close links, through Alliance membership or formalised partnership relationships,[2] to both the US and most EU Member States; these relationships enable it to work relatively seamlessly with the two most important non-NATO contributors to that effort.[3] NATO is thus well suited to contribute to the sustained multinational military effort off Somalia.

It is important in understanding NATO's role to appreciate that its institutions and capabilities, including its military planning and operational capabilities, are essentially tools to be employed, or not, according to the wishes of the states which comprise the Alliance. Allies often choose to take coordinated action through NATO, but there is no obligation on them to take foreign policy or national security action through NATO. If the Allies collectively consider it useful to employ Alliance mechanisms to

---

[2] Most notably, the Partnership for Peace, which structures NATO cooperation with almost all non-NATO European states, including among others Russia, Ukraine and all but one non-Allied EU Member States.

[3] Some three-quarters of the EU's and NATO's memberships overlap, and the EU's procedures and methods for managing its multinational military missions are based on and closely congruent with NATO's.

advance common foreign policy objectives, they may do so; if they do not choose that course, no collective action is taken by the Alliance and the Allies remain free to take action individually or in coordination outside the NATO context.

Implicit in this characteristic is that, unlike in the case of the other major participants in naval operations off Somalia, NATO as an organisation does not have an autonomous foreign policy. The Secretary General may suggest policy responses to various potential security challenges, and is charged with carrying out policy decisions made by the Council, but he cannot establish or conduct a NATO policy that has not been agreed by the Allies, nor can he or SACEUR[4] direct the taking of military action by NATO forces without specific authorisation by the Council.[5]

NATO is thus a specialised resource available to and employed by its Member States in conducting their foreign and security policies rather than an independent foreign policy actor. Consistent with this status, it lacks the full array of foreign policy tools available to states and to the EU. In particular, NATO has no foreign assistance programme or substantive technical expertise outside its principal military area of competence. This means that NATO has only a marginal ability (primarily through training of coast guards and related personnel) to contribute to building the capacity of state institutions either in Somalia or in other states of the region. NATO is further constrained in contributing to regional capacity building (RCB) by its ineligibility to participate in or benefit from the funding of the UN Trust Fund created to support RCB to address piracy-related issues.[6]

NATO's internal rules also have an impact on its approach to piracy. Decisions at NATO are made by consensus of all 28 Allies; there is no procedure allowing the taking of action by the Alliance over the opposition of any of its members. The consensus decision-making mechanism is a powerful organisational asset, ensuring that NATO operations enjoy at least the nominal, and in most cases the active, support of all Allies. The process of building consensus, moreover, increases the likelihood that all relevant factors will be considered carefully and that reservations or uncertainties will be addressed and reflected in Council decisions rather than being disregarded or downplayed. A concomitant disadvantage is that Council decisions may be taken less rapidly, and be more cautious and less ambitious than some may consider desirable.

Alliance operations are carried out by national forces placed temporarily under NATO command; there are virtually no 'NATO' as opposed to national operational assets.[7] The necessary forces are volunteered by individual Allies, or by non-Allied states which have elected to participate in a NATO-led operation.[8] In part because under long-standing NATO practice the costs of deploying these forces fall largely or

---

[4] NATO military operations fall under the direction of SACEUR (Supreme Allied Commander, Europe), who heads Allied Command Operations (ACO), located in Mons, Belgium, and informally known by its historical name, SHAPE (Supreme Headquarters, Allied Powers in Europe). SACEUR is directly accountable to the Council.

[5] The limited exceptions to this rule have little bearing on the counter-piracy operation.

[6] The UN Trust Fund Supporting Initiatives of States Countering Piracy off the Coast of Somalia provides funds only to UN bodies and their implementing partners. See http://www.thecgpcs.org/trustfund. do?action=trustFund

[7] Exceptions include specialised capabilities including limited AWACS and air transport capacities.

[8] The participation of non-Allied states in operations led by NATO is quite common, even standard—the NATO-led operation in Afghanistan, for example, includes 22 states in addition to the 28 Allies.

entirely on the state contributing them, it may at times be difficult to obtain commitments of the forces necessary to ensure full resourcing of an operation.[9]

III. CHRONOLOGY OF NATO'S PARTICIPATION IN COUNTER-PIRACY OPERATIONS

A. Initial Contributions

NATO's contribution to the counter-piracy effort predated its military operations, when the NATO Shipping Centre—an element of the Allied Maritime Command Headquarters at Northwood, UK—began gathering and disseminating to the international shipping community information on piracy and armed robbery in the Gulf of Aden and, later, offered to coordinate assistance to ships under attack. NATO has continued to play a coordinating role in other contexts as well. It has participated actively in the Shared Awareness and Deconfliction (SHADE) initiative since its inception in 2008 and in the International Recommended Transit Corridor (IRTC) since its creation in early 2009, and contributes its expertise to the development and continual refinement of BMPs. It has played a particularly useful role in providing a framework for coordination with individual national participants, including several South and East Asian states which operate independently of Ocean Shield, Atalanta, Combined Task Force 151 and other multinational efforts.

The first engagement of NATO military forces in the counter-piracy effort followed from a request by the UN Secretary General[10] that it provide, on an interim basis, escorts for World Food Programme vessels transporting food supplies to Somalia during a period between Canada's provision of escorts and assumption of that responsibility by the EU. NATO conducted two short-term military operations in response to this request and a subsequent one several months later, for this purpose diverting one or the other of its two Standing NATO Maritime Groups (SNMGs)[11] en route to and from deployments in the Gulf and South Asia.[12]

B. Ocean Shield

Long-term NATO deployments began in August 2009, with initiation of Operation Ocean Shield. Initially intended to end in 2012, the operation has since been extended for a further two years. Ocean Shield is carried out by the two SNMGs operating in

---

[9] Although this has at times threatened to be a significant operational issue for the NATO counter-piracy operation, sufficient naval forces have at all times been made available to Ocean Shield.

[10] Letter from UN Secretary-General Ban Ki-Moon to NATO Secretary General Jaap de Hoop Scheffer dated 25 September, 2008.

[11] The SNMGs are standing NATO naval groups resourced by Allies and available for a variety of Alliance purposes.

[12] Operations Allied Provider (October–December 2008) and Allied Protector (March–August 2009), respectively.

rotation. Depending on the time of year, the operation has been supported by between two and six naval vessels at any one time.[13]

Ocean Shield operates largely beyond the traditional limits of the territorial sea,[14] and almost exclusively defensively. One major area of focus is surveillance and deterrence, tracking both potential pirate vessels and maritime commerce in order to provide appropriate guidance and monitor status in real time. Ocean Shield participates in escort of commercial vessels, primarily in the IRTC, as well as in prevention and disruption of hijackings. Force may be used to stop and board suspect vessels or intervene in hijackings in progress (including 'citadel situations' in which crews are barricaded within armored interior locations within a vessel), but generally not recapture of vessels already in pirate hands.[15]

Unlike in the earlier short-term Operations Allied Provider and Allied Protector, under Ocean Shield NATO forces may detain pirates and turn them over to national law enforcement authorities of participating states or land them on shore in Somalia; in the absence of prisoner transfer agreements, however, suspects are not turned over to national or regional authorities in Somalia or other states in the region.

Ocean Shield participating vessels have been able to provide some incidental capacity-building support. As there is no special Alliance programme or funding for this purpose, such support is as a practical matter provided primarily during port visits by Ocean Shield vessels, and in the context of those vessels' normal operational functions.

C. 2012 Strategic Review and Subsequent Operations

In early 2012, NATO conducted a major strategic review of Ocean Shield, with the intention of assessing its continuing appropriateness as an Allied activity. The review confirmed that it provided significant 'value added' in light of increasing counter-piracy activity under EU or US leadership and by individual nations, including China, India, the Republic of Korea and Russia. It also determined whether any existing or potential elements should be modified in an extended mission.[16]

The 2012 strategic review reflected NATO's experience to date, and in particular since counter-piracy operations had become a standing element in the NATO operational landscape. The reassessment broadly reaffirmed the existing operation and resulted in extension of the mission through the end of 2014.

Among the contributions of Ocean Shield to the broader international counter-piracy effort identified by Allies as being of particular importance were NATO's overall professional authority, reputation and capabilities. These were seen as especially important in the context of facilitating smooth collaboration among the many

---

[13] Vessels have been provided by Canada, Denmark, Greece, Italy, the Netherlands, Portugal, Turkey, the UK and the US.

[14] Somalia's claim of a 200-mile territorial sea limit has been recognised by no major maritime power, nor is the author aware of any other state which has recognised it.

[15] For general information regarding Operation Ocean Shield, see http://www.nato.int/cps/en/natolive/topics_48815.htm?

[16] For general information regarding the results of the March 2012 strategic assessment, see http://www.nato.int/cps/en/SID-8A004662-3D0E9802/natolive/news_85230.htm

national forces involved in counter-piracy operations off Somalia. The Council also recognised the importance of specific counter-piracy assets that were not accessible through the EU but that could be made available in the context of a NATO operation; such assets include maritime patrol aircraft from Norway (which is not an EU member) and naval vessels, aircraft and special forces from Denmark (which does not participate in EU security operations). Equally important, NATO provides a unique and well-tried mechanism for facilitating the participation of the US and integration of its capabilities into a multi-national operation.

Operationally, the 2012 reassessment recommended an increased focus on disabling pirate logistics and support bases, including motherships, skiffs and bases, as a more efficient approach than simply waiting for events to occur and responding to them.[17] As a direct result of this recommendation, NATO requested and obtained approval by the Somali Transitional Federal Government (TFG) to conduct operations in Somali internal waters, including the beach area between the low- and high-water marks—a modification that facilitates direct attack on pirate vessels preparing to go to sea.[18]

IV. OPERATIONAL ISSUES

The most fundamental issue facing NATO, of course, is that Somali governmental institutions have been incapable of addressing the circumstances in that country which have allowed piracy to develop and continue unchecked. As noted above, NATO's contribution to the restoration of effective Somali public authority comes primarily in the form of military efforts directed at the symptoms of this breakdown, and not as direct support for Somali institutions themselves. NATO is thus dependent on Somalia and other members of the international community to provide effective forces of public order and courts, prisons and related judicial institutions, and to create an economy offering plausible alternatives to piracy.

Institutional shortcomings and weaknesses of other partners and potential partners in the region reduce the efficiency and effectiveness of Ocean Shield. As discussed below, NATO and many other participants in counter-piracy military operations find it highly desirable to make arrangements with states in the region to hold, try and imprison suspected or convicted pirates. The US and the EU have successfully negotiated prisoner transfer agreements with states such as Seychelles, Kenya and Mauritius;[19] implementation of such agreements has not always been smooth, but they have nonetheless permitted prompt transfer of many prisoners following their capture to the territory and jurisdiction of those states. States of the region have, however, only limited capacity to try and imprison suspected or convicted pirates—particularly as such transfers are invariably conditioned on requirements for their treatment that may be more demanding than is the norm within those countries.

Having in place a legal framework, including development of appropriate prisoner transfer agreements, could provide important support to NATO military operations.

---

[17] Ibid.

[18] 28 March 2011 letter from Somali Permanent Representative to President of UN Security Council, corrected copy.

[19] See G Swiney, Chapter 8 below, on US policy and D Thym, Chapter 6 above, on transfer agreements concluded between the EU and third countries.

Such support could also be provided by building a limited network of military liaison offices to facilitate cooperation with countries of the region. However, no formal liaison arrangements are in place at this time.

The lag in development of prisoner transfer agreements and liaison arrangements referred to above can be attributed, in significant part, to NATO's inability to address capacity issues through linked assistance programmes, which makes it a less attractive partner for such states than the EU or other players able to support such agreements with programmes aimed at building partner capabilities to hold, try and, following conviction, imprison transferred persons under conditions acceptable to the transferring states and their publics.

The practical consequence is that NATO commanders must normally choose among unsatisfactory alternatives, each of which materially diminishes the effectiveness of the counter-piracy operation. Returning prisoners for prosecution in national courts (or for transfer to another non-regional state for prosecution) involves considerable cost and administrative inconvenience, and will likely remove the concerned vessel or key members of its crew from operational availability for some period both immediately and later at the time of trial. Moreover, it is uncertain of ultimate success in light of the difficulties of ensuring, in an operational context, that sufficient evidence is gathered and properly preserved to allow conviction under the procedural standards applied in the courts of NATO Allies or partners. The principal alternative is to disarm the pirates, confiscate or destroy their equipment, and allow them to return to shore. This practice, commonly known as 'catch and release', has the virtue of allowing vessels to return immediately to counter-piracy duties, but for obvious reasons neither diminishes the number of pirates nor gives them any reason to fear the consequences of returning to piracy.

Directly related to the question of how to handle detained piracy suspects in-theatre are the requirements of Allies' domestic legal systems relative to their treatment before, during and after trial. The reluctance of states participating in Ocean Shield to try persons for piracy—a crime that in earlier times was viewed as so exceptionally threatening to society that all states were expected to punish its perpetrators without mercy—derives largely from the perceived risk that prosecutions will fail due to procedural or evidentiary failures following from the operational circumstances in which they were detained. An additional concern is that, once in a country subject to the ECHR, the Convention against Torture, the International Covenant on Civil and Political Rights or similar treaties a person detained for piracy may be able to apply successfully for political asylum or invoke the principle of non-refoulement upon release either due to completion of a term of imprisonment or to failure to be convicted at trial—a concern compounded by the political potency of immigration and refugee issues in many Western countries. As a result, suspects detained for eventual prosecution are likely to include primarily those suspected of involvement in attacks on the nationals or flag vessels of the detaining state or those of Allies or other states which themselves wish to prosecute and transfer to which can be made with few or no legal difficulties.

An operational challenge of a different character is the fact that the forces of states participating in Ocean Shield normally operate under two sets of Rules of Engagement (RoE)—NATO's and their own national ones—and must comply with both sets. In the case of some states, the NATO RoE may be more restrictive than the national ones; for others, national RoE or other 'caveats' may limit their ability to carry out certain activities that in principle are permitted by the NATO RoE.[20] The NATO RoE are those determined by the military chain of command to be necessary to conduct the mission as mandated by the Council; all NATO RoE must be consistent with applicable international humanitarian and human rights law. The RoE are devised in light of the Council mandate to conduct a mission and are approved by the Council at the time it approves the mission's operations plan. However, it is impossible as a matter of practice for an operation to be approved in cases where it could not be carried out due to national restrictions precluding its effective prosecution. Nonetheless, limited disjuncture between national and NATO RoE is a normal and predictable feature of NATO and NATO-led operations which is accommodated through practices developed and honed over decades of cooperation in such multinational military operations.

V. BROADER LEGAL ISSUES

As noted earlier, NATO is a political-military alliance of sovereign states the forces of which participate in NATO operations on a voluntary basis and under national command. In considering NATO's approach to legal issues affecting Alliance operations, it is essential to realise that NATO's legal perspective is derived from the perspectives of its members as reflected most importantly in the decisions of the Council; the Organization cannot adopt legal doctrines or positions that would override the national legal positions of Allies. It is nonetheless important for operational reasons that members of the Alliance have coordinated views on basic legal issues related to any operation in which they participate, and the NATO civilian and military legal staffs may play a significant role in shaping or articulating those views.

In the case of Somalia, the principal legal issues have related to the requirements of the series of UNSCRs which create the framework for the international community to take action against piracy off the coast of that country.

Those Resolutions, in particular UNSCRs 1816, 1846 and 1851,[21] were adopted under Chapter VII to address the existence of a threat to international peace and security.[22] They authorise the use of force,[23] and set forth a framework for engagement with the TFG (since August 2012, Federal Government of Somalia/FGS, whereas UNSCR 2077/2012 uses the term 'Somali authorities', operative paragraph 12), exercising

---

[20] RoE are classified and are therefore not discussed in detail.

[21] These resolutions are only a few of the many UNSCRs relating to piracy off the coast of Somalia adopted since 2008. In particular, UNSCRs 1897 (2009), 1950 (2010), 2020 (2011) and, most recently, 2077 (2012) continue the authorisations for action within Somali territorial waters and on Somali territory first set forth in UNSCRs 1846 (2008) and 1851 (2009).

[22] Stating that 'the situation in Somalia . . . continues to constitute a threat to international peace and security in the region' and '*Acting* under Chapter VII of the Charter of the United Nations, . . .' UNSCR 1816 (2008), preambular para 12. See similar provisions in UNSCRs 1838 (2008), 1846 (2008) and subsequent UNSCRs.

[23] UNSCR 1816 (2008), operative para 7 reads as follows: '*Decides* that for a period of six months . . . States cooperating with the TFG in the fight against piracy and armed robbery at sea off the coast of Somalia, for which advance notification has been provided by the TFG to the Secretary-General, may . . . (b) Use, within the territorial waters of Somalia, in a manner consistent with action permitted on the high seas with respect to piracy under relevant international law, all necessary means to repress acts of piracy and armed robbery at sea'. See similar provisions in UNSCRs 1846 (2008), 1851 (2008) and subsequent UNSCRs.

Somalia's sovereign rights.[24] Although all describe the conventional and customary law of the sea as the applicable legal framework for use of force in counter-piracy operations,[25] some hint at the applicability of international humanitarian law[26] while also requiring compliance with international human rights law.[27]

The most important substantive legal question for the NATO operation is what body of law applies to its activities conducted under the regime established by the UNSCRs. Use of force may be appropriate under any of multiple bodies of international law, including in the context of law enforcement operations.[28] The body of law that most frequently comes to mind in the context of Security Council authorisation to states to use force (take 'all necessary means') in another state is international humanitarian law (IHL); the applicability of IHL, in turn, is closely linked with the existence of an armed conflict.

Reference to IHL cannot in this case be read as implying that counter-piracy activities under the UNSCRs should be considered as 'armed conflict', with all that may imply legally. While the 'threat to international peace and security', which provides the basis for adopting the resolutions under Chapter VI, is the overall social and political situation in Somalia, of which piracy is only a symptom, it is piracy alone against which 'all necessary means' are authorised to be taken.[29] It should also be noted that the UNSCRs make no reference to terrorism, nor do they characterise the situation in Somalia as an armed conflict. Piracy constitutes a distinct category of activity in international law, one most comprehensively addressed in the UN Convention on the Law of the Sea (UNCLOS).[30] As noted in the resolutions themselves, the framework under international law applicable to combating piracy is found in the UNCLOS, Article 105 of which unambiguously authorises use of force to seize pirate vessels;[31]

---

[24] Ibid. NATO's practice, like that of other participants in the counter-piracy operation, has been periodically to request TFG/FGS representatives at the UN to provide broad authorisation to engage in specified categories of activity, and to do so only after those representatives have notified the UN Secretary General or President of the Security Council of their agreement on behalf of Somalia. To date, these requests have normally been made following adoption of new UNSCRs or when seeking to expand the authorised operations.

[25] For instance, UNSCR 1851 (2008), preambular para 14 reads as follows: '*Reaffirming* that international law, as reflected in the United Nations Convention on the Law of the Sea of 10 December 1982 . . . sets out the legal framework applicable to combating piracy and armed robbery at sea'. See also UNSCR 1838 (2008), preambular para 4 and similar provisions in UNSCR 1846 (2008) and subsequent UNSCRs.

[26] UNSCR 1851 (2008), operative para 6 reads as follows: '[A]ny measures [ie 'all necessary means' to suppress piracy and armed robbery at sea] . . . shall be undertaken consistent with applicable international humanitarian and human rights law'. See provisions to similar effect in UNSCR 1897 (2009) and subsequent UNSCRs.

[27] Ibid.

[28] See A Proelss, Chapter 3 above.

[29] UNSCR 1816 (2008), preambular para 12 reads as follows: '*Determining* that the incidents of piracy and armed robbery against vessels in the territorial waters of Somalia and the high seas off the coast of Somalia exacerbate the situation in Somalia which continues to constitute a threat to international peace and security in the region'. In its operative para 7, UNSCR 1816 then authorises states to take all necessary measures specifically against piracy and armed robbery at sea. A similar structure is continued in UNSCR 1838 (2008) and subsequent UNSCRs. By extending the legal regime applicable to actions on the high seas to actions taken in Somali territorial waters, this formulation obviates the potential which would otherwise exist for differences to arise over the precise legal regime applicable in the 200-mile zone claimed as territorial seas by Somalia but not recognised as such by other states.

[30] The UNCLOS provisions on piracy (Arts 101–07) are widely accepted as restating the terms of customary law. For an analysis of the UNCLOS provisions on piracy, see R Churchill, Chapter 1 above.

[31] 'On the high seas, or in any other place outside the jurisdiction of any State, every State may seize a pirate ship . . . and arrest the persons and seize the property on board . . . .' (UNCLOS, Art 105).

the specification of UNCLOS as the relevant and legally fully satisfactory basis for use of force against piracy at sea further confirms that the UNSCRs cannot be read as characterising the situation in Somalia or specifically relating to piracy as one of armed conflict.

This situation is unfortunately somewhat muddied by UNSCR 1851. While UNSCR 1846 had authorised use of force at sea, UNSCR authorised the use of force to suppress piracy through actions 'in Somalia'—in other words, on its land territory. These measures are in turn required to be undertaken consistently with applicable international humanitarian and human rights law.[32] While it is clear that UNCLOS cannot be the basis for actions on land and that some other body of law must therefore provide the framework for such actions, there is no clear reason to refer to IHL in the context of actions taken against criminals and for law enforcement purposes. By definition, piracy is undertaken by persons acting out of private motives;[33] pirates, moreover, are not organised for or capable of conducting military operations. For these reasons, as well as the fact that the character of any use of force by or against pirates is unlikely to achieve the level of intensity required for armed conflict, it is difficult to imagine how international humanitarian law could be considered as applying to such actions. This reference is thus perhaps best understood as directed at a hypothetical evolving situation in which linkage between the pirates and parties to the fighting elsewhere in Somalia resulted in a fundamentally different understanding of the nature of pirate activity.

The appropriate conceptual paradigm for use of force in counter-piracy operations is thus that of law enforcement, and the RoE for military forces engaged in such operations must therefore correspond to the limitations on use of force associated with law enforcement action. There is, of course, a large overlap in the rules relating to use of force in armed conflict and for law enforcement, but there are important differences as well. Among the most important of these are that in law enforcement use of lethal force must be avoided as far as possible and used only when reasonable and necessary in the circumstances, and must be preceded by escalatory warning signals.[34] Moreover, the primary purpose of law enforcement activity is the arrest and prosecution of those suspected of criminal actions, placing a correspondingly high priority on the gathering and preservation of evidence capable of sustaining successful prosecutions in national courts. It is thus important that the RoE and associated procedures applied in counter-piracy operations be particularly clear where there may be a disjuncture between these objectives and requirements and the normal training and experience of involved military forces.

---

[32] 'States and regional organizations . . . may undertake all necessary measures that are appropriate in Somalia, for the purpose of suppressing acts of piracy and armed robbery at sea . . . provided, however, that any measures undertaken pursuant to the authority of this paragraph shall be undertaken consistent with applicable international humanitarian and human rights law' (UNSCR 1851 (2008), operative para 6).

[33] UNCLOS, Art 101 ('Definition of piracy'): 'Piracy consists of any of the following acts: '(a) any illegal acts of violence or detention, or any act of depredation, *committed for private ends*' (emphasis added).

[34] See *M/V Saiga (No2)*, Judgment (ITLOS), 1 July 1999, paras 153–59.

VII. CONCLUDING OBSERVATIONS

NATO has viewed piracy in progressively broader terms over the years. Consistent with its original perception of piracy as primarily a 'national' problem, to be responded to by individual states, NATO's response to the UN Secretary-General's 2008 request for assistance was a narrowly tailored mission carried out through relatively minor adjustments to an existing programme of port visits by an SNMG in order to bridge a short-term gap in protection for such relief shipments.[35] The follow-on operation, also of limited duration, involved a limited expansion of the SNMG's mission to include escorts for general commercial shipping as well as humanitarian shipments, and expanded its scope to include limited surveillance, deterrence and disruption of pirate activities.

With the initiation of the longer-term Ocean Shield, and its inclusion as part of the SNMGs' routine, core duties, NATO's counter-piracy operations became a standing element of the NATO operational landscape. The requirement for deployment to the Somali Basin was built into the SNMGs' annual schedules, and all states participating in the SNMGs were thus expected to participate in the operation. With the 2012 strategic review, NATO further expanded its scope of activities to include proactive efforts to disable pirate assets on shore, although not (yet) to include military action above the high-water mark. Albeit with only limited success to date, NATO seeks to augment its strictly military activities through political arrangements with regional states to facilitate prisoner transfers and establish liaison offices.

Nevertheless, NATO's role in countering piracy off the coast of Somali remains a specifically military one. The scope of its activities is limited in particular by its character as a mechanism for collective military action rather than as an independent actor, and, relatedly, by a consensus-based decision-making methodology that in its nature promotes more cautious policies.

These limitations, however, are counterbalanced by a number of unique capabilities. As a many-sided military organisation, NATO brings to bear not only naval vessels, aircraft and other 'hard' military resources, but also command and control structures and institutions such as the NATO Shipping Center. NATO's most notable contribution to the effort is its unparalleled experience and its mechanisms, continually tested in real-world operational contexts, for structuring multilateral military operations. Through those mechanisms it is able to organise contributions in particular from states with relatively limited individual military resources, sustaining an effective, consistent and coordinated operation drawing on the resources of many states which are not able or prepared, individually, to sustain a consistent counter-piracy presence.

Operation Ocean Shield and its predecessor operations have confirmed the continuing effectiveness of the Alliance as a means of structuring and conducting substantial and long-lasting multinational military operations to address problems of concern to the broader international community. NATO's counter-piracy activities also illustrate the Alliance's political as well as military ability to sustain an extended and relatively low-visibility 'policing' operation that differs in important ways from the more intense

---

[35] See http://www.nato.int/cps/en/SID-622BDA96-The fE52A73CB/natolive/news_46388.htm,

military operations, such as those conducted in Afghanistan and Libya, with which NATO is commonly associated. Whether and when these capabilities may be employed in future will depend on both the desires of the larger international community and the readiness of the Allies themselves to support such operations.

8

International Law and US Responses to Piracy off the Coast of Somalia

GABRIEL SWINEY*

I. INTRODUCTION

T HE UNITED STATES of America has been one of the most active participants in the international response to pirate attacks based out of Somalia. US
warships patrol the waters off the coast of Somalia and in the Indian Ocean,
US courts have convicted pirates, and the US has taken a leading role in authorising
new tools for the fight against piracy at the UN. In all of these endeavours, questions
of international law have played a prominent role. This chapter sets forth US thinking
on a few of the most pressing piracy-related international legal questions.

The chapter begins with an examination of the definition of piracy, and focuses
in particular on recent US jurisprudence relating to domestic and international legal
definitions of this crime. It discusses the relationship between universal jurisdiction
and piracy, and examines questions about what body of law applies to counter-piracy
operations. The chapter then focuses on prosecutions, and in particular whether there
is a need for novel, international mechanisms for trying piracy suspects. The applicability of piracy laws to organisers and financiers follows, and the chapter concludes
with brief remarks about the broader question of 'root causes' of piracy.

II. DEFINITION OF PIRACY

A. Jurisprudence and US Government Views

It is appropriate to begin this chapter with US views regarding the definition of piracy.
The question of definition is obviously important background for the remainder of
this discussion, but, more interestingly, the definition of piracy has been the subject

---

* Any views expressed herein are solely those of the author, and do not necessarily reflect those of the US
Department of State or the US Government.

of a pair of cases considered by a US federal appellate court.[1] These cases involved a particularly neat intersection of domestic and international law, and for that reason alone, they are worth of examination.

The first case is *United States v Said*.[2] *Said* was a prosecution for, among other counts, piracy resulting from a failed attack on the American warship USS *Ashland*. The second case, *United States v Dire*,[3] was similar: it arose out of an attack against the USS *Nicholas*, which was lit to disguise itself as a merchant vessel. In both cases, US forces captured the pirates as they attempted to board the vessel and they were transferred to the US for prosecution. These defendants were charged with a range of crimes, but the charge carrying the heaviest penalty—a mandatory life sentence—was 'piracy as defined by the law of nations'.[4]

The statute creating the domestic crime 'piracy as defined by the law of nations' dates back to 1819.[5] As described by the court in *Dire*, a significant body of evidence suggests that in 1819 the crime of piracy under international law required some actual taking of property, either by seizing or robbing a ship.[6] On the other hand, the current definition of piracy—reflected in the UN Convention on the Law of the Sea (UNCLOS)—clearly encompasses a much broader range of conduct, including attempted seizure or robbery of a ship. The defendants in *Said* and *Dire/Hasan* argued that the US piracy statute incorporates the international law definition of piracy at the time of its adoption, and therefore, because they had not taken any property, they could not be convicted of piracy.

The trial court in *Said* agreed with this argument and dismissed the piracy charge.[7] A different trial court reached the opposite conclusion in *Dire/Hasan*.[8] Notably, Harold Koh, the US State Department's Legal Adviser, submitted a declaration in *Hasan* at the trial level in which he set out the US government's view that 'piracy as defined by the law of nations'—that is, international law—means the definition set out in the High Seas Convention and UNCLOS, which the US considers to reflect customary international law.[9]

The US Court of Appeals for the Fourth Circuit, which is the intermediate court of appeals with jurisdiction over both cases, heard the *Said* and *Dire/Hasan* appeals and issued its opinions on 23 May 2012.[10] The Court of Appeals accepted the modern definition of piracy as set out by UNCLOS, and ultimately held that this modern

---

[1] Both cases were ultimately appealed to the US Court of Appeals for the Fourth Circuit, an intermediate appellate court in the US federal judicial system. The first case is United States v Said, 680 F.3d 374 (2012); the second is United States v Dire (which was US v Hasan at the trial level), 680 F.3d 446 (2012).

[2] At the trial level, the case was 757 F Supp 2d 554 (ED Va 2010).

[3] At the trial level, the case was 747 F Supp 2d 599 (ED Va 2010).

[4] 18 USC, § 1651.

[5] Act of March 3, 1819, ch 77, § 5, 3 State 510, 513–14. 'That if any person or persons whatsoever, shall, on the high seas, commit the crime of piracy, as defined by the law of nations, and such offender or offenders, shall afterwards be brought into or found in the United States, every such offender or offenders shall, upon conviction thereof . . . be punished'.

[6] *US v Dire*, 453–67.

[7] 757 F Supp 2d, 556.

[8] 747 F Supp 2d, 640–41.

[9] Koh Declaration, see 747 F Supp 2d 599, note 2.

[10] The reasoning is set out in *US v Dire*. In *US v Said*, the Fourth Circuit simply vacated the trial court's decision and remanded the case for further proceedings consistent with the Fourth Circuit's opinion in *US v Dire*. 680 F.3d, 375.

definition is what should be applied when trying defendants for piracy in the US.[11] The Court reasoned that Congress intended, back in 1819, to fully exercise universal jurisdiction over the crime of piracy as provided by international law, and therefore intentionally adopted a standard that would change over time to reflect international law. Any other result, the Court reasoned, would mean that the US could not actually exercise universal jurisdiction over piracy to the full extent permitted by customary international law, because US domestic law would only cover a narrow slice of piratical conduct.[12] The decision by the Circuit Court is consistent with the views of the US Executive as articulated by Legal Adviser Koh.

B. Universal Jurisdiction

Closely tied to the definition of piracy is the idea of universal jurisdiction. The concept of universal jurisdiction is often controversial, and countries have widely divergent views regarding what universal jurisdiction means and to which crimes it applies. One point of international agreement, however, seems to be that, whatever universal jurisdiction is, it applies to piracy. Member States' submissions to the Sixth (Legal) Committee of the UN General Assembly on this topic demonstrate this clearly.[13] The fact that universal jurisdiction exists for piracy has profound implications for how the international community can respond to the resource, logistic and legal challenges that arise when prosecuting alleged pirates.

The US suggested a working definition of universal jurisdiction in remarks at the Sixth Committee in 2010. Its remarks were that

> for purposes of this discussion, the United States understands universal jurisdiction to refer to the assertion of criminal jurisdiction by a State for certain grave offenses, where the only link to the particular crime is the presence in its territory of the alleged offender.[14]

It is helpful to keep this idea of universal jurisdiction in mind as we consider other aspects of the international response to piracy.

III. SUPRESSING PIRACY

A. Applicable Law

Although much of this chapter addresses how the US supports efforts to prosecute pirates (both in the US and elsewhere), the reality is that, before suspected pirates can be brought to trial, they must first be captured. There is also the very real need to protect ships operating off the coast of Somalia and in the Indian Ocean from pirate attacks. The upshot of these realities is that, in practice, naval forces are often used to

---

[11] See *US v Dire*, 469.

[12] Ibid, 468–69.

[13] See http://www.un.org/en/ga/sixth/67/ScopeAppUniJuri.shtml and related links from previous sessions of the Sixth Committee (last checked 6 November 2012).

[14] Remarks by the author. http://usun.state.gov/briefing/statements/2010/149640.htm.

suppress and respond to incidents of piracy. In this context, one of the issues that the US has faced is: what are the legal limits on counter-piracy operations?

For operations on the high seas, customary and treaty law provide a relatively clear answer. Articles 105 and 110 of the UNCLOS, which reflect customary international law, provide that, if a warship has reasonable grounds for suspecting that a vessel is engaged in piracy, it may stop, board and inspect the vessel.[15] States may then seize pirate vessels, arrest suspected pirates and confiscate property on board pirate ships. The courts of the state which carried out the seizure may decide upon the penalties to be imposed, and may also determine the action to be taken with regard to the seized ship.

The rules differ closer to shore, and here UN Security Council resolutions are relevant. Operative paragraph 10 of Resolution 1846 (2008) authorised states cooperating with Somali authorities in fighting piracy (and meeting certain notification requirements) to enter Somali territorial waters[16] and use, within those waters, 'all necessary means to repress acts of piracy and armed robbery at sea' consistent with such actions as they are permitted on the high seas.[17] This authorisation has been renewed each year, most recently in Resolution 2077 (2012).[18] The authorisation to use 'all necessary means' is language the Security Council uses to authorise the use of force; unusually, here, that authorisation is to be 'consistent with such actions as they are permitted on the high seas'. Taking this authorisation as a whole, the US interprets paragraph 10 of Resolution 1846 as essentially importing the high seas legal regime into Somali territorial waters. Accordingly, naval ships can take the same measures within Somali territorial waters that they can take in the high seas (such as to stop, board, and inspect) to combat piracy.

Two weeks after adopting Resolution 1846, the Security Council took another step with Resolution 1851 (2008). Responding to concerns about the need to pursue pirates who might flee towards Somalia, the Security Council authorised states cooperating with Somali authorities, subject to request and notification requirements, to 'undertake all necessary measures that are appropriate in Somalia, for the purpose of suppressing acts of piracy and armed robbery at sea'. These measures 'shall be undertaken consistent with applicable international humanitarian and human rights law'.[19] This authorisation was renewed most recently by Resolution 2077 (2012).[20]

There are a few particularly noteworthy aspects to the authorisation contained in Resolution 1851 (2008). First, it is an authorisation to use force on land in Somalia. As mentioned above, the Security Council uses the phrase 'all necessary measures' when it is authorising member states (or a peacekeeping operation) to use force. This authori-

---

[15] Available at   http://www.un.org/Depts/los/convention_agreements/texts/unclos/closindx.htm   (last accessed on 7 November 2012).

[16] Somalia has a 200 nautical mile territorial sea claim, which the US (and most other states) do not recognise. From a US perspective, 'Somali territorial waters' extends 12 nautical miles from shore.

[17] Available at http://www.un.org/en/sc/documents/resolutions/2008.shtml (last accessed on 7 November 2012).

[18] Available at http://www.un.org/en/sc/documents/resolutions/2012.shtml (last accessed on 4 December 2012)

[19] Operative para 6. Available at http://www.un.org/en/sc/documents/resolutions/2008.shtml (last accessed on 7 November 2012).

[20] Available at http://www.un.org/ga/search/view_doc.asp?symbol=S/RES/2077(2012) (last accessed on 28 June 2013).

sation marked a major expansion of the legal powers available to states combating piracy. In addition to activities permitted under the high seas regime provided for under customary and conventional international law and, in territorial waters, Resolution 1846, states can now take the fight to shore and use 'all necessary means' when they get there, should states choose to do so. When acting under this authorisation, states are not limited to the board/inspect/seize/arrest framework of the high seas.

This expanded power comes with important restrictions, and these raise interesting and difficult legal questions. Resolution 1851 requires that the measures which it authorises 'shall be undertaken consistent with applicable international humanitarian and human rights law'. This 'consistent with applicable law' language is quite common in Security Council resolutions: this phrase is used when the Council authorises the use of force in a range of contexts, particularly in regard to peacekeeping missions.[21] But what does it actually mean in the piracy context? What is the applicable law? Is it international human rights law? International humanitarian law? Both? I will try to suggest some of the complexities the US has been dealing with in addressing these questions.

On the one hand, pirates are criminals. They are not, in most circumstances, members of a party to an armed conflict, but instead are civilian bandits. They may be captured, arrested, tried and sentenced, all through the criminal justice systems of individual states. Seen through this framework, the applicable law and guiding principles would seem to be those of the human rights and law enforcement world.

The Security Council has authorised states to use 'all necessary means' to suppress piracy. In the language of the Council, this includes the use of force if necessary. This authorisation is unprecedented; the Security Council has never before provided an authorisation of this type targeting a particular criminal enterprise. Often, when the Security Council authorises the use of 'all necessary means', military forces are using force in an armed conflict, either on behalf of individuals states or as part of a UN peacekeeping mission, and international humanitarian law (IHL) applies to at least some conduct (such as the selection of lawful targets and decisions regarding appropriate weapons and levels of force). So what law guides military forces when they use force to suppress piracy? Military forces are accustomed to thinking in terms of IHL when using force. But how does that line up with a counter-piracy mission? And how does it interact with a human rights and law enforcement framework?

An example illustrates the question. Imagine a warship is chasing suspected pirates. Assume that there is proof that these individuals are indeed engaged in piracy but, for whatever reason, the warship cannot manage to capture the pirate ship, or cannot do so safely (for instance, perhaps because it is in shallow water) before the pirates land their ship and escape to shore. What options does the warship have? In situations of armed conflict, combatants may attack and destroy targets, including members of the enemy force, provided they comply with IHL, including the principles of distinction and proportionality.[22] Even though pirates are not combatants (and would

---

[21] See, eg operative para 12(b) of Resolution 2098 (2013), available at http://www.un.org/ga/search/view_doc.asp?symbol=S/RES/2098(2013), and operative para 1 of Resolution 2093 (2012), available at http://www.un.org/ga/search/view_doc.asp?symbol=S/RES/2093(2013) (both last accessed on 28 June 2013).
[22] These two principles are found in the Protocols Additional (1977) to the Geneva Conventions of 1949. See, eg Additional Protocol I, Art 51. The US has not ratified these Protocols, but it has affirmed that these fundamental principles are part of customary international law. See MJ Matheson, 'The United States

thus be protected from attack under IHL), one could read Resolution 1851 (2008) as converting pirates into legitimate targets, thus rendering them subject to attack. The argument would be that, since the Security Council has authorised the use of force against pirates, they must be or now are lawful targets.[23] A human rights or law enforcement framework, on the other hand, would not necessarily approach the use of force in the same way. So the options available to counter-piracy forces may differ depending on the legal framework under which they are operating, and how one interprets the 'all necessary measures' language.

The negotiating history of Resolution 1851 does not shed much light on how the Security Council intended the authorisation contained in operative paragraph 6 to be read. When the resolution was adopted, British Foreign Minister David Miliband stated that 'The United Kingdom considers that any use of force must be both necessary and proportionate. These concepts include an assessment that the measures taken must be appropriate to the circumstances to which they are directed.'[24] The US, which was represented by Secretary of State Condoleezza Rice, did not address this point in its remarks at the time, nor did any other state. In practice, the US has applied an IHL to its counter-piracy operations. Although it has used force against pirates, those instances have involved self-defence or the rescue of hostages,[25] where both human rights law and international humanitarian law would permit the use of lethal force.

B. Cooperation and Coordination

Piracy suppression is very much a cooperative mission. The US participates in a number of counter-piracy missions, most of which involve working closely with other countries. It established Combined Task Force 151 in 2009, which brings together naval forces from a number of countries to operate under a unified structure to protect against, deter and respond to piracy. This task force operates in the Gulf of Aden and off the eastern coast of Somalia, and covers more than one million square miles of sea in that area. The US commanded this force for a time in 2009, but command has since rotated to a number of other countries, including Denmark, the Republic of Korea, Pakistan, Turkey and Thailand. The US also participates in NATO's Operation Ocean Shield, and ships under direct US command patrol the region as well. All of this takes place alongside and in close coordination with forces from many other states, as well as the European Union's Operation Atalanta.[26] Operational coordination between all

---

Position on the Relation of Customary International Law to the 1977 Protocols Additional to the 1949 Geneva Conventions', (1987) 2 *American University Journal of International Law and Policy* 419, 426.

[23] It is unclear whether under these circumstances it is appropriate to think in terms of there being an armed conflict between pirate groups and states authorised by the Security Council to use force against them, and how the Security Council authorisation interacts with that question.

[24] Available in UN Doc S/PV.6046, a record of remarks made at the meeting of the Security Council on 16 December 2008.

[25] Self-defence situations include attacks on the USS *Ashland* (which resulted in *US v Said*) and on the USS *Nicholas* (which resulted in *US v Hasan*). Hostage rescue situations include the rescue of Capt Philips of the *Maersk Alabama* in 2009 and of two aid workers (Jessica Buchanan (American) and Poul Thisted (Danish)) on shore in Somalia in January of 2012.

[26] For an analysis of Operation Atalanta, see R Gosalbo-Bono and S Boelaert, Chapter 5 above.

of these forces takes place largely in a military-to-military forum that convenes in Bahrain, known as SHADE ('Shared Awareness and Deconfliction'). Participation in these efforts is entirely voluntary, but it is established that even naval commanders from countries with strained relationships work well together in this collaborative environment. Finally, it is important to note that navies participating in multi-national missions retain the right to act according to national rules of engagement.

IV. PROSECUTING ACCUSED PIRATES

A. Prosecuting and Imprisoning Pirates

A military response is only the first step in dealing with piracy. When US or other naval forces respond to pirate attacks, they often end up capturing suspected pirates. The question then becomes one of criminal justice. Although the international community has been dealing with these questions in some form for hundreds of years, the prosecution and imprisonment of pirates continues to be one of the most controversial issues faced in its efforts to combat piracy.

If there is a single principle that guides US efforts in this regard, it is that the US is a strong proponent of prosecution of suspected pirates in national courts of regional and other affected states. 'Affected states', in this context, refers to the flag state of a pirated (or targeted) vessel, as well as the state of its crew, passengers or cargo, or its state of shipownership and operation. The US takes the position that these affected states are particularly well placed to prosecute accused pirates, while other states assist these states in shouldering the burden of prosecution. This does not imply that other states do not have the legal authority to prosecute; piracy is after all a universal jurisdiction crime, as described earlier. Nevertheless, affected states, whose interests are most directly implicated, should take primary responsibility for piracy prosecutions.

For the US, a focus on such cases means that the US Department of Justice has prosecuted suspected pirates for attacks on US vessels and interests; there have been several dozen US prosecutions in recent years, including the two cases mentioned at the beginning of this chapter, resulting in 27 convictions to date, with one case ongoing.[27] The US has also encouraged other affected states to pursue prosecutions, with mixed results. In the region, Kenya and the Seychelles are leaders in prosecutions and both have successfully convicted pirates that were apprehended by US forces.

Ideally, a large portion of piracy trials would take place in the pirates' home country: Somalia. Obviously there are capacity and other problems with that, including a lack of appropriate legislation, so the US supports international efforts to help Somalia increase its ability to prosecute pirates and imprison convicted pirates. In order to increase regional and Somali capacity, the UN and individual countries provide advisory, in-kind and sometimes direct budgetary support for efforts to increase local Somali prison capacity, develop a prisoner transfer framework and support regional

---

[27] As of November 2012.

prosecution efforts. In 2011, a new maximum security prison opened in northern Somalia to hold general convicts as well as convicted pirates.[28]

Yet efforts to build Somali domestic capacity cannot change the situation overnight, so the international community has been forced to think creatively. Some countries and commentators have suggested establishing an international piracy tribunal, while a UN adviser has floated the idea of a Somali court operating outside of the territory of Somalia itself.[29] Understanding the pros and cons of these and other options has been an important focus for the US in recent years.

On the question of an international tribunal, the US agrees that international courts can be useful and appropriate in certain circumstances, but not with regard to piracy. Piracy is a very old crime, one that has been handled by domestic criminal justice systems for hundreds of years. The fact that it is a crime of universal jurisdiction means that questions about domestic jurisdiction are minimal, and domestic prosecutors and courts have the technical competence to handle these sorts of cases. Domestic prosecutions offer an immediate and proven means of trying and convicting pirates; as of 2012, more than 1,100 pirates are in custody in 20 countries around the world.

On the other hand, many countries have expressed increasing reluctance to accept pirates for prosecution or incarceration, so it is not surprising that some states have voiced a desire for alternative or additional options for prosecution.

Nevertheless, international tribunals have proven to be expensive to operate and slow to get started. International tribunals '[need] judges, a prosecutor, a registrar, investigative and support staff, an extensive interpretation and translation system, a legal aid structure, premises, equipment, courtrooms, detention facilities, guards and all the related funding'.[30] Hiring appropriate staff and securing the necessary real estate and resources takes time and coordination.

International tribunals also expend substantial resources to create the legal framework within which they conduct their daily investigatory and judicial work.[31] Tribunals draft, develop, adopt and revise internal procedural rules, as well as a body of substantive legal precedent. The International Criminal Tribunal for Yugoslavia (ICTY), for example, spent four months drafting and adopting rules of procedure, evidence and detention (which were subsequently revised and amended numerous times); guidelines on assignment of counsel; a headquarters agreement; and a working framework for

---

[28] UNODC and the Chair of Working Group 2 of the CGPCS have been engaged in law and prison reform, and capacity building work to develop legal institutions and prison capacity and standards throughout the territory of Somalia. Regional authorities have law reform groups that have been meeting with UNODC and the WG2 Chair to move forward new prison laws and piracy laws, and the new laws are already in force in Somaliland.

[29] Letter dated 24 January 2011 from the Secretary-General to the President of the Security Council, with Annex, S/2011/30.

[30] S/1994/1007, para 30; see also H Holthuis, 'Operational Aspects of Setting Up the International Criminal Court: Building on the Experience of the International Criminal Tribunal for the Former Yugoslavia' (2001) 25 *Fordham International Law Journal* 708, 713 (enumerating the systems the ICTY had to set up as 'a court-archiving system, rules of detention, rules governing assignment of defense counsel, regulations regarding visits to and communication with detainees, model agreements on enforcement of sentences and relocation of witnesses, investigation protocols, information security directives, security directives and protocols for staff in the field, codes of conduct for defense counsel, procedures and protocols for the handling of evidence, a framework within which to deal with claims by wrongly accused or convicted persons, and, as a final example, a code of ethics for interpreters').

[31] S/1994/1007, para 38; see also L Raub, 'Positioning Hybrid Tribunals in International Criminal Justice' (2008–09) 41 *New York University Journal of International Law and Policy* 1013, 1044.

the Victims and Witnesses Unit.[32] In the case of hybrid tribunals, even determining the applicable substantive law for certain issues has been challenging. Domestic statutes and regulation must be reconciled with sometimes conflicting sources of international law.[33]

International tribunals—especially those created by the UN Security Council—confront jurisdictional hurdles to hearing cases, namely legal challenges to the body's international authority to carry out its mandate. The ICTY, for example, expended much time and significant resources simply persuading its detractors of the validity of its existence.[34] Finally, international tribunals require continual oversight, and would divert precious resources—both financial and otherwise—away from building national capacities. For these reasons, the US has not supported the idea of an international piracy court.

Another option that the international community has considered is the idea of an extraterritorial Somali court. In January of 2011, Jack Lang, Special Adviser to the UN Secretary General on legal issues related to piracy, advocated creating a court operating under Somali law but located outside of that country, possibly in Arusha, Tanzania.[35]

In October 2011, the Security Council asked the Secretary-General to examine that possibility, along with other ideas, for specialised piracy courts operating within the domestic legal systems of countries in the region.[36] The Secretary-General's report, which was circulated in January 2012, explained that there are serious questions about any extraterritorial Somali Court.[37] Most fundamentally, Somali authorities are adamantly opposed to creating an extraterritorial court, and Somalia lacks adequate anti-piracy legislation even for prosecutions within Somalia itself.

Ultimately, the international community is faced with a lack of Somali capacity coupled with continuing difficulty in finding states that are willing to prosecute suspected pirates. One solution to this dilemma, which the US strongly supports, is a focus on courts operating within the normal, domestic criminal law systems of countries in the region. Prior to the issuance of the 2012 UN Report, Seychelles had offered to host a regional prosecution center, if sufficient prison capacity could be found elsewhere to imprison convicted pirates. To date, 67 convicted pirates have been transferred to prisons in Somaliland and Puntland which were built and are being supported by the UN Office on Drugs and Crime (UNODC). UNODC has developed a proposal for

---

[32] S/1994/1007.

[33] Raub, n 31 above, 1044 ('reconciling the application of national and international law has not always proven an easy task'). Raub illustrates her point with a domestic East Timorese regulation that states that East Timor law prior to 25 October 1999 would apply in the Special Panels for Serious Crimes (SPSC) to the extent that 'it did not conflict with either the standards referenced in section two of the International Legal Standards or the fulfillment of the mandate given to UNTAET by the UN Security Council resolution'. The SPSC found it difficult to determine which parts of domestic East Timorese law were conflicting with the International Legal Standards or the UNTAET mandate.

[34] S/1994/1007, para 44; see also *Prosecutor v Tadic, Decision on the Defence Motion for Interlocutory Appeal on Jurisdiction* (2 October 1995), available at http://www.iilj.org/courses/documents/Prosecutor. Tadic.pdf (holding that the ICTY had jurisdiction to determine its jurisdiction and that the Security Council acted within its authority in the UN Charter to establish the tribunal).

[35] S/2011/30.

[36] UN Security Council Resolution 2015 (2011), available at http://www.un.org/en/sc/documents/resolutions/2011.shtml (last accessed on 16 November 2012)

[37] Report of the Secretary-General on specialized anti-piracy courts in Somalia and other States in the region, S/2012/50.

building additional courtrooms in Seychelles, and construction is well under way. In March 2012, the US transferred 15 suspected pirates to Seychelles to face prosecution for their alleged roles in an attempted attack on the Bahamian-flagged vessel M/V Sunshine and a successful attack and hostage-taking of the Iranian fishing dhow Al Molai.

Finding a place to try suspects is not the end of the story, of course. The UN Report explained that availability of sufficient and suitable prison facilities, including in Somalia, remains a key need, and it is not realistic to expect a small country such as Seychelles to house all of the pirates that it convicts. Once again, the ideal solution is a Somali one, and here there has been significant progress. In 2012, Seychelles enacted a new prison law and signed a prisoner transfer agreement with Somaliland.[38] Seventeen prisoners were transferred under that agreement immediately thereafter. Seychelles has also entered into a prisoner transfer arrangement with Puntland, and Mauritius has entered into arrangements with Somalia and the region of Puntland. The US believes that this sort of burden-sharing, cooperative arrangement, based on domestic systems but drawing on international expertise, offers the best chance for meeting the demand for bringing pirates to justice.

B. Organisers and Financiers

The preceding discussion regards how the international community can and should go about prosecuting and imprisoning pirates. Another question is: which pirates? For those pirates caught in the act—the 'foot soldiers' of the piracy world, so to speak—anti-piracy laws clearly apply. But what about the organisers and financiers of piracy? International law reaches them, too, and the US is increasingly focusing on pirate networks. After a review of the US piracy strategy in 2011, Secretary of State Hillary Rodham Clinton approved a series of recommendations which, taken together, constituted a new strategic approach, and a focus on piracy networks is at the heart of this strategy.[39] Like all other aspects of the fight against piracy, reaching those who fund, enable and direct piracy operations requires cooperation among states.

As the international community goes after pirate financiers and organisers, one question that will need to be answered is whether states have the necessary laws in place.[40] The US believes that the international law definition of piracy clearly encompasses financing and organising. As recognised in operative paragraph 15 of UN Security Council Resolution 1976 (2011), 'individuals and entities who incite or intentionally facilitate an act of piracy are themselves engaging in piracy as defined under international law'. Pursuant to customary international law, as reflected in Article 101 of UNCLOS, '[a]ny act of inciting or intentionally facilitating' an act of piracy, as

[38] At a February 2012 London Conference.

[39] The US has also been a strong proponent of international efforts to investigate, apprehend and prosecute piracy financiers, facilitators and organisers. Working Group 5 of the Contact Group on Piracy off the Coast of Somalia, chaired by Italy, began work on a number of initiatives in this arena in 2011. Further, the UK has partnered with Seychelles to stand up a 'Regional Anti Piracy Prosecution Coordination Center', an intelligence fusion center focused on targeting piracy financiers and facilitators. The US is supportive of these efforts.

[40] For the US rules on ransoms, see A Skordas, Chapter 13 below.

defined in that same article, is itself an act of piracy. As a result, to the extent that an individual ashore in Somalia or in the territory of another state can be proven to have incited or intentionally facilitated a pirate attack,[41] that individual is as much a pirate as his or her cohorts at sea who directly participated in the attack. Moreover, just as with suspected pirates captured at sea, a strong argument exists that all states are authorised as a matter of international law to assert universal jurisdiction over the suspect for his conduct.

As a domestic matter, not all states have incorporated the complete definition of piracy—in particular, subparagraph (c) of Article 101 on incitement and facilitation—into their domestic criminal law. In the event that states have defined piracy under their domestic law in a limited manner as consisting only of acts at sea, states may still be able to charge an act ashore intended to support a pirate attack by relying on theories such as conspiracy or aiding and abetting.

In addition to the crime of piracy, each state may have other domestic criminal statutes that prosecutors could use to charge an organiser, financier or facilitator of piracy, and there will often be multilateral agreements that also might apply, some of which will have provisions regarding extradition and other important issues.[42]

V. SPECIFIC DETERRENCE

So far this chapter has discussed how governments—and in particular the US—take action against pirates. Industry also has a crucial role, though a complete consideration of that topic would require a separate chapter entirely. First, the US strongly believes that the shipping industry should follow the best management practices developed by the International Maritime Organization. This set of practices makes pirate attacks more difficult and less successful. Secondly, the US supports the appropriate use of embarked armed security teams, which are effective in deterring and foiling pirate attacks.

VI. RESPONDING TO 'ROOT CAUSES'

Finally, it is worth quickly considering the idea of 'root causes' of piracy. That phrase can mean a number of different things, but at the very least it suggests that a crucial way to reduce piracy is by addressing the broader problems facing Somalia: in particular, a security vacuum, a lack of state institutions and the undeveloped economy.

The US supports a range of efforts to address these problems. It has been a consistent supporter of the Somali peace process, and continues to be deeply engaged in that process as it moves into a new phase. It also supports the African Union peacekeeping force in Somalia, AMISOM, politically through its position on the UN Security Council and materially through bilateral assistance to some of the countries

---

[41] Notably, the high seas law of piracy is imported to the exclusive economic zone (12–200 nm) by the LOS Convention (Art 58.2). Therefore, pirate attacks can legally occur anywhere outside of territorial seas (usually 12 nm).

[42] See, eg the Convention for the Suppression of Unlawful Acts of Violence Against the Safety of Maritime Navigation, 1988.

participating in that mission. AMISOM and Somali security forces are having real success, bringing stability to portions of Somalia that have not known peace in a long time.

VII. CONCLUDING THOUGHTS

The US continues to mount a robust response to the challenge of pirate attacks based out of Somalia. When necessary, the US is willing to use its Coast Guard and Navy to secure vital shipping routes and prevent pirate attacks. Yet naval response is only one step, and an increasing focus on investigation, prosecution and deterrence, as well as a recognition that stopping piracy means finding ways to target those who finance and organise it, has marked US policy in recent years. These efforts have been firmly situated in a multilateral context, with the US preferring to act in concert with other states—including Somalia—whenever possible.

9

Piracy and the UK

ANDREW MURDOCH*

I. INTRODUCTION

THERE ARE A number of factors which have contributed to shaping the UK's response to piracy off the coast of Somalia. Certainly, the UK has been mindful of its obligation to cooperate in the repression of piracy on the high seas,[1] but the exact nature of this legal duty is far from clear. Whatever its contours,[2] the UK has nevertheless, through the various mechanisms outlined in this chapter, been extremely active in the international community's response to these international crimes. There is also a clear national interest in countering the threat of piracy including the UK's security, prosperity and values. As the UN Security Council has determined,[3] piracy in this region exacerbates the situation in Somalia, a situation which constitutes a threat to international peace and security. In terms of energy security, the threat to the shipping routes off the coast of Somalia is a major concern. As well as the effect of any disruption to energy supplies,[4] a successful piracy attack on an oil tanker in these environmentally important waters has the potential to be extremely serious. Furthermore, the impact on the shipping industry more generally from the constriction of major maritime trade routes off Somalia could be significant, globally and in the UK, with the UK shipping industry turning over £10.7 billion per annum. Piracy also represents a threat to UK nationals, whether seafarers transiting

---

* The views expressed in this chapter are those of the author and do not necessarily represent those of the Foreign and Commonwealth Office or Her Majesty's Government.

[1] 1982 UN Convention on the Law of the Sea, Art 100 (1833 UNTS 3).

[2] The International Law Commission in its commentary on the equivalent provision in the High Seas Convention noted that 'any State having an opportunity of taking measures against piracy, and neglecting to do so, would be failing in a duty laid upon it in international law. Obviously, the State must be allowed a certain latitude as to the measures it should take to this end in any individual case . . .'. Doubt has been expressed as to whether this duty extends to requiring that states have an adequate national law addressing piracy (Harvard Research in International Law: Draft Convention on Piracy, (1932) 26 *American Journal of International Law Supplement* 755, 760. See D Guilfoyle, 'Treaty Jurisdiction over Pirates: A Compilation of Legal Texts with Introductory Notes', paper presented at the 3rd Meeting of Working Group 2 on Legal Issues, The Contact Group on Piracy off the Coast of Somalia, Copenhagen, 26–27 August 2009, 1.

[3] UNSCR 1816 (2008).

[4] In 2010, 35% of the UK's total gas imports arrived by sea of which 79% came from Qatar: see 'Royal Navy in the Middle East' (2011), available at http://www.royalnavy.mod.uk/About-the-Royal-Navy/~/media/Files/Navy-PDFs/About-the-Royal-Navy/RN%20and%20the%20Middle%20East.pdf.

the Gulf of Aden, tourists aboard vessels in the wider Indian Ocean or, indeed, British citizens at threat from other risks that benefit from the financial spoils of piracy.[5]

Piracy off the coast of Somalia is a symptom of the instability in Somalia, and it is generally accepted that tackling the cause of the instability on land is the way to bring about long-term security in the waters off Somalia. However, when the incidents of piracy started to increase rapidly in 2008, it was recognised that achieving such order on land throughout Somalia was not achievable in the short term. Addressing the root causes of piracy on land was a priority, but a more immediate effect was needed through tackling the pirates at sea. The efforts by the UK to contribute to addressing the underlying stability issues in Somalia will be discussed, but first it is appropriate to focus on the multifaceted efforts by the UK to tackle the symptom itself.

II. INTERNATIONAL COORDINATION AND COOPERATION

Piracy has been on the agenda of numerous multinational organisations from the UN (Security Council and the General Assembly)[6] and NATO, to the EU, Council of Europe, African Union and League of Arab States. Such efforts are in addition to numerous national efforts, whether military, political or diplomatic. The need for a comprehensive approach to tackling piracy off Somalia was recognised by Member States of the UN, particularly if efforts to tackle the symptom of piracy were to complement efforts to address the root causes.[7] This understanding and an escalation in piracy led to creation of the Contact Group on Piracy off the Coast of Somalia (CGPCS) on 14 January 2009.[8] Its formation was consistent with the UN Security Council's encouragement for cooperation and coordination amongst states, regional and international organisations. The rapid creation of the CGPCS was made possible by its lack of formal legal status and authority. It has met consistently since its creation, holding its fourteenth meeting in May 2013. Despite its lack of legal status, it has been an effective forum for more than 60 states, regional and international organisations, and has proved influential in shaping the international response to piracy. It has also shown the flexibility to expand its remit in response to new challenges,[9] and is able

---

[5] For example, British nationals have been: yacht crew, including the Chandlers (husband and wife held by Somalia pirates for over one year after being captured in their yacht in the Indian Ocean in 2009), 'Timeline: Paul and Rachel Chandler Kidnap', *BBC News*, 14 November 2010, available at http://www.bbc.co.uk/news/uk-10338484; passengers on cruise ships, 'Cruise Ship Repels Somali Pirates', *BBC News*, 5 November 2005, available at http://news.bbc.co.uk/1/hi/4409662.stm; and crew of merchant ships, 'Sirius Star Oil Tanker Released after $2m Ransom Paid', *The Telegraph*, 9 January 2009, available at http://www.telegraph.co.uk/news/worldnews/piracy/4208438/Sirius-Star-oil-tanker-released-after-2m-ransom-paid.html.

[6] Including UN On Drugs and Crime (UNODC), UN Development Programme (UNDP) and UN Political Office for Somalia (UNPOS).

[7] UN Secretary General, 64th meeting of the UN General Assembly, 14 May 2010.

[8] http://www.thecgpcs.org/about.do?action=background.

[9] CGPCS originally consisted of four working groups: Group 1, on Military and Operational Coordination, Information Sharing and Capacity Building; Group 2 looked at Legal Issues; Group 3 tackled Commercial Industry Coordination; and Group 4 looked at Public Information. Group 5 was later created to focus on how to advance information sharing internationally and between industry and government authorities. It works with key partners, such as INTERPOL, to better understand how illicit financial flows associated with piracy move.

to highlight areas where there is a duplication of effort as well as identifying priority capacity building needs.[10]

The UK has continually chaired the key CGPCS working group with responsibility for military operational coordination and has supported the building of the judicial, penal and maritime capacity of regional states to ensure that they are better equipped to tackle piracy and maritime security challenges. This working group relies on the strong coordination at sea between military counter-piracy forces. Such tactical coordination has improved since 2008 as a result of the Shared Awareness and Deconfliction (SHADE) mechanism. SHADE meetings were initially hosted by the Combined Maritime Forces (CMF) based in Bahrain, and were instigated and chaired by the UK Deputy CMF Commander. SHADE sought to ensure better coordination and deconfliction of military units operating under different command structures (such as NATO, EU and independent nations) in the same waters off Somalia, including through agreement to patrol in designated areas to maximise the overall spread of naval forces. The meetings have proved hugely successful and have grown in size as the scope of the operational activities being coordinated has expanded.[11] Cooperation with the merchant community and other nations (including China, Russia and Republic of Korea) that deploy independent forces to the Indian Ocean has substantially increased. Through its leading role in SHADE and significant UK national commitment, the UK Ministry of Defence is able to support the efforts of international counter-piracy operations to help ensure unity of effort and to avoid duplication wherever possible.

The UK military has consistently committed scarce naval assets to counter-piracy operations. Notwithstanding the competing and changing demands on the UK military within the strategic global context and following the Strategic Defence and Security Review, the UK has retained its intention to provide two frigates or destroyers to Middle East maritime security operations on an enduring basis.[12] Of these, one will be available for either counter-terrorism or counter-piracy duties dependent on relative threat levels, availability of other assets, intelligence and seasonal conditions. Warships are deployed to one of the CMF task force,[13] the EU's counter-piracy mission Operation Atalanta[14] or NATO.[15] In addition to the provision of warships, the UK has provided military facilities in Northwood (London) as the operational headquarters for Operation Atalanta, and its operational commander since the operation commenced in 2008. Politically, the UK has supported Operation Atalanta from the outset, including the

---

[10] The UK chaired WG1 has introduced a web-based Capacity Building Coordination Platform, which is overseen by a capacity building coordination group of key implementing partners. This builds on previous WG1 work to coordinate international capacity building activity.

[11] For example, at the 25th SHADE meeting in September 2012 the 110 delegates included representatives from 27 states including military, law enforcement agencies, the shipping industry and other government officers: see http://combinedmaritimeforces.com/2012/09/23/combined-maritime-forces-host-25th-international-meeting-of-shade/.

[12] Secretary of State for Foreign and Commonwealth Affairs, 'Tenth Report from the Foreign Affairs Committee of Session 2010–2012 "Piracy off the Coast of Somalia"—Response of the Secretary of State for Foreign and Commonwealth Affairs', March 2012, 8–9, available at www.official-documents.gov.uk/document/cm83/8324/8324.pdf.

[13] Combined Task Force 151, available at http://combinedmaritimeforces.com/ctf-151-counter-piracy/.

[14] On Operation Atalanta, see R Gosalbo-Bono and S Boelaert Chapter 5 above.

[15] NATO Operation Ocean Shield, available at http://www.manw.nato.int/page_operation_ocean_shield.aspx.

extension to its mandate[16] to permit operations ashore in Somalia, as authorised by the UN Security Council.[17]

Lastly, the UK Maritime Trade Operations (UKMTO) office in Dubai, which is manned by the UK military, including those with merchant shipping experience, has made a significant contribution to assisting merchant vessels transiting through high-risk waters off the coast of Somalia. They act as the primary point of contact for merchant vessels and liaison with military forces in the region. UKMTO Dubai also administers the Voluntary Reporting Scheme under which merchant vessels are encouraged to send regular reports, providing their position/course/speed and estimated time of arrival at their next port whilst transiting the region. UKMTO Dubai subsequently tracks vessels and the positional information is passed to the CMF, the NATO Shipping Centre and the EU Maritime Security Centre—Horn of Africa[18] (MSC(HOA)). Emerging and relevant information affecting commercial traffic can be passed directly to ships rather than via company offices, which improves the responsiveness to any incident.

III. TACKLING THE SYMPTOM

In 2009, a representative of the UN Office on Drugs and Crime (UNODC) stated that

> any lasting solution to the problem of piracy involves ensuring stability, development and an effective criminal justice system in Somalia. Until that is achieved, it is critical to assist in the prosecution of suspected pirates in order to deter further acts and to avoid these crimes being treated with impunity.[19]

The UK has supported the provision of a criminal justice disposition mechanism for suspected pirates captured at sea. Since UK naval forces first detained suspected Somali pirates and transferred them to Kenya for the purposes of prosecution,[20] the UK government's policy has been to support regional prosecutions as well as the principle of increasing the capacity of anti-piracy courts located in the region and operating within their own territories under their national law. Capacity building in the region, including in Somalia when conditions are right, is considered by the UK to be the most sustainable model.

Considerable scrutiny was given to the recommendation of the Special Adviser to

---

[16] Council Decision 2012/174/CFSP of 23 March 2012 amending Joint Action 2008/851/CFSP [2012] OJ L89/69.

[17] UNSC Resolution 1851 (2008), which provides the authorisation has been renewed annually, most recently by Resolution 2125 (2013).

[18] The Maritime Security Centre—Horn of Africa (MSC(HOA)) is an initiative established by EU NAVFOR with close cooperation from industry. The MSC(HOA) centre provides 24 hour manned monitoring of vessels transiting through the Gulf of Aden whilst the provision of an interactive website enables the Centre to communicate the latest anti-piracy guidance to industry and for shipping companies and operators to register their vessel movements through the region: see http://www.mschoa.org/on-shore/about-us/eu-operation-atalanta.

[19] UNODC Counter Piracy Programme Report, programme coordinator, November 2009.

[20] In November 2008 HMS *Cumberland* transferred eight suspected pirates to Kenya for prosecution: see http://www.guardian.co.uk/world/2008/nov/18/piracy-somalia-kenya-royal-navy.

the UN Secretary General on the legal aspects of piracy,[21] Mr Jack Lang, to establish an extraterritorial Somali court in Arusha, Tanzania (the site of the current International Criminal Tribunal for Rwanda) to deal exclusively with piracy cases. The UK made clear at the time that such an approach would be costly and would not address the fundamental capacity gap.[22] In a follow-up report of 15 June 2011,[23] the Secretary-General identified the modalities for the establishment and effective functioning of an extraterritorial Somali court, which included: consideration of the views of the Somali authorities and of potential host states; the need for an appropriate criminal and procedural legislative framework for piracy prosecutions; the need for trained judges, prosecutors and other legal professionals; and the need for security and premises. In response, the UK stated that the Secretary-General's report made clear that Somali authorities did not support the establishment of an extraterritorial Somali court, and that it would be wrong to disregard their view. In addition, the practical and legal difficulties of establishing such a court made the option unworkable in the near future, and not cost-effective compared to prosecution in national courts in the region.[24]

Support for the proposal for an extraterritorial Somali court declined after publication in 2012 of the UN Secretary General's report on specialised anti-piracy courts in Somalia and other states in the region.[25] This report indicated that the Somali authorities continued not to favour the establishment of a Somali court outside the territory of Somalia, preferring any assistance for new courts to be implemented within Somalia. Further concerns about the proposal were also identified in the report in respect of shortfalls in the legislative basis for piracy prosecutions, the availability of a trained and qualified Somali judiciary and legal profession, and security in Uganda.

In line with government policy, the UK has directed its short- to medium-term assistance to the creation of sufficient prosecution and prison capacity in the region to support the investigation and prosecution of suspected pirates. At the same time, regional prosecuting states have been encouraged to enter into arrangements with Somali authorities for the repatriation of convicted pirates to Somalia to serve their sentence.[26] Such repatriations help regional states who do not wish to hold foreign prisoners in the long term, and enable Somali prisoners to have access to their own culture, their families and appropriate skills training during their prison sentences. The most obvious and urgent need to support this prisoner transfer model is to increase the availability of suitable prison facilities in Somalia.[27] The provision of modern penal

---

[21] Report of the Special Adviser to the Secretary-General on Legal Issues Related to Piracy off the Coast of Somalia, 25 January 2011, UN Docs S/2011/30.

[22] UK response, 6473rd UN Security Council meeting record, 25 January 2011, UN Doc S/PV.6473.

[23] 'Report of the Secretary-General on the Modalities for the Establishment of Specialized Somali Anti-piracy Courts, 15 June 2011, UN Docs S/2011/360.

[24] UK response, 6560th UN Security Council meeting record, 21 June 2011, UN Docs S/PV.6560.

[25] Report of the Secretary-General on specialized anti-piracy courts in Somalia and other States in the region, 20 January 2012, UN Docs S/2012/50.

[26] The Government of the Republic of Seychelles has signed Prisoner Transfer Arrangements (PTAs) with the Transitional Federal Government of Somalia (TFG), and the governmental authorities of Puntland and Somaliland. See House of Commons, Foreign Affairs (Select) Committee, 'Piracy off the coast of Somalia', Tenth Report of Session 2010–12, HC 1318 (5 January 2012) 54. In 2012 the Republic of Mauritius also signed PTAs with the TFG and Puntland authorities.

[27] Including reference to such instruments as the Standard Minimum Rules for the treatment of prisoners, adopted by the first UN Congress on the Prevention of Crime and the Treatment of Offenders, Geneva, 1955.

facilities provides not only the near-term capacity for piracy prosecution purposes but will leave a legacy to support the longer term governance and rule of law projects of the UN Development Programme in Somalia.[28]

In delivering these objectives, the UK has strongly supported the work of the UNODC's counter-piracy programme. The programme, which started in 2009, established a strategic plan with three objectives. The first is to support four regional prosecution hubs (in Seychelles, Mauritius, Kenya and Tanzania) to conduct fair and efficient trials of suspected pirates with humane and secure prison facilities for pirates. The second is to create humane and secure prison facilities in Somalia for convicted pirates. The third and final objective is to provide fair and efficient trials of suspected pirates in Somalia. The UK will have provided almost £11.5 million to the UNODC's counter-piracy programme in FY2012–13.

The UK has provided funding support to UNODC work in Kenya focusing on: the refurbishment of prisons to improve health and welfare facilities and the training of prison staff to ensure good prison practice; support to the police by equipping police stations to effectively gather evidence and prepare case work on piracy-related cases; and support to prosecutions by training Kenyan officials on prisoner handover agreements, the law of the sea, advocacy and evidential issues. In Seychelles, UK support has focused on the courts, police and prisons. Assistance has been given to promote effective trials and ensure that prosecutors and judges receive training specific to piracy prosecutions and international law. In particular, the UK has seconded lawyers from the UK's Crown Prosecution Service (CPS) to Seychelles to assist in the prosecution of piracy trials, and prison experts from the UK's National Offender Management Service to assist in prison management. More broadly, the UK has provided funding to the UNODC counter-piracy programme to facilitate the attendance of foreign witnesses at piracy trials and to develop assistance frameworks for all other regional states willing to undertake piracy prosecutions (e.g. Tanzania and Mauritius).

Within Somalia, the UK has funded UNODC activities in both Puntland and Somaliland. In Puntland this support has contributed to the construction of a courtroom and equipment for Boosaaso prison and the provision of capacity building and training programmes for piracy prosecutions. It has also assisted in the building of a new prison designed to add considerable prison capacity to support the prisoner transfer programme. In Somaliland the UNODC focus, with UK assistance, is on improving prison conditions, including staff housing, providing capacity building and training programmes to prison staff, and improving prison security and welfare standards. A new Ministry of Justice building in Somaliland is being constructed with UK funding and UNODC project implementation. The UK has also provided funding for UNODC's Somali law reform project, which covers the incorporation of piracy provisions into Somali law and the brokering of post trial transfer agreements (PTTs), such as the PTTs signed between the Government of Seychelles and Puntland, Somaliland and the then Transitional Federal Government of Somalia. In March 2012, the first prisoner transfers took place, with 17 transferred from Seychelles to Somaliland to serve the remainder of their sentence in Hargeisa prison. A further group of pirates

---

[28] UNDP in Somalia: see http://www.so.undp.org/index.php/G1Governance-Rule-of-Law-Security.html.

was transferred to a prison in Boosaaso, Puntland, in December 2012, with more transfers expected in 2013.[29]

The UK government has not ruled out prosecuting pirates in the UK,[30] and has the domestic legal framework in place to do so.[31] However, the priority has remained to support regional states in their wish to deal with the problem of piracy themselves, as expressed through instruments such as the 2009 Djibouti Code of Conduct.[32] The UK government has therefore sought to negotiate transfer arrangements with states in the region in the event that UK forces capture suspected pirates at sea. At the time of writing, the UK has entered into memoranda of understanding with Seychelles, Tanzania and Mauritius. The UK continues to work with the Kenyan government to re-establish the transfer arrangement with the UK which was terminated by Kenya in 2010, noting that Kenya has indicated its willingness to consider transfers on an ad hoc basis.

When appropriate, the UK has also cooperated with flag states wishing to exercise jurisdiction over piracy incidents. On 10 October 2011, UK forces transferred to Italian naval forces nine suspected pirates who had been detained by the Royal Navy following a boarding of the Italian registered vessel MV *Monte Cristo* which was under the control of pirates.[33] The nine are being prosecuted in Italy.

The practice of 'catch and release' of individuals suspected of committing acts of piracy but where no option of a prosecution is available owing to a lack of evidence, capacity or willingness to prosecute can have a disruptive effect on pirate action groups by seizing the equipment they rely on to launch attacks. However, the UK government has acknowledged that it is a generally unsatisfactory outcome as it is likely to have only a temporary effect. To reduce incidents of catch and release, the UK, working with international partners, has focused on addressing the challenges of evidence collection and prosecution practice. The UK drafted the first detailed guidance for naval units on evidence and handling which has been used subsequently as a template by UNODC and other states. The UK CPS has also worked with regional states to improve case management and prosecutorial decision making, and provided feedback to naval units to improve the quality of the evidence they provide to regional states. However, it is not simply a matter of securing sufficient evidence. More important is ensuring that there is sufficient ability, capacity and willingness in the region to prosecute cases where there are reasonable prospects of securing a conviction. To this end the UK

[29] As of March 2013, 59 pirates had been transferred to Somalia: 29 to Hargeisa in Somaliland and 30 to Bosasso in Puntland. The UNODC projects in Somalia focus on utilising local resources and personnel, enabling facilities to be sustainable and reduce dependency on external funding and expertise. See UNODC Counter Piracy Programme Report, March 2013.

[30] 'The United Kingdom is willing to consider prosecuting pirates in its national courts on a case-by-case basis, especially where our nationals have been affected', UK response, n 24 above.

[31] The UK is able to assume extraterritorial jurisdiction for piracy offences under its domestic law, where the offence of piracy is part of the common law (*R v Jones & others* [2006] UKHL 16). Section 26 and sch 5 to the 1997 Merchant Shipping and Maritime Security Act provide a statutory definition of the offence by incorporating the 1982 UN Convention on the Law of the Sea's definition of piracy in Art 101. In addition, there are other relevant offences, such as hijacking and hostage-taking, over which the UK courts have extraterritorial jurisdiction.

[32] Code of Conduct concerning the Repression of Piracy and Armed Robbery against Ships in the Western Indian Ocean and the Gulf of Aden, signed on 29 January 2009, available at http://www.imo.org/ourwork/security/piu/pages/dcoc.aspx.

[33] 'UK and US Forces Rescue Pirate-Held Italian Ship', *BBC News*, 11 October 2011, available at http://www.bbc.co.uk/news/uk-15261734.

government signed a statement of Principles on Regional Burden Sharing with Kenya, Mauritius, Seychelles and Tanzania at the London Conference on Somalia in February 2012, a stated aim of which was to increase prosecution capacity in the region.[34] The agreement paves the way for looking at the standards of evidence needed for prosecution in the region by engaging with regional directors of public prosecutions.

IV. ADDRESSING THE ROOT CAUSE

Establishing rule of law and governance in Somalia is key to fighting land-based piracy networks. However, the scale of the problem in rebuilding a properly functioning state of Somalia is considerable after 20 years of conflict, and with no effective central government since 1991. It requires long-term concerted action by the international community in order to assist the Somali people who have borne the brunt of the violence that has affected the country for so long. The UK's overarching aim in Somalia is to build a more stable, peaceful and prosperous country. Building such stability also remains critical for the UK's national security. As the British Prime Minister has said, the situation in Somalia 'directly threatens British interests'. Similarly, in giving evidence to the Foreign Affairs Committee, an FCO Minister remarked that 'in addition to counter-terrorism, we have a range of interests in the country, including piracy/maritime security threats'.[35] In 2011, the UK Department for International Development (DFID) announced that it was substantially increasing aid to Somalia to an average of £63 million per year. This funding is in addition to FCO funding of counter-piracy related programmes, and EU donor aid to which the UK contributes. The EU is a major donor to Somalia, committing €215.4 million for development aid for the period 2008 to 2013.[36] The UK has also contributed significant sums to the 2011 UN administered Consolidated Appeal for Somalia in view of the humanitarian crisis in 2011. In FY 2011/12 the UK allocated nearly £80 million towards humanitarian assistance in Somalia to a range of trusted and experienced partners who are still able to deliver in this most challenging of environments, and in 2013 committed an additional £145 million over four years (2013–17) to help prevent famine.[37] The UK also provides significant funding for the African Union Mission in Somalia bilaterally, through the UN and through the EU.

The UK, together with international partners and working through the UN Security Council, has worked to achieve a peaceful and stable Somalia. The UK supported the Djibouti Peace Process, encouraging the Somali Transitional Federal Government to maintain momentum in the roadmap leading to the end of transitional administration

---

[34] Written Ministerial Statement, Secretary of State for Foreign and Commonwealth Affairs, 27 February 2012, col 13WS, available at http://www.publications.parliament.uk/pa/cm201212/cmhansrd/cm120227/wmstext/120227m0001.htm.

[35] House of Commons, Foreign Affairs (Select) Committee, n 26 above, 65, available at http://www.parliament.uk/business/committees/committees-a-z/commons-select/foreign-affairs-committee/inquiries1/parliament-2010/piracy-off-the-coast-of-somalia/.

[36] EU External Action Service, 'EU Engagement in Somalia', April 2011.

[37] House of Commons, Foreign Affairs (Select) Committee, n 26 above, 65–66, para 135. At the 2013 Somalia Conference the Department for International Development (DFID) announced a major new humanitarian programme with an additional £145 million over four years to help prevent famine, available at https://www.gov.uk/government/news/uk-commits-to-help-somalia-improve-security-and-prevent-famine.

on 20 August 2012. On 23 February 2012 the UK hosted the London Conference on Somalia, which brought together 55 delegations from Somalia and the international community.[38] The Conference demonstrated the UK's efforts to bring international actors together to work in a coordinated, cooperative and strategic manner, and gave impetus to ending the period of transitional administration in Somalia. The conference participants agreed a new action-oriented international approach to Somalia and injected important momentum into the political process. They also agreed: to help develop Somali security and justice structures; measures to bring pirates to justice and target pirate financiers; to step up action against terrorists; to increase support to local areas of stability to build legitimate and peaceful authorities, and improve services to people living in those areas; to sustain efforts to end famine; and to improve international coordination on Somalia. Importantly, the UN Security Council adopted Resolution 2036 (2012) on 22 February, which increased troop numbers and the support package for AMISOM[39] to enable it to move outside Mogadishu.

Following the conference, the UK has continued to galvanise international action on Somalia and to ensure that the conference commitments are implemented.[40] Against a backdrop of substantial gains by AMISOM forces against Al-Shabaab, the UK welcomed the adoption by the Somali National Constituent Assembly of a new provisional Constitution for Somalia and the subsequent formation of a government following elections of a president by the newly formed Somali Parliament. The end of the transition administration in August 2012 and the formation of a Somali government was a major milestone in the journey towards greater stability in Somalia. The UK is now working closely with the Somalis and is committed to supporting them to deliver their priorities. In September 2012, Foreign Secretary William Hague announced that the UK would provide an additional £10 million to help the new government of Somalia with its immediate needs, such as promoting governance and accountability, increasing the capacity of government institutions, helping resolve constitutional issues, security and justice, and developing a free media.[41] Building on the momentum of the London Conference, the governments of the UK and Somalia co-hosted an international conference on Somalia on 7 May 2013. This conference built on the progress since the last 2012 conference and brought the international community together to agree practical measures to support the federal government's plans in three key areas—security, justice and public financial management. The international community endorsed Somali plans for developing its armed forces, police, justice sector and public financial management systems, and committed over $300 million to deliver them.[42] The conference also commended the Somalis and international partners for

---

[38] London Conference on Somalia: Communique, 23 February 2012, available at https://www.gov.uk/government/news/london-conference-on-somalia-communique-2?id=727627582&view=PressS.

[39] African Union Mission in Somalia (AMISOM) has been deployed in Somalia since 2007 (UNSC Resolution 1744 (2007)).

[40] For example, the Mogadishu Stabilization Plan, a partnership between the US Agency for International Development and the UK DFID, supported by $9.5 million of US and UK funding: see http://ukinsomalia.fco.gov.uk/en/about-us/working-with-somalia/humanitarian-response.

[41] 'The UK will provide an additional £10 million to help the new government of Somalia', FCO Announcement, 27 September 2012, available at https://www.gov.uk/government/news/the-uk-will-provide-an-additional-10-million-to-help-the-new-government-of-somalia.

[42] 'Somalia Conference 7 May 2013: Key Outcomes', 13 May 2013, available at https://www.gov.uk/government/news/somalia-conference-7-may-2013-key-outcomes.

progress made in combating piracy over the previous year, and welcomed the Somali federal government's Maritime Resource and Security Strategy.

In terms of programme assistance in Somalia, the UK government has generally preferred implementation through partners as it provides the best value for money and delivers results. Indeed, one of the recommendations of the Foreign Affairs Committee, having scrutinised UK assistance in Somalia, was for the UK government to continue to act through the UN and European programmes to pursue peace and stability in Somalia.[43] The UN is an important implementing partner in Somalia, but the UK also strongly supports EU efforts in this area, in line with the new EU Strategic Framework for the Horn of Africa.[44] In particular, the EU has launched EUCAP NESTOR, a mission under the Common Security and Defence Policy, in order to enhance the maritime capacities of five states in the Horn of Africa and the Western Indian Ocean.[45] One of the two main objectives of the mission is to strengthen the rule of law sector in Somalia.

The UK also prioritises engagement with civil society organisations in Somalia, although conditions on the ground pose significant challenges. To this end, the Foreign Secretary announced, during a trip to Mogadishu on 2 February 2012, that there will be a UK Ambassador to Somalia—the first in 21 years. This demonstrates the commitment of this government to strengthening local engagement. On 25 April 2013 a new British Embassy in Mogadishu was opened by the Foreign Secretary, who also met with prominent members of Somali civil society during his visit.[46] The British government is committed to ensuring strong links with the diaspora as an important means of engaging with the Somali community, and to this end there have been periodic meetings arranged with ministers and senior officials. The Prime Minister hosted an event on the morning of 7 May to meet Somali Youth representatives in advance of the 2013 Somalia Conference. The year before, the Prime Minister hosted an event on the 20 February 2012 for the Somali diaspora to hear the views of Somalis. Such engagement is essential in order to fully take account of the views of Somali people in the UK and to explain UK policy on Somalia. The importance of engagement with civil society organisations is why the government announced £2 million worth of funding in October 2011 for community development projects delivered by UN agencies in Somalia. The UK has supported two piracy-related projects in particular. The first helps fund the UNODC's Somalia Beyond Piracy: Anti-Piracy Advocacy Campaign, the goal of which is to make piracy unappealing to Somalis and to offer an alternative vision and strategy for a future Somalia beyond piracy by working with community elders, government leaders, religious leaders, media outlets, locals and members of the Somali diaspora. The second contributes to the UNDP Somalia's Alternative Livelihoods to Piracy project, to strengthen community resilience against piracy through stimulating local economic growth, creating jobs and improving productive assets and

---

[43] House of Commons, Foreign Affairs (Select) Committee, n 26 above, 65.

[44] See Council Conclusions on the Horn of Africa, Doc No 16858/11 (Brussels, 14 November 2011).

[45] See Council Decision 2012/389/CFSP of 16 July 2012, [2012] OJ L187/40; Political and Security Committee Decision EUCAP NESTOR/1/2012 of 17 July 2012, [2012] OJ L198/16.

[46] 'Foreign Secretary Opens New British Embassy in Mogadishu', 25 April 2013, available at https://www.gov.uk/government/news/foreign-secretary-opens-new-british-embassy-in-mogadishu. The Foreign Secretary discussed preventing sexual violence in Somalia: see http://www.flickr.com/photos/foreignoffice/8681336064/in/photostream/.

capabilities, with a particular focus on coastal and rural communities and on poor and marginalised groups, youth and women, and where unemployment is highest and the potential for growth is greatest. Research certainly indicates that coastal communities are disappointed with the economic benefits of hosting pirates, and they may therefore be receptive to solutions which provide more attractive alternatives.[47] The value of providing sustainable and lawful alternatives to piracy is well recognised by industry, and the UK government welcomed the announcement at the London Conference on Somalia that four companies were providing $2 million to support projects with this objective.[48]

V. SUPPORTING INDUSTRY'S ROLE IN RESPONSE

In the first nine months of 2012, there were 99 attacks against ships in waters off the coast of Somalia, resulting in the hijacking of 13 ships. This compares with 269 reported attacks and 30 ships hijacked during the same period in 2011. However, piracy continues to pose a serious threat, since 224 seafarers and 17 vessels were held hostage as late as September 2012. As the UN Secretary-General's 2012 report[49] indicates, this declining trend is attributable to, or may be affected by, the changing behaviour of the shipping industry, in particular: the improved implementation of the International Maritime Organization's (IMO) guidance and industry-developed best management practices (BMP)[50] for Protection against Somalia-based Piracy; better application of self-protection measures and situational awareness by merchant ships, including through the use of fortified safe rooms; and the deployment of privately contracted armed security personnel on board ships.

The UK, international partners, insurers and naval operators all believe that following all BMP self-protection measures guidelines remains industry's best and first line of defence against a successful hijacking. The purpose of BMP is to assist ships to avoid, deter or delay piracy attacks in the high risk area (HRA).[51] It includes recommendations on speed, information on typical pirate attacks and self-protection measures, including watch keeping, manoeuvring practice and use of safe citadels in the event of a boarding. It advises ships transiting the HRA to register with the appropriate military authorities (MSC(HOA) and UKMTO Dubai) so that military forces are best able to protect vessels as they transit through this area of highest risk of attack. The current military effort combined with BMP compliance by industry has, according to the UK government[52] and the UN Secretary-General,[53] reduced the rate of

---

[47] A Shortland, 'Treasure Mapped: Using Satellite Imagery to Track the Developmental Effects of Somali Piracy', Chatham House Africa Programme Paper AFP PP 2012/01 (January 2012), available at http://www.chathamhouse.org/publications/papers/view/181277.

[48] More companies have since joined the consortium and, as of 1 January 2013, seven companies are supporting this initiative.

[49] Report of the Secretary-General pursuant to Security Council Resolution 2020 (2011), 22 October 2012, UN Docs S/2012/783, available at http://www.un.org/ga/search/view_doc.asp?symbol=S/2012/783.

[50] Best Management Practice (version 4), http://www.shipping.nato.int/Pages/BMP.aspx.

[51] The HRA is an area bounded by Suez and the Strait of Hormuz to the North, 10°S and 78°E.

[52] Secretary of State for Foreign and Commonwealth Affairs, Response, n 12 above, 2.

[53] Report of the Secretary-General pursuant to Security Council Resolution 1897 (2010), 27 October 2010, UN Docs S/2010/556, 13, available at http://www.un.org/ga/search/view_doc.asp?symbol=S/2010/556.

successful piracy attacks. The CGPCS have repeatedly underlined the importance of full adherence to BMP as the first and most effective line of self-protection, and they have noted the conclusion of the SHADE co-chairs that successful hijacks are four times more likely if BMP measures are not in use.[54]

In responding to the threat posed to shipping off the coast of Somalia, the UK government changed its policy in 2011 to allow the use of privately contracted armed guards on board UK flagged ships. The policy applies to internationally trading passenger ships and cargo ships of 500 gross tonnage and above, in certain exceptional circumstances:

- when the ship is transiting the high seas throughout the HRA;
- when the latest BMP is being followed fully but, on its own, is not deemed by the shipping company and the ship's master as sufficient to protect against acts of piracy; and
- when the use of armed guards is assessed to reduce the risk to the lives and well-being of those on board the ship.

The change in policy was in step with the general shift in the attitude of the shipping industry towards being in favour of embarking armed security to protect crews, and reflected the persuasive statistic that, to date, there have been no successful attacks against ships carrying private armed security. To support the policy, the UK Department for Transport published Interim Guidance to UK flagged shipping on the use of armed guards to defend against the threat of piracy.[55]

The UK recognised that this change in policy, and existing UK criminal law on the licensing of firearms held on board UK ships,[56] needed to be supplemented by an appropriate accreditation system for the private security companies (PSCs) using the firearms. The need for such a framework forms part of the UK government's aim to raise the global standards of private security companies working in complex and high-risk environments overseas. The objective has been to work closely with interested partners, including industry and civil society, to establish a voluntary, independently audited and internationally recognised accreditation system that is practicable, effective and affordable.

In 2010, an International Code of Conduct for private security service providers (ICOC)[57] was created. This provides a set of principles to guide companies. In particular, the ICOC mandated the development of auditable standards to ensure that signatory companies are implementing their commitments under the code. The ICOC has now been signed by over 500 PSCs, around a third of them British. After reviewing

---

[54] CGPCS, 12th plenary session Communique, 25 July 2012, available at http://www.state.gov/t/pm/rls/othr/misc/195964.htm.

[55] Department for Transport's 'Interim Guidance to UK Flagged Shipping on the Use of Armed Guards to Defend against the Threat of Piracy in Exceptional Circumstances', Version 1.1 (November 2011). Version 1.2 was published in May 2013 and is available at https://www.gov.uk/government/uploads/system/uploads/attachment_data/file/204123/use-of-armed-guards-to-defend-against-piracy.pdf.

[56] It is an offence for a person to have in his possession, including on board a UK registered ship, a weapon prohibited under s 5 of the Firearms Act 1968 without the authority of the Secretary of State. See 'Guidance to Applicants for Section 5 Authorization to Protect UK-Registered Ships', March 2012, available at http://www.homeoffice.gov.uk/publications/police/firearms/section-5-authorisation.

[57] ICOC, 9 November 2010, available at http://www.dcaf.ch/Project/International-Code-of-Conduct-for-Private-Security-Service-Providers.

options on setting new professional standards to make the code effective, the government announced its intention to issue a publication specifying that ASIS PSC 1-2012[58] is the applicable standard for UK-based PSCs working in complex environments on land overseas.[59] The next stage in the process is for companies, independent auditors and the UK Accreditation Service (UKAS) to take steps to enable auditing against these standards to begin.

The ICOC was drafted with land-based PSCs in mind and therefore the resultant ASIS PSC 1 was similarly land orientated. Since 2010, however, there has been a rapid rise in the number of PSCs working on anti-piracy operations at sea, the majority being based in the UK. Although many of the principles relating to PSCs working on land and at sea are similar, there are important legal[60] and practical differences. The demand for tailored guidance and standards for the private maritime security company (PMSC) sector led to the adoption of interim guidance for PMSCs (based on draft text developed by a UK-led sub-group of CGPCS Working Group 3) by the IMO's Maritime Safety Committee (MSC).[61] The IMO Secretary-General said that

> the use of PMSCs on board ships was an exceptional measure to be used only in exceptional circumstances in the high risk area, and should not become institutionalised. However, guidance was needed to assist policy development at the national level and facilitate greater harmonisation of policies in international shipping related to the issue of arms on board.[62]

The MSC also requested the International Standards Organisation (ISO) to develop a more detailed standard for armed private security companies working in the maritime environment. The ISO was able inter alia to draw upon work already produced by the UK government's trade association partners, the Security in Complex Environments Group. The ISO presented its draft standard to the IMO in November 2012, where it was welcomed, but not formally endorsed.[63] The ISO subsequently published the ISO PAS 28007 standard,[64] which can now be used as the basis for auditing. The British government has accepted this ISO standard as appropriate for PMSCs and is,

---

[58] The international security trade association (ASIS) was funded by the US Department of Defense to develop the standard—'PSC1'—for the regulation of private security companies operating on land in complex environments overseas. This standard was drafted in a multinational and multi-stakeholder forum in which the UK government, UK industry and UK civil society fully participated. It was published in March 2012 as an approved American National Standard. It was published in March 2012 as an approved American national standard.

[59] The Parliamentary Under-Secretary of State for Foreign and Commonwealth Affairs (Mr Mark Simmonds), Written Ministerial Statement, 17 December 2012, col 72WS, available at http://www.publications.parliament.uk/pa/cm201213/cmhansrd/cm121217/wmstext/121217m0001.htm.

[60] Most notably jurisdictional issues concerning investigation of incidents while ships transit through ports, territorial waters and the high seas. See, eg the dispute between Italian and Indian authorities concerning jurisdiction over an incident at sea following the shooting by Italian marines of two Indian fishermen, 'India Allows Italian Ship *Enrica Lexie* to Leave', *BBC News*, 2 May 2012, available at http://www.bbc.co.uk/news/world-asia-india-17920840. See also http://www.bbc.co.uk/news/world-asia-india-21781993 and http://www.bbc.co.uk/news/world-asia-india-21999318.

[61] 'Interim Guidance to Private Maritime Security Companies Providing Privately Contracted Armed Security Personnel on Board Ships in the High Risk Area', IMO MSC.1/Circ 1443 (25 May 2012), available at http://www.imo.org/OurWork/Security/PiracyArmedRobbery/Pages/Private-Armed-Security.aspx.

[62] IMO Maritime Safety Committee (MSC), 90th session, 16–25 May 2012, available at http://www.imo.org/MediaCentre/PressBriefings/Pages/16-msc90-highlevel.aspx.

[63] Meeting Summary of Maritime Safety Committee, 91st session, 30 November 2012, available at http://www.imo.org/MediaCentre/MeetingSummaries/MSC/Pages/MSC-91.aspx.

[64] ISO PAS 28007 Guidelines for Private Maritime Security Companies (15 December 2012).

at the time of writing, running a pilot audit process with UKAS and several certification bodies. The pilot process will seek to ensure the certification process is outcome focused and reaches appropriate standards on training, including in human rights. In addition to the specific restrictions on the embarkation and use of firearms on UK ships, there are controls on the removal from the UK (export) of firearms, ammunition and other military and paramilitary equipment, and the involvement of UK persons in moving, or arranging the movement of, such items between overseas countries (trade). The UK Export Control Organisation (ECO) is responsible for these controls. In most cases export or trade in such items is prohibited unless authorised by a licence issued by the ECO. To make it less bureaucratic for UK companies to move weapons from country to country to provide private armed maritime security to ships off the coast of Somalia, the UK introduced a new Open General Trade Control Licence (Maritime Anti-Piracy).[65] This makes the licensing process more straightforward while maintaining strict conditions to ensure the appropriate use of weapons and increasing awareness of companies' actions. Licences will contain conditions, such as a requirement that weapons may only be stored on land in designated secure armouries. The licensing process can, if necessary, respond to new developments in the PMSC operating model, such as the use of floating armouries to act as holding stations at sea to avoid the delays and costs associated with storing weapons on land.

VI. TACKLING THE PIRACY BUSINESS MODEL

The CGPCS established a new Working Group 5 in July 2011, chaired by Italy, to coordinate international efforts to identify and disrupt the financial networks of pirate leaders and their financiers.[66] This decision reflects the view in CGPCS that successful eradication of piracy is impossible without dismantling the illicit funding and financial flows related to piracy taking place on shore.[67] The UK is an active participant in Working Group 5 and hosted a meeting with representatives of the UK industry on 13 January 2012 to ensure that the role that the shipping and insurance industries can play is properly understood and tapped into. Working Group 5 has identified INTERPOL as the principal international single point of contact with the shipping industry, and has recommended that each country identifies a single point of contact to strengthen domestic coordination and to facilitate liaison with the private sector.[68]

During the 2012 London Conference on Somalia, the UK pledged over 1 million USD to establish a Regional Anti-Piracy Prosecutions and Intelligence Co-ordination Centre (RAPPICC) in Seychelles. Temporary offices were functional on 1 June 2012, with a permanent building opening on 1 March 2013. It has co-directors from the UK (Serious Organised Crime Agency (SOCA)) and Seychelles, and will be staffed by

---

[65] OGTCL (Maritime Anti-Piracy) entered into force on 23 February 2012, available at https://www.gov.uk/open-general-trade-control-licences.

[66] The UK has considered whether the proceeds of piracy are making their way into the UK financial system and has found no evidence that this is occurring. However, the issue is being monitored and, should the assessment change, the government will consider the appropriate channels for communicating this to partners.

[67] CGPCS, Working Group 5, available at http://www.thecgpcs.org/work.do?action=workAd.

[68] Report of the Secretary-General, n 49 above, 5.

experts from the region and international partners. RAPPICC is an information fusion centre, which aims to facilitate the capture and prosecution of the financiers, investors and ringleaders of Somali piracy. This UK–Seychelles-led initiative is the most significant practical step made so far by the international community to specifically target the pirate hierarchy. It will coordinate and analyse intelligence to inform tactical law enforcement options, including the turning of intelligence into useable evidence for prosecutions both in the region and further afield. RAPPICC will benefit from a hub based in SOCA in London, which will provide a further link to intelligence sources from international partners. One of the primary benefits of this will be the links that can be drawn with industry. It is expected that, through the cell, RAPPICC will become an effective conduit for information on piracy held by the London-based maritime industry to flow to relevant law enforcement authorities.

The key challenges faced in tackling the pirate leaders and money flows are information sharing, the lack of a formal banking system in Somalia, and ensuring the admissibility of information in those courts asserting jurisdiction over suspected pirate leaders and financiers. In addition, prosecutions must be underpinned by appropriate domestic law, including offences relating to the proceeds of crime and money-laundering. The Financial Action Task Force has looked at the challenges for law enforcement authorities,[69] and is working with countries in the region to ensure anti-money-laundering legislation is implemented effectively.

VII. RANSOMS

The UK government's policy is not to make, facilitate or encourage substantive concessions to hostage-takers, including by payment of ransoms. The London Conference on Somalia underlined the importance of taking decisive action to tackle piracy, in particular on the financial flows that support it. Ransom payments are the key driver in pirate business models and thus encourage further piratical activity. If the pirate business model is to be broken, attention must be given to exploring what action can be taken to curtail ransoms and, ultimately, shut them off.

Despite the obvious benefit of preventing ransom payments to pirates, there are problems in seeking to do so.[70] For example, the shipping industry strongly maintains that paying a ransom is the only reliable method for securing the safe release of captured vessels and their crew,[71] and asserts that if payments are shut off then lengths of captivity and frequency, as well as the frequency and seriousness of mistreatment of crews held captive, may increase in order to extract a payment. It is also recog-

---

[69] See 'Organised Maritime Piracy and Related Kidnapping for Ransom', FAFT Report (July 2011), available at http://www.fatf-gafi.org/documents/documents/organisedmaritimepiracyandrelatedkidnappingfor-ransom.html.

[70] A Anyimadu, 'Coordinating an International Approach to the Payment of Ransoms: Policy Options for Preventing the Payment of Ransoms', Chatham House, Africa Programme Discussion Document (May 2012). See also discussion of ransom payments in A Murdoch, 'Recent Legal Issues and Problems Relating to Acts of Piracy off Somalia' in C Symmons (ed), *Selected Contemporary Issues in the Law of the Sea* (Leiden, Nijhoff, 2011) 165.

[71] In the UK Court of Appeal case of *Masefield AG v Amlin Corporate Member Ltd* [2010] EWCA 280 (Comm), it was argued that the only real option to ensure the release of crews was to pay a ransom, adding that failure to do so could jeopardise the safety of other seafarers.

nised that if only some states take action to stop payments then those private actors wishing to pay a ransom may still be able to do so by locating to a more permissive jurisdiction.

In view of the imperative need to look at the payments of ransoms to pirates, the complexities of the issues and recognising that a multilateral approach may be more effective, the Prime Minister announced at the London Conference on Somalia that the UK would be establishing an international task force on ransom payments. The 14-nation task force brought together experts from some of the world's largest flag states, states whose seafarers are most commonly at risk and those at the forefront of responding to the threat. The views of industry, the Somali diaspora and policy options prepared by Chatham House[72] were considered by the task force. Their meetings examined, amongst other matters, options for preventing the payment of ransoms; options for avoiding the payment of ransoms/alternative strategies to paying ransoms; and options for reducing the size/frequency of ransom payments.

On 11 December 2012, the task force published its recommendations:[73]

- develop a new strategic partnership between flag states, the private sector and law enforcement agencies that brings together those tackling piracy and those subjected to it in a united effort to break the piracy business model;
- develop a more co-ordinated approach to information-sharing to provide evidence to pursue and prosecute all involved in piracy;
- strengthen co-ordination between flag states, the private sector and military responders to prepare for potential hostage situations; and
- encourage implementation of anti-piracy measures, including greater compliance with BMP.

The UK initiative on this complex and multi-stakeholder issue has led to a clear recognition that a multilateral approach to the problem is appropriate, including a partnership between the public and private sectors. While much work is still required to bring about concrete responses to the recommendations, the creation of RAPPICC is wholly consistent with the thrust of the task force's work.

VII. CONCLUSIONS AND BUILDING ON EXPERIENCES TO FACE EMERGING CHALLENGES

Responding to the threat of piracy off the coast of Somalia has required a comprehensive cross-departmental approach within the UK government based on a strategy

---

[72] Anyimadu, n 70 above.

[73] 'Piracy Ransoms Task Force Publishes Recommendations', 11 December 2012, available at https://www.gov.uk/government/news/piracy-ransoms-task-force-publishes-recommendations. On publication of the recommendations, the Foreign Office Minister, Alistair Burt, said that the 'UK Government firmly supports and endorses the conclusions of the Piracy Ransoms Task Force. Only through the international community working together to break the pirates' business model will we reach a position whereby pirates are no longer able to receive or profit from ransom payments. The Government will continue to work as a leading member of the Contact Group and with industry in taking forward the implementation of the task force's recommendations.'

that tackles the problems both ashore and at sea.[74] The Foreign and Commonwealth Office has the overall lead on coordinating the government's response to piracy off the coast of Somalia and facilitates discussion amongst the key departments,[75] including the Department for Transport, Home Office, Ministry of Defence, Ministry of Justice, HM Treasury and Department for International Development. The requirement for such a comprehensive approach reflects the immensely complex issues that have arisen, as well as the need to coordinate action to maximise its effect and avoid duplication of effort. The identification of policy leads for all the relevant strands of piracy work and a department with responsibility for overall coordination has enabled the UK government to respond to emerging challenges promptly.

As well as the declining trend in successful piracy attacks in 2012, 1190 Somali pirates are now awaiting trial, or serving custodial sentences, in over 20 states.[76] While the UK recognises that positive trends in tackling counter-piracy are reversible unless the momentum of action is maintained, the strategy of responding to piracy using a comprehensive and coordinated approach, including both state and private actors, has proven successful. In adopting and promoting such a comprehensive approach, the UK has played a leading role in shaping the international community's response to piracy.

The UK can usefully draw upon its experience in responding to Somali piracy when considering the appropriate response to threats to maritime security in other regions. For example, incidents of piracy and armed robbery at sea in the Gulf of Guinea are of increasing concern, spreading along the coast from Nigeria and further out to sea. The Gulf of Guinea is an important trade route for both West African and international markets, and currently contributes to global energy security.[77] Clearly, all elements of the Somali counter-piracy strategy are not appropriate in this region as the nature of the maritime threat in the Gulf of Guinea is very different from that off the coast of Somalia. First, the general stability in West Africa is very different from Somalia, so does not present the same opportunities for pirates to hold ships and crew hostage for long periods of time. Secondly, the attacks take place mainly in territorial waters, and are focused on the theft of cargo, usually on ships carrying products which can easily be unloaded and sold onto the black market, such as oil and gas. Lastly, the level of violence used against crew members is much higher, with crews often injured and in a small number of instances killed.

The UK is therefore developing a bespoke cross-Whitehall UK strategy to address maritime security in West Africa. The UK is working closely with states in the region, international partners, regional and international institutions and industry to

---

[74] Adopting such an approach has been endorsed by the House of Commons, Foreign Affairs (Select) Committee, n 26 above, 42.

[75] The Department for Transport leads on engagement with the shipping industry, compliance of UK flagged vessels with BMP and the guidance to shipping companies on the use of private armed guards for counter-piracy purposes; the Home Office leads on the issuing of section 5 authorities under the Firearms Act and contributes through the Metropolitan Police, SOCA, HQ to RAPPICC and piracy ransoms task force; the Ministry of Defence leads on the military response to piracy; the FCO leads on international coordination, regional capacity building (including prosecutions), work to undermine the piracy business model, ransom payments linked to piracy, the provision of travel advice and UK consular cases; and the Department for International Development leads on longer term development, such as employment creation.

[76] UNODC County Piracy Programme, Support to the Trial and Related Treatment of Piracy Suspects, Issue 10, December 2012.

[77] Some 11.8% of global oil and gas production comes from the Gulf of Guinea, and it is expected that more reserves will be brought online over the next few years.

coordinate action and build capacity. This approach relies, in the West African context, on states in the region taking ownership of the problem and the active involvement of regional organisations.[78] As a practical and significant step, the UK is working with industry to create a regional Maritime Trade Information Sharing Centre (MTISC), similar to UKMTO Dubai, which will build up a picture of trade and shipping routes in the area. The centre will be the first initiative to collate and disseminate information to provide support to industry and to allow states to respond with what little resources are available. It is hoped that it will become an integral part of the ECOWAS comprehensive maritime security strategy. The UK has also welcomed industry efforts to develop an equivalent to the Somali-focused BMP for West African piracy. However, the potential for publication of more than one guidance document by the shipping industry[79] suggests that seeking IMO recognition of a single publication for this region would be the appropriate way forward.

The UK's approach to the threats to maritime security off the coast of West Africa demonstrates that, while each situation will be approached on an individual basis, elements of previous successful strategies to counter other maritime attacks can be adapted to face new challenges. The creation of MTISC is a clear example of where experience gained in one context—in this case, UKMTO Dubai's impact in countering Somali piracy—can be successfully used in other regions. The production of West African BMP is another example. It is likely that other elements of the UK comprehensive approach to counter the complex issues concerning Somali piracy can also be successfully adapted to meet the threats to maritime security in other regions as they arise.

---

[78] For example, the Economic Community of West African State (ECOWAS) and Economic Community of Central African States (ECCAS).

[79] Interim Guidance for Owners, Operators and Masters for protection against piracy in the Gulf of Guinea region has been developed by BIMCO, ICS, INTERCARGO and INTERTANKO to supplement BMP4: see https://www.bimco.org/en/Security.aspx. However, separate guidance is being developed by a large industry association.

10

Fighting Piracy—The German Perspective

DORIS KÖNIG AND TIM RENÉ SALOMON

I. INTRODUCTION

T HE STRUGGLE AGAINST modern-day piracy is a cause shared by many nations. As such, it seems a very narrow approach to concentrate on the legal regime of one nation only. However, while many issues of national law may indeed have a limited relevance to the international sphere, others, albeit based on national law, are reflexes of legal challenges and obstacles that potentially every nation may encounter, but that may or may not have materialised yet. This contribution will focus on German law controversies connected to fighting piracy, which, despite the decrease of piracy off the coast of Somalia, remains an international security concern.[1] The analysis will concentrate on three key areas. First, it will address the constitutional law background and its implications for the German participation in the struggle against piracy. Secondly, German criminal law will be analysed with a focus on the types of piracy-related crimes that fall under German criminal jurisdiction. Thirdly, the legal regime governing private security providers will be outlined with a focus on the recent changes.

II. CONSTITUTIONAL LAW BACKGROUND AND IMPLICATIONS FOR ANTI-PIRACY OPERATIONS

This section will address the legal basis of deployments of the German Armed Forces outside the borders of Germany (out-of-area) under constitutional law and other ways in which constitutional law influences the participation of Germany in counter-piracy efforts worldwide.

---

[1] For a short official description of counter-piracy actions taken by Germany and entailing, for example, financial support of the UN Office on Drugs and Crime (UNODC) programme, participation in the Contact Group on Piracy off the Coast of Somalia and Operation Atalanta, see UN, 'Compilation of Information Received from Member States on Measures They Have Taken to Criminalise Piracy under their Domestic Law and to Support the Prosecution of Individuals Suspected of Piracy off the Coast of Somalia and Imprisonment of Convicted Pirates', Annex to UN Doc S/2012/177 (26 March 2012) 32.

A. Constitutional Prerequisites for a Deployment of the Bundeswehr

There has been a decade-long academic and political discussion on the possibilities and need of amending the German Constitution to create an explicit legal basis for out-of-area operations by the German Armed Forces.[2] In view of the ongoing military commitments undertaken by the Federal Republic of Germany worldwide, including but not limited to the Atalanta mission, it may come as a surprise that such out-of-area-deployments are typically accompanied by challenges based on German constitutional law.

1. Developments from 1945 to Today

These doubts are firmly rooted in the German history. The current constitutional framework has to be understood against this background, especially the Conference of Yalta in February 1945, in which the 'complete disarmament and demilitarisation of Germany and the elimination or control of all German industry that could be used for military production'[3] after the German capitulation was agreed upon.[4] However, soon after the capitulation, the beginning cold war led to Germans being armed again for border control purposes in 1951. In 1955, the Bundeswehr—the German Armed Forces—were officially founded. Subsequently, in 1956, Germany's Basic Law (Grundgesetz—GG) was amended and Article 87a GG, the norm of primary importance in the Constitution when discussing a deployment of the armed forces, was introduced. It was amended in 1968 as part of the state-of-emergency-amendment (Notstandsverfassung), which was primarily concerned with the use of the armed forces within Germany in a state of emergency.[5] Article 87a GG still contains the constitutional basis for the deployment of troops.[6] Its first two paragraphs read:

> The Federation establishes armed forces for purposes of defence . . .
>
>   Apart from defence, the armed forces may be employed[7] only to the extent expressly permitted by this Basic Law.

This article expresses the determination of the German people after the Second World War to be a peaceful nation within the international community and to abstain from

---

[2] For a constitutional law analysis of Art 87a GG see also D König, 'Legal Problems of Fighting Piracy: The German Perspective' (2012) *Zeitschrift für Japanisches Recht* Special Issue 6—Germany and Japan: A Legal Dialogue between Two Nations 145.

[3] Tripartite Agreement by the United States, the United Kingdom and Soviet Russia concerning Conquered Countries, 2 August 1945, quoted part reprinted in S Wolff, *The German Question since 1919: An Analysis with Key Documents* (Westport, CT, Praeger, 2003) 184.

[4] *Cf* I Couzigou, 'Yalta Conference (1945)' in R Wolfrum (ed), *The Max Planck Encyclopedia of Public International Law*, 2010, online edition www.mpepil.com, visited on 13.12.2011; W Benz, 'Yalta, Potsdam and the emergence of the cold war: an overview from Germany in the light of the latest research', in Council of Europe (ed), *Crossroads of European histories—Multiple outlooks on five key moments in the history of Europe* (Strasbourg, Council of Europe Publishing, 2006) 279.

[5] See D König, 'Putting an End to an Endless Constitutional Debate? The Decision of the Federal Constitutional Court on the "Out of Area" Deployment of German Armed Forces' (1995) 38 *German Yearbook of International Law* 103, 113, with further references.

[6] For a comprehensive overview of the textual history see O Depenheuer, 'Art 87a' in T Maunz/G Dürig, *Grundgesetz*, 53. EGL 2008.

[7] While the translation (see n 9 below) mentions the term 'employment', the term 'deployment' will be used in the following as it is closer to the actual meaning of the German term 'Einsatz'.

military activities.[8] In addition, Article 24(2) GG formed part of the Constitution since its adoption in 1949, reading:

> With a view to maintaining peace, the Federation may enter into a system of mutual collective security; in doing so it shall consent to such limitations upon its sovereign powers as will bring about and secure a lasting peace in Europe and among the nations of the world.[9]

On the basis of these two norms rests the participation of the German Armed Forces in multilateral military operations today. In contrast to operations for the purpose of defence, which Article 87a(2) GG explicitly allows, the constitutional modalities of out-of-area operations are very controversial. These legal insecurities even related to Germany's NATO self-defence commitments.[10] In its *AWACS* judgment of 1994, which dealt with the constitutionality of the participation of German troops in UN peacekeeping operations in the Adriatic, Bosnia-Herzegovina and Somalia, the Federal Constitutional Court (Bundesverfassungsgericht) stated that Article 24(2) GG contains a military dimension[11] and Article 87a GG does not preclude the deployment of troops within a system of mutual collective security.[12] In the Court's opinion, the constitutional permission to enter a system of mutual collective security includes an authorisation to fulfil the tasks typically arising from such membership. According to this interpretation, Article 24(2) GG allows the use of the armed forces within all frameworks of mutual collective security, be it in operations under a NATO mandate, in peacekeeping operations based on resolutions of the UN Security Council, in Chapter VII operations beyond peacekeeping or under the mandate of other systems of mutual collective security. Apart from the legality under Article 87a GG, the German parliament (Bundestag) has to give its prior explicit consent to any deployment of the Bundeswehr, since the armed forces have to be firmly integrated into the democratic constitutional order.[13]

At first sight, this legal situation seems to be a sensible compromise, weighing a country's need to defend itself and its allies with the need to contribute to collective security against the political sensitivity of troop deployment abroad, while giving credit to the value of international cooperation. Yet it has in fact proven to be a minefield of legal insecurity. There are several controversial issues, which will be touched upon in the following.

2. Territorial Scope of Article 87a GG

The first controversy concerns the territorial scope of Article 87a GG. When the

---

[8] For a comparison of the legal provisions in Japan, Germany and the USSR see L Fisler Damrosch, 'Constitutional Control of Military Actions: A Comparative Dimension' (1991) 85 *American Journal of International Law* 92, 99ff. She speaks of 'the basic antiwar philosophy behind the two clauses' (ie the Japanese 'Renunciation of War' clause and its German equivalent).

[9] Translations by C Tomuschat and DP Currie, available at http://www.gesetze-im-internet.de/englisch_gg/englisch_gg.html.

[10] Depenheuer, n 6 above, para 79.

[11] Judgment of 12 July 1994, 90 BVerfGE 286, 345ff.

[12] Ibid, 355ff.

[13] The need for explicit parliamentary consent was elaborated by ibid, 384ff, and is not expressly stipulated in the Basic Law, but finds itself in the Parliamentary Participation Act of 2005: see Depenheuer, n 6 above, para 143. For more details see König, n 5 above, 124ff; M Zöckler, 'Germany in Collective Security Systems—Anything Goes?' (1995) 6 *European Journal of International Law* 274, 282ff.

norm was introduced in the German Basic Law in part VIII, on the 'Enforcement of Federal Laws and the Federal Administration', the systematic structure of the Basic Law suggested that it was only intended to govern the use of the armed forces within the German borders.[14] Indeed, it was hardly conceivable at that time that German Armed Forces would ever again be deployed in other countries to conduct combat operations—a taboo which was broken only much later, with Germany's participation in the NATO humanitarian intervention in Kosovo in 1999. Limiting the scope of Article 87a(2–4) GG to German territory would mean that out-of-area deployments were subject only to international law.[15] They would not be subject to any constitutional law restrictions other than the ban of wars of aggression in Article 26 GG. In contrast to the historical background and the systematic structure, the wording of Article 87a(2–4) GG certainly allows for a broader interpretation that includes out-of-area deployments.[16] Its purpose—to prevent acts of aggression against other states—has been argued to speak for a more restrictive interpretation excluding anti-piracy-operations.[17] However, the object and purpose of the norm may also be convincingly seen to support a broader scope, which would encompass the regulation and control of any kind of military action by the German Armed Forces.[18]

The German Federal Constitutional Court evaded the question regarding the territorial scope of Article 87a(2) GG in its *AWACS* judgment of 1994.[19] The court simply decided that, if it was applicable to an out-of-area deployment of German troops under UN control and consequently an express constitutional authorisation was needed, then Article 24(2) GG would grant such authorisation.[20] Accordingly, it did not touch upon the controversial question whether Article 87a(2–4) GG is at all applicable.

The German Federal Administrative Court (Bundesverwaltungsgericht) has since adopted the broader view by stating that each deployment of the German Armed Forces is regulated by Article 87a(2) GG. Consequently, out-of-area operations are not only subject to international law, but need an express authorisation in the Basic Law. The court then agrees with the Constitutional Court in that Article 24(2) GG is a provision expressly allowing out-of-area operations in the sense demanded by Article 87a(2) GG.[21] Today this is the prevailing view in practice and scientific discourse alike.

---

[14] See V Epping, 'Art 87a' in V Epping and Christian Hillgruber (eds), *BeckOK-GG*, 18th edn (Munich, Verlag CH Beck, 2013) paras 18ff.
[15] See G Nolte, 'Bundeswehreinsätze in kollektiven Sicherheitssystemen' (1994) 54 *Zeitschrift für ausländisches öffentliches Recht und Völkerrecht* 652, 655 with further references.
[16] See Epping, n 14 above, para 18.
[17] R Wolfrum, 'Terrorismus-Bekämpfung auf See' (2003) 140 *Hansa* 12, 14 is of the opinion that, in view of its main objective, namely to prevent acts of aggression against other states, Art 87a GG is not applicable to the fight against piracy; see also R Wolfrum, 'Fighting Terrorism at Sea: Options and Limitations under International Law' in JA Frowein et al (eds), *Negotiating for Peace, Liber Amicorum Tono Eitel* (Berlin, Springer, 2003) 648, 656ff; M Allmendinger and A Kees, 'Störtebeckers Erben' [2008] *Neue Zeitschrift für Wehrrecht* 60 argue for a restrictive interpretation in this specific case relying on the fact that anti-piracy operations were clearly not in the minds of the drafters.
[18] *Cf* Epping, n 14 above, para 1.
[19] 90 BVerfGE 286, 286ff.
[20] See König, n 5 above, 117ff.
[21] BVerwG, [2007] NVwZ-RR 257, 259.

3. The Notion of 'Deployment'

The second issue refers to the concept of 'use' (*Verwendung*) or 'deployment' (*Einsatz*) of the armed forces. It is generally agreed that merely technical, logistical and humanitarian support for UN- or other operations are not 'deployment' in the sense of Article 87a(2) GG.[22] Whilst such cases are non-controversial, the meaning of the term deployment is far from clear and this shows, for example, in the fight against piracy. It has been argued by German scholars that the operation against Somali pirates is chiefly a law enforcement operation and thus does not qualify as a deployment in the sense of Article 87a GG.[23] This would again mean that Article 87a GG does not limit such operations. However, taking into consideration the legislative history and the purpose of Article 87a GG, namely the regulation and control of any kind of enforcement action by the German Armed Forces as part of the executive power,[24] it seems preferable to see law enforcement actions conducted by the military encompassed by the term 'deployment', especially when military means are used,[25] as is the case in the Atalanta operation.

4. The Notion of 'Defence'

The third issue that has come up with regard to the fight against piracy concerns the notion of 'defence'.[26] The German Navy operating in Atalanta may indeed be seen as defending vital German commercial interests and the security of supply chains, yet it would be an unreasonably broad reading of Article 87a(2) GG to include the protection of commercial interests in the constitutional law notion of defence.[27] It also runs counter to the spirit of the norm, which emanates, as stated, a determination for peace. However, while the whole operation cannot be deemed a defence, single actions may qualify as defence in a constitutional law sense. For example, concrete action against pirates attacking a German-flagged merchant vessel goes beyond defending abstract interests and attacking a German-flagged vessel may be seen to be similar to an attack on the country itself.[28] However, the object and purpose of Article 87a GG, to restrict the use of the armed forces to defence operations unless otherwise permitted, in order to prevent a resurgence of German militarism, imply an even more restrictive interpretation of the term defence. A convincing argument can be made to

---

[22] See König, n 5 above, 111.

[23] See U Fastenrath, 'Zur Verfassungsmäßigkeit unilateraler Piratriebekämpfung durch die Deutsche Marine' in HP Hestermeyer et al (eds), *Coexistence, Cooperation and Solidarity, Liber Amicorum Rüdiger Wolfrum*, vol 2 (Leiden, Nijhoff, 2012) 1935, 1944ff; see also K Braun and T Plate, 'Rechtsfragen der Bekämpfung der Piraterie im Golf von Aden durch die Bundesmarine' (2010) *Die öffentliche Verwaltung* 203, 205.

[24] BVerwG, [2007] NVwZ-RR 257, 260; M Schultz, *Die Auslandsentsendung von Bundeswehr und Bundesgrenzschutz zum Zwecke der Friedenswahrung und Verteidigung, Völker- und verfassungsrechtliche Analyse unter besonderer Berücksichtigung der Entscheidung des Bundesverfassungsgerichtes zum Einsatz deutscher Streitkräfte vom 12. Juli 1994* (Frankfurt am Main, Lang, 1998) 160ff; Epping, n 14 above, para 17; M Bothe, 'Völkerrecht und Verfassungsrecht', *Frankfurter Allgemeine Zeitung*, 30 June 2008, 9.

[25] Depenheuer, n 6 above, paras 102ff.

[26] Depenheuer, n 6 above, paras 59ff.

[27] See more generally for defence of interests Depenheuer, n 6 above, paras 116ff.

[28] Depenheuer, n 6 above, para 108.

reduce the notion to situations covered by the provision on individual and collective self-defence, as codified in Article 51 of the UN Charter.[29]

5. Express Authorisation—Scope of Article 24(2) GG

In sum, the following conclusions can be drawn: (i) Article 87a GG most likely applies to out-of-area operations;, (ii) the troops are actually 'deployed' in the sense of Article 87a GG in Atalanta; and (iii) the operation against Somali pirates is not for defence purposes. Consequently, Article 87a(2) GG demands an express authorisation in the Basic Law for this operation.

As stated, Article 24(2) GG is pertinent for permitting military operations that form part of a 'system of mutual collective security'. If the EU were such a system, Atalanta would be allowed by Articles 87a(2) and 24(2) GG. The precise interpretation of this term, however, has proven to be yet another challenge. For decades, constitutional law scholars have fought over the correct interpretation. Many were of the opinion that only classical collective security systems are covered by Article 24(2) GG, ie systems to deter and combat the use of force by one member of the system against other members and, as such, internally. Defence alliances which are targeted at the use of force by external aggressors would have been left out.[30] In the *AWACS* judgment, the Federal Constitutional Court adopted a more extensive interpretation which covers both kinds of security systems.[31] Nowadays, it is agreed that the UN—specifically with actions based on Security Council resolutions—forms such a system. This means that the Bundeswehr may be deployed on the basis of the UN Security Council authorisation. The same would apply to NATO.[32] But what about the EU?

The status of the EU as a 'system of mutual collective security' seemed settled, but has arisen again because of an *obiter dictum* in the 2009 German Constitutional Court's judgment on the Treaty of Lisbon. Whereas the German government and Parliament implicitly acknowledged the EU to that extent, the Federal Constitutional Court and some scholars seem to have doubts.[33] In view of the development of the Common Security and Defence Policy in the Treaty of Lisbon,[34] a convincing argument can be made, however, in favour of the EU having at least grown into a 'system of mutual collective security' in the sense of Article 24(2) GG.[35] This means that Article 24(2) GG permits Germany's participation in the Atalanta operation.

---

[29] See also Epping, n 14 above, para 6.

[30] For details see König, n 5 above, 112ff; Zöckler, n 13 above, 276ff.

[31] 90 BVerfGE 286, 347ff; confirmed by 104 BVerfGE 151, 209ff and 121 BVerfGE 135, 157.

[32] 90 BVerfGE 286, 349ff; for UN, NATO and the EU see W Heintschel von Heinegg, 'Art 24' in *BeckOK-GG*, n 14 above, para 33.

[33] 123 BVerfGE 267, 361: 'Auch wenn die Europäische Union zu einem friedenserhaltenden regionalen System gegenseitiger kollektiver Sicherheit im Sinne des Art 24 Abs. 2 GG ausgebaut würde . . .' (translation: 'Even if the EU were to be further developed into a peacekeeping regional system of mutual collective security within the meaning of Article 24(2) of the Basic Law . . .'), see M Trésoret, *Seepiraterie* (Baden-Baden, Nomos, 2011) 551.

[34] Cf eg Art 42 (7) Treaty of the European Union.

[35] See, eg S 'Schmahl, 'Die Bekämpfung der Seepiraterie' (2011) 136 *Archiv des öffentlichen Rechts* 44, 84; Braun and Plate, n 23 above, 207ff; D König, 'Der Einsatz von Seestreitkräften zur Verhinderung von Terrorismus und Verbreitung von Massenvernichtungswaffen sowie zur Bekämpfung der Piraterie: Mandat und Eingriffsmöglichkeiten' in A Zimmermann et al (eds), *Moderne Konfliktformen—Humanitäres Völkerrecht und privatrechtliche Folgen, Berichte der Deutschen Gesellschaft für Völkerrecht 44* (Heidelberg, Müller, 2010) 203, 231ff, with further references.

6. Article 25 GG as Express Authorisation

The provisions of the Basic Law, independent from Article 24(2) GG, that can also serve as express authorisations in the sense of Article 87a(2) GG are a topic of debate. This issue is especially relevant in cases where collective action has not (yet) been agreed upon. Before Operation Atalanta was started in December 2008, there was discussion about whether the German Navy could take unilateral action against Somali pirates on the basis of Article 87a(2) GG read together with Article 25 GG, which states that 'the general rules of public international law constitute an integral part of federal law'. This provision has been interpreted to mean that the Bundeswehr may be deployed in all cases in which customary international law permits military action.[36] This would certainly allow unilateral military action against piracy, the fight against which can be based on a long-standing customary international law regime (codified in Articles 100–10 of the United Nations Convention on the Law of the Sea Convention (UNCLOS)). It is, however, doubtful if the very general reference in Article 25 GG can be taken to fulfil the requirement set up by Article 87a(2) GG—express authorisation. The wording as well as the object and purpose of Article 87a(2) GG are against such a broad interpretation. Therefore, unilateral action against piracy by the German Navy cannot be based on Article 87a (2) in connection with Article 25 GG.[37]

7. Separation of Police and Armed Forces

A further topic has caused controversy regarding Atalanta: it is a general principle in Germany that police and military powers shall be separated. This doctrine again is a response to Germany's dark history, namely the practice of paramilitary police units in the Third Reich. There is a debate among legal scholars whether the so-called separation doctrine (*Trennungsgebot*) applies to out-of-area operations or whether it is only applicable within the borders of Germany. If this principle were rigidly applied to out-of-area operations, military actions would be strictly constrained to military measures, and law enforcement duties would be out of line.[38] Accordingly, it has been argued that the German Navy is not competent to arrest pirate suspects and transfer them to states in the region, such as Kenya and Seychelles, for detention and prosecution.[39] Such measures are clearly in the realm of law enforcement and fall within the competence of the German Federal Police (Bundespolizei), which is competent to act in maritime areas beyond the territorial sea.[40] Currently, the Bundespolizei is, however, not adequately equipped to combat piracy off the Somali coast.

---

[36] JA Frowein, 'Deutschlands Marine darf schon jetzt Piraten verfolgen', *Spiegel Online*, 26 November 2008, available at http://www.spiegel.de/politik/deutschland/0,1518,592618,00.html.

[37] This conclusion is shared by Schmahl, n 35 above, 83; Braun and Plate, n 23 above, 206; S Schiedermair, 'Piratenjagd im Golf von Aden' (2010) 135 *Archiv des öffentlichen Rechts* 185, 215ff and note 173; A Fischer-Lescano, 'Bundesmarine als Polizei der Weltmeere, Völker-, europa- und verfassungsrechtliche Grenzen der Piraterriebekämpfung' (2009) *Zeitschrift für öffentliches Recht in Norddeutschland* 49, 53.

[38] Fischer-Lescarno, n 37 above, 54ff; A Fischer-Lescano and T Tohidipur, 'Rechtsrahmen der Maßnahmen gegen Seepiraterie' (2009) *Neue Juristische Wochenschrift* 1243, 1246; Schmahl, n 35 above, 88ff; Braun and Plate, n 23 above, 208ff.

[39] See, eg Fischer-Lescarno and Tohidipur, n 38 above, 1246.

[40] Cf § 6 (1) of the Federal Police Act (Bundespolizeigesetz), which states (in translation): 'Without prejudice to the competence of other authorities or the armed forces, the federal police takes those measures at sea outside the territorial sea to which the Federal Republic of Germany is entitled under international law.

Applying the separation doctrine strictly would have severe consequences for Germany's ability to participate in multilateral military operations in the framework of collective security systems. The mandates for such multilateral operations usually do not distinguish between police and military powers. Consequently, the Bundeswehr would not be able to participate in these operations as soon as it would have to fulfil law enforcement duties. Such result runs counter to Article 24(2) GG, which foresees German participation in multilateral operations according to the prevalent interpretation. This makes it preferable to not apply the separation doctrine beyond the borders of Germany.[41] Limiting the doctrine to inside German borders is also justified by its object and purpose. Its aim was to outlaw the dangerous situation within the borders of Germany, if the police force would be granted military powers or vice versa. Applying it to the military undertaking out-of-area operations comes close to turning the purpose of the doctrine on its head, since it would mean that the German Navy would be constitutionally allowed to shoot at and sink pirate vessels, while employing less harmful police powers, such as intersecting and arresting the perpetrators would be prohibited. Consequently, the separation doctrine should, in principle, be limited to the internal organisation of the military and police within German borders.

8. Implications

To sum up, the German Navy is only allowed to operate against Somali pirates within a system of mutual collective security, namely within the EU Operation Atalanta, as authorised by the Bundestag. Apart from assistance in the case of an imminent attack (Article 98 UNCLOS), which may be seen to be a general principle in which the military may act, unilateral action is prohibited by the Constitution. While, in the case of the Operation Atalanta, the constitutional framework seems to be working at first sight, it leads to peculiar consequences in the fight against piracy at large.

One of these rather absurd consequences is that the German Navy may not free vessels which are already in the hands of pirates outside of the operational area of Atalanta. Freeing a vessel would be a deployment, as it would be undertaken by using military means and it would not be defence, as the notion is arguably limited to defending the state and not single citizens, especially since a German-flagged vessel may or may not actually have German citizens on board. Furthermore, it would not be expressly authorised by the Basic Law, since the act is not part of a system of mutual collective security and such action would exceed the scope of assistance against an imminent attack. This case arose when the German-flagged vessel *Taipan* was seized by Somali pirates outside of the Atalanta area of operations, and thus outside the scope of the Bundeswehr's mandate. Fortunately, the Netherlands Navy was closer to the vessel and up for the task of freeing the ship, yet this example shows possible and bizarre consequences of the current legal situation.

This does not apply to measures that are assigned by federal law to other authorities or agencies or that are reserved solely for warships'; see also Fischer-Lescarno and Tohidipur, n 38 above, 1246.

[41] See also Schiedermair, n 37 above, 217; T Marauhn, 'Streitkräfte zur Friedenssicherung im Ausland: zwischen militärischem und polizeilichem Einsatz' in A Zimmermann et al (eds), *Moderne Konfliktformen— Humanitäres Völkerrecht und privatrechtliche Folgen, Berichte der Deutschen Gesellschaft für Völkerrecht 44* (Heidelberg, Müller, 2010) 249.

The current situation can be summarised as follows: the German Navy is able and equipped to operate against pirates. However, it is either unnecessarily restricted by the Constitution in this case or, at the very least, is subjected to great legal insecurity. Meanwhile, the German Federal Police is competent by law to operate, but does not have the means to do so. This paradox situation needs to be remedied, which could be achieved by an amendment to Article 87a GG that takes into account the changed circumstances from 1968 until today and acknowledges the active role that the Bundeswehr plays in operations for the maintenance of peace all over the world.

B. Constitutional Duties of the Bundeswehr

The Constitution affects the actions of the Bundeswehr beyond the scope of Article 87a GG. Interesting questions concern duties laid upon the armed forces by constitutional law.

1. Protecting the Victims

One subject that is of interest is the basis of this contribution is the question whether there is a duty to protect the victims of piracy under international law in line with the comments made by the UN Special Rapporteur on Terrorism.[42] In Germany, this issue is addressed mainly in connection with constitutional law, which provides a much stricter standard for the state's duties to protect its subjects.[43] There are two plausible ways to arrive at a constitutional duty to protect: the rights of life and well-being, codified in Article 2(2) GG (as an example for other fundamental rights, such as property), and Article 27 GG, which acknowledges the existence of a German mercantile marine.[44] Both have been invoked by shipowners, and industry in general, to push for vessel protection detachments supplied by the Bundeswehr or the Bundespolizei for German vessels. Yet a duty to supply such specific protection has no basis in constitutional law. The very broadly worded Article 27 GG does not even codify a subjective right of shipowners to protection by the state.[45] Article 2(2) GG obliges Germany to protect its subjects when their lives and well-being are threatened, but, as with all duties to protect, the state has a wide margin of appreciation as to how to fulfil that duty and bring about such protection,[46] and Germany can invoke its participation in the Operation Atalanta as a means of fulfilling this duty. Therefore, there exists no specific duty to train and make available soldiers or policemen to escort trade vessels,

---

[42] See, eg 'Promotion and Protection of Human Rights and Fundamental Freedoms while Countering Terrorism', UN Doc A/66/310 (18 August 2011) 5ff.

[43] With reference to diplomatic protection see A Kolb, T Neumann and TR Salomon, 'Die Entführung deutscher Seeschiffe: Flaggenrecht, Strafanwendungsrecht und diplomatischer Schutz' (2011) 71 *Zeitschrift für ausländisches öffentliches Recht und Völkerrecht* 191, 234ff.

[44] For this see D König, 'Arbeitskreis VIII: Moderne Piraterie—Seeschifffahrt unter Beschuss, Schutz vor Piraterie—hoheitlich oder privat?', 50. *Deutscher Verkehrsgerichtstag*, 25–27 January 2012, 299, 302ff.

[45] König, n 44 above; U Mager, *Einrichtungsgarantien* (Tübingen, Mohr Siebeck, 2003) 386ff; M Herdegen, 'Art 27' in T Maunz/G Dürig, *Grundgesetz*, 47. EGL 2007, para 6.

[46] For the margin of appreciation concept vis-à-vis duties to protect see König, n 44 above; M Hilf and TR Salomon, 'Margin of Appreciation Revisited: The Balancing Pole of Multilevel Governance' in M Cremora et al (eds), *Reflections on the Constitutionalization of International Economic Law—Liber Amicorum Petersmann* (Leiden, Brill, 2013) 34ff.

notwithstanding singular cases when this might be the only way to protect an exceptionally vulnerable subject.[47]

2. Protecting the Perpetrators

Referring to fundamental rights, it has to be pointed out that the perpetrators and suspects are also subject to the basic rights guaranteed in the German Constitution. This topic is of great importance and potentially has a very significant influence on Germany's ability to participate in the ongoing fight against piracy, especially with regard to the transfers of suspects to third states. According to Article 1(3) GG, the 'basic rights shall bind the legislature, the executive and the judiciary as directly applicable law'. In contrast to the sometimes problematic application of human rights to extraterritorial state action, Article 1(3) GG states that basic rights are binding with regard to all state actions, no matter where they take place. This might seem obvious at first, but the applicability of basic rights to out-of-area operations by the Bundeswehr is still being contested by the literature and practice alike.[48] The Ministry of Defence took the position that actions undertaken by the German Navy in the Atalanta mission are not attributable to Germany and, consequently, are not acts by the German executive pursuant to Article 1(3) GG.[49] The Ministry also argued, in a case before the Administrative Court in Cologne, that, if applicable, the Basic Law did not intend to reduce the effectiveness of out-of-area operations by the military by demanding that the basic rights were to be adhered to.[50] This argument was rightly rejected by the court.

Although a rule that effectiveness trumps guarantees of basic rights outside of Germany does not form part of the law, the Federal Constitutional Court has accepted that, when applying these constitutional guarantees to state actions out-of-area, some modifications may be necessary.[51] First, this is the case when international law demands a modification of these rights.[52] For example, a duty to protect derived from the basic rights cannot justify unauthorised actions on foreign soil, so that the constitutional rights could not be used to justify or mandate such breaches of the territorial integrity of other states. Further grounds for modification are due to the nature and purpose of the specific guarantee concerned, which determines how far it is eligible to be applied extraterritorially.[53] An example of a widely accepted modification is the right

---

[47] König, n 44 above; Final Report of the Working Group 'Bekämpfung der Seepiraterie' of the Conference of Interior Ministers, 'Rechtliche und tatsächliche Möglichkeiten zum Schutz deutscher Handelsschiffe' (29 November 2011) 24, available at http://www.bundesrat.de/DE/gremien-konf/fachministerkonf/imk/Sitzungen/11-12-09/Anlage14,templateId=raw,property=publicationFile.pdf/Anlage14.pdf.

[48] See for an overview over the discussion D Wiefelspütz, 'Auslandseinsatz der Streitkräfte und Grundrechte' [2008] *Neue Zeitschrift für Wehrrecht* 89.

[49] See the position of the Ministry in the case before the Administrative Court in Cologne, Az 25 K 4280/09, Judgment of 11 November 2011, para 20f; for an in-depth study of the operation, including the command structures, see R Gosalbo-Bono and S Bolaert, Chapter 5 above.

[50] Administrative Court in Cologne, Az 25 K 4280/09, Judgment of 11 November 2011, para 23.

[51] See, eg 100 BVerfGE 313, 362f.

[52] See, eg A Zimmermann, 'Grundrechtseingriffe durch deutsche Streitkräfte im Ausland und das Grundgesetz' [2012] *Zeitschrift für Rechtspolitik* 116, 117; A von Arnauld, 'Das (Menschen-)Recht im Auslandseinsatz. Rechtsgrundlagen zum Schutz von Grund- und Menschenrechten' in D Weingärtner (ed), *Streitkräfte und Menschenrechte* (Baden-Baden, Nomos, 2008) 61, 71.

[53] See, eg 31 BVerfGE 58.

in Article 104(3) GG to be brought before a judge within 48 hours after arrest. This time-frame is very restrictive when it comes to arresting pirate suspects on the high seas.[54] Honouring it unconditionally would arguably mean to render the German Navy unable to participate in vital parts of the Atalanta operation. Consequently, scholars widely agree that this time-frame may be modified in line with international human rights law to mean 'promptly' in the sense that the suspect has to be brought before a judge without undue delay and as soon as possible under the given circumstances.[55]

In doing so, scholars approve the current practice of transferring suspects to countries in the region and thus also allow a second modification of Article 104(3) GG, which orders bringing the suspects before a German judge. It may be worth noting that other states, such as Italy, have taken steps to at least provide the arrested suspects with a video link to an Italian judge, in order to introduce some kind of judicial oversight over the transfers. Germany has not yet taken steps to that effect—a somewhat problematic omission against the backdrop of Article 13 ECHR as well as Articles 19(4) (right of recourse to the courts) and 103(1) GG (right to a hearing). It should be stressed that, while modifications of the fundamental constitutional guarantees are possible in an out-of-area-setting, the state remains under a duty to safeguard these rights as far as possible.[56]

Article 104(3) GG is not the only right that is possibly infringed in the current transfer strategy. In extradition cases, which the transfers bear a certain similarity to, the Federal Constitutional Court has stated that there are non-refoulement-type guarantees in constitutional law rendering extraditions illegal, when it can be reasonably expected that the circumstances in the country to which the person is to be extradited or the specific treatment of the extradited person falls short of the minimum standards guaranteed by international law or the indispensable principles of German constitutional law.[57] This means that the international standards form part of the constitutionally guaranteed standards as well. On this basis, a transfer of piracy suspects to Kenya in 2009 has been held to have been illegal by the Administrative Court of Cologne because the conditions of detention in Kenya did not accord to international standards, as guaranteed by the Constitution.[58] There is ongoing concern whether the regional partners of the current strategy supported by the UN mainly through the UNODC meet these standards. The human rights situation in Seychelles, Kenya, Mauritius and Tanzania, as well as ultimately Somalia itself, where the suspects will—in some cases—be transferred to after their conviction to serve their time, casts serious doubts on the human rights compliance of the previous transfers, especially with a view to children's rights. It also pulls into question the constitutionality of transfer-

---

[54] See König, n 35 above, 236; A von Arnauld, 'Die moderne Piraterie und das Völkerrecht' (2009) 47 *Archiv des Völkerrechts* 454, 472; C Kreß, 'Die moderne Piraterie, das Strafrecht und die Menschenrechte' in D Weingärtner (ed), *Die Bundeswehr als Armee im Einsatz* (Baden Baden, Nomos, 2010) 95, 114.

[55] See especially König, n 35 above, 236; Kreß, ibid, 114; von Arnauld, bid, 472; D Wiefelspütz, 'Die Beteiligung der Bundeswehr am Kampf gegen Piraterie' [2009] *Neue Zeitschrift für Wehrrecht* 133, 149, but also the Administrative Court in Cologne, Az 25 K 4280/09, Judgment of 11 November 2011, para 44; for the opposing view see C Walter and A von Ungern-Sternberg, 'Piratenbekämpfung vor Somalia—Zum Zusammenspiel europäischer und deutscher Grundrechte' [2012] *Die Öffentliche Verwaltung* 861, 867; A Fischer-Lescarno and L Kreck, 'Piraterie und Menschenrechte' (2009) 47 *Archiv des Völkerrechts* 481, 495.

[56] See especially Kreß, ibid, 115; for a study on the ongoing transfers see D Thym, Chapter 6 above.

[57] See, eg 16 BVerfGK 491.

[58] Administrative Court Cologne, Az 25 K 4280/09, Judgment of 11 November 2011.

ring suspects to these states under German law. It is likely due to these doubts that the German Navy has been reluctant to transfer suspects to these regional states for prosecution and instead releases most captured suspects.

III. GERMAN CRIMINAL LAW AND PIRACY

After the account of German constitutional law, criminal law has to be addressed at least briefly, if only for the recent judgment by the Landgericht Hamburg on 19 October, 2012 and for the very recent prosecution of a pirate suspect who was arrested when entering Germany illegally on 8 May 2013 and was identified by his fingerprints as one of the suspects in the case of the *Marida Marguerite*, which was hijacked in May 2010. The suspect in the latter case is in pre-trial detention for suspicion of causing bodily harm by dangerous means and abduction for the purposes of black-mail. He is thought to have supplied food and water for the people on the vessel and kept the books on which basis the ransom payment was split up.[59]

A. Prosecuting Pirates in Hamburg—The *Taipan* Case

In the former case before the Landgericht Hamburg, the adult perpetrators were sen-tenced to six to seven years' imprisonment, while the juveniles and the defendants who were under 21 years of age at the time of the perpetration were handed a two-year prison term. They walked free and continue to go to school in Germany after having already served their time during the extended period of pre-trial detention. The Land-gericht started trial proceedings against a group of 10 pirate suspects in 2010. These came to a close after 105 days of trial.[60] This proceeding has left many people dissatis-fied especially because of its long duration, but it may serve as a reminder that piracy trials, while usually not being overly complex when it comes to the act itself, may indeed take a long time. What seemed to be a rather clear-cut case at the start ended up being a very challenging and long-lasting endeavour for the Hamburg court, which led the trial with great care. The problems that occurred in Hamburg may appear in every prosecution of pirates worldwide. An example would be the burdensome, though important, duty of verifying the ages of the accused claiming to be under 21, 18 or even 14 years of age—which took a long time and three expert testimonies to solve with the necessary certainty. Another obvious problem concerned reaching witnesses based in Somalia and the surrounding regions called by the defence. This trial has also served as a reminder concerning the importance of individual defence. There have been allegations that the defence has engaged in dilatory tactics and some of these may be well-founded but, during the trial, the accused independently chose to testify against each other in order to gain an advantageous position over the others.

---

[59] For this case see the press release of the State Office of Criminal Investigation Lower Saxony, 'Mutmaßli-cher somalischer Pirat in Deutschland festgenommen' (13 May 2013), available at http://www.presseportal. de/polizeipresse/pm/105578/2470155/lka-ni-mutmasslicher-somalischer-pirat-in-deutschland-festgenommen.

[60] For a brief account of the trial and the Taipan incident see TR Salomon, 'Long Road to Justice. The German Piracy Trial', *Communis Hostis Omnium*, 21 October 2012, available at http://piracy-law. com/2012/10/21/long-road-to-justice-the-german-piracy-trial.

This helped the search for truth and thus the trial, but it was only possible because the accused each had defence attorneys of their own.

When one looks at the circumstances of trials, for example, in Seychelles and in Kenya, they are led fundamentally differently. Not only has the age of the accused regularly not had an impact on the penalty,[61] there is also just one defence attorney for up to 11 defendants. The trials are certainly much shorter, but the duration of the trial may well indicate the lack of effectiveness of the defence. This is not to say that every trial should last 105 days to accord to minimum standards, but effective defence is part of the international minimum standards and it is not adhered to in these trials on a regular basis.

B. German Practice: To Prosecute or not to Prosecute

The trial against the *Taipan* pirates and the recent case of the *Marida Marguerite* pirate suspect are exceptions rather than the rule in Germany. Usually, state attorneys open investigations into pirate attacks and, in most cases, close the proceedings again, because the suspects can be put on trial elsewhere and are transferred to that jurisdiction or because there is a perceived lack of evidence.[62] In addition, there is a working group, consisting of representatives of several government ministries, that decides whether there is a German interest in a given case. Although this is not a legal prerequisite for a prosecution and the state attorneys would be well equipped to determine whether to open investigations or not by themselves, this political predetermination is seen as some kind of necessity for trying pirates in Germany.[63] After the pirates attacked the *Taipan*, the Netherlands Navy boarded the vessel, arrested the suspects and freed the hostages. Subsequently, the Netherlands Navy brought the suspects to the Netherlands and the authorities indicated to Germany that they wanted to extradite them, since the *Taipan* was a German-flagged vessel. Consequently, Germany was under obvious political pressure to accept the transfer and acted accordingly.[64] This shows that Germany is not actively seeking to prosecute and try pirate suspects, but does so only when there are no politically defensible alternatives.

C. The Scope of German Criminal Law

When it comes to criminal jurisdiction, German law is lacking a clear-cut approach, which renders criminal law applicable to all piratical acts *iure gentium*. The applicability of German criminal law needs to follow from the clear wording of a national law act, thus the universality principle in international law is not sufficient to render the

---

[61] See the judgment of the Supreme Court of Seychelles, *The Republic v Houssein Mohammed Osman & ten others*, Criminal Side No 19/2011, 12 October 2011, para 8.

[62] § 153c of the Criminal Procedure Code (StPO) allows the closing of proceedings in case of crimes committed outside of Germany in certain cases.

[63] See critically Kolb et al, n 43 above, 214; König, n 35 above, 238.

[64] For an extended analysis on the following topic see TR Salomon, 'Die Anwendung des deutschen Strafrechts auf Piraterie. Reichweite und Lücken' [2012] *Deutsche Richterzeitung* 307; Kolb et al, ibid, 211ff.

criminal code applicable.[65] § 3 StGB (German Criminal Code) codifies the territoriality principle and applies German criminal law to acts conducted on German territory. Yet ships do not belong to the territory of a state. § 4 StGB fills the gap and applies German law to every act undertaken on board a German-flagged vessel. Acts committed *on board* a ship, however, do not necessarily cover acts committed against ships, especially when they adhere to the imperative of a strict interpretation of the wording of the criminal code.[66] This potential gap is filled by § 6 StGB, the national law codification of the universality principle, which renders German criminal law applicable to acts pursuant to § 316c StGB—attacks on air and maritime traffic—everywhere in the world without the need for a link between the act and Germany pursuant to § 6 No 3 StGB.[67] For purposes of completeness, § 7 StGB needs mention, which codifies the personality principle and orders the applicability of German criminal law to acts perpetrated against a German national, 'if the act is a criminal offence at the locality of its commission or if that locality is not subject to any criminal jurisdictions' (§ 7(1) StGB) or by German nationals in certain circumstances (§ 7(2) StGB).

This regime covers the main areas of modern-day piracy. If a ship is attacked, the act in question would likely qualify as a crime under § 316c StGB and German criminal law would apply universally, independent of the ship's flag. If a criminal act, such as a violent crime, occurs on a German-flagged vessel, then German criminal law would apply by virtue of § 4 StGB. If the vessel of a German-based shipowner that does not fly the German flag is hijacked and the shipowner blackmailed, German criminal law applies pursuant to § 3 StGB, since the result of the blackmail would occur on German territory.[68] However, there are tangible gaps in this regime. This is the case especially when it comes to acts committed against non-Germans no longer on board a German ship. Somali pirates have regularly moved hostages to other ships or to Somali territory. Acts committed there against non-German-nationals, who worked on a German-flagged vessel before they were taken hostage, would not be covered by German criminal law, which makes potential future proceedings in Germany against pirate suspects in these cases unnecessarily ineffective.

D. Substantive Law: The Narrow German Approach vs. Piracy *Iure Gentium*

Some aspects of substantive law have already been mentioned. The universally applicable § 316c StGB played a central role in the case of the *Taipan* pirates and will do so in potential piracy cases to come. The other offence that the pirates were found guilty of in Hamburg is abduction for the purpose of blackmail pursuant to § 239a StGB. With these two norms, German criminal law covers many aspects of Somali piracy and its scope is quite unambiguous. German criminal law does not, however,

---

[65] See Salomon, n 64 above, 307; Kolb et al, ibid, 211.

[66] Kolb et al, ibid, 217; but see G Werle and F Jeßberger, *Leipziger Kommentar-StGB*, 12th edn (Berlin, de Gruyter Recht, 2007) § 4, para 59ff.

[67] Nevertheless, in practice, courts sometimes demand a genuine link when basing jurisdiction on § 6 StGB: see, eg BGH, [1994] *Neue Zeitschrift für Strafrecht* 232.

[68] The locus of the crime is either 'where the offender acted' or the place 'in which the result if it is an element of the offence occurs or should have occurred according to the intention of the offender' (§ 9(1) StGB); see also Salomon, n 64 above, 307.

contain a notion of piracy itself, and it also lacks a criminal law notion of conspiracy or planning of piratical attacks, in contrast to the criminal law regime of many other states.[69] Indeed, for a criminal act such as § 316c or § 239a StGB, German law demands that the perpetrator has taken 'steps which will immediately lead to the completion of the offence',[70] while the preparation stage for such a crime is usually not subject to criminal penalty. It is therefore very narrow in scope, when compared to other national legal systems and also the definition of piracy in Article 101 UNCLOS. This is especially true in view of the recent discussions, which have featured an increasingly broad piracy notion. The 'private ends' requirement is read as possibly including actions by ecological activists against scientific whaling or illegal dumping,[71] and Articles 101(b) and (c) UNCLOS are increasingly seen as not being limited to the locus of Article 101(a) UNCLOS—the high seas and exclusive economic zones (EEZ).[72] As such, the operation of a vessel that has just started from the Somali beach and is heading to the high seas may be deemed piracy *iure gentium*. Even fuelling up a skiff on the beach may possibly constitute piracy in itself according to the wording of Article 101(b) UNCLOS and its broad conception. Moreover, under Article 101(c) UNCLOS, the intentional facilitation of piracy is piracy in itself, meaning that, pursuant to this new and possibly overly broad understanding, even charitable donations to ecological activists who act in the described way may now be deemed piracy under international law itself. Such an extensive notion of piracy will be found only in the criminal law regimes that define piracy by reference to piracy *iure gentium*, if that broad notion is in fact part of international law, which will ultimately have to be determined by state practice.[73] It certainly finds no basis in German law.

---

[69] See Sterio, who lists a number of states that explicitly criminalise conspiracy to commit piracy and identifies: US, France, Argentina, Belgium, Cyprus, Israel, Norway, Poland, Seychelles, Singapore and New Zealand. She also lists Denmark, Kenya, Turkey and South Korea as criminalising conspiracy to ship-hijacking, M Sterio, 'Prosecuting Conspiracy to Commit Piracy' (29 March 2013), available at http://ilg2.org/2013/03/29/prosecuting-conspiracy-to-commit-piracy/ (last accessed on 5 June 2013).

[70] See § 22 StGB.

[71] See SP Menefee, 'The Case of the Castle John, or Greenbeard the Pirate?: Environmentalism, Piracy and the Development of International Law' (1993) 24(1) *California Western International Law Review* 1, 14; D Guilfoyle, *Shipping Interdiction and the Law of the Sea*, (Cambridge, Cambridge University Press, 2009) 35; T Garmon, 'International Law of the Sea: Reconciling the Law of Piracy and Terrorism in the Wake of September 11th' (2002) 27 *Tulane Maritime Law Journal* 257, 265; Kreß, n 54 above, 96, note 12; M Bahar, 'Attaining Optimal Deterrence at Sea: A Legal and Strategic Theory for Anti-Piracy-Operations' (2007) 40 *Vanderbilt Journal of Transnational Law* 1, 28ff. On piracy and environmental protest see also R Churchill, Chapter 1 above.

[72] D Guilfoyle, 'Committing Piracy on Dry Land: Liability for Facilitating Piracy', *European Journal of International Law:Talk*, 26 July 2012, available at http://www.European Journal of International Lawtalk.org/committing-piracy-on-dry-land-liability-for-facilitating-piracy/; see, however, the contrary opinion expressed by J Bellish, 'Breaking News from 1932: Pirate Facilitators Must Be Physically Present on the High Seas', *European Journal of International Law:Talk*, 19 September 2012, available at http://www.European Journal of International Lawtalk.org/breaking-news-from-1932-pirate-facilitators-must-be-physically-present-on-the-high-seas/.

[73] This seems to be the common ground between the two rivalling opinions, see the discussion under Bellish, n 72 above.

IV. PRIVATELY COTRACTED ARMED SECURITY PROVIDERS IN GERMAN LAW

The final issue this chapter will deal with—privately contracted armed security providers—has been a controversial topic worldwide.[74] Since Germany is playing an interesting role, it is appropriate to introduce the German way of regulating this new and thriving industry. Private armed guards have been used on German vessels for quite some time now. It remains a highly questionable policy to do so,[75] although the current drop in successful hijackings off the Horn of Africa has to be attributed at least in part to the increased use of armed security providers. Supporters and critics of this practice alike, however, should agree that the implementation of a high-quality standard among armed guards is key to protecting the security of the crew, vessel and cargo alike.[76]

A. The Legal Regime Regarding Private Security up to 2012

Initially, shipowners were reluctant to consider private armed guards and deemed the employment of armed guards on German-flagged trade vessels forbidden by German law on the basis of correspondence with the Ministry of the Interior.[77] As the discussion advanced, it became clear that the law on private security providers, governed mainly by the German Trade Regulation Act (Gewerbeordnung—GewO), indeed allowed such employment in general terms, since the law until the end of 2012 did not draw a distinction between security guards on land and guards on vessels.[78] § 34a GewO states that whoever protects the life or property of others in a commercial manner is required to be permitted to do so by the competent German authority. Such permission may be subject to conditions and subsequent amendments to the extent necessary to protect the public or the respective clients. The authority shall refuse the permission if, for example, the facts justify the assumption that the applicant does not meet the required reliability or does not produce the required documentation issued by a chamber of commerce to show that the applicant was informed about the legal requirements of the trade and is familiar with them. If these prerequisites are fulfilled, the authority is under a constitutional law duty to issue the authorisation.[79] Moreover, a security company may only employ guards who meet these (rather vague) requirements. A more thorough examination is required for guards patrolling in public areas or in areas with public traffic, protecting shops

---

[74] For a helpful publication on the topic as a whole see P Cullen and C Berube (eds), *Maritime Private Security: Market Responses to Piracy, Terrorism and Waterborne Security Risks in the 21st Century* (London, Routledge, 2012).

[75] See D König and TR Salomon, 'Private Sicherheitsdienste auf Handelsschiffen—Rechtliche Implikationen', PiraT-Working Paper No 2 (2011) 35, available at http://www.maritimesecurity.eu/ fileadmin/content/ news_events/workingpaper/PiraT_Arbeitspapier_Nr2_2011_Koenig-Salomon.pdf.

[76] See also H Jessen, 'Der Einsatz privater bewaffneter Sicherheitsunternehmen auf Handelsschiffen unter deutscher Flagge' [2013] *Recht der Transportwirtschaft* 125, 127.

[77] J Ritter, 'Die Piraten haben den Bootsmann erschossen', interview with Niels Stolberg, FAZnet, 1 February 2011, available at http://www.faznet/-01nyjt.

[78] See König and Salomon, n 75 above, 25.

[79] TR Salomon and S tho Pesch, 'License to Kill?—Staatshaftung und die Zertifizierung von maritimen Sicherheitsdiensten' [2012] *Zeitschrift für Rechtspolitik* 1; F Jungk and C Deutschland, in J-C Pielow (ed), *BeckOK-GewO*, 12th edn (Munich, Verlag CH Beck, 2010) § 34a, para 28.

against shoplifters or employed as doormen in entrance areas of hotels and restaurants.[80] This, however, did not apply to maritime security providers, as they arguably do not fall into any of these categories.

Also, the individual guards may only exercise the rights that everyone is entitled to in the case of self-defence or an emergency, as well as such rights that are contractually transferred upon them by the respective clients, as § 34a(5) GewO clarifies.

Security guards using arms need further permission by the competent authorities pursuant to the Weapons Act (Waffengesetz—WaffG). § 28 WaffG allows the individual security provider to carry weapons 'if they can credibly demonstrate that security contracts are being or are to be performed which require guns in order to protect a person in danger . . . or an endangered property' and if the general legal requirements of gun possession, reliability (§ 5 WaffG), personal aptitude (§ 6 WaffG) and specialised knowledge (§ 7 WaffG) are met.

This regime was drafted with traditional security occupations in mind (unarmed security guards in front of nightclubs, but also armed personnel, such as cash transport services). Generally speaking, the legislative body did not deem higher standards necessary for these traditional activities of security providers. This explains why such guards basically only have to show that they are reliable in order to be permitted to work, while the interpretation of 'reliability' has been left largely to the administration and the courts.

B. Steps to Regulate Maritime Security Providers

The above rules applied to maritime security providers, since German law is applicable on a German-flagged vessel (Article 92 UNCLOS), and neither the Trade Regulation Act nor the Weapons Act is limited in scope to German territory. However, with the increased use of private armed guards on vessels, the German authorities, led by the Federal Ministry of Economics and Technology, rightly deemed the existing regulation insufficient and the Bundestag adopted new legislation on 13 December 2012, in order to guarantee that only sufficiently qualified security providers, who meet the factual requirements of such operations, will be employed.[81] This legislation has also been demanded by the shipping industry, which at first advocated for military or police protection, but, when recognising that such measures were unlikely to be adopted, called for more legal security regarding the use of private armed guards on board their vessels in an attempt to limit their liability risks.

Key parts of this new legislation entered into force in March 2013 and the new regulation involves a number of federal authorities: the BAFA (Federal Office of Economics and Export Control), the Bundespolizei and the BSH (Federal Maritime and Hydrographic Agency).[82]

---

[80] See § 34a(1) GewO for the regime outlined above.

[81] See Federal Ministry of Economics and Technology press release, 'Kabinett beschließt Gesetzentwurf zur Zulassung privater Sicherheitskräfte zur Pirateriebekämpfung' (18 June 2012), available at http://www.bmwi.de/DE/Presse/pressemitteilungen,did=499738.html.

[82] For the draft proposal see Bundestag printed paper 17/10960 of 10 October 2012, available at http://dipbt.bundestag.de/dip21/btd/17/109/1710960.pdf; for the adopted version see Bundestag printed paper 17/11887 of 12 December 2012, available at http://dip21.bundestag.de/dip21/btd/17/118/1711887.pdf.

C. Requirements of the BAFA Authorisation

The new mechanism establishes a legal duty of maritime security providers working on German-flagged ships to be authorised by German authorities pursuant to the new regulation, if they operate seawards of the German EEZ and guard the vessel against dangers coming from the outside.[83] The competent authority is the BAFA, in consultation with the Bundespolizei.[84] This duty is laid down in the newly introduced § 31(1) GewO and came into force in December 2013, in order to allow for a transitional period in which a sufficient number of providers could be authorised. The detailed requirements, which security companies and their employees have to meet, are specified in two ordinances (*Rechtsverordnungen*): the Ordinance on the authorization of security companies on seagoing vessels (Authorisation Ordinance) and the Ordinance on the execution of the ordinance on the authorization of security companies on seagoing vessels (Execution Ordinance). These regulations are closely adapted to the IMO guidelines[85] as well as the new ISO standard,[86] although the latter still needs to be refined by practice.[87]

It is important to note that only the security companies and not the individual employees will need to be authorised under the new regime. However, the new legislation includes responsibilities of the companies concerning the safeguarding of the minimum age of 18 years,[88] as well as the reliability,[89] personal aptitude[90] and sufficient qualification of their employees.[91] The necessary qualifications include nautical, maritime and technical knowledge, knowledge of the English language, the ability to recognise and evaluate hazards caused by pirates, knowledge of life-saving measures at sea and the necessary legal knowledge, eg of the actions they may legally perform with regard to the use of firearms for self-defence.[92] The new regulation also specifies how the company shall ensure that these requirements are met, namely by regulating modalities of choosing,[93] monitoring[94] and training personnel.[95]

An authorisation will be denied by the BAFA if the security company does not meet the requirements of internal organisation, especially with regard to the procedures

---

[83] This can be criticised, since the legislation specifically wanted to exclude security guards on ferries in the North and Baltic Sea. Many of these routes, however, go beyond the German EEZ. Accordingly, such security providers may fall under the new legislation, although it could be argued that those services are mainly employed to protect the shipping operation from disturbances from the inside not from external dangers. See TR Salomon and S tho Pesch, 'Das Zulassungsregime für bewaffnete Sicherheitsdiensten auf Handelsschiffen' (Die Öffentliche Verwaltung, 2013) 760.

[84] The Federal Police will evaluate the maritime competence of the companies applying for authorisation and the rules of engagement or rules of force proposed by the company, Jessen, n 76 above, 131.

[85] 'Especially Revised Interim Guidance to Shipowners, Ship operators and Shipmasters on the Use of Privately Contracted Armed Security Personnel on Board Ships in the High Risk Area', IMO Doc MSC.1/Circ 1405/Rev.2 (25 May 2012).

[86] ISO/PAS 28007, 'Guidelines for Private Maritime Security Companies (PMSC) Providing Privately Contracted Armed Security Personnel (PCASP) On Board Ships' (2012).

[87] Jessen, n 76 above, 127.

[88] § 7 No 2 Authorisation Ordinance.

[89] Ibid, § 7 No 1 and § 8.

[90] Ibid, § 7 No 3 and § 9.

[91] Ibid, § 7 No 4 and 10.

[92] See § 10(1) of the Authorisation Ordinance and its annex.

[93] § 4 Execution Ordinance.

[94] Ibid, § 5.

[95] Ibid, § 6 and 7.

that guarantee these requirements.[96] The authorisation will further be denied if the executive level of the whole company or of a branch thereof does not meet the requirements for management, the person charged with executive duties does not have the required specialised knowledge, personal aptitude or reliability, or if no evidence of public liability insurance is provided.[97] The admission procedure will be subject to a fee[98] to be paid by the security company. The Federal Ministry of Economics and Technology expected 50–75 applications per year, although early numbers suggest that such estimates are too high. Up to the end of January 2014, seven companies had been admitted.[99] For the security companies, the Ministry estimates a minimum of €500 in training costs per guard per year and, for companies just entering the market, the non-recurring maximum total costs necessary to satisfy the admission requirements are estimated to be around €1.1 million.[100] Once a company is authorised, it will be published on a list available online at the BAFA's webpage pursuant to § 31(6) GewO, if it consents.

With regard to the period of validity of the authorisation issued by the BAFA, a previous draft suggested that short periods (ie one year) need to be adopted in order to guarantee a certain degree of control and regularity of inspection, since the possibilities of inspection and control are limited by the nature of the trade of maritime security providers. However, it is now settled that the period of validity will be two years, apparently in order to find a balance with practical demands.[101]

Finally, the new regulation also includes the recognition of authorisations by EU Member States, if such authorisations are based on requirements equivalent to the German mechanism.[102]

D. Other Modalities and Duties

Parallel to the duty of security providers to be authorised by the BAFA when working on a German-flagged vessel, shipping companies are under a duty to employ, if they choose to employ them at all, security providers authorised under the new scheme for their German-flagged vessels. This is administered by the BSH and laid down in an amended version of the Maritime Personal Safety Ordinance (See-Eigensicherungsverordnung).

Additional duties of shipping companies and security providers are again closely modelled after the IMO guidelines. They include duties such as keeping documentation of specific jobs and documenting incidents in which weapons were used, including written testimony of witnesses to the incident.[103] Furthermore, security companies are also under a duty to report incidents as well as the loss of weapons or ammunition to the BAFA as soon as possible.[104] If they themselves used weapons, a report has to be made to the BAFA and the Bundespolizei, although there is no duty to report

---

[96] § 31(2) No 1 GewO.
[97] § 31(2) No 2 and 3 GewO; § 11f Authorisation Ordinance.
[98] Seeschiffbewachungs-Gebührenverordnung, Federal Law Gazette 2013 I 4110.
[99] See www.bafa.debafa/en/other_tasks/pmsc/list_of_licensed_companies/index.html.
[100] See the explanations to the draft for the data listed, n 82 above, 3.
[101] See the draft, n 82 above, 3 and now § 3 Authorisation Ordinance.
[102] § 15 Authorisation Ordinance.
[103] Ibid, § 13.
[104] Ibid, § 14(1, 2 and 4).

information that would cause the reporting individual to be in danger of being sub-jected to criminal prosecution or an administrative offence.[105]

In addition, the companies are required to introduce internal control,[106] documen-tation[107] and communication procedures,[108] guarantee 24 hour availability of a legal advisor,[109] and regulate in advance which rules and standards are to be adhered to, when a security team is dispatched to a vessel and what to do when an incident occurs.[110] Minimum standards laid down by the new regulations are the avoidance of the use of force and the adherence to the escalation pyramid in the case of an attack, referring to the internationally accepted sequence: warning shots in the air, warning shots in the sea, shots against the attacking skiff and, as a measure of last resort, shots targeted directly against the attacker.[111]

Furthermore, the new regulation also lays down minimum requirements regarding equipment that the security company has to bring on board the vessel.[112] It also speci-fies the minimum number of security guards, namely four, needed to conduct the protection, including a certified first responder.[113]

One of the most important aspects of the legislation, however, is what it does not change. It leaves untouched the rule that security providers are only allowed to exercise self-defence and the help of others in emergency situations, so there are no clear rules of engagement for maritime security providers, but the general rules of self-defence and self-help remain applicable.[114]

E. Amending the Weapons Act

The Weapons Act has also been amended as part of the new regulation. As outlined, the Weapons Act demands that each individual be scrutinised before the possession and carriage of a gun by security providers is allowed by the German authorities. Pursuant to § 28 WaffG, the individual security guard needs to show a necessity for using the weapon on the job, and the general requirements for possession of weapons (outlined in § 4 WaffG[115]) need to be met. The new § 28a(1) WaffG now provides

---

[105] Ibid, § 14(3a).
[106] § 9 Execution Ordinance.
[107] Ibid, § 10.
[108] Ibid, § 11.
[109] Ibid, § 8.
[110] Ibid, § 12, 13.
[111] Ibid, § 12(4).
[112] Ibid, § 14(2).
[113] Ibid, § 2(2).
[114] See § 31(2) No 3; in practice the most important rule will be that of self-defence in § 32 StGB; see König and Salomon, n 75 above, 31ff.
[115] '(1) In order to be granted a licence, applicants shall

1. be at least 18 years of age (Section 2 (1)),
2. have the necessary reliability (Section 5) and personal aptitude (Section 6),
3. demonstrate the necessary specialized knowledge (Section 7),
4. demonstrate a need (Section 8), and
5. enclose proof of liability insurance cover of one million euros for personal injury and property damage when applying for a weapons licence or shooting licence.

(2) Applicants not ordinarily resident for at least five years in the territory governed by this Act may be refused a licence to acquire, possess, carry or shoot a weapon.

that the existing § 28 WaffG applies only with modifications to security companies on German-flagged vessels. § 28a(1) WaffG regulates that the necessity to carry a weapon for the specific contract, which is otherwise needed for the authorisation pursuant to § 28 WaffG, is assumed in cases of guards protecting German-flagged vessels and employed by maritime security companies that have been admitted by the BAFA. This means that this requirement does not need to be proven by the maritime security company. Moreover, the permission to carry weapons is granted to the owner of the company under the condition that the company shall only employ guards that meet the general requirements of § 4(1) Nos 1–3 WaffG.[116] The company shall prove that this is the case by submitting documentation when requested by the authorities, and it shall communicate the personal data of the guards that are deployed on the vessels. The authorisation under the Weapons Act will then extend to the employees of the company (ie the specific armed guards) until the admission under § 31 GewO expires. The wording of the new § 28a WaffG, however, leaves some space for the inspection of individual guards, in contrast to the company-oriented approach of the BAFA authorisation. Indeed, early practice suggests that the individual guards are inspected by the competent authority. The authorisation, if granted, includes in its scope the right to transfer guns or ammunition into the territory governed by the new act, as mandated by § 29 WaffG. Finally, a new sentence in § 48(1) WaffG provides that the authorities of the Free and Hanseatic City of Hamburg will be competent for issuing weapon licenses to persons that conduct armed protection on German-flagged vessels.

Concerning the general constraints with regard to the category of weapons that may be used, there was widespread agreement by the political actors that no amendments should be made in this regard. While Belgium has allowed the use of automatic weapons for maritime security providers under certain circumstances,[117] guards on German-flagged vessels will remain confined to using semi-automatic guns, since automatic guns remain forbidden under the Weapons of War Control Act (Kriegswaffenkontrollgesetz).[118]

F. Sanctions and Compliance

The former draft provision of the new legislation, which penalised shipowners that hired non-authorised guard companies when these acts resulted in a risk that a gun or ammunition would be lost, stolen or subject to unauthorised access with a prison term of up to three years or a fine, has been retracted in the final adopted version. Such acts

---

(3) The competent authorities shall verify the reliability and personal aptitude of licence holders and, in the cases covered by subsection 1 no. 5, shall require proof of liability insurance at regular intervals of no more than three years.

(4) The competent authorities shall verify that a need still exists three years after the first licence is granted under the Weapons Act. This may be done at the same time as the verification referred to in subsection 3. The competent authorities may also verify that a need still exists after the period referred to in the first sentence has expired.' Translation provided by the Language Service of the Federal Ministry of the Interior, available at http://www.gesetze-im-internet.de/englisch_waffg/englisch_waffg.html.

[116] However, the standard for specialised knowledge will not be drawn from the general § 7 WaffG, but from the specific requirements set up by the ordinances under § 31 GewO.

[117] Jessen, n 76 above, 132.

[118] See König and Salomon, n 75 above, 31.

were downgraded from criminal offences to mere administrative offences under § 144 GewO, carrying fines only, and will be under the administration of the BSH. This may prove to be too lenient, seeing that the big difference in price between reliable and authorised security providers on the one hand and less reliable, non-authorised companies on the other hand may drive shipowners to hire non-authorised companies, save money and simply pay the fine in the event that German authorities actually gain knowledge of this circumstance, which will probably be the exception rather than the rule.

Similarly, violations concerning post-incident reporting and other duties may only result in the revocation of the authorisation and will be subject to a fine of up to €5,000.[119] As stated, the legislative body rightly acknowledged that the principle of *nemo tenetur* has to be observed regarding post-incident reporting and, accordingly, a person is exempted from presenting incriminating information that places the person or close relatives in danger of criminal prosecution.[120] These rules may in practice prove to be too weak to ensure compliance, especially since the new regulations fail to implement means that enable the public authorities to investigate suspicious incidents apart from the cooperation and information-sharing by the shipowner and the security company. Against this backdrop, the need for a close monitoring of compliance and, if necessary, the introduction of a more rigid mechanism of control and supervision needs to be stressed.[121]

It remains to be seen how the industry complies with the new rules. The widespread use of private armed guards bears risks. It is not only since the *Enrica Lexie* incident,[122] in which an Italian vessel protection detachment mistook fishers for pirates and killed innocents, that the possibility of errors and their fatal consequences have materialised. The practice of employing guards may be seen to be justified because of their overall success in protecting trade vessels. However, in the event of incidents like *Enrica Lexie*, the possibility of investigations should not depend solely on the cooperation of the individual security provider that is under the suspicion of criminal behaviour. Instead, better control mechanisms need to be implemented. Ways that have been discussed include helmet cameras, which are already used by many security providers to be able to prove, in possible prosecutions against them, that there was no misconduct on their part in a specific case. The implementation of anonymous complaint mechanisms may also further the degree of possible supervision over armed security providers. With such mechanisms, which already form part of the Maritime Labour Convention that entered into force on 20 August 2013, the master or crew of a trade vessel may, for example, contact the flag state anonymously and inform them of specific cases of misconduct.[123]

---

[119] § 16 Authorisation Ordinance, in connection with § 144(2) No 1 and (4) GewO.

[120] Ibid, § 14(3a).

[121] See Salomon and tho Pesch, n 79 above, 4; TR Salomon and S tho Pesch, 'Zertifizierung bewaffneter Sicherheitskräfte auf deutschen Handelsschiffen und Staatshaftung' [2012] *Zeitschrift für öffentliches Recht in Norddeutschland* 65, 70.

[122] See, eg Jessen, n 76 above, 128f.

[123] For these suggestions see Salomon and tho Pesch, n 79 above, 4; Salomon and tho Pesch, n 120 above, 70.

A big issue on the horizon is the conflict between the new German legislation and coastal state legislation, especially concerning piracy and maritime violence in the Gulf of Guinea. Certain countries, such as Nigeria, forbid—in contrast to the law of the sea[124]—vessels passing through their territorial seas to have armed guards of a nationality other than Nigerian on board. Nigerian armed guards will, however, most likely not have undergone the authorisation procedure demanded by the German government. German flagged vessels thus find themselves caught between a rock and a hard place if travelling though Nigerian waters—they must take on board Nigerian security teams and violate German law; travel under armed protection by BAFA-authorised security guards and violate Nigerian law; or travel without armed protection at all and be the defenceless target of maritime violence. It remains to be seen if Nigeria will uphold its policy on armed guards, despite growing international pressure.

G. Outlook

Legally, the new mechanism does not represent a huge shift. It does not come close to the current discussions in the Netherlands, where maritime private security was forbidden, which is now starting to change. Although the maritime coordinator of the German government stated in 2011 that he was planning to change the traffic light from red to yellow for maritime private security[125] when he talked about his plans to amend the law, the traffic light was in fact green all along. The new legislation does not legalise private maritime security guards; rather, it regulates a sector that was not previously regulated sufficiently and only existed legally because the drafters of § 34a GewO had not considered a maritime security dimension of the norm. The new legislation now introduces much needed specific guidelines, which are a good first step to implementing higher standards in the maritime security industry. A second step should be a stronger enforcement regime. Generally, the assessment leads to a conclusion ending on a positive note: the German mechanism might even have the potential to elevate the overall quality in the maritime security industry. Major players on the market will seek authorisation by the BAFA, if only for purposes of public relations. Security companies have long sought to become members of international and national initiatives and codes of conduct, etc. One of the reasons for this has always been to project reliability to their potential clients. Being authorised by the German authorities may well be seen as a desirable quality indicator for shipowners, leading many security companies to seek authorisation. As a result, they may well implement higher standards in their businesses.

---

[124] See König and Salomon, n 75 above, 12ff. Art 21 UNCLOS allows certain coastal state legislation regulating innocent passage (which a passage generally remains pursuant to Art 19 UNCLOS, even when private security teams are on board). The national regulation may not, however, regulate manning pursuant to Art 21, para 2 UNCLOS, and the aspects a coastal state may regulate according to Art 21, para 1 UNCLOS do not entail security measures. Naturally, a state may pass and enforce Nigerian-type rules for ships entering its ports.

[125] *Gelbes Licht für private Piratenabwehr, Deutsche Verkehrs-Zeitung*, 23 July 2011.

V. CONCLUSION

It is a curious development that such a historic crime as piracy is catching the legal regime of a developed nation such as Germany off guard to some extent. The constitutional law regime regarding out-of-area deployment of the Bundeswehr has long been recognised to be in need of reform. However, the political sensitivity of this issue has so far proven to be a very effective stumbling block for progress. The role of Germany in the world has changed significantly since the introduction of Article 87a GG in 1956 and its overhaul in 1968, and today Germany is determined to participate in out-of-area operations under international mandates. Hopefully, the Constitution will soon reflect this determination in a way that is appropriate given the importance of the issue. Besides Article 87a(2) GG, there are a host of other issues with a constitutional law nexus in connection with the fight against piracy. Above all, it seems that the importance of basic and human rights for actions by the Bundeswehr vis-à-vis suspected pirates, especially with regard to the transfer of suspects to regional states for purposes of prosecution and detention and the procedure of such transfers, need more attention in discussion and practice alike.

With regard to criminal law, German law has what is needed to try pirates, with the notable exception of a jurisdictional gap regarding hostages from foreign countries who are removed from a German-flagged ship and taken to other places. The first trial in Hamburg has shown, however, that there are problems, eg when trying to contact witnesses located in Somalia or other neighbouring countries. A prosecution closer to the *locus delicti* in regional states will certainly alleviate some of these issues, yet the standards of these trials and of the subsequent detention deserve close scrutiny to ensure compliance with international and European human rights, as well as constitutional rights and specific human rights of vulnerable groups such as children.

While effective prosecution in accordance with human rights is a necessity in reaching satisfactory long-term results in the fight against piracy not only off the coast of Somalia, but also beyond, the demand for short-term solutions offering immediate relief for seafarers and shipowners is high. Private armed security has proven to be an effective way to guard vessels. Despite well-founded doubts and fears concerning their long-term effect on the modus operandi of pirates, they will continue to be part of the security portfolio of shipowners, most likely as long as the threat lasts. To turn a blind eye to this development and leave it as it is would mean to accept the significant risks posed by low-standard service providers and free-riders. As such, the introduction of binding higher standards for security providers is a cause that should be shared by supporters and opponents of private armed security alike. On the professionalism of the service providers hinge the security of the crews, the effectiveness of the defence, and their acceptance by coastal and port states. Accordingly, this question should not be left to chance. The complex German regulatory approach is certainly not a universal solution. It is, however, a step in the right direction, although oversight and control mechanisms raise concerns when it comes to their effectiveness. A downside may be that unilateral action contributes to a fragmentation of flag state policies. Yet the German approach resembles the IMO recommendations and takes into account the new ISO standard on the issue, so that it in fact may be understood as giving (some) teeth to these internationally accepted instruments.

11

Piracy and the East African Region

EDWIN EGEDE*

I. INTRODUCTION

ALTHOUGH PIRATES ARE sometimes romanticised in fiction books and films as swashbuckling Robin Hood-type characters, in reality under international law individuals who carry out the act of piracy at sea are regarded as committing a heinous crime. In the *Le Louis* case, it was said that pirates are 'enemies of the human race, renouncing every country, and ravaging every country in its coasts and vessels indiscriminately, and thereby creating an [sic] universal terror and alarm'.[1] Piracy is one of the oldest international crimes, and also one of the first subject to universal jurisdiction. Viscount Sankey LC, in the *In re Piracy Jure Gentium* case, pointed out that the states were allowed to exercise universal jurisdiction for piracy because 'a person guilty of such piracy has placed himself beyond the protection of any State. He is no longer a national, but 'hostis humani generis' and as such he is justiciable by any State anywhere.'[2]

Although piracy has for a long time attracted the attention of the international community, it has assumed particular prominence off the coast of East Africa, especially around the coast of Somalia. According to the International Maritime Bureau (IMB), a specialised division of the International Chamber of Commerce (ICC), the Somali pirates operate not only in the northern, eastern and southern coast of Somalia, but also in the Western Indian Ocean, the Gulf of Aden and the Arabian Sea.[3] The IMB, which provides figures on incidents of piracy and armed robbery at sea, reported that in 2012 there were a total of 297 attacks worldwide, of which 28 were hijackings. Of these, there were 75 total incidents, 14 hijackings and, as at 31 December 2012, a total

---

* The author expresses his special thanks to Prince Emmanuel for the support and inspiration—you are a friend who sticks closer than a brother does. Email: EgedeE@cardiff.ac.uk (all URL sites referred to in this chapter were visited on 5 August 2013, unless otherwise stated).
    [1] (1817) 2 Dods 210.
    [2] [1934] AC 586, 589. See also the Kenyan Court of Appeal decision in the *In re Mohammed Hashi et al* [2012] HC Misc App 434 of 2009, Judgment of 18 October 2012 (CA) case, where the court, endorsing the *In re Piracy Jure Gentium* case, held that Kenya has universal jurisdiction to try piracy suspects for piratical acts committed outside Kenya's territory, including its territorial sea, para 39, *per* Maraga JA, available at http://piracylaw.files.wordpress.com/2012/10/kenya-hashi-appeal-opinion.pdf.
    [3] http://www.icc-ccs.org.uk/piracy-reporting-centre/prone-areas-and-warnings.

of 127 hostages reported for Somalia piracy.[4] Piracy worldwide has been estimated to cost the international economy \$7–12 billion per year, with a large chunk of the costs from the piracy incidents in the East African region, and as such it is currently a major security challenge faced by the international community.[5]

This chapter explores the recent upsurge of piracy off the coast of East Africa. It begins by exploring the definition of piracy, particularly with regard to certain difficulties faced with applying the traditional conception of piracy under international law to the situation off the coast of East Africa. It will then examine whether there is a distinction between the piracy situation in East Africa and that in other regions, in particularly Southeast Asia and West Africa. Further, the chapter will examine the various approaches to dealing with piracy in East Africa with a view to determining how effective they are in curbing piracy incidents in this region.

II. DEFINITION OF PIRACY AND EAST AFRICAN PIRACY

Since the definition of piracy has been explored in detail in some other chapters in this book,[6] this section shall confine itself to examining some rather stimulating definitional issues that are particularly relevant to East African piracy. As has been mentioned in other chapters, Article 101 of the United Nations Convention on the Law of the Sea Convention (UNCLOS) 1982, a virtual copy of the provision of the High Seas Convention 1958, defines piracy.[7] One of the issues arising from this definition is whether an individual who does not actually participate in the piratical acts on the high seas but provides financial support as an 'investor' to the actual pirates, and sometimes acts as a negotiator for the ransom money, could be regarded as a pirate under UNCLOS. This is a particularly noteworthy issue in East Africa, as the piracy 'business' there involves an intricate network of both the actual pirates and their backers, who provide the necessary finance to enable the former to obtain the equipment and weaponry to carry out the piratical operation, and are sometimes even involved in the negotiation on behalf of the pirates for the release of captured vessels and hostages. These financial backers get profitable returns on their 'investments' when the ransom monies are paid. According to Dr Keene, the Director of the Security Economics Programme of the Institute for State Craft:

> Maritime piracy in Somalia has become a profitable business, attracting not only 'internal' investment from the pirate communities, but a variety of international investors through the establishment of a specialist 'stock exchange' dedicated to investment in piracy operations in addition to diaspora support from around the world.[8]

---

[4] http://www.icc-ccs.org/news/836-piracy-falls-in-2012-but-seas-off-east-and-west-africa-remain-dangerous-says-imb.

[5] A Bowden, K Hurlburt, E Aloyo, C Marts and A Lee, 'The Economic Cost of Maritime Piracy: One Earth Future', working paper (December 2010), available at http://oceansbeyondpiracy.org/sites/default/files/documents_old/The_Economic_Cost_of_Piracy_Full_Report.pdf.

[6] See especially R Churchill, Chapter 1 above.

[7] Art 15 of The High Seas Convention (HSC) 1958 substantially adopted the definition of piracy in Art 3 of The Harvard Research in International Law Draft Convention on Piracy: Harvard Research in International Law, 'Part IV: Piracy' (1932) 26 *American Journal of International Law Supplement* 739, 743.

[8] S Keene, 'Maritime Piracy, Somalia' (The Institute for State Craft, 12 November 2012), available at http://www.statecraft.org.uk/research/maritime-piracy-somalia.

The role of these so-called 'investors' in the piracy 'business' in the upsurge of piracy in the East African region has been acknowledged by the Security Council. It recognised that to effectively deal with the piracy situation in this region there was

> the need to investigate and prosecute not only suspects captured at sea, but also anyone who incites or intentionally facilitates piracy operations, including key figures of criminal networks involved in piracy who illicitly plan, organise, facilitate, or finance and profit from such attacks.[9]

The question is whether these backers who do not participate in the actual high seas piracy operations could be rightly prosecuted for piracy under UNCLOS.

This issue was explored in two recent US Court of Appeals decisions, *United States of America v Ali Mohammed Ali, also known as Ahmed Ali Adan, also known as Ismail Ali*[10] and *United States of America v Mohammad Saaili Shibin, a/k/a Khalif Ahmed Shibin, a/k/a Mohammad Ali, a/k/a Ali Jama*.[11] In these cases the US Court of Appeals had to examine the American law that allowed for the prosecution of '[w]hoever, on the high seas, commits the crime of piracy as defined by the law of nations'.[12] The two decisions held that conduct violating Article 101(c) UNCLOS does not have to be carried out on the high seas, but it suffices if it incites or intentionally facilitates acts committed against ships, persons and property on the high seas.[13] In essence, this would mean that a person who is located within a national jurisdiction when involved in inciting or intentionally facilitating piracy may actually be deemed to be a pirate.

While the act of financing piratical acts is reprehensible and is certainly a criminal act, it is argued that the well-intentioned attempt by the US Court of Appeals to interpret Article 101(c) independently of Article 101(a) UNCLOS is erroneous. Article 101(c) is intended to be ancillary to Article 101(a) and should be regarded as dealing with incitement or intentional facilitation committed either on the high seas or in a place outside the jurisdiction of any state, since the essence of piracy, a crime that attracts universal jurisdiction, is that it is committed outside the territorial jurisdiction of any state.[14] The Court of Appeals in these cases sought to make out that Article 101(c) was clear and unambiguous, and was rather scathing about the use of preparatory materials, including the Harvard Research in International Law Draft Convention on Piracy, to seek to interpret Article 101(c).[15] However, in reality there is some ambiguity with regard to this provision, and therefore such preparatory materials may be used under Article 32 of the Vienna Convention on the Law of Treaties (VCLT) 1969.[16] This provision states:

---

[9] Para 4, S/RES/2020 (2011) of 22 November 2011.
[10] *USA v Ali Mohamed Ali* Case No 12-3056 (CA, DC Circ, 11 June 2013), available at http://www.cadc.uscourts.gov/internet/opinions.nsf/16778EF07896TTB085257B8700507F47/$file/12-3056-1440653.pdf.
[11] *USA v Shibin* Case No 12-4652 (CA, 4th Circ, 12 July 2013), available at http://www.gpo.gov/fdsys/pkg/USCOURTS-ca4-12-04652/pdf/USCOURTS-ca4-12-04652-0.pdf.
[12] 18 USC 1651.
[13] See *Ali*, n 10 above; *Shibin*, n 11 above, 17.
[14] Art 101(a)(i) and (ii) UNCLOS
[15] *Ali*, n 10 above, 15, where the Court stated: 'Effectively, Ali would have us ignore UNCLOS's plain meaning in favour of eighty-year-old scholarship that may have influenced a treaty that includes language similar to UNCLOS Art 101. This is a bridge too far.' See also *Shibin*, n 11 above, 12–30.
[16] 1155 UNTS 331.

Recourse may be had to supplementary means of interpretation, including the preparatory work of the treaty and the circumstances of its conclusion, in order to confirm the meaning resulting from the application of article 31, or to determine the meaning when the interpretation according to article 31:

(a) leaves the meaning ambiguous or obscure; or . . .

Resort may therefore be had to the *travaux preparatoires* of the International Law Commission (ILC) in respect of the 1958 Geneva Convention on High Seas, since Article 15 of this treaty is identical to Article 101. Although the ILC did not specifically comment on Article 15(3), the provision equivalent to Article 101(c) UNCLOS, in the final draft treaty it submitted to the General Assembly as a prelude to UNCLOS I, it did refer to and generally endorse the comments of the authoritative Harvard Research in International Law Draft Convention on Piracy, from which it copied certain provisions on piracy that were eventually included in the 1958 High Seas Convention (HSC).[17] Harvard Research, in its commentary on a similar provision in the Draft Convention to Article 15(3) of the HSC and now Article 101(c) UNCLOS, was clear that such an act or facilitation should not be 'subjected to the common jurisdiction unless it takes place outside territorial jurisdiction'.[18] Persons involved in inciting or intentionally facilitating piratical acts that at the time of the commission of the crime were not located on the high seas or a place outside national jurisdiction fall outside the ambit of, and cannot be prosecuted as pirates under, Article 101(c). On the other hand, they may be prosecuted under the 1988 Convention for the Suppression of Unlawful Acts against the Safety of Maritime Navigation (SUA Convention) provided the prosecuting state has taken such measures as required by the Convention to establish jurisdiction.[19] Article 3(2)(b) of the SUA Convention states that a person is guilty of an offence if such person 'abets the commission of any of the offences set forth in paragraph 1 perpetrated by any person or is otherwise an accomplice of a person who commits such an offence'. Also, such individuals may be prosecuted on the basis of territoriality by the state in whose territory they have committed the offence, provided such state has national legislation which criminalises such act of incitement or intentional facilitation done within its territory.[20] Undoubtedly, for effective counter-piracy action, more needs to be done to prosecute the backers of the pirates who contribute to piracy from locations outside that stated by UNCLOS. However, as UNCLOS presently stands, such individuals may not be prosecuted as pirates under universal jurisdiction. Only two things could change this: first, a separately negotiated treaty with explicit and unambiguous provision of this intention is entered into by states; or, secondly, if subsequent state practice provides sufficient evidence of an intention to modify the meaning of Article 101(c).[21]

Another significant definitional issue that arises with regard to piracy in East Africa

---

[17] Report of the International Law Commission on the Work of its Eighth Session, 4 July 1956, Official Records of the General Assembly, Eleventh Session, Supplement No 9, (A/3159), [1956] 2 *Yearbook of the International Law Commission* 282, available at http//untreaty.un.org/ilc/documentation/english/a_cn4_104.pdf.

[18] See Harvard Research in International Law Draft Convention on Piracy, n 7 above, 822.

[19] See Art 6, SUA Convention, available at http//cns.miis.edu/inventory/pdfs/aptmaritime.pdf. For parties to SUA 1988 see http://www.imo.org/About/Conventions/StatusOfConventions/Pages/Default.aspx.

[20] See para 114 of S/2012/50.

[21] Art 31(3)(a) and (b) VCLT 1969.

is in respect of the 'private ends' requirement of UNCLOS.[22] Piratical acts committed on behalf of a state would certainly not be piracy under international law, though such an act would undoubtedly be an internationally wrongful act for which there could be state responsibility.[23] In the case of the East African piracy, there is no evidence, nor any suggestion, that the acts of piracy are committed under the authorisation of the Federal Government of Somalia (FGS), the internationally recognised government of Somalia, which has limited authority beyond the capital Mogadishu and is therefore unable to maintain law and order within a large part of Somali land territory and territorial sea.[24] Whilst the failure of governance has prompted the rise of warlords and armed militias controlling various parts of Somalia[25] and some of the warlords are sometimes involved in piracy, there is no suggestion that they do so as insurgent groups or for any political reason. Their involvement appears to be strictly commercial and for the private benefit of such warlords.[26] There is no indication that the Somali pirates have the push for the establishment of a stable and effective government in Somalia as part of their agenda. On the contrary, they would appear to be satisfied with the current position, which provides the right environment for them to continue with their criminal acts.

On the other hand, the so-called 'Robin Hood' or 'coast guard' narrative would appear to suggest that pirates commit the piratical acts for the public benefit of the Somali people because they seek to remedy the injustice of illegal fishing and dumping of toxic waste in their waters, and that they play some type of coast guard role to prevent such illegal acts.[27] For instance, in Gettleman's interview of Sugule Ali, the spokesman for the Somali pirates holding hostage the MV *Faina* (a Ukrainian freighter loaded with weapons), the latter declared that:

> We don't consider ourselves sea bandits ['sea bandit' is one way Somalis translate the English word pirate]. We consider sea bandits those who illegally fish in our seas and dump waste in our seas and carry weapons in our seas. We are simply patrolling our seas. Think of us like a coast guard.[28]

---

[22] See Art 101(a) LOSC.

[23] See M Bahar, 'Attaining Optimal Deterrence at Sea: A Legal and Strategic Theory for Naval Anti-Piracy Operations' (2007) 40(1) *Vanderbilt Journal of Transnational Law* 1, 12. However, see A Rubin, 'Is Piracy Illegal?' (1976) 70(1) *American Journal of International Law* 92, 93, who argues that it is difficult to believe that the similar provision of Art 15 of the HSC 1958 was intended to revive the archaic international law norm of privateering which had since been prohibited under international law.

[24] M Silva, 'Somalia: State Failure, Piracy and the Challenge to International Law' (2009–10) 50 *Virginia Journal of International Law* 554, 555–59.

[25] F Onuoha, 'Piracy and Maritime Security off the Horn of Africa: Connections, Causes, and Concerns' (2010) 3 *African Security* 191, 200.

[26] Ibid, 200–01.

[27] See P Schneider and M Winkley, 'The Robin Hood Narrative: A Discussion of Empirical and Ethical Legitimizations of Somali Pirates' (2013) 44(2) *Ocean Development & International Law* 185; C Bueger, 'Practice, Pirates and Coast Guards: Deconstructing the Grand Narrative of Somali Piracy' (2013) 34(10) *Third World Quarterly* 1811, available at http://www.academia.edu/2089360/Practice_Pirates_and_Coastguards_The_Grand_Narrative_of_Somali_Piracy.

[28] J Gettleman, 'Q & A with a Pirate: 'We Just Want the Money'' *New York Times*, 30 September 2008, available at http://thelede.blogs.nytimes.com/2008/09/30/q-a-with-a-pirate-we-just-want-the-money. See interesting analysis of this interview by Bueger, ibid. See also interview of former Prime Minister of Somalia Abdiweli Mohamed Ali criticising illegal, unreported and unregulated fishing and dumping of toxic waste off the coast of Somalia: T McConnell, 'Somali Pirates' Rise Linked to Illegal Fishing and Toxic Dumping', *Global Post*, 16 March 2012, available at http://www.globalpost.com/dispatch/news/regions/africa/120306/pirates-Somalia-how-it-started%20.

Bueger points out that this 'coast guard' narrative appears to suggest that Somali piracy is 'a normal practice of protecting against environmental crime, resource robbery and the violation of borders and as contributing to the economic development of Somali regions'.[29] This would appear to suggest that piratical acts in this region are not carried out for private ends, but rather for a public purpose, thereby excluding it from the definition of piracy under UNCLOS. However, it is difficult to accept this since there is no evidence that such piratical acts are directed only against vessels that are engaged in illegal fishing, dumping toxic waste or acts that are detrimental to the sovereignty of the Somali state. Rather, the attacks have been indiscriminate and directed against any vessel in the region.[30]

Moreover, the Secretary-General of the United Nations in his report to the Security Council pointed out that there was little evidence to support the claim that illegal fishing and dumping of toxic waste off the coast of Somalia was the cause of the upsurge of piracy in the region. He indicated that, though dumping of toxic waste may have occurred a few years ago, there was no evidence that it was still ongoing. Furthermore, he mentioned that, even though there was a significant potential for the fisheries and aquaculture sector to contribute to the economy of Somalia, in reality only a small percentage of the population (2%) were actually engaged in coastal fishing. In fact, the bulk of the population (65%) were engaged in the livestock sector instead.[31] He warned that the concern for the protection of the marine environment and resources should not be allowed to be used to cover the real essence of the Somalia piracy, 'which is a transnational criminal enterprise driven primarily by the opportunity for financial gain'.[32] Nonetheless, the Security Council has urged states either individually or within the framework of competent international organisations to consider investigating any new allegations of illegal fishing and illegal dumping of toxic substances off the coast of Somalia with a view to prosecuting persons within their jurisdiction who commit such offences.[33]

To the knowledge of the author, there has been no specific case where the courts have had to explicitly consider whether the issue of illegal fishing and dumping of toxic waste off the coast of Somalia would validly exclude piratical acts from the realm of 'private ends' as required by Article 101(a) LOSC. However, in the Supreme Court of Seychelles' decision in *Republic v Abdukar Ahmed & 5 ors*,[34] the court rejected the argument of the defence counsel that the prosecution had failed to prove the accused were acting for private ends. The court held as follows:

> the evidence reveals that the accused were motoring an unregistered boat on the high seas. The boat was also flying no flag. In their own statements, the accused said it was their

[29] Bueger, n 27 above, 1812.

[30] Para 64, S/2012/783 of 22 October 2012.

[31] Paras 65–66, ibid.

[32] Para 65, ibid.

[33] Para 28, S/RES/2077 (2012) of 21 November 2012. Further, the Council pointed out the responsibility of the Somali authorities to declare an exclusive economic zone (EEZ) in accordance with the Law of the Sea Convention (LOSC) 1982. See para 4, ibid. On the EEZ see LOSC 1982, ch V; R Churchill and V Lowe, *The Law of the Sea* (Manchester, Manchester University Press, 1999) 160–62.

[34] Criminal Side No 21 of 2011, available at http//law.case.edu/grotian-moment-blog/documents/CR21-2011-Judgment.pdf. See also *The Republic v Mohamed Ahmed Dahir & 10 ors*, Criminal Side No 51 of 2009, available at http//law.case.edu/grotian-moment-blog/documents/CR51-2009-Judgment.pdf, where the court pointed out that private ends does not include acts with governmental objectives.

joint decision to attack the *Gloria*. And further, that some accused were recruited by one Ahmed Hussein and others by Hassan Ali. They also stated that the boat was owned by Farahan (deceased) who also supplied the group with the fuel, food, engines, weapons and other equipment. Generally, apart from names of individuals, there was no mention of any government or international organization or authority of some sort that was attributed to being responsible for this mission. Indeed, none has come forward to claim so. These factors can only confirm that the accused were acting on their own and for their own private ends.[35]

From this it would appear that the court was of the view that, once there was evidence that those committing piratical acts were operating with a private vessel on the high seas and had no authority from any government or international organisation, that would suffice to establish that they were acting for 'private ends'. While these factors are clearly relevant in determining whether the acts of the Somali pirates are for their own private ends, they merely raise a rebuttable presumption of such, which shifts the burden on the accused to provide valid evidence that such piratical acts were actually intended to achieve political or ideological goals.[36] In spite of the obviously grave issues arising concerning illegal fishing and dumping of toxic waste, the Somali pirates appear to be primarily motivated by private monetary gains. Even if it is accepted that there is some political motivation behind the actions of the Somali pirates as their primary aim is to demand ransom monies for the personal gain of both the pirates and their backers, this would cause their actions to fall squarely within the realm of 'private ends' as required by the LOSC.[37]

III. PIRACY IN EAST AFRICAN REGION—A PECULIAR PHENOMENON?

Although piracy is certainly not limited to the East African region—there are other piracy prone areas in the world, such as Southeast Asia and the Gulf of Guinea region[38]—the Somali pirates have been said to have developed a 'specific brand of piracy'.[39] An understanding of this so-called 'specific brand of piracy' in comparison to piracy in other parts of the world, particularly Southeast Asia and the Gulf of Guinea, would provide a better understanding of the various approaches and the challenges sometimes faced in dealing with piracy in the East African region. Davenport, for instance, identified geopolitical and tactical differences between piracy occurring in the Southeast Asia and the East African region.[40] She pointed out that the latter was primarily due to the fact that Somalia is a failed state, while, in contrast, in the case of the former, the bordering states in the region have functioning governments and

---

[35] Ibid, 16.

[36] JD Peppetti, 'Building the Global Maritime Security Network: A Multinational Legal Structure to Combat Transnational Threats' (2008) 55 *Naval Law Review* 73, 92; M Sterio, 'The Somali Piracy Problem: A Global Puzzle Necessitating a Global Solution' (2009–10) 59 *American University Law Review* 1449, 1467.

[37] T Garmon, 'International Law of the Sea: Reconciling the Law of Piracy and Terrorism in the Wake of September 11th' (2002) 27 *Tulane Maritime Law Journal* 257, 265.

[38] International Maritime Bureau (IMB), 'Piracy and Armed Robbery Prone Areas and Warnings', available at http//www.icc-ccs.org.uk/piracy-reporting-centre/prone-areas-and-warnings.

[39] M. Kingsley, 'An Analysis of Pirate Incidents in Africa', CNA Analysis & Solutions (June 2011), available at http://www.cna.org/sites/default/files/OTA%20Pirate%20Incidents%20in%20Africa%20 D0023395%20A2.pdf.

[40] T Davenport, 'Legal Measures to Combat Piracy and Armed Robbery in the Horn of Africa and in Southeast Asia' (2012) 35 *Studies in Conflict & Terrorism* 570, 570.

legal systems. Consequently, these governments, through regional cooperation, such as the highly successful Regional Cooperation Agreement on Combating Piracy and Armed Robbery against Ships in Asia (ReCAAP),[41] have been able to deal with this issue without direct Security Council involvement.

With respect to tactics, the Somali pirates adopt a hijack, kidnap and ransom model. The usual method of operation for the East African piracy is for heavily armed Somali pirates with automatic weapons and rocket-propelled grenades to use large 'mother ships' to follow the targeted ship, and on approaching such ship to launch smaller speedboats ('skiffs'), which move in closer to enable the pirates to board the ship.[42] Once the pirates have successfully boarded the target ship they hijack it, along with the crew and passenger. Thereafter, they sail the vessel towards the Somali coast and demand a ransom for the release of the vessel and crew. By contrast, pirates in Southeast Asia primarily adopt 'opportunistic hit and run attacks of robbery' of cash or property, usually when the ships are anchored or berthed.[43] Similarly, the situation in the Gulf of Guinea, which has recently witnessed an upsurge in piracy that has attracted the attention of the Security Council,[44] may be said to be different from that in the East African region. Neethling contends that the piracy in the Gulf of Guinea should be viewed, first, against the background of a large population in the region and abundant energy resources produced by a number of states in the area. Secondly, he identifies the link between oil development and poor socio-economic, as well as environmental, conditions for some of the inhabitants of the oil producing areas, notably the Niger Delta area of Nigeria, as being crucial to the upsurge of piracy in the Gulf of Guinea.[45] He points out that:

> there is a clear link between a feeling of alienation and marginalisation on the part of some inhabitants of the Niger Delta region and the occurrence of militancy and criminality in the Delta region, with specific reference to hostage-taking (especially that of employees of foreign oil multinationals) as a common criminal activity—and this extends to piracy in the Gulf of Guinea on a broader scale.

Again, like piracy in Southeast Asia, we see geopolitical and tactical differences between piracy occurring in the Gulf of Guinea and the East African region. Yet again, none of the states bordering the Gulf of Guinea is a failed state. Also, in terms of tactics, there appears to be some divergences. The IMB identifies that the pirates/armed robbers in the Gulf of Guinea region, who are usually well armed and very violent, attack ships and hijack them, forcing the master of the hijacked ship to sail to an unknown location, where the ship is ransacked and its properties and oil cargo are stolen.[46] While hostages are sometimes taken, it would appear that, unlike the piracy

---

[41] See 'Regional Cooperation Agreement on Combating Piracy and Armed Robbery against Ships in Asia, 28 April 2005' (2005) 44 *International Legal Materials* 829.

[42] T Neethling, 'Piracy around Africa's West and East Coasts: A Comparative Political Perspective' (2010) 38(2) *South African Journal of Military Studies* 89, 94.

[43] Davenport, n 40 above, 570–71.

[44] S/RES/2018 (2011) of 31 October 2011.

[45] Neethling, n 42 above, 98.

[46] http://www.icc-ccs.org.uk/piracy-reporting-centre/prone-areas-and-warnings. See also United Nations Secretary-General Report to the Security Council, S/2012/45 of 19 January 2012. However, see K Hurlburt and D Conor Seyle, 'The Human Cost of Maritime Piracy 2012', Oceans Beyond Piracy working paper, available at http://oceansbeyondpiracy.org/sites/default/files/hcop2012forweb.pdf, which identified that,

in East Africa, the demand for ransom is not always the driving goal for all attacks.[47] Also, in this region we actually see states around the region taking the initiative with military actions to seek to reduce piracy in this region.[48]

In spite of the differences between the piracy in East African region and that in Southeast Asia and the Gulf of Guinea, there are some common features with regard to the root causes of piracy. It would appear that an analysis of the situation in all these regions would suggest that piracy flourishes in regions where there are challenges with governance, either because of failed state(s) in the region or because of states which, though not failed, have rather weak political and governance systems. Further, piracy blossoms in regions where there are issues concerning poverty affecting a huge percentage of the populace. It is therefore not surprising that regions within the more developed parts of the world, which have relatively strong governments and a decent standard of living for a large segment of its populace, do not have incidents of piracy.[49]

IV. MEASURES AGAINST PIRACY IN EAST AFRICAN REGION

As mentioned above, piracy in the East African region is a peculiar type of piracy, unlike those in other regions, due to the crucial linkage between Somalia state failure, leading to a complete breakdown of governance, and the piracy situation in the region. The pirates use the failed state as a launch pad to carry out the piratical acts on the high seas, as well as a haven for them to bring back captured vessels and hostages.[50] Consequently, the approaches to dealing with the scourge of piracy in this region have been primarily based on initiatives of the international community. Various measures have been taken by the international community to deal with the scourge of piracy in East Africa, which this section will examine under three main heads: namely military, judicial prosecutions and peaceful cooperative approaches.[51]

A. Military Approach

With the consent of the TFG/FGS, the Security Council has adopted several resolutions to deal with the situation of piracy in Somalia.[52] Some of these resolutions were

---

although hijacking and hostage-taking was not the main aim of pirates in the Gulf of Guinea, this does occur from time to time (see 12–17).

[47] S/2012/45, ibid. See also Hurlburt and Seyle, ibid.

[48] See 'Ghana's Navy Intercepts Suspected Pirate Ship and Arrests Crew', *Reuters*, 2 August 2013, available at http://www.reuters.com/article/2013/08/02/us-ghana-pirates-idUSBRE9710FA20130802; 'Nigerian Navy Gets Tough', *Maritime Security Review*, 5 August 2013, available at http://www.marsecreview.com/2013/08/piracy-and-oil-theft-nigerian-navy-gets-tough.

[49] See ICC, 'Piracy and Armed Robbery Prone Areas and Warnings', available at http//www.icc-ccs.org.uk/piracy-reporting-centre/prone-areas-and-warnings.

[50] See Silva, n 24 above, 555–59; and Onuoha, n 25 above, 200.

[51] Para 3, Report of the Secretary-General Pursuant to Security Council Resolution 2020 (2011), S/2012/783 of 22 October 2012.

[52] S/RES/1816 (2008) of 2 June 2008; S/RES/1838 (2008) of 7 October, 2008; S/RES/1844 (2008) of 20 November 2008; S/RES/1846 (2008) of 2 December, 2008; S/RES/1851 (2008) of 16 December 2008; S/RES/1897 (2009) of 30 November, 2009; S/RES/1918 (2010) of 27 April, 2010; S/RES/1976 (2011) of 11 April 2011; S/RES/2015 (2011) of 24 October 2011; S/RES/2020 (2011) of 22 November 2011; S/RES/2077 (2012) of 21 November 2012.

adopted by the Security Council utilising its Chapter VII powers because piracy and armed robbery at sea hinder the prompt, safe and effective delivery of humanitarian aid to Somalia and the region; is a threat to the safety of seafarers and other persons at sea around the region; affects international navigation and the safety of commercial maritime routes in the region; and is a threat to other vulnerable ships, including those engaged in fishing activities in conformity with international law, and also because it is generally a threat to the peace and security of the region. Recently, the Security Council has also expressed concerns about the involvement of children in piracy off the coast of Somalia.[53] While urging states to cooperate with the FGS, amongst themselves and with appropriate international organisations, notably the IMO, to fight the menace of piracy in the East African region, the Security Council authorises states to use 'all necessary means' to repress acts of piracy and armed robbery in the Somalia territorial sea and the high seas off its coast, including foreign military and law enforcement action.[54] Based on these resolutions, there have been several coalition military forces set up to fight against piracy in the East African region, such as the EU's Operation Atalanta force, the NATO's Operation Open Shield and the Combined Maritime Forces, a US-led international naval coalition of 27 states. These coalition forces are complemented by several naval ships and aircrafts deployed by several UN Members States, such as China, India, the Islamic Republic of Iran, Japan, Kenya, Malaysia, Saudi Arabia, Republic of Korea, Russian Federation, South Africa and Yemen.[55] Much literature, including certain chapters of this book, has been devoted to exploring the various military coalitions put together under the auspices of the Security Council resolutions and how effective they are, so this section will not explore this issue in much detail.[56] However, despite the relative success of the current naval operations, there is no doubt that they are grossly inadequate to cover the vast area in the Gulf of Aden and the Indian Ocean where the pirates operate.[57] Interestingly, although the piracy activities are right in the African Union (AU)'s 'backyard', there is an absence of an AU joint naval task force, even though the AU, with its fundamental responsibility to promote peace, security and stability in Africa, has piracy in the East African region high on its agenda[58] and is also meant to have an African Standby

---

[53] See preamble of S/RES/2077 (2012).

[54] See, eg para 7, S/RES/1816; paras 2 and 3, S/RES/1838 (2008); paras 6–9, S/RES/1846; para 10, S/RES/2077 (2012). See Art 42 of the United Nations Charter, which permits the Security Council to impose military measures.

[55] For details on the activities of the various multinational coalition military forces and the independent forces of UN Member States see paras 39–56, Report of the Secretary-General Pursuant to Security Council Resolution 1950 (2010), S/2011/622 of 25 October 2011; paras 33–39, Report of the Secretary-General Pursuant to Security Council Resolution 2020 (2011), S/2012/783 of 22 October 2012

[56] See, however, D Guilfoyle, 'Piracy off Somalia: UN Security Council Resolution 1816 and IMO Regional Counter-piracy Efforts' (2008) 57 *International & Comparative Law Quarterly* 690; T Treves, 'Piracy, Law of the Sea, and Use of Force: Developments off the Coast of Somalia' (2009) 20(2) *European Journal of International Law* 399. See also PM Olson, Chapter 7 above; R Gosalbo Bono and S Boelaert, Chapter 5 above; G Swiney, Chapter 8 above; A Murdoch, Chapter 9 above; A Proelss, Chapter 3 above.

[57] See para 3, S/2012/783 of 22 October 2012; para 9 of S/2012/50 of 20 January 2012.

[58] See, eg the African Union Durban Resolution on Maritime Safety, Maritime Security and Protection of the Marine Environment in Africa, AU/MT/MIN/DRAFT/Res.II of 16 October 2009; press statement of the AU's Peace and Security Council held on 4 October 2010, available at http//pages.au.int/sites/default/files/Communiqu__Eng__FINAL[1]-1.pdf. See also Art3(f) of the African Union Constitutive Treaty 2000 and Art 3 of the Protocol Relating to the Establishment of the Peace and Security Council of the African Union 2002, available at http//au.int/en/treaties.

Force (ASF).[59] This is all the more striking as the AU is actively involved in onshore peacekeeping in Somalia through the African Union Mission in Somalia (AMISOM), a regional peacekeeping mission set up by the AU's Peace and Security Council and operating with the approval of the UN Security Council.[60] The reason for the absence of AU naval operation to combat piracy is the lack of capacity and the non-inclusion in the ASF framework of the possibility of joint AU naval operations.[61] This gap has been recognised by the AU. In its recent African Integrated Maritime Strategy (AIMS) 2050, it included as one of the strategies to be implemented the following:

> Steps toward promoting inter-agency and transnational cooperation and coordination on maritime safety and security shall include the development of an inter-agency approach, a Naval Component capacity within the framework of the African Standby Force (ASF), and the establishment of a representative continental working group of Chiefs of African Navies and/or Coast Guards (CHANS) to scrutinize issues of situational awareness and collaborate towards the enhancement of Africa's Maritime Domain Awareness (MDA), and to uphold cooperative efforts between Navies/Coast Guards of the AU Member states and international partners.[62]

Despite this, some have stressed that, while naval operations are no doubt important in dealing with piracy, what is more crucial, based on the adage that 'the land conquers the sea', is for the international community to give more priority to reinforcing and supporting the AMISOM onshore operations and ensuring that the FGS is adequately empowered to take up its responsibility of ensuring that its territory is not used as a base for launching piracy attacks offshore.[63]

Another issue that affects the effectiveness of the naval operations is the so-called 'capture and release' policy of some of the naval forces.[64] According to Jack Lang, the UN Secretary-General's Special Adviser on legal issues related to piracy off the coast of Somalia, while, at one time, only certain navies opted to 'catch and release' pirates, such a policy has now become the rule; judicial prosecution is now the exception.[65] A number of states involved in the naval operations have been reluctant to prosecute the Somali pirates in their national courts because of the logistical difficulties and expense involved in such prosecution, as well as the sheer lack of political will to engage in

---

[59] See http://www.africa-union.org/root/AU/AUC/Departments/PSC/Asf/asf.htm.

[60] http://amisom-au.org/about/amisom-background/. See also the following United Nations Security Council Resolutions: S/RES/1772; S/RES/1801; S/RES/1831; S/RES/1863; S/RES/1910; S/RES/1964; S/RES/2072; S/RES/2073; S/RES/2093.

[61] See ASF Framework 2004, available at http//www.peaceau.org/uploads/asf-policy-framework-en.pdf. The AU Commissioner for Peace and Security, Ambassador Lamamra, after identifying various threats faced by Africa, including piracy, admitted that the capacity of the AU to respond to such security challenges was limited. See the Report of the Tenth Conference of the Committee of Intelligence and Security Services of Africa (CISSA), 1–8 May 2013 in Harare, Zimbabwe, available at http://www.peaceau.org/uploads/final-cissa-10th-conf-harare-commissioner-s-statement-final.pdf.

[62] Para 31, available at http//pages.au.int/sites/default/files/2050%20AIM%20Strategy%20(Eng)_0.pdf.

[63] G Grewal, 'African Union Can Remove Pirates Says Uganda', *Maritime Security Review*, 15 November 2010, available at http://www.marsecreview.com/2010/11/african-union-can-remove-pirates-says-uganda/; see also World Bank press release, 'Ending Somali Piracy will need on-shore solutions and international support to rebuild Somalia' (11 April 2013), available at http://www.worldbank.org/en/news/press-release/2013/04/11/ending-somali-piracy-will-need-on-shore-solutions-and-international-support-to-rebuild-somalia.

[64] See the Jack Lang Report, annexed to Letter dated 24 January 2011 from the Secretary-General to the President of the Security Council, S/2011/30 of 25 January 2011.

[65] Para 43, ibid.

such prosecution in their domestic courts.[66] Although a handful of Somali pirates have been prosecuted by the courts of arresting developed states, such as the US and the Netherlands, these cases have been rather few and far between. Moreover, most of these cases were ones directly affecting their national interests, either in the form of a pirate attack against their vessels or a hijack of their nationals.[67]

The 'catch and release' policy is utilised by some navies because their flag states do not have adequate legislation to deal with piracy, especially those that do not involve or affect their nationals or national interest. For others it is simply the concern with the human rights implications of capturing and detaining suspected pirates for a period of time until the naval ship is able to get to its flag state. Others are merely concerned with the cost and political implication of actual prosecution of pirates that are non-nationals.[68] Clearly, for effective counter-piracy action in the East African region there has to be an operative nexus between naval operations and effectual judicial prosecution of the captured pirates. According to Lang, to avoid the 'catch and release' practice 'there is a need to streamline the transfer of prisoners to the competent judicial authorities'.[69] These competent authorities must, however, also be willing and able to prosecute such pirates—an issue that is explored in the next section.

B. Judicial Prosecution Approach

Under international law, any state may prosecute pirates by reason of the notion of universal jurisdiction.[70] Ordinarily, under UNCLOS 1982 the state which has carried out the seizure of the pirate ship or aircraft and the arrest of the pirates may prosecute them.[71] However, as has been mentioned above, a number of the capturing states are reluctant to do so.[72] Although some pirates have been prosecuted in Puntland and Somaliland, in general Somalia, as a failed state, currently lacks the capacity to effectively prosecute all the pirates. Certain developed states involved in the various naval enforcement operations in the East African region have recently entered into memoranda of understanding with some states within the region, such as Comoros, Kenya, Seychelles, Madagascar and Tanzania, for the transfer of arrested pirates to the latter states so that the pirates may be prosecuted based on universal jurisdiction before their national courts.[73] These regional states, however, face certain challenges, including in

---

[66] E Kontorovich, 'International Legal Responses to Piracy off the Coast of Somalia', *ASIL Insights*, 6 February 2009, available at http://www.asil.org/insights090206.cfm.

[67] See, eg *USA v Abdi Wali Dire*, Case No 11-4310 (CA, 4th Circ, 23 May 2012), where Somali pirates were prosecuted in the USA for attacking the American navy frigate, the USS *Nicholas*, thinking it was a merchant ship.

[68] Paras 42–76 of S/2011/30 of 25 January 2011.

[69] Para 44, ibid.

[70] E Kontorovich and S Art, 'An Empirical Examination of Universal Jurisdiction for Piracy' (2010) 104 *American Journal of International Law* 436.

[71] See Art 105 of UNCLOS, which allows the courts of the state that carried out the seizure to prosecute.

[72] See the discussion on the 'catch and release' policy in Section IV(A) above.

[73] See S Hodgkinson, 'International Law in Crisis: Seeking the Best Prosecution Model for Somali Pirates' (2011) 44 *Case Western Reserve Journal of International Law* 303, 304–08; Report of the Secretary-General on Specialized Anti-Piracy Courts in Somalia and Other States in the Region, S/2012/50 of 20 January 2012.

some cases the inadequacy or lack of domestic legislation criminalising piracy.[74] Some of the national legislation have actually expanded the scope of piracy as going beyond piratical acts committed on the high seas to include such acts committed within the national jurisdiction. For instance, Section 69(1) of the Penal Code of Kenya provides that the offence of piracy is committed when the piratical acts are committed either in the territorial sea or upon the high seas.[75] However, this provision has been repealed by the Kenyan Merchant Shipping Act of 2009, which states that for such piratical acts to be piracy they must be committed 'in a place outside the jurisdiction of any state'.[76] Seychelles, in the revised section 65(4) of its Penal Code, after listing out a definition which is substantially in line with the LOSC 1982, also adds as part of this definition that the piratical acts which 'except for the fact that it was committed within a maritime zone of Seychelles, would have been an act of piracy under either of those paragraphs'.[77] On the other hand, Article 205 of the 1959 Somali Maritime Code, as amended, which is headed 'piracy', states that

> the Master or officer of Somali or foreign vessels who commit acts of depredation to the damage of a Somali or foreign vessel or its cargo, or for this purpose commit violence against persons on board Somali or foreign vessels, are punished by imprisonment from 10 to 20 years.[78]

This rather dated provision is unclear as to whether it extends to territorial waters or is limited to the high seas.

Moving to Tanzania, previously section 66(1) of its Penal Code (1981) provided that:[79]

> Any person who—
> (a) does any unlawful act of violence against a ship or vessel registered in Tanganyika or against persons or property on board that ship or vessel; or
> (b) being a citizen of Tanganyika does any unlawful act of violence against any ship or vessel or against any person or property on board that ship or vessel; or
> (c) voluntarily participates in the operation of a ship, vessel or aircraft for the purpose of doing any act referred to in paragraph (a) or (b), shall be guilty of the offence termed 'piracy' and shall be liable on conviction to imprisonment for life.

This provision was rather restrictive since jurisdiction was limited to acts against ships or vessels having Tanzanian nationality, or instances where the perpetrators were Tanzanian nationals. Further, it is not too clear if this legislation covers piratical acts committed within the national jurisdiction as well. Therefore, in May 2010 the Penal Code of Tanzania was amended to give the Tanzanian court the jurisdiction over piracy

---

[74] United Nations Secretary-General Compilation of Information on Measures Taken by Some States against Piracy, S/2012/177 of 26 March 2012.

[75] *Penal Code* (Laws of Kenya, ch 63).

[76] Section 369. For a detailed analysis of Kenya's piracy prosecutions see JT Gathii, 'Kenya's Piracy Prosecutions' (2010) 104(1) *American Journal of International Law* 416.

[77] See M Sterio, 'Piracy off the Coast of Somalia' (2012) 4(2) *Amsterdam Law Forum* 105, 116.

[78] Cap 195, Art 205. See http://www.somalilandlaw.com/Somali_Maritime_Code.pdf. Contrast this with Art 2 of the so-called Republic of Somaliland Law on Combatting Piracy (Piracy Law) Law No 52/2012, which generally adopted the definition in UNCLOS.

[79] Cap 16 of the Laws (Revised).

committed by any person on the high seas, with the high seas defined as 'the open seas of the world outside the jurisdiction of any state'.[80] The amendment defines piracy as

> (a) any act of violence or detention or any act of degradation, committed for private ends;
> (b) participation in the operation of a ship with knowledge that the ship was intended was has [sic] been used in acts of piracy; or (c) incitement or intentional facilitation of either (a) or (b).[81]

This definition criminalises not only the actual piratical acts, but also acts that incite or facilitate the commission of the piracy, such as financing and planning the crime. Under the amendment, unless a pirate ship is registered in Tanzania, 'no prosecution shall be commenced unless there is a special arrangement between the arresting state or agency and Tanzania'.[82] Further, the Director of Public Prosecutions of Tanzania is required to consent to every piracy trial.[83] It has been said that this is to prevent Tanzania being a dumping ground for piracy committed on the high seas.[84]

Djibouti, under its Code of Maritime Affairs 1982, also limits the definition of piracy to (i) piratical acts committed by a crew member (both nationals and non-nationals) of a ship flying the Djiboutian flag or (ii) a foreign ship who commits such acts against either Djiboutian ships, crew or cargo or ships, crew or cargo belonging to a state with which Djibouti is not at war.[85] The recently enacted Piracy and Other Maritime Act 2011 of Mauritius, which came into force 1 June 2012,[86] makes a distinction between piracy and maritime attack.[87] Piracy under this legislation is as defined under UNCLOS, while maritime attack is defined as such piratical acts committed within the territorial sea, or the internal, historic and archipelagic waters of Mauritius, a term which appears to be synonymous with what the SUA designates as armed robbery against ships. According to Sterio, this new legislation appears to have 'blended UNCLOS and SUA' by criminalising both piracy and armed robbery.[88]

Further, states within the region face the challenge of coping with a large number of cases on rather limited resources, as well as difficulties in investigating and conducting sometimes complex prosecutions of the pirates. While support has been provided by various UN agencies, such as the UN Office on Drugs and Crime and the UN Development Programme, as well as partner developed states, this support is clearly inadequate. A number of states in the region, notably Kenya, have expressed concerns that they are carrying an unfair weight of prosecuting Somali pirates, which is causing a strain on their justice system, and that other states should share the burden

---

[80] RL Phillips, 'Tanzania—a Case Study', *Communis Hosti Omnium*, 3 March 2011, available at http://piracy-law.com/2011/03/03/tanzania-%E2%80%93-a-case-study.

[81] Section 66(1).

[82] Section 66(3).

[83] Section 66(4).

[84] Phillips, n 80 above.

[85] Arts 208 and 209. Arts 385 and 387 of the Criminal Code of Djibouti 1995 also creates the offence of hijacking when any aircraft, ship or other mode of transportation with people on board is deemed to have been hijacked within the territory of Djibouti. See S/2012/177 of 26 March 2012.

[86] Act No 39 of 2011. See Letter dated 23 March 2012 from the Secretary-General to the President of the Security Council, S/2012/177 of 26 March 2012, 58–66.

[87] See s 3.

[88] Sterio, n 77 above, 118.

of such prosecution.[89] Various suggestions have been put forward to seek to promote such burden sharing, including the establishment of a Somali extraterritorial court in one of the neighbouring states in the region, with funding and administration by the international community;[90] an ad hoc international tribunal to deal with piracy;[91] the possibility of amending the International Criminal Court (ICC) Statute to include piracy as one of the offences within the jurisdiction of the ICC;[92] and the establishment of specialised anti-piracy courts in Somalia and certain neighbouring states, with a regional prosecution centre and more assistance from the international community.[93]

However, there has been a lack of support for an Somali extraterritorial court by the Somali authorities, who actually prefer that assistance be provided for such piracy courts to be located within Somalia.[94] Also, the call for an ad hoc piracy tribunal similar to the International Criminal Tribunal for the Former Yugoslavia and the International Criminal Tribunal for Rwanda has not gained significant support amongst Member States of the UN because these courts are very costly to maintain. Similarly, the proposal to amend the Statute of the ICC is problematic: while piracy could be said to be a serious crime of 'concern to the international community',[95] the practicality of adding piracy to the ICC's jurisdiction (which, obviously, would apply globally rather than being limited to the East African region) is rather doubtful. First, Somalia is not a party to the Rome Statute, and even if the Security Council, acting under Chapter VII, refers this to the ICC,[96] it is unlikely that this court, with its busy and full docket under the current jurisdiction, would be able to cope with the number of piracy cases and to dispose of these cases as swiftly as domestic courts.[97]

On the other hand, there appears to be more of a support for establishing the specialised piracy court in Somalia and other neighbouring states in the region with more international community support.[98] This would be complemented by ongoing prisoner transfer arrangements between the states hosting the specialised piracy court and Somalia, whereby the convicted Somali pirates may be transferred to Somalia to serve their prison terms in prisons built with the assistance of the international community.[99]

---

[89] 'Kenya Ends Trials of Somali Pirates in its Courts', *BBC News*, 1 April 2010, available at http://news.bbc.co.uk/1/hi/8599347.stm.

[90] Lang Report, n 64 above; paras 122–29.

[91] R Geiß and A Petrig, *Piracy and Armed Robbery at Sea: The Legal Framework for Counter-piracy Operations in Somalia and the Gulf of Aden* (Oxford, Oxford University Press, 2011) 180–81.

[92] Y Dutton, 'Bringing Pirates to Justice: A Case for Including Piracy within the Jurisdiction of the International Criminal Court' (2010) 11(1) *Chicago Journal of International Law* 201.

[93] Report of the Secretary General on specialized anti-piracy courts in Somalia and other States in the region, S/2012/50 of 20 January 2012.

[94] Para 38, ibid.

[95] See Art 5 of the Rome Statute, available at http//untreaty.un.org/cod/icc/statute/romefra.htm.

[96] See Art 13(b) of the Rome Statute. For parties to the ICC see http://www.icc-cpi.int/en_menus/asp/states%20parties/Pages/the%20states%20parties%20to%20the%20rome%20statute.aspx.

[97] For situations and cases currently before the ICC see http://www.icc-cpi.int/en_menus/icc/situations%20and%20cases/Pages/situations%20and%20cases.aspx.

[98] S/2012/50.

[99] Ibid, paras 39–113.

C. Peaceful Cooperative Approach

UNCLOS encourages all states to cooperate to the fullest possible extent in the repression of piracy.[100] One of the most notable documents signalling peaceful regional cooperation in the East African region, *the Djibouti Code of Conduct*,[101] emulating the rather successful East Asian ReCAAP, was piloted by the IMO and adopted on 29 January 2009 by the representatives of Djibouti, Ethiopia, Kenya, Madagascar, Maldives, Seychelles, Somalia, the United Republic of Tanzania and Yemen. It seeks to promote regional efforts to deal with piracy and armed robbery against ships in the East African region, and has been described as 'a milestone development and a central instrument in the development of regional capacity to combat piracy'.[102] The Code seeks to promote cooperation by improving communication between states in the region (eg by setting up information sharing centres) and increasing their capacity in relation to arresting and prosecuting pirates, and also to enable these states to improve their coast guard capabilities.[103] In addition to the original signatories, other states in the region, such as Comoros, Egypt, Eritrea, Jordan, Mauritius, Mozambique, Oman, Saudi Arabia, South Africa, Sudan and the United Arab Emirates, have since signed the Code of Conduct, thereby bringing the total number of signatories to 20 states. It has been suggested that the Code would be more effective if it were signed not only by regional states, but by all stakeholders, including states with large international maritime global interests.[104] However, this would seem to miss the point of the code: it is intended to be a regional agreement that seeks to promote regional capacity building. Moreover, there are other cooperative forums that provide a meeting point for both the regional states and the stakeholders in other parts of the world.[105] Presently the Code is merely declaratory and not legally binding.[106] Even though the Code allows the parties to consult two years after its adoption with a view to making it a binding document, it still remains non-binding. At the recent London Conference in May 2012 it was agreed that the Code would remain non-binding with a proviso that the status of the Code will be reviewed in two years' time.[107] Clearly its non-binding nature of the Code makes the cooperation merely voluntary.

---

[100] Art 100.

[101] http://www.imo.org/OurWork/Security/PIU/Documents/DCoC%20English.pdf.

[102] Geiß and Petrig, *Piracy*, n 91 above, 49.

[103] http://www.imo.org/OurWork/Security/PIU/Pages/DCoC.aspx.

[104] VC Figliomeni, 'Countering Piracy and other Organised illicit Activities in East Africa: Piracy, Illicit Activities of Organised Crime and Failed States' in SC Galletti (ed), *Piracy and Maritime Terrorism: Logistics, Strategies, Scenarios* (Amsterdam, IOS Press BV, 2012) 166.

[105] See, eg the Contact Group on Piracy off the Coast of Somalia, available at http//www.thecgpcs.org/about.do?action=background. See also D Guilfoyle, 'Prosecuting Pirates: The Contact Group on Piracy off the Coast of Somalia, Governance and International Law' (2013) 4(1) *Global Policy* 73.

[106] See Arts 13 and 15(a) of the Djibouti Code.

[107] See 'IMO Signs Strategic Counter-piracy Capacity Building Partnerships with UN Agencies and EU', IMO Press Briefing 15 (17 May 2012), available at http//www.imo.org/mediacentre/pressbriefings/pages/15-capacitypartnerships.aspx.

V. CONCLUSION

Piracy in the East African region has played a key role in bringing modern-day piracy into the limelight. With the spate of hijacking, taking of hostages and demands for huge amounts in ransom money by the pirates, the international community has engaged with this threat in the East African region, which is an outcome of the failure of the Somali state. Various Security Council resolutions have been adopted on the basis that these piratical acts are threats to international peace and security. Consequently, various naval coalitions and navies of several UN Member States, acting under the Security Council resolutions, have become involved in law enforcement operations in the combat against this international crime. In addition, there have been several prosecutions of arrested pirate suspects, a number of whom have been convicted. Further, the Djibouti Code of Conduct provides a platform for regional cooperation in counter-piracy efforts amongst states located in the region. Are all these measures effective? By and large, though there have been a few shortcomings, as explored in this chapter, the various legal initiatives have been quite effective. The proof of this is in the significant drop in piracy attacks in the East African region last year, the lowest since 2009.[108]

---

[108] http://www.icc-ccs.org/news/811-imb-reports-drop-in-somali-piracy-but-warns-against-complacency; United Nations Secretary-General report, paras 3–7, S/2012/783 of 22 October 2012.

12

Alternative Approaches to Piracy and Armed Robbery in Southeast Asian Waters and off the Horn of Africa: A Comparative Perspective

DAVID M ONG

I. INTRODUCTION

INTERNATIONAL LEGAL APPROACHES to tackling Somali-based sea piracy off the African Horn and Gulf of Aden coastlines typically focus on the conceptual and practical issues of exercising enforcement jurisdiction at sea and facilitating adjudication on land. The maritime aspect revolves around issues of universal, as well as concurrent coastal and flag state, enforcement jurisdiction. The terrestrial focus tends to be limited to the legal prospects for prosecution, adjudication and penal incarceration of convicted pirates, whether within the enforcing states or the home states of the pirates concerned. Wider issues relating to the historical roots, as well as political, socio-economic and cultural connections to the causes and effects of piracy, are usually mentioned as an aside, but are arguably neglected within such legal analyses. In contrast, this chapter deliberately takes on a set of comparative geographical and historical legal perspectives to assess how far the roots of Somali-based piracy are similar to previous historical incidences of mass piracy and contemporary geographical piracy incidence elsewhere in the world today. The main historical and geographical comparisons in this context will be with Southeast Asian regional pirate activity, which peaked on either side of the millennium (2000) and continues to this day. The aim here is to recast piracy not only as an international legal problem in and of itself, but also as a symptom of a wider and deeper malaise that is best addressed as a set of international, regional, national and local governance issues revolving around state-building, rule of law, and socio-economic and cultural development.

Prior to African Horn-based pirate activity becoming a global issue, the main geographical hot spot for piracy and armed robbery at sea was in Southeast Asian waters, with the Malacca and Singapore Straits taking centre stage. This contribution will apply a comparative perspective on the piracy phenomena within these two maritime regions. Similarities and differences between Southeast Asian and African Horn-based piracy will be highlighted according to the following criteria: (i) numbers and types of piracy incidents occurring; (ii) economic, social and cultural (including religious) backgrounds to pirate activity; and (iii) regional and extra-regional (including global) responses to piracy incidents in each of these regions. Finally, an exploration of possible syntheses in the policy and legal approaches to piracy in both these regions will be undertaken.

Before we embark on this comparative analysis of the incidence, causes and responses of Southeast Asian and African Horn-based piracy, two contextual points need to be made. First, while the increasing numbers of piracy incidents worldwide, and especially off the African Horn coast and in the Gulf of Aden region, is significant, overall piracy numbers still constitute only a very small proportion of the global total of seaborne vessels. Secondly, there is often cited expert commentary in news media reports on the connection between piracy and terrorism, especially Islamic fundamentalist-based terrorism (for Al-Shabaab in Somalia, read Jemaah Islamiyah in Indonesia),[1] which are themselves based on official US government policy statements on these links.[2] However, there is little concrete evidence of any meaningful relationship between these two activities, serious transnational crimes though they both are. As Young and Valencia write, 'Since the events of 11 September 2001, the conflation of "piracy" and "terrorism" has become common in the mass media and government policy statements, both within and outside [Southeast Asia]'.[3] Hamilton reports on research into the motivations of Somali pirates conducted in Kenya, where over 100 Somalis are being prosecuted for piracy, and argues that the weight of current evidence strongly suggests that piracy off the East African coast is strictly an economic crime.[4]

This is not to suggest that there are no underlying political reasons at all for the rise in piracy, both in Southeast Asia and in the African Horn. As Teitler notes unequivocally, 'all instances of piratical phenomena only occur in weak or failed states'.[5] Indeed, as elaborated below, the more salient connection here may well relate to the fact that the higher than usual incidence of piracy in both Southeast Asia and the Horn of Africa can be attributed to the serious political instability afflicting a major country in the area during the relevant periods of high incidence of piracy. These are, respectively, Indonesia in the late 1990s and Somalia during the past couple of decades. Historically, too, this accords with Teitler's observation that piracy thrives during periods of domestic political instability, coupled with the nearby presence of burgeoning international trade, mainly conducted via shipping and thus affording

---

[1] See, eg J Bolton, 'Treat Somali Pirates like Terrorists: Viewing Sea Raids as Law Enforcement Issue Hasn't Worked', *Washington Times*, 14 October 2011, available at http://www.washingtontimes.com/news/2011/oct/14/treat-somali-pirates-like-terrorists/.

[2] For example, the White House's National Strategy for Maritime Security, issued by the Bush Presidency administration in 2005, links piracy with terrorism by suggesting that 'the capabilities to board and commandeer large underway vessels—demonstrated in numerous piracy incidents—could also be employed to facilitate terrorist acts'. See White House, *National Strategy for Maritime Security* (2005) 5.

[3] A Young and M Valencia, 'Conflation of Piracy and Terrorism in Southeast Asia: Rectitude and Utility' (2003) 25 *Contemporary Southeast Asia* 269.

[4] K Hamilton, 'The Piracy and Terrorism Nexus: Real or Imagined?', Proceedings of the 1st Australian Counter Terrorism Conference, Edith Cowan University, Perth Western Australia, 30 November 2010, available at http://ro.ecu.edu.au/act/3.

[5] G Teitler, 'Piracy in Southeast Asia: A Historical Comparison' (2002) 1 *Maritime Studies* 67, 73, available at http://www.marecentre.nl/mast/documents/GerTeitler.pdf.

plentiful opportunities for plunder.[6] This latter aspect of the appropriate conditions for a preponderance of piracy, namely, proximity to major international trade shipping routes, is very much the case in both maritime regions examined here. The Straits of Malacca and Singapore, and the South China Sea region in general, is home to the most important international shipping lane between Europe, the Middle East and India on the one hand, and China, (South) Korea and Japan on the other. As for the waters off the African Horn, Mark Brownrigg, Director General of the UK Chamber of Shipping, has recently highlighted Somalia's positioning at the edge of the Gulf of Aden in terms of energy imports and energy security for the world.[7]

II. NUMBERS AND TYPES OF PIRACY INCIDENTS OFF THE AFRICAN HORN AND SOUTHEAST ASIA

International attention on piracy and its impact on global shipping have shifted in the last few years from Southeast Asian waters to the waters off the African Horn region and the Gulf of Aden. This shift seems justified both by the sharp and continuing growth in the number of successful pirate attacks in and around the Gulf of Aden and the sustained fall-off in such incidents in Southeast Asia since the turn of the millennium. Figures from the International Maritime Bureau's Piracy Reporting Centre show that piracy incidents in Southeast Asia waters peaked in 2000 at 242 (over half of the 469 recorded globally), while incidents off the coast of Somalia and the Gulf of Aden then only accounted for 22 (less than 5% of the global total).[8] However, by 2009, the situation was reversed. Southeast Asian waters accounted for only 45 out of 406 reported incidents (11%), while the Gulf of Aden area accounted for 217 incidents (53% of the global total). In fact, the 2009 figure for Southeast Asia is the lowest recorded by the Bureau for this region since 1994. In 2010, at least 219 attacks occurred in the Horn of Africa region, with 49 successful hijackings. This compares with 120 incidents of piracy and armed robberies at sea reported in Southeast Asia in 2010, of which 87 attacks were successful, including seven hijackings of tugs and fishing vessels.[9] The first three months of 2011 then saw pirate attacks worldwide hit an all-time high, largely driven by piracy off the coast of Somalia. From January to March 2011, the International Chamber of Shipping recorded 97 attacks by Somali pirates, averaging more than one a day. Fifteen ships were successfully hijacked and 299 crewmen taken hostage. The rise in attacks coincided with an increase in violence, with seven seafarers killed and 34 injured worldwide. This steep upward trajectory in

---

[6] Teitler, ibid, 67–68.

[7] House of Commons (UK), Foreign Affairs (Select) Committee, 'Piracy off the Coast of Somalia', Tenth Report of Session 2010–12, HC 1318 (5 January 2012) 16, para 16.

[8] The IMB Piracy Reporting Centre follows the definition of piracy as laid down in Art 101 of the 1982 United Nations Convention on the Law of the Sea (UNCLOS) and armed robbery as laid down in Resolution A.1025 (26), adopted on 2 December 2009 at the 26th Assembly Session of the International Maritime Organisation (IMO). Information on the IMB is available at http://www.icc-ccs.org.uk/icc/imb and on the IMB's piracy reporting centre at http://www.icc-ccs.org.uk/piracy-reporting-centre.

[9] K von Hoesslin, 'Piracy and Armed Robbery against Ships in the ASEAN Region: Incidents and Trends' in R Beckman and JA Roach (eds), *Piracy and International Maritime Crimes in ASEAN: Prospects for Cooperation* (Cheltenham, Edward Elgar, 2012) 121, citing Risk Intelligence, '2010 Statistics Fact File' (31 December 2010), accessed from the MaRisk website, http://www.marisk.dk.

piracy incidents off the Somali coast continued throughout 2011 and into 2012, with 239 actual and attempted hijackings reported in 2011, and a further 69 attacks in the first six months of 2012.[10] Although the rate of attacks has declined in recent months, the western reaches of the Indian Ocean remains the world's most pirated waters.[11] Indeed, Somali-based piracy has become a world-wide media phenomenon. So much so that, in its recent report on this issue, a UK Parliamentary Committee also noted with concern that some observers have attributed the recent rise in piracy off the west coast of Africa in the Gulf of Guinea to copycat attacks inspired by Somali piracy. Ultimately, the Committee concluded that, while lessons should be learned from experience in dealing with Somali piracy, such as the importance of swift intervention, piracy in the Gulf of Guinea has on the whole followed a different model to that of Somali piracy.[12] When compared to the high Somali/Gulf of Aden piracy figures today, it would seem that domestic (particularly, Indonesian) and regional anti-piracy efforts are paying dividends in Southeast Asia. Having said this, the IMB's 'live' piracy map covering the most recent incidents suggests that all is still not well in Southeast Asia.[13] Indeed, the early part of 2013 showed a significant spike in piracy/robbery at sea activity in Southeast Asian waters.

Considering now the types of vessels that are subject to piracy, Southeast Asian pirates typically attack any type of vessel, nationality and cargo, with the exception of very large vessels, such as the very large crude (oil) carriers that traverse the Malacca and Sunda Straits between major Middle Eastern oil producers and the equally major East Asian economies. Small and medium-sized cargo vessels are much the preferred targets.[14] According to von Hoesslin, the most common incident type of piracy/ armed robbery in Southeast Asia still takes the form of onboard theft against ships at anchor within territorial waters. Targeted vessels are usually robbed at night, when perpetrators use the element of surprise and generally seek to steal engine parts, crew effects, cash or other portable high-value items. Incidents involving robbery at berth (when the ship is in port, engaged in loading or unloading cargo operations) are more seldom attempted.[15] This type of piracy/armed robbery is in contrast with that practised by Somali pirates, who favour the vast ocean, targeting vessels on the high seas, while Southeast Asian pirates and robbers are limited to operations in littoral territorial waters as well as in exclusive economic zones (EEZ).[16] However, there is evidence suggesting that Somali pirates based in and around the Horn of Africa attack a wide range and different types of vessels, including the taking of large cargo or tanker ships, as well as individually owned/operated leisure craft. For example, the UK Parliamentary House of Commons report observed that since 2007 only three British

---

[10] International Chamber of Commerce (ICC), IMB 'Piracy and Armed Robbery Against Ships—Annual Report, 2011' (IMB, 2012a); ICC, IMB 'Piracy and Armed Robbery Against Ships—Report for the Period 1 January–30 June, 2012' (IMB, 2012b). Both these Reports are accessible from: http://www.icc-ccs.org.uk/ piracy-reporting-centre/piracynewsafigures.

[11] IMB, 2012b, ibid, 7, as cited in ER Lucas, 'Somali's Pirate Cycle: The Three Phases of Somali Piracy' (2013) 6 *Journal of Strategic Security* 55, 55, available at http://scholarcommons.usf.edu/jss/vol6/iss1/8.

[12] House of Commons, Foreign Affairs (Select) Committee, n 7 above, 11.

[13] A regularly updated IMB 'live' piracy incidents map is available at http://www.icc-ccs.org.uk/ piracy-reporting-centre/live-piracy-map.

[14] IMB, 2012b, n 10 above, 31.

[15] Von Hoesslin, n 9 above, 122.

[16] Ibid, 138.

owned and registered ('flagged') ships and two further vessels that were managed by UK companies but sailed under different states' flags were hijacked in 2009 and 2010. However, the range of vessels hijacked is remarkable, as listed below:

- the yacht *Lynn Rival* was hijacked on 23 October 2009, with the yacht's British owners, Paul and Rachel Chandler, taken hostage and held on shore for over a year before being released on 14 November 2010;
- the chemical tanker MV *St James' Park* was hijacked on 28 December 2009 with a non-British crew of 26 on board. It was released on 14 May 2010; and
- the vehicle carrier MV *Asian Glory* was hijacked on 1 January 2010 with a non-British crew of 25 on board. It was released on 11 June 2010.[17]

Further evidence of the wide range of vessels attacked off the African Horn/Gulf of Aden area can be seen in two further cases of vessels that are managed by UK companies but sailed under the flags of other states, namely, the *Ariana*, a bulk cargo carrier flying the Maltese flag was hijacked in 2009, and the *Talca*, a refrigerated cargo ship sailing under a Bermudan flag was hijacked in 2010.[18] Lucas explains this shift in the type and size of vessels attacked by Somali-based pirates as indicating the movement from the initial phase of Somalia's piracy cycle to the second and third phases of this cycle, corresponding to the historical cycle of piracy first enunciated by Gosse.[19] According to Lucas, the second and third phases of the Somali piracy cycle (since 2005 and 2007, respectively) are characterised by a higher frequency of attacks by larger and more organised pirate groups.[20] This level of organisation can also be contrasted with the Southeast Asian variant, which has been labelled 'subsistence'-type piracy by Schofield.[21]

Significantly, unlike piracy in other parts of the world, hostage-taking for ransom is another hallmark of Somali piracy.[22] The IMB reports that more hostages—over 1,180—were taken at sea in 2010 than any year since records began.[23] Over 86% of these captives were taken by Somali pirates. In December 2011, 11 international vessels and 193 seafarers remained in the hands of these pirates,[24] although these numbers have now reduced to seven vessels and 113 hostages.[25] Further differences that clearly distinguish Somali from Southeast Asian piracy, according to von Hoesslin, include: the use of hijacked vessels as mother ships from which to launch their skiffs at other target ships; and the fact that Somali pirates have no qualms about threatening to kill hostages on board these mother ships when confronted by patrolling naval forces or armed security teams on board their target vessels.[26]

Moving on from comparisons of the numbers and types of piracy incidents, an

---

[17] House of Commons, Foreign Affairs (Select) Committee, n 7 above, 17, para 18.

[18] Ibid, 17, note 35.

[19] Lucas, n 11 above, 56–57, citing P Gosse, *The History of Piracy* (New York, Burt Franklin, 1932).

[20] Lucas, ibid, 57.

[21] Ibid, 56, citing C Schofield, 'Plaguing the Waves: Rising Piracy Threat off the Horn of Africa' (2007) 19(7) *Jane's Intelligence Review* 45.

[22] L Ploch, CM Blanchard, R O'Rourke, RC Mason and RO King, 'Piracy off the Horn of Africa' Congressional Research Service Report 7-5700.R40528 (Washington, US Library of Congress, 2011) 5.

[23] ICC, IMB, 'Piracy and Armed Robbery Against Ships: 2010 Annual Report' (IMB, 2011).

[24] IMB, 2012a, n 10 above, 20–24.

[25] See ICC, Piracy News & Figures webpage, http://www.icc-ccs.org/piracy-reporting-centre/piracynewsafigures.

[26] Von Hoesslin, n 9 above, 136.

initial and major difference that should be noted between piracy in Southeast Asian waters and off the African Horn is the highly different geographical circumstances in which they are conducted. The relatively wide area of sea/ocean where Somali-based pirates are active testifies to the vast geographical reach of this brand of piracy. According to Leipziger, this reach now extends over an immense area from the Red Sea into the Gulf of Aden and along the Horn of Africa off Somali shores.[27] It stretches down the coastlines of Kenya and Tanzania, reaching as far south as Madagascar and Mozambique. Somali-based pirate activities have expanded into the Arabian Sea off Oman and deep into the Indian Ocean as far as the Indian coast.[28] Although the number of successful attacks carried out has declined since 2011, Somali pirates have increased both the range of their attacks and the size of their targets. As Lucas observes, Somali pirates are capable of hijacking large merchant vessels located hundreds of miles offshore.[29] This lies in stark contrast with Southeast Asian-based piracy, which is still largely confined to the near shore areas lying within easy reach from their island bases situated in the Malacca and Singapore Straits; between Hong Kong and Macau islands, in the so-called 'H-L-H' (Hong Kong–Luzon–Hainan) island 'terror' triangle; and finally within the wider Indonesian archipelago of islands, as Liss catalogues in a recent monograph.[30] In this sense, it is significant to note that most Southeast Asian 'piracy' is technically speaking 'robbery at sea' from an international legal perspective, taking place as it does within the maritime jurisdictions of one or more of the littoral coastal/island states in this region.

A second discernible difference between Southeast Asian and Somali-based piracy lies in the nature of the global and regional institutional responses to piracy in both regions. Writing in 1998, close to the height of Southeast Asian-based piracy incidence, Chalk analysed the contemporary dynamic of maritime piracy in the Southeast Asian region. Having first discussed the main trends in terms of incidence, type of attack, geographic location and facilitative factors, he then examined the main counter-measures that have been initiated in an attempt to control this particular maritime threat. Chalk argued that there was considerable scope for further improving regional and international action against piracy—especially with regard to creating effective multilateral joint patrol areas; consolidating the work of the Regional Piracy Centre; institutionalising the issue of piracy on the future Southeast Asian security agenda; and creating more favourable conditions for the provision of regionally applied international assistance. He concluded by stating that, in the absence of movement in these directions, there was little to prevent piracy from growing into a more destabilising influence than it already is.[31] Since his calls for increased and improved institutionalisation of piracy prevention and abatement efforts, new regional initiatives have indeed been undertaken by the littoral states, with support from interested extra-regional

---

[27] A Leipziger, 'Somali Piracy: Lessons from 19th Century China', MA thesis in Law and Diplomacy and Occasional Paper #6 (Institute for Global Maritime Studies, 5 December 2012) 31, available at http://www.igms.org/sites/default/files/publishedworks/Alex%20Leipziger%20-%20Somali%20Piracy_Lessons%20from%2019th%20century%20China.pdf.

[28] Leipziger, ibid, citing IMB, 2012a, n 10 above, 20–24.

[29] Lucas, n 11 above, 57.

[30] C Liss, *Oceans of Crime: Maritime Piracy and Transnational Security in Southeast Asia and Bangladesh* (Singapore, ISEAS, 2011).

[31] P Chalk, 'Contemporary Maritime Piracy in Southeast Asia' (1998) 21 *Studies in Conflict & Terrorism* 87, 111–12.

powers. This is unlike the almost unprecedented and global scale of the international institutional approach to tackling Somali piracy, as mediated through the UN and otherwise. The contrast between the global approach to Somali piracy and the mainly sub-regional and domestic approaches to Southeast Asian piracy will be elaborated below.

It is also interesting to juxtapose the real and relative decline in piracy and armed robbery incidents occurring in and around the Strait of Malacca with the overall state of domestic government control during this time period over the local communities from where the pirates are said to hail. In particular, the loss of control by the Indonesian central government in the immediate aftermath of the 1997 Asian financial crisis and the downfall of the Soeharto regime certainly represent two significant factors explaining the relatively higher piracy and armed robbery rates in Indonesian waters during this period. In *Oceans of Crime*, Carolin Liss chronologically charts three different Southeast Asian sub-regional hot spots as follows: between 1990 and 1992, the waters in the Straits of Malacca and Singapore were the most pirate-infested. Following the initiation of anti-piracy patrols in this area, the focus of piracy shifted from 1993 to 1995 to the H-L-H terror triangle, encompassing the waters between Hong Kong island, Luzon island in the northern Philippine archipelago and Hainan island off the southern coast of the PRC. Finally, since the mid-1990s, as the authoritarian Soeharto regime unravelled in Indonesia, the waters of this wide-ranging archipelago became the most pirate-infested in the Southeast Asian region. Liss also notes the 1997 Asian financial crisis inter alia as another reason for the lack of resources provided to local marine enforcement agencies, which in turn was a major factor for the rise in piracy during this period.[32]

III. ECONOMIC, SOCIAL AND CULTURAL (INCLUDING RELIGIOUS) BACKGROUNDS TO PIRACY IN SOUTHEAST ASIA AND SOMALIA

Liss offers an integrated analysis of the root causes of piracy within the Southeast Asia and Bangladesh maritime regions, linking declining fish stocks, organised crime networks, radical political groups, the use of flags of convenience, the lack of state control over national territory and the activities of private security companies, and identifies their wider security implications.[33] This cause and effect list is similar to that provided by Adam Young.[34] In an earlier work, Young describes three particular discontinuities between modern and historical piracy: the static territorial borders introduced by nation state consciousness; the fact that in the past piracy had some conditional legitimacy whereas in the present it is considered completely illegal; and the material, political, social and cultural changes of the modern era.[35]

Here the relatively more professionally oriented approach of Somali/Horn of Africa

---

[32] Liss, n 30 above, 26 and 29.

[33] Ibid.

[34] AJ Young, *Contemporary Maritime Piracy in Southeast Asia: History, Causes and Remedies* (Leiden, International Institute for Asian Studies, 2007).

[35] AJ Young, 'Roots of Contemporary Maritime Piracy in Southeast Asia' in D Johnson and M Valencia (eds), *Piracy in Southeast Asia: Status, Issues and Responses* (Singapore, Institute of Southeast Asian Studies, 2005) 16.

pirates can be contrasted with the categorisation by Liss of the types of pirates active in the Southeast Asian maritime region as mainly divided into two groups: (i) opportunistic sea-robbers, involved in small scale attacks; and (ii) more sophisticated organised pirate gangs, responsible for hijackings and other major pirate attacks.[36] Somali-based pirates seem almost exclusively to belong to the latter kind, with Baker, for example, noting that, towards the end of 2010, Somali pirate ring-leaders were operating five mother ships and launching successful attacks more than 1,000 miles from Somalia itself,[37] and certainly much further than any Southeast Asian/South China Sea pirate would venture into the seas, as noted above. On the other hand, von Hoesslin points out that 'professional' criminal enterprises or syndicates are increasingly playing a key role in the overall picture of piracy and armed robbery at sea in Southeast Asia, regardless of the financial crises and higher unemployment levels. He notes that

> since 2008, a sophisticated campaign of piracy and armed robbery at sea has been waged off the Anambas Islands, orchestrated by experienced syndicates running business enterprises that in many ways operate independently of global economic conditions. By 2010, the main perpetrating group had fine-tuned its operations, increased its hunting grounds and begun recruiting seasoned, 'career-oriented' members—persons who steadily make a living off piracy rather than merely being out of work tradesmen and fishermen.[38]

Many of the reasons for Southeast Asian piracy are similar to those identified as the causal effects of Horn of Africa-based piracy, including the more contentious allegations of links between piracy and fundamentalist Muslim terrorism.[39] According to the final report of the experts group convened in 2008 by the UN Special Representative to Somalia, 'poverty, lack of employment, environmental hardship, pitifully low incomes, reduction of pastoralist and maritime resources due to drought and illegal fishing and a volatile security and political situation all contribute to the rise and continuance of piracy in Somalia'.[40] Pirate activity and ransom revenues have increased significantly in the past three years, and many now assert that Somalia's economy and its population are increasingly dependent on piracy. The average ransom paid in 2010 has been estimated at over US$5.4 million; with more than 50 reported hijackings in the last year, this places the 2010 ransom revenues of the Somali pirates at over US$250 million.[41] Indeed, certain eminent observers on Somali/Horn of Africa piracy issues have even suggested that some of the ransom money is going to the al-Qaeda-linked terrorist group Al-Shabaab to fund its fight against the UN-backed Transitional Federal Government (TFG) in Somalia,[42] which, since August 2012, has been recognised as the

[36] C Liss, 'Roots of Piracy in Southeast Asia', available at Nautilus Institute for Security and Stability website: http://nautilus.org/apsnet/the-roots-of-piracy-in-southeast-asia/.

[37] See ML Baker, 'Smarter Measures in Fight against Piracy' (US Council of Foreign Relations, 10 December, 2010), available at http://www.cfr.org/somalia/smarter-measures-fight-against-piracy/p23611.

[38] Von Hoesslin, n 9 above, 121–22.

[39] See, eg P Lehr (ed), *Violence at Sea: Piracy in the Age of Global Terrorism* (New York, Routledge, 2007).

[40] International Expert Group on Piracy off the Somali Coast, commissioned by the Special Representative of the Secretary General of the UN to Somalia, Ambassador Ahmedou Ould-Abdallah, Final Report, Nairobi, 21 November, 2008, available at http://www.asil.org/files/somaliapiracyintlexpertsreportconsolidated1.pdf.

[41] General Insurance Research Organizing Committee estimate, as referenced in A Bowden et al, 'The Economic Cost of Maritime Piracy', One Earth Future Working Paper (December 2010).

[42] For example, senior US and EU public figures, such as former CIA director Leon Panetta (see 'Somali Militants Aiming to Attack Abroad: CIA Chief', *AFP*, 8 June 2011) and Baroness Ashton, the EU Foreign

Federal Government of Somalia (FGS). A recent note by the International Institute for Strategic Studies has also observed a 'growing synergy' between pirates and Al-Shabaab, stating that, although the groups remained separate in aims and ideology, Al-Shabaab's need for new funding sources and its control of the port of Kismayo has allowed for 'taxation and limited co-operation between the groups'.[43] However, direct connections/linkages between piracy and terrorism have so far not been proven, merely strongly alleged. For example, the UK House of Commons Foreign Affairs Committee received no evidence of a link between piracy and terrorism, and reported that Dr McCafferty, Head of Counter-terrorism and UK Operational Policy at the UK Ministry of Defence, had informed the Committee that 'there has not been any evidence of a link between the pirates and al-Shaba[a]b, the terrorists in Somalia'.[44]

Delving into past incidences of mass piracy within a wider geographical context, Leipzinger has chartered historical parallels between contemporary Somali piracy off the African Horn, when compared with piracy off the southeastern coast of mainland China during the eighteenth and nineteenth centuries. The first of these similarities is proximity to burgeoning international trade conducted by shipping. In historical China, this was due to the legalisation and encouragement of seaborne trade by the Qing dynasty government in 1684. This official authorisation to trade led to bur-geoning commerce along China's coastline, thriving particularly in the South China Sea. This region, comprising the Chinese provinces of Guangdong and Fujian, handled as much as 75% of China's maritime domestic and international trade between 1735 and 1812, with Canton as its hub, having officially become the sole port through which outsiders were permitted to trade with China in 1757.[45] According to Leipziger, this developing maritime trade stimulated the Chinese economy along its coast. While this trade led merchants, shopkeepers and the landed gentry into an age of prosperity, the wealth generated by such commerce was unevenly distributed. Those at the margins of society—small-scale farmers, fishermen, sailors and labourers—had little access to economic opportunities. Rising population density exacerbated these conditions. Many of those at the bottom of the Chinese social hierarchy were driven deeper into poverty by rising prices and deteriorating job prospects. Compounding these socio-economic changes, the Guangdong region experienced an unusually high number of natural disasters—floods, droughts and locusts—throughout the period 1780–1810. These environmental catastrophes caused famines, intensified unemployment and added to the sense of dislocation and disorder that poverty had cultivated.[46] Official

Minister, who told the UK House of Commons Foreign Affairs Committee that links between Al-Shabaab and pirates were 'a worry at the present time' in oral evidence taken before the Foreign Affairs Committee on 21 November 2011, HC (2010–12) 1642-i, Q 41.

[43] International Institute for Strategic Studies, 'IISS Strategic Comments', vol 17, comment 40 (November 2011).

[44] House of Commons, Foreign Affairs (Select) Committee, n 7 above, 16, para 16.

[45] Leipziger, n 27 above, 5–6, citing R Antony, *Like Froth Floating on the Sea: The World of Pirates and Seafarers in Late Imperial South China* (Berkeley CA, University of California Institute for East Asian Studies, 2003) 53 and 56–59; and R Antony, 'Piracy and the Shadow Economy in the South China Sea, 1780–1810' in R Antony (ed), *Elusive Pirates, Pervasive Smugglers: Violence and Clandestine Trade in the Greater China Sea* (Hong Kong, Hong Kong University Press, 2010) 101.

[46] Leipziger, ibid, 6–7, citing Antony, *Like Froth Floating on the Sea*, ibid, 81; Antony, 'Piracy and the Shadow Economy in the South China Sea', ibid, 100; and R Antony, 'Piracy on the South China Coast through Modern Times' in B Elleman, A Forbes and D Rosenberg (eds), *Piracy and Maritime Crime: Historical and Modern Case Studies* (Newport RI, Naval War College Press, 2010) 39.

correspondence in the late eighteenth century recognised the causal effects that these natural disasters and rising unemployment had on piracy.[47]

The second historical parallel and similarity between the roots of eighteenth/nineteenth-century Chinese piracy and contemporary Somali piracy, as drawn by Leipziger, relates to the conditions of government neglect, absence and eventual political instability. He observes that piracy grew as a result of the inadequate government response to the dire economic conditions charted above. Political instability increased in the late eighteenth century as a result of a debilitated central government unwilling and unable to cope with the problems of peripheral provinces. This was a time of rising crime and disorder throughout southern China, with increasing poverty, social unrest and banditry only a sample of the problems that the region faced in addition to piracy. The Qing government initially ignored the socio-economic maladies and mounting lawlessness in the region, due at least in part to a number of major internal rebellions.[48] Leipziger concludes that it was economic dislocation, aggravated by natural disasters and the inability and unwillingness of the Qing government to adequately address this economically depressed population, that catalysed piracy's rise.[49]

IV. GLOBAL, REGIONAL AND SUB-REGIONAL LEGAL RESPONSES TO PIRACY IN SOUTHEAST ASIAN AND AFRICAN HORN WATERS

Having charted the similarities and differences between piracy phenomena and their causes in both the Horn of Africa and Southeast Asian situations, the next question to address is whether there have been any similarities and differences in the legal responses to piracy incidence in each of these maritime regions. Here it is possible to discern several commonalities of approach, ranging from: (i) an initial emphasis on clarifying the nature and extent of the international or universal jurisdiction exercisable by states over pirates,[50] whether to interdict, board, arrest and prosecute them; to (ii) efforts by regional and extra-regional states to cooperate in relation the above clarification; and (iii) further cooperative efforts to address the grassroots issues laid bare by the high levels of piracy incidence in the relevant geographical regions, especially in the Horn of Africa. The similarities and differences in the international policy and legal approaches towards piracy in both these regions will be examined in turn. To begin with, however, it should be noted that what Singh and Bedi have labelled 'the turbid legal regime of counter-piracy' allows for confusion in the legal treatment of pirates, as with terrorists. This is because

> Like the War on Terror, the War on Piracy entails the construction of legal architecture in its support. Given the muddle of international and domestic laws on piracy, and [the fact]

---

[47] Leipziger, ibid, 7, citing M Leung, 'Piracy in South China in the Nineteenth Century' in L Kawamura and K Scott (eds), *Buddhist Thought and Asian Civilization: Essays in Honor of Herbert v Guenther on His Sixtieth Birthday* (Emeryville CA, Darma Publishing, 1977) 153–64.

[48] Leipziger, ibid, 7, citing Antony, 'Piracy on the South China Coast through Modern Times', n 46 above, 35–49.

[49] Leipziger, ibid.

[50] In this regard, Dubner and Greene have recently highlighted the historical reasons for contemporary jurisdictional problems over piracy. See BH Dubner and K Greene, 'On the Creation of a New Legal Regime to Try Sea Pirates' (2010) 41 *Journal of Maritime Law & Commerce* 439.

that prosecuting captured pirates in Somalia is not entirely viable, piracy is becoming legally conflated with terrorism. UN agreements and resolutions are the legal platform for the War on Piracy, but its proponents have pursued law-making and prosecutions amid considerable legal ambiguity, which opens the door to exceptional legal practices and rights violations, as the War on Terror has proven.[51]

Thus, it is vital to enumerate the relevant international legal issues arising from piracy before examining the policy and legal responses to these issues within Southeast Asia and the African Horn. This is the subject of the following discussion:

- Significantly, any interdiction at sea raises important questions of jurisdiction, including the following: how permission to board a foreign vessel is obtained; whether boarding state or flag state law applies during the interdiction (or whether both apply); and which state has jurisdiction to prosecute any crimes discovered. In his comparative study of the legal scope for intervention at sea, Guilfoyle considers all the possible actions by states in stopping, searching and arresting foreign flag vessels and crew on the high seas in cases of piracy, slavery, drug smuggling, fisheries management, migrant smuggling, the proliferation of weapons of mass destruction and maritime terrorism. Legal issues such as the applicable rules on the use of force, the status of boarding state officers under flag state law, protection of human rights of individuals in the boarded ship and compensation for wrongful interdiction are also considered by Guilfoyle, who argues that underlying every lawful interdiction there must be jurisdiction to undertake enforcement not only through the acts of boarding and inspection themselves, but also through prosecution and confiscation, disposal or return. However, the exercise of these different types of jurisdiction may be distributed among different states.[52] Responding to this point, Crawford perceptively notes that it is more sustainable, and usually simpler from an operational point of view, to use existing recognised jurisdictions (especially that of the flag state) rather than to assert or invent new ones, via Chapter VII of the United Nations Charter or otherwise.[53]
- In this regard, Klein has observed that the threat to international peace and security which precipitated the relevant UNSC Resolution 1816 of 2008 related to the precarious situation in Somalia specifically, as opposed to the increasing numbers of piracy and armed robberies at sea generally.[54] Nevertheless, she suggests that a precedent has been set whereby continuing or especially violent acts of piracy could be viewed from now on as amounting to a threat to international peace and security, necessitating UN Chapter VII Security Council action. Moreover, according to Klein, the fact that the Security Council has authorised interdictions to respond to maritime security threats is in itself a significant international law development.[55] Karim, however, sees this simply as an acknowledgement that combating piracy at sea and apprehending pirates have been long-standing problems for the global com-

---

[51] C Singh and A Singh Bedi, '"War on Piracy": the Conflation of Somali Piracy with Terrorism in Discourse, Tactic and Law', Working Paper No 543 (The Hague, Institute of Social Studies, May 2012) 27, available at http://repub.eur.nl/res/pub/32374/wp543.pdf.

[52] D Guilfoyle, *Shipping Interdiction and the Law of the Sea* (Cambridge, Cambridge University Press, 2009).

[53] J Crawford, foreword to Guilfoyle, ibid, xv–xvi.

[54] N Klein, *Maritime Security and the Law of the Sea* (Oxford, Oxford University Press, 2011) 280.

[55] Ibid, 281.

munity.[56] More generally, Crawford observes that the search for sustainable solutions for this problem helps to explain the quite high levels of cooperation revealed in state practice, for example in the various ship-rider schemes, and the conclusion of a range of bilateral and regional treaties and arrangements on such matters as drug trafficking (supplementing the UN Narcotics Convention of 1988) and interdiction of weapons of mass destruction and precursor material.[57] Progressing along these lines, Karim notes that the UN Security Council also adopted a resolution urging all states to fully implement relevant international conventions in their domestic legal systems.[58]

- Moreover, and implicitly accepting the current unviability of Somali-based judicial enforcement and incarceration capacity over apprehended pirates, a related strand of international legal doctrine has been concerned with exploring just how far coastal states are either obliged—or, indeed, even responsible—under international law to enforce their respective maritime jurisdiction over piracy and especially armed robbery acts at sea.[59] For example, the fact that armed robberies within the territorial sea can occur with impunity has led to suggestions for the geographical scope of universal jurisdiction over piracy to be extended beyond the high seas and EEZ to include the territorial waters of (other) states.[60] Apart from arguments of necessity, it has also been argued that the requirement of international cooperation against piracy allows action to be taken/continued within the maritime jurisdiction zones of (other) coastal states.[61] As Karim notes in this regard, the most significant aspect of the successive UNSC resolutions on this issue in Somalia has been the authorisation of action against armed robbery in Somali territorial waters, albeit on a temporary (six months) and renewable basis.[62] Indeed, Todd highlights that UNSC resolution 1851 (2008) even allows for the possibility of states undertaking measures in Somalia itself, for the purpose of suppressing not only acts of piracy, but also armed robbery at sea.[63]

- Going further down this legal pathway, it has even been argued that coastal states that are unable or unwilling to take action against piracy/armed robbery in their own maritime jurisdiction zones could be held responsible under international law for their failure to protect foreign shipping adequately.[64] Taking into consideration the relevant Security Council resolutions and existing international law, Karim examines whether there is an international obligation to criminalise piracy under

---

[56] MS Karim, 'Is There an International Obligation to Prosecute Pirates?' (2011) 58(3) *Netherlands International Law Rev* 387.

[57] Crawford, n 53 above.

[58] Karim, n 56 above, 390, citing para 14 of UNSC Resolution 1950 (2010).

[59] Klein, n 54 above, 81–82.

[60] JL Jesus, 'Protection of Foreign Ships against Piracy and Terrorism at Sea: Legal Aspects' (2003) 18 *International Journal of Marine & Coastal Law* 363, 382–84. Such an extension to the exercise of enforcement jurisdiction, especially in the context of 'hot pursuit', is currently prohibited under Art 111(3) of the 1982 UNCLOS.

[61] Jesus, ibid; RC Beckman, 'Combatting Piracy and Armed Robbery against Ships in Southeast Asia: The Way Forward' (2002) 33 *Ocean Development and International Law* 317, 333–34.

[62] Karim, n 56 above, 391–92, citing para 7 of UNSC 1816 (2008).

[63] P Todd, *Maritime Fraud and Piracy*, 2nd edn (London, Lloyd's List, 2010) 11, para 1.041, citing para 6 of UNSC Resolution 1851 (2008).

[64] TM Sittnick, 'State Responsibility and Maritime Terrorism in the Strait of Malacca: Persuading Indonesia and Malaysia to Take Additional Steps to Secure the Strait' (2005) 14 *Pacific Rim Law and Policy Journal* 743.

domestic legal frameworks and to prosecute pirates in domestic courts. He concludes that existing international law arguably imposes an obligation to prosecute pirates, at least in certain circumstances, and that the Security Council resolutions reinforce this obligation. However, Karim also observes that, despite the Security Council's interventions on this critical issue in the international response to African Horn-based piracy, most states are still reluctant to prosecute Somali pirates in their domestic courts.[65] He notes that prosecuting pirates appears to be more difficult than apprehending them, except when the national interests of the capturing countries are directly involved.[66] The last word on this complex set of legal issues should belong to Dubner and Henn, as they note that: 'Naturally, the best way to solve piracy is to solve the problems in a lawless society such as Somalia'.[67] They go on to conclude that the poor living standards in Somalia, such that basic necessities are scarce, coupled with evidence of illegal fishing and toxic dumping operations offshore Somalia, which contribute to an abiding sense of social injustice, render efforts to secure more domestic piracy prosecutions futile.[68]

A further response to the jurisdictional stalemate highlighted above has been the increasing employment by shipping and cargo owners of private security companies (PSCs) as a proactive means to prevent the boarding and taking of their ships by pirates. The significance of the extra-state, and indeed extra-judicial, aspects of these private security operations should be highlighted. As Liss observes, PSCs have emerged in the past 20 years, offering a vast menu of military and security services that were in the past largely the responsibility of government enforcement agencies. While PSC operations are often thought to be largely confined to war/conflict zones and failed states in Africa and the Middle East, this issue has come to popular media attention due to the use of such security firms against piracy activities off the African Horn. However, there are also many PSCs that are currently active in Southeast Asia, where they operate within the context of growing economies and comparatively stable polities. The demand for private military and security services in this region comes in part from the maritime sector, where PSCs are today employed to secure ports, vessels and offshore energy installations. According to Liss, the increasing use of anti-piracy services provided by PSCs to secure shipping in Southeast Asia has implications for the already nominal control of force exerted by certain states within their waters.[69] Notwithstanding the effectiveness of such innovative means to ensure shipping security, the use of private firms in this way throws up wider issues for public international law.[70] As Dickinson has noted: 'International law does not prohibit states from using

---

[65] Karim, n 56 above, 392.

[66] Ibid, 393, citing E Kontorovich, 'A Guantanamo on the Sea: The Difficulties of Prosecuting Pirates and Terrorists' (2010) 98 *California Law Review* 243, 244–46.

[67] BH Dubner and JP Henn, 'On Selecting a Judicial System(s) to Try Sea Pirates—An Interesting/Necessary Exercise but is it Enough to Deter the Attack/Hijackings?' (2011) 42(4) *Journal of Maritime Law and Commerce* 569, 583.

[68] Dubner and Henn, ibid, citing BH Dubner and LM Diaz, 'Foreign Fishing Piracy vs Somali Piracy—Does Wrong Equal Wrong?' (2010) 14 *Barry Law Review* 73; and MA Waldo, 'Somali Piracy, the Other Side of the Coin', *African Prospect* (October 2009) 8.

[69] C Liss, 'Losing Control? The Privatisation of Anti-piracy Services in Southeast Asia' (2009) 63(3) *Australian Journal of International Affairs* 390.

[70] See, eg S Chesterman and C Lehnardt (eds), *From Mercenaries to Market: The Rise and Regulation of Private Military Companies* (Oxford, Oxford University Press, 2007).

private contractors to provide military and security services'.[71] However, as she goes on to observe,

> treaty law does prohibit some forms of mercenarism [*sic*] and denies mercenaries combatant or POW status. The definitions of a 'mercenary' are narrow, however, and may not encompass the activities undertaken, for example, by PSCs employed by the United States in Afghanistan and Iraq.[72]

Moreover, the jurisdictional implications of the use of PSCs against piracy at sea are arguably different from their use within recent armed conflict situations on land. These issues are currently being played out in the aftermath of the *Enrica Lexie* incident between India and Italy, in which two Italian marines seconded to a private Italian cargo flagship shot and killed two Indian fishermen on an unflagged but Indian-registered fishing boat within Indian maritime jurisdiction zones.[73] An extended discussion of the international legal issues arising from this incident is beyond the scope of this paper.

A. Extra-regional, Regional and Sub-regional Efforts at Curbing Piracy and Robbery at Sea in Southeast Asian Waters

In stark contrast to the globalised aspect of international community engagement with piracy off the African Horn, particularly via UN Security Council action, piracy within Southeast Asian waters has remained a regional issue to be addressed mainly by the littoral states concerned even at the height of its notoriety. Despite the expressed willingness of extra-regional powers to assist, a marked reluctance on the part of certain countries in the region—notably, Indonesia and Malaysia—prevented external involvement, except when expressly invited on specific issues. This was mainly due to the implicitly known yet not widely acknowledged fact that most incidents of Southeast Asian piracy take place within the extended maritime jurisdictions of the littoral states. This fact initially confounded regional cooperation efforts to address this problem. These instances of armed robbery at sea, rather than piracy within international waters, should be subject to the relevant national maritime jurisdictions involved for their enforcement.

However, domestic and bilateral political sensitivities between the neighbouring states in the region prevented even an acknowledgement of perceived failures in national jurisdiction enforcement, let alone any cooperative action to remedy these failures. Indeed, it is arguably no coincidence that Southeast Asian regional cooperation to combat piracy and armed robbery at sea only began in earnest once the littoral states of the Strait of Malacca had acquired the necessary tactical assets and weaponry, as well as human capacity, along with matching confidence in their deployment, to adequately enforce their penal codes within their extended maritime jurisdictions. On this score, for example, it is only recently that Chun has been able to observe that

---

[71] LA Dickinson, 'Accountability of Private Security Contractors under International and Domestic Law' (2007) 11 *ASIL Insights*, issue 31, available at http://www.asil.org/insights071226.cfm.

[72] Ibid.

[73] For an initial assessment of the relevant legal issues see KS Harisankar, 'Jurisdictional and Immunity Issues in the Story of *Enrica Lexie*: A Case of Shoot & Scoot Turns Around!', available at http://ssrn.com/abstract=2240738.

the coastal states have all taken steps at the national level. The Indonesian Navy is reforming its operations and modernising to increase effective patrols against criminal activities. It has set up command centres, contactable by shipping, and deployed special forces that can respond to piracy. The Royal Malaysian Navy has built radar stations along the Malacca Straits to monitor traffic and acquired new patrol boats. Special anti-piracy task forces have been set up and vulnerable vessels like tugs and barges are protected. It has also formed a coast guard, the Malaysian Maritime Enforcement Agency (MMEA), to bring together all the agencies involved in maritime security under one command. Singapore has introduced an integrated surveillance and information network for tracking and investigating suspicious movements; increased naval and coast guard patrols; and re-designated shipping routes to minimise merchant vessel interaction with small craft.[74]

A further, political economy-oriented reason for the change in attitude among the Southeast Asian states towards cooperative anti-piracy efforts followed the listing of the Strait of Malacca and some parts south of the Philippines (as well as Somalia, Iraq and Lebanon) as a 'war-risk' area in July 2005, by the Joint War Committee of the Lloyd's Market Association. The effect of a 'war-risk' listing is that insurance premiums for vessels passing through the region are higher,[75] thereby creating a disincentive for shipping companies to use the Strait of Malacca. The negative international trade implications of this 'war-risk' listing for the economies of the littoral states in the region have arguably had the positive effect of incentivising these countries to address piracy and armed robbery at sea issues at a higher level of prioritisation than previously obtainable.

Initial progress in Southeast Asian regional maritime security and cooperation to combat piracy has also been impaired by historical distrust, different national interest priorities and clashes between the national interests of some of the neighbouring countries.[76] In addition, Southeast Asian governments appear to have different levels of interest and policy approaches towards piracy. Coastal state priority is often given to issues of national sovereignty,[77] protection of marine resources within the EEZ[78] and disputes over claims of certain ocean areas,[79] as opposed to the threat of terrorism per se, which is arguably more of an extra-regional concern than an intra-regional one.[80] As Liss observes,

---

[74] CK Ho, 'Contemporary Piracy in Southeast Asia and Somalia: An Analysis of Causes, Effects, and Current Counter-piracy Approaches' (2011) 21(2) *The Southeast Asian Review* 293, 315–16.

[75] N Passas and A Twyman-Ghoshal, 'Controlling Piracy in Southeast Asia—Thinking Outside the Box' in Beckman and Roach, n 9 above, 76, citing D Rosenberg, 'The Political Economy of Piracy in the South China Sea' (2009) 62(3) *Naval War College Review* 43, 51.

[76] Ibid, 76, citing J Mo, 'Options to Combat Maritime Piracy in Southeast Asia' (2002) 33 *Ocean Development & International Law* 343, 350; and JN Mak, 'Unilateralism and Regionalism: Working Together and Alone in the Strait of Malacca' in GG Ong-Webb (ed), *Piracy, Maritime Terrorism and Securing the Strait of Malacca* (Singapore, ISEAS Publishing, 2006) 135.

[77] Ibid, 76, citing E Barrios, 'Casting a Wider Net: Addressing the Maritime Piracy Problem in Southeast Asia' (2005) 28(1) *Boston College International and Comparative Law Review* 149, 159; and MN Murphy, 'Piracy and UNCLOS: Does International Law Help Regional states Combat Piracy?' in Lehr, n 39 above, 167.

[78] Ibid, 76, citing JN Mak, 'Pirates, Renegades and Fishermen: The Politics of 'Sustainable' Piracy in the Strait of Malacca' in Lehr, ibid, 216.

[79] Ibid, 76, citing D Rosenberg and C Chung, 'Maritime Security in the South China Sea: Coordinating Coastal and User state Priorities' (2008) 39 *Ocean Development & International Law* 51.

[80] Ibid, 76, citing J Dela Pena, 'Maritime Crime in the Strait of Malacca: Balancing Regional and Extra-regional Concerns' (2009) 2 *Stanford Journal of International Relations* 1, 4.

even in countries such as Indonesia and Malaysia, where the number of reported pirate attacks was comparatively high, piracy was one of the least pressing of many security risks, which included natural disasters, the threat posed by separatist and terrorist groups, and the high incidence of crimes committed on land.[81]

Indeed, regional commentators have sought to downplay the significance of Southeast Asian piracy numbers as well as talk-up regional and sub-regional efforts to tackle its incidence.[82]

Thus, Southeast Asian regional states still tend to deal with piracy and other maritime crimes as primarily a national law enforcement issue (trilaterally, to a limited extent, in the case of Straits of Malacca and Singapore). Individual Southeast Asian countries have met previously to discuss security, cooperation and joint anti-piracy efforts. For instance, in 2003 Malaysia and Thailand began coordinated patrols along their joint maritime border, followed in 2004 by MALSINDO (Malaysia–Singapore–Indonesia) coordinated patrols. These coordinated patrols were not joint patrols; each naval power would patrol their own territorial waters, with no right to enter another nation's waters and no right of pursuit. In September 2005, MALSINDO was expanded to air patrols over the straits under the 'Eyes-in-the-Sky' (EiS) initiative, providing combined and coordinated aerial surveillance of the Singapore and Malacca Straits.[83] These coordinated patrols have been said to be of limited value and have even been described as being a public relations exercise.[84] However, by August 2006, following both the MALSINDO and the EiS initiatives in 2004–05, the Lloyd's Joint War Risk Committee had dropped the classification of the Strait of Malacca as a war-risk area. Moreover, according to the 'Oceans beyond Piracy' project,[85] the International Maritime Bureau (IMB) recorded the number of pirate attacks in the Strait of Malacca per se as having dropped from 38 in 2004 to zero in 2011.[86] Chun has confirmed that

> The co-ordinated Malacca Straits Patrols, running since July 2004, despite their limitations mentioned earlier, have had a positive effect, and Thailand and India look set to join later this year to improve the security of the northern sector. A Joint Co-ordinating Committee between the participating countries has been established, an Information Exchange Group has been set up between naval intelligence agencies, and joint standard operating procedures have been developed. As a result, the number of attacks has substantially declined in the Straits. However criminal activity has not been completely eradicated and concentrating on the Malacca Straits may have only succeeded in pushing attacks elsewhere.[87]

More generally, in relation to continuing suggestions of links between Southeast Asian piracy and terrorism, Singh and Bedi observe that '(t)he withdrawal of the Strait of Malacca as a war risk area signals that despite the fear that pervades the discourse of maritime terrorism, most analysts concur it constitutes a less than credible threat'.[88]

---

[81] Liss, n 30 above, 8.

[82] See, eg JH Ho, 'The Security of Sea Lanes in Southeast Asia' (2006) 46(4) *Asian Survey* 558.

[83] Ibid, 76. See Singapore Ministry of Defence, 'Launch of Eyes in the Sky (EiS) Initiative', available at http://www.mindef.gov.sg/imindef/news_and_events/nr/2005/sep/13sep05_nr.html.

[84] Ibid, 77, citing JN Mak, 'Unilateralism and Regionalism: Working Together and Alone in the Strait of Malacca' in Ong-Webb, n 76 above, 156.

[85] The Oceans Beyond Piracy project was launched in 2010 on the initiative of the One Earth Future Foundation, an NGO located in Colorado, USA. See www.oneearthfuture.org/.

[86] http://oceansbeyondpiracy.org/matrix/activity/malacca-strait-patrols.

[87] Ho, n 74 above, 316.

[88] Singh and Bedi, n 51 above, 13.

There is a further cooperative sub-regional arrangement between Indonesia, Malaysia and Singapore through the 2007 Cooperative Mechanism between Littoral States and User States on Safety of Navigation and Environmental Protection in the Straits of Malacca and Singapore.[89] Established in 2007, in line with Article 43 of 1982 UNCLOS, the Cooperative Mechanism 'provides an opportunity to cooperate, contribute and play a role in maintaining and enhancing the safety of navigation and protection of the marine environment in the Straits which is of strategic importance for regional and global trade'. The three main components of the Cooperative Mechanism include: (i) a Cooperation Forum for dialogue on issues of common interest; (ii) a Project Coordination Committee for the implementation of joint projects; and (iii) an Aids to Navigation Fund that will finance the renewal and maintenance of navigational aids along the Straits. The Cooperative Mechanism operates in parallel to the coordinated patrols undertaken by all three countries under the MALSINDO in 2004 as well as through the 2005 EiS initiative, which focused on securing the Malacca and Singapore Straits—said to have contributed to the significant decrease of reported attacks in the area.[90] Also at the sub-regional level, Indonesia, Malaysia and the Philippines signed the 2002 Trilateral Agreement on Information Exchange and Establishment of Communication Procedures,[91] and have subsequently been joined by Brunei, Cambodia and Thailand. The agreement provides a framework for cooperation by: facilitating proper coordination during border and/or security incidents, transnational crimes and other illegal activities; establishing common understanding and approaches; strengthening capacities; and reviewing and enhancing internal rules, linkages, dialogues and response mechanisms. Significantly, three out of the 11 cooperation areas pertain to maritime security: terrorism, piracy/robbery at sea and hijacking. Theft of marine resources and marine pollution are also included as cooperation areas.[92] Jurgen Ruland, however, has noted that the 2002 Agreement is non-binding and does not have 'integrative potential'.[93] This observation highlights a truism in the evolution of international legal frameworks on any particular issue area, including, for our purposes here, piracy: it is the domestic implementation and enforcement of key international instruments, rather than the adoption of a plethora of documents, whether binding or non-binding, that ensures progress on the ground (or, in this case, in the water!).

On the other hand, the high numbers of incidents in the region and the transnational nature of the crimes point to the need for concerted efforts at a regional level to combat maritime crimes effectively. More recently, therefore, these bilateral, sub-regional, regional and extra-regional cooperation measures on maritime piracy and

---

[89] 2007 Singapore statement on the Enhancement of Safety, Security and Environmental Protection in the Straits of Malacca and Singapore, IMO/SGP1/4, issued on 6 September 2007 in Singapore, accessible from The Maritime and Port Authority of Singapore (MPA) website, at http://www.mpa.gov.sg/sites/pdf/spore_statement.pdf.

[90] T Chalermpalanupap and M Ibañez, 'ASEAN Measures in Combating Piracy and Other Maritime Crimes' in Beckman and Roach, n 9 above, 156, citing S Jayakumar, 'UNCLOS: Two Decades On' (2005) 9 *Singapore Yearbook of International Law* 1.

[91] 2002 Trilateral Agreement on Information Exchange and Establishment of Communication Procedures (adopted on 7 May 2002 by Philippines, Indonesia and Malaysia), accessible from the ASEAN Secretariat website at www.aseansec.org/17346.pdf.

[92] Chalermpalanupap and Ibañez, n 90 above, 156–57.

[93] See J Ruland, 'Traditionalism and Change in the Asian Security Discourse' in S Hoadley and J Ruland (eds), *Asian Security Reassessed* (Singapore, ISEAS, 2006)

terrorism have been assisted by the efforts of the pre-eminent Southeast Asian-based regional inter-governmental organisation, namely, the Association of Southeast Asian Nations (ASEAN). As Chun has observed, at the wider regional level, there are now a number of programmes and agreements in force to close the jurisdictional and informational gaps and to increase regional cooperation,[94] especially within and through ASEAN.

For example, along with 10 other ASEAN dialogue partners and external parties, eight ASEAN Member States entered into the 2004 Regional Cooperation Agreement on Combating Piracy and Armed Robbery against Ships in Asia (ReCAAP).[95] With 18 state parties altogether, comprising 14 regional states and four external states to the Southeast Asian region,[96] this treaty entered into force in September 2006. According to Zou, ReCAAP is the first binding international legal instrument that recognises the IMO definition of armed robbery at sea, in addition to the UNCLOS definition of piracy.[97] Moreover, this includes armed robbery in the territorial sea, archipelagic waters and internal waters, as well as a broader definition of 'attacks' directed 'against a ship' and not only those 'against another ship', according to Hayashi.[98] Chalermpalanupap and Ibañez observe that ReCAAP established a system of information sharing relating to incidents of piracy and armed robbery among Member States with the aim of improving the exchange of information through an Information Sharing Centre (ISC) in Singapore, and assisting in capacity-building and inter-state cooperation.[99] The ISC collects, collates and analyses information as well as provides alerts in case of imminent threats, and circulates inter-country requests for information and action among the contracting countries. Information sharing is made possible through focal points in each party. Requests for cooperation may be for detection, appropriate measures (arrest or seizure) and rescue operations, which may be made either directly to the requested country or through the ISC. Requests for extradition and mutual legal assistance in criminal matters, however, should be made directly to the requested party.[100] Given the underlying regional tensions based on sovereignty and enforcement jurisdiction over pirates and especially armed robbers, ReCAAP represents a clear advance in terms of legal cooperation on these issues. However, it would

---

[94] Ho, n 74 above, 315–16.

[95] ReCAAP was adopted in Tokyo, Japan on 11 November 2004 and entered into force on 4 September 2006. The 10 non-ASEAN states party to it are: Bangladesh, China, Denmark, India, Japan, Republic of Korea, Netherlands, Norway, Sri Lanka and the UK. Indonesia and Malaysia are not signatories or parties. Sources: 2398 UNTS 199, 44 ILM 839 (2005), accessible from the CIL documents database, at http://cil.nus.edu.sg/2004/2004-regional-cooperation-agreement-on-combating-piracy-and-armed-robbery-against-ships-in-asia/. ReCAAP Information Sharing Centre available at http://www.recaap.org/Portals/0/docs/About%20ReCAAP%20ISC/ReCAAP%20Agreement.pdf.

[96] The 18 contracting parties to ReCAAP are the People's Republic of Bangladesh, Brunei Darussalam, the Kingdom of Cambodia, the People's Republic of China, the Kingdom of Denmark, the Republic of India, Japan, the Republic of Korea, the Lao People's Democratic Republic, the Republic of the Union of Myanmar, the Kingdom of the Netherlands, the Kingdom of Norway, the Republic of the Philippines, the Republic of Singapore, the Democratic Socialist Republic of Sri Lanka, the Kingdom of Thailand, the Socialist Republic of Vietnam and the United Kingdom.

[97] Z Keyuan, 'New Developments in the International Law of Piracy' (2009) 8(2) *Chinese Journal of International Law* 323, 327.

[98] M Hayashi, 'Introductory Note to the Regional Cooperation Agreement on Combating Piracy and Armed Robbery against Ships in Asia' (2005) 44 *International Legal Materials* 828.

[99] Chalermpalanupap and Ibañez, n 90 above, 157.

[100] Ibid.

be a mistake to attribute the notable decline in attacks against shipping in the Strait of Malacca solely to the innovations introduced by this agreement, as Tuerk appears to do.[101] This is because, as Chun notes, the potential effectiveness of the agreement is diminished because of its limited applicability due to the fact that two of the key states, Malaysia and Indonesia, are not parties to this agreement due to their concerns about its implications for national sovereignty and jurisdiction over their maritime zones.[102] As Murphy explains, one of the reasons that the coastal states in this region are so sensitive to issues of sovereignty is because their borders are mostly young and artificial, based on colonial-era territories.[103]

Regionally, therefore, ASEAN still has no binding legal instrument providing for anti-piracy cooperation. Instead, piracy is discussed in the context of transnational crimes, as part of the transnational challenges affecting maritime security in the region. However, according to Chalermpalanupap and Ibañez, despite these challenges and limitations, ASEAN has made progress in developing a regional response to piracy and maritime crimes.[104] As they go on to note, maritime security officially became part of ASEAN's discussions only in the period 1997–98,[105] coinciding with the highest levels of piracy and armed robbery in the region. Despite the inclusion of 'piracy' within the expanded scope of transnational crimes addressed by the 1997 ASEAN Declaration on Transnational Crime adopted in Manila,[106] as well as the 1998 Hanoi Declaration,[107] the 1998 Hanoi Plan of Action (1999–2004) did not specifically mention piracy or maritime security.[108] It was only in the 2003 Bali Concord II, where maritime security cooperation was identified as a 'matter of common concern', that ASEAN members declared a 'willingness to share information' as part of nurturing its common values.[109]

Maritime security was also designated as one of the seven areas where political and security cooperation should be heightened, because 'maritime issues and concerns are transboundary in nature, and therefore shall be addressed regionally in [a] holistic, integrated and comprehensive manner'.[110] It was envisioned that 'maritime cooperation between and among ASEAN Member states shall contribute to the ASEAN Security

---

[101] H Tuerk, *Reflections on the Contemporary Law of the Sea* (Leiden, Martinus Nijhoff, 2012) 86.

[102] Ho, n 74 above, 316.

[103] MN Murphy, 'Piracy and UNCLOS: Does International Law Help Regional States Combat Piracy?' in Lehr, n 39 above, 167.

[104] Chalermpalanupap and Ibañez, n 90 above, 139–40.

[105] Ibid, 140.

[106] 1997 ASEAN Declaration on Transnational Crime, 20 December 1997, signed in Manila, the Philippines by the Ministers of Interior/Home Affairs and Representatives of ASEAN Member States, accessible from the National University of Singapore, Centre for International Law (NUS/CIL) documents database, at http://cil.nus.edu.sg/1997/1997-asean-declaration-on-transnational-crime-signed-on-20-december-1997-in-manila-philippines/.

[107] 1998 Hanoi Declaration (adopted on 16 December 1998 in Hanoi, Vietnam by the Heads of state and Governments of ASEAN), accessible from the NUS/CIL documents database, at http://cil.nus.edu.sg/1998/1998- hanoi- declaration/.

[108] 1998 Hanoi Plan of Action (adopted on 15 December 1998 in Hanoi, Vietnam by the Heads of state and Governments of ASEAN), accessible from the CIL documents database, at http://cil.nus.edu.sg/1998/1998-ha-noi-plan-of-action-signed-on-15-december-1998-in-ha-noi-viet-nam-by-the-heads-of-state-government/.

[109] 2003 Declaration of ASEAN Concord II (adopted on 7 October 2003 in Bali, Indonesia by the Heads of state/Governments of ASEAN), accessible from the CIL documents database, at http://cil.nus.edu.sg/2003/2003-declaration-of-asean-concord-ii-signed-on-7-october-2003-in-bali-indonesia-by-the-heads-of-stategovernment/; ASEAN Secretariat, www.aseansec.org/15159.htm.

[110] Bali Concord II, ibid, A5.

Community'.[111] It was also in this context that the ASEAN Regional Forum officially included maritime security as part of its agenda in 2003.[112] Following the 2003 Bali Concord II, subsequent ASEAN plans and programmes became more specific in addressing maritime security matters. For example, the 2004 ASEAN Security Community Plan of Action sought to promote maritime security cooperation as part of ASEAN's cooperation in non-traditional security issues.[113] This aim was reiterated in the 2004 Vientiane Action Programme (2004–2010), which further developed the idea by proposing to 'explore the establishment of an ASEAN maritime forum' and strengthen cooperation to address non-traditional security concerns.[114] More recently, Chalermpalanupap and Ibañez have noted that the primary ASEAN instrument spelling out ASEAN's plans as regards maritime security cooperation and related mechanisms for enhancing such cooperation is the 2009 ASEAN Political-Security Community Blueprint (APSC Blueprint),[115] which provides a roadmap and timetable to establish the ASEAN Political-Security Community by 2015.[116]

Apart from establishing the ASEAN Maritime Forum to apply a comprehensive approach to navigational safety, including search and rescue[117] and security concerns,[118] the key provisions of the APSC Blueprint on non-traditional maritime security cooperation involving piracy and armed robbery at sea are as follows: to strengthen cooperation, particularly in combating transnational crimes and other transboundary challenges, including forging 'closer cooperation in fighting against sea piracy, armed robbery against ships, hijacking and smuggling, in accordance with international laws'.[119] As Chalermpalanupap and Ibañez observe, as well as mandating closer cooperation to deal with transnational crimes in general, the APSC Blueprint specifically calls for the close cooperation of ASEAN Member States in fighting piracy, armed robbery against ships and hijacking in accordance with international law. It also encourages ASEAN Member States to enhance cooperation in extradition and mutual legal assistance,[120] which is crucial for the effective apprehension and prosecution of

---

[111] Ibid.

[112] Chalermpalanupap and Ibañez, n 90 above, 141, citing RC Severino, *The ASEAN Regional Forum*, 1st edn (Singapore, ISEAS Publishing, 2009).

[113] 2004 ASEAN Security Community Plan of Action, adopted on 29 November 2004 in Vientiane, Laos by the Heads of state and Governments, accessible from the ASEAN Secretariat website, at http://www.aseansec.org/16826.htm.

[114] 2004 Vientiane Action Programme 2004–2010, adopted on 29 November 2004 in Vientiane, Laos by the Heads of state and Governments, accessible from the CIL documents database, at http://cil.nus.edu.sg/2004/2004-vientiane-action-programme-2004-2010-signed-on-29-november-2004-in-vientiane-laos-by-the-heads-of-stategovernment-vap/.

[115] 2009 ASEAN Political-Security Community Blueprint, adopted on 1 March 2009 at 14th ASEAN Summit in Cha-am, Thailand, accessible from the CIL documents database, at http://cil.nus.edu.sg/2009/2009-blueprint-on-the-asean-political-security-community/.

[116] Chalermpalanupap and Ibañez, n 90 above, 142.

[117] 2010 Declaration on Cooperation in Search and Rescue of Persons and Vessel in Distress at Sea, adopted on 27 October 2010 in Hanoi, Vietnam by ASEAN Foreign Ministers, accessible from the CIL documents database, at http://cil.nus.edu.sg/2010/2010-asean-declaration-on-cooperation-in-search-and-rescue-of-persons-and-vessels-in-distress-at-sea/.

[118] The ASEAN Maritime Forum (AMF) was launched during the 1st AMF meeting in Surabaya, Indonesia in July 2010.

[119] See 2009 APSC Blueprint, n 115 above, under B.4. Non-Traditional Security Issues, B.4.1, xv.

[120] For example, through ratification of the Treaty on Mutual Legal Assistance in Criminal Matters among ASEAN Member States; see 2009 APSC Blueprint, ibid, under B.4. Non-Traditional Security Issues, B.4.1, ii.

perpetrators of serious maritime crimes, ensuring ultimately that no Member State in the region can be used as a safe haven.[121] All these institutional efforts have arguably been successful in Southeast Asia due mainly to the multiple levels of governmental engagement and joint efforts among officials from the relevant neighbouring states. As Bradford was able to observe by 2008,

> In the past few years, significant progress appears to have been made in the fight against piracy. Regional states are displaying greater-than-ever commitments to address both the causes and manifestations of the criminal phenomenon. Regional co-operation is growing and extra-regional powers that rely on trade transiting the region have expanded their contributions to the fight. This improved anti-pirate activity correlates to the reduced piracy rates revealed in the statistics documented since 2003.[122]

As we shall see below, this regional level of institutional cooperation is notably absent in the Somalia situation.

However, it is also important to note that these regional, sub-regional and even bilateral institutional initiatives have so far stopped short of actually allowing neighbouring states to exercise their criminal jurisdiction over armed robbery at sea within the maritime jurisdictions of other states. Instead, the previous discussion centred around how extra-regional, regional (focusing on ASEAN) and sub-regional efforts within Southeast Asian waters improve the utilisation of individual coastal state jurisdiction and domestic enforcement of such jurisdiction over pirates, especially by littoral states adjacent to maritime areas that are susceptible to pirate activity. Given that most pirate activity within Southeast Asian waters constitute armed robbery at sea incidents rather than high seas piracy, the legal provision for multiple enforcement jurisdiction over such activities may not be necessary in any case, unlike within the considerably more open maritime spaces off the Horn of Africa. Thus, despite the manifestly high levels of regional and sub-regional cooperation on piracy in general, Southeast Asian countries have maintained their individual autonomy to tackle such armed robbery incidents within their own waters according to their domestic legal systems.

B. International Efforts at Curbing Piracy and Robbery at Sea off the Horn of Africa

The almost total reliance on international (global and regional) efforts to address the prevention, enforcement, prosecution and even the root causes of African Horn piracy constitutes the major difference to the multi-level institutional engagement with piracy (and armed robbery at sea) incidence within the Southeast Asian region. According to the US Congressional Research Service study on piracy off the Horn of Africa,

> in the short term, the international community has primarily responded to the threat of piracy in the waters off the Horn of Africa with multinational naval patrols, diplomatic coordination, and enhanced self-protection and private security efforts by members of the commercial shipping industry. These efforts address two of the three lines of action identified in the US government's action plan to address piracy, namely, prevention and disruption of attacks. The third line of action, the prosecution of pirates, is considered by many to be

---

[121] Chalermpalanupap and Ibañez, n 90 above, 143.
[122] JF Bradford, 'Shifting the Tides against Piracy in Southeast Asian Waters' (2008) 48(3) *Asian Survey* 473, 491.

a critical step toward addressing a perception of impunity among would-be offenders and making piracy less attractive. The challenge of locating and sustaining jurisdictions willing and able to prosecute piracy suspects and imprison those convicted, however, persists, despite some regional capacity building efforts . . . By all accounts, pirates are likely to continue to find sanctuary in Somalia until basic governance and security conditions improve.[123]

More generally, there is now an explicit recognition that 'the international community cannot rely solely on its law enforcement agencies to defeat pirates, whether at sea or on land'.[124] As Klingebiel had previously observed in relation to African regional security issues generally, 'short-term, "myopic" military responses should not be allowed to obscure the fact that long-term development goals must be assigned high priority'.[125]

Thus, in order to move toward a long-term solution for Horn of Africa piracy, it should be recognised that: 'Ultimately, piracy is a problem that starts ashore and requires an international solution ashore'.[126] This raises the question of how far efforts to combat Horn of Africa piracy at sea should in fact focus on improving the humanitarian situation on land first.[127] As Oliver et al observe, '[a]lmost all pirate activity in Somalia originates from territories claimed by the self-governing region of Puntland, which stretches around the Horn of Africa from Bosaso in the north to Galkayo in central Somalia'.[128] These 'on-the-ground' facts raise pertinent issues such as: (i) the extent of the FGS's control over both Puntland and Somaliland—another autonomous region located to the west of Puntland with a coastline bordering the Gulf of Aden; and (ii) the focus of international and domestic efforts to secure law and order, restore the rule of law and establish alternative socio-economic development pathways that, inter alia, reconnect with the traditional pastoral economy of these regions, based on livestock production and maintenance.[129] Commentators on this latter issue are almost united in their recommendations. Singh and Bedi, for example, propose a shift from military to developmental responses to piracy, with an emphasis on respecting local institutions of law enforcement and governance in Somalia. Specifically, they advocate the quite radical solution of drawing down the naval counter-piracy forces currently operating off the Horn of Africa, and then utilising the financial resources thus saved towards building the capacities of locally owned and culturally acceptable law enforce-

[123] US Library of Congress, n 22 above, 42.

[124] Q-T Do et al, 'The Pirates of Somalia: Ending the Threat, Rebuilding a Nation' (Washington, DC, World Bank, April 2013), available at http://documents.worldbank.org/curated/en/2013/01/17672066/pirates-somalia-ending-threat-rebuilding-nation

[125] S Klingebiel, 'Regional Security in Africa and the Role of External Support', (2005) 17(3) *European Journal of Development Research* 446, cited in Singh and Bedi, n 51 above, 35–36.

[126] United States Navy, Commander, Combined Maritime Forces Public Affairs, 'Combined Maritime Forces Issues New Alert to Mariners', in *Piracy off the Horn of Africa*, US Library of Congress, 7 April 2009, n 22 above, 41–42.

[127] See, eg C Bueger, J Stockbruegger and S Werthes, 'Pirates, Fishermen and Peacebuilding: Options for Counter-piracy Strategy in Somalia' (2011) 32(2) *Contemporary Security Policy* 356.

[128] S Oliver, R Jablonski and J Hastings, 'The Tortuga Disease: How Maritime Piracy Undermines Economic Development', paper presented at the International Studies Association 2012 Annual Meeting, San Diego, California, USA. April 2012, available at http://ssrn.com/abstract=2233959.

[129] AA Elmi, 'Livestock Production in Somalia with Special Emphasis on Camels' (1991) 29 *Nomadic Peoples* 87, available at http://agris.fao.org/agris-search/search-do?f=1992/SE/SE92007.xml;SE9210370.

ment in Somaliland, Puntland and South-Central Somalia, on the basis that this would better prevent piracy at sea.[130]

These terrestrial-based issues of Horn of Africa piracy have also been assessed by a number of important official bodies, among them the UK Parliament House of Commons, the US Congressional Research Service and, initially, an International Expert Group convened by the UN's Special Representative of the Secretary-General (SRSG) to Somalia. The views expressed in these reports and their assessments of current international efforts, as well as their suggestions on how best to address Somali piracy issues on land in the long term, will be outlined and examined here. To begin with, the UN's SRSG issued a public statement in September 2008 addressing the fact that piracy constitutes a risk for peace and stability in Somalia. This was followed on 3 October 2008 with a meeting of the diplomatic community in Nairobi, Kenya where the SRSG launched his initiative for coordinated international response.[131] This land-based action is mainly coordinated between the UN, the Somali TFG (now FGS), the governing authorities of Somaliland and Puntland respectively, and certain large international non-governmental organisations (NGOs), such as CARE, the Danish Refugee Council and the Norwegian Refugee Council. The UN Transitional Plan (UNTP) is the framework document used by the UN as a common plan for the work of all UN agencies, funds and programmes in Somalia from 2008–09 onwards. The UNTP is in turn firmly based on objectives set out in the Reconstruction and Development Programme (RDP), the five-year national plan for Somalia (2006–11), which was produced by a Joint Needs Assessment for Somalia carried out by the UN, the World Bank and Somali partners. In summary, the RDP is built around three pillars:

1. Deepening peace, improving security and establishing good governance.
2. Investing in people through improved social services.
3. Creating an enabling environment for private sector-led growth to expand employment and reduce poverty.

The UNTP has then used these pillars as the basis for their planning and has identified five overall outcomes which are:

1. Strengthening of key federal, Somaliland and Puntland institutions.
2. Improved service delivery by local governance in selected locations.
3. Improved security and protection under the rule of law.
4. Better access to education and health.
5. Improved food security and economic opportunities (livelihoods).[132]

In the short term, the UN International Expert Group recommended that, in order to effectively curb piracy off Somalia, a minimum capability of effective law and order be established in Puntland and in the coastal areas of Somalia.[133] Moreover, the establishment of the rule of law in the whole Somalia is deemed a necessary condition for the success of a development initiative in Puntland and coastal areas. The re-establishment of state legitimacy through the rule of law must progress in parallel

---

[130] Singh and Bedi, n 51 above, 36.
[131] International Expert Group on Piracy off the Somali Coast, above n 40, 38.
[132] Ibid, 39.
[133] Ibid, 41.

with the reconstruction of the (state) security sector, as an important condition is to enable and allow the state to control its security system.[134] Ultimately, the international community goal is to uproot piracy altogether. For this to happen, the international community will have to be sure that a sustainable state is established in Somalia and that it is fully integrated into the community of nations.[135] Thus, to establish the rule of law in Somalia, the Expert Group recommended, inter alia, the following actions:

1. Support for IMO efforts to establish regional anti-piracy arrangements.
2. Strengthening the operational capacity of the regional Somali law enforcement authorities.
3. Strengthening the Puntland coastguard.
4. Developing and upgrading the capacity of the Somali prison service.
5. Incorporating piracy offences into Somali penal law.
6. Strengthening the general legal system in Somalia.[136]

However, the Expert Group noted that even if this short-term recommendation to curb piracy by establishing a minimum capability of effective law and order in Puntland and in the coastal areas of Somalia is successfully implemented, piracy will not be suppressed unless coastal populations are provided with alternative occupation and revenue. Such goals could only be reached through establishing a minimum state of law throughout Somalia, which would allow business, trade and other economic activities to flourish. The primary actors in these measures should be the regional (Somalia, Somaliland and Puntland) community.[137] Thus, this reconstruction effort must focus on the coastal areas, especially in Puntland, to prevent Puntland becoming a pirate state. According to the International Expert Group, this reconstruction effort should include the following actions:

1. Development of the fishing industry in Somalia.
2. Building up of the local infrastructure in Somalia coastal communities through the creation of labour-intensive jobs.
3. Vocational training for unemployed youth.
4. Support to youth groups.
5. Engagement with Somali diaspora for greater socio-economic benefits of Somalia.
6. Support to pastoralists in Puntland.[138]

These proposed actions can be seen as a response to the fact that, while naval counter-piracy measures off the Somali coastline have been successful of late, they have failed to change the socio-economic incentives for piracy, especially among the young adult Somali male population, raising calls for land-based approaches to replace piracy as a source of income. Shortland has gone further in her analysis of the socio-economic impacts of Somali piracy, arguing that, at least in the short-term, positive developmental effects may be felt in the immediate vicinity of pirate communities, notably

---

[134] Ibid, 43.
[135] Ibid, 43.
[136] Ibid, 43.
[137] Ibid, 42.
[138] Ibid, 43–44.

in the Puntland region at the tip of the Horn of Africa.[139] Kraska, too, notes a ripple effect from the local communities that harbour pirates through to the Somali diaspora abroad as ransom money 'percolates through the local economy'.[140] However, these relatively immediate developmental effects have been discounted by Oliver et al, who argue instead that these short-term economic gains in piracy-prone areas due to the influx of illicit wealth have negative long-term structural consequences for both the local and the global economy.[141] For example, much of the ransom money obtained from hostage-taking 'is spent on consumption or re-invested into predation, rather than into productive and sustainable economic activity'.[142]

Recognition of the socio-economic background for Somali piracy has prompted the most recent World Bank study on this issue to conclude that

> the solution to Somali piracy is first and foremost political. Pirates rely on onshore support to conduct negotiations and to secure safe access to coastal territories. In turn, politically powerful figures capture large portions of the profits associated with piracy. Any solution therefore will involve forging a political contract with local stakeholders—a shift in attention, in other words, from the perpetrators to the enablers of piracy.[143]

However, both the RDP and the UNTP have been criticised for their failure to 'engage with Somali society to provide a sense of legitimacy and local ownership of the political settlements and development projects'.[144] In submissions to the UK Parliamentary Committee, both Saferworld, an NGO that works with Somali civil society organisations, and World G18 Somalia, a UK-based diaspora group, noted the lack of trust between the local Somali communities and the international community. According to Saferworld, the lack of structured and substantive consultation with Somali civil society has created a 'trust deficit' between local, national and international actors. Furthermore, Saferworld argued that this 'impacts negatively on the effectiveness of aid programmes, undermines Somali civil society, and contributes to a sense of alienation among Somali communities from the decision-making processes that affect their lives'. More specifically, Saferworld and World G18 Somalia also criticised the UK's approach in channelling its funding through international NGOs, seeing this as a 'lack of meaningful engagement' with Somalis and the Somali diaspora.[145] In terms of what measures should be taken to improve the situation in Somalia, and thus reduce the scope for resort to piracy off its coastline, both World G18 Somalia and Saferworld mentioned the need to provide employment and development alternatives to piracy, with the fishing industry being suggested by an expert as having 'huge potential' to offer alternative employment. However, other experts were more sceptical, arguing that there was limited opportunity to develop sources of legitimate income, and that 'even if there were, the income [per capita] generated by these alternative professional activi-

---

[139] A Shortland, '"Robin Hook": The Developmental Effects of Somali Piracy', DIW Discussion Papers 1155 (2011).
[140] J Kraska, 'Freakonomics of Maritime Piracy' (2010) 16(2) *Brown Journal of World Affairs* 109, 116.
[141] Oliver et al, n 121 above.
[142] Ibid.
[143] Do et al, n 124 above.
[144] House of Commons, Foreign Affairs (Select) Committee, n 7 above, paras 136, 66.
[145] Ibid, para 138, 66.

ties would pale compared to the cash generated via piracy ransom payments', and that the solution to piracy lies in a more comprehensive 'nation [re]building process'.[146]

With a similar goal in mind, across the Atlantic, some members of the US Congress have called on the US federal government administration to develop a comprehensive approach to Somalia that responds to the threat of piracy in the context of a broader effort to stabilise the country and support transitional government institutions.[147] Several US officials have publicly supported such a holistic approach, arguing that a sustainable resolution to the threat of piracy off the Horn of Africa would require a combination of efforts to improve the security, governance, rule of law and economic opportunity in Somalia.[148] The scope for greater and better US federal government engagement with the Somali government has been improved with the recent official US recognition of the 'government of Somalia' (although, controversially, not the governmental authorities of Somaliland and Puntland) on 17 January 2013.[149] However, a more cautionary note is expressed by the UK Parliamentary Committee report, which observes as follows:

> The ongoing problems in Somalia are of such scale that no single state can hope to have a meaningful impact alone. The UK should be very wary of international claims to deliver a solution on land in Somalia. International capacity to rebuild a Somali state is extremely limited. We conclude that the UK should continue to act through the United Nations and European Union programmes to pursue peace and stability in Somalia. We urge the Government to push for a concerted international effort to capitalise on the African Union Mission in Somalia's (AMISOM) recent military gains against al-Shabab by supporting the Transitional Federal Government (TFG) in its efforts to extend its control, build the rule of law combat corruption and encourage development.[150]

In his statement to UN's International Contact Group (ICG) on Somalia, the UN's SRSG, Augustine Mahiga, has referred to both the Kampala Accord[151] and the Road Map, which, respectively, establish the means by which the four priority tasks for ending the transition—security, constitution, reconciliation and good governance—can be achieved in order that key targets on addressing Somali-based piracy can be met in the transitional period.[152] Significantly, in light of the NGO criticism of previous UN efforts at Somali reconstruction, among the principles implemented by the Road Map is that of Somali ownership of the process, in that the TFG (now the FGS) is called upon to lead the process of the implementation of the roadmap, working with the

---

[146] Para 139, 67.

[147] US Library of Congress, n 22 above, 41.

[148] Ibid, 42, citing Dr Jun Bando, Maritime Security Coordinator/US Africa Command Liaison, US Department of State Bureau of African Affairs, 'International Response to Piracy Expanded, Unified', DipNote, 30 January 2009.

[149] Remarks of US Secretary of State, Hillary Rodham Clinton, with President of Somalia, Hassan Sheikh Mohamud, after their meeting in the Treaty Room, US Department of State, Washington, DC, 17 January 2013, PRN: 2013/0040, available at http://www.state.gov/secretary/rm/2013/01/202998.htm.

[150] House of Commons, Foreign Affairs (Select) Committee, n 7 above, 65, para 132. On the EU's approach to piracy off the coast of Somalia, see R Gosalbo-Bono and S Boelaert, Chapter 5 above.

[151] Full title: Agreement between the President of the Transitional Federal Government of Somalia and the Speaker of the Transitional Federal Parliament of Somalia, Made in Kampala on 9 June 2011 (The Kampala Accord).

[152] SRSG statement on Piracy to ICG, Copenhagen, 29 September 2011, available at http://eunavfor.eu/wp-content/uploads/2011/10/SRSG-STATEMENT-ON-PIRACY-TO-Copenhagen-ICG.pdf.

Transitional Federal Parliament, regional entities and all sectors of society, including women, the business community, religious leaders, elders and youth.[153]

These international efforts are continuing on a more well-grounded basis with the re-established central government of Somalia, led by President HE Hassan Sheikh Mohamud. This is evidenced by the Six Pillar Policy instituted by the newly entitled Federal Government of the Somali Republic (also known as the Federal Republic of Somalia), which has been defined by the President in a speech delivered on his behalf to the International Organization for Migration (IOM) Council meeting in Geneva, as follows:

> My administration's goal over the next four years is to put in place the necessary mechanisms to: 1) create stability in the country; 2) speed up economic recovery, 3) build peace and remove the main drivers of conflicts; 4) vastly improve the Government's capacity to respond to the needs of its people by improving service delivery; 5) increase our international partnerships and create closer ties with our neighbours and friends of Somalia; 6) last but not least, Mr Chairman, I believe that unity at home is what will propel Somalia forward.[154]

More recently, an international conference on Somalia convened by the UK and Somali governments was described in a communiqué as occurring at a pivotal moment for Somalia, first, with its eight-year transition ending and the establishment of a new, more legitimate parliament, president and government; and secondly, as the security situation is improving, as AMISOM forces,[155] and their Ethiopian allies, recover towns and routes from Al-Shabaab.[156] More significantly for our purposes here, the communiqué also noted the following trends: '*The number of pirate attacks committed off the coast of Somalia has drastically reduced.* The famine has receded. The diaspora have begun to return. The economy is starting to revive.'[157] The conjunction between the positive domestic governance and the security trends noted in the communiqué, and the reduction of sea piracy off the Somali coast, is arguably not unconnected. This allows us to empirically confirm, albeit on the basis of only two contemporary case studies, that it is the absence of effective domestic government structures that contributes most to the propensity for pirate activity in coastal areas lying beside international shipping lanes. As Leipziger has previously noted, this conjunction between weak state institutions and the endemic incidence of piracy was also evident historically off the southern Chinese coastal region during the Qing dynasty period. More recently, when comparing Somali piracy with similar activities in the Gulf of Guinea, Biziouras has shown that increases in the enforcement capacity of states in the

---

[153] Full title: Statement on the Adoption of the Roadmap, at the (1st) Consultative Meeting on Ending the Transition in Somalia, Mogadishu, 6 September 2011. See also 'Somalia: UN-Backed Meeting Endorses Roadmap to End Transition, Restore Stability', accessible from UN New Centre, at http://www.un.org/apps/news/story.asp?NewsID=39467.

[154] HE Hassan Sheikh Mohamud, President of the Federal Republic of Somalia's Keynote address to the International Organization for Migration (IOM) at the 101st session of the Council in Geneva on 28 November 2012, available at http://www.iom.int/files/live/sites/iom/files/About-IOM/governing-bodies/en/council/101/H-E-Hassan-Sh-Mohamud-President-of-the-Somali-Republic.pdf.

[155] Under UNSC Resolution 2093, AMISOM has been authorised to continue its deployment for a further year, until 28 February 2014. See AMISOM press release, 'The African Union Welcomes the Extension of the Mandate of AMISOM by the UN Security Council', available at http://amisom-au.org/2013/03/the-african-union-welcomes-the-extension-of-the-mandate-of-amisom-by-the-un-security-council/.

[156] See Final Communique of Somalia Conference, London, 7 May 2013, available at https://www.gov.uk/government/news/somalia-conference-2013-communique.

[157] Ibid (emphasis added).

Gulf are necessary but not sufficient tools to combat the emergence, growth and institutionalisation of piracy in that region. He, too, argues that, in addition to improvements in state enforcement capacity, more generic state-building measures dealing with youth unemployment, income inequality and environmental degradation are required to reduce the incentives for individuals to join piracy organisations.[158]

V. CONCLUSIONS

The comparative analysis undertaken here between piracy off the coast of Somalia/ Horn of African/Gulf of Aden region and Southeast Asian regional waters (including the Strait of Malacca and the South China Sea) has highlighted several similarities as well as differences. Among the most significant differences are, first, the wider geographical range and scope of pirate attacks from Somalia and, secondly, the higher propensity for hostage-taking during such attacks in the Horn of Africa/Gulf of Aden region. Focusing on the latter, according to Baker, the consensus among commentators on Somali piracy is that

> the international community has to increase the rewards and decrease the risks ashore while simultaneously increasing the risks and decreasing the rewards at sea. To do this effectively means not only focusing on the pirates operating at sea but also changing the risk-reward equation for the ringleaders sitting in plush villas in Nairobi, clans providing support to pirates in the semi-autonomous Somali state of Puntland, and agents providing intelligence from African ports.[159]

The dual aspect nature of this approach—increasing rewards and reducing risks for onshore economic activities, while increasing risks and reducing rewards for offshore piracy—is imperative, especially bearing in mind the intrinsic link between these two sides of the piracy issue.

Proceeding on the basis of the insights derived from the legal and policy-oriented studies and reports covered in the above analysis, I suggest that successful legal measures for addressing piracy phenomena, whether in Southeast Asia or Somalia, or indeed anywhere else around the world today, requires the adapted application of a very well-known international law of the sea principle forming the legal basis for continental shelf/seabed jurisdiction claims in a number of cases before the ICJ, namely, the principle that the 'land dominates the sea'. Most recently, when considering the issue in dispute before it in the Romania/Ukraine maritime delimitation dispute in the Black Sea, the Court recalled two principles underpinning its jurisprudence on this issue, only the first of which is relevant for our purposes here, namely, that the 'land dominates the sea in such a way that coastal projections in the seaward direction generate maritime claims'.[160] While this adage has proved useful in establishing a basic legal principle for justifying coastal states' claims to extend their jurisdiction from their relevant coastlines over the adjacent areas of seabed and superjacent waters, it is

---

[158] N Biziouras, 'Piracy, State Capacity and Root Causes: Lessons from Somali Experience and Policy Choice in the Gulf of Guinea' (2013) 22(3) *African Security Review* 111.

[159] See Baker, n 37 above.

[160] Citing *North Sea Continental Shelf (Federal Republic of Germany/Denmark; Federal Republic of Germany/Netherlands)*, Judgment, ICJ Reports 1969, 51, para 96.

submitted here that it is equally applicable to piracy issues in terms of ensuring that international law and policy address the underlying root causes of piracy on land, rather than the multiple jurisdictional and other legal issues arising from enforcement activities against piracy incidence at sea. Thus, future legal research should not only be devoted to the jurisdictional and other enforcement-related legal issues noted above, but should also, and arguably more profitably, be directed at addressing the means by which political and legal institutions can act to turn around local communities that nurture and support piracy as a semi-legitimate business and/or personal career development choice. Moreover, it would be a mistake to presume that the rule of law can somehow be imposed or otherwise applied without due consideration of the relevant socio-economic and cultural–religious backgrounds of these local communities. Ultimately, therefore, the problem of sea piracy as a set of inter-linked legal issues should perhaps be viewed through the prism of the international law of development and also of transitional justice, rather than, strictly speaking, a problem of allocation of enforcement jurisdiction under international law.

Part III

Rethinking the Main Tenets of Counter-piracy Approaches

13

The Dark Side of Counter-piracy Policies

ACHILLES SKORDAS

I. PIRACY AS A PROBLEM OF WORLD SOCIETY

A. Purposes and Objectives of the Study

THERE IS AN invisible, dark side in counter-piracy policies. It is widely believed that the response of the international community to piracy has been well calibrated and well planned, and there are no major controversies among major powers and regional states on how to manage the related risks. The US, the EU, NATO, Russia, China, India and Iran are all in the same boat.[1] States are authorised to use force both under Chapter VII of the UN Charter, and with the consent of the Somali authorities, in order to protect the freedom of navigation, to enforce the relevant provisions of the law of the sea and to avoid the deterioration of the situation in Somalia, and law enforcement mechanisms were put in place that should guarantee the punishment of those apprehended.

In addition, the problem seems to be progressively brought under control, which could be evidence of the effectiveness of the concerted action. Since 2008, the international community has embarked on the huge effort to repress piracy off the coast of Somalia, and by 2013 it seems that it has achieved most of its goals. As the Monitoring Group for Somalia and Eritrea indicated in its 2013 report on Somalia, 'it appears that the heyday of Somali piracy may be over'.[2] A similar conclusion was reached by the latest piracy report of the International Maritime Bureau (IMB) of the International Chamber of Commerce (ICC), confirming a 'significant drop in the frequency and range of attacks by Somali pirates'.[3] All in all, counter-piracy could almost be celebrated as a success story of international coordination and cooperation, if the debacle of the US's Iraq 'mission accomplished' had not made policy-makers reluctant to declare victory in the murky post-9/11 environment.

---

[1] On the EU, see R Gosalbo-Bono and S Boelaert, Chapter 5 above; on NATO, PM Olson, Chapter 7 above; on the US, G Swiney, Chapter 8 above; on the UK, A Murdoch, Chapter 9 above; and on Germany, D König and TR Salomon, Chapter 10 above.

[2] 'Report of the Monitoring Group on Somalia and Eritrea pursuant to Security Council Resolution 2060 (2012): Somalia', S/2013/413 (12 July 2013), para 53.

[3] ICC, IMB, 'Piracy and Armed Robbery Against Ships, Report for the Period 1 January–30 June 2013' (July 2013) 22; see also 18.

The present chapter tells a different story, because it identifies a blind spot lying between policies and results, and explained by the evolutionary change in the patterns and practices of piracy in the era of world society. The chapter stands critical to the significance and impact of two main approaches followed by the international community for the repression of piracy: (i) the use of military force authorised under Chapter VII of the UN Charter, and with the consent of the Somali authorities; and (ii) law enforcement, in particular criminal prosecution of individuals suspected of involvement in piracy and related crimes, including hostage-taking. The authorisation to use force for counter-piracy purposes under Chapter VII and the focus on law enforcement appear to be the obvious avenues for the re-establishment of authority and for the implementation of the rule of law in the strategy of restoration of peace and repression of piracy. In reality, the postulated policies were neither designed nor implemented as the narrative would have anticipated.

There is also a third counter-piracy approach, consisting in the use of private maritime security companies (PMSCs) and best management practices for the defence of vessels and crews, and for the deterrence and disruption of pirate activities. The argument is that this third approach, in particular the private security at sea, which was considered as supplementary or occasionally unattractive in terms of official policies, proved to be the most effective and promising, and should be given preference, despite the legal complexities that may arise. Use of military force and law enforcement should be still used as complementary policies, but targeted to the achievement of specific policy objectives.

This chapter argues that piracy off the coast of Somalia appears to be defeated, at least for the time being, despite the failure or non-implementation of declared core policies of the international community. It contends that the use of military force has not been, and was not meant to be, a major factor in counter-piracy, and law enforcement has not been a success, to put it mildly. Reflecting on the various components of counter-piracy, the conclusion can be drawn that private security at sea has been the decisive factor contributing the most to the successful management of piracy risks.

An assessment of policy instruments at this point makes sense, because it is not clear how to proceed at a time when Somali piracy is in decline. The big question is whether the international community should put an end to the mandate of the international naval forces or should maintain a strong military presence for the indefinite future. The easy answer offered by the precautionary principle, namely that in view of risks and uncertainties it would be prudent not to demobilise, does not take into account the cost factor for the maintenance of the existing counter-piracy system in place.

B. Core Assumption and Contradictions of the Mainstream Narrative

The main counter-piracy policies of the international community are based on a core assumption underpinning the mainstream narrative: that piracy is causally linked to the situation on the land ('land dominates the sea'). Though there obviously exists a link between land and piracy, its significance has been overrated, and has led to debatable policy proposals and expectations. If the assumption were true, it would then be almost intuitive to recognise the wisdom of liberal interventionism and the primacy of the military solution for the restoration of peace. In closer view, though, reality frustrates the narrative, though this is not always discernible by policy-makers and planners.

The 2013 Report of the World Bank on the Somali piracy (the Report) is a good source for the detection of the mainstream's frame of mind. The Report considers that piracy caused a loss of US\$ 18 billion to the world economy in 2010, with a margin of error of US\$ 6 billion, amounting to a 'tax' on trade affected by piracy between 0.75 to 1.49 percentage points.[4] It draws the conclusion that it is a rational policy to devote resources to the repression and deterrence of piracy. In the same line of thought, it tries to navigate through the more complex issue of future policies in view of the decline of pirate activities:

> While offshore initiatives such as navy patrols and onboard security are believed to explain why piracy plunged in 2011 and 2012 . . . these are only effective as long as they remain in place: they would have to be permanent to prevent any resurgence of piracy. Because of their high cost, in the long run they may simply be unsustainable.[5]

In the first place, the implicit assumption that naval presence and onboard security, mainly private security, should be dealt with as two facets of a single issue is flawed. There is no reason to presume that the two policies should be treated as one—in fact, as will be seen later, there are important reasons why they should be differentiated. Secondly, the Report recognises that, because of the cost, the maintenance of a security presence 'in the long run' is unsustainable. Thirdly, the World Bank purports to offer a solution by making a 'democracy argument', and contends that it is necessary to shift the focus from the 'perpetrators' to the 'enablers' of piracy, eg from the pirates themselves to the 'diffuse group of individuals and communities whose interactions with one another go well beyond the realm of piracy'. If negotiation with this group is part of the process of normalisation, and if the prerequisite for the negotiation is the legitimate representation of the affected communities, then, according to the World Bank, 'the long-term solution to piracy off the Horn of Africa cannot be dissociated from construction of a Somali state that is viable at both central and local levels'.[6] Not many would disagree with this conclusion, even though, if scrutinised, it appears as being no more than a platitude: the Report fails to explain how the objective of reconstruction of a democratic Somali state as 'the' solution to piracy is anything other than a recipe for the maintenance of the counter-piracy 'alert' for an indefinite time, considering the successive failures to establish a viable Somali statehood since the early 1990s.

Indeed, though there is clearly a linkage between land and piracy, the Report is here trapped in the thinking of territoriality, and overrates the relevance of the 'land factor' for the choice of the appropriate counter-piracy policies. On this point, the World Bank does not draw the necessary conclusions from the nature of Somali piracy as a transnational activity involving cooperation between sophisticated networks in Somalia and in the metropolitan centres of world society, in particular in London, which was

---

[4] World Bank, 'The Pirates of Somalia: Ending the Threat, Rebuilding a Nation' (2013) 15.
[5] Ibid, xxv.
[6] Ibid, xxv and ch 10.

characterised as the 'capital' of Somali pirates' intelligence.[7] Though the Report offers an excellent analysis of the various factors that build the system of Somali piracy and provides ample evidence of its transnational dynamics, the ultimate conclusion that apparently represents the consensus of the international community can be criticised as falling short of the complexity of the reality it describes.

There are at least three reasons that highlight the shortcomings of the mainstream approach. First, the question of how to deal with the increasing cost of counter-piracy measures in the long-term cannot be framed in terms of generally maintaining or phasing out naval presence and onboard private security. A rational policy should differentiate depending on who pays for the repression and deterrence of piracy—the states involved, or the beneficiaries of the affected activities, eg private business and the consumer. It may be unjustified to externalise the cost of preventive and open-ended counter-piracy operations and missions to the taxpayer, but it can be acceptable or even advisable to internalise the cost of security to the maritime business, to the insurer, and to the end-user of the related goods and services.

Secondly, a relatively recent phenomenon, the 'diversification' of pirate interests via the so-called 'spoiler networks', shows that piracy may be effectively repressed before the completion of state-building if the pirate groups consider it to be no longer profitable. The Monitoring Group describes how, in view of the decline of the fortunes of piracy, pirate groups are already turning to other forms of transnational crime in which they have engaged in the past, including the provision of armed guards to illegal fishing vessels from Iran and Yemen, and involvement in other forms of illegal investment and possibly the arms trade, in cooperation with individuals in Oman, Yemen and Kenya.[8] Such activities may be undesirable and further destabilise Somalia and the region, but they are not piracy. Piracy effectively ends even if, or because, such networks shift their activities to other areas of domestic or transnational crime, build alternative criminal infrastructures and, as a result, cease obstructing international navigation. These new activities can be dealt then within the framework of restoration of peace and the re-establishment of the rule of law in Somalia.

Thirdly, the implicit conclusion that mobilisation could still be necessary as long as networks may shift their activities away from or back to piracy raises a different set of questions: first, whether there is some evidence for the contention that piracy patterns can reoccur once the activities of the criminal groups have shifted to other areas, and secondly, if this is confirmed, whether the continuation of the current levels of mobilisation at sea is necessary if the problem is reduced in scale and quality. After all, it is not plausibly explained why some reduced level of criminal activities at sea should be a matter of collective security in the Horn of Africa but not in Southeast Asia, where piracy is endemic.[9] The potential argument that collective security replaces for now—and for the foreseeable future—the missing state authority in Somalia is

---

[7] G Tremlett, 'This is London—the Capital of Somali Pirates' Secret Intelligence Operation', *The Guardian*, 11 May 2009, available at http://www.theguardian.com/world/2009/may/11/somalia-pirates-network (last accessed on 26 September 2013); see also Reuters, 'Somali Pirates Using London Contacts: Report' (11 May 2009), available at http://www.reuters.com/article/2009/05/11/us-spain-pirates-idUSTRE54A4GF20090511 (last accessed on 26 September 2013).

[8] Report of the Monitoring Group, S/2013/413, above n 2, paras 63–64, and Annex 3.1.

[9] *Cf* DM Ong, Chapter 12 above.

not convincing, because the main issue is whether it is necessary to 'eradicate' piracy, as some acts and declarations indicate, or whether it is sufficient to reduce piracy and armed robbery to the level of an organised crime that causes some concern to maritime commerce but can be managed without disproportionate efforts, cost and risks.

In discussing the counter-piracy policy, the current chapter does not have the ambition to offer a policy blueprint, but has set itself the objective of reflecting on the suitability, intrinsic rationale, coherence and effectiveness of the main policy instruments in the sense of 'legal policy'. The diagnosis of the causal chains between policies and results, and the evaluation of the contribution of each instrument, are primordial for designing future policies and for committing resources to counter-piracy operations. From the perspective of legal policy, it is important to discuss the risks of alternative legal instruments, explore their chances of success and failure, and prioritise and integrate them into a coherent policy scheme. Further, Somali piracy should be viewed as a phenomenon of world society, where land is a factor though not the decisive one, at least for reasons of policy. It should be assumed that piracy can be defeated by preventing or making it unprofitable with practical measures or 'smart' responses.

II. MILITARY FORCE IN COUNTER-PIRACY OPERATIONS

This section will discuss whether the use of military force has been a significant normative and factual element in the fight against piracy and armed robbery at sea. Assuming that, under the conditions of Somalia as a failed state, counter-piracy operations would potentially threaten or violate, at least prima facie, the territorial integrity or political independence of the country, policy-makers on national, regional and international levels can be expected to design their policies taking into account the principle of prohibition of the use of force (Article 2, pararaph 4 UN Charter), and the relevant exceptions. Moreover, it is to be examined whether the presence and activities of the international naval forces, as provided for in the respective UN Security Council resolutions, have constituted a significant factor in reaching the objectives set for them by the international community at a reasonable cost, including the opportunity cost: as military resources are finite, the issue of alternative uses should also be considered.

In terms of the relationship between normativity and policy, it is not sufficient that the Security Council formally implements Chapter VII of the UN Charter, but it is necessary to further explore whether the state addressees were granted legal authority that they would not otherwise have; in addition, it is worth reflecting whether and under what circumstances alternative legal bases of international law, in particular the consent of Somalia or self-defence (Article 51 UN Chapter), have played a role in providing ancillary bases of legality to counter-piracy operations. Thus, it has to be assessed whether the law of force is an autonomous factor in counter-piracy policy or whether the application of the respective rules and exceptions in addition to the rules of the law of the sea merely facilitates coordination among states and strengthens consensus on the level of the 'political' without influencing the implementation of policies *qua* normativity.

As far as counter-piracy operations are considered as law enforcement action,[10] it has been argued that they lie outside of the scope of the prohibition of the use of force.[11] The question of which operations should be properly characterised as law enforcement and which should be qualified as use of military force[12] does not need to be addressed in detail in the context of the present 'law and policy' analysis. Suffice it to note that, even if some of the measures for the repression of piracy are law enforcement measures,[13] at least the entry and presence of powerful international navies in the territorial sea of Somalia in a state of alert and with the preparedness to use force, the potential engagement with well-armed pirate groups, and the use of force on Somali land territory for the rescue of hostages or by air for the destruction of pirate infrastructure should be considered as use of military force and fall prima facie within the scope of the prohibition of threat or use of force.

Less intrusive measures of law enforcement could be exempted, under the above approach, from the scope of Article 2, paragraph 4 UN Charter, if they are reasonable and necessary; alternatively, if they are considered to fall within the scope of the above principle, their compatibility with the law of force is to be assessed on the basis of consent,[14] or on the basis of the other exceptions provided for by the Charter and by customary international law. Policy-makers interested in acting within the framework of international legality are expected to plan their activities in a way that fulfils at least the customary standards of reasonableness, necessity and proportionality, whereby the criterion of necessity should be covered by a UN Security Council resolution under Chapter VII.[15]

A. International Law of Force as Autonomous Normative Factor

1. *The Implementation of Chapter VII*

Since 2008, the UN Security Council has adopted Chapter VII resolutions in view of authorising the use of force against piracy in the sea, as well as on land. The Security Council activated Chapter VII in order to facilitate counter-piracy operations within

---

[10] On this point, Major General Howes stated that 'we are engaged in a constabulary task, and that is the fundamental guiding principle that constrains what we can do. So force can only be applied in self-defence and in a wholly proportionate and minimal fashion', House of Commons—Foreign Affairs Committee, Piracy off the Coast of Somalia, Tenth Report of Session 2010–12, HC 1318 (January 2012), Ev 14, response to Q85.

[11] See generally O Corten, *The Law against War—The Prohibition on the Use of Force in Contemporary International Law* (Oxford, Hart Publishers, 2010) 52–66. With regard to the law of the sea, see also PJ Kwast, 'Maritime Law Enforcement and the Use of Force: Reflections on the Categorization of Forcible Action at Sea in the Light of the *Guyana/Suriname* Award' (2008) 13 *Journal of Conflict and Security Law* 49.

[12] From the case law, see *Fisheries Jurisdiction Case (Spain v Canada)*, Judgment, ICJ Reports 1998, 432; ITLOS, *The M/V 'Saiga' (No 2) case (Saint Vincent and the Grenadines v Guinea)*, Judgment of 1 July 1999, paras 153–59; Arbitral Tribunal, *Guyana and Suriname*, Award of 17 September 2007, paras 425–47.

[13] See the Djibouti Code of Conduct, in IMO C 102/14, 3 April 2009, Attachment 1, Resolution 1, Annex, Art 4, para 3.

[14] See, eg D Guilfoyle, 'Interdicting Vessels to Enforce the Common Interest: Maritime Countermeasures and the Use of Force' (2007) 56 *International & Comparative Law Quarterly* 69, 81.

[15] On law enforcement and use of force, see Proelss, Chapter 3 above.

the territorial sea of Somalia and on land, as such operations might violate the prohibition of the use force (Article 2, paragraph 4 UN Charter). In Resolution 1816/2008, the Council authorised states cooperating with the Transitional Federal Government (TFG) to 'enter the territorial waters of Somalia for the purpose of repressing acts of piracy and armed robbery at sea', and to 'use, within the territorial waters of Somalia, in a manner consistent with action permitted on the high seas with respect to piracy under relevant international law, all necessary means to repress acts of piracy and armed robbery'. The authorisation was adopted with the consent of the TFG, was valid for six months,[16] and was renewed for another 12 months by Resolution 1846/2008.[17] Soon after, Resolution 1851/2008 extended the scope of the authorisation on land and in the airspace, by enabling cooperating states to 'undertake all necessary measures that are appropriate in Somalia, for the purpose of suppressing acts of piracy and armed robbery at sea, pursuant to the request of the TFG' for a period of 12 months from the date of adoption of Resolution 1846/2008.[18] These authorisations were consolidated by Resolution 1897/2009,[19] and have been renewed by subsequent resolutions.[20]

Chapter VII resolutions determine the existence of a threat to the peace, and include measures for the restoration of peace. The latter are expected to be tailored to the specific features of the former: the measures for the restoration of peace should focus on the source of the threat and establish a process through which the regional system regains its stability. Thus, it is the existence of the threat that establishes the competence of the Council to authorise the use of force under Articles 42 and 53 UN Charter with the legal effects of Article 103 UN Charter, according to which 'in the event of a conflict between the obligations of the Members of the United Nations under the present Charter and their obligations under any other international agreement, their obligations under the present Charter shall prevail'. It is held that only authorisations that constitute a real delegation of Security Council powers and have the purpose, for instance, to suppress a threat to the peace, can deploy the effect of Article 103, so that states do not incur responsibility for the violation of international law.[21] In the absence of a clear determination of a threat to the peace under Article 39 UN Charter, the measures adopted by the Council, including an authorisation for recourse to force, belong to the category of recommendations that do not relieve state addressees from international responsibility.

A careful reading of the counter-piracy resolutions reveals that the Council did not determine that piracy constituted a threat to the peace. The Council expressed its grave concern for 'the threat that acts of piracy and armed robbery against vessels

---

[16] UNSC Resolution 1816/2008, operative paras 7(a) and (b), 9.

[17] UNSC Resolution 1846/2008, operative paras 10–11.

[18] UNSC Resolution 1851/2008, operative para 6. According to the preamble of this resolution, the Somali President requested the international community to assist the TFG 'in taking all necessary measures to interdict those who use Somali territory and airspace to plan, facilitate or undertake acts of piracy and armed robbery at sea' (para 6).

[19] UNSC Resolution 1897/2009, operative para 7.

[20] Last renewed by UNSC Resolution 2125/2013, operative para 12.

[21] See R Kolb, 'Does Article 103 of the Charter of the United Nations Apply only to Decisions or also to Authorizations Adopted by the Security Council?' (2004) 64 *Zeitschrift für ausländisches öffentliches Recht und Völkerrecht* 21. Cf D Sarooshi, *The United Nations and the Development of Collective Security* (Oxford, Oxford University Press, 1999) 151.

pose to the prompt, safe and effective delivery of humanitarian aid to Somalia, the safety of commercial maritime routes and to international navigation' and determined 'that the incidents of piracy and armed robbery against vessels in the territorial waters of Somalia and the high seas off the coast of Somalia exacerbate the situation in Somalia which continues to constitute a threat to international peace and security in the region'.[22]

The resolutions therefore distinguish between the threat to international navigation and the exacerbation of the situation in Somalia, which continues to constitute a threat to the peace. The threat to international navigation is not directly related to Somalia, apart from the escort of the World Food Program (WFP) vessels delivering humanitarian aid, and the Council has avoided determining that the threat to navigation is indeed a 'threat to the peace' in the technical sense. The determination that piracy exacerbates the situation in Somalia is also not a threat to the peace in the sense of Chapter VII, and this means that the policy instruments available for the restoration of peace in Somalia are applicable to piracy only as far as the related activities are an integral part of the threat to the peace in Somalia—for instance, with regard to the arms embargo; on the contrary, the authorisation for the use of force granted by the Security Council to the African Union Mission in Somalia (AMISOM) is not, at least prima facie, applicable to the repression of piracy.[23] The distinction between the resolutions on the threat to the peace in Somalia, as initiated by the UNSC Resolution 733/1992, and the counter-piracy resolutions that followed the adoption of UNSC Resolution 1816/2008[24] offer another indication that piracy is not conceived by the Council as fully integrated in the threat to the peace in Somalia, but as a relatively autonomous disruptive factor not reaching *eo ipso* the threshold of the threat to the peace.

In the absence of a determination of a threat to the peace, the authorisations for the use of force cannot constitute delegation of authority, and necessarily take the form of recommendations deprived of the legal effect of Article 103 UN Charter. Therefore, states cooperating with the TFG or its successor, the Federal Government of Somalia (FGS), are not authorised to take measures, apart from those permitted in principle by the law of the sea, though the resolutions closed some jurisdictional gaps and extended the application of the rules on piracy to armed robbery at sea.[25] Therefore, Chapter VII is not a significant factor in counter-piracy operations, because it does not broaden the range of measures that states can take consistently with the law of force in the absence of an authorisation. Moreover, it does not offer an unequivocal legal justification for the entry of international naval forces into the territorial waters of Somalia, which constitutes a violation of that country's territorial integrity, or for

---

[22] UNSC Resolution 1816/2008, first and penultimate paras of the preamble; see also the similar formulations of the preamble of the other counter-piracy resolutions, inter alia, UNSC Resolutions 1846/2008, 1851/2008 and 2077/2012.

[23] See, eg UNSC Resolution 2093/2013, which does not make any reference to the counter-piracy resolutions in its preamble.

[24] *Cf*, however, operative para 11 of UNSC Resolution 1814/2008, calling upon states 'to take action to protect shipping involved with the transportation and delivery of humanitarian aid to Somalia', but without mentioning piracy by name.

[25] See Proelss, Chapter 3 above; R Churchill, Chapter 1 above; R Geiß and A Petrig, *Piracy and Armed Robbery at Sea* (Oxford, Oxford University Press, 2011) 70–87.

military action in the territorial sea or on land, whether for the destruction of pirate infrastructure[26] or for the rescue of hostages and the arrest of pirates.[27]

2. Consent of the Somali Authorities

The international law of force can nevertheless be a normative factor in counter-piracy if counter-piracy operations in the territorial sea, land and airspace of Somalia are covered by the consent of the Somali authorities. The Security Council resolutions have also stressed the role and importance of consent, by clearly indicating that collective action was undertaken upon the invitation of the TFG.[28] As intervention by invitation is a valid exception to the prohibition of the use of force,[29] it is arguable that, as long as the international naval forces have the consent of the Somali government for specific instances of use of force, which can be also signified by the absence of objection,[30] the international law of force can indeed facilitate the planning and conduct of counter-piracy operations, even if the role of the Security Council is normatively less pivotal than generally assumed.

Here, again, the situation is more complex than assumed, because the granting of consent presupposes the existence of authorities acting as a 'government' with the capacity to express the will of the state. It should be therefore examined whether the TFG/FGS can be considered as the government of Somalia. In the UK practice, the relevant criteria include the constitutionality of the government, the degree, nature and stability of administrative control, the existence of 'dealings' between the authorities in question and the British government, and, marginally, the extent of international recognition.[31] It is difficult to conclude that the TFG, which was replaced by the FGS in August 2012, fulfilled these criteria. The Monitoring Group for Somalia and Eritrea has questioned the effectiveness and constitutional and democratic legitimacy of the TFG and of all previous administrations since 1991, and has provided ample evidence for the mismanagement and misappropriation of state funds, endemic corruption, and the looting and theft of national wealth by the officials of the above bodies and the elites that supported them.[32]

Following the Libyan crisis, there appears to be a change in the practice of recognition, as reflected in the treatment of the National Transitional Council and in the case *British Arab Commercial Bank PLC and the National Transitional Council of*

---

[26] On the relevant action of the EU NAVFOR, see EU NAVFOR press release, 'EU Naval Force Delivers Blow against Somali Pirates on Shoreline' (15 May 2012), available at http://eunavfor.eu/eu-naval-force-delivers-blow-against-somali-pirates-on-shoreline/ (last accessed on 18 October 2013).

[27] *Cf* the French action that was carried out on Somali territory before the Security Council had adopted the counter-piracy resolutions, D Guilfoyle, 'Piracy off Somalia: UN Security Council Resolution 1816 and IMO Regional Counter-piracy Efforts' (2008) 57 *International & Comparative Law Quarterly* 690, 692.

[28] See Section II.A.1 above.

[29] See generally G Nolte, *Eingreifen auf Einladung* (Berlin, Springer, 1999).

[30] See also *Armed Activities on the Territory of the Congo (DR Congo v Uganda)*, Judgment, ICJ Reports 2005, 168, para 46.

[31] [1993] QB 54, 68; see also *Sierra Leone Telecommunications C Ltd v Baclays Bank plc* [1998] 2 All ER 821.

[32] See, eg 'Report of the Monitoring Group on Somalia and Eritrea pursuant to Security Council Resolution 2002 (2011)', S/2012/544 (13 July 2012), para 15, Annex 1.1, para 34; 'Report of the Secretary-General on the Situation in Somalia', S/2008/709 (17 November 2008), para 24; Report of the Monitoring Group, S/2013/413, above n 2, Annex 5.2, para 1.

the State of Libya,[33] that may facilitate the recognition of the FGS as a government[34] despite the doubts that were expressed on whether such practice is consistent with international law.[35] The US, which had recognised the TFG not as the government of Somalia but as the 'governing body in Somalia',[36] ultimately recognised the FGS as the government as late as January 2013.[37]

Even if the FGS is considered as the government of Somalia in the sense of international law, this does not by itself affect the legality of the use of force that has already taken place with the 'consent' of the previous administrations that did not have governmental capacity. This is additional evidence of the limited role of the international law of force in the counter-piracy operations conducted off the Somali coast or in Somalia proper. In fact, the members of the UN Security Council were unwilling to directly determine that piracy was a threat to the peace, and they sought an additional basis of legitimacy for their action in the consent of the local authorities that were the 'interlocutors' of the UN but not the government of Somalia. Adding two shaky legal grounds for intervention does not generate legality, though it does provide some degree of legitimacy for the exercise of hegemonic authority and evidence for the limited relevance of the international law of force under the circumstances of Somali piracy.

3. Self-defence (Article 51 UN Charter)

According to the jurisprudence of the ICJ, the right of self-defence can be exercised 'in case of an armed attack by one state against another state'.[38] It is therefore improbable that a situation might emerge under which the right of self-defence, as provided for by the UN Charter and customary international law, could play a role in counter-piracy operations. Self-defence in the international law of force should be clearly distinguished from the right of self-defence as recognised by the domestic legal orders, and can be invoked when the crew, private maritime security guards or vessel protection detachments use force in the case of an attack against the vessel.[39] The invocation of the right of self-defence under Article 51 UN Charter can be a difficult theoretical exercise, even under the assumption that self-defence can be used against violent non state actors, such as terrorists. The reason is that pirate groups do not have the degree

---

[33] [2011] EWHC 2274 (Comm).

[34] See, however, the critique of the latest report of the Monitoring Group to the FGS with regard to public finances and corruption, S/2013/413, paras 70–79, 23–25.

[35] P Capps, 'British Policy on the Recognition of Governments' [2014] *Public Law* (forthcoming). It should be noted that such reservations should not affect the legitimacy of the related institution of 'premature recognition' of states for the advancement of the objectives of the international community. On that institution see generally S Oeter, 'Selbstbestimmungsrecht im Wandel' (1992) 52 *Zeitschrift für ausländisches öffentliches Recht und Völkerrecht* 741.

[36] US Supreme Court, *Samantar v Yousuf*, No 08-1555, 1 June 2010, 3, note 3.

[37] See remarks of Secretary of State Hillary Clinton with President of Somalia Hassan Sheikh Mohamud, 17 January 2013, available at http://www.state.gov/secretary/rm/2013/01/202998.htm; see also remarks of Assistant Secretary Johnnie Carson on the visit of the Somali President, 16 January 2013, available at http://www.state.gov/p/af/rls/rm/2013/202926.htm.

[38] *Legal Consequences of the Construction of a Wall in the Occupied Palestinian Territory*, Advisory Opinion, ICJ Reports 2004, 136.

[39] See below under IV.

of organisation, structure and capability required for violence reaching the threshold of an armed attack, or for the conduct of hostilities over a protracted period of time.[40]

Under the mainstream approach and as adopted by the ICJ, self-defence can be exercised against violent non-state actors if their acts can be attributed to a state.[41] There are some possible constructions under which pirates could either be considered as acting on behalf of Somalia[42] or as exercising elements of governmental authority in the absence or default of official authorities;[43] for instance, when there is collusion of pirate groups with the local authorities in Puntland,[44] or when pirates argue that they act as a Somali 'coastguard' in defence of the food resources of Somalia against illegal, unreported and unregulated (IUU) fishing, or against the dumping of hazardous waste by foreign vessels.[45] However, the opaque links and dealings of pirate groups with local administrations can be better explained as forms of criminal activity rather than as acts of a state in the sense of international law, whilst the claims regarding IUU and dumping of waste are elements of a stereotypical 'post-colonial' narrative dismissed by the UN Secretary-General, the Security Council and the World Bank as baseless.[46]

Self-justifications by pirates could be used by third states to validate the use of force as self-defence; however, this has not happened because such reasoning would lack any legitimating effect, and would discredit those invoking it. Self-defence under the Charter has not played any meaningful part in counter-piracy operations and policies.

4. Conclusion

The law of force does not appear to be a major factor in counter-piracy operations because, under the circumstances, its rules are formally applicable but lack the capacity to steer the conduct of the intervening powers. The application of Chapter VII despite the absence of a determination of a threat to the peace, the recommendatory nature of the pertinent resolutions, the lack of a Somali government capable of conveying the valid consent of the state and the irrelevance of self-defence in the meaning of the UN Charter define an area of indeterminacy, where the rules on force cease to be operational. This is the result of the unwillingness of the Security Council to authorise the systematic use of 'hard' military force for the restoration of peace and security in Somalia in view of repressing piracy, and of its decision to encourage the use of

---

[40] See the contributions of T Marauhn, Chapter 4 above; Proelss, Chapter 3 above; *cf*, however, E Kontorovich, '"A Guantánamo on the Sea": The Difficulty in Prosecuting Pirates and Terrorists' (2010) 98 *California Law Review* 243, 259–62, discussing the question of whether pirates are 'combatants'.

[41] See generally C Gray, *International Law and the Use of Force*, 3rd edn (Oxford, Oxford University Press, 2008) 128–40.

[42] Art 8 of the ILC Articles on the Responsibility of States for Internationally Wrongful Acts (ARSIWA), A/RES/56/83 (28 January 2002), Annex.

[43] Ibid, Art 9 ARSIWA.

[44] See, eg J Lunn, 'Does Somali Piracy Have Any "Developmental Effects"?', House of Commons Standard Note SN06238 (28 February 2012); A Shortland, 'Treasure Mapped: Using Satellite Imagery to Track the Developmental Effects of Somali Piracy', Africa Programme Paper AFP PP 2012/01 (Chatham House, January 2012).

[45] C Bueger, 'Practice, Pirates and Coast Guards: The Grand Narrative of Somali Piracy' (2013) 34(10) *Third World Quarterly* 1811.

[46] On this latter issue see UNSC Resolution 2077/2012, operative para 28; 'Report of the Secretary-General on the Protection of Somali Natural Resources and Waters', S/2011/661 (15 October 2011), paras 38–48; 'Report of the Secretary-General Pursuant to Security Council Resolution 2020 (2011)', S/2012/783 (22 October 2012), paras 63–68; World Bank, n 4 above, 57–63.

large naval forces but permit only recourse to 'soft' military power for safeguarding the freedom of navigation. The policy implications of the imperfect implementation of Chapter VII do not need to be necessarily seen in a negative light. The Security Council avoided the militarisation of the sea, intending counter-piracy operations to affect the freedoms of navigation and maritime communication as little as possible. The use of hard military power at sea would threaten the very freedoms that the international community is expected to safeguard.

To achieve the double goal of counter-piracy and the safeguarding of maritime communication, the Security Council tolerates the potential violations of the principle of prohibition of the threat or use of force by making sure that formal, but legally 'empty', resolutions are adopted and are legitimised by the 'consent' of a Somali governing body, acting in partnership with the international community, even if it does not have the capacity to be the government of the state in terms of international law. Nonetheless, from the overall context of counter-piracy efforts and the international consensus, the use of force can be routinely expected to be both 'necessary' and 'reasonable', and it is obviously proportionate, due to the inherent limitations of the counter-piracy mission. It is a normative paradox that the Security Council legitimises the Somali authorities in Mogadishu, which, in turn, legitimise the resolutions of the Council on the use of force. As a consequence, a grey area of normativity is formed where legality is not secured but objection is not expected.

B. Military Force as a Factual Element and the Question of Cost

If the law of force is not a significant factor, the next question is whether the use of force itself is an important factual element in the efforts to restore peace off the coast of, and in, Somalia, in particular if the question of costs and benefits is taken into account. The question here is not whether the international naval forces have succeeded in implementing the military dimension of their mandate, because it was never put into doubt that they could prevail over the pirates in any asymmetrical encounter. They question is rather to establish a relationship between the cost of the mission and the expected benefits, and to assess whether the contribution of the military has been indispensible and cost-effective.

Both the 2013 report of the Monitoring Group and the ICC IMB piracy report of January–June 2013 make positive references to the necessity and effectiveness of the international naval presence, as well as to the contribution of private maritime security companies. The Monitoring Group stated the following:

> During 2012, the number of successful attacks by Somali pirates continued to decline, with 14 registered hijackings. This trend, already apparent in 2011, can largely be attributed to the increasing use of private maritime security companies on board merchant vessels and the ability of international naval forces to contain the operational environment.[47]

The ICC IMB report is more detailed in explaining a similar assessment:

> IMB attributes this significant drop in the frequency and range of attacks by Somali pirates to actions by international navies, as well as preventive measures by merchant vessels, including

---

[47] Report of the Monitoring Group, S/2013/413, above n 2, para 53.

the deployment of privately contracted armed security personnel. The navies continue to play a vital role in ensuring this threat is kept under control. The two vessels hijacked were recovered by naval action before the pirates could take them to Somalia. Only the navies can take such remedial action after a hijack.[48]

The presence and action of international naval forces have indeed contributed to the fight for the repression of piracy. The question is how, in what context and at what cost. The IMB report offers two reasons for the significance and necessity of military action: the remedial action of the naval forces and the containment of the operational environment. However, both reasons appear somehow questionable. If preventive action by private security at sea could be expanded, remedial action might become redundant to a large degree. Containment of the operational environment can be a more important argument, though it depends on the precise meaning given to these terms. According to a 2011 report by the UN Secretary General, as pirates operated on the high seas at distances up to 1750 nautical miles covering about 2.8 million square miles, 'the geographical spread of pirate activities . . . put increased strain on scarce naval forces'.[49] Thus, the justification for the necessity of sustained military presence on the above grounds is rather shaky.

Furthermore, the effectiveness of naval action should be measured in the light of the achievement of broader objectives. In the case of counter-piracy, it is arguable that there are no 'broader objectives', because the UNSC decided to separate the threat of piracy from the threat to the peace in Somalia. Despite the conceptual and policy-related distinction between the '733/1992' resolutions on the threat to the peace in Somalia and the '1816/2008' resolutions on piracy, there is one exceptional issue where the differentiation is lifted and the threat of piracy is integrated into the threat to the peace in Somalia: this issue is relevant to the humanitarian crisis and humanitarian aid, whereby pirate activities against WFP vessels directly threaten the provision of humanitarian aid and therefore constitute a threat to the peace in Somalia. One of the justifications for the implementation of Chapter VII with regard to piracy was the need to secure the 'prompt, safe and effective delivery of humanitarian aid to Somalia' by protecting WFP vessels.[50] Escorting WFP humanitarian shipments for the achievement of the above objectives has been one of the main elements of the European Union Naval Force Somalia (EU NAVFOR)[51] and NATO[52] mandates.

Here the principle that 'land dominates the sea' is fully applicable, in the sense that the assessment of the success of the action at sea is subordinate to the achievement of safe and effective delivery of humanitarian aid to the Somali population. Therefore, the effectiveness and necessity of naval escort action has to be measured taking into account the broader context of restoration of peace in Somalia. The naval mission cannot be considered as 'effective' merely because the vessels reached their harbour of

---

[48] ICC IMB, above n 3, 22.

[49] 'Report of the Secretary-General Pursuant to Security Council Resolution 1950 (2010)', S/2011/662 (25 October 2011) para 7; on the correspondence between distance and square miles, see Report of the Secretary-General, S/2012/50 (20 January 2012), para 9.

[50] UNSC Resolution 1816/2008, paras 2 and 8 of the preamble; UNSC Resolution 1838/2008, which is devoted to this aspect of the crisis; see also recently UNSC 2077/2012, para 2 of the preamble.

[51] Art 2(a) Council Joint Action 2008/851/CFSP of 10 November 2008, L 301/33, 12 November 2008, as amended by Art 1(2)(a) Council Decision 2012/174, 23 March 2012, L89/69, 27 March 2012.

[52] http://www.nato.int/cps/en/natolive/topics_48815.htm? (last accessed on 1 October 2013).

destination safely, but only if the objective of 'effective delivery' has been secured. The cost of maintaining strong naval forces responsible for the fulfilment of this mandate cannot be justified unless the conditions that permit humanitarian aid to reach the recipients exist and there is an effective system in place in Somalia that can safeguard the delivery. If these conditions are not fulfilled, escorting vessels of a specific category is the wrong allocation of resources.

This is indeed what happens in Somalia. The system of delivery of humanitarian aid is dysfunctional, due in particular to the diversion and misappropriation of funds, as the reports of the Monitoring Group demonstrate.[53] In the first place, international aid resources are diverted to Al-Shabaab and 'taxes' are paid to the terrorist group by the humanitarian agencies involved in aid distribution. Indeed, such taxes are paid by the beneficiaries of the humanitarian assistance to the terrorist group with the full knowledge of the donors, as well as of local and international agencies, whilst many agencies 'admit off the record to having reimbursed their national staff when they did, or to having actually increased national salaries to make up for the taxes imposed on them by Al-Shabaab authorities'.[54] Secondly, other networks of groups and individuals ('gatekeepers') exploit vulnerable populations in the areas controlled by the TFG, by stealing and diverting aid.[55] Thirdly, the Monitoring Group has sharply criticised not only the acquiescence of the agencies to such practices, but also the lack of accountability of, and the fraud by, the staff and partners of the UN agencies and NGOs. The Monitoring Group has exercised a scathing critique of the humanitarian agencies and civil society organisations involved for being more interested in maintaining access to funding than providing the expected assistance to those in need.[56]

The deep systemic problems in the provision of humanitarian services and aid

---

[53] On the problems of delivery of humanitarian assistance, see Report of the Monitoring Group, S/2013/413, above n 2, paras 117–128 and Annex 7.2; see also Report of the Monitoring Group, S/2012/544, above n 32, paras 79–92, and Annex 6.

[54] Report of the Monitoring Group, S/2013/413, ibid, Annex 7.2, para 3, 364.

[55] Ibid, Annex 7.2, paras 4–10.

[56] 'The subject of gatekeepers is a sensitive one amongst the international humanitarian community as agencies are often reluctant to confront protection and accountability issues for fear of losing access or funding. While some agencies respond by conducting thorough assessments involving local authorities and establishing stringent monitoring of their programmes, others continue to deal with gatekeepers without realising or questioning their modus operandi. Security concerns associated with gatekeepers have all too often justified the degree of diversion and exploitation in Somalia. In the words of a senior humanitarian official: 'The narrative of many agencies has nothing to do with the reality, where non-delivery and sub-standard programmes are the rule, not the exception' Report of the Monitoring Group, S/2013/413, above n 2, Annex 7.2, para 7, 365–66. 'Although such cases are often documented and known to humanitarian agencies, they sometimes ignore them due to preoccupations with spending existing funds and securing future grants rather than ensuring accountability either to donors or beneficiaries. In the absence of common operating standards or even informal agreements amongst the aid community on addressing gatekeepers, agencies willing to adopt a principled approach feel they are taking the major risks without any benefits. Indeed, while donors have stressed the need for increased transparency and accountability, they have not supported or promoted principled actors or provided many incentives for agencies to systematically tackle the problems of diversion', ibid, para 9, 366. 'Ground observations and greater third party monitoring have often revealed shocking truths about the lack of implementation and low quality of programmes. According to a senior UN official, 'the disconnect between the rhetoric of some UN agencies and NGOs and what has actually been happening at local level is enormous', ibid, para 11, 367. 'Furthermore, since the terms of contracts vary greatly across agencies, many contractors are not required to provide information on their partners or subcontractors, creating a major loophole in the risk management system and undermining its ability to monitor the supply chain of implementation, a sensitive issue that had been a main rationale for establishing the RMU [Risk Management Unit] in the first place', ibid, para 20, 369–70.

are confirmed from other sources as well, including the Médecins Sans Frontières (MSF) and the UK Department for International Development (DFID). A statement announcing the termination of the MSF presence in Somalia reads:

> Over its 22-year history in Somalia, MSF has negotiated with armed actors and authorities on all sides. The exceptional humanitarian needs in the country have pushed the organization and its staff to tolerate unparalleled levels of risk—much of it borne by MSF's Somali colleagues—*and to accept serious compromises to its operational principles of independence and impartiality.*[57]

The UK government recently acknowledged that humanitarian materials and supplies of a value of £480,000 were stolen by Al-Shabaab between November 2011 and February 2012. According to the DFID, its 'partners had no prior warning of the confiscations being carried out and therefore had no time to prevent loss by relocating goods'. Strangely enough, the report talks about 'confiscations' (without a quotation mark!), a term reminiscent of the Al-Shabaab 'taxes'. In a second case, another £260,000 was lost because of non-performance of a project in the period 2006–2012. The statement adds that the costs 'could not be recouped'.[58] There is no further information in the report about the partner organisations involved, the precise circumstances and potential responsibility/accountability for the losses, or any plans to conduct an inquiry. There is a visible lack of transparency when this report is compared to the reports of the Monitoring Group.

This is shocking information that provides evidence for a sustained systemic failure in the delivery of aid, and substantiates the lack of security. It also demonstrates the entrenchment of a culture of institutional malfunction and corruption in the aid system, which ultimately leads to the deterioration of the situation and the exacerbation of the threat to the peace by, inter alia, providing resources of the international community to those groups that are targeted by the international action as the source of the threat to the peace. In terms of policy, it is difficult to justify an expensive naval mission with the mandate to protect aid shipments at the beginning of the pipeline if the movement of goods and services collapses at its end for reasons that are mostly within the responsibility of the UN.

In terms of efficiency, the cost of escorting and protecting these shipments is relatively high because the WFP uses 'small, slow ships requir[ing] greater military protection resources', and this had created uneasiness in the House of Lords.[59] If the protection of WFP vessels was a primary objective of the international naval missions, it is not evident that the same objective could not have been achieved by private maritime security. Furthermore, the benefits from the action of the international naval forces should be measured against the cost. According to one set of assessments, the total cost of military operations in 2012 was around $1.09 billion, including $691,079,446 for naval vessel deployment and $19,656,000 for the cost of vessel protection detachments for WFP and AMISOM ships. However, not all cost linked to the international naval operations could be independently calculated and assessed, and, if such incre-

---

[57] Statement of 14 August 2013, available at http://www.doctorswithoutborders.org/press/release. cfm?id=6985 (last accessed on 1 October 2013) (emphasis added).

[58] Department for International Development, Annual Report and Accounts 2012–2013, 208.

[59] House of Lords, European Union Committee, 'Combating Somali Piracy: The EU's Naval Operation Atalanta', 12th Report of Session 2009–2010, HL Paper 103, 13.

mental costs were added, then the overall cost of the operations off the Somali coast could rise to $3 billion.[60]

In addition, the opportunity cost of naval deployment should be taken into account, in particular under the conditions of the UK Strategic Defence and Security Review. According to the Review, the Department of Defence plans to reduce the number of frigates by four, but would still continue to support the EU NAVFOR with one frigate for some period of time.[61] According to the report of the House of Commons on Somali piracy, a significant number of warships were dedicated to EU and NATO counter-piracy operations between January 2007 and July 2011 as their primary task, and to Royal Navy operations in the area off the coast of Somalia, the Gulf of Aden and the Arabian Gulf as a complementary task.[62] Considering the upheavals and armed conflicts in the Southern and Eastern Mediterranean as a consequence of the insurgencies and violent regime changes across North Africa and the Middle East, counter-piracy missions limited the capacity of the UK to deploy its naval capabilities in areas of greater strategic concern.

C. Conclusion

The policy of fighting piracy by means of the use of military force appears to have had mixed results, due to the asymmetrical conditions under which the use of force was planned and implemented. Despite the fact that piracy incidents are on the wane as a result of international efforts, the international law of force was not among the main factors that influenced or determined the conduct and strategy of the states involved. The cooperating states implemented policies that were not legally irreproachable from the perspective of the law of force, although they had gained the consensus of the vital players, including the permanent members of the UN Security Council and, crucially, the Somali authorities. Violations of the law of force were not directed against Somalia's statehood, but were caused by the collapse of state structures[63] and the absence of a government that could grant valid consent.

Moreover, the impression arising from the various elements of the practice is that the overall benefits do not necessarily justify the cost of the military deployment and mobilisation of international navies. The observer cannot avoid thinking that, as long as the main purpose of the counter-piracy resolutions is indeed the safeguard of maritime communication and not the restoration of peace in Somalia, other policies, namely private security, could be more efficient; and when the purpose is to contribute to the restoration of peace, then the results are also meagre because of the failure of the methods and policies implemented in Somalia.

The second main policy adopted by the international community, law enforcement,

---

[60] J Bellish et al, 'Oceans Beyond Piracy, The Economic Cost of Somali Piracy 2012', 13–18, available at http://oceansbeyondpiracy.org/cost-of-piracy/economic (last accessed on 1 October 2013).
    [61] 'Securing Britain in an Age of Uncertainty: The Strategic Defence and Security Review', Cm 7948 (October 2010) 22, 62–63.
    [62] House of Commons—Foreign Affairs Committee, n 10 above, 35.
    [63] On the legal problems associated with the failure of the Somali state, see MD Evans and S Galani, Chapter 15 below.

also exhibits deep systemic problems that put into question the significance of its impact on the repression of piracy.

III. THE FAILINGS OF LAW ENFORCEMENT

Apart from the use of force, law enforcement is the second core dimension of counter-piracy, not least because piracy is a criminal offence under the law of the sea. The Djibouti Code of Conduct provided that the participants intended to cooperate by 'arresting, investigating, and prosecuting persons who have committed piracy or are reasonably suspected of committing piracy'.[64] Furthermore, the Security Council authorised the use of force for the repression of piracy as a transnational crime, and therefore the question of criminal law enforcement has become a crucial element of the Council's agenda. UNSC Resolution 2015 (2011), for instance, emphasised the significance of prosecution and elaborated on the principles and actions that the states were expected to take in that regard.[65] As successful criminal prosecution is the cardinal 'moment' of law enforcement, whether individuals arrested in the course of counter-piracy operations have been successfully prosecuted by the authorities of the states concerned is an issue to be further explored.

Some UN reports create an impression of positive developments. A report from March 2012 includes information on legislation concerning criminalisation and prosecution provisions from 42 states.[66] Another report by the Secretary-General assesses that, of 1186 suspects held between 2006 and October 2012, 623 were convicted, ie a success rate of 52,5%, and only 115 were released for various reasons after being handed over to a state.[67] A closer look, though, reveals a number of methodological shortcomings; for instance, only a small number of the above 42 states offered any information on the actual practice of arrests and prosecution. The report of the Secretary-General on arrests and convictions was based on the information provided by only 21 states, and makes no reference to individuals released immediately after they were arrested.

Other sources offer a more realistic and disappointing picture. According to the assessment of the EU NAVFOR, adopted by the Lang Report, more than 90% of pirates arrested are released without being prosecuted.[68] Kontorovich and Art concluded that prosecution of piracy under universal jurisdiction is limited to a meagre 1.47% of all cases where this legal basis could clearly have been used.[69] The lack of effectiveness of criminal law enforcement is to be attributed to normative and policy reasons.

The UNCLOS provisions on the repression of piracy are weak for two main

---

[64] Art 4(3)(a) of the Code; see n 13 above.

[65] UNSC Resolution 2015/2011.

[66] Compilation of information received from Member States, S/2012/177 (26 March 2012).

[67] Report of the Secretary-General, S/2012/783, n 46 above, para 44 with table.

[68] 'Report of the Special Adviser Jack Lang to the Secretary-General on Legal Issues Related to Piracy off the Coast of Somalia', S/2011/30 (25 January 2011) para 14.

[69] E Kontorovich and S Art, 'An Empirical Examination of Universal Jurisdiction for Piracy' (2010) 104 *American Journal of International Law* 436; but see also E Kontorovich, 'The Penalties for Piracy: An Empirical Study of National Prosecution of International Crime', Faculty Working Papers, Paper 211 (Northwestern University School of Law, 2012).

reasons: first, because the Convention does not require states to make piracy a crime under their domestic law; and secondly, because it does not introduce the principle *aut dedere aut judicare*.[70] The Security Council did not change these aspects of the jurisdictional basis but, instead, called for increased cooperation between states, and proposed an alternative of shiprider agreements.[71] This did not resolve the structural problem because the EU—perhaps the most important player in the efforts to suppress Somali piracy—did not conclude any agreements of that kind.[72] As a consequence, the release of pirates without trial frustrates the achievement of the objectives of the UN Security Council but does not breach the international law of the sea.

The difficulties in the repression of piracy are linked to the state of the law in the developed states, but also to the unwillingness of some of them to prosecute. The evolution of law—in particular, of human rights law—has created conditions discouraging the prosecution of piracy. The high threshold of evidence required, and the difficulties in collecting evidence in the course of the counter-piracy operations, complicate criminal processes, though the Foreign Affairs Committee of the House of Commons was apparently not persuaded by the arguments of the government.[73] Even when criminal trials take place and result in the conviction of the accused, the sentences cannot be considered as having any serious deterrent effect. In the *Hamburg* trial in Germany, for instance, which is indicative of the approach of the German legal order, the 10 suspects received sentences between two and seven years, and those with the lighter sentences were freed after the judgment was announced.[74]

Even more important in this regard is the development of a certain version of interpretation of human rights law, which clearly obstructs the efforts to successfully prosecute the crime of piracy. At the centre of this evolutionary trend is the extensive interpretation of the principle of non-refoulement and of the prohibition of degrading or inhuman treatment or punishment by the European Court of Human Rights (Article 3 ECHR). The EU and its Member States in particular are worried that the states where the suspects could be transferred for trial, or deported after the end of criminal proceedings or the serving of the sentences, in particular Somalia, are not 'safe' in the sense of human rights law and might be persecuted, or face a real risk of the death penalty or degrading or inhuman treatment or punishment. Though the EU concluded 'transfer agreements' with some of these regional states that should facilitate the transfer of those arrested,[75] the obstacles have not been overcome, because the courts of the individual Member States may make their own assessments. In Germany, for instance, the Administrative Court of Cologne considered the transfer of piracy suspects to Kenya as illegal because the detention conditions did not, in its assessment, correspond to international standards.[76]

As a result, Somali pirates appear to enjoy a paradoxical impunity, whereby race and

---

[70] See Churchill, Chapter 1 above; J Klabbers, Chapter 14 below.

[71] Geiß and Petrig, n 25 above, 165–68; 85–95.

[72] See D Thym, Chapter 6 above.

[73] House of Commons—Foreign Affairs Committee, n 10 above, 45, para 81.

[74] *LG Hamburg*, 3. Große Strafkammer, Judgment of 19 October 2012, 603 KLs 17/10. See also König and Salomon, Chapter 10 above.

[75] See Thym, Chapter 6 above.

[76] See König and Salomon, Chapter 10 above; see also Art 12 Council Joint Action 2008/851/CFSP.

religion may also have influenced the lack of a more active response.[77] Taken together, the above factors strengthen the motivation to engage in piracy, because the worst outcome for pirates can be the transfer to the EU and imprisonment for a relatively brief period of time, followed by the expectation of a permanent stay in the country. It is thus reported that the juvenile pirates who were freed after their conviction by the Hamburg Court and the completion of their time in jail were not deported back to Somalia, but receive schooling and are resocialised and integrated in Germany.[78]

This pattern of response is the result of a misconceived interpretation of international refugee law and human rights law. It is not possible to make a detailed analysis of the relevant issues in this chapter; only a brief presentation of the main arguments can be given.[79] First, it is questionable whether pirates could be considered as refugees, because they are accused of criminal acts and are not engaged in Somalia's civil conflict, apart from being involved in corruption and collusion networks with the regional administrations. Secondly, even in the rare cases where they would fulfil the conditions of Article 1A of the Geneva Convention Relating to the Status of Refugees,[80] they would be excluded from refugee protection under Article 1F, because they act 'contrary to the purposes and principles of the United Nations'. Thirdly, the deporting states may request assurances from the Somali authorities to prevent the risk of torture or inhuman treatment; the policy of deportation with assurances should be encouraged, because the UN Security Council emphasised the primary responsibility of Somalia for the prosecution of pirates.[81] Thus, the refusal to transfer suspects or convicted pirates to Somalia contradicts the official policy of the UN that 'the transfer of individuals convicted of piracy-related crimes to Somalia is crucial to the strengthening of the counter-piracy efforts off the coast of Somalia and in the Indian Ocean'.[82] Human rights law should not be applied in a way that leads to the marginalisation and impairment of the counter-piracy efforts of the international community, but some form of 'comity' should be established between the two sets of norm complexes.[83]

The evolution of interpretive patterns of law and case law throughout Europe and the selection of some alternatives at the expense of others are to some extent accessible to explanation. Various factors play a role in the process of legal evolution—the activities and interests of business, civil society organisations and human rights groups play a significant role in that respect. Here is some brief, but illustrative information

---

[77] Kontorovich argued that allegations of torture or mistreatment can be put forward by pirates and can be effectively used against Western states bringing into collective memory the patterns of abuse in Guantánamo Bay, Cuba. A media-effective campaign could thus link counter-piracy to an alleged offence by the West against Islam: Kontorovich, above n 40, 266–67.

[78] See König and Salomon, Chapter 10 above.

[79] On this issue see further Y Dutton, 'Pirates and Impunity: Is the Threat of Asylum Claims a Reason to Allow Pirates to Escape Justice?' (2011) 34 *Fordham International Law Journal* 233.

[80] 189 UNTS 150.

[81] See, eg UNSC Resolution 2077/2012, operative para 6, according to which the Security Council is 'calling upon the Somali authorities to interdict, and upon interdiction to investigate and prosecute pirates', in combination with para 8 of the preamble, where the SC underlined 'the primary responsibility of the Somali authorities in the fight against piracy and armed robbery at sea off the coast Somalia'. See also UNSC Resolution 2125/2013, para 24 of the preamble.

[82] Report of the Secretary-General, S/2012/783, n 46 above, para 55; on the support and funding of the related projects see ibid, paras 56–58.

[83] On 'comity' between legal regimes, see A Skordas, 'Völkerrechtsfreundlichkeit as Comity and the Disquiet of Neoformalism' in P Koutrakos (ed), *European Foreign Policy—Legal and Political Perspectives* (Cheltenham, Edward Elgar Publishing, 2011) 115–44.

from some EU Member States and non-state groups. In Germany, for instance, left-wing groups and organisations linked to Christian Churches actively questioned the rationale of the criminal processes and acted in support of the pirates,[84] and one commentator characterised the Hamburg trial as a 'pointless and expensive circus'.[85] Powerful non-state actors demonstrably ignore pleas for information and assistance by the international community. Facebook has never responded to requests and official correspondence from the Monitoring Group on information contained in Facebook accounts on hijacking and hostage-taking; such behaviour blocks crucial evidence from reaching police and the courts, and puts human lives at risk,[86] but apparently this is not an issue that can negatively affect the company's reputation.[87] Even more important is the sharp critique by the Monitoring Group of the UK for its failure to prosecute pirates.[88] This practice cannot be adequately explained by the authorities' concerns that the accused could advance asylum claims,[89] and it can be presumed that the policy is also attributed to a combination of factors relating to the interests of the maritime and banking business. Indeed, there is sufficient evidence substantiating this assumption.

The Monitoring Group's critique regarding the inconsistent practices and policies of the UK for the repression of piracy is instructive of the 'state of affairs' in the hegemonic country of maritime business. The 2012 report first criticises countries unwilling to prosecute and investigate piracy, such as Greece, which, even though it 'reportedly owns more ships than any other country in the world', failed to initiate proceedings in 'at least 22 hijacking cases'.[90] The report next praises the contribution of the UK to the counter-piracy naval task forces, and its related intelligence and diplomatic initiatives and activities.[91] It then makes some dramatic accusations against the UK regarding its failure to prosecute and the reasons behind this policy:

> Conversely, the UK has failed to pursue law enforcement investigation against alleged Somali pirates and their associates in at least 6 different opportunities where it has potential criminal jurisdiction. Furthermore, the British Government has blocked UN Security Council efforts to designate senior Somali pirate leaders for targeted sanctions, apparently at the behest of powerful domestic interests in shipping, crisis and risk management consultancies, maritime law and insurance, and private maritime security companies (PMSCs) who indirectly derive significant profits from the Somali piracy phenomenon. These enterprises, which

---

[84] See, eg C Rath, 'Kalaschnikows und Geiselhaft', *Die Tageszeitung*, 21 October 2012, available at http://www.taz.de/!103991/ (last accessed on 5 October 2013); see also the information and opinions on the blogspot Somali Piraten Prozess, available at http://somali-piraten-prozess-hamburg.blogspot.de/ and, in English language, http://reclaim-the-seas.blogspot.com/ (last accessed on 6 October 2013).

[85] B Lacotta, 'Germany's Somali Pirate Trial is Pointless', *Spiegel Online*, 9 December 2012, available at http://www.spiegel.de/international/germany/german-trial-of-somali-pirates-turns-into-pointless-and-expensive-farce-a-855252.html (last accessed on 18 October 2013).

[86] Report of the Monitoring Group, S/2013/413, above n 2, para 69, note 39.

[87] In comparison, when Twitter's reputation suffered real damage as a consequence of the trolling of female activists in the UK, the company amended its regulations to control abuse on line: M Townsend and L Moon, 'Twitter Boss Says Sorry to Targets of Troll Abuse', *The Guardian*, 3 August 2013, available at http://www.theguardian.com/technology/2013/aug/03/twitter-clamps-down-on-abuse (last accessed on 6 October 2013).

[88] See below, following para.

[89] KJ Heller, 'Pirates are People, Too', Opinio Juris blog, 13 April 2008, available at http://opiniojuris.org/2008/04/13/pirates-are-people-too/ (last accessed on 18 October 2013).

[90] Report of the Monitoring Group, S/2012/544, above n 32, Annex 4, para 28, 209.

[91] Ibid, para 29.

predominate with respect to Somali hijacking cases, also possess much valuable information and intelligence on Somali pirate groups, negotiators and networks—including details of financial and communication arrangements. This information is rarely, if ever, released for the purposes of criminal prosecution or the imposition of targeted sanctions, whether inside or outside the UK, raising serious questions and concerns, especially when UK residents or nationals are found to be involved in Somali piracy activities.

The UK Government's ambivalent posture with respect to Somali piracy is illustrative of a more general international reluctance to tackle Somali piracy as a form of international organized crime, rather than as a sui generis product of Somali statelessness requiring custom-made military and custodial responses. Unless and until this attitude changes, international counter piracy efforts will continue to treat the symptoms of Somali piracy rather than the cause.[92]

Thus, the Monitoring Group accused the UK of undermining the international efforts to repress piracy under the pressure of powerful domestic groups. Most importantly, though, it confirmed the reluctance of many states to consider the international and transnational dimensions of piracy, and criticised the conventional approach to Somali piracy as the product of a failed state that requires a military solution. At this point, the Monitoring Group's report touched the cardinal flaw of counter-piracy policies.

The 2012 report goes on to criticise the UK government's policies on ransom payments. The UK opposed the US's policy of banning ransoms,[93] with the reasoning that this would complicate the efforts to release hostages and would put their lives at risk.[94] However, the Monitoring Group suspected other motives:

Nevertheless, the British Government decided to place a technical hold on an April 2010 US proposal to also sanction pirate leaders under Security Council Resolution 1844 in order to ensure that ransom payments remain legal—apparently in deference to concerns raised by elements of Britain's influential shipping and counter piracy industries. The UK's technical hold against designation of pirate leadership by the Security Council has remained in force until to date.[95]

The contentions of the Monitoring Group about the responsibility of the UK were not contradicted by the World Bank report of 2013 on Somali piracy. The World Bank stated that 'London is at the epicenter of pirate ransom negotiations', noting that 'London has been the world center of the maritime underwriting market since the late 17th century'.[96] The report also emphasised that individuals in the Somali diaspora are involved in moving ransoms across the financial centres of the world,[97] including through the Hawala system, often acting in tandem with terrorist groups.[98]

All these factors strengthen the capacities of pirates by enabling them to use the

---

[92] Ibid, paras 30–31, pp 209–10.
[93] See Executive Order 13536 concerning Somalia—Blocking Property of Certain Persons Contributing to the Conflict in Somalia of 13 April 2010, available at http://www.whitehouse.gov/the-press-office/executive-order-concerning-somalia (last accessed on 5 October 2013); see also Clyde & Co—US LLP, 'Impact of President Obama's April 13, 2010 Executive Order on Somalia and Piracy on US and non-US Insurance Companies, April 2010', available at http://www.clydeco.com/uploads/Files/Publications/2010/US%20INSURANCE%20PERSPECTIVE_2010.pdf (last accessed on 5 October 2013).
[94] House of Commons—Foreign Affairs Committee, n 10 above, paras 111–15.
[95] Report of the Monitoring Group, S/2012/544, above n 32, Annex 4, para 34, 211.
[96] World Bank, n 4 above, 93–94.
[97] Ibid, 96–97.
[98] Ibid, 77.

mechanisms of the world financial system, but do not seem to greatly impress upon policy-makers in London. The discussion in the Foreign Affairs Committee of the House of Commons revealed the evasive answers of the representative of the government to questions on the payment of ransoms. It also showed that the maritime industry was against the ban of ransoms,[99] and demonstrated that, as a consequence of insurance policies covering the risk of ransom, the level of the ransom price increased dramatically.[100] As to the information, or worry, that at least some of the ransoms end up in London, the Parliamentary Undersecretary of State, Henry Bellingham MP, answered that the government is 'trying to understand much more about the financial flows'. He added that the UK has 'very advanced money-laundering laws' and that the government funds the UN Office on Drugs and Crime.[101] Asked specifically about the government's activities within the territory of the UK, he said that, though it 'certainly do[es] all [it] can in the UK',[102] it '[was] possibly slow to look at this area as a priority',[103] and that the SOCA (Serious Organized Crime Agency) would be involved if there was evidence of ransom money laundered through the UK, but it does not have such evidence.[104] In his supplementary written evidence, Stephen Askins of Ince & Co LLP stated that ransom money is sometimes collected in London, but also in other places, and sent to the hostage-takers, and that 'movement through London is done with the consent of SOCA and [the UK Border Agency]'.[105]

As a conclusion, it can be confirmed that the call of the Security Council for states to take the necessary measures for criminal law enforcement did not have the expected resonance. Pirates are often released upon their arrest, and the legal-structural conditions in Europe, including the action of non-state groups and the dominant assumption on the scope of human rights law, complicate the enforcement of criminal law. Moreover, major corporate and insurance interests in the UK do not welcome more effective action against the economic infrastructure of the pirate business, and reject the criminalisation of the payment of ransoms. As a result, the authorities step back, preferring to pursue counter-piracy policies in international fora rather than in domestic jurisdiction. Thus, the contribution of criminal law enforcement to the repression of piracy has been generally rather modest.

IV. COUNTER-PIRACY AND SELF-HELP: A GLOBAL LAW PERSPECTIVE

As neither the use of military force nor law enforcement can effectively resolve the problem of piracy, private security at sea takes over the primary role. Private security at sea is provided for by PMSCs, which have the capacities to afford protection to international navigation and to deter pirate attacks. An analysis of the incidents between 2011 and 2013 is instructive on the role of the PMSC and of best management anti-piracy practices, including citadels, razor wire rigging and the manoeuvring

---

[99] House of Commons—Foreign Affairs Committee, n 10 above, paras 112–13; Ev 48, Q294.
[100] Ibid, Ev 4–5, Q20–30.
[101] Ibid, Ev 49, Q297.
[102] Ibid, Ev 49, Q298.
[103] Ibid, Ev 49, Q299.
[104] Ibid, Ev 49, Q302.
[105] Ibid, Ev 66. On the UK position on ransom, see Murdoch, Chapter 9 above.

of ships to prevent and deter pirate attacks. An analysis of the ICC IMB reports for the years 2011–13 shows that 2012 saw not only the swift decline of piracy incidents, but also the increasing contribution of the above methods and practices.

In 2011, 47 actual attacks took place in the area of Somalia, the Gulf of Aden and the Red Sea, but in 15 cases naval forces interfered and rescued the crew before or after the pirates had left the ship. In all cases, no armed guards were reported as being present on the hijacked vessels.[106] In the same period, 189 attempted attacks took place: in 88 cases, armed security guards or vessel protection detachments were on board the attacked ships, including one case where international naval forces also played an important role; in 12 cases, the pirate attacks were obstructed by the naval forces; and in 89 cases, the attacks failed as a result of preventive anti-piracy measures.[107]

According to the 2012 report, 16 vessels where attacked and hijacked, and there is no mention of an armed presence on any of them; the interference of the international naval forces in four cases resulted in the rescue of the crews or the flight of the pirates.[108] In the same period, 59 attacks failed, and in 43 cases the attacked vessels had armed security guards on board. No vessel with armed security guards on board was hijacked, and in five of the 43 cases, international naval forces also provided assistance. The navies also took action in another five cases, where the attacked ships were not reported to have armed security guards. In the other 11 cases, the attacks failed due to anti-piracy measures and the responses of the attacked ships without the use of armed force or the involvement of international naval forces.[109]

The report of the ICC IMB for the months January–June 2013 informs that one vessel was hijacked, with a second attacked and rescued on the same day, in the above-mentioned area.[110] Also, six attempted attacks in the same area failed without the ships coming under the control of pirates at any time; in all these cases the vessels were under the protection of onboard armed security guards.[111] On 11 October 2013, a fully laden supertanker was attacked in the Indian Ocean, but the attack was thwarted because of the response of the armed security team.[112]

The reports provide convincing evidence for the successful use of PMSCs and for the declining role of the international naval forces. Indeed, pirate attacks failed in all cases where private guards were used, and warning shots were usually sufficient to put an end to the attack. The use of PMSCs initially met serious reservations, and was opposed from many sides. The 2010 report of the European Union Committee of the House of Lords, for instance, showed that the major constituencies of maritime commerce, including business and public actors, were reluctant to recommend the use of private security guards:

> We endorse the view of the shipping industry, the IMO and the Government that private security guards should not be placed on commercial shipping as this would increase the

---

[106] ICC IMB, 'Piracy and Armed Robbery Against Ships—Annual Report 2011', 60–68.
[107] Ibid, 78–107.
[108] ICC IMB, 'Piracy and Armed Robbery Against Ships—Annual Report 2012', 56–58.
[109] Ibid, 70–80.
[110] ICC IMB, above n 3, 41.
[111] Ibid, 48–49.
[112] EU NAVFOR press release, 'EU Naval Force Confirms Super Tanker Safe after Attack by Suspect Pirates off Somali Coast' (11 October 2013), available at http://eunavfor.eu/eu-naval-force-confirms-super-tanker-safe-after-attack-by-suspect-pirates-off-somali-coast/ (last accessed on 18 October 2013).

risks to which the ships and crew were subject. However, military personnel from national armed forces are occasionally placed on commercial shipping on a case-by-case basis, and we believe this should continue. The Government and the EU should ensure that any such personnel receive prior specialised training to a high standard for this role.[113]

Less than two years later, the climate had changed. In the House of Commons report, the Foreign Affairs Committee reached the following conclusion:

> We conclude that for too long the Government failed to respond to the urgent need for armed protection. However, we welcome the Prime Minister's recent announcement that the Government's position would be reversed and that private armed guards will be permitted on UK-flagged vessels. We agree that the evidence in support of using private armed security guards is compelling and, within legal limits and according to guidance, shipowners should be allowed to protect their ships and crew by employing private armed security guards if they wish to do so.[114]

The Government responded to this report of the House by adopting the Interim Guidance on the Use of Armed Guards.[115] The Guidance permits the use of private security guards 'in exceptional circumstances', that is, when three cumulative conditions apply: (i) the ship transits the area between the Suez Canal and the Straits of Hormuz; (ii) it implements the latest best management practices, as determined by the industry; and (iii) 'the use of armed guards is assessed to reduce the risk to the lives and well being of those onboard the ship'.[116]

The use of PMSCs is justified by a number of reasons. First, there is evidence of the practical difficulties the international naval forces face in their efforts to disrupt and deter piracy off the Somali coast, due to the extensive geographical space where pirate activities are undertaken compared to the scarcity of the available resources.[117] Secondly, if states cannot provide the necessary protection to property rights or to the right to life, it can be expected that individuals and companies should not only be allowed, but would also be entitled, to take measures of self-defence and self-protection. The third reason is linked to the budgetary implications of the operation of international naval forces, and to the need to internalise security costs to the shipping industry and the consumer. A fourth related reason is that, if piracy can be effectively deterred or disrupted by the use of PMSCs, the international naval presence can be minimised, so that warships can be made available for other operational priorities.[118]

---

[113] House of Lords, European Union Committee, above n 59, para 50.

[114] House of Commons—Foreign Affairs Committee, n 10 above, para 31.

[115] Department of Transport, Interim Guidance to UK Flagged Shipping on the Use of Armed Guards to Defend Against the Threat of Piracy in Exceptional Circumstances, Version 1.2, updated May 2013.

[116] Interim Guidance, 1.6. For the German legislation on this issue, see the contribution of König and Salomon, Chapter 10 above.

[117] A Petrig, 'The Use of Force and Firearms by Private Maritime Security Companies Against Suspected Pirates' (2013) 62 *International & Comparative Law Quarterly* 667, 668–72; H-G Ehrhart and K Petretto, 'The EU and Somalia: Counter-piracy and the Question of a Comprehensive Approach', study for the Greens/European Free Alliance, Hamburg (February 2012) 35, referring to the 'partial failure of the EU NAVFOR'.

[118] See on this point House of Commons—Foreign Affairs Committee, n 10 above, Rory Stewart MP (Q153–59), Ev 25–26; see in particular the question/comment of Dave Watts MP (Q285), Ev 46: 'Isn't the whole policy in a mess? Let me give an example. It seems to me that, ideally, you would like to resolve the matter on land, as you have said, but that is not going to happen in the foreseeable future. We see from the figures that arresting pirates and bringing them to trial is not successful. The only thing that seems to be successful is having armed guards on ships. We can see that the pirates do not target ships from

The use of PMSCs for purposes of self-defence has to adjust to, and comply with, international law, and, in particular, with the law of the sea, but the appropriate interpretation of the respective rules can resolve most of these questions and offer practical solutions.[119] Here, the focus is on the issue of broader evolutionary change in the law of force, as signalled by the turn towards private security on the high seas. Indeed, it is not only about the protection of actors, such as crews, hostages or companies, and their property, but also about the protection of maritime communication as a fundamental freedom in world society.

Indeed, the reason why Somali piracy has acquired such notoriety as a global issue cannot be explained merely by the threat to persons or to property. Piracy is a persistent or endemic phenomenon in other parts of the world as well, including West Africa, South Asia and South China Sea, and in strategic sea lanes such as the Straits of Malacca and Singapore.[120] The Somali piracy developed into a global business enterprise by using advanced negotiation strategies, intermediaries and facilitators, and moving financial capital and ransoms through the financial centres of the world. This evolutionary moment can explain the strength of the 'piracy as business' model, which is also a system of sustainable economic activity for the affected local communities. It can also illustrate the magnitude of threat to the freedom of navigation and maritime communication, as well as the inconsistencies and impasse of conventional counter-piracy approaches. The institutionalised use of private security guards corresponds both to the particular features and risks of piracy as an activity with world societal dimensions and to the need to protect the freedoms of maritime communication and navigation.

Thus, piracy is a 'risk activity' to maritime communication as a fundamental principle of the law of the sea and an indispensable pillar of world trade. In the Corfu Channel case, the first judgment after its establishment, the ICJ recognised the principle of freedom of maritime communication, from which concrete legal obligations may arise.[121] In his Individual Opinion, Judge Alvarez stressed that, between 1941 and 1945, the freedom of the seas and oceans had been recognised as a fundamental principle both by international practice and by public opinion, and 'it may therefore be said to form part of the new international law'.[122]

In the *Saiga II* case of the International Tribunal for the Law of the Sea, Judge Laing extensively discussed issues relevant to the function of the freedom of navigation and freedom of maritime communication in world society. Acknowledging the lack of clarity in the law of the sea, he stated that:

> currently the more widely accepted, yet somewhat unclear, notion about the basis of the institution of freedom of navigation is that it is subsumed under the freedom of the high seas, which is itself based and dependent on a broader freedom of maritime communication and intercourse, given the fact that the sea is essentially an indispensable global highway.[123]

India, Russia and China; they leave those ships alone and concentrate on those that have no armed guards. Wouldn't it be better to stand down the Navy, stop doing all the other things, and just put some armed guards on all of our ships?'

[119] See the excellent analysis of Petrig, n 117 above.
[120] See Ong, Chapter 12 above; E Egede, Chapter 11 above.
[121] *The Corfu Channel Case*, ICJ Reports 1949, 4, 22.
[122] Ibid, 46.
[123] ITLOS, *The M/V 'Saiga' (No 2) case*, n 12 above, Separate Opinion of Judge Laing, para 21.

Judge Laing then emphasised the links of the law of the sea with the global economy and stressed that the 'freedom of the high seas and related freedoms subserve the needs of international trade and commerce and . . . they have been, and remain, an indispensable factor in the development of the world economy and international commerce'.[124] He further argued that the freedom of the high seas, taking into account their links with the global economy, should be considered as a 'peremptory norm' and 'fundamental principle of international law as a whole':

> Whether the basis of freedom of the high seas is the institution of maritime communication, or is an integral aspect of the global economy, the freedom has been described as 'an obligatory binding norm;' a 'fundamental principle, which has also had great influence on other branches of international law, particularly space law and the regime of the Antarctic Treaty', and 'a fundamental principle of international law as a whole'. The subsumed freedom of navigation has also been described as a peremptory norm of the law of nations.[125]

Notwithstanding any doctrinal controversies on *jus cogens*, the freedom of high seas and the broader freedom of maritime communication are fundamental normative pillars of world trade and world economy, and there is no doubt that piracy can cause serious prejudice to these activities. At the same time, piracy does not lead to armed conflict, and the use of conventional 'hard' military power is not an effective tool for its suppression; in fact, even if it were, military force would also threaten the freedom of maritime communication in the long term. Furthermore, instead of the 'full eradication' of piracy as an objective of the UNSC[126] and of the Conference on Somalia,[127] the management of the 'risk of piracy' and the protection of sea lanes of strategic importance is a more feasible alternative,[128] fully compatible with the freedom of maritime communication.

The use of PMSCs is therefore appropriate in reaching the basic aims of counter-piracy, which are deterrence[129] and self-defence. The harmonisation of the rules on the use of private security enables states and the shipping industry to fight piracy without the involvement of the military, without violating the international law of force and without necessarily resolving the problems on the land. These rules are set up by numerous stakeholders, including state and non-state actors, who regulate various aspects of the activities of the PMSC. The IMO, for instance, adopted guidelines regarding the Somali piracy addressed to three categories of stakeholders, the shipping industry, the port and coastal states, and the flag states.[130] According to the

---

[124] Judge Laing, ibid, para 23.

[125] Ibid, para 27.

[126] See, eg UNSC Resolution 1846/2008, para 10 of the preamble.

[127] 'We reiterated our determination to work with Somalia to eradicate piracy and other maritime crimes', Somalia Conference Communiqué, 7 May 2013, available at https://www.gov.uk/government/news/somalia-conference-2013-communique (last accessed on 13 October 2013).

[128] See the statement of J Potgieter, Senior Researcher, Institute for Security Studies, South Africa, in G Martin, Piracy Can Never Be Conquered—Expert', *defenceWeb*, 24 July 2013, http://www.defenceweb.co.za/index.php?option=com_content&view=article&id=31306%3apiracy-can-never-be-conquered-expert&catid=108%3amaritime-security&Itemid=233 (last accessed on 13 October 2013).

[129] On deterrence as comprehensive strategy of counter-piracy, see M Bahar, 'Attaining Optimal Deterrence at Sea: A Legal and Strategic Theory for Naval Anti-piracy Operations' (2007) 40 *Vanderbilt Journal of Transnational Law* 1.

[130] 'Revised Interim Guidance to Shipowners, Ship Operators and Shipmasters on the Use of Privately Contracted Armed Security Personnel on Board Ships in the High Risk Area', MSC.1/Circ.1405/Rev.2 (25 May 2012); 'Revised Interim Recommendations for Port and Coastal States Regarding the Use of Privately

IMO Guidance for the shipping industry, 'the absence of applicable regulation and industry self-regulation coupled with complex legal requirements governing the legitimate transport, carriage and use of firearms gives cause for concern'.[131] Similarly, the ISO has also adopted guidelines for PMSCs,[132] as well as organisations of the shipping industry, such as BIMCO[133] and Intertanko.[134]

Self-regulation should be at the heart of the system of rules pertaining to private security at sea. It would establish the foundations for the safeguard of the freedom of maritime communication, and integrate private security in the overall system of activities and risk management of the maritime industry, forming 'model guidelines' for the protection of shipping beyond the confines and specific features of the East African region. The security of maritime communication is an issue broader than just Somalia, and the maritime industry should take the lead in formulating globally applicable rules[135] and best management practices. Self-regulation should be underpinned by domestic legislation and backed up by recommendations of international organisations—and, if necessary, by a plurilateral agreement to be drafted and adopted by the main maritime powers.

The institutionalisation of private security at sea for purposes of deterrence and self-defence cannot per se resolve the problem of risk management; states must vigorously prosecute the crime of piracy, and it is occasionally necessary for the military to use force against pirate vessels. Though in individual cases 'smart' approaches may lead to the arrest of pirate leaders without extraterritorial action,[136] the use of force for the arrest of pirates and the seizing of pirate ships is a component of counter-piracy policies. Because of the practical complexities in the use of naval forces for the fulfilment of these tasks, it has been suggested that PMSCs could be entrusted with the comprehensive package of counter-piracy operations, including arrests, seizing of pirate vessels and interdiction. These proposals are based on the issuance of 'letters of marque' by states and on the idea of reprisals and forcible countermeasures as a form

---

Contracted Armed Security Personnel on Board Ships in the High Risk Area', MSC.1/Circ.1408/Rev.1 (25 May 2012); 'Revised Interim Recommendations for Flag States Regarding the Use of Privately Contracted Armed Security Personnel on Board Ships in the High Risk Area', MSC.1/Circ.1406/Rev.2 (25 May 2012).

[131] Revised Interim Guidance, MSC.1/Circ.1405/Rev.2, ibid, Annex, para 1.2.

[132] ISO/PAS 28007:2012, 'Guidelines for Private Maritime Security Companies (PMSC) Providing Privately Contracted Armed Security Personnel (PCASP) On Board Ships (and Pro Forma Contract)', available at http://www.iso.org/iso/home/store/catalogue_tc/catalogue_detail.htm?csnumber=42146; revised by ISO/CD 280071 (under development, according to the ISO website), available at http://www.iso.org/iso/home/store/catalogue_ics/catalogue_detail_ics.htm?csnumber=63166 (last accessed on 18 October 2013).

[133] BIMCO, 'Guidance on Rules for the Use of Force (RUF) by Privately Contracted Armed Security Personnel (PCASP) in Defence of a Merchant Vessel (MV)', available at https://www.bimco.org/Chartering/Documents/Security/~/media/Chartering/Document_Samples/Sundry_Other_Forms/Sample_Copy_Guidance_on_the_Rules_for_the_Use_of_Force.ashx (last accessed on 18 October 2013).

[134] See the so-called '100 Series Rules' for the use of force, available at https://100seriesrules.com/ (last accessed on 18 October 2013).

[135] *Contra* Petrig, n 117 above, 701, advocating a 'leading role' for states and international organisations.

[136] A Higgins and N Kulish, 'A Proposed Movie Deal for a Piracy Suspect Has a Surprise Ending: His Arrest', *New York Times*, 15 October 2013, A4, available at http://www.nytimes.com/2013/10/15/world/europe/a-proposed-movie-deal-for-a-piracy-suspect-has-a-surprise-ending-his-arrest.html?_r=0 (last accessed on 15 October 2013).

of recourse of force,[137] which, even though formally illegal, is tolerated as self-help, or as advancing the fundamental interests of the international community.[138]

The authorisation to private maritime companies to interdict piracy would constitute a return to the 'letters of marque' as one of the earliest practices of reprisals. By these letters, the sovereign used to authorise private persons to seize goods belonging to individuals from another jurisdiction, if necessary by entering into the territory of another sovereign, in order to secure compensation, under the condition that all other means had failed.[139] It has thus been proposed that this instrument be used to authorise PMSCs to interdict pirate vessels, given that the US Constitution still permits Congress 'to declare War, grant Letters of Marque and Reprisal, and make Rules concerning Captures on Land and Water' (Article I, section 8). There is an ongoing discussion on these issues, and it cannot yet be foreseen whether private security will take over the function of interdiction and be allowed to act in a quasi-official capacity. For the time being, it seems that, in exercising self-defence, private security guards are not restricted in merely repelling the attack but, if they subdue the attackers, they may arrest them, seize the pirate vessel and hand them over to the authorities of coastal states or to international naval forces. There are, however, formidable legal and political obstacles in the adoption of a policy of active interdiction and full privatisation of counter-piracy operations.[140]

Therefore, a body of rules on private security at sea is currently taking shape as a combination of hard and soft law, public and private law, and international and domestic law. This normative complex of global law fulfils the function of an idiosyncratic self-help of the shipping industry, and it generates practices that are linked to the idea of reprisals and forcible countermeasures, in particular when the PMSCs are fulfilling official or semi-official acts.

V. TAKING PIRACY SERIOUSLY: POLICY CONCLUSIONS

Piracy as an organised business activity is a phenomenon of world society, and the situation on the land is only one factor among others. Counter-piracy should adapt to the nature of piracy as transnational crime supported by networks that are active not only in the territory of a failed state, but also in the metropolitan centres of world society. The transnational dimension is both the strength and the weakness of contemporary piracy. It is its strength because pirate activities, at least in East Africa, have ceased being acts of isolated 'sea bandits', and have been integrated into the global

---

[137] TE Hutchins, 'Structuring a Sustainable Letters of Marque Regime: How Commissioning Privateers Can Defeat the Somali Pirates' (2011) 99 *California Law Review* 819; T Richard, 'Reconsidering the Letter of Marque: Utilizing Private Security Providers Against Piracy' (2010) 39 *Public Contract Law Journal* 411; A Schwarz, 'Corsairs in the Crosshairs: A Strategic Plan to Eliminate Modern Day Piracy' (2010) 5 *New York University Journal of Law & Liberty* 500.

[138] See T Franck, *Recourse to Force* (Cambridge, Cambridge University Press, 2002) 109–34; D Bowett, Reprisals Involving Recourse to Armed Force' (1972) 66 *American Journal of International Law* 1; A Skordas, 'Hegemonic Intervention as Legitimate Use of Force' (2007) 16 *Minnesota Journal of International Law* 407.

[139] G Clark, 'The English Practice with Regard to Reprisals by Private Persons' (1933) 27 *American Journal of International Law* 694.

[140] Petrig, n 117 above, 692–94.

economic cycle; it is its weakness because piracy can be defeated if the business can be made unprofitable either by the increase of the cost or by the decrease of the revenue, and because key players are exposed to international police cooperation as they move across borders.

Grand armadas are not the most appropriate structures in the fight against piracy, and the international law of force, including Chapter VII of the UN Charter and state consent, is not a major and autonomous factor in counter-piracy policies. Instead, there is a shift towards private security at sea and self-help of maritime business. A rule-complex, or 'global assemblage',[141] composed of rules, norms, regulations and guidelines from various formal and informal sources, is taking shape as the global law of counter-piracy, and it fulfils the function of safeguarding the freedom of maritime communication and global commerce.

The deeper change in this new format of counter-piracy operations is its integration into the routine operation of the affected maritime business in a way that secures deterrence and self-defence. In this way, business not only internalises the cost of its own security and preserves the freedom of navigation in strategic areas, but also re-establishes the symmetry that had been upset in the relationship between pirates and international naval forces. Evidently, PMSCs should be legally responsible for their actions, and should be obliged to surrender all arrested pirates and seized pirate vessels to national or international naval forces or to regional states as soon as possible, to report incidents and to take all reasonable measures for the rescue of life at sea. Hard military force should be used only exceptionally, for the rescue of hostages or for the destruction of major pirate infrastructures.

Law enforcement in Europe should be streamlined and strengthened, and clear priorities should be set. Prosecution should focus on pirate kingpins and intermediaries, and on money laundering; the payment of ransom should be prohibited by law, and measures should be taken to track the movement of pirate funds. Justice should interfere at the heart of the pirate business and criminal law should introduce deterrent sentences. Arrested suspects of inferior rank in the criminal networks should preferably be extradited or transferred to Somalia, under the terms of a memorandum of understanding, to be negotiated with the involvement of the UN that would also take over the responsibility for monitoring the situation of the individuals concerned.

From a realist perspective, piracy will not be eradicated in the foreseeable future, but it can be effectively marginalised. The most prominent obstacle for the attainment of this goal is not the collapse of authority in Somalia, but the capacity of pirate networks to stabilise their activities by locating themselves as 'parasites' on the dark side of the political, financial and legal institutions of the developed world.[142]

---

[141] On the term see S Sassen, *Territory—Authority—Rights. From Medieval to Global Assemblages* (Princeton, NJ, Princeton University Press, 2006).

[142] On the concept of 'parasite' see M Serres, *The Parasite* (Minneapolis, MN, University of Minnesota Press, 2007, 1st edn 1980).

14

Piracy in Global Law and Global Governance

JAN KLABBERS

I. INTRODUCTION

DURING THE MOST recent municipal elections in Helsinki (2012), one of the participating political parties called itself the Pirate Party, therewith happily and proudly appropriating a label it considered reflective of its political programme. The illicit radio stations operating from outside the territorial waters during the 1960s and 1970s (Radio Caroline in the UK, Radio Veronica and Radio Noordzee in the Netherlands), breaking through public broadcasting monopolies, were self-styled 'pirate stations'.[1] Ever since Robert Louis Stevenson published his *Treasure Island* in the late nineteenth century, pirates have been a staple of popular culture, with many a children's bookshelf filled with books starring pirates. Young women in the 1940s would swoon over a buccaneering Errol Flynn; my own generation grew up with the televised adventures of *Sandokan*, while today's youth may be absorbed by *Pirates of the Caribbean* (or Johnny Depp perhaps).

In short, while pirates are often depicted as enemies of mankind, there is also a certain romanticism attached to them and to piracy in ways that do not apply to other enemies of mankind: it is difficult to think of radio broadcasters labeling themselves as Nazi stations, or to imagine *genocidaires* as popular heroes, or to have a political party refer to itself as the Terrorist Party.[2] This ambivalence has always attached to piracy, it seems: reportedly, even the ancient Greeks and Romans 'tended to view pirates as heroes rather than as offenders',[3] and while Grotius deplored piracy as banding

---

[1] For a brief discussion, see RR Churchill and AV Lowe, *The Law of the Sea*, 3rd edn (Manchester, Manchester University Press, 1999) 211–12.

[2] Although terrorism too is not free from ambivalences. See, eg I Porras, 'On Terrorism: Reflections on Violence and the Outlaw' (1994) 19 *Utah Law Review* 119; J Klabbers, 'Rebel with a Cause? Terrorists and Humanitarian Law' (2003) 14 *European Journal of International Law* 299.

[3] See W Rech, *Enemies of Mankind: The Doctrine of International Law Enforcement in Vattel's Droit des Gens* (Leiden, Martinus Nijhoff, 2013). Note, however, that some caution may be well advised: it is by no means certain that the terms used by the likes of Cicero carried the same connotations as they do nowadays, while it may also be the case that debatable translations distort the historical record. The point is well made by AP Rubin, 'The Law of Piracy' (1987) 15 *Denver Journal of International Law and Policy* 173, esp 178.

together 'for wrongdoing', he nonetheless admiringly acknowledged that pirates, much like the citizens of a state, exhibited the kind of group solidarity and mutual bonds 'without which no association can exist'.[4] Moreover, Grotius astutely noted that states too sometimes engage in uncommendable activities, rendering the distinction between states and pirates into one of degree rather than of kind.[5]

The aim of this chapter is to address the fight against piracy in terms of global law and global governance, with twofold inspiration. First, in doing so, I hope to shed some light on how piracy is dealt with by the international community, focusing on the most visible action: the fight against piracy off the coast of Somalia. Secondly, a closer look at piracy may also help sharpen our understanding of global law and global governance. The reason why piracy in particular may be of use is the classic one, according to which pirates tend to operate in the interstices of the international system. The pirate is often said to fall between the cracks of the system of sovereign states, each with their own system of jurisdiction. Operating on the high seas, pirates do not fall within anyone's territorial jurisdiction in an obvious manner. Being composed, typically, of a variety of individuals of different nationality, pirate groups tend also to evade all too obvious applications of jurisdiction based on nationality and, given that the victims of piracy tend to be private persons rather more often than public entities, protective jurisdiction can usually not plausibly be invoked either.[6]

It is for this reason, so it is often claimed, that international law developed its universality principle of jurisdiction. This presupposes that pirates can be deemed 'enemies of mankind' subject to universal (or at least quasi-universal) approbation and condemnation.[7] As noted above, this depiction of pirates as enemies of mankind comes with its ambivalences and might on occasion provoke dissent, which renders piracy an even more interesting laboratory with respect to possibilities for global law and, as we shall see, in particular global governance.

II. GLOBAL LAW AND GLOBAL GOVERNANCE

It remains, as yet, uncommon to speak of 'global law'; indeed, it is questionable whether there exists a generally accepted definition of what the term might mean. The leading comparativist William Twining, for example, is sceptical, pointing out that the adjective 'global' is often utilised rather too quickly. Terms such as 'global law', he writes, 'are abused and over-used in many ways, often as part of generalisations that are false, exaggerated, misleading, meaningless, superficial, ethnocentric, or a com-

---

[4] See Grotius, *On the Law of War and Peace*, Neff edn (Cambridge, Cambridge University Press, 2012; first published 1625), book III, ch 3, s 2.

[5] Ibid.

[6] Useful on jurisdiction and its links with the traditional requirements of statehood is B Simma and AT Müller, 'Exercise and Limits of Jurisdiction' in J Crawford and M Koskenniemi (eds), *The Cambridge Companion to International Law* (Cambridge, Cambridge University Press, 2012).

[7] Rubin cogently argues that assertions of jurisdiction over pirates had little to do with universal conceptions of property or universal condemnation of thievery, but stops short of arguing against the functionalist point that piracy would fall through the cracks in the system without universal jurisdiction. See Rubin, n 4 above. Notably, Kontorovich suggests that universal jurisdiction over piracy was usually thought to be based on the heinousness of the crime, a construction he deplores. He too, however, refrains from addressing the functionalist point. See E Kontorovich, 'The Piracy Analogy: Modern Universal Jurisdiction's Hollow Foundation' (2004) 45 *Harvard International Law Journal* 183.

bination of all of these'.[8] From a strict (or even not so strict) positivist perspective, Twining has a point, of course: few rules are globally accepted, and even those that are tend to be applied in rather different ways in different places.

International law contains a few rules that, it would seem, are globally accepted. Some of these are technical (for want of a better term) and based on reciprocity. Thus, states universally respect the sanctity of diplomatic mail, and coastal states (not a universal group) tend universally to grant passing ships the right of innocent passage, under conditions that would seem to be universally accepted. In this sense, global law is by no means impossible, even if fairly rare. Any possible disputes tend to be done away with swiftly by domestic courts, if they ever even reach the local judiciary. It would seem, for instance, that the right to innocent passage is sometimes invoked by defendants accused of drugs trafficking, in the hope that courts overlook the traditional exception with respect to this particular line of work.[9]

In addition, there are some norms of international law that are globally accepted as part of an international 'ordre public': so-called *jus cogens* norms. While this is an open-ended group, most observers agree that it includes the prohibitions of genocide, apartheid, torture, slavery and slave trade. Even so, universal application hardly exists: while some courts have exercised universal jurisdiction over violations of such norms— perhaps most famously the US Court of Appeals for the Second Circuit in *Filartiga*, addressing torture[10]—others have not, and whether or not they should do so depends first and foremost on whether domestic law allows local courts to apply jurisdiction over international crimes and, if so, which specifically. The most that can be said is that international law does not, generally, resist the exercise of universal jurisdiction; but it would be too strong to say that international law obligates states to exercise universal jurisdiction.[11]

And then, of course, there are a number of rules from domestic law that would seem to be more or less universally accepted: prohibitions of murder and theft, for example, or the sanctity of contract. To refer to these as 'global law' would, however, be awkward: not only may local definitions of what constitutes theft vary considerably, but so too do penalties. There may be fairly little uniformity here, and it would seem cumbersome to describe rules springing from local communities as having somehow attained global status without there being some global recognition of the propriety of these norms. Moreover (but arguably less to the point), the classic dualist Westphalian structure divides law into domestic and international orders, and has a hard time accepting as universally valid the aggregate contents of domestic law without a further transboundary element: while customary international law typically involves the aggregate of domestic laws and practices, these become *international* law by virtue of there being a transboundary element.

One reason for the scarcity of global law, then (at least on positivist premises),

---

[8] See W Twining, *General Jurisprudence: Understanding Law from a Global Perspective* (Cambridge, Cambridge University Press, 2009) 14.

[9] The 1958 Convention on the Territorial Sea (in Art 19) and the 1982 UN Convention on the Law of the Sea (Art 27) allow for the exercise of criminal jurisdiction by coastal states if necessary for the suppression of illicit traffic in narcotic drugs. See, eg the cases reported in 73 ILR 182–83 and 283–86.

[10] See *Filártiga v Pena-Irala*, 630 F.2d 876, US Court of Appeals, 2d Circuit, 30 June 1980.

[11] For a fine monograph, see M Kmak, *The Scope and Application of the Principle of Universal Jurisdiction* (Helsinki, Erik Castrén Institute, 2011).

resides in the necessity of such law coming with strict validity requirements. By contrast, global governance is generally considered a much more fluid phenomenon, especially if not limited to successful, or immediately successful, exercises alone. Hence, it might be easier to identify global governance than it is to identify global law. It is by no means eccentric, for instance, to regard the creation and functioning of the International Criminal Court as an exercise in global governance:[12] the mere circumstance that a large number of states, backed by an active civil society movement, aims to lay down the law on war criminals and *genocidaires* by stipulating what is proper and what is improper behaviour may not amount to global law, but it does amount to global governance, or at least to a simulacrum thereof.[13] The circumstance that some of the largest military powers are not part of the project does little to undermine it: the ICC represents an attempt to govern the globe and set the relevant standards, and those that have chosen not to participate are clearly on the defensive, condemned to making counter-moves, the most well known of which was the US initiative to conclude many bilateral agreements creating immunities from the ICC's jurisdiction for US troops.

Likewise, it is not uncommon to think of the work of the International Organization for Standardization (ISO) as an exercise in global governance, despite ISO's unclear legal status in international law, and despite the circumstance that many of the standards developed are to be complied with on a voluntary basis. In short, global governance can be exercised as a matter of fact by whoever is in a position to exercise it, regardless of legal status, legal competences or whether the instruments used are recognisably legal instruments. This places quite a challenge on international law: it has to come to terms with amorphous actors utilising elusive instruments lest it becomes largely irrelevant. One response has been to posit the existence of a global administrative law,[14] whereas others have found inspiration in constitutionalist thought.[15]

Either way, typical for global governance (and often difficult to capture in legal terms, regardless of the adjective) is that it involves either the work of entities of unclear status or the work of specialised powerful organs subjected to little legal regulation: the Security Council is perhaps the best possible example. The next section will pay some attention to the Council as well as the Contact Group on Piracy off the Coast of Somalia (the Contact Group), exercising institutional authority and capacity-based authority respectively.[16]

---

[12] For instance, Danner and Voeten's work on the agency of international criminal judges is premised on the idea of international criminal law as manifesting global governance. See A Danner and E Voeten, 'Who is Running the International Criminal Justice System?' in DD Avant, M Finnemore and SK Sell (eds), *Who Governs the Globe?* (Cambridge, Cambridge University Press, 2010).

[13] See J Klabbers, 'Hannah Arendt and the Languages of Global Governance' in M Goldoni and C McCorkindale (eds), *Hannah Arendt and the Law* (Oxford, Hart Publishing, 2012).

[14] See B Kingsbury, N Krisch and RB Stewart, 'The Emergence of Global Administrative Law' (2005) 68 *Law and Contemporary Problems* 15; A von Bogdandy et al (eds), *The Exercise of Public Authority by International Institutions: Advancing International Institutional Law* (Heidelberg, Springer, 2010).

[15] For discussion, see J Klabbers, A Peters and G Ulfstein, *The Constitutionalization of International Law* (Oxford, Oxford University Press, 2009).

[16] Avant et al have developed a useful framework, further identifying delegated authority, expert authority and principle-based authority. See DD Avant et al, 'Who Governs the Globe?' in Avant et al, n 12 above, 11–14.

III. PIRACY AND GLOBAL LAW?

As the various other contributions to this volume suggest, piracy can hardly be considered as an emanation of global law. In Malcolm Evans's pithy phrase, piracy is 'not that important a problem'.[17] As Robin Churchill underlines, many states lack piracy legislation, and those states that do have some laws on the books may have widely divergent laws.[18] Hence, to think of piracy as somehow part of global law would seem feasible only upon a very relaxed—too relaxed—definition of what global law might stand for.

As far as international law goes, moreover, international law contains a definition of piracy, but does not spell out what consequences attach to acts of piracy.[19] Article 101 UNCLOS defines piracy as 'any illegal acts of violence or detention' taking place on the high seas,[20] but does not say what the illegality consists of or how it ought to be punished. Hence, Guilfoyle suggests that the norm against piracy is not so much a substantive norm of criminal law, but rather a jurisdictional device: 'every State may seize a pirate ship or aircraft', as Article 105 UNCLOS puts it. Moreover, the courts of the apprehending state may decide on penalties and determine which action ought to be taken with regard to the ships or property, Article 105 continues. In other words, the relevant articles in the Law of the Sea Convention spell out not so much what precise behaviour is prohibited as which states are allowed to do something about it.[21]

It is here, arguably, that the vaguely romantic appeal of piracy plays an important role: it precludes piracy from being regarded as the sort of activity that demands universal condemnation in the strongest terms. Neil Boister has usefully distinguished between international criminal law and what he proposes to refer to as 'transnational criminal law'.[22] The former would comprise activities such as genocide or crimes against humanity: these are strong norms condemning acts that shock mankind's sense of morality. By contrast, transnational criminal law would cover criminal activities which have a transnational element but which do not shock mankind in quite the same way. Drugs trafficking and money laundering might fall into this category, and, while Boister does not refer to it, so might piracy.

After all, one of the hallmarks of transnational criminal law is that enforcement is usually left to domestic authorities. Since there is no international tribunal for piracy, and since piracy does seem to evoke vaguely romantic sentiments in addition to concern, it would seem to follow that piracy is best seen as coming under transnational criminal law, in Boister's classification, and therewith can hardly be regarded as an element of global law.[23]

Finally, it may be useful to be reminded that, even if it were true that states can

---

[17] MD Evans and S Galani, Chapter 15 above, 365.

[18] See R Churchill, Chapter 1 above, note 86 and text.

[19] For a brief but solid overview, see I Shearer, 'Piracy' in R Wolfrum (ed), *Max Planck Encyclopedia of Public International Law* (Oxford, Oxford University Press, 2012), vol VIII, 320–27.

[20] This also covers, under UNCLOS, the maritime zones in which states exercise functional jurisdiction (such as the exclusive economic zone), but not territorial waters. See Shearer, ibid, 323.

[21] See D Guilfoyle, Chapter 2 above. See also D Guilfoyle, *Shipping Interdiction and the Law of the Sea* (Cambridge, Cambridge University Press, 2009).

[22] See N Boister, '"Transnational Criminal Law"?' (2003) 14 *European Journal of International Law* 953.

[23] Elsewhere Boister tentatively classifies piracy as 'arguably a prototype transnational crime'. See N Boister, *An Introduction to Transnational Criminal Law* (Oxford, Oxford University Press, 2012) 29.

prosecute pirates based on universal jurisdiction,[24] it does not follow that piracy is, or even ought to be, regarded as universally prohibited. This is so for two reasons. First, the distinction between substance (piracy) and procedure (prosecution), however difficult to flesh out, has met with long-standing recognition in international law, and, while manifested in different settings, has repeatedly been confirmed by the ICJ. Thus, the ICJ has held that the existence of *erga omnes* obligations does not mean that states can seize the ICJ without a sufficiently established jurisdictional link.[25] It has held that *jus cogens* rules and the rules on state immunity cannot be in conflict with one another because they deal with different aspects (substance versus procedure);[26] and in a recent environmental dispute it held that breaches of procedural norms need to be separated from allegations concerning breaches of substantial provisions, even in a setting in which, arguably, substantive norms are largely made up of bundles of procedural obligations.[27]

The second reason is this. While international law does not prohibit the exercise of adjudicative jurisdiction based on the principle of universality, it does not demand it either, not even when it comes to genocide. The Genocide Convention grants jurisdiction to the state where the genocide was committed or to some international tribunal, as agreed (Article VI), but is careful not to go further. In other words, international law is permissive, in this respect: it allows for states to exercise universal jurisdiction but does not demand it, and states are free not to exercise their right. Even those crimes which are subject (on the basis of a treaty) to the *aut dedere, aut judicare* principle do not properly mark emanations of the universality principle because, as Boister puts it, jurisdiction in such situations is 'subsidiary to the failure to extradite and thus has a limiting territorial element: it depends on the presence of the accused within the territory of the state establishing jurisdiction'.[28]

In short, it cannot convincingly be argued that the fight against piracy is a matter of global law, if that term is to have any independent meaning beyond 'transnational' or 'international' law. States retain too much freedom with regard to piracy to apply the label 'global law' in any meaningful way. There is a lack of clarity as to what the illegality of piracy consists of, and too much divergence in enforcement.

IV. PIRACY AND GLOBAL GOVERNANCE

To some extent, piracy has attracted the attention of the global governance agency *par excellence*: the UN Security Council. In a series of resolutions adopted in 2008, the Council established a comprehensive anti-piracy regime relating to Somalia. In the first relevant resolution, Resolution 1814 of 15 May 2008, little of this was visible. The resolution was aimed first and foremost at establishing a political process in Somalia,

---

[24] Some have expressed considerable hesitation on this point. See, eg AP Rubin, *Ethics and Authority in International Law* (Cambridge, Cambridge University Press, 1997) 24.

[25] See *East Timor (Portugal v Australia)*, [1995] ICJ Reports 90.

[26] See *Jurisdictional Immunities of the State (Germany v Italy)*, Judgment of 3 February 2012, nyr.

[27] See *Pulp Mills on the River Uruguay (Argentina v Uruguay)*, Judgment of 20 April 2010, nyr. The point about the substance of international environmental law consisting largely of procedural obligations was at the heart of the powerful dissent by judges Al-Khasawneh and Simma.

[28] See Boister, n 22 above, 964. Hence he coins the phrase 'subsidiary universality'.

with a view to the promotion of peace and stable state institutions. Nonetheless, the preamble expressed serious concern about the worsening humanitarian situation, noting difficulties for humanitarian organisations 'including humanitarian access and security for humanitarian personnel'.[29] The operative paragraphs do not specifically refer to piracy in any form, but express support for the protection of World Food Programme maritime convoys and calls upon states to protect shipping relating to the transportation and delivery of humanitarian aid.[30] Moreover, it demands that access to humanitarian assistance is ensured, and urges the countries in the region to facilitate the passage of essential relief goods.[31]

Two and a half weeks later, the Council zoomed in more closely on piracy by means of Resolution 1816 (2008). It linked the problems with delivery of humanitarian assistance to piracy, and also expressed grave concern about the safety of commercial maritime routes and international navigation more generally.[32] The resolution urges states to be vigilant with respect to acts of piracy, encourages them to increase and coordinate their efforts to deter such acts, and urges further cooperation and information-sharing.[33] More to the point, perhaps, the resolution allows states to enter the territorial waters of Somalia in order to repress acts of piracy, and authorises the use of 'all necessary means to repress acts of piracy' within those territorial waters.[34] Essentially, it would seem, the regular means of combating piracy on the high seas are being extended to Somalia's territorial waters for a period of six months and are dependent on a form of cooperation with the Transitional Federal Government (TFG) of Somalia.[35] Two subsequent resolutions added some detail and extended the period of authorisation.[36]

Of greater policy relevance is Resolution 1851 (2008), which in its preamble notes that 'lack of capacity, domestic legislation, and clarity how to dispose of pirates after their capture, has hindered more robust international action',[37] and consequently invites states to conclude so-called shiprider agreements (using foreign law enforcement officials on ships)[38] and encourages the establishment of an international cooperation mechanism.[39] This cooperation mechanism would become the so-called Contact Group on Piracy off the Coast of Somalia, a network cum organisation (it is a bit unclear which) comprising some 60 states and a number of intergovernmental organisations and other international actors, established in January 2009.[40]

The Contact Group is explicitly set up pursuant to SC Resolution 1851 (2008), but,

---

[29] See SC Resolution 1814, 15 May 2008, preambular para 17.

[30] Ibid, para 11.

[31] Ibid, para 12.

[32] See SC Resolution 1816, 2 June 2008, preambular para 2.

[33] Ibid, paras 2 and 3.

[34] Ibid, para 7.

[35] The language used is decidedly opaque: the chapeau of para 7 refers to 'States cooperating with the TFG in the fight against piracy and armed robbery at sea off the coast of Somalia, for which advance notification has been provided by the TFG to the Secretary-General'. Since August 2012, Somalia has been governed by a President and a Cabinet, according to SC Resolution 2077, 21 November 2012.

[36] See SC Resolutions 1838, 7 October 2008, and 1846, 2 December 2008.

[37] See SC Resolution 1851, 16 December 2008, preambular para 9.

[38] Ibid, para 3.

[39] Ibid, para 4.

[40] Much of what follows is derived from the Contact Group's website, www.thecgpcs.org (last accessed on 14 January 2013).

while it reports regularly to the UN and its plenary meetings (three per year) are held at UN Headquarters, it is not considered part of the UN.[41] Instead, it operates as an independent entity, and has divided its work between five working groups. The first addresses issues of capacity building in countries neighbouring Somalia, in particular judicial and penal capacity building. Working Group 2 is labelled the Working Group on Legal Issues and deals with anti-piracy, while Working Group 3 deals with defensive action and protection on behalf of industry and labour groups. Working Group 4 addresses public diplomacy issues, while Working Group 5 concentrates on identification and disruption of the financial networks of pirates and their financiers. In January 2010, moreover, a Trust Fund was established within the UN (apparently upon recommendation from the Contact Group) to help finance legal capacity building and the prosecution of piracy.

For students of the legal niceties involved in global governance, the Contact Group and Resolution 1851 (2008) provide interesting examples of global governance. I will argue that the regime thus established is best seen as an exercise in global governance, albeit on a (very) limited part of the globe, and addressing a (very) limited policy issue.

To start with the resolution, one of its most eye-catching features is the legal disclaimer it contains in paragraph 10, which is interesting enough to be cited at length. The Council:

> Affirms that the authorization provided in this resolution apply only with respect to the situation in Somalia and shall not affect the rights or obligations or responsibilities of Member States under international law, including any rights or obligations under UNCLOS, with respect to any other situation, and underscores in particular that this resolution shall not be considered as establishing customary international law, and affirms further that such authorizations have been provided only following the receipt of the 9 December 2008 letter conveying the consent of the TFG.[42]

This is interesting for several reasons. First, the resolution makes it clear that it applies only with respect to the situation in Somalia, and thus cannot justify any counter-piracy action taken elsewhere in the world. The precise reason for this is not immediately self-evident, but may well reside in several factors simultaneously. It might be that the piracy situation off the Somali coast was considered worse than elsewhere, although reportedly piracy has also been on the rise in the South China Sea and the Malacca and Singapore Straits.[43] It might be the case that the economic interests of shipping and oil industries were considerably more affected by Somali piracy than by piracy elsewhere, or that piracy interfered to a far greater extent with the provision of basic services and humanitarian assistance in Somalia than elsewhere. And the assent

---

[41] See W Hoge, 'Interview with Henk Swarttouw, Chairman of the Contact Group on Piracy off the Coast of Somalia', available at www.theglobalobservatory.org/interviews/167-interview-with-henk-swart-touw-chairman-of-the-contact-group-on-piracy-off-the-coast-of-somalia.html (last accessed on 14 January 2013).

[42] See Resolution 1851, 16 December 2008, para 10. To be sure, the same disclaimer was already present in SC resolution 1816 (2008), para 9, and repeated in SC Resolutions 1838 and 1846 (paras 8 and 11, respectively). Moreover, the claim that political action should have no precedential value has been heard in earlier contexts as well, eg in connection with NATO's intervention over Kosovo in 1999.

[43] See Guilfoyle, n 21 above, 53–61. Here also an entity was created under a 2005 Regional Agreement on Combating Piracy and Armed Robbery at Sea against Ships in Asia (ReCAAP). See DM Ong, Chapter 12 above.

of the TFG may also have been a factor—while there can be little doubt that, under Chapter VII of the Charter, the Security Council has the power to authorise actions within a Member State's territorial waters, the assent of the TFG may be presumed to add considerably to the legitimacy of such an authorisation.[44] More intriguingly, it helps to dissolve possible problems relating to the precise limit of Somalia's territorial waters. In 1972, Somalia claimed a territorial sea extending to 200 miles off the coast and, while it has since become a party to UNCLOS and is thus bound to respect a maximum of 12 miles, it would seem that the 200 mile claim has never been revoked. By insisting on the participation of the TFG, the width of the territorial sea is all but guaranteed not to become an issue.[45]

Secondly, the resolution specifies in paragraph 10, as cited above, that the authorisation shall not affect the rights, obligations or responsibilities of UN Member States under international law '. . . with respect to any other situation'. The position of the comma in the sentence just quoted creates some interpretative issues, but is probably the result of a reference, between commas, to UNCLOS, and thus an indication that the regime is allowed to override those rights, obligations and responsibilities as far as the situation off the Somali coast is concerned, but not elsewhere. As Treves points out, the reference to existing rights, obligations and responsibilities was considered necessary by many smaller nations to safeguard the integrity of UNCLOS: it was thought necessary to prevent the Somali piracy regime from being regarded as an attempt to rewrite the rules of UNCLOS.

Thirdly, and most curiously, the resolution provides that it 'shall not be considered as establishing customary international law'. Again, it is not immediately self-evident what this means, but the most likely explanation is the desire to prevent a precedential effect. This in itself opens up tricky jurisprudential issues in international law. One may wonder, for instance, whether UN authorised action can ever become customary international law, or even whether the activities of international organisations themselves can become customary international law applicable between states.[46] At least thus far, the ICJ has been reluctant to view the practice of international organisations as anything more than the collective practice of states,[47] and if that still holds true, then the practice of the Security Council is, at best, the practice of three handfuls of states, and therewith not quite general enough to ground a customary rule.[48] Then again, it cannot be excluded that some of the members of the Security Council with potential piracy problems of their own desired an explicit guarantee that the Somali action could not be used later against them—it is probably no coincidence that the point about not contributing to the formation of customary international law was

---

[44] It has the added benefit of bolstering the status of the TFG.

[45] See T Treves, 'Piracy, Law of the Sea, and Use of Force: Developments off the Coast of Somalia' (2009) 20 *European Journal of International Law* 399, 407–08.

[46] A different question is whether organisational practices may become customary law applicable in international institutional law or governing relations between international organisations.

[47] See J Klabbers, 'International Organizations in the Formation of Customary International Law' in E Cannizzaro and P Palchetti (eds), *Customary International Law on the Use of Force* (Leiden, Martinus Nijhoff, 2005).

[48] There is a preceding conceptual question here: is the relevant action that of the Council, or that of states based on Council authorisation?

made most explicitly by Indonesia and Vietnam.[49] Moreover, there might be merit in the suggestion that, by expressing a non-lawmaking intent, the Council catered to the wishes of states who deemed it necessary to protect the integrity of UNCLOS.[50] Finally, there is the scope of Resolution 1851 (2008) to be considered: it speaks consistently of not only piracy but also armed robbery at sea, as do the previous resolutions mentioned above. The reason for this is no doubt that piracy in international law is rather narrowly defined: acts are only acts of piracy if committed on the high seas, and if they involve two or more ships or aircraft. Thus, acts taking place on one ship only would not constitute piracy, but may well classify as armed robbery at sea, as would, possibly, acts taking place in territorial waters. Moreover, it is noteworthy that Resolution 1851 (2008) also authorises action 'in Somalia': this was reportedly a response to a pursuit of pirates into mainland Somalia, but may also be seen to cover acts related to the preparation or aftermath of piracy.[51]

The establishment of the Contact Group raises other intriguing issues. For one thing, it is unclear whether the Contact Group must be seen as an international organisation. It lacks some of the formal characteristics of an international organisation. For instance, there seems to be no foundational document. Some of the participants (major flag states, for the most part) have signed the 2009 New York Declaration, recognising the desirability of concerted action and adoption of 'best management practices' against piracy, but this declaration contains no institutional provisions.[52] The Contact Group seems to have no rules on admission (or expulsion or suspension) of members, although its website notes that the Contact Group 'offers participation to any country or international organisation making a tangible contribution to the counter-piracy effort, or to any country significantly affected by piracy off the coast of Somalia'.[53] Other stakeholders may be invited to join as observers. In addition, there is little evidence of the Contact Group being able to adopt instruments, and little information concerning the sorts of powers that have been conferred upon it.

On the other hand, the Contact Group does seem to have a plenary organ (meeting three times a year) and five working groups—from this perspective, at least, it looks not unlike an international organisation. Its membership, however fluid, consists predominantly of states and international organisations (including the UN, EU, IMO, NATO, Arab League and INTERPOL), with a handful other entities thrown in, such as the Seafarers International Union and the International Chamber of Shipping.

Perhaps the most sensible taxonomic conclusion to draw is that the Contact Group is best seen as a network, with all that this entails.[54] It is generally held that networks

---

[49] Indonesia did so most clearly when discussing SC Resolution 1816 (2008); see S/PV.5902, 2. See also, with respect to SC Resolution 1851 (2008), the statements by Indonesia and Vietnam, S/PV.6406, 6.

[50] See Treves, n 45 above, 405, who suggests that Security Council practice might contribute to a new customary rule. He deems the expression of non-intent to be of debatable value: it would provide 'a strong, although perhaps not insurmountable, argument' against the formation of a new rule of customary international law.

[51] See Resolution 1851 (2008), para 6.

[52] It was signed by the Bahamas, Cyprus, Japan, Liberia, the Marshall Islands, Panama, Singapore, the UK and the US, with the UK even making a reservation (a sign that the declaration is taken seriously indeed). The text can be found at http://www.state.gov/r/pa/prs/ps/2009/sept/128767.htm (last accessed on 14 January 2013).

[53] See www.thecgpcs.org (last accessed on 14 January 2013).

[54] The seminal study is A-M Slaughter, *A New World Order* (Princeton, NJ, Princeton University Press, 2004).

offer flexibility and a 'can do' mentality, rather than the lengthy and protracted procedures often associated with formal international organisations.[55] Their drawbacks, however, are also well recorded: they offer little transparency, and accountability (democratic, judicial or otherwise) is difficult to achieve. It is also difficult to get a precise handle on what the Contact Group is actually doing: documents on its website are hidden behind a password.

V. FRAGMENTATION OR CONCERTED EFFORTS?

The Security Council and the Contact Group are not the only bodies involved in the fight against piracy off the Somali coast. The Maritime Safety Committee of the IMO has issued a number of guidelines and instructions both on the prevention of piracy and armed robbery at sea (dating back to 1984) and on the use of privately contracted armed security personnel. Moreover, the IMO has sponsored the conclusion of the so-called SUA Convention, addressing the suppression of unlawful acts against the safety of maritime navigation. This SUA Convention has, to date, 156 parties, and is generally referred to as being among the relevant legal instruments, despite not being specifically directed against piracy—its main inspiration was combating terrorism, in particular the hijacking of the *Achille Lauro* in 1985.[56]

Since 2008, the EU contributes by having established the European Naval Force Somalia (EU NAVFOR), in order to protect the delivery of food and humanitarian assistance, as well as to deter, prevent and repress acts of piracy generally.[57] NAVFOR was accompanied by a coordination cell, reportedly consisting of five individuals and operating on a minimal budget. This initially met with some scepticism, and was considered by some as 'more symbolic than practical'.[58] Nevertheless, NAVFOR itself is regularly instrumental in arresting piracy suspects, and the operation has been joined by several non-EU Member States: Norway, Croatia[59] and Ukraine have provided ships or personnel, and transfer agreements have been concluded with Montenegro, Seychelles and Kenya.[60] The EU has an obvious economic interest at stake: reportedly, almost a third of Europe's oil supply is transported through the Gulf of Aden.[61] EU NAVFOR also operates a register of ships passing through the area, and urges all ships to register in advance.

NATO operates a counter-piracy task force that is operative in the area, currently under the title Operation Ocean Shield and consisting of three ships. Its main role is

---

[55] See M Hajer, *Authoritative Governance* (Oxford, Oxford University Press, 2009).

[56] On the *Achille Lauro* affair, see A Cassese, *Law and Violence in the Modern Age*, Greenleaves trans (Princeton, NJ, Princeton University Press, 1988). See also Guilfoyle, Chapter 2 above.

[57] See Joint Action 2008/851/CFSP [2008] OJ L301/33. See the analysis by R Gosalbo-Bono and S Boelaert, Chapter 5 above.

[58] See R Middleton, 'Piracy in Somalia: Threatening Global Trade, Feeding Local Wars', Chatham House briefing paper 08/02, available at www.chathamhouse.org.uk (last accessed on 14 January 2013), 8.

[59] Croatia has since joined the EU, as of 1 July 2013.

[60] See Council Decision 2009/199/CFSP concluding the agreement with Montenegro [2009] OJ L88/1, and Council Decision 2009/877/CFSP concluding the agreement with Kenya [2009] OJ L315/35. For the Agreement with Kenya, which has now been revoked, see [2009] OJ L79/49. For an analysis of the transfer agreements, see D Thym, Chapter 6 above. See generally www.eunavfor.eu (last accessed on 15 January 2013).

[61] According to the chairman of Lloyd's of London, speaking in 2009. See http://www.lloyds.com/lloyds/press-centre/speeches/2009/04/todays_piracy_problem (last accessed on 15 January 2009).

to provide naval escorts and deterrence,[62] and occasionally NATO ships are involved in arresting suspected pirates, sometimes in conjunction with EU NAVFOR.[63]

The shipping industry too is involved. A group of interest organisations comprising, amongst others, Intertanko, Intercargo and the International Chamber of Shipping, adopted best management practices (fourth edition) with respect to piracy in the Gulf of Aden and off the Somali coast in 2011, and used this as something of a blueprint for the adoption of a set of interim guidelines in December 2012 addressing piracy in the Gulf of Guinea region.[64]

In short, there is a lot of action going on, with many stakeholders being involved in the formulation of guidelines and in protection and deterrence. This is, no doubt, one of the reasons why the Contact Group was established: to facilitate coordination and harmonisation. Yet it also suggests that sometimes the left hand may have difficulty working out what the right hand is doing and may even, as in other walks of life, lead to turf wars between the various stakeholders involved.

There may also be other factors at stake: it is notable, for instance, that the private insurance industry does not seem to have developed any high-profile anti-piracy initiatives—the insurance providers involved with the Contact Group, in the form of the International Group of P&I Clubs, are all non-profit mutual insurance associations.[65] The Chairman of Lloyd's of London, speaking about piracy in 2009, noted that shipowners using risky waters should expect to pay higher premiums, and that piracy was now being reclassified into the category of insurance against war, presumably also against higher rates. He also noted, more generally, that rerouting ships around the calmer Horn of Africa would delay transport considerably, and would thus result in higher costs for consumers.[66]

Moreover, it has been observed that one of the factors contributing to the rise in piracy off the Somali coast resides in the collapse of Somalia's fishing industry, with its waters being heavily fished by European, Asian and African ships.[67] If so, this represents (yet again) the truism that global issues need a holistic approach. While many have urged the international community to bring peace and stability to Somalia, it might also not be a bad idea to create or maintain legitimate economic opportunities for local populations.

In the end, the international community seems to have taken over the provision of law and order in and around Somalia, though to a limited extent geographically (territorial waters, occasionally mainland Somalia) and for a limited purpose (the fight against piracy and armed robbery at sea, but nothing else). This is a curious exercise of global governance, somewhere between regular enforcement action under UN auspices and international territorial administration. There is little doubt that the Security Council can do so, either under Chapter VII of the Charter or under a vari-

---

[62] See PM Olson, Chapter 7 above.
[63] For instance, on 5 January 2013 a NATO ship and a NAVFOR ships together apprehended twelve suspects. For more details, see www.eunavfor.eu.
[64] See http://www.ics-shipping.org/piracybmp.htm (last accessed on 15 January 2013).
[65] See http://www.igpandi.org/Home (last accessed on 15 January 2013). P&I, incidentally, stands for protection and indemnity.
[66] See http://www.lloyds.com/lloyds/press-centre/speeches/2009/04/todays_piracy_problem.
[67] See Middleton, n 58 above, 5.

ation of the responsibility to protect doctrine,[68] all the more so given the consent of the local authorities.

Several questions still remain. For instance, why focus on piracy off the Somali coast and nowhere else? More pressingly, perhaps, given the repeated insistence by most stakeholders (including the Council itself) that the stabilisation of Somalia would in itself be an important element in the fight against piracy, why not focus more specifically on peace building? It is notable that the tone of the relevant Council resolutions has changed over time: while Resolution 1814 (2008) was replete with references to 'establishing peace and security in Somalia',[69] Resolution 1851 treats Somalia solely as a breeding ground for piracy, as does the lengthy Resolution 2077 (2012).[70]

While various explanations for this changing tone are possible, there is always the nagging suspicion that focusing on piracy is easier to organise and much easier to find support for—also given the concrete interests at stake—than trying to stabilise a country in disarray. And if romance is usually a two-sided affair (no pun intended), perhaps the romantic appeal of fighting piracy rather outweighs the romantic appeal of muddling through in peace building. Either way, the downside is that the work on piracy is concentrating on symptoms rather than underlying causes. This is not automatically to say that Somalia ought be subjected to full territorial administration under UN auspices; what it does mean, however, is that there seems to be little coherent justification for the partial and limited administration (law and order relating to piracy) that is currently in place.

VI. BY WAY OF CONCLUSION

In a sense, the terms 'global law' and 'global governance' are best seen as metaphors, describing with greater or lesser accuracy the existence of legal norms or the exercise of authority on a global level by global actors. Neither has a well-defined content, and perhaps this applies even more strongly to global law than to global governance.

It would seem to follow from the above that piracy is not subjected to anything resembling global law. Instead, legal approaches remain decidedly local, and while there are attempts to help strengthen local capacity, there is no global regime against piracy. Put in quasi-Kelsenian terms,[71] international law by and large delegates the treatment of pirates to local authorities: it allows for prosecution on the basis of the thought that piracy falls under the universality principle of jurisdiction, but does not oblige states to take action.

It would also seem to follow from the above, though, that one particular mani-

---

[68] On the latter see A Orford, *International Authority and the Responsibility to Protect* (Cambridge, Cambridge University Press, 2011).

[69] See SC Resolution 1814 (2008) in almost all of the first 12 preambular paras, with only the penultimate para zooming on piracy-related concerns.

[70] See Security Council Resolution 2077 (2012) 21 November 2012: of its 29 preambular paras and 36 operative paras, only two can charitably be said to refer to peace building: preambular para 26 emphasises the importance of peace and stability, with the next para welcoming Somalia's presidential elections of September 2012 and subsequent cabinet formation.

[71] See in particular H Kelsen, *Principles of International Law* (New York, Rinehart & Co, 1952). Kelsen's conception of the relationship between states and international law would possibly deserve renewed consideration in the context of global governance.

festation of piracy is subjected to quite a bit of global governance. The UN Security Council is involved in the fight against piracy off the Somali coast, as are a variety of other actors, operating within the broad limits set by the Security Council. Thus, the international community concentrates on a particular piece of the globe, and aims to manage it to the best of its ability. As with all exercises of power, this ought to provoke the question why this particular situation has been singled out.

Harold D Lasswell famously defined politics as 'who gets what, when, how'.[72] While this is an impoverished definition of politics, focusing solely on the distributional side of politics and not on its responsible side (*vel non*), it is nonetheless also a useful starting point for the scrutiny of global governance. Somali piracy has triggered a set of responses that have not been witnessed elsewhere, and while those responses may be perfectly legitimate in and of themselves, one nonetheless has to wonder why these particular responses were singled out and not others. Moreover, while in legal terms there is little wrong with the action authorised by the Security Council, the large variety of actors involved and their sometimes nebulous status and modus operandi do raise concerns about accountability. Then again, that is only fitting: arguably the main current challenge to global governance resides in how it can be controlled[73]—and the fight against piracy off the Somali coast proves no exception.

---

[72] See HD Lasswell, *Politics. Who Gets What, When, How* (Cleveland OH, Meridian Press, 1958 [1936]).
[73] For further reflections on this theme, see J Klabbers, 'Law, Ethics and Global Governance: Account-ability in Perspective' (2013) 11 *New Zealand Journal of Public and International Law* forthcoming.

15

Piracy and the Development of International Law

MALCOLM D EVANS AND SOFIA GALANI

I. INTRODUCTION

T
HIS CHAPTER SEEKS to step back from the detail of the debates concerning the current international responses to piracy in order to consider
some of the more general questions which those responses raise. Since it is
impossible to deal fully with such questions in a short chapter such as this, its purpose
is limited to offering some general observations concerning the manner in which the
current concerns regarding piracy, and the responses to them, may raise questions of
more general significance for a number of key areas of international law and their
future direction. Of the many such areas which could have been chosen, this chapter
focus chiefly on issues concerning jurisdiction, human rights and soft law, though
others will also be touched on too. The choice is eclectic, but is designed in part to
illuminate just how far-reaching the potential implications of practice arising from the
responses to Somali piracy might be.

Although the purpose of this chapter is to focus on the future, it is worth recalling
at the outset that piracy and the responses to it have played a critical role in shaping
our understanding of international law.[1] At the same time, some of the problems we
face with tackling piracy today are a direct result of the structuring of contemporary
international law itself. The entire point about piracy from an international law perspective is that it 'does not fit' with the basic organising principle around which the
subject is structured, this being the existence of a system of states exercising territorial
sovereignty. Piracy is 'special' because it sits outside of that framework—comprising
illegal acts by private persons 'on the high seas or in any other place outside the juris-

---

[1] Indeed the challenges of tackling violence at sea lie close to the very foundations of international law
and contemporary legal structuring in relation to it. See, eg A Clapham, *Brierly's Law of Nations*, 7th edn
(Oxford, Oxford University Press, 2012) 225; see generally A Rubin, *The Law of Piracy* (Newport, RI, Naval
War College Press, 1988); A Rubin, *Ethics and Authority in International Law* (Cambridge, Cambridge
University Press, 1997). For a short, helpful, historical account see R Geiss and A Petrig, *Piracy and Armed
Robbery at Sea: The Legal Framework for Counter-piracy Operations in Somalia and the Gulf of Aden*
(Oxford, Oxford University Press, 2011) 37–54.

diction of any State'.[2] It is, then, not surprising that we should see our responses to piracy as a testing ground for evolution and innovation in developing the international order. This is important, since this is, ultimately, what is at stake. To be clear at the outset, this chapter does not aim to explore the impact of Somali (or any other) piracy on international law and international order. Rather, it seeks to highlight a number of questions concerning the future direction of international law—some of which are quite challenging—which merit reflection in the light of the responses to piracy in recent times.

II. PIRACY AND JURISDICTIONAL ISSUES

Piracy challenges the traditional paradigms of international law, so the responses to it deserve to be carefully considered as they too tend to challenge the orthodoxies of the international legal framework, and as a result can have a significant impact upon it. The most obvious example of this is the idea that pirates are 'hostis humani generis'—enemies of mankind as a whole[3] who, because their actions take themselves outside of the state-centred jurisdictional framework, become subject to the jurisdiction of all states: the quintessential example of universal jurisdiction.[4] The concept of universal jurisdiction which this idea has spawned has now developed a life of its own and is deeply embedded in contemporary international law thinking.[5] Yet one might wonder if the supposition on which it is founded was ever really true. From a factual perspective, pirates might have been beyond the reach of those states which might otherwise have exercised jurisdiction over them—and this might justify the vesting of a general jurisdiction over all those who engaged in such acts. Nevertheless, over time it has become the case that it is the nature of the act, rather than the lack of jurisdictional competence over the actors, which has become the defining feature of

---

[2] 1982 Law of the Sea Convention, Art 100. This contrasts with such acts which take place within zones of national jurisdiction, which are classed by the IMO as 'armed robbery at sea'. See N Klein, *Maritime Security and the Law of the Sea* (Oxford, Oxford University Press, 2011) 81. For a discussion of the ambiguities surrounding 'armed robbery at sea' and its relationship to piracy see Geiss and Petrig, n 1, 72–75.

[3] See the classic statement by Judge Moore in *The Lotus* case: 'Piracy . . . is an offence against the law of nations; and as the scene of the pirate's operation is the high seas, which it is not the right or duty of any national to police, he is denied the protection of the flag which he may carry, and is treated as an outlaw, as the enemy of mankind—"hostis humani generis"—whom any nation may in the interest of all capture and punish'. See PCIJ, Ser A No 10 (1927) 70. For an alternative rationale—that it is because piracy endangers a common interest that the flag state does not have exclusive jurisdiction—see D Guilfoyle, *Shipping Interdiction and the Law of the Sea* (Cambridge, Cambridge University Press, 2009) 28–29.

[4] Most of the seminal domestic cases concerning universal jurisdiction have drawn on the piracy analogy either to justify an extension or a restriction upon the scope of universal jurisdiction. See, eg in the US *Filartiga v Pena Irala*, 630 F.2d 876 (2nd cir 1980) at 890; *Sosa v Alvarez Machain*, 542 US 692 (2004); and most recently *Kiobel v Royal Dutch Petroleum Co*, 153 S.Ct 1659 (2013), 10–12. In the UK see, eg the *Pinochet* case, [1999] UKHL 17, where Lord Brown Wilkinson refers to the torturer as the 'common enemy of mankind' when discussing universal jurisdiction. For a critical discussion of the analogy between jurisdiction over piracy and universal jurisdiction based on the supposed heinousness of the acts in question see E Kontorovich, 'The Piracy Analogy: Modern Universal Jurisdiction's Hollow Foundation' (2004) 45 *Harvard International Law Journal* 183. See also Geiss and Petrig, n 1, 145–47, who also reject the 'heniousness' approach and favour the '*locus delicti*' argument.

[5] For an overview see L Reydams, *Universal Jurisdiction* (Oxford, Oxford University Press, 2003). For his subsequent trenchant critique of universal jurisdiction see L Reydams, 'The Rise and Fall of Universal Jurisdiction', Leiden Centre for Global Governance Studies, Working Paper 37 (2010). See also C Ryngeart, *Jurisdiction in International Law* (Oxford, Oxford University Press, 2009) 100–27.

universal jurisdiction today. Nowhere is this change in focus clearer than in the 2001 Princetown Principles on Universal Jurisdiction.[6] Piracy is the first of the seven serious crimes to which it says universal jurisdiction attaches,[7] the Commentary to the Principles observing that '"Piracy" is a crime that paradigmatically is subject to prosecution by any nation based on principles of universality, and it is crucial to the origins of universal jurisdiction, so it comes first'.[8] Yet it goes on to say that 'the whole point of universal jurisdiction would seem to be to permit or even encourage prosecution when states find within their territory a non-citizen accused of serious crimes under international law'.[9] Today, there is no doubt at all that states can exercise jurisdiction over certain categories of acts which, but for their having been made subject to universal jurisdiction, they would not have, nor, crucially, they would need to have, since other states are able, and capable, of exercising jurisdiction over them.[10] Rather than 'filling a gap' in the jurisdictional framework, universal jurisdiction has become a means of highlighting forms of conduct which attract the opprobrium of the international community and broadening the range of states which are capable of taking action against those responsible, rather than it being a means of ensuring that domestic jurisdiction could reach out to those who might otherwise be beyond its reach. Whilst universal jurisdiction may have had its origins in the need to tackle serious illegal activities which took place beyond the jurisdictional reach of *any* state, it has become a means of bringing those responsible for serious illegal activities within the jurisdictional reach of *every* state.

It is, however, noteworthy that the actual exercise of universal jurisdiction in its pure form still remains surprisingly infrequent, despite the emphasis which seems to be placed upon it. Although widely acknowledged, it has not been widely utilised.[11] Even in the context of piracy itself, universal jurisdiction does not appear to be exercised as frequently as might be expected, and the rise in piracy off the coasts of Somalia has not been matched by a commensurate similar increase in the exercise of universal jurisdiction over acts of piracy. Indeed, and as will be commented on later, what is most notable has been the desire of those states whose forces have apprehended pirates to find alternatives to their use of universal jurisdiction to prosecute.

A. Universal Jurisdiction and Somali Piracy

It may be helpful here to address some of the prevailing myths surrounding the international response to Somali piracy. Whilst it is true that the concerted nature of the response at an institutional level has been unprecedented, the innovatory nature of

---

[6] The Princetown Principles were drafted and adopted by a group of scholars in 2001 in an attempt to crystallise emergent practice. For the text, commentary and further consideration see S Macedo, *Universal Jurisdiction* (Philadelphia, PA, University of Pennsylvania Press, 2004).

[7] Princetown Principles, Principle 2(1).

[8] Commentary, 45.

[9] Ibid, 43.

[10] Thus, for example, the Princetown Principles include a lengthy Principle 8 on 'Resolutions of Competing Jurisdictions'. See also Ryngeart, n 5, 127–33.

[11] For a rare example in the UK see *R v Zardad*, unreported, July 2005, [2007] EWCA Crim 279, in which an Afghan warlord was convicted of torture on non UK nationals in Afghanistan. See T Kelly, *This Side of Silence* (Philadelphia, PA, University of Pennsylvania Press, 2011).

reactions of the UN Security Council in authorising international action on the basis of Chapter VII of the UN Charter has tended to be overstated. The first UN Security Council Resolution, Resolution 1816, was adopted in June 2008 and authorised states to[12]

   (a) Enter the territorial waters of Somalia for the purposes of repressing acts of piracy and armed robbery at sea, in a manner consistent with such actions permitted on the high seas with respect to piracy under relevant international law;

   (b) Use, within the territorial waters of Somalia, in a manner consistent with action permitted on the high seas with respect to piracy under relevant international law, all necessary means to repress acts of piracy and armed robbery.

This seemingly startling extension of the powers of states to exercise jurisdiction over piracy and armed robbery within the territorial sea of a state is, however, qualified in two important ways. First, it is not always remembered that, although it ratified the UNCLOS in 1989, it appears that Somalia is yet to revoke its Law No 37 on the Territorial Sea and Ports of 10 September 1972, Article 1 of which provides for the establishment of a 200 nautical mile territorial sea.[13] Indeed, it has recently reaffirmed its continuing applicability.[14] Yet the impermissibility of so extensive a territorial sea under international law is clear, 12 nautical miles being the maximum which a state party to the 1982 Law of the Sea Convention might lawfully claim.[15] Nevertheless, it is certainly helpful to have it made clear, as Resolution 1816 does, that states have the right to take action in the area beyond the 12 nautical miles which international law permits them to do without having to face the prospect of testing the legitimacy of the Somalia's extended maritime claim. To the extent that this is one of the purposes of the resolution, it is more about 'good housekeeping' than expanding the jurisdictional reach in relation to piracy and is merely facilitating the application of the pre-existing orthodoxies.

   On the face of it, however, the extension by Security Council resolution of the power of all states to apprehend pirates and armed robbers within the undoubted 12 nautical mile territorial sea does appear revolutionary—as does the subsequent extension in December 2008 by Resolution 1851 (2008) to undertake 'all necessary measures that are appropriate in Somalia for the purposes of suppressing acts of piracy and armed robbery at sea'.[16] However, Resolutions 1816 (2008) and 1851 (2008) and all subsequent resolutions authorising such action[17] have all made it clear that the Transitional Federal Government of Somalia (TFG) has consented to the Security Council doing so. In other words, the Security Council has been used as the vehicle through which the TFG has expressed and manifested its willingness for other states to take actions within its territorial sea, and territory. As Treves argues 'The reference to the

---

[12] UNSC Resolution 1816 (2 June 2008), para 7.

[13] UN Division for Ocean Affairs and the Law of the Sea, 'Maritime Space: Maritime Zones and Maritime Delimitation—African States—Somalia', available at www.un.org/Depts/los/LEGISLATION-ANDTREATIES/africa.htm.

[14] See the Government Statement of 6 June 2013, reported at horseedmedia.net/2013/06/06/somalia-somali-federal-government-clarifies-its-position-on-territorial-waters/.

[15] See 1982 LOSC, Art 3, which is reflective of customary international law.

[16] UNSC Resolution 1851 (16 December 2008) para 6.

[17] The resolutions were initially valid for 6 months, and then 12 months and thus need to be renewed, and sometimes adapted, on a regular basis.

authorization of the coastal state take away all, or much of, the revolutionary content of the resolutions'.[18]

In 2012 the UN Secretary General issued a report in which it is stated that 1063 persons had been prosecuted for piracy off the coast of Somalia in some 20 countries since 2006. Of these, approximately 400 had been in Somalia (or Puntland or Somaliland), meaning that a little over 650 were being prosecuted before the courts of other countries.[19] What the report does not make clear is how many of such prosecutions in third states are on the basis of universal jurisdiction, as opposed to situations in which there is a jurisdictional nexus with the prosecuting state. Even more interesting for current purposes is its failure to make clear how many of the prosecutions in which there might be no jurisdictional nexus were taking place in the arresting states. Although there are doubtless examples of such cases, they are swamped by the number of cases in which the arresting state has transferred the suspect to the jurisdiction of a third state for the purposes of prosecution. Of course, this does not mean that such prosecutions are not taking place on the basis of universal jurisdiction, but it does suggest that the paradigmatic idea of jurisdiction over the 'hostis humani generis', as provided for in customary international law and the 1982 Law of the Sea Convention, has not proved a popular means of tackling piracy off the coasts of Somalia. At best, the rules of international law have come to be used as a means of apprehending pirates as a preventive measure, though the apprehending states seem to feel little compunction to exercise universal jurisdiction over them. Rather, they are keen to 'pass the prosecutorial buck' to others, and it has become an orthodoxy that it is preferable to ensure that prosecutions take place—and sentences are served—within the region (which, for these purposes, includes Kenya, Seychelles, Mauritius and others). There may be good reasons for doing so: for example, other states may be much better placed to bring the prosecution, hear witnesses, assess the evidence, etc. But it is not at all clear why these states are in fact better placed to exercise jurisdiction over those who are passed into their custody than are the states which arrested them. Moreover, it is clear that there is no preference towards local regional prosecution when there is a clear jurisdictional nexus with, for example, a European, US or Japanese vessel or interest.[20] This again reinforces the impression that there is an underlying reluctance to prosecute those apprehended solely on the basis of universal jurisdiction, an unwillingness that appears to be borne out by the replies to the Secretary General's request for information from states concerning their approaches to anti-piracy initiatives.[21] It is also borne out by reports that nine out of ten of those detained for piracy are released

---

[18] See T Treves, 'Piracy and the International Law of the Sea' in D Guilfoyle (ed), *Modern Piracy* (Cheltenham, Edward Elgar, 2013) 130.

[19] See 'Report of the Special Adviser to the Secretary-General on Legal Issues Related to Piracy off the Coast of Somalia, "Summary: A Plan of 25 Proposals"', S/2011/30, 20–21, paras 42–43; 'Report of the Secretary-General on Specialised Anti-piracy Courts in Somalia and Other States in the Region', S/2012/50, 5, para 10.

[20] See, eg the *Shebelle* case, in which Germany requested the extradition of 10 Somali nationals who had been arrested by the Dutch navy when rescuing a German flagged vessel. See UN Doc S/2012/177 (26 March 2012) 68. The 10 were convicted in October 2012 and sentenced to between two and seven years in prison in what is said to have been Germany's first piracy trial for 400 hundred years. See www.spiegel.de/international/germany/hamburg-court-hands-down-somali-pirate-sentences-a-862350.html.

[21] See UN Doc S/2012/177 (26 March 2012). Of the 42 countries which gave information on the action they had taken regarding the criminalising of Somali piracy, only one seems to indicate that it has undertaken prosecutions on the basis of universal jurisdiction, this being the Netherlands (68). In all other cases

soon after being apprehended for the want of anyone willing to take them off the hands of the detaining state.[22] Indeed, the media and related literature are replete with examples of such cases.

The political and practical difficulties, alongside the human rights constraints related to the prosecution of suspect pirates, which will be considered in more detail below, seem to have taken the heart out of efforts to tackle piracy through the medium of universal jurisdiction in the form envisaged in classical international law and the Law of the Sea Convention. Unless there is some very pressing reason to do so, even as regards piracy, states seem reluctant to prosecute without a jurisdictional nexus—and being a 'hostis humani generis' does not seem to be enough. As a result, one major—and salutary—subject for reflection is whether universal jurisdiction really is as useful and practical a tool, as opposed to a useful rhetorical claim or potential threat,[23] in the fight against individuals who commit wrongs under international law as is so frequently claimed.

One of the most notable aspects of the current approach to piracy off the coasts of Somalia is the considerable sums of money which are being spent on enabling Somali pirates to be tried in the domestic courts of countries in the region, notably Kenya, Mauritius and Seychelles, as well as in Somalia itself.[24] Many of the states which responded to the Secretary General's request for information pointed to the sums of money which they have given to facilitate this.[25] According to their most recent information bulletin, since 2009 UNODC have facilitated the construction of four court rooms and provided or refurbished 1400 prison places to international standards, as well as providing judicial and legal capacity building in order to allow trials to take place in the region.[26] Increasingly, the additional prison capacity is being constructed in Somalia (including Puntland and Somaliland), and there is a trend towards repatriating those convicted of piracy in neighbouring countries to serve their sentences in Somali prisons.[27] Whilst this may be desirable on many fronts, what is therefore actually happening is that the international forces detain suspects and transfer those which they do not wish to prosecute themselves to regional countries for investigation and prosecution, following which they will most likely, in time, be transferred to a

where prosecutions were brought by states outside of the region there appears to have been some other form of jurisdictional nexus.

[22] Congressional Research Service, 'Piracy off the Horn of Africa' (2011) 30; House of Commons Foreign Affairs Committee, *Piracy off the Coast of Somalia* (London, The Stationery Office Limited, 2012) 43–44, paras 74–76.

[23] It may be going too far to agree with Reydams (2010), n 5 above, 29, that 'Bad ideas never die and universal jurisdiction probably is one'.

[24] The costs of the UN strategy for assisting the domestic anti-piracy courts in Somalia, Seychelles, Kenya, Mauritius and Tanzania cover a range of activities, such as training personnel, constructing prisons and interpretation services, and are expected to reach $30.49 million between early 2012 and mid-2014, of which $9.38 million has already been contributed. See the 'Economic Cost of Somali Piracy' (2012) 27–30, available at oceansbeyondpiracy.org/sites/default/files/eco2012final_2.pdf, which assesses the total costs of the project presented in Specialised Courts Report, n 19; UNODC, 'Counter Piracy Programme (CPP)—Support to the Trial and Related Treatment of Piracy Suspects' (2013).

[25] For examples see UN Doc S/2012/177 (26 March 2012).

[26] UN Doc S/2012/177 lists, in Somaliland, a 380-bed facility in Hargeisa; in Puntland, the construction of a new 500-bed prison in Garowe, and an additional 240 beds at Bossaso prison; in Kenya, the refurbishment of five prisons; in Seychelles, a 60-bed high security block and other works; and in Mauritius, an additional 36 beds in the principle prison.

[27] Ibid, including 29 from Seychelles to Somaliland and five to Puntland.

prison in Somalia to serve their sentences. De facto, the domestic criminal jurisdiction of Somalia over its nationals committing piracy or armed robbery at sea is being internationalised (or at least regionalised). Not only does this reinforce the challenge to traditional thinking concerning pirates as persons who are beyond the jurisdictional reach of any state and so subject to the jurisdiction of all—these are, in effect, Somali nationals who are committing offences and who are being dealt with on Somalia's behalf until it can do so itself—it also challenges thinking concerning the ideas of 'international criminal law' and 'international criminal justice' more generally.

B. The Role of the International Criminal Court (ICC)

It is, of course, quite ironic that the quintessential 'international crime' is not within the jurisdiction of the ICC,[28] which, on the face of it, might have seemed to be an ideal venue for such 'hostis human generis' to be tried. The option of doing so, or of establishing a new bespoke court along the lines of the special courts or tribunals, has not been seriously contemplated (or contemplated only in order to be rejected).[29] The ICC itself has so far considered cases concerning eight countries, four of which themselves have referred cases to the ICC.[30] The Security Council has brought two situations before the ICC,[31] whilst the Prosecutor has been given permission to consider cases arising out of a further two situations.[32] This is not the place for an examination of the work of the ICC, but it is difficult to avoid noting that there appears to be a trend towards its focusing on the more totemic cases arising out of major international incidents and on key figures, rather than on the less prominent offenders, no matter how serious the offence in question might be.[33] It may well be that the infrastructure of international criminal justice, and its attendant procedures, have become so time consuming[34] and expensive[35] that it may be thought simply inappropriate for anything less than the most high profile of offenders. It is difficult to imagine how the infrastructure and processes at the Hague could have handled the over 1000 people

[28] The jurisdiction of the ICC is limited by Art 5 of the ICC Statute to the crime of genocide, crimes against humanity, war crimes and the crime of aggression. The origins of the ICC in fact lay in attempts to establish a court with jurisdiction over illicit trafficking in narcotic drugs, something which did not find its way in the Statute. See P Robinson, 'The Missing Crimes' in A Cassese, P Gaeta and J Jones (eds), *The Rome Statute of the International Criminal Court* (Oxford, Oxford University Press, 2002) 497–525. At no time does it appear to have been suggested that the court should have jurisdiction in respect of piracy.

[29] For an exploration of the various options see the UN Report of the Secretary-General, S/2010/394 (2010). In the same report it is indicated that members of the CGPS did suggest that the ICC Statute be amended to include the crime of piracy, but this was rejected as not feasible (p37). For a thorough-going presentation and review see Geiss and Petrig, n 1, 168–86. See also the discussion in D Guilfoyle, 'Prosecuting Somali Pirates: A Critical Evaluation of the Options' (2012) 10 *Journal of International Criminal Justice* 780.

[30] These being Uganda, the Democratic Republic of Congo, the Central African Republic and Mali.

[31] These concerning the situation in Darfur (Sudan) and Libya.

[32] These being Kenya and Cote d'Ivoire.

[33] For an overview of its work, see the '8th Annual Report of the International Criminal Court, 2011–12', UN Doc A/67/308 (14 August 2012).

[34] The first judgment of the ICC, in the *Lugamba* case, was given in March 2012 after a trial which lasted over 3 years and nearly 6 years from after his was received into the custody of the ICC. An appeal is currently pending.

[35] The ICC has over 750 staff and an annual budget in the region of $140 million, and has cost approximately $900 million since its establishment.

already detained for Somali piracy, though, given the sums which are being expended on making 'in country' trials within the region viable, it is unlikely to be merely a question of cost.

C. Conclusion

When thinking about the more systemic questions which arise from tackling piracy, it may, then, be worth reflecting on what this says about our understanding of international criminality and how it is tackled. It may be that the lesson is that only major figures in high-profile situations will in future be destined for international criminal tribunals, whereas those who are merely involved in such criminal activity are more likely to continue to be dealt with in national courts. This, in a sense, has been the general experience of most of the major criminal tribunals—such as the Nuremburg and Tokyo Tribunals following the Second World War and, although they did not start out in this way, the International Tribunals for the former Yugoslavia and Rwanda. It may be that one lesson to be learnt from the experience of tackling Somali piracy is that we need to moderate our understanding of, and expectations for, the ICC, as well as for universal jurisdiction.

III. HUMAN RIGHTS

A. The Human Rights of Pirates

One of the most interesting features of the response to Somali piracy has been the slow but steady rise of human rights questions,[36] many of which do not appear to have been seriously raised in similar contexts in the past. It is difficult to speculate, but it may be that the debates concerning the rendition of terrorist suspects and the prominence given to the legitimacy or efficacy of 'deportation with assurances' may have had an unexpected part to play here. As is well known, the UK embarked on a fairly aggressive policy of entering into agreements with a range of countries to which it wished to return terrorist suspects but to which return was prohibited by the existence of a real risk of torture or ill-treatment.[37] This highlighted the problem of the extent to which a country might be in breach of its human rights commitments should it hand over a person to the jurisdiction of another state where their

---

[36] For considerations of human rights implications see D Guilfoyle, 'Counter-piracy Law Enforcement and Human Rights' (2010) 59 *International & Comparative Law Quarterly* 152; T Treves, 'Human Rights and the Law of the Sea' (2010) 28(1) *Berkeley Journal of International Law* 7; S Piedimonte Bodini, 'Fighting Maritime Piracy under the European Convention on Human Rights' (2011) 22 *European Journal of International Law* 840; E Papastavridis, 'European Convention on Human Rights and the Law of the Sea: The Strasbourg Court in Unchartered Waters?' in M Fitzmaurice and P Merkouris (eds), *The Interpretation and Application of the ECHR—Legal and Practical Implications* (Leiden, Martinus Nijhoff Publishers, 2013) 122–26.

[37] Agreements, in the form of a Memorandum of Understanding (MOU) or an Exchange of Letters, are currently in place with Jordan (August 2005), Lebanon (December 2005), Algeria (July 2006), Ethiopia (December 2008) and Morocco (September 2011). An earlier MOU with Libya is no longer in operation. See also A Murdoch, Chapter 9 above.

rights might be violated. This includes not only the risk of being subjected to torture, inhuman or degrading treatment (which includes prison conditions),[38] but also to situations in which there is a risk of a flagrant denial of justice which violate the right to a fair trial.[39] The problem is obvious: can detaining states—and particularly European states subject to the jurisdiction of the European Court of Human Rights—hand over pirates apprehended to countries in which there is a real risk that they may face conditions of detention which amount in inhuman or degrading treatment, or legal systems in which they might face a flagrant denial of justice? The short answer is no, they cannot. A solution to this problem would be for the apprehending state to simply release the pirates whom it does not itself wish to prosecute. Non-refoulement considerations have led states to order their naval forces to release captured pirates in the past[40] and the UK Foreign Office, for instance, has repeatedly warned the Royal Navy against detaining captured pirates out of fear that the UK might be left with any apprehended pirates who cannot be deported after prosecution or imprisonment due to claims of asylum or non-refoulement obligations.[41] The Danish navy has also been reported to have released captured pirates due to Danish law prohibiting extradition to countries where they may face torture, inhuman or degrading treatment or the death penalty.[42] States are further discouraged from detaining pirates because they can be held responsible for breaching the pirates' human rights through the conduct of their naval forces, and also face particular challenges as regards the requirement

---

[38] The origins of this jurisprudence within the European Human Rights system lie in the case of *Soering v UK*, 7 July 1989, Series A No 161. In *Chalal v UK*, 15 November 1996, RJD 1996-V, it was determined that this approach was to be adhered to even if the person was believed to pose a risk to national security, since the prohibition of torture and ill-treatment is absolute and, when challenged in the light of the 'war on terror', was confirmed by the European Court in *Saadi v Italy* [GC], No 37201/06 ECHR (2008).

[39] See *Othman (Abu Qatada) v UK*, No 8139/09, 17 January 2012, where the court decided that returning Abu Qatada to Jordan under the terms of the UK MOU would not prevent his being convicted on the basis of evidence acquired through the torture of others, and this would amount to a flagrant denial of justice and hence his return would be in breach of Art 6 of the Convention. Abu Qatada was eventually returned to Jordan in July 2013, following the conclusion of a treaty between the UK and Jordan, the terms of which prevented the use of such evidence in proceedings and thus met the concerns of the European Court of Human Rights. See 'Treaty on Mutual Legal Assistance in Criminal Matters between the United Kingdom of Great Britain and Northern Ireland and the Hashemite Kingdom of Jordan' (2013), Art 27(3)–(5).

[40] GS Goodwin-Gill, 'The Right to Seek Asylum: Interception at Sea and the Principle of Non-Refoulement' (2001) 23(3) *International Journal of Refugee Law* 443.

[41] The British government confirmed in 2012 that in the past two years 21 pirates have been transferred to other states by the Royal Navy for prosecution, in 2012 seven pirates were transferred to Seychelles for prosecution, and between April 2010 and November 2011 a further 60 suspected pirates were released. The official justification for the release of pirates was that a successful prosecution was unlikely. See Piracy off the Coast of Somalia, n 22, 43–44, paras 74–76 and 53–55, paras 104–10. See also E Kontorovich, 'International Legal Responses to Piracy off the Coast of Somalia' (2009) 13(2) *American Society of International Law Insights*, available at www.asil.org/insights/volume/13/issue/2/international_legal_responses_piracy_coast_somalia; E Kontorovich, '"A Guantanamo on the Sea": The Difficulty of Prosecuting Pirates and Terrorists' (2010) 98 *California Law Review* 265. For an analysis of the lack of a legal basis for the asylum claims on behalf of suspected pirates see YM Dutton, 'Pirates and Impunity: Is the Threat of Asylum Claims a Reason to Allow Pirates to Escape Justice?' (2011) 34 *Fordham International Law Journal* 240.

[42] M Hand, 'Danish Navy Release 10 Somali Pirates' (Lloyd's List, 25 September 2008); T Treves, 'Piracy, Law of the Sea, and the Use of Force: Developments off the Coast of Somalia' (2009) 20(2) *European Journal of International Law* 408; A Murdoch, 'Recent Legal Issues and Problems relating to Acts of Piracy off Somalia' in CR Symmons (ed), *Selected Contemporary Issues in the Law of the Sea* (Leiden, Brill, 2011) 150–51.

that those detained be brought before a judicial authority 'promptly'.[43] Even though there do not appear to be, as yet, any cases in which those prosecuted for piracy have alleged that the naval forces have been responsible for human rights violations,[44] it is now established in the case law of the European Court of Human Rights and other international human rights bodies that those arrested at sea by state agents and held on or transferred to or from vessels are within the jurisdiction of the flag state for the purposes of human rights law.[45] It is, then, clear that states have to respect the human rights of those they apprehend at sea, irrespective of where that might be. It would also seem to be the case that the state will be held responsible for the actions of their naval forces when operating in the context of multinational forces, such as those conducted under the umbrella of NATO or EUNAVFOR.[46] This could prove a problem for those contributing to international forces that could easily end up in an invidious position as a result.

One 'solution' to the human rights dilemmas might be to simply release those captured—and, as has been seen, this is a fairly common practice. It is also worth recalling that, in addition to any constraints posed by the human rights framework, naval forces are faced with numerous practical and operational dilemmas. The transfer of pirates to ports following their capture may require lengthy and expensive diversions, and, therefore, other vessels might remain exposed to the danger of being attacked in the meantime.[47] Therefore, on grounds of overall effectiveness, military forces might prefer to be engaged in 'catch and release' strategies, in which pirates are disarmed but released after being captured, instead of leaving vessels unprotected for a considerable period of time.[48] The pressure of human rights compliance should they be detained might add even greater weight to such practical considerations.

Another solution has already been alluded to, this being the injection of considerable

---

[43] See, eg *Medvedyev and Others v France*, Application No 3394/03, [GC] 23 March 2010, where it was ultimately decided that the exceptional circumstances of arrest at sea justified on board detention for a period of two weeks, on the specific facts of the case.

[44] It is reported that, in 2010, a Dutch court, which was the first European court to examine a Somali piracy related case, agreed with the defendants that a 40-day detention aboard was against Art 5 of the ECHR, but the court found this claim irrelevant to the criminal law proceedings. See Marine Log, 'Netherlands Court Convicts Somali Pirates' (2010), available at www.marinelog.com/DOCS/NEWSMMIX/2010jun00172.html.

[45] See *Medvedyev and Others v France*, n 44 above, paras 50–51; *Hirsii Jamaa and Others v Italy*, Application No 27765/09, Judgment of 23 February 2012; *Rigopoulos v Spain*, Application No 37388/97, inadmissibility decision of 12 January 1999; *Xhavara and others v Albania*, Application No 39473/98, inadmissibility decision of 11 January 2001; Inter-American Commission of Human Rights, Case 10.675 v United States (*Haitian Interdiction Case*), Report No 51/96 of 13 March 1997; *PK et al v Spain*, Communication No 323/2007, UN Doc CAT/C/41/D/323/2007 of 21 November 2008.

[46] *Al-Jedda v United Kingdom* (2011), Application No 27021/08, paras 80, 83–85; *Al-Saadoon and Mufdhi v United Kingdom* (2009), Application No 61498/08, paras 85, 88–89. See also Art 48 of the Articles on the Responsibility of International Organisations (ARIO) 2011, adopted by the International Law Commission at its sixty-third session, in 2011: *Yearbook of the International Law Commission, 2011*, vol II; MD Evans and P Okowa, 'Approaches to Responsibility in International Courts' in MD Evans and P Koutrakos (eds), *The International Responsibility of the European Union: European and International Perspectives* (Oxford, Hart Publishing, 2013) 101; E Cannizzaro, 'Beyond the Either/Or: Dual Attribution to the European Union and to the Member State for Breach of the ECHR' in Evans and Koutrakos. ibid, 295; Papastavridis, n 36 above, 139. See also the decision of the Supreme Court of the Netherlands in *Netherlands v Muhanovic*, 6 September 2013 (the 'Dutchbat' case).

[47] Piracy off the Coast of Somalia, n 22, 44, para 77.

[48] For a detailed analysis of the 'catch and release' approach see Guilfoyle, n 37, 141–42; and Kontorovich (2009), n 41 above. For a discussion on 'deter and disrupt' see A Murdoch and D Guilfoyle, 'Capture and Disruption Operations: The Use of Force in Counter-piracy off Somalia' in Guilfoyle, n 18 above, 163.

sums of money to construct new or renovate existing facilities and to ensure that the functioning of the justice system is such as to render them human rights compliant and thus safe from the perspective of the transferring state. It might be noted that in 2011 the Administrative Court in Cologne refused to allow the transfer of suspects to Shimo la Tewa, the largest remand prison in Kenya, where some 80 suspected Somali pirates were being held, because of the conditions of detention.[49] In its latest CPP communication in March 2013, UNODC details the work it is doing to improve facilities in this prison.[50] To the extent that such funds are dedicated to building bespoke facilities for those being transferred, this has the bizarre consequence of privileging the 'enemies of mankind' in comparison to domestic suspects and offenders, whose conditions and fate appear to remain of relatively little concern to the broader international community.[51] A parallel approach is to enter into transfer agreements in the form of MOUs. The leading example is the Transfer Agreement between the EU and Kenya,[52] which has since been used as a model for agreements with other countries in the region, and has also been adapted for use by a number of countries entering into bilateral MOUs, such as with Seychelles, Tanzania and Mauritius.[53] Whilst seeking to ensure that those transferred are treated in a human rights compliant fashion by providing for appropriate capacity building, it also seeks to broaden the scope of the definition of piracy or acts related to piracy, and to legitimate the arrest of those suspected of such acts (which fall outside the international law definition) and their transfer to the states in question.[54]

Monitoring has also emerged as an important tool that can be used to ensure that there are both effective prosecutions and effective human rights protection, and has been used by both the UN and EU as a response to concerns regarding the conditions of detention in the states of the region, including issues of overcrowding, lack of proper medical treatment and allegations of ill-treatment.[55] The EU–Kenya agreement, for example, contains a number of specific human rights guarantees, including legal safeguards against torture, guarantees regarding the conducting of prompt and fair

---

[49] The case is discussed in Treves, n 18 above, 194. For the conditions of detention in Kenya see Specialised Courts Report, n 19 above, 21, paras 69–70; JT Gathii, 'Kenya's Piracy Prosecutions' (2010) 104 *American Journal of International Law* 430.

[50] CPP, n 24, 4. It may be that it is having some effect: see, for example, the news story concerning life in the prison, 'Somali Pirates Find Life in Kenyan Jail more Comfortable than on Ocean Waves', *The Guardian*, 16 August 2013, available at www.theguardian.com/world/2013/aug/16/somali-pirates-kenya-jail-indian-ocean.

[51] But *cf* CPP, ibid, 1, which emphasises the benefits to the general Kenyan criminal justice system of the new court rooms it has constructed at Shanzu to facilitate the trial of pirates held at Shimo La Tewa.

[52] Exchange of letters for the conditions and modalities for the transfer of persons having committed acts of piracy and detained by the European Union-led Naval Force (EUNAVFOR), and seized property in the possession of EUNAVFOR, from EUNAVFOR to Kenya, [2009] OJ L79/49 as annexed to European Council Decision 2009/293CFSP, [2009] OJ L79, 47. See also D Thym, Chapter 6 above.

[53] Piracy off the Coast of Somalia, n 22, 49–50, paras 93–103. See also the consideration of the EU–Kenya and EU–Seychelles Transfer Agreements in Geiss and Petrig, n 1, 200–07. They also record that the UK and the USA have entered into transfer agreements with Kenya and Seychelles, and Canada, China and Denmark with Kenya, all of which were unpublished (ibid, 198–99). In March 2013, the UK also entered into an MOU with Nigeria, focusing on counter-terrorism and maritime security, against the background of increasing pirate activity in the Gulf of Guinea.

[54] Ibid.

[55] Council of Europe Parliamentary Assembly, 'The Necessity to Take Additional International Legal Steps to Deal with Sea Piracy' (2010) para 2. The Specialised Courts Report, n 19 above, provides information for the different states of the region concerning their prison facilities and conditions of detention.

trials,[56] and provisions to ensure the effective monitoring of the situation of pirates following their transfer to the state in which they are to be prosecuted.[57] It can be concluded, therefore, that, whilst it has taken some time, there is now an acute awareness of the need to ensure that those apprehended for piracy must be treated in accordance with international human rights standards, and considerable efforts have been made to ensure that this is the case. However, serious questions remain about the long-term effectiveness of this, particularly as regards those prisoners who are transferred back to Somalia to serve their sentences—and just how long the international community will be prepared to continue to exercise oversight of the treatment of those serving sentences remains to be seen.

B. The Human Rights of the Victims of Piracy

Whilst issues concerning the human rights of those detained have received considerable attention, it has taken rather longer for another human rights issue to achieve the prominence it deserves: the rights of the victims of piracy, and in particular those taken hostage. In 2012, 851 seafarers were attacked by pirates, 381 came into close contact with pirates when the latter boarded their vessels and 349 seafarers were taken hostage off the coasts of Somalia.[58] At the time of writing, some 113 hostages seized by Somali pirates remain in captivity.[59] The crew and passengers on vessels which have armed security guards on board can find themselves caught up in crossfire, as if in a warzone.[60] Yet those who may be taken hostage not only face the threat of personal injury or death during the violent seizure of their vessels, but continue to run that risk throughout the period of captivity, in addition to facing the fear and stress that attends not knowing what is happening or what may be about to happen to them. In the last few years, more information has become available concerning the treatment which many of those taken hostage have had to endure— and this offers a stark comparison with the situation of many of those whose failed attempts to seize vessels has resulted in their arrest for piracy. Even more worrying than the general levels of welfare of those taken hostage is the increasing evidence of the extent to which they may be subjected to forms of violence at the hands of their abductors. Until about 2010, there seems to have been something of a general belief, by both maritime officials and the media, that there was some kind of 'gentlemen's agreement', according to which pirates treated their hostages with respect. This is premised largely on the assumption that the identity of the hostages was relatively

---

[56] Provisions on the conditions of transfer of suspected pirates and seized property from the EU-led naval force to the Republic of Kenya, [2009] OJ L79/51, para 3.

[57] Council of Europe, Parliamentary Assembly, Resolution 1722 (2010), 'Piracy—A Crime and a Challenge for Democracies', para 16.2.

[58] While the figures show that there was a significant drop in successful hijackings—the 42 reported successful hijackings in 2010 reduced to three in 2013—the number of hostages remains high. The figures also show that a large number of hostages remained in captivity for a long period of time. In 2012 a total of 589 mariners were in captivity, among whom 133 had been hostage since 2010 and 107 since 2011. See Oceans Beyond Piracy, 'The Human Cost of Maritime Piracy' (2012) 17, available at oceansbeyondpiracy.org/sites/default/files/hco2012forweb_6.pdf; CPP Report, n 24 above, 10.

[59] CPP Report, ibid, 10; CGPS: Quarterly Update (2013).

[60] Oceans Beyond Piracy, 'The Human Cost of Somali Piracy' (2011) 8–9, 20, available at oceansbeyondpiracy.org/sites/default/files/hcop_2011.pdf.

unimportant to the hostage takers, whose primary interest was in the vessels and their cargos, so there was nothing to be gained from treating hostages badly.[61] This myth has been exploded as a result of more becoming known of the manner in which hostages have been treated, through interviews with hostages and testimonies given by those who have been released. This information refutes the theory that Somali pirates are 'humane captors'.[62]

For example, hostages have described the physical and psychological abuse they have suffered in captivity, disclosing that they were beaten and tortured, forced to stay in freezers, hung up from masts, exposed to the sun on shipdecks for prolonged periods of time, made to phone their relatives to beg for help at gunpoint, and suffered from malnutrition and from a lack of drinkable water.[63] Maritime officials have also become more forthright in describing the physical abuses which hostages have been subjected to. For example, Royal Marines Major General Buster Howes reported that, if naval forces approached too close to pirate vessels, the pirates might drag hostages on deck and beat them until the warship went away.[64] The Major General also acknowledged that 'pirates have recently tied hostages upside down and dragged them in the sea, locked them in freezers, beaten them and used plastic ties around their genitals'.[65] The Assistant Secretary of the US Bureau of Political-Military Affairs, Andrew Shapiro, further stated that 'The attacks are more ruthless, more violent and wider ranging. Hostages have been tortured and used as human shields'.[66]

In the light of this, it is striking that, until very recently, little thought seems to have been given to the rights of the victims of piracy. One reason is that they seem to fall—at first sight—outside the human rights frame of reference. Pirates are not state agents, and the state is not responsible for the manner in which pirates treat their victims.[67] Whilst it is becoming increasingly the case that non-state actors are believed to be capable of being responsible for human rights violations,[68] pirates are not easily equated to 'non-state actors', as traditionally understood. Nevertheless, there is an alternative route available through the recognition of the positive obligation of the state to protect the rights of those who it knows, or ought to know, are at risk.[69] It is

---

[61] Ibid 24.

[62] Ibid 12.

[63] Ibid 6–7.

[64] D Howden, 'Somali Pirates Are Using Torture as Defence Shield' (2011) *The Independent*, 3 February 2011, available at www.independent.co.uk/news/world/africa/somali-pirates-are-using-torture-as-defence-shield-2202614.html; K Houreld, 'AP Interview: Somali Pirates Torturing Hostages', *The Guardian*, 1 February 2011, available at www.guardian.co.uk/world/feedarticle/9479830.

[65] Ibid; 'AP: SKorean Crew Recount Beatings by Somali pirates', *Asian Correspondent*, 3 February 2011, available at asiancorrespondent.com/47610/skorean-crew-recount-beatings-by-somali-pirates/.

[66] A Shapiro, 'US Approaches to Counter-piracy' (2011), available at www.state.gov/t/pm/rls/rm/159419.htm.

[67] Art 2 of the International Law Commission's Articles on Responsibility of States for Internationally Wrongful Acts (2001) prescribes that: 'There is an internationally wrongful act of a State when conduct consisting of an action or omission: (a) is attributable to the State under international law; and (b) constitutes a breach of an international obligation of the State': *Yearbook of the International Law Commission*, vol II.

[68] For detailed considerations of the different aspects of the role of non-state actors and state responsibility see, eg P Alston, *Non-state Actors and Human Rights* (Oxford, Oxford University Press, 2005); A Clapham, *Human Rights Obligations of Non-State Actors* (Oxford, Oxford University Press, 2006); J Crawford, A Pellet and S Olleson, *The Law of International Responsibility* (Cambridge, Cambridge University Press, 2010).

[69] The international and regional human rights bodies have expanded the human rights obligations of states. It is now widely accepted that states have negative, positive (to prevent and react) and procedural (to investigate effectively and independently human rights violations) obligations.

incontrovertible that those lawfully engaged in passage on the high seas in areas off Somalia are known to be at risk;[70] the question then emerges of the obligations which might be owed to them—and by whom?[71] Interestingly, the 'international community'—a much used expression—is not itself an addressee of human rights obligations per se. However, international organisations, including the EU, may be subject to human rights obligations, and this opens up some important questions for the future of human rights protection in a world in which the interrelationship between the roles and responsibilities of the state and of the international organisations which they create (and of which they are a part) are becoming increasingly complex.[72]

The UN Secretary General Ban Ki-moon has acknowledged that the welfare of seafarers, and particularly hostages, is at stake.[73] Looking beyond the context of piracy, the UN Human Rights Council has also recognised that terrorist hostage-taking has an impact on the human rights of hostages, and in 2011 tasked the Human Rights Council Advisory Committee with producing a report on human rights and issues related to terrorist hostage-taking.[74] In its report to the Human Rights Council, the Advisory Committee commented that:

> 23. . . . acts of terrorist hostage-taking generate multiple violations of human rights of these different categories of victims. Violations are mainly committed by the hostage-takers; in some cases, however, they occur during counter-terrorism activities. According to the specific circumstances of a terrorist hostage-taking situation, appropriate responses should take into account the interests and concerns of all affected members of society. Responses to hostage-taking situations should respect everyone's right to life, liberty and security of person as enshrined in numerous human rights instruments and reaffirmed in the preamble to the International Convention against the Taking of Hostages.

---

[70] Piedimonte Bodini, n 36 above, 838 also argues that when a state is aware that a vessel which is flying its flag has been hijacked it also knows of the real and imminent risk that those taken hostage on board face, so it has a positive obligation to protect them under Art 2 of the ECHR, 838. See also the discussion in Papastavridis, n 3 above, 129–30.

[71] This question becomes even more complicated when examined under the rubric of extraterritoriality. The attacks on and detention of seafarers take place well beyond the borders of the states themselves, and there is a marked reluctance on the part of many states to accept the extraterritorial application of human rights obligations. To argue, for example, that the UK is in breach of its obligations because it has failed to do all it might to prevent a Somali pirate from ill-treating a UK national does, admittedly, remain challenging. For discussion of the problem see O De Schutter, *International Human Rights Law* (Cambridge, Cambridge University Press, 2010), where he concludes that 'in the currently state of development of international law, a clear obligation for States to control private actors operating outside their national territory, in order to ensure that these actors will not violate the human rights of others, has not crystallized yet' (162).

[72] Art 7 of the ARIO provides that 'The conduct of an organ of a State or an organ or agent of an international organisation that is placed at the disposal of another international organization shall be considered under international law an act of the latter organization if the organization exercises effective control over that conduct'. As a result, international organisations may be held responsible separately or jointly with states that place their agents at its disposal. See *Netherlands v Muhanovic*, n 46 above.

[73] Foreign Commonwealth Office, 'London Conference on Somalia-Speeches' (2012), available at www.youtube.com/watch?v=FgsydbMEzXsandfeature=results_mainandplaynext=1andlist=PL355FA9D26E47A9B0.

[74] See Human Rights Council Resolution 18/10 (29 September 2011) and the Report of the Human Rights Council Advisory Committee on the Human rights and issues related to terrorist hostage-taking, A/HRC/24/47 (4 July 2013). Both the HRC Resolution and the Advisory Council Report tend to stress the possible human rights implications for broader society when action is taken against hostage takers. Once again, therefore, the rights of the hostages themselves are not centre stage and, arguably, are compromised by the need to respect the rights of the general society within which they might be being held.

The UN Special Rapporteur on Counter Terrorism and Human Rights has further emphasised the positive obligation upon the state to protect the rights of potential victims of terrorism.[75] His 2012 report is worth quoting at length. The Special Rapporteur comments that:

> 11. . . . the Special Rapporteur strongly urges states to recognize that the deliberate infliction of lethal or potentially lethal violence by non-state actors in the course of an act of terrorism amounts, in all cases where death or serious physical or psychological injury results, to a grave violation of the human rights of the victim, irrespective of the question of direct or indirect state responsibility.
>
> 12. . . . Some of the gravest violations of human rights are nowadays committed by, or on behalf of, non-state actors operating in conflict situations of one kind or another, including by domestic and international terrorist networks. If international human rights law is to keep pace with these changes, the victims of acts of terrorism must now be recognized as victims of grave violations of international human rights law.
>
> 13. . . . Certainly, when viewed from a victim's perspective, the mass killing of civilians which is the objective of most terrorist campaigns, involves the deprivation of the most fundamental human right of all. The Special Rapporteur acknowledges that there is a responsible body of opinion to the effect that only states and comparable entities can violate human rights. However, he does not share this view. Indeed, it can be argued that allowing victims of terrorism to remain as legally ossified 'prisoners of doctrine' is an outdated and retrograde analysis that can lead to various forms of secondary victimization.
>
> 14. It is a striking fact that despite the proliferation of international agreements concerned with the suppression of terrorism, there is none that specifically addresses the human rights of the victims and the corresponding obligations of states . . .

Whereas the reports are speaking of terrorism, it is suggested that the same general analysis could be made as regards victims of piracy, although there are clearly additional issues as regards the extraterritoriality of human rights obligations to be taken into account in the piracy context. The question is probably no longer one of whether states might have positive obligations to the victims of piracy when they engage with pirates in hostage situations. The question is what does that obligation entail? This is an important question which requires urgent consideration. It seems safe to assume that a human rights-conscious approach which takes account of the interests of the victims of piracy as well as the interests of the perpetrators of piracy is an emergent issue which, if properly engaged with, could have a significant impact upon human rights thinking. Taken together with a more general victim-oriented approach, it may be that the general understanding of human rights within the international community is undergoing a subtle, but significant, transformation.

---

[75] 'Report of the Special Rapporteur on the Promotion and Protection of Human Rights and Fundamental Freedoms while Countering Terrorism, Ben Emmerson', A/HRC/20/14 (2012).

IV. PIRACY AND INTERNATIONAL SOFT LAW

A further issue arising from the response to Somali piracy concerns the role of 'soft' law.[76] Whilst there is nothing new about the use of soft law to provide frameworks within which to conduct co-ordinated activities through MOUs and to develop and determine applicable standards through guidance or codes of conduct, the range and reach of such instruments in this context seems to mark a significant development. What is equally significant is the extent to which this has been driven by the shipping industry as well as states, and the manner in which they have come together in order to forge a web of quasi-legal commitments to deal with the problem. For example, mention has already been made to the numerous MOUs that have been entered into to facilitate the transfer and prosecution of those apprehended for piracy within the region. It is beyond the scope of this chapter to look in detail at the wealth of such arrangements, but it is worth drawing attention briefly to a number of examples of practice.

A. The Contact Group on Piracy off the Coast of Somalia (CGPS)

The CGPS was established on 14 January 2009 under UNSC Resolution 1851 (2008), which

> encourage[d] all states and regional organizations fighting piracy and armed robbery at sea off the coast of Somalia to establish an international cooperation mechanism to act as a common point of contact between and among states, regional and international organizations on all aspects of combating piracy and armed robbery at sea off Somalia's coast.[77]

The creation of the CGPS was based on a US recommendation, and its institutional structure reflects the 2005 US National Strategy for Maritime Security, which acknowledged that maritime security can be best achieved by a hybrid actor that combines public and private maritime security activities on an international scale.[78] The mixture of the various activities of the CGPS is illustrated by the work of its five working groups (WGs), which are assigned to accomplish one of the following tasks: to promote military and operational coordination (WG1, chaired by the UK), to provide judicial guidance vis-à-vis the prosecution of pirates (WG2, chaired by Denmark),[79] to raise self-awareness and improve self-defensive mechanisms within the shipping industry (WG3, chaired by the Republic of Korea), to enhance diplomatic and public information initiatives (WG4, chaired by Egypt), and to promote information sharing

---

[76] For general discussions of the various meanings of soft law see C Chinkin, 'The Challenge of Soft Law: Development and Change in International Law' (1989) 38 *International & Comparative Law Quarterly* 850; C Chinkin and A Boyle, *The Making of International Law* (Oxford, Oxford University Press, 2007) 211–29; A Boyle 'Soft Law' in M Evans (ed), *International Law*, 4th edn (Oxford, Oxford University Press, 2014) ch 5.

[77] UN Security Council Resolution 1851 (2008) para 4.

[78] Oceans Beyond Piracy, 'Burden-Sharing Multi-Level Governance: A Study of the Contact Group on Piracy off the Coast of Somalia' (2013) 18–20, available at oceansbeyondpiracy.org/sites/default/files/burden_sharing_apr29.pdf

[79] This task is further assisted by the Counter Piracy Programme, which is an initiative coordinated by the UNODC. See www.unodc.org/easternafrica/en/piracy/index.html.

among the various stakeholders fighting against piracy (WG5, chaired by Italy).[80] The CGPS lacks regulatory powers,[81] and can only adopt recommendations by consensus in its meetings held by the CGPS participants.[82] It does, however, provide a platform for international cooperation, and acts as a 'useful model for collective efforts that addresses problems requiring fast and adaptive responses to changing situations on the ground, and on issues where power imbalances between actors will not scuttle the collaborative execution of collective goals'.[83] The activities of the CGPS are funded by the Trust Fund to Support the Initiatives of States to Counter Piracy off the Coast of Somalia, which was established by the UN Secretary-General, Ban Ki-moon, on 27 January 2010. The Trust Fund is another voluntary mechanism open to contributions from governments, industry and others that seeks to 'help defray expenses associated with the prosecution of suspected pirates and other activities related to implementing contact group objectives'.[84]

B. Regional Cooperative Mechanisms

Two more initiatives, which, similarly to the CGPS, act as forums, but at a more regional level, are the Somali Contact Group on Counter-piracy, also known as the Kampala Process, and the Shared Awareness Deconfliction process (SHADE). The Kampala Process was established by the TFG in 2010 on a request of the WG1, and is a 'Somali initiative focussed on Somalis' that brings together the Somali regions and provides a forum for discussions among them.[85] The aims of this group are articulated in the Somali Maritime Resource and Security Strategy, which, inter alia, stressed the need for 'a coordinated and coherent approach to Somali maritime challenges, issues, and capacity building'.[86] The meetings of the SHADE process, which are held in Bahrain, bring together representatives from governments and the maritime industry from 27 countries and 14 international organisations that work together with the aim of coordinating the various military counter-piracy operations.[87] The significance of its role is indicated by the comment of the UN Secretary General that 'the magnitude and complexity of the various military operations currently conducted . . . evidently require a lead role and coordination arrangements that go beyond the operational capacity and resources of the United Nations Secretariat'.[88]

The Djibouti Code was the product of a sub-regional meeting convened by the

---

[80] See Geiss and Petrig, n 1 above, 26–27. For more information on the activities of the five WGs see www.thecgpcs.org/work.do?action=work.

[81] D Guilfoyle, 'Prosecuting Pirates: The Contact Group on Piracy off the Coast of Somalia, Governance and International Law' (2013) 4(1) *Global Policy* 75.

[82] The term 'participants' replaced the term 'members', since the membership criteria were abolished with a view to permitting more states to participate in the international forum of the CGPS. Today, the CGPS brings together over 80 countries, organisations and industry groups that have a common interest in battling piracy. See n 78 above, 20; CGPS: Quarterly Update (2013) para 1.

[83] Above n 78, 7.

[84] Trust Fund, www.thecgpcs.org/trustfund.do?action=trustFund.

[85] Kampala Process: A Draft Somali Maritime Strategy—Communique No 1, para 4.

[86] Ibid, para 7.

[87] See Geiss and Petrig, n 1 above, 27–28.

[88] 'Report of the Secretary-General Pursuant to Security Council Resolution 1846 (2008)', S/2009/146, 13, para 54.

International Maritime Organization (IMO) and represents the response of states from the Western Indian Ocean, Gulf of Aden and Red Sea to calls from the IMO that they should implement a code of practice for the investigation of the crimes of piracy. It has been adopted by 20 countries in the region and has been effective since 29 January 2009,[89] but it remains a non-binding agreement.[90] In summary, by virtue of the Djibouti Code of Conduct (Resolution 1), states have undertaken to cooperate in a manner consistent with international law in the investigation, arrest and prosecution of persons; the interdiction and seizure of suspect ships; the rescue of ships, persons and property, along with the care and treatment of seafarers; and in the conduct of shared operations. In addition, and picking up on the human rights themes considered in the previous section, through the Code, those states most affected by piracy not only acknowledged the 'grave dangers'[91] that seafarers face, but have committed themselves by consensus to rescue hostages and offer proper treatment to victims of piracy.[92] The Djibouti Code gave birth to further voluntary, ad hoc mechanisms that plan and fund its implementation. The Project Implementation Unit was formed to assist the signatories with the effective implementation of the Code, and it is funded by the establishment of a multi-donor voluntary fund, the Djibouti Code of Conduct Trust Fund, the main donor to which is Japan.[93]

Another notable initiative is the Declaration condemning the violence against seafarers by the three largest flag states, Marshall Islands, Liberia and Panama, which between them represent around 40% of the world's shipping tonnage.[94] In March 2012, the Commonwealth of Bahamas became the fourth state to sign this non-binding joint declaration. The Declaration recognises that the increasing violence against seafarers remains underreported and that the relevant information is extremely sensitive.[95] The Declaration affirms the commitment of the flag states to collect and provide information on the levels of violence against seafarers with a view towards determining the human cost of piracy.[96] The coordinated collation of information by four of the largest flag states offers an invaluable tool to stakeholders, who might use this information to develop new strategies against piracy with a view to better protecting vessels and seafarers.

C. Self-defence Initiatives by the Shipping Industry

The shipping industry has responded to pirate attacks by implementing a number of

---

[89] IMO, 'Djibouti Code of Conduct—Project Implementation Unit', 2nd edn (February–August 2012). For an overview see Geiss and Petrig, n 1 above, 48–51.

[90] The Djibouti Code of Conduct (Resolution 1), Art 15(a). Art 13 provided for consultations regarding the conclusion of a legally binding agreement, but this has not yet come about.

[91] Ibid, Annex, Attachment 1, 5.

[92] Ibid, 3 and Art 2, Annex, Attachment 1.

[93] Ibid. Japan has contributed to the fund almost $14 million, while the total of the rest of the contributions is about $500,000.

[94] ICC Commercial Crime Services, 'Flag States Sign Declaration Condemning Acts of Piracy against Seafarers' (2011), available at www.icc-ccs.org/news/451-flag-states-sign-declaration-condemning-acts-of-violence-against-seafarers.

[95] 'Declaration Condemning Acts of Violence Against Seafarers' (2011), available at oceansbeyondpiracy. org/content/declaration-condemning-acts-violence-against-seafarers-full-text.

[96] Ibid.

robust self-defence measures. Best management practices (BMPs) are the most prominent example of the self-protective measures that the shipping industry has adopted
for the protection of vessels. These include practices and tools such as watchkeeping,
manoeuvring, citadels, alarms and armed guards, to name but a few.[97] BMPs are
supplemented by the New York Declaration, by virtue of which the signatories have
committed themselves to 'avoid, deter or delay acts of piracy',[98] and also by Reporting
Procedures, by virtue of which the shipping companies have agreed that their ships
will constantly report their whereabouts.[99] Among BMPs, the detailed regulation of
private maritime security companies (PMSC) requires special mention, as it has been
the product of numerous soft law initiatives. The use of PMSCs was originally opposed
because of concerns that the employment of lethal force could put human lives at
risk. Whereas a general sense of discomfort regarding their use remains, international
responses show that there is a move towards authorising their use. The IMO, which
had initially expressed concerns about the use of PMSCs, has now issued a number
of guidelines on their use, while expressly stating that these recommendations must
not have the effect of institutionalising the use of armed guards on board vessels.[100]
Another set of guidelines has been issued by the Baltic International Maritime Council,
which delineates the use of PMSCs and the use of lethal force by armed guards. Due
to their nature, PMSCs fall within the broader category of private security contractors, and hence they are further regulated by the International Code of Conduct for
Private Security Service Providers.[101]

The upsurge of counter-piracy soft law initiatives further substantiates the argument
that the current international legal framework cannot effectively respond to Somali
piracy. This has led states to explore new avenues that have given rise to a number of
radical and innovative mechanisms. The examination of the operational effectiveness
of these mechanisms does not fall within the purposes of this chapter. However, in the
light of the significant drop in successful pirate attacks off the Somali coasts, it could
be reasonably argued that these mechanisms have significantly contributed to that end.

---

[97] Best Management Practices for Protection against Somalia Based Piracy, Version 4 (August 2011).

[98] Third Plenary Session of the Contact Group on Piracy off the Coast of Somalia, para 3.

[99] The EU and the UK have contributed to the implementation of BMPs by establishing the Maritime
Security Centre—Horn of Africa (MSCHOA) and the UK Maritime Trade Operations (UKMTO) respectively, which collect the reports of the ships and assess their vulnerability: see n 97 above, 11–13, 19.

[100] IMO, 'Revised Interim Recommendations for Flag States Regarding the Use of Privately Contracted
Armed Security Personnel On Board Ships in the High Risk Area', MSC.1/Circ.1406/Rev.2 (25 May 2012)
Annex, r 1 (IMO Flag State Recommendations); IMO, 'Revised Interim Recommendations for Port and
Coastal States Regarding the Use of Privately Contracted Armed Security Personnel On Board Ships in the
High Risk Area', MSC.1/Circ.1408/Rev.1 (25 May 2012) Annex (IMO Port and Coastal State Recommenda-
tions); IMO, 'Revised Interim Guidance to Shipowners, Ship Operators, and Shipmasters on the Use of
Privately Contracted Armed Security Personnel On Board Ships in the High Risk Area' MSC.1/Circ.1405/
Rev.2 (25 May 2012) Annex (IMO Shipowner Recommendations).

[101] For a detailed analysis of the soft law documents that regulate the PMSCs see A Petrig, 'The Use of
Force and Firearms by Private Maritime Security Companies against Suspected Pirates' (2013) 62 *Interna-
tional & Comparative Law Quarterly* 667; J Kraska, 'International and Comparative Regulation of Private
Maritime Security Companies Employed in Counter-piracy' in Guilfoyle, n 18 above, 219–49.

V. CONCLUSION: LAW OF THE SEA OR THE LAW OF STATEHOOD?

Other contributions to this volume look at the implications for the experience of tackling Somali piracy on aspects of the law of the sea in general and piracy in particular.[102] This chapter has looked at some wider implications for international law. This reflects a broader tension within the approach to the problem. The very language that is used—focusing on Somali piracy, jurisdiction over pirates, the rights of pirates and of victims of piracy, and so on—reinforces the impression that the problem really is about the shortcomings in the regulatory and jurisdictional frameworks established in accordance with the overarching framework of the law of the sea. By way of conclusion, however, it is worth reflecting on whether this really is the appropriate lens through which to examine—and address—the problem: why has the international community chosen to approach this as a matter of 'piracy'?

Had Somalia not been a failed state, it is highly unlikely—probably inconceivable—that events would have unfolded as they have. This applies both to the emergence of the problem of piracy in the region itself and to the nature of the international response. The very idea of a 'failed state' is disturbing for an international system that has come to suppose that every area and every person is, or ought to be, subject to the effective jurisdiction of a state or state-like entity.[103] In that sense, there is something deeply right about the idea of piracy being the fulcrum for the international community's engagement with the criminal consequences of the lack of effective apparatus of government, since this draws on the idea that piracy is an activity which is beyond the reach of national jurisdiction. At the same time, it also feels deeply wrong. As the successive UNSC resolutions have demonstrated,[104] over time it has become ever more apparent that the solution to the problem of 'piracy' does not lie at sea. From a jurisdictional perspective, policing piracy is obviously within the purview of the law of the sea—but quite why preventing piracy is seen through the lens of the law of the sea is mystifying. The sea is the locus of the offence, no more.[105] House robbers may rob houses, but the solution to the problem of house-breaking is not a matter of land law. This is not a trivial point: indeed, it goes to the heart of the problem that needs to be faced. There is a danger that in conceptualising the problem as one of 'piracy' we are simply missing the point. The 'piracy' element here is the product of a series of systemic failures rather than the actions of 'rouges' operating beyond the limits of national jurisdiction. Whilst hugely fascinating and hugely important from the perspective of the law of the sea, this is not where the solution lies. Indeed, the fixation

---

[102] See, in particular, R Churchill, Chapter 1 above. For further reflections on this see generally Guilfoyle, n 18 above.

[103] Cf J Crawford, *The Creation of States in International Law*, 2nd edn (Oxford, Oxford University Press, 2006) 720–22, who prefers to speak of a 'crisis of government' rather than the failure of the state. But although Crawford himself also acknowledges that in Somalia there is 'a virtual absence of central government' (233), he does not see this as a reason to accept the extinction of the state (722).

[104] See, eg UNSC Resolution 1851 (2 June 2008) and subsequent resolutions referring to activities within the territory of Somalia, rather than the territorial seas. See n 17 above.

[105] This is underlined by the decision of the *US v Ali*, US Court of Appeals, District of Colombia, 13 June 2013, in which it was determined that aiding and abetting acts of piracy, even where those acts did not take place on the high seas, nevertheless fell within the international definition of piracy, and so were within the jurisdiction of the US courts (20). It was stressed that, although some act needed to take place on the high seas, this did not mean that only those acts which took place on the high seas fell within the scope of piracy under the law of nations.

with 'piracy' here runs the risk of diverting attention from the unwillingness—or inability—of the international community to seriously engage with the bigger questions relating to international law which lurk in the background.

For all the wealth of engagement by the international community and despite the potential significance that this has for some key concepts of international law, as suggested in this chapter, the most notable thing is what has *not* happened—and this concerns the implicit challenge to statehood itself. The underlying premise of the international action is that although Somalia is called a state and treated as a state, both diplomatically and within the political organs of the international community, it is not considered to be able to function as a state.[106] Admittedly, there is little new in this: many states lack the capacity to effectively exercise control over all parts of their territory yet still remain incontrovertibly sovereign. But here the situation is more akin to an inability to effectively exercise control over any of its territory—and one cannot help but wonder at the willingness of the international community to countenance such a lacuna in its system of international order, particularly when the consequences of doing so are most manifestly affecting international peace and security. Put this way, it is entirely right that the problem should be the subject of UN Chapter VII resolutions that address the situation: but why do so by expanding international jurisdiction over piracy to the territory of Somalia? Rarely can there have been a more obvious example of the international community addressing the symptoms rather than the causes of a problem.

The unwillingness to respond to realities in the arena of statehood is surely the root cause of the problems here. But, in the absence of a willingness to reallocate jurisdictional competences in a manner which is just too reminiscent of grand reorderings of the nineteenth and early twentieth centuries—in the traditions of the Congress of Vienna, the Treaty of Berlin or the League of Nations Mandates—to be countenanced in anything other than a decolonising context (which is clearly inapplicable here), it seems as if there is nothing to be done except wait for the time to come when the failed entity can resume its functions and can command credibility.

Meanwhile, the reluctance of the international community to engage in a modern form of state-making is matched only by its hesitancy to formally embrace the emergent entities of Somaliland and Puntland.[107] As has already been mentioned in

---

[106] On 17 January 2013 the US formally recognised the Federal Government of Somalia, noting that as a result the US and Somalia were moving to a 'normal sovereign nation to sovereign nation relation'. See comments of Secretary of State Clinton, available at www.state.gov/secretary/rm/2013/01/202998.htm. A month later, and quoting this comment, the Federal Government of Somali invoked sovereign immunity on behalf of the former prime minister of the Barre government, Samantar Mohamad Ali Samantar, in proceedings before the US Supreme Court; proceedings in which the US Department of State had previously declined to make a suggestion of immunity. See *Yousuf v Samantar*, 699 F.3d 763 (4th Cir 2012): see the Letter of the Office of the Prime Minister of the Federal Government of the Somali Republic to the US Secretary of State, Ref OPM/00128/13, 26 February 2013. It remains to be seen how the Department of State and the Supreme Court respond to this consequence of resuming 'normal' relations.

[107] Space precludes an extended discussion of the status of these entities. In brief, however, Somaliland is the former British Protectorate which enjoyed four days of autonomous existence in 1960 before uniting with Somalia on 1 July 1960. It formally declared independence from Somalia in 1991 but, whilst recognised as having 'a high degree of autonomy' (Crawford, n 103 above, 414), it is not formally recognised as a state—though it is classified by Crawford as a territorial entity 'proximate' to a state (ibid, 740). Puntland does not claim to be a state separate from Somalia but since 1998 has claimed to be a separate state within a Somali Federal State, which does not as yet exist. Its first Constitution was adopted in 2001, describing itself as the Puntland State of Somalia, and this reaffirmed its commitment to participation in

the context of UNODC's CPP programme, the international community is building prisons and returning those convicted of piracy to the authorities of these entities to serve their sentences—something which should only be countenanced if there is a belief in the legitimacy and long-term stability of those entities. This seems well founded, and the levels of engagement with the de facto authorities in these entities suggests they are at least as able to provide a degree of practical governance as any other entity; yet the idea of the international community facilitating the dissolution of even a failed state into its embryonic entities remains controversial, to say the least.[108] Nature may abhor a vacuum, but at least the laws of physics ensure that the gap be filled. International law also abhors a vacuum, but it abhors filling it too. Meanwhile, however, it does not really remain empty. Where states lose control, or ultimately fail in part or in whole, it is not self-evident that waiting for—or even working towards— the restoration of the status quo ante or the emergence of a effective successor to the whole is the most sensible policy option in the face of the blunt reality.[109] Nor does 'soft' engagement with the emergent entities within the Somali legal space really address the issue. Would a more robust response to the failure of the restoration of effective governance in Somalia have proven a better solution for the difficulties which we are now facing?

There are now more states than there have ever been, and the number will continue to rise. More states have come into being in the last 50 years than in any other period of history. For all practical purposes, however, the international community seems to have lost the willingness to accept that it is also possible to lose states, in the sense that the state ceases to have the capacity to function effectively within its territory. It seems that we are yet to generate effective means of dealing with the consequences when a state just 'goes', or ceases to provide an effective means of governance, and there are far more states which hover on the margins of effectiveness than is generally admitted. One of the lessons, then, is that it may be necessary to reflect on why we reify statehood when it is unable to provide solutions to the problems which need answers. On that basis, there is a lot to be said for the forms of soft engagement with Somaliland and Puntland which have been taking place, even if this can only be said very softly.

What if there are no such emergent entities? In Somalia, the international com-

a Federal Somalia, if and when this comes into being (see www.so.undp.org/docs/Puntland%202001%20 English.pdf). A revised Constitution was adopted in 2012. A new Federal Government of Somalia was established in September 2012, but the legitimacy of this has now been challenged by the authorities in Puntland, who have suspended all cooperation and relations with it. See the press release of 5 August 2013 (www.puntlandpost.com/press-release-official-position-of-puntland-government-on-relations-with-federal-government-of-somalia). Puntland State of Somalia is not recognised internationally.

[108] The only real analogy would seem to be the break up for the Socialist Federal Republic of Yugoslavia, characterised by Crawford (n 103 above, 707) as 'extinction by involuntary dissolution'.

[109] There has, of course, been a great deal of work undertaken by the international community, flowing from the 2004 Transitional Federal Charter, which was to pave the way for the construction of a federal state. The Kampala Accords of 2011 ultimately paved the way for the election of a new president in September 2012 who, under the Charter, would be tasked with this function, but it is evident that this process has already failed to constructively engage with Puntland (see n 107) and fails also to begin to address the de facto independence of Somaliland which, according to the Charter, remains within the Somali Republic. Thus for all its willingness to engage with the situation, neither the UN nor the international community more generally has been willing to work outside of its preferred paradigm of the continuity of Somali statehood, in the teeth of all the evidence that this is simply not going to work.

munity has been lucky in that the depth of the weakness of the Somali state and the existence of strong emergent entities.[110] To that extent, it is an easy case. How this may play out in other places—where the state is not so weak and the emerging governing entities are not so welcome—remains to be seen, but it is doubtful whether extending and utilising the concept of piracy is the answer when the problem manifests itself in that form.

And if we cannot effectively handle such problems when they manifest themselves in the form of piracy, how are we going to handle those which manifest themselves in the form of international terrorism? Perhaps that provides a better paradigm than the allocation of jurisdictional competences within the framework of the Law of the Sea? Or perhaps, whilst it is obviously a very important problem, piracy is not actually considered to be *that* important a problem?

---

[110] But *cf* Crawford, n 103 above, 417, who suggests that the lack of an effective Somali government has been a hindrance to Somaliland achieving independence, since it is unable to signal to the international community that it accepts that this should occur.

Index